Practical Project Management with

Microsoft Project

Bonnie Biafore

and John Riopel

Cold Press Publishing

Practical Project Management with Microsoft Project

by Bonnie Biafore and John Riopel

Published by Cold Press Publishing
PO Box 1553, Conifer, CO 80433
www.coldpresspublishing.com
Email: info@coldpresspublishing.com

Cover graphics and interior layout by Scott Baird

978-0-9982943-8-4

Contents

Credits

Bonnie Biafore has always been a zealous organizer of everything from software demos to gourmet meals, with the occasional vacation trip to test the waters of spontaneity. As an engineer, she's fascinated by how things work and how to make things work better. Ironically, fate, not planning, turned these obsessions into a career as a project manager. When Bonnie realized she was managing projects, her penchant for planning and follow-through kicked in and she earned a Project Management Professional (PMP)® certification from the Project Management Institute.

When she isn't helping clients wrangle their software into submission, Bonnie writes about and teaches project management, bookkeeping, and technology. She has a knack for mincing these dry subjects into easy-to-understand morsels and then spices them to perfection with her warped sense of humor.

Bonnie records courses on project management, Microsoft Project, and QuickBooks for LinkedIn Learning. She is also the author of *Successful Project Management*, which won an International Award of Merit from the Society of Technical Communication, *QuickBooks: The Missing Manual*, *Your Project Management Coach*, and several other award-winning books.

When unshackled from her computer, she hikes in the mountains, ties herself up in fabric à la Cirque du Soleil, improv comedy, cooks gourmet food, and mostly tries not to act her age. She has also published a novel, Fresh Squeezed, featuring hit men, stupid criminals, and a great deal of political incorrectness.

Website: www.bonniebiafore.com
Email: info@bonniebiafore.com
Twitter handle: @BBiafore
Linkedin: linkedin.com/in/bonniebiafore
Instagram: bonniebiafore

John Riopel has been managing projects since before computers became the mainstay of managing schedule information. As a Berklee College of Music musician, he began managing projects by handling scheduling and delivery of gigs. He graduated to managing projects for a major defense contractor on the Extra Low Frequency (ELF) program for GTE Government Systems, working on microelectronics circuit boards for the ELF radio's delivery. He was program manager for the Wire and Cable Services (WACS) program delivering fiber optics network infrastructure for Cape Canaveral and the Supreme Court among others.

He is now a project management consultant and owner of PM Providers, a Microsoft Silver Partner and Project Management Institute (PMI) Registered Education Provider (REP). He presents and records courses on project management, Microsoft Project, and Project Online/Project Server for LinkedIn Learning and speaks at PMI Global and Chapter meetings, and many other project management events. John holds a Project Management Professional (PMP)® certification, and Microsoft Certified Technical Specialist (MCTS) and Microsoft Certified Professional (MCP) certifications from Microsoft in Enterprise Project and Portfolio Management. He was awarded Community Leader for the Microsoft Project User Group. He provides coaching, training, and project management services for government and commercial customers.

Website: www.pm-providers.com
Email: jriopel@pm-providers.com
Twitter handle: @JARPM

About the Team

Scott Baird (production editor) is the chief creative officer of Baird Enterprises, LLC. He has over 20 years of graphic design experience, including web design, logo design, corporate marketing and branding, as well as book design and layout. He has a BS in Business with an emphasis in Marketing from the University of Colorado, Boulder, and an AA in Visual Art from the Art Institute of Dallas.

Introduction

People have been managing projects for centuries. The construction of the mountaintop city of Machu Picchu was a project—although no one's really sure whether the ancient Inca had a word for "project manager." In fact, you may not have realized you were a project manager when you were assigned your first project to manage. Sure, you're organized and good at making sure people get things done, but consistently managing projects to successful conclusions requires specific skills and know-how. Whether you're building an enclave on a cliffside or aiming for something more mundane, Microsoft Project helps you document project tasks, build a schedule, assign resources, track progress, and make changes until your project is complete.

Perhaps you've launched Project, and now you're staring at the screen, wondering about the meaning of the program's Gantt Chart and Resource Usage views. Or maybe you already have dozens of Project schedules under your belt. Either way, some Project features can be mystifying. You know what you want to do, but you can't find the magic combination that makes Project do it.

This book helps you find your way around Microsoft Project and provides step-by-step guidance on how to use it. This book comes with exercise files for each chapter, so you can follow along and practice techniques. For more experienced project managers, this book can help you take your Project prowess to a new level with tips, time-saving tricks, and mastery of features that never quite behaved the way you wanted.

What's New in Project Desktop Client

Here's an overview of the new Project features and where to learn about them in this book:

- **Multiple timelines**: The Timeline view can summarize key info about a project, whether you want to highlight key tasks and milestones or show when project phases start and finish. Now, you can display more than one timeline at the same time, for example, to show project phases in one timeline and crucial tasks and milestones in another. These timelines are more flexible than they were in the past. You can control bar labels and display task progress in timelines. See Chapter 20 to learn more.

- **Recent File and Folder locations:** The Open and Save screens in the backstage view list recent files and folders you've used so you can easily access the locations you want. Chapter 3 describes these features.

- **Link tasks using a drop-down menu:** When you select a cell in the Predecessors or Successors column and click the down arrow, the drop-down list displays the task names for all the tasks in your project, including the hierarchy and order. See chapter 5 for the details.

- **Agile features with Project Online Desktop client:** You can manage agile projects with task boards, Scrum, and Kanban. Chapter 30 provides the whole scoop.

- **Project Online includes features such as:** Resource Engagements for controlling resource scheduling. See chapter 29 for more info.

- **Link a Project task to Planner:** You can link tasks in a Project file to Planner to collaborate with your team and update status in a task board view. See chapter 29.

- **Roadmap:** This new tool can provide a view of information from multiple waterfall and Agile projects that you can share with co-workers. You can download a document about Roadmap from www.coldpresspublishing.com.

Where Microsoft Project Fits In

Any project manager who has calculated task start and finish dates by hand knows how helpful Project is. By calculating dates, costs, and total assigned work, the program eliminates a mountain of grunt work and helps prevent carpal tunnel syndrome, so you'll have time and stamina left over to actually manage your projects.

In the planning stage, Project helps you develop a project schedule. You add the tasks and people to a Project file, link the tasks together in sequence, assign workers and other resources to those tasks, and poof!—you have a schedule. Project calculates when tasks start and finish, how much they cost, and how many hours each person needs to work each day. The program even helps you develop **better** project plans, because you can revise the schedule quickly to try other strategies until the plan really works. Views and reports help you spot problems, like too many tasks assigned to the same beleaguered team member.

Once your project is under way, you can add actual dates, hours, and costs to the Project file. With actual values, you can use Project to track progress to see how actual progress and cost compare to the project plan. If problems arise—like tasks running late or over budget—you can use Project's tools, views, and reports to look for solutions and quickly make changes until you find a way to get the project back on track.

Of course, plenty of project-management work goes on outside Project. Touchy-feely tasks like identifying project objectives, negotiating with vendors, and building stakeholder buy-in are all about people skills (although Project's reports can certainly help you communicate status with these folks). And projects typically require a lot of documents besides the project schedule. For example, a project plan may include financial-analysis spreadsheets, requirements and specifications documents, change request databases, and diagrams to show how the change-management process works. In addition, thousands of email messages, memos, and other correspondence could change hands before a project finishes.

Communication, change management, and risk management are essential to successful project management, but they don't occur in Project, either. For example, you may have a risk-management plan that identifies the risks your project faces and what you plan to do if they occur. You may also develop a spreadsheet to track those risks and your response if they become reality. In Project, you can link the risk-tracking spreadsheet or risk-response document to the corresponding tasks, but that's about it.

> **Note:** The enterprise features in Project Server or Project Online help you track risks, issues, changes, and more. But smaller teams can collaborate on topics like these on an Office 365 team site. Chapter 28 describes Office 365 and SharePoint collaboration features in more detail.

Choosing the Right Edition

This book covers Project 2019 Standard and Project 2019 Professional, which have about the same capabilities if you manage projects independently and aren't trying to work closely with other project managers, teams, and projects. (Chapter 29 provides a brief introduction to Project Server so you can see whether they make sense for your organization.)

> **Note:** This book also covers Project Online Desktop client (a subscription product) as that edition stood at the time this book was written. However, because it updates more frequently than the desktop versions, differences between that edition and this book will increase over time.

Project Standard works for most one-person shows, even if you manage several projects at the same time. It lets you communicate with your team via email and share documents on a network drive, or the cloud.

Project Professional adds the Team Planner view, and the abilities to inactivate tasks and synchronize Project tasks to a task list in SharePoint. If you manage project teams with hundreds of resources, share a pool of resources with other project managers, or manage your project as one of many in your organization's project portfolio, then you need Project Professional, along with Microsoft Project Portfolio Management Solution. (You can set up your own Project Server environment or subscribe to a hosted solution, such as Project Online.)

Project Online Desktop client, a subscription-based version of Project, gives you the convenience of an always-up-to-date version of the program and also works with Project Server and Project Online.

Project Server (On Premise) and **Project Online** (Cloud) are great if your organization wants to manage an entire portfolio of projects. (This book focuses on the subscription and non-subscription desktop clients, although it has a brief overview of working with Project Server and SharePoint.)

Complementary Software

Managing a project requires other programs in addition to Project. Word and Excel are great for working with the documents and financial-analysis data you produce. PowerPoint is ideal for project presentations and status meetings. And Outlook keeps project communication flowing. This book includes instructions for using these programs in some of your project-management duties.

Office Home and Business includes Word, Excel, PowerPoint, OneNote, and Outlook. Office Professional adds Office Web Apps, Publisher, and Access to the Office Home and Business suite. Here are some of the ways you might use these products in project management:

- **Word**: Producing documents like the overall project plan, work-package descriptions, requirements, specifications, status reports, and so on.

- **Excel**: Creating spreadsheets for financial analysis or tracking change requests, risks, issues, and defects reported.

- **PowerPoint**: Putting together presentations for project proposals, project kickoff, status, change control board meetings, and so on.

- **Outlook**: Emailing everyone who's on the project team.

- **Publisher**: Publishing newsletters, fliers, invitations to meetings, and so on.

- **Access**: Tracking change requests, requirements, risks, and issues. Access is a database program that's a more robust alternative to Excel.

Visio Professional is another program that comes in handy, whether you want to document project processes in flowcharts or to generate Visio-based visual reports from within Project. Visio isn't part of the Office suite, so if you want to use Visio, you have to purchase it separately.

About This Book

Over the years and versions, Project has collected improvements the way sailboat keels attract barnacles. To use Project successfully, you need to understand something about project management, but that's an exercise Microsoft leaves to its customers. The program's Help feature is at least organized around the activities that project managers perform, but Help still focuses on what *Project* does rather than what *you're* trying to do.

> **Note:** Although each version of Project adds new features and enhancements, you can still use this book if you're managing projects with earlier versions of Project. Of course, the older your version of the program, the more discrepancies you'll run across. Because Project 2010 switched to the Office ribbon, this book won't be as useful if you still use Project 2007 or earlier editions.

The book focuses on managing projects with Project desktop clients, with the aid of a few other Microsoft programs like Word and Excel. The book points out some of the power tools that come with Microsoft's enterprise project-management software, and briefly explains how to use Project Server/Online and Project Web App. This book explains which features are useful and when to use them. From time to time, this book also includes instructions for using other programs—like Word and Excel—in your project-management duties.

This book provides step-by-step instructions for using Project features (minus the ones that require Project Server/Online). In fact, by using the downloadable exercise files available on the website (www.coldpresspublishing.com), you can follow along to build and manage a project schedule from start to finish. You can create your own practice file and use it for every chapter. Each chapter has its own sample files, so you can use them if you want to jump into a chapter in the middle of the book.

Practical Project Management with Microsoft Project contains 30 chapters:

- **Chapters 1 through 7** introduce you to building a project schedule. These chapters take you through each aspect of planning a project, including breaking work down into manageable pieces, estimating work and duration, building a schedule, assembling a team, and assigning resources to tasks.

- **Chapters 8 through 12** explain how to refine your plan until everyone is (mostly) happy with it, and then how to prepare it for the execution phase of the project. It describes how to review your plan and fine-tune it, whether you want to modify resource assignments, shorten the schedule, or reduce cost. Chapter 12 describes how to save the schedule.

- **Chapters 13 through 16** take you from an approved project plan to the end of a project. These chapters explain how to track progress once work gets under way, evaluate that progress, manage your budget, and manage changes. Of course, during project execution, you'll jump back to earlier chapters as you need to modify the schedule.

- **Chapters 17 through 23** explain how to customize every aspect of Project to fit your needs—even the ribbon. After all, every organization is unique, and so is every project. Chapter 23 shows you how to save time by reusing Project elements (including templates).

- **Chapters 24 through 30** help you get the most out of Project. These chapters talk about how to work on more than one project at a time, share data with other programs, record macros to automate work, and collaborate on projects with colleagues.

- At the end of the book, three **appendixes** provide a guide to help resources for Project, a quick review of the most helpful keyboard shortcuts, and a reference guide to all the options you can set in the Project Options dialog box (which is available as a download from coldpresspublishing. com).

Downloading Sample Files

As you read through this book, you'll find references to samples files that you can use to follow the steps in the book. To download these files, you need to hop online and visit this book's web page (www.coldpresspublishing.com).

Our Books and Training Courses

Bonnie has written several books on project management and Microsoft Project. Bonnie and John both record training courses for LinkedIn Learning. If you're looking for more information on project management or Microsoft Project, this section lists their books and online training resources.

You can go to Bonnie's website (www.bonniebiafore.com) or John's website (www.pm-providers.com) for a link that provides a free trial to LinkedIn Learning.

Bonnie's Project Management Books

Project 2013: The Missing Manual, O'Reilly Media

Practical Project Management with Microsoft Project 2016

Your Project Management Coach: Best Practices for Managing Projects in the Real World, Wiley

Successful Project Management: Applying Best Practices, Proven Methods, and Real-World Techniques with Microsoft Project, Microsoft Press

Bonnie's LinkedIn Learning Project Management Courses

Project Management Fundamentals

Managing Project Schedules

Managing Small Projects

Learning Microsoft Project

Microsoft Project 2019 and Project Online Desktop Essential Training

Microsoft Project Tips Weekly

Microsoft Project Quick Tips

Microsoft Project 2016 Essential Training

Microsoft Project 2013 Essential Training

Microsoft Project 2010 Essential Training

Advanced Microsoft Project

Agile Project Management with Microsoft Project

Managing Resource-Constrained Projects with Microsoft Project

Managing Subcontractor Projects with Microsoft Project

Managing Actual Values in Microsoft Project

Selecting and Managing a Project Portfolio with Microsoft Project

Modeling Work Schedules with Calendars in Microsoft Project

John's LinkedIn Learning Project Management Courses

Project Online Reporting with Power BI

Microsoft Project Server 2016 Administration

Microsoft Project Web Application 2016

Managing Time-Constrained Projects with Microsoft Project

Managing Budget-Constrained Projects with Microsoft Project

Mastering Microsoft Project Graphical Reports

Visualizing a Report in Microsoft Project

Working with Custom Fields and Formulas in Microsoft Project

1

Projects 101

Microsoft Project has lots of features to help you manage any kind of project, but you have to know something about project management to make those features sing. If your boss hands you a project to manage, you might ask what "project" and "manage" really mean. If so, this chapter is for you.

A project is different from day-to-day work, and this chapter explains how. You'll learn what project management is at a high level—and why it's worth the effort. Project management helps you deliver the right results on time, within budget, and without going into crisis mode. When a project falters, project management techniques also help you get it headed back in the right direction.

What's So Special About Projects?

Projects come in all shapes and sizes, from hosting a dinner party to launching a new product for your company. What's the common thread that unites all projects and makes them different from other kinds of work? Here's one definition: *A project is a unique endeavor with clear-cut objectives, a starting point, an ending point, and (usually) a budget*. Here's a breakdown of the definition's main points:

- **Unique** is the most important word in that definition, because every project is different in some way. Events in different cities, in different venues, during different times of year, and organized by different teams constitute different projects. The event's venue, site conditions, weather, and team members make every event unique, even if they have the same basic structure. In contrast, a crew that fields technical support requests performs the *same* work every day; this kind of work is typically called *operations*.

- **Clear-cut objectives** are necessary if you want any hope of reaching the end, staying within budget, and making stakeholders happy. Whether you call them specific, quantifiable, or unambiguous, objectives define what the project is supposed to accomplish so everyone knows when it's done. "Train the cat" isn't a good objective. It doesn't specify what you're trying to train the cat to do—or not do. (With a cat, the objective may not even be feasible.) On the other hand, an objective that you *can* complete (albeit with some physical risk) is "Remove the cat from the Thanksgiving turkey carcass." For a product kickoff event, you might have objectives like reaching 100,000 potential customers, obtaining press coverage from five top industry trade magazines, and snagging 1,000 product orders.

- A project **begins** at one point in time and **ends** when it achieves its objectives (although some projects *seem* never-ending). When the road crew unloads the equipment back at the office and the product kickoff tour is officially over, the product kickoff project team is ready to move on to its next project. However, if the end of the project always seems just out of reach, poorly defined objectives are usually to blame.

- **Budgets** play a role in most projects, because few people consider money irrelevant. In addition to achieving the objectives within the desired timeframe, you also have to keep the price tag within an acceptable range. For example, the management team might want to keep the kickoff's budget to less than 5 percent of forecast sales. In addition, time may be as important as money for some projects, so you might budget time as well.

> **Note:** Dr. Joseph M. Juran, best known for his work on quality management, was the impetus for today's Six Sigma process-improvement methodology; he described a project as a *problem scheduled for solution*. The concept is the same as the definition described in the preceding list: Working with stakeholders to identify and agree upon the problem that needs solving helps identify the project's objectives. When you schedule the problem for solution, you determine the project's start and end dates.

What Is Project Management?

Project management is the art of balancing project objectives against the constraints of time, budget, resource availability, and quality. Achieving that balance requires skill, experience, and a boatload of techniques. This section gives you a glimpse of what happens from a project's infancy to its old age.

Novices sometimes think of project management as building a sequence of tasks, but those in the know recognize that project management starts *before* a project officially begins and doesn't end for a while after the project's objectives are achieved. There's no single "right" way to manage projects (the note titled "Picking a Project Management Methodology" identifies a few different project management methodologies), but most methodologies cover the following five phases (illustrated in Figure 1-1):

- **Getting started**: Often called *initiating*, this first phase of project management is short but important. It's your only opportunity to get the project off to a good start. In this phase, you answer questions like "Why are we doing this project?" and "Do we really want to do it?" The initial attempts to describe the purpose of a project may produce vague results like "Hold event to introduce our new product." But as you identify the project stakeholders, you learn what the project is about and what the stakeholders hope to achieve. The more specific you are when you describe a project's objectives, the greater your chances for success.

Neglecting to line up support for a project is all too common, and it's **always** a big mistake. A project needs buy-in from its sponsor and stakeholders to survive challenges like contradictory objectives, resource shortages, funding issues, and so on. What's more, **you**, the project manager, need official support too, so everyone knows the extent of your authority.

- **Planning**: This phase is where you draw your project road map: defining objectives to achieve, the work to perform, who's going to do that work, when and how much the whole thing will cost. Moreover, you set out the rules of the game, including how people will communicate with one another, who has to approve what, how you'll manage changes and risks, and so on.

> **Note:** Most IT projects, whether they are agile or predictive (also known as waterfall), include requirements and design processes in the planning phase.

- **Performing the project**: Also referred to as **executing**, this part of project management lasts a long time, but it boils down to following the plan. As the project manager, your job is to keep the project team working on the right things at the right times.

- **Keeping things under control**: In a perfect world, performing the project would be enough, because things would always run according to plan. But because the world isn't perfect, project managers have to monitor projects to see whether they're on schedule, within budget and achieving their objectives. Whether someone gets sick, a truck breaks down, or the convention center is plagued with locusts, something is bound to push your project off course. In the **controlling** phase, you measure project performance against the plan, decide what to do if the project is off track, make the necessary adjustments, and then measure again. Chapters 10 and 11 explain how to use Project to control things.

- **Gaining closure**: Like personal relationships, projects need closure. Before you can call a project complete, you have to tie up loose ends like closing out contracts, transitioning resources to their new assignments, and documenting the overall project performance. The **closing** phase is when you ask for official acceptance that the project is complete—your sign that your job is done.

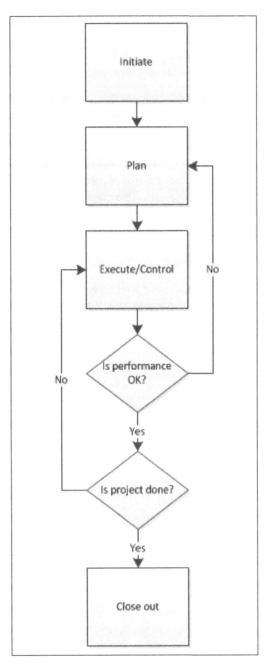

Figure 1-1. *Planning isn't a one-time event, because no project runs exactly according to plan. Whether changes, issues, or full-blown disasters arise, you regularly revisit and revise the plan.*

Picking a Project Management Methodology

Companies that perform project after project usually pick a project management methodology, such as PRINCE2 or Agile, and stick with it. That way, all their projects follow approximately the same project management processes. Teams learn what works and what doesn't, and everyone learns what to do and expect.

The approach you choose depends a lot on the environment in which you work. Complex environments with large projects, widely distributed teams, or multiple vendors usually need a robust project management methodology with formal, well-documented procedures, standardized forms and documents, and project management software like Microsoft's Enterprise Project Management Solutions to keep track of everything. Simpler, smaller projects would bog down with that kind of overhead but run just fine with a more informal approach.

This book introduces the basic steps of project management, which you can use as a starting point. If you want a ready-made methodology to adopt, check out the following resources:

- Many organizations have developed methodologies based on the project management principles outlined in the Project Management Institute's® **Project Management Body of Knowledge** (affectionately known as PMBOK®). Project Management Institute® (PMI®) is a registered mark of the Project Management Institute, Inc.

- **PRINCE2** (PRojects IN Controlled Environments) is a methodology used to manage government projects in the United Kingdom as well as private-sector projects around the world.

- **Iterative, rolling wave, and agile methodologies** work well when the solution for the project isn't clearly defined. You use iterations to gradually identify the solution as you work on the project.

- **TenStep, Inc.** offers a project management approach that (predictably) takes 10 steps from start to finish. This approach can be adapted to large, medium and small projects. If you register with the website www.tenstep.com (for free), you can mine a mother lode of additional project management wisdom.

- *Project Planning, Scheduling & Control* by James P. Lewis (McGraw-Hill) bucks the trend in project management books by providing an easy-to-read, and even amusing, description of one way to manage projects.

- *A Management Framework for Project, Program, and Portfolio Integration* by R. Max Wideman (Trafford Publishing) tries to simplify project management—and for the most part succeeds.

Why Manage Projects?

The five phases of an ***unmanaged*** project go something like this: wild enthusiasm, dejected disillusionment, search for the guilty, punishment of the innocent, and promotion of those not involved. An unmanaged project is like a black hole that sucks up every person, resource, and dollar—and still doesn't deliver what it's supposed to. Despite all that, many organizations fear that project management requires bureaucratic and inflexible procedures and will make projects take longer. On the contrary, planning projects and managing the plan provides many benefits, including the following:

- **Happy customers**: Whether a project is for outside customers or groups within your organization, customers like to get ***what*** they want ***when*** they want it. Because the first step in project management is finding out what your customers and stakeholders want to accomplish with the project, your customers are more likely to get the results they expect. And by keeping the project under control, you're also more likely to deliver those results on time and at the right price.

- **Achieved objectives**: Without a plan, projects tend to cultivate their own agendas, and people tend to forget the point of their work. A project plan ties a project to specific objectives, so everyone stays focused on those goals. Documented objectives also help you rein in the renegades who try to expand the project scope.

- **Timely completion**: Finishing a project on time is important for more than just morale. As work goes on for a longer duration, costs increase and budgets get blown to bits. In addition, you may lose the resources you need or prevent other projects from starting. On-time completion should be one of your objectives, like when you're trying to get a product to market before the competition.

- **Flexibility**: Contrary to many people's beliefs, project management makes teams ***more*** flexible. Project management doesn't prevent every problem, but it makes problems that occur easier to resolve. When something goes wrong, you can evaluate your plan to quickly develop alternatives—now that's flexibility! More importantly, keeping track of progress means you learn about bad news when you still have time to recover.

- **Better financial performance**: Most executives are obsessed with financial performance, so most projects have financial objectives—increasing income, lowering costs, reducing expensive recalls, and so on. Project management is an executive-pleaser because it can produce more satisfying financial results.

- **Happier, more productive workers**: Skilled workers are hard to come by and usually cost a bundle. People get more done when they can work without drama, stress, and painfully long hours. Moreover, happier, more productive workers don't abandon ship, so you spend less on recruiting and training replacements.

Project Planning in a Nutshell

Project planning is like other types of planning—you figure out what you're going to do before you do it. Project plans are destined to change, because the projects they guide never happen exactly as planned. But the inevitability of change shouldn't scare you off planning. What you learn during the planning process can help you keep a project on course even when changes occur.

Project planning involves two main elements: **why** you're doing the project, and **how** you're going to do it. You begin by identifying what the project is supposed to accomplish. Only then can you start planning how to achieve the project's goals.

Veteran project managers have official names for each part of a project plan, but any plan boils down to a series of questions. Here are the basics:

- **Why are we going to perform this project?** The answer to this question describes the point of the project. You can also rephrase this question as "What's the problem we want to solve or the opportunity we want to leverage?" You describe the problem that the project is supposed to solve in the *problem statement*.

- **What are we going to achieve?** By definition, a project eventually ends. You have to know what the project is supposed to achieve so you can tell when it's done. The first step is to spell out all the goals, or *project objectives*. Projects usually have several goals, which can fall into different categories. For example, a project may have a financial objective to earn more than a specific amount of money, a business objective to raise awareness of a product, and a performance objective to deliver the project before the biggest selling season.

- **What approach are we going to take?** The problems that projects solve usually have more than one solution. Part of project planning is figuring out which solution—or *project strategy*—is best. Then, the project plan documents the strategy you're going to use to address the problem and why you chose it.

- **What are we going to do?** Based on the strategy that's selected, the project plan describes how the project will achieve its objectives in a few other forms, each of which plays a specific role. The *project scope statement* lists what is and isn't part of the project. It delineates the boundaries of the project so stakeholders know what to expect. The scope statement also helps you rein in pressures to expand the project (*scope creep*).

  Intimately linked to project scope are *deliverables*—the tangible results the project needs to produce—and the *success criteria* you use to judge whether the deliverables are acceptable. Every section listed in the project scope statement has corresponding deliverables and success criteria, and vice versa. With the scope, deliverables, and success criteria in hand, you're ready to describe the work that needs to be performed. As its name implies, a *work breakdown structure* or *WBS* breaks down the work that people do on a project into manageable pieces.

In addition to the work specific to achieving project objectives, projects need a few project management processes (for things like managing risk, controlling changes, communicating, and managing quality) to keep the project under control. A project plan outlines how these processes will work.

- **When will the project start and finish?** Projects have starting and ending points, so the plan documents these dates. In addition, the **_project schedule_** actually shows the sequence of tasks and when each one starts and finishes (see Chapter 5 to learn how to build one).

- **Who will work on the project?** People and other resources actually do the work, so the project plan includes a **_responsibility assignment matrix_** (RAM) and a **_project organization chart_** to identify the team. Depending on the size of the project and where resources come from, the plan might also include a detailed staffing plan. If you don't have approval for the project yet and can't assign specific people, you can identify the skill sets or roles that you'll need to complete work. Chapter 6 describes how to add resources to your Project file.

- **How much will it cost?** Blank checks are rare in any environment, so the project plan includes a budget (Chapter 15) showing where all the money goes. Chapter 9 explains how Project helps you calculate and track project costs.

- **How good do the results need to be?** Given constraints on time, money, and resources, you usually don't have the luxury of doing a spectacularly better job than required. The project plan outlines how you intend to achieve the level of quality the project requires, and how you'll measure that quality.

- **How do we know when we're done?** Part of project planning is to clearly define success. For each objective and deliverable you identify, specify how you're going to determine whether they're done. Otherwise, you could have trouble bringing closure to your project.

Project planning is an iterative process, not a one-time deal. You may run through the planning steps several times just to get a plan that stakeholders approve. Then, once you begin to execute the plan, you'll have to rework it to accommodate changes and glitches that come up. In addition, for projects with goals that aren't clear-cut, you might use an even more iterative approach: planning and executing small portions of the project until the entire solution is complete. Figure 1-2 shows the project-planning steps and the path you take the first time through.

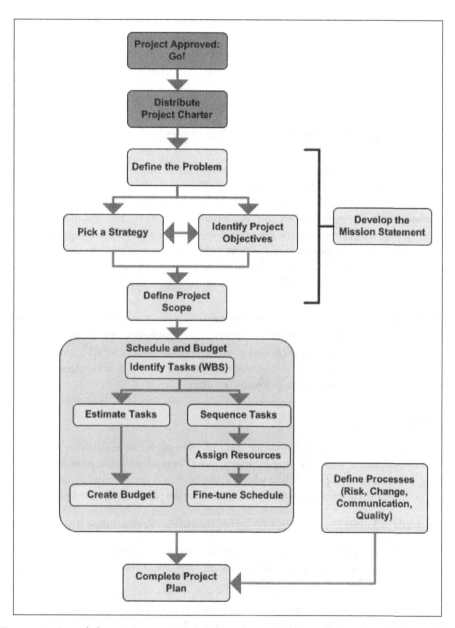

Figure 1-2. *Several planning steps may occur at the same time. For example, you can work on identifying project objectives and project scope simultaneously. Then you might jump back and forth between steps, as you learn more about different aspects of the project. If the problem, objectives, or scope change significantly, you may have to change the strategy and mission as well.*

> **Tip:** Not every project plan requires detailed write-ups for every component described in this section. For example, a small project may need only a sentence or two about how you're going to communicate with your two other team members. Use your judgment to decide how much detail to include.

Laying Out Project Processes

As you manage a project, some activities keep running for as long as the project does, such as the support-type activities usually referred to as *level of effort*. For example, you have to keep an eye on changes that people ask for and run them through a change-management process to prevent scope creep. A *change-management process* includes steps for requesting changes, deciding whether to include changes in the project, and tracking the changes. Similarly, *risk-management*, *communication-management*, and *quality-management* processes also run until the project is complete. Defining these processes has to occur while you're still planning the project, or your team will mill about like sheep without a border collie. This section introduces the four processes you define and document in the project plan.

> **Tip:** How you approach change management, risk management, and other processes depends on your project. Small projects can survive with relatively informal procedures, whereas large, global projects require more rigor. Moreover, corporate culture has an effect on how team members view the processes you define.

Communicating

As a project manager, you already know that most of your job is communicating with people. But everyone else working on a project communicates, too. A *communication plan* describes the rules for sharing information on a project, like whether people should email status updates, post them on a website, or scratch them on white-boards. A communication plan answers the following questions:

- **Who needs to know?** For instance, who should receive the list of pending change requests?

- **What do they need to know?** The change control board may receive the full documentation of change requests, whereas a team leader receives only info about the associated work tasks and when the work is due.

- **When do they need to know it?** Do status reports come out every week, every other week, or once a month? And do they come out on Friday or a different weekday?

- **How should they receive it?** The methods for distributing information depend on what your organization has available, as well as how people like to communicate. Some organizations place more weight on paper documents, while others prefer the convenience of email or collaboration websites.

- **Where do they need to keep information?** Establish a common file structure and location to make it easy for a project team to find, save, and archive vital project plans, data and other information.

Managing Change

When you plan a project, you define its scope, the deliverables it will produce, and the objectives it will achieve. Once the scope, objectives, budget and timetable are established, you can set your baseline to which all change is compared. Inevitably, when the project starts, someone remembers one more thing they need, and someone else finds a better way to tackle a problem. These changes can dramatically affect the plan you so carefully prepared, so you need to evaluate requested changes to decide whether they belong in the project. If they do, then you adjust the project plan accordingly.

A *change management plan* (CMP) describes how you handle change requests: how people submit them, who reviews them, the steps for approving them, and how you incorporate them into your plan. (It doesn't, however, describe how you manage the extra work that those change requests entail.) For modest projects, an Excel workbook and email may be enough to handle change-management activities. But most projects need a *change control board* (CCB)—a group of people who decide the fate of change requests. Chapter 16 gets into the nitty-gritty of managing changes, but here are the basic activities involved:

- Submit change requests via a change log

- Receive and record change requests

- Evaluate the effects of change requests on cost, schedule, and quality

- Decide whether change requests become part of the project

- Update project documents to incorporate accepted changes

- Track changes as you do other project task work

- Maintain and review the change log

Managing Quality

Most projects have objectives that relate to quality, whether you need to attain satisfaction ratings from sponsors or hit a particular decibel level of audience applause. A *quality management plan* starts with a project's quality objectives. Then, for each objective, you define how you plan to achieve those quality levels, which is called *quality assurance* (QA). Quality assurance defines what to measure and the process of measuring to meet those standards. Later, you execute the plan where you monitor and measure quality performance, which is called *quality control* (QC).

Managing Risk

Things can and will go wrong on your projects. It's easier and faster to recover from troublesome events if you anticipate them and have a plan for how to respond. Risk management starts with identifying what could go wrong. Then you analyze those risks and decide what you'll do if they actually happen. As the project progresses, you monitor risks to see whether they're becoming more threatening or going away. Finally, if a risk does become reality, you launch your counter-attack and monitor the results.

> **Note:** If you want to learn more, consider reading Project and Program Risk Management: A Guide to Managing Project Risks and Opportunities by R. Max Wideman (PMI) or Risk Management: Tricks of the Trade for Project Managers by Rita Mulcahy (RMC Publications).

Project Execution

Project execution is what you do to get project work going. You bring your core project team on board and explain the project rules. Of course, this is also when you start to put your plans to work: you look at your baselined project schedule, hand out assignments to the team, and they start cranking through the tasks in the project WBS.

Monitoring and Controlling a Project

You continually monitor your project to see whether it's following your plan. If it isn't, you analyze the issues and come up with ways to get the project back on track (in other words, control the project). Here's what you do to monitor and control a project:

- Implement communication, quality, risk, and change management plans.

- Track progress and compare the actual performance to the baselined schedule within your project plan, which helps you determine whether you need to correct course.

- Report performance and status to the appropriate audiences.

- Solve problems.

- If your project is not running according to plan, determine the corrective actions you're going to use to control scope, schedule and cost.

In the end, you deliver on your promises to your customer as defined in your scope and begin the closeout process.

Closing a Project

Closing a project means tying up all the loose ends after the project work is complete. First, you get approval from the project customer that the project truly is complete. You might transfer ownership of deliverables to the customer, for example, for a project to build a new software system. If the project involved contracts with other companies, you have to close those contracts along with any billing accounts you used to track project finances. In addition, you also document the final performance and lessons learned, and release the resources so they can move on to their next assignments.

2

Getting to Know Microsoft Project

This chapter provides a quick introduction to Microsoft Project. The journey begins with launching the program. The chapter then takes you on a tour of Project's ribbon tabs and the Quick Access Toolbar (QAT). After that, you'll explore panes that appear in the Project window and learn how to work with views you use as you work on projects. You'll also discover tips on using the QAT and ribbon effectively. The chapter wraps up by describing how to use Screen Tips to learn about Project features and how Smart Tags help you tell Project what you're trying to accomplish.

Launching Project

How you launch Project depends on the Windows operating system you use:

* **Windows 8**: Open the Start screen by pressing the Windows key (or by pointing the mouse pointer at the screen's bottom-left, and then clicking the Start icon when it appears). If you see the Project tile, click it to launch the program. If you don't see the tile, point at the screen's right edge to scroll through additional tiles, and then click the Project tile. (If you still don't see the Project tile, right-click a blank area of the Start screen, and then choose All Apps from the shortcut menu.)

* **Windows 10**: Open the Start screen by pressing the Windows key or by clicking the Start icon at the screen's bottom-left. If you see the Project tile, click it. If you don't see the tile, click "All apps" just above the Start icon, scroll to the Project entry, and then click it.

Project opens to the Backstage view, which is where you create new Project files (from scratch or from a template), open existing ones, and perform a few other actions. If you've opened Project files before, you see them listed under the Recent heading on the left side of the view. For the purposes of this tour, click Blank Project on the right side of the view to create a new, blank project. Chapter 3 provides the full scoop on creating and opening Project files.

Using the Ribbon and the Quick Access Toolbar

Project's ribbon is like a cyber border collie, herding related features onto tabs to make them easier to find, as shown in Figure 2-1. As you schedule and manage a project, you shift your focus from tasks to the resources who work on them to the big picture of the entire project, so the Task tab, Resource tab, and Project tab make perfect sense. You'll also turn to a few other tabs as you work with your Project files and look at your projects in different ways. This section steps through the seven tabs that appear when you launch Project for the first time and explains how to use and customize the Quick Access Toolbar. (See Chapter 22 to learn how to add other tabs to the ribbon and how to create your own custom tabs.)

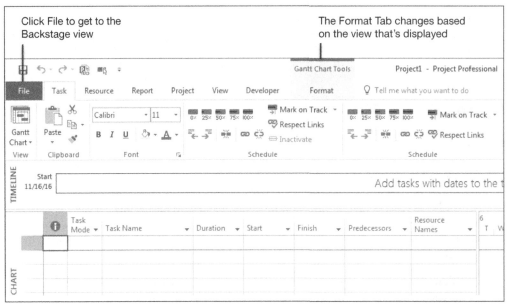

Figure 2-1. *Click the File tab, and the Backstage view takes over. Click any other tab, like the Task tab shown here, and you see the ribbon across the top of the program window while a Project view fills the rest.*

Managing the Backstage View

When you click the File tab, Project opens the ***Backstage view***. When you click a command on the left side of the Backstage view, it takes over the entire Project window, as you can see in Figure 2-2. For example, when you click New, the Backstage view presents several ways to create a new file (see Chapter 3).

Figure 2-2. *When you click the File tab, the ribbon tabs disappear and the Backstage view takes over. After you finish working in the Backstage view, you can return to the Project ribbon by clicking the arrow in a white circle at the top left of the screen.*

Some commands listed in the Backstage view should be familiar: Save, Save As, Open, Close, and Exit. For the most part, they do what they've always done. The other entries in the Backstage view let you do even more. You'll learn about them in other chapters of the book, but here's a quick intro:

- **Info**: Clicking this entry opens the Info page, which displays information about the active Project file (such as start and finish date) on the right side of this page. This page also includes an Organizer button that lets you copy project elements between files (Chapter 23). And if you use Project Server and Project Web App (Chapter 29), you can access Project Web App accounts, assign permissions, and publish project progress to Project Web App from this page.

- **New**: This page offers several ways to create a new file, including starting from scratch with a blank project; using a template; creating an agile or waterfall project; or creating a file from an existing project, an Excel workbook, or a SharePoint Tasks List. If you want some serious handholding to get started, you can use templates that are installed with the application or you can search for templates online.

- **Open**: The Open page, shown in Figure 2-3, makes it easy to access your Project files, whether they're stored on your computer or in the cloud. Click Recent to see a list of all the projects you've opened lately. If you open a lot of Project files—say, as you write a book about Project— this is the quickest way to reopen a file. File locations in the cloud, such as OneDrive, appear below the Recent entry. You can add other storage locations by clicking "Add a Place." For files stored on your trusty computer, click This PC. If you work on a project for months at a time, you can pin it to the top of the Recent list by clicking the pushpin icon to the right of the file name.

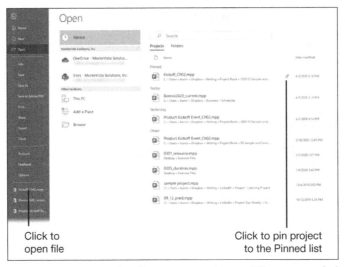

Figure 2-3. *For even easier access, a few of your most recently opened files appear at the bottom of the Backstage menu. Simply click a file's name to open the file.*

Tip: To change how many projects appear at the bottom of the Backstage menu, display the Backstage view by clicking the File tab, and then click Options. On the left side of the Project Options dialog box, click Advanced, and then scroll to the Display section. Turn on the "Quickly access this number of Recent Projects" checkbox and then, in the box to its right, type the number you want.

- **Save**: Clicking Save simply saves the active Project file. (If you've created a new file, clicking Save opens the Save As page instead.) If you use SharePoint, Project Server, or subscribe to Project Online (an online Microsoft service for managing project portfolios and collaborating with project teams), you can also save your file to SharePoint, Project Server or Project Online.

- **Save As**: On the Save As page, you can choose to save the file in the cloud, on your computer, or other locations. The right side of the Save As page lists locations where you've recently saved files.

- **Print**: The Print page looks like a spiffed-up version of the familiar Print dialog box. This page lets you select a printer, specify print settings like paper orientation, and choose page setup options like margins (Chapter 18). If you rarely touch any of those settings, you can simply choose the number of copies and click the big Print button at the top of the page.

Tip: Print settings are typically set to Portrait orientation. To view Gantt Charts more easily, switch to Landscape orientation.

- **Share**: As its name implies, this page offers features for sharing Project files. You can synchronize your Project file with a SharePoint Tasks List (see Chapter 28) or send it as an email attachment (Chapter 25).

- **Export**: Despite its name, this page offers several methods for saving a project in other file formats, such as PDF, XPS, older Project formats, project templates, Excel, XML, and so on.

- **Close**: Click this command to close the active Project file.

- **Account**: This page (available in Project Professional) displays the information about the Microsoft account you use to log into Project Server or Project Online and access connected services like OneDrive. (You set up a Microsoft account during installation, if you don't already have one.) Click the About Project button on this page to see which version of the program you have.

- **Options**: Click Options to open the Project Options dialog box and choose settings to tell the program how you'd like it to behave.

A Tour of the Ribbon Tabs

Project management's focus on projects, tasks, and resources is a natural fit for tabs on the ribbon. The ribbon gathers features into tabs that, for the most part, are logically organized. Here's a quick introduction to the tabs on the Project ribbon besides the File tab (you'll learn about each one in detail throughout this book).

- The **Task tab** is your first stop after creating a Project file. It's home to commands for creating tasks (subtasks, summary tasks, and milestones), linking them to one another, and rearranging them into an outline. The first section on this tab lets you choose popular task-oriented views like the Gantt Chart. You can also use this tab to format tasks, copy and paste them, or look at their details. This tab also includes the incredibly useful "Scroll to Task" command, which scrolls the view timescale (described later in this chapter) until the selected task's task bar is visible. While the project is under way, you can use commands on this tab to move tasks to new dates, to update task progress, and to investigate scheduling issues.

- The **Resource tab** is next up in the project-scheduling lineup, because you need resources to complete the work. This tab has a section for choosing popular resource-oriented views, like the Resource Sheet and the Team Planner (Chapter 7). Whether you're adding resources to a project, assigning them to tasks, or leveling them to remove overallocations, this is the tab you want. It also contains commands for setting up, refreshing, and updating a resource pool (Chapter 24) so you can share resources among several projects. If you use Project Server, this tab has commands for accessing the Enterprise Resource Pool.

- The **Report tab** includes several categories of built-in reports, such as Dashboards, Resources, and Costs. You can also create visual reports, create your own customized reports, or compare two Project files. Chapters 18 and 19 have the complete details on running and customizing reports.

- The **Project tab** is a catch-all for commands to fine-tune your project: viewing project information, defining work calendars, setting project baselines, inserting subprojects, creating links between projects, and so on. This is also the tab to select if you want to work on custom fields or your WBS codes. In addition, you can find commands here to set the project's status date and to update the project in certain situations (Chapter 13).

- The **View tab** starts with buttons for the most popular task and resource views, but you can also access the More Views dialog box to choose any views you've customized or that come standard with Microsoft Project. This tab has commands for controlling what information you see in a view: how many levels in the outline; the table applied; highlighting; how the view's contents are filtered, grouped, or sorted; and the time periods used in the timescale. You can turn the Timeline pane and Details pane on or off and choose the view that appears in the Details pane (described later in this chapter). You can also switch between windows and arrange windows from this tab. The only command that doesn't seem to belong on this tab is in the last section: You choose Macros to run Visual Basic for Applications (VBA) macros.

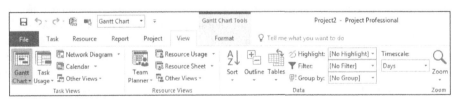

- The **Format tab** is a chameleon that offers different formatting commands depending on the view that's active. For example, when the Gantt Chart view is applied, the Gantt Chart Tools | Format tab lets you insert columns in the table, format task bars and text styles, display elements like summary tasks or critical tasks, and so on. When you switch to the Timeline view, the Timeline Tools | Format tab lets you add tasks to the timeline and format them. For the Resource Usage view, the Resource Usage Tools | Format tab has checkboxes that let you control which fields you see in the time-phased data grid.

Work Quicker with the Quick Access Toolbar (QAT)

The Quick Access Toolbar is so small that you might not notice it above the File and Task tabs (see Figure 2-4). But it's always visible, so it's a handy place for your favorite commands. (In addition, it keeps you from having to jump from tab to tab to get to your favorites.) Out of the box, it has icons for Save, Undo, and Redo, because people use these commands so often. To add more commands, click the down arrow on the right end of the toolbar, and then, on the drop-down menu (shown in Figure 2-4), choose the command you want to add. For example, to make views easy to select, click View on the drop-down menu. When you do, Project turns on the checkmark to the left of the entries name and adds the View box to the Quick Access Toolbar. Then you can click the down arrow in the View box and choose the view you want to display. (The View box on the Quick Access Toolbar displays the name of the view that's currently active.)

> **Tip:** To make the Quick Access Toolbar even easier to reach, click the down arrow on the right end of the toolbar, and then, on the drop-down menu, choose "Show Below the Ribbon." When you do that, the toolbar snuggles up underneath the left side of the ribbon. Once you have all your favorite tools in the QAT, you can roll up the ribbon by double-clicking one of the tabs. To open a ribbon just click on that tab, and to leave it open again, double click a tab.

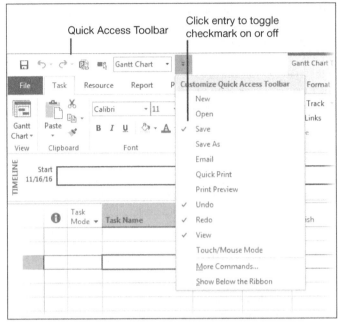

Figure 2-4. *To position the Quick Access Toolbar below the ribbon instead of above it, choose "Show Below the Ribbon."*

Note: You can add any command you want to the Quick Access Toolbar. On the ribbon, right-click the command you want to add, and then choose "Add to Quick Access Toolbar."

Working with Views

Managing projects means looking at information in many different ways, which explains all the built-in views Project offers. These views come with a lot of moving parts. This section explains what each component of a view does and how to choose the view you want.

Note: If you want to follow along, use the file Product Kickoff Event_Ch02.mpp, which you can download from the book website, www.coldpresspublishing.com.

The Anatomy of Project Views

Many views have a left and a right pane that show different perspectives of a project, but some views have only one pane. Then again, combination views show two views at the same time, one above the other. Usually, the top pane of this double-decker arrangement is called the primary pane, whereas the bottom pane is called the Details pane. This section describes the various components you might run into depending on the views you look at. By definition, a view is comprised of a table, filter and a group.

- **Table**: For views like the Gantt Chart (shown in Figure 2-5) and Task Usage, the left side of the view is a table with field values in the columns. (To display the Gantt Chart view, on the left side of the Task tab, click the top half of the Gantt Chart button.) Depending on the view, the rows show tasks, resources, or assignments. (The Gantt Chart view displays tasks in the table rows.) You can add or edit values directly in the table or use it simply for reviewing. Some views, like the Resource Sheet view and Task Sheet view, are like giant tables, similar to Excel worksheets. Chapter 20 describes how to customize tables.

- **Timescale or time-phased grid**: If a view has a pane on the right side, it shows values by time period. In the Gantt Chart view, task bars in the timescale show when tasks begin and end, as shown in Figure 2-5. The Task Usage view's timescale uses a time-phased table instead, in which the columns represent time periods. (To display the Task Usage view, on the left side of the Task tab, click the bottom half of the Gantt Chart button, and then choose Task Usage on the drop-down menu. After you look at the Task Usage view, click the top half of the Gantt Chart button to display the Gantt Chart view.)

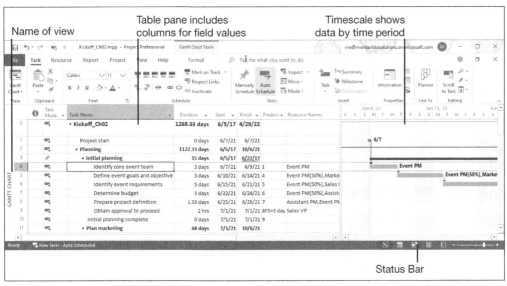

Figure 2-5. *Many views have a left and a right pane, as shown here. The left pane is a table with rows for tasks, resources, or assignments, and columns for field values. The right pane is a timescale that shows data over time.*

> **Note:** The status bar runs along the bottom edge of the overall Project window (Figure 2-5). You can switch between Manually Scheduled mode and Auto Scheduled mode (see Chapter 4) on the left side of the status bar. On the right side of the status bar, you can click icons for popular Project views or drag the Zoom slider to change the timescale in the current view.

- **Details pane**: The Details pane appears in the lower portion of the Project window and shows detailed information about the task, resource, or assignment that's selected in the top pane (called the primary pane). To display the Details pane, in the View tab's Split View section, turn on the Details checkbox, and then choose the view you want in the Details pane from the drop-down list (Resource Graph, in this example). (If the Resource Graph doesn't appear in the drop-down list, choose More Views, and then double-click Resource Graph in the More Views dialog box.) Figure 2-6 shows the Gantt Chart view in the primary pane and the Resource Graph view in the Details pane.

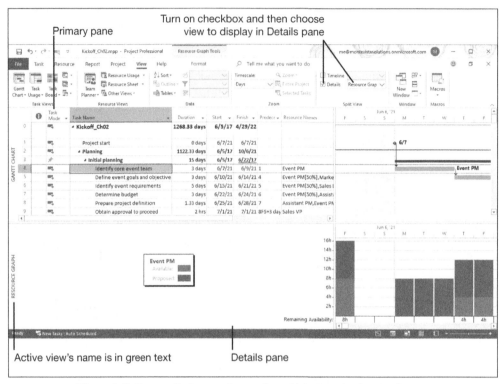

Figure 2-6. *You can display two views at the same time, one in the primary pane and another in the Details pane.*

Note: The actions you can perform in Project depend on whether the primary or Details pane is active. If you select a new view, then Project replaces the view in the active pane with the one you selected. You can tell which pane is currently active because its name is displayed to the left of the pane in green text (see Figure 2-7); the inactive pane's name is displayed in gray text.

- **Timeline pane**: The Timeline view appears in its own special pane above the primary pane (in the view tab's Split View section, turn on the Timeline checkbox). The Timeline view can display key tasks and milestones along a horizontal timeline. (See Chapter 20 to get the full story on the Timeline view.) However, you can see only two panes at a time, which means you have to choose between the Timeline view pane and the Details pane. If the Details pane is visible and you turn on the Timeline checkbox, then Project automatically hides the Details pane (and turns off the Details checkbox). Similarly, if the Timeline view pane is visible and you turn on the Details checkbox, Project hides the Timeline view pane. After you look at the Timeline view, in the View tab, turn off the Timeline checkbox to display only the primary pane.

> **Note:** Just to keep life interesting, Project also has task panes (no relation to view panes) for different project-related activities. For example, when you choose Task Tasks Inspect, the Task Inspector pane appears to the left of your views (see Chapter 10).

- **Combination view**: Project's views come in single and combination variations. A single view is simply one Project view that you can choose to display in the primary pane or the Details pane, such as the Gantt Chart view shown in Figure 2-6. Combination views, on the other hand, contain *two* single views: one on top and one in the Details pane. The built-in Task Entry view, for example, has the Gantt Chart view (a single view) on top and the Task Form view (another single view) in the Details pane. To display the Task Entry view, on the Task tab, click the bottom half of the Gantt Chart view, choose More Views on the drop-down menu, and then double-click Task Entry in the More Views dialog box's list. In combination views, the active view is the one whose name (on the left side of the window) appears in green text; the inactive view's name appears in gray text (Figure 2-7).

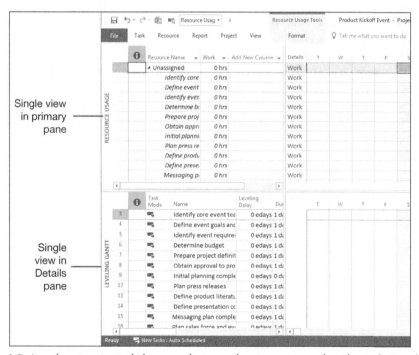

Figure 2-7. *A combination view includes one single view in the primary pane and another in the Details pane.*

Choosing a View

Over the life of a project, you need to look at its data in different ways, so it's no surprise that you frequently change the view you're looking at. For that reason, Project has buttons for choosing views in several locations on the ribbon. Here are your choices:

- **The Task tab**: To choose a view in this tab, head to the View section, click the bottom half of the Gantt Chart button, and then choose the view you want from the drop-down menu. If the view you want isn't listed, then choose More Views at the bottom of the menu. In the More Views dialog box, double-click the view you want to apply, such as Task Entry.

- **The Resource tab**: In this tab's View section, click the bottom half of the Team Planner button if you use Project Professional (it's the Gantt Chart button if you use Project Standard), and then choose the view you want from the drop-down menu, such as Resource Sheet. You can also choose More Views at the bottom of the menu to open the More View dialog box so you can choose *any* view that's in your Project file or global template (Chapter 23).

    > **Tip:** If you want to have a view appear in the drop-down menu, edit that view and select the "Show in menu" check box.

- **The View tab**: This tab (shown in Figure 2-8) has two sections devoted to choosing views. The Task Views section contains buttons to display the Gantt Chart view, Task Usage view, Network Diagram view, Calendar view, and Task Form view. (In this example, click Gantt Chart.) In the Resource Views section, click the appropriate button to apply the Team Planner view, Resource Usage view, or Resource Sheet view. If you want to apply a view that doesn't have a button, click the down arrow on any of these buttons, and then choose More Views on the drop-down menu that appears.

    > **Note:** When the primary pane and Details pane are both visible and you select a single view like the Gantt Chart, Project applies the view to the active pane and keeps the other pane as it is.

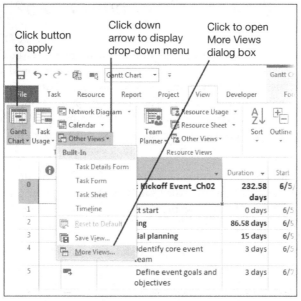

Figure 2-8. *Click a button to apply the corresponding view, or click the button's down arrow to choose a view from the drop-down menu.*

Note: If you've created any custom views (Chapter 20), the view drop-down menus on the Task, Resource, and View tabs include two headings: Custom and Built-In. (If you haven't created any custom views, you see only the Built-In heading.) The views listed below the Custom heading are custom views that you've created or copied into your Project file from another file. The views listed below the Built-In heading are the views that come with Project.

Tip: If you're a Project old-timer, you might wonder what happened to the View Bar, a narrow bar that contains buttons for many popular views. It's still available as long as you know how to retrieve it. Right-click just inside the left border of the main Project window (for example, right-click the view name that's positioned vertically on the left side of the view), and then choose View Bar at the bottom of the view shortcut menu that appears. The View Bar appears on the left side of the window. Click an icon to apply the corresponding view.

Displaying One Pane or Two?

When you have one view in the primary pane and another view in the Details pane, you can tell Project whether you want to see both the primary pane and the Details pane, or only the primary pane. For example, suppose you apply a combination view like Task Entry (on the Task tab, click the bottom half of the Gantt Chart button, choose More Views on the drop-down list, and then double-click Task Entry in the More Views dialog box's list). The Gantt Chart view appears on top and the Task Form appears in the Details pane. You can hide the Details pane to concentrate on task dependencies in the Gantt Chart view or restore the Details pane to simplify editing tasks.

To hide the Details pane, in the View tab's Split View section, turn the Details checkbox off. To restore the Details pane, turn the Details checkbox on. After you turn the checkbox on, in the drop-down list, choose the view you want to see in the Details pane, such as Tracking Gantt.

Less obvious controls are also available to hide and show panes. If both panes are visible, you can hide the Details pane by double-clicking the horizontal divider between the two panes. To bring the Details pane back, you can double-click the box immediately below the vertical scroll bar on the right side of the Project window, shown in Figure 2-9. You can also adjust the height of the panes by moving your cursor over the horizontal divider; when the cursor turns into a two-headed arrow, drag up or down until the panes are the height you want.

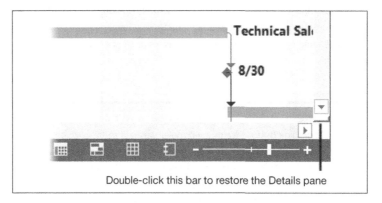

Double-click this bar to restore the Details pane

Figure 2-9. *When you hide the Details pane, you can change the view in the primary pane as many times as you want. When you restore the Details pane, it shows the view it contained when you hid it.*

Resetting a View

Suppose you modified a built-in view, such as the Gantt Chart, in several ways, such as adding columns and altering the timescale, and now you want to return the view to its original state. Here's how to reset a built-in view to the settings it had when you installed Project:

1. Display the view you want to restore to its original settings, in this example, Gantt Chart.

2. On the Task tab, click the bottom half of the Gantt Chart button, and then, on the drop-down menu, choose "Reset to Default."

   The built-in view reverts to the settings it had when you first installed Project.

> **Note:** You can't reset custom views that you create. If a custom view is active, "Reset to Default" is grayed out on the drop-down menu.

Taming the Project Ribbon

Now that you've finished your Project tour, you might want to master a few handy tricks to simplify working with the ribbon. The ribbon takes up a broader swath at the top of the main Project window than the menu bar used to. If you want to reserve your screen real estate for your project schedule, the ribbon will obligingly take up less space. This section describes a couple of methods for reducing the size of the ribbon.

Once you're familiar with which commands reside on which tabs, you can collapse the ribbon to a trimmer profile. To collapse the ribbon to something more like the old menu bar, use any of these methods:

- Double-click the active ribbon tab.

- Right-click the ribbon and then choose Minimize or "Collapse the Ribbon" (depending on what version you have).

- Click the up arrow at the bottom right of the ribbon.

Choosing commands when the ribbon is collapsed is almost the same as choosing them when the ribbon is visible. To choose a feature on a tab, click the tab's name (the tab appears). Choose the command you want, and the tab disappears. The only difference is that you have to click the tab to open it each time you want to choose a command on it, even if you want to use two commands in a row that are on the same tab. For example, to change the task mode to Auto Scheduled and then insert a new task, you would first click the Task tab, and then, in the Tasks section, click Auto Schedule. Project would then collapse the ribbon, so you'd have to click the Task tab again, and in the Insert section, click Task.

To switch back to keeping the ribbon in view, double-click anywhere on the collapsed ribbon, or right-click any tab name, and then choose "Collapse the Ribbon" which toggles the feature off.

The ribbon also contorts itself to fit as you resize the Project window. For example, if you narrow the window (for example, by dragging the right edge of the window), the ribbon makes some buttons smaller by shrinking their icons or leaving out the icons' text. If you narrow the window dramatically, an entire section may be replaced by a single button, such as Insert, Properties, and Editing on the

Task tab shown in Figure 2-10. When you click the button, a drop-down panel displays all the hidden commands. In this example, after you examine the ribbon in a narrow window, drag the right edge of the Project window to the right to widen it.

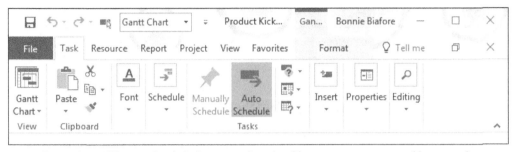

Figure 2-10. *When you shrink the Project window, the ribbon rearranges sections and buttons to fit.*

> **Tip:** If you prefer to keep your fingers on the keyboard, you can trigger ribbon commands without the mouse. To unlock these shortcuts, press the Alt key. Letters appear below each tab on the ribbon. Press a key to pick a tab, and Project then displays letters under every button on that tab. Continue pressing the corresponding keys until you trigger the command you want. For example, to insert a task with the Insert Task command, press Alt, and then press the H key to open the Task tab. You see the letters "TA" below the Task button in the Insert section, so press the T key followed by the A key to display the drop-down menu. To insert a task, press T again.

Finding Commands on the Ribbon

If you can't find the command you want on the ribbon, you may be looking in the wrong place—or the command simply might not *be* on the ribbon. To see where a command resides on the ribbon, do the following:

1. Right-click anywhere on the ribbon, and then choose "Customize the Ribbon" on the drop-down menu.

   The Project Options dialog box opens to the Customize Ribbon screen.

2. Click the down arrow to the right of the "Choose commands from" box, and then choose All Commands.

   The list box below the "Choose commands from" box displays the complete list of Project commands.

> **Tip:** To determine whether you can't find a command because it isn't on the ribbon, in the "Choose commands from" drop-down list, choose "Commands Not in the Ribbon." If you find the command you're looking for in the list, you have to add it to a custom group (Chapter 22) to use it.

3. Scroll to the command you're looking for and position your pointer over the command's name.

A tooltip appears that tells you the ribbon tab, group, and name of the command. For example, if you point at the Assign Resources command, the tooltip reads "Resource tab | Assignments | Assign Resources (ResourcesAssign)," which means that the command is on the Resource tab in the Assignments section, and the command is labeled Assign Resources. The text in parentheses ("ResourcesAssign" in this example) is the name of the command if you're using Visual Basic.

> **Tip:** Chapter 22 explains how you can customize the ribbon to add tabs, sections (technically called custom groups), and commands.

ScreenTips and Smart Tags

ScreenTips and Smart Tags are two Project features that make only temporary appearances. ScreenTips pop into view when you position the mouse pointer over certain items onscreen, like the icons in the Indicators column in a table (that's the column whose header is an i in a blue circle). The ScreenTip for a date constraint icon tells you the type of constraint and the date. A Task Note icon displays a ScreenTip with part of the note. When you put your pointer over a button on the ribbon, a ScreenTip appears with a description of the command and the keyboard shortcut for triggering it. To learn about the purpose of a Project field or how it's calculated, position the pointer over a column header and read the ScreenTip that appears.

Smart Tags, on the other hand, appear when you perform certain Project actions that have a reputation for confusing beginners. For example, if you select a Task Name cell (for example, "Identify core event team") in a table and then press the Delete key, a Smart Tag appears to the left of the cell. When you click the Smart Tag's down arrow, Project displays options for deleting just the task name or the entire task, as illustrated in Figure 2-11. (In this example, click the "Delete the task name" option to clear the value in the Task Name cell. After you do that, press Ctrl-Z to restore the task name.) The Smart Tag icon you see depends on what you're trying to do. For example, if you edit a task's duration, then the icon is an exclamation point inside a yellow diamond.

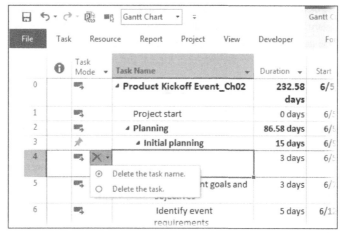

Figure 2-11. *When you press the Delete key when a task name cell is selected, a Smart Tag appears with options for deleting just the task name or deleting the entire task.*

Once you know Project inside and out, you probably don't need the help that Smart Tags offer. In that case, you can turn off different types of Smart Tags. To do that, click the File tab, and then choose Options. On the left side of the Project Options dialog box, choose Display. In the "Show indicators and options buttons for" section, turn off the checkboxes for the Smart Tags you don't want:

- Turning off the **"Resource assignments"** checkbox removes the Smart Tags that appear when Project needs more info about how to adjust a task when you change its resource assignments (such as shortening duration or increasing work).

- Turning off the **"Edits to work, units, or duration"** checkbox hides the Smart Tags that appear when you change a task's work, duration, or units and Project needs to know what you're trying to accomplish.

- The **"Edits to start and finish date"** checkbox controls whether Smart Tags prompt you for more info when you change a task's date.

- The **"Deletions in the Name column"** controls the Smart Tag that asks if you want to delete the task name or the entire task when you select a Task Name cell and then press the Delete key.

3

Setting Up a Project File

For days, weeks, sometimes months, you build the foundation of your project plan—the project's goal, objectives, scope, requirements, and so on. At long last, you're ready to build the project schedule, the map that guides what happens and when, from beginning to end. It tells everyone what work is required, who's supposed to do it, when it should be done, and how much it should cost. Something this fundamental to project management takes some preparation—and the next several chapters of this book—to construct.

The project schedule is where Microsoft Project becomes indispensable. In Project, you build a list of project tasks, link them to define their sequence, and assign resources and costs. This chapter is the first leg of this schedule-building journey. It begins with describing Project options you might want to change before you start working on any projects. Then, the chapter delves into creating and saving a new Project file, and defining calendars—that is, the working days and times for your project and resources.

When you're ready to learn more about managing Project files, the latter part of this chapter describes other ways to create Project files—whether you want to start from an existing project or template, or create a project from an Excel workbook or SharePoint Tasks List. You'll also discover shortcuts for opening and saving files. This chapter also provides tips on working with calendars: how to create new calendars and work weeks, modify existing ones, and set up recurring exceptions to working time.

Getting Started with Project Options

Microsoft Project comes with dozens of options so you can tell the program how you want it to behave. It automatically picks option settings, and many of those out-of-the-box settings may be just what you need. But you may want to change some of Project's default settings, such as making new tasks automatically scheduled or specifying the folder where you want to store your Project files. This section describes settings that you'll probably want to change.

To open the Project Options dialog box, click the File tab, and then, on the left side of the dialog box, choose Options. Although project options can be changed at any time, it's helpful to set them at the beginning. You can apply options to the active Project file or to all new projects. If you apply them to all new projects, then Project handles applying those settings each time you create a new Project file.

> **Note:** You'll find descriptions of Project options and tips for when you might want to change the standard settings scattered throughout this book. As you dig deeper into Project's features, you can adjust options to match how you work. To read about all the program's options in one place, head to online Appendix C, Project Options Reference.

Scheduling Options

The options in the Schedule category control how Project calculates schedules and other scheduling features. The Schedule category's "Scheduling options for this project" section contains several settings that you'll probably want to change from the ones that Project sets by default.

To access these options, on the left side of the Project Options dialog box (choose File→Options), click the Schedule category. Scroll down to the "Scheduling options for this project" section. In the box to the right of the section label, choose All New Projects, so these setting changes will apply to every project you create going forward. Here are the settings you might want to adjust:

- **New task created**: This box is initially set to Manually Scheduled, which means that you have to fill in the tasks' start and finish dates. That's fine if you're planning to import dates or want to type in dates without Project calculating them for you. Because you usually want Project to calculate the schedule based on task dependencies, resource assignments, and other factors, choose Auto Scheduled instead. If you choose Auto Scheduled, then in the "Auto scheduled tasks scheduled on" drop-down list, choose the date you want Project to use for new auto-scheduled tasks. Typically, you'll choose Project Start Date so new auto-scheduled tasks start on the project's start date. (Auto-scheduled tasks' dates change automatically when you link them to other tasks.)

- **New tasks are effort driven**: This setting is turned on initially. With effort driven scheduling turned on, you add resources to decrease task duration or want duration to increase when you remove resources. Effort-driven scheduling means the total work for a task remains the same when you add or remove resources. With this option turned off, Project handles task work the way meetings run—adding resources to a task increases the number of work hours and removing resources from a task decreases the number of work hours.

- **Autolink inserted or moved tasks**: This setting is turned on initially, so Project automatically adds and removes links between tasks as you create, move, or delete tasks. If you aren't watching closely, you might not notice that task dependencies have been added or removed. If you want to be in control of task dependencies, be sure to turn this checkbox off.

- **Tasks will always honor their constraint dates**: Although this checkbox is initially turned on, it's a good idea to turn it off. Here's why: Suppose a task has an inflexible date constraint (see Chapter 5) and a finish-to-start task dependency (Chapter 5); if the predecessor task runs late,

Project can't obey both the date constraint and the task dependency. When this setting is turned on, Project honors the date constraint, which means the two tasks overlap instead of following each other, but you *don't* get a warning that the overlap exists. By turning this checkbox off, Project maintains the task dependency so the tasks follow one another. If the task dependency pushes the successor task past its date constraint, Project warns you with a Missed Date indicator (as long as the Indicators column is included in a table).

Save Options

The options in the Save category control where Project saves files. To access these options, in the Project Options dialog box (choose File→Options), click the Save category, and then scroll to the "Save projects" section. Here are the settings you might want to adjust:

- **Default File location**: This option is particularly helpful when you don't save files in the Backstage. If you specify a folder in this box, and then later press F12 to save a new project, Project automatically displays the contents of the folder you specify here in the Save As dialog box.

- **Save to your computer**: Initially, this checkbox is turned off, which means that Project selects your OneDrive location automatically when you save a file. If you store your files on your computer, turn on this checkbox. That way, when you jump to the Backstage's Save As page, the program automatically selects Computer instead.

Creating a New Project File

Before you can build that schedule you're itching to get started on, you have to create a new Project file. This file is like a container that holds the project's tasks, its resources, and the relationships between them. This section describes a couple of ways to create a new Microsoft Project file.

> **Note:** See the section "More About File Management" later in this chapter to learn how to create new Project files using predefined templates, from an Excel workbook, or from an existing Project file.

Creating a Blank Project File

If you're starting an unconventional project or want to unleash your maximum creativity, a new blank Project file is like an empty canvas. Here are two easy ways to create a blank file:

- **From the Backstage**: Choose File→New. On the New page, at the top left of the set of template icons, click Blank Project, and voilà—Project creates a new blank file, called something like Project1.

- **With a keyboard shortcut**: Anytime the ribbon tabs are visible, simply press Ctrl+N to create a blank Project file.

Creating a Project from a SharePoint Tasks List

If you use Microsoft SharePoint, creating a list of tasks on a SharePoint site is an easy way to start a project schedule. For simple projects, creating and managing tasks on the SharePoint site may be enough. If your simple project morphs into something bigger, you can create a new Project file from a SharePoint Tasks List, and then use Project's more comprehensive tools to manage the schedule.

Here are the steps for creating a Project file from a Tasks List:

1. Click File→New.

2. On the New page, click the "New from SharePoint Tasks List" icon.

3. In the "Site URL" box, type the SharePoint URL for the site that contains the Tasks List you want to save to Project. Then, click Check Address.

    Don't include the name of the Tasks List in the URL. You specify that in the next step.

    When you click Check Address, Project connects to the SharePoint server and fills in the Tasks List drop-down list with the existing Tasks Lists on the site.

4. In the Tasks List drop-down list, choose the Tasks List you want to sync the Project file to.

5. Click Save.

    When the synchronization is complete, the tasks from SharePoint appear in the current Project view.

From now on, you can synchronize any changes you make in Project or SharePoint. See Chapter 28 to learn more.

Setting the Project Start Date and Other Properties

Projects rarely start on the day you create your Microsoft Project file. You usually have some business to take care of before the work begins, like obtaining project plan approvals or lining up funding. The project start date is the setting you're most likely to change in any Project file. This section describes how to set the project start date and a few other properties.

> **Tip:** To receive a reminder to set the project start date and other file properties, you can tell Project to ask you for that information whenever you create a new file. Choose File→Options, and then, on the left side of the Project Options dialog box, choose Advanced. In the General section, turn on the "Prompt for project info for new projects" checkbox, and then click OK to close the dialog box. Choose File→Close and restart Project. After that, whenever you create a new project, the Project Information dialog box appears.

Setting the Project Start Date

In Project, the project start date is the earliest date on which tasks are scheduled. When you create tasks in your Project file, the program automatically schedules them to start on the project start date (until you link them to other tasks). By default, Project sets the project start date for new projects to the date that you create the Project file. If work will begin on a different day, set the project start date to that day instead. If a task does start before the project start and you have scheduling messages turned on (they are by default), Project notifies you that the task starts before the project start.

Here's how to set the project start date for your Project file:

1. With the Project file open and active, in the Project tab's Properties section, click Project Information.

   The Project Information dialog box opens, as shown in Figure 3-1. If you created the file from scratch, Project sets the "Start date" box to today's date. If you create a new Project file from a template or an existing project, the "Start date" box contains the start date that was set in the original file.

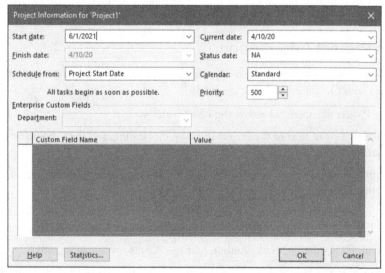

Figure 3-1. *Out of the box, the "Schedule from" box is set to Project Start Date, which is almost always what you want. When you set the start date, Project calculates the finish date for you.*

2. Most of the time, you'll want to keep the "Schedule from" box set to Project Start Date. With that setting in place, when you set the start date, Project calculates the finish date for you.

   You can schedule a project by entering a start date and working forward, or by entering a finish date and working backward. Although customers and executives always seem to have a finish date in mind, scheduling projects from the start date is usually the best approach. Entering a specific

---

Chapter 3: Setting Up a Project File

end date cripples one of Project's most powerful features—the ability to calculate a realistic end date based on tasks, resources, and work time.

If you know when the project can start, how long tasks should take, and the sequence in which tasks occur, Project spits out when the project should end. With a calculated end date, the first advantage is that you can show the stakeholders when the project can realistically finish. Armed with this information, you may be able to negotiate for a different deadline.

If the end date can't move, schedule from the start date anyway. That way, if the project deadline is earlier than the finish date that Project calculates, you can evaluate whether techniques like crashing or fast-tracking (described in Chapter 11) can shorten the schedule sufficiently.

3. In the "Start date" box, type or choose the date on which you expect work to begin, and then click OK. For example, to follow along with the sample project in this book, choose 6/21/2021.

If you choose a weekend day or other non-workday, Project adjusts the start date you entered to the next business day.

The "Finish date" box shows the date Project calculates for when the project will finish. If the Project file doesn't have any tasks yet, then the "Finish date" value is the same as the "Start date" value. The date in the "Finish date" box isn't meaningful until you've completely defined your project schedule.

Filling in Project Information

You can also add information about the project, like a title and keywords, to the Project file's properties as you can with files for other Office programs.

1. With the Project file open and active, choose File→Info.

2. Click the down arrow next to the Project Information heading, and then choose Advanced Properties.

3. In the "[project name] Properties" dialog box ([project name] is the filename prefix), fill in a title for the project, such as Product Kickoff Event.

When you save your file, Project automatically fills in the Title box with the filename prefix you specify. This Title box is also the Project Summary task or row 0 in a Project file.

4. If you want, fill in other fields like Author, Manager, Company, Category, and Keywords.

You can include the Title and Author fields in Project report headers; then, if this information changes, your report headers use the current values automatically. Any text in the Comments box appears in a note attached to the project summary task, so this box is a good place to write a brief summary of what the project is about. You can also search these fields in Windows Explorer (type keywords in the Search box).

Defining Working and Non-working Times with Calendars

The amount of available working time has a big impact on how quickly a project finishes. A mission-critical project to beat the competition to market might opt for longer workdays during the week with some weekend overtime as well. On the other hand, if you're building a vacation house on a tropical isle, you might have to adjust the working time for the more relaxed work schedules that hot sun and siestas induce. You need a calendar to indicate which days and times are available for work.

In Microsoft Project, *calendars* spell out working and nonworking days and times. You can use one of the program's built-in calendars, modify existing calendars, or build brand-new ones for unusual work schedules. Then you can apply a calendar to an entire project to set the standard working times, which is perfect for specifying the holidays for your organization. You can also define and apply calendars to individual people or to tasks.

To keep Project's work and duration calculations accurate, it's important that the number of hours Project uses for duration match the hours those durations represent in your organization's typical work schedules. Project's calendar options control how the program converts durations into hours of work.

This section covers selecting the project calendar you want to use, defining its working and non-working times, and then setting calendar options to match your project's working times. To learn how to customize calendars even more, see the section "More About Calendars" later in this chapter.

Choosing a Project Calendar

Assigning a calendar to a project sets the standard working days and times for the entire project. For most projects, the project calendar looks a lot like your organization's work schedule—its standard workdays, the official start and end of the workday, the time off for lunch, and official holidays. But some projects follow a different drummer. For instance, construction work on a busy highway might take place from 9 p.m. to 5 a.m. to minimize agonizing gridlock during rush hour.

Project comes with three built-in *base calendars*, which are calendar templates you can use as-is or modify to represent your organization's work schedule:

- **Standard**: Sets working time to Monday through Friday from 8 a.m. to 5 p.m. with an hour for lunch from 12 p.m. to 1 p.m., shown in Figure 3-2.

- **Night Shift**: Sets working times from Monday through Friday from 11 p.m. to 8 a.m. with lunch from 3 a.m. to 4 a.m.

- **24 Hours**: Schedules work 24 hours a day, 7 days a week. Although many high-pressure projects *feel* like they run on 24-hour schedules, this calendar is suitable for projects that *actually* run three shifts or tasks that run 24 hours a day.

Tip: When you customize one of these built-in calendars, such as Standard, Project stores the customized calendar in your Project file. If you send the file to someone who has their own customized version of the calendar, your file will still use the calendar you set up.

Note: When using Project Online or Server, an enterprise calendar will override local calendars by default. Enterprise calendars control organization-wide project scheduling

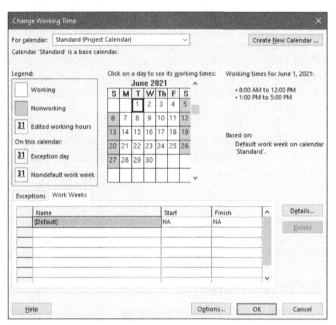

Figure 3-2. *Project automatically assigns the Standard calendar to new projects you create. This calendar comes without any days off for holidays, so you should change this calendar to add holidays or tweak working times.*

When you create a new project, Project automatically assigns the Standard calendar to it. To use a different project calendar, follow these steps:

1. With the project open, in the Project tab's Properties section, click Project Information.

    The Project Information dialog box opens.

2. In the Calendar drop-down menu, shown in Figure 3-1, choose the calendar you want, whether it's a built-in calendar or one you've customized, and then click OK.

    If you open the Change Working Time dialog box (on the Project tab in the Properties section, click Change Working Time), then in the "For calendar" box, you see "(Project Calendar)" to the right of the name of the calendar that the entire project uses. The working and nonworking time for all tasks and resources without special calendars conform to the project calendar work schedule.

What Resource and Task Calendars Do

You can also apply calendars to resources and tasks (which you'll learn more about later in this book):

- **Resource calendar**: A resource calendar is ideal when an individual or several resources work specialized schedules. If your project spans multiple shifts, then you can define a calendar for each shift and apply the shift calendar to the folks who work that shift. For the ultimate in schedule accuracy, you can edit a resource's calendar to reserve dates for scheduled vacations. That way, you can see whether your schedule needs tweaking to deliver a deadline before a key resource heads out of town. Chapter 6 describes how to assign a calendar to a resource.

- **Task calendar**: Most tasks run according to the project calendar and any resource calendars applied to the assigned resources. But occasionally, tasks follow their own schedules, like performing server maintenance when it causes the least disruption. Applying a calendar to a task is ideal to specify offbeat work times that apply only to that task. Chapter 5 explains how to assign a calendar to a task.

Defining Work Weeks and Holidays

Resources aren't at your beck and call 24/7. Team members take vacations, attend training and conferences, and get sick. They may also work part time or work 4 long days and take Fridays off. Incorporating nonworking time and specialized work arrangements into calendars makes a Project schedule more likely to forecast how the project will actually play out. This section describes how to define working and non-working time in Project calendars.

Project calendars offer two features for defining working and nonworking time: work weeks and exceptions. The following sections explain what each one does and how to use them to specify workdays and non-workdays and times.

Understanding Work Weeks

Work weeks identify the workdays and non-workdays in a 7-day week, as well as the work hours for each workday. The [Default] work week, which Project adds to a calendar by default, applies to all dates. When a work schedule lasts several weeks or months, with different workdays and times—like a stint of 10-hour days Monday through Saturday to meet a crucial deadline, you can set up an additional work week for that. You tell Project the date range within which that work week schedule applies and define the work week (by clicking the Details button in the Change Working Time dialog box). Project then modifies the current calendar to use that work week between the start and stop dates you specified.

You can set up more than one work week within the same Project calendar, which is great if your organization has different work schedules at different times during the year. Here are some examples of why you might create additional work weeks:

- **Company-wide work schedules**: Create additional work weeks when your company has a summer-schedule work week, a winter-schedule work week, and the standard work week in force the rest of the year.

- **Extended company-wide nonworking time**: You can also set up a work week for company-wide *nonworking* time that lasts one or more weeks—for example, a factory shutdown for the last two weeks of the year.

> **Note:** You can't create a work week that applies to several non-adjacent time periods. For example, suppose you set up a summer-schedule work week. You can't create the work week to recur every summer. Instead, you have to define a summer work week for the summer of 2020, another summer work week for the summer of 2021, and so on.

- **Resource work schedules**: Work weeks in a resource calendar are great when someone works an altered schedule for a few weeks or months; for example, when someone works half-days for two months while recuperating from an illness. You simply select the resource calendar and then create a work week for the recuperation schedule.

Understanding Exceptions

Exceptions are primarily for nonworking time, like company holidays, but you can also use them for alternate work schedules that run for a shorter period of time. In a Project calendar, you create a separate exception for each company holiday or other special day. Later in this chapter, you'll see how to set up recurring exceptions—for example, to schedule a non-workday once a quarter for the ever-popular all-hands meeting.

Consider using calendar exceptions for the following situations:

- **Single days with a different schedule**: A company holiday and a half-day for a corporate meeting are perfect examples of single-day exceptions.

- **Multiple days with a different schedule**: For example, you can set a modified schedule for a multiday training class that someone attends or a series of short days when the auditors are in town.

- **Recurring changes**: Use exceptions to specify altered work times that occur on a regular schedule, like company meetings or monthly server maintenance.

- **Altered work schedules longer than a week**: You can use an exception for a schedule change that lasts longer than a week as long as all the days of the exception are either nonworking days or have the same working times. (For that reason, work weeks and exceptions work equally well for factory shutdowns and people's vacations.)

Defining a Work Week's Working and Nonworking Days and Times

Every calendar in a Project file comes with one work week. When you select a calendar and select the Work Weeks tab, the name of the first entry is [Default]. The Start and Finish cells are set to NA, which means that the work week applies to all dates.

> **Note:** Initially, the [Default] work week considers weekdays as workdays and weekends as non-workdays. To set different work times on specific days, you have to specify those work times in calendar work weeks. Also, when you specify start and end times for work hours for calendar days, make sure the start and end work times you specify in Project's calendar options (see the section "Setting Calendar Options") are set to the same times.

Suppose your organization's standard work week is Monday through Friday from 9 AM to 6 PM with lunch from noon to 1 PM. Here's how you define workdays and work hours for a work week using that example:

1. In the Change Working Time dialog box, select the calendar, and then click the Work Weeks tab.

2. In the Work Weeks table, click the cell that contains the name of the work week you want to modify (for example, the built-in workweek "[Default]").

    If you haven't added any additional work weeks, the only entry you see in the Work Weeks tab is "[Default]" in the Name cell of Row 1.

3. To specify the workdays and times, click Details.

    The Details dialog box appears with the heading "Details for <work week name>" as shown in Figure 3-3.

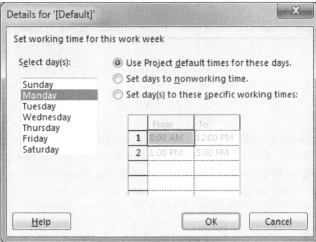

Figure 3-3. *If you select a workday, you see the current work hours in the working-time table. If you select a nonworking day, the table is empty.*

4. In the "Select day(s)" list, select the day(s) you want to modify. In this example, drag over Monday through Friday.

    To select a single day, click it. To select several adjacent days, drag over the days (or click the first day and Shift-click the last). To select nonadjacent days, Ctrl-click each day you want to select.

    If you select multiple days that use different settings, none of the options in the dialog box are selected and the working-time table is blank. When all selected days use the same settings, Project shows the common work times in the working-time table.

5. Select the appropriate working-time option.

    When you're modifying the [Default] work week, the initial setting for every day of the week is "Use Project default times for these days," which sets weekdays as workdays and weekends as non-workdays, and sets the work times from 8 AM to 5PM with lunch from 12 PM to 1PM. If you're modifying another work week, the label reads "Use times from the default work week times for these days."

    To change a workday to a non-workday (for example, to change Friday to a non-workday), select the "Set days to nonworking time" option.

    To change the work hours for any workday, select the "Set day(s) to these specific working times" option. This option makes the working-time table editable, so you can change the work hours for the selected days. In addition to changing work hours, use this option to change a non-workday (like a weekend day) to a workday. Because the example work week uses different work hours, in this example, select this option to edit the working times.

> **Note:** Project recognizes a few shortcuts in the working-time table. For example, if you type 8 in a cell, Project fills in 8:00 AM. In fact, Project switches to an a.m. time whenever you type a number from 7 to 11. Project changes the number 12 and the numbers from 1 to 6 to p.m. times; for instance, 12 becomes 12:00 PM. To enter a time including a.m. or p.m., simply type a value like 8 pm.
>
> If you type a time in a From cell that's later than the To time, Project automatically adjusts the To time to be one hour later than the From time. For example, suppose the first set of work times run from 8:00 a.m. to 12:00 p.m. If you change the From cell to 1:00 PM, then Project changes the To cell to 2:00 PM.
>
> Overlapping times in different rows are a problem. For instance, suppose you enter work times of 1:00 PM to 5:00 PM in the first row and 4:00 to 5:00 PM in the second row. Project doesn't complain until you click OK, when it warns you that the start of one shift has to be later than the end of the previous shift. Click OK and remove the overlap.

6. To change the work hours in an existing entry in the table, click the cell, and then type the new time. In this example, click the first From cell, type 9, and then press Enter. In the second row, click the To cell, type 6, and then press Enter.

When you click a cell in the working-time table, Project selects the cell's entire contents, so you can simply start typing to change the value. Working-time text boxes behave like all other text boxes. You can edit times by clicking to position the insertion point, or by dragging to select the text you want to edit.

7. To specify working times for other days, repeat steps 4–6. You don't have to do this in the example.

> **Note:** To add a new row of working times, click the first blank From cell, and then type the starting time. For example, suppose you switch to 14-hour days and add a second break in the late afternoon. You can add a new row for the third set of work hours. In this example, you don't have to add another row.
>
> To remove a row of work times, click either the From or To cell, and then press Delete. Project removes the times in both the From and To cell. For example, to change a full workday to a half workday, you can delete the after-lunch work hours.

8. When you're done, click OK to close the Details dialog box.

Setting Aside Holidays and Other Exceptions to the Work Schedule

Work weeks assign the same schedule of workdays and times over a specific period of time. As their name implies, calendar *exceptions* are better for shorter changes to the work schedule. Here are the steps for defining an exception in a calendar:

1. In the Change Working Time dialog box, in the "For calendar" drop-down list, select the calendar (in this example, Standard), and then click the Exceptions tab.

    Project doesn't set up any exceptions automatically, so all the rows in the Exceptions table start out blank.

2. On the Exceptions tab, click the first blank Name cell, and then type a name for the exception, like *Thanksgiving*.

    You can create as many exceptions in a calendar as you need—to set each company holiday in the year, to reserve vacation time for a team member, or to specify different work hours for a particular day.

3. Click the Start cell in the same row, click the down arrow that appears in the cell, and then choose the first date to which the exception applies, for example, 11/25/2021. Click the Finish cell in the same row, and then choose the last date for the exception, in this example, the next day, 11/26/2021.

    Start and finish dates can be the same day, a few days apart, or any two dates you want. The only restriction is that all the days within that date range must be either non-workdays or have the same working times.

4. To define the days and times for the exception, click Details.

    The "Details for <calendar name>" dialog box opens. Because many exceptions are holidays and other days off, Project automatically selects the Nonworking option at the top of the dialog box.

5. For one nonworking day, simply click OK. If the exception represents more than one adjacent days, in the "Range of recurrence" section, select the "End by" option, and then choose the last date for the exception in the date box (11/26/2021, in this example). Then, click OK.

The Details dialog box closes, and the exception is waiting for you on the Exceptions tab.

Exceptions can also represent short exceptions to working time, for example, two long work days to set up and run the product kickoff event. To create a working time exception, do the following:

1. On the Exceptions tab, click the first blank Name cell, and type the exception name, such as *Product kickoff*.

2. Click the Start cell in the same row, click the down arrow that appears in the cell, and then choose the first date to which the exception applies, in this example, 4/11/2022.

3. Click the Finish cell in the same row, and then choose the last date for the exception, in this example, the next day, 4/12/2022.

4. Click Details to open the Details dialog box.

5. Select the "Working times" option.

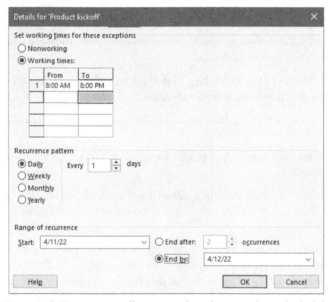

Figure 3-4. *Exceptions usually represent short changes to the work schedule.*

6. Set the working times in the "Working times" table, as shown in Figure 3-4.

For example, to set the two days to an 8 AM to 8 PM schedule, click the label in the second row, and then press Delete. Click the first From cell and type "8". Then, click the first To cell, and type 8 pm. Press Enter.

7. In the "Range of recurrence" section, select the "End by" option, and then choose 4/12/2022 in the date box.

8. Click OK to close the Details dialog box.

The exception appears in the Exceptions table.

Setting Calendar Options

Calendars specify working days and times. But calendar options, stored in the Project Options dialog box, tell Project how to translate durations for those working times into hours of work. For example, if the "Hours per week" option is set to 40, a task with a 2-week duration represents 80 work hours. But if "Hours per week" is set to 35, then a 2-week task represents only 70 hours of work. Because calendar options and calendar work times have to match, calendar options can be different for each project, as Figure 3-5 shows.

> **Warning:** Project doesn't warn you when your calendar options and project calendar don't jibe, so it's a good idea to make sure they do. Project uses the calendar options to convert one time period into another—for instance, to calculate the work hours that correspond to a duration you enter in weeks. If the calendar options and the calendar disagree, Project's duration conversions will create confusing results in resource assignments.
>
> Suppose the Hours Per Day option is set to 6 hours. For a task with a 5-day duration, Project multiplies the 5 days by 6 hours per day to get task work of 30 hours. Someone assigned to the task at 100 percent may work 8-hour days according to the project calendar. But when Project converts workdays into work hours, it thinks he's working only 6 hours a day because of the Hours Per Day option. The solution is to set the number of work hours per day in your calendar options to match the number of work hours per day in the default work week in the calendar.

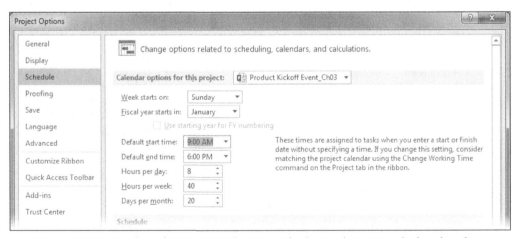

Figure 3-5. *You can choose the project to apply settings to by choosing the project in the drop-down list to the right of the "Calendar options for this project" label.*

Project's out-of-the-box calendar options are perfect for your typical 8-to-5 operation. Usually, a quick glance at these options confirms that they fit your organization's schedule, and you can move on to other project-management duties. To view Project's calendar options, choose File→Options. In the Project Options dialog box, click Schedule. Here are the options you can set and what each one does:

- **Week starts on**: This option specifies the first day of the week in your schedule and is initially set to Sunday, which is usually fine. You might change this option when you exchange actual project values with your corporate time-tracking system, for example, so both programs start work weeks on the same day of the week.

> **Tip:** If your organization uses an unusual work schedule for all its projects and you want to adjust the calendar options to follow suit, then in the drop-down list to the right of the "Calendar options for this project" label, choose All New Projects to apply the current calendar options to all new (not existing) projects. If you want to change the settings for existing projects, you have to open each project and follow the instructions in this section to change the calendar options.

- **Fiscal year starts in**: You need to change this option only when your organization's fiscal year starts in a month other than January *and* you want to produce fiscal-period reports in Project. When you set the month for the fiscal year, the Gantt Chart timescale displays the fiscal year. For example, if the fiscal year begins in July, then September 30, 2020, appears under the 2021 fiscal year. If you set the "Fiscal year starts in" box to a month other than January, the "Use starting year for FY numbering" checkbox springs to life. Turning on this checkbox sets the fiscal year to the calendar year in which the fiscal year begins. For example, with this checkbox turned on and the fiscal year set to start in July, July 2020 is in fiscal year 2020. With this checkbox turned *off* and the fiscal year set to start in July, July 2020 is the beginning of fiscal year 2021. For more on fiscal years, see Chapter 15.

- **Default start time**: For most tasks, the start time depends on when predecessor tasks finish. The time in this box affects a task's start time only when you create a task and specify a start date without a start time. This option is set to 8:00 a.m. initially. If your workday starts earlier or later, adjust the value of this box accordingly, in this example, 9:00 AM.

- **Default end time**: The finish time for most tasks depends on when the task begins and how long it takes. The time in this box becomes the finish time for a task only when you specify a task's finish date without specifying a finish time. This box is set to 5:00 p.m. initially. If your workday ends earlier or later, adjust this value accordingly, in this example, 6:00 PM.

- **Hours per day**: Sets the number of working hours for a single workday. For example, with the standard setting of 8.00, one workday represents 8 hours of work. Chapter 10 discusses approaches you can take when people aren't productive the entire workday.

- **Hours per week**: Defines the number of working hours in one week and is set to 40.00 initially.

- **Days per month**: This option is the conversion between days and months and is set to 20 workdays (4 weeks each with 5 workdays) per month initially.

Saving a Project File

Whether you create a file with a blank project or a template, you save it the first time by choosing File→Save. Project opens the Backstage view's Save As page so you're sure to save a new file. Project, like other Microsoft programs, automatically uses the Save As command whenever you save a file created from a template, so you can name the new file whatever you want. Most of the time, you choose a location, folder, and filename, and you're done. But Project mavens know that there are other handy tools for saving files in special ways, which are described later in this chapter.

> **Tip:** If you want to bypass the Backstage view's Save As page and jump directly to the Save As dialog box, simply press F12.
>
> Pressing Ctrl+S to open the Save As dialog box is a time-saving shortcut for saving files for the first time. (If you press Ctrl+S while working on a file that you've saved previously, Project simply re-saves the file.) To tell Project to do that, choose File→Options, and then, on the left side of the Project Options dialog box, choose Save. Turn on the "Don't show the Backstage when opening or saving files" checkbox, and then click OK.

Here are the steps for saving a new project, whether you store your files on your computer or in the cloud:

1. Choose File→Save.

    The Backstage view's Save As page appears (Figure 3-6).

Figure 3-6. *The Save As page includes a list of file-storage locations, including your computer, your One-Drive cloud storage, and SharePoint in case you use that program for collaborating with team members. You can add other locations by clicking "Add a Place."*

> **Tip:** If you opened an existing project and want to save it as a new one, then choose File Save As instead of File Save. Otherwise, all Project will do is save any changes you made to the existing project.

2. On the left side of the Save As page, select where you want to save the new file, such as This PC.

When you select a location, a list of recent folders appears on the right side of the page. (In case you grow weary of these file-saving steps, the section "File Saving Shortcuts" later in this chapter offers several timesavers for saving files.)

3. Select the location where you want to save your file.

If the name of the folder you want appears on the right side of the Save As page, simply click its name, and the Save As dialog box opens to that folder.

If the folder where you want to save the project *isn't* in the Recent Folders list, then click Browse to open the Save As dialog box. Then navigate to the folder (in this example, the folder where you store the sample files).

4. In the "File name" box, type a name for the project.

Short but meaningful filenames—like ***ProductKickoffEvent***—help you and your colleagues find the right files. In addition, it's best to not use spaces in filenames. Spaces can lead to issues, such as seeing "%20" in place of a space, in applications such as SharePoint and Project Server.

> **Tip:** Don't include a date in your working Project file. That way, files pinned to the file list (and other shortcuts based on the file name) will always access your latest copy. On the other hand, when you save an archive version of the file, it's a good idea to append the save date to the file name.

5. Leave the "Save as type" drop-down list set to Project to create a regular Project .mpp file, and then click Save.

If Windows Explorer is set up to show file extensions, the "Save as type" drop-down list includes the file extension, such as "Project (*.mpp)." See the section "Saving Projects to Other File Formats" later in this chapter to learn about the different file formats in which you can save Project files, and when to use them. If you suspect that your file is corrupt, save it to an earlier version of Project, re-open it, and save it to the current Project format. That process might eliminate the corruption.

> **Tip:** To automatically associate your name and initials with files you create, in Project, choose File Options. In the Project Options dialog box, choose General. Under "Personalize your copy of Microsoft Office," type your name and initials in the "User name" and Initials boxes.

Opening a Project File

This section explains how to open files in the Backstage view. Later in this chapter, you can learn about shortcuts for opening files.

> **Tip:** To bypass the Backstage view's Open page and jump straight to the Open dialog box, press Ctrl+F12.

Here's how you open files using Project's Backstage view:

1. Choose File→Open.

   The Backstage view's Open page appears and displays a list of recent projects, as shown in Figure 3-7.

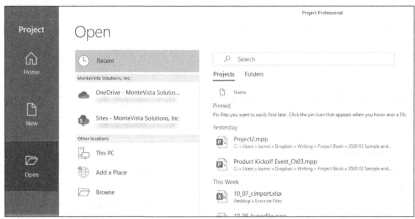

Figure 3-7. *The Open page initially shows projects you've worked on recently. If the project you want to open appears in the list, simply click its name to open it.*

2. If you recently worked on the project you want to open, click its name on the right side of the Open page.

   Project immediately opens the file, so you can skip the rest of the steps in this list.

3. If the project you want to open isn't listed, on the left side of the Open page, select where you stored the file, such as This PC or OneDrive. Alternatively, to show a list of recent folders, click Folders underneath the Search box.

   Depending on the location you select, the right side of the Open page might display a list of recent folders or a list of recent Project files.

4. If the Open page displays a list of folders, choose the folder where the file is stored to open it.

   If the folder *isn't* in the Recent Folders list, click Browse. In the Open dialog box, navigate to the folder.

5. In the file list on the right side of the dialog box, click the name of the project you want to open.

More About File Management

Working with Project files is a regular occurrence when you use Microsoft Project to manage projects, so it's worth learning the tricks of the Project file-management trade. This section dishes out helpful tips about managing Project files.

More Ways to Create Project Files

Projects, by definition, are unique endeavors, so you might think that a template won't be much help for creating a new Project file. But it turns out that the basic tasks for similar projects are often pretty much the same, even if the dates, team members, and results are different. If you have a task list or other project info in an Excel workbook, you can populate a new Project file with that data. Even an existing Project file can be called into play to create a Project file for a new project. This section explains how to create a Project file using all these methods.

Using a Template to Create a Project File

Templates can jumpstart a new file, because they contain elements that are common to many other projects. Just edit the tasks, names, dates, and so on to match your current project. Templates usually include typical tasks linked to one another in a logical sequence. Sometimes, they include durations if the work almost always takes the same length of time. You can create your own templates, not only with a sequence of tasks with estimated durations, resources, and resource assignments, but also to include customized elements like your company's working calendar, views, tables, reports, and so on, as Chapter 23 explains.

> **Tip:** Microsoft Project displays numerous templates on the Backstage's New page (File New). If you don't see a template that sounds like your project, you can search online for additional templates. Type keywords in the "Search for online templates" box, and then click the magnifying glass icon. For example, if you're planning to start a new business, type a keyword like "startup." Project displays a list of the templates it finds. To start a new Project file from one of these templates, click its icon and then click Create.
>
> If you use older files or templates to get started, don't switch between opening the files in older and newer versions of Project. Doing so can cause data corruption over time as well as losing functionality.

No matter where you get the template you want to use, the steps for creating a new project file from a template are similar:

1. Click File→New.

   The Backstage's New page appears with commands for creating Project files in different ways and choosing featured templates, as shown in Figure 3-8.

2. If a template's name sounds like it describes your project, click its icon.

If you choose a featured template, a dialog box opens, showing a thumbnail of the project, the name of the person or company that developed it, and a brief description.

> **Tip:** If you've created your own templates and set up a folder for them (described in Chapter 23), click the Personal heading below the search box, and then click the icon for the personal template you want to use. In the dialog box that appears, click the Create button to create a new Project file from that template. The section "Save Options" earlier in this chapter explains how to specify your templates folder in Project.

3. In the dialog box, click the Create button.

    If the template is an online template, Project downloads it and then creates a new file from it.

Presto! You're ready to work on or save your new file (described later in this chapter).

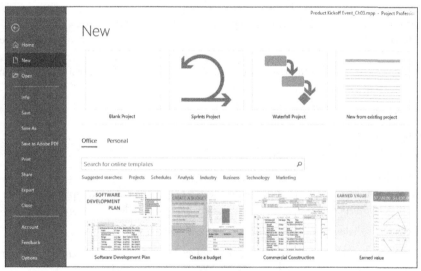

Figure 3-8. *The New page includes different ways to create a new project: a blank Project file, from an existing project, from an Excel workbook, and from a SharePoint Tasks List.*

Creating a Project File from an Excel Workbook

If you define tasks in an Excel workbook, you can import those tasks into Project. Here's the easiest way to do it:

1. Choose File→New.

2. Click the "New from Excel Workbook" icon.

    The Open dialog box appears. In the box to the right of the "File name" box, choose the file type for your Excel file: Excel Workbook, Excel Binary Workbook, or Excel 97-2003 Workbook. You can also choose Text (Tab delimited), CSV (Comma delimited), and XML Format, if the data is in one of those formats.

3. Double-click the name of the workbook.

    The Import Wizard opens. Chapter 25 explains how to bring tasks into Project from Excel.

You can also create a Project file from an Excel workbook with the Open command. Choose File→Open, and then select the location where you stored the Excel workbook (such as This PC and the folder). When the Open dialog box appears, in the file type drop-down list to the right of the "File name" box, choose Excel Workbook, click the Excel file you want, and then click Open. The Import Wizard launches to help you import tasks into Project (as described in Chapter 25).

Creating a New Project from an Existing Project

If you're scheduling a project similar to one you've done in the past, why not borrow those ready-made tasks and dependencies? However, you might not use the same people, monetary values, and other details of that old project. You could clear the values from all those fields, but that would take just as long as creating the new project from scratch. Although Project's New page contains a "New from existing project" command, clicking it simply opens the file you select so you can save it as a new file with a different name. This command doesn't remove any of the old values you want to leave behind.

The best way to turn an existing project into a *clean* new project is to create a template from the existing project. Here's what you do:

1. Open the existing project.

2. Immediately choose File→Save As.

3. Choose a location for the new file.

    For example, choose This PC or your OneDrive location, and then choose the folder where you want to store the file. If you plan to use the file as a new project and a template for future projects, then choose your personal templates folder (see Chapter 23 to learn how to specify it).

4. In the Save As dialog box's "File name" box, type a new name.

5. In the "Save as type" drop-down list, choose Project Template ("Project Template (*.mpt)" if you have Windows Explorer set to show file extensions), and then click Save.

6. In the Save As Template dialog box that opens, turn on the checkboxes for the data you want to *remove* from the project (not the data you want to keep). You can remove baseline values, actual values, resource rates, fixed costs, and whether tasks have been published to Project Web App—typically, you want to remove all of those.

7. Click Save to close the dialog box. Project creates a template file, which uses an *.mpt* file extension, and opens it.

8. Now, to save that template as a new squeaky-clean Project file, choose File→Save As. Choose the location for the new Project file. In the Save As dialog box, make sure that the "Save as type" box is set to Project, and then save the file in the folder you want, with the name you want.

File-Opening Shortcuts

Although File→Open is the tried and true method for opening Project files, the program offers several shortcuts for opening a file:

- **Jump directly to the Open dialog box**: Pressing Ctrl+F12 bypasses the Backstage and opens the Open dialog box. If you want Ctrl+O to open the Open dialog box the way it did in earlier versions of Project, choose File→Options, and then, on the left side of the Project Options dialog box, choose Save. In the "Save projects" section, turn on the "Don't show the Backstage when opening or saving files" checkbox and then click OK.

- **Open recent projects**: When you choose File→Open, the Backstage's Open page displays several recent projects (shown earlier in Figure 3-7). Simply click a filename in this list to open it. Or underneath the Search box, click Folders to display a list of recently accessed folders.

- **Specify how many recent projects appear in this list**: Choose File→Options. In the Project Options dialog box, choose Advanced. Scroll to the Display section. Change the value in the "Show this number of Recent Projects" box to control how many projects appear on the Backstage's Open page.

- **Pin projects to the Recent Projects list**: If you work on a few projects for months at a time, you can pin them to the top of the Open page so they won't be replaced by other files. Point to the filename in the recent projects list, and then click the angled pushpin icon that appears to the right of the filename. The project name leaps into the Pinned category at the top of the page, as shown in Figure 3-9.

- **Choose recent projects on the Start page**: The Start page is like the Backstage's New and Open pages rolled into one. You'll see files you've worked on recently. To select a recent project, click its name. To open other projects, click "more projects" at the screen's bottom right.

  To tell Project to display the Start page when you launch the program, choose File→Options. On the left side of the Project Options dialog box, click General, and then, in the "Start up options" section, turn on the "Show the Start screen when this application starts" checkbox.

- **Display projects on the Backstage's menu**: When you click the File tab, the Backstage view opens with a menu on its left side. You can display projects on that menu so you don't have to choose Open in the menu. To set this shortcut up, choose File→Options. In the Project Options dialog box, choose Advanced. Scroll to the Display section, and then turn on the "Quickly access this number of Recent Projects" checkbox and type the number you want. Project displays that number of recent projects, starting with projects that are pinned to the Recent Projects list. Click a filename to open that Project file.

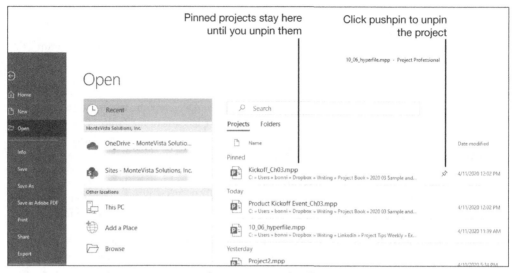

Figure 3-9. *When you pin projects to the Recent Projects list, they remain in the Pinned section of the Open page for quick access until you unpin them (click the pushpin to unpin a project).*

- **Open the last file you worked on when Project launches**: If you work on only one project at a time, a slick shortcut is to have Project open the last file you worked on automatically. That way, each time you launch Project, your latest project is waiting for you. Choose File→Options. In the Project Options dialog box, choose Advanced. In the General section, turn on the "Open last file on startup" checkbox and then click OK.

File-Saving Shortcuts

After you save a file for the first time, you can prevent untold grief by getting into the habit of frequently pressing Ctrl+S to save your file as you work. The old adage "Save early, save often" applies just as much to Project as it does to old favorites like Word and Excel. This section describes options and keyboard shortcuts that can help you save files in no time. To access the options described in this section, choose File→Options, and then on the left side of the Project Options dialog box, choose Save.

Setting File Format and Location

You can tell Project the file format and storage location to use when you create and save your projects. These settings are located below the "Save projects" heading:

- **File format**: Initially, Project is set up to save files using the Project (*.mpp) format. However, you can specify another file format if, for example, your colleagues still use Project 2007. In the "Save files in this format" drop-down list, choose the format you want, such as Microsoft Project 2007 (*.mpp). You can also choose Project Template (*.mpt) if, for instance, it's your job to create template files for the project managers in your organization.

- **File location**: If you specify a folder in the "Default File location" box, whenever the Save As dialog box opens, it automatically opens to that folder.

Setting up Project to Save Automatically

If you've lost work in the past because you forgot to save files often enough, you'll be happy to know that Project can automatically save your work every so often. You can tell the program to ask you whether you want to save, as well as which projects to save. Use these options below the "Save projects" heading to control how Project automatically saves projects:

- **Auto save frequency**: To tell Project to save your files automatically without any action on your part, turn on the "Auto save every __ minutes" checkbox, and then type a number of minutes in the box. For example, 45 minutes is a good trade-off between security and interruption.

  > **Note:** Auto Save saves your Project files with any changes you've made. That means that if you're playing what-if with a schedule, Auto Save could make the current scenario permanent. In addition, you won't be able to undo any changes after Project auto-saves the file. However, Auto Save is indispensable if you get lost in schedule work and forget to save for hours.

- **Active or all files**: Unless you change it, Project selects the option to save only the *active* file (the one you're currently working on). If you work on several files simultaneously and want to save them all, select the "Save all open projects" option instead.

- **Prompt before saving**: If you want Project to ask permission before saving a file, keep the "Prompt before saving" checkbox turned on so the program asks whether or not to save a project.

Settings for Saving to your Computer and the Cloud

Project makes it easy to work with files whether they're stored on your computer or in the cloud. So it's no surprise that the program has a few options related to opening and saving files. Here's what the options at the end of the "Save projects" section do:

- **Open the Open and Save As dialog boxes directly**: If you store files on your computer, you don't need more steps for opening and saving files. Initially, the "Don't show the Backstage when opening or saving files" checkbox is turned off, which means that choosing File→Open takes you to the Backstage's Open page, and choosing File→Save As displays the Backstage's Save As page. To open the Open and Save As dialog boxes with a single keyboard shortcut, turn this checkbox off. Then, you can press Ctrl+O to jump straight to the Open dialog box, and press F12 to jump right to the Save As dialog box.

- **Show all storage locations**: Out of the box, the "Show additional places for saving, even if sign-in may be required" checkbox is turned on. With this setting on, the Save As page shows *every* location you've set up for file storage, even if you have to sign in to access it. If you're working offline and don't want to be distracted by file locations you can't use, then turn this checkbox off.

- **Save to your computer**: Initially, when you try to open or save a file, Project selects your One-Drive location automatically. If you store your files on your computer, turn on the "Save to Computer by default" checkbox to make the Backstage view's Save As page automatically select Computer instead and show the recent folders you've used to save files.

> **Note:** The Cache section includes two additional settings, which let you save projects locally to a cache in case you're disconnected from Project Server or Project Online, for example. When you're back online, you can publish your updates from the cache to Project Server or Project Online. You can specify the size of the cache and where it's stored.

Saving Projects to Other File Formats

The most common file format for a Project file is the .mpp file extension, which stands for Microsoft Project Plan. Project can open .mpp files created in Project 2010, 2007, 2003, 2002, 2000, and 1998. However, people with earlier versions of Project can't always open .mpp files created in more recent Project versions, so you may have to save your files in these *legacy formats* (Microsoft's term for earlier file formats). In addition, you can save Project files in other formats to do things like use Excel to analyze costs, or to publish project information to the Web. (Chapter 25 covers exporting from and importing to Project using different file formats.)

To save a Project file in another format, choose File→Save As, and then select the location and folder in which you want to save the file. Then, from the "Save as type" drop-down list, choose the format you want. Here are some occasions when you might choose other formats:

- **Working with earlier versions of Project**: If a colleague uses an earlier version of Project, you can save a Project file that opens in those versions by choosing Microsoft Project 2007. Project warns that you may lose data from Project's new enhanced features and lists the changes or omissions that come with saving to the earlier format. If you use Project to open files created in Project 2007 or earlier, you can edit them, although with reduced functionality.

- **Exporting data to Excel**: If you want to export data from Project fields to a spreadsheet (to create a budget from estimated costs, say), then choose Excel Workbook, Excel Binary Workbook, or Excel 97-2003 Workbook. When you save in these formats, Project launches the

Export Wizard, which steps you through selecting and exporting the data you want in the way you want. You can also *import* Excel spreadsheets into Project. Chapter 25 has the full scoop on importing and exporting.

- **Exporting Project data to use in other programs**: As you manage projects, other programs are sometimes better tools for working with data—creating a WBS, estimating, or managing risk, for example. Depending on the format that the other program reads, choose "Text (Tab delimited)" or "CSV (Comma delimited)" to create a file in a generic text format. When you save in these formats, Project saves just the active table (the table area in the left pane of the view), not the entire project.

- **Publishing to the Web or interchanging data**: If you want to publish a project online or use extensible markup language (XML) to exchange structured data, choose "XML format."

- **Creating a viewable file:** Choose PDF Files or XPS Files when you want to share or print a view of your project.

> **Tip:** Saving a file to an earlier version of Project or to XML and then saving it back to the most recent Project file format might eliminate corruption in the file.

Project's factory settings don't let you open or save files in older (legacy) Project file formats or to other formats like database-file formats (called *non-default formats*). So if your and your compatriots' files are in older formats, one of the first actions to take after installing Project is to tell it to work with these older files. To save and open legacy and non-default formats, do the following:

1. Click File→Options→Trust Center.

2. In the Trust Center dialog box, click the Trust Center Settings button.

   The Trust Center lets you sprinkle your trust onto publishers, add-ins, macros, legacy formats, and more. In addition to the options for working with file formats, you can clear a few file properties when you save a file. On the left side of the Trust Center, click Privacy Options and then turn on the "Remove personal information from file properties on save" checkbox. This setting removes Author, Manager, Company, and Last Save By, presumably to cover your tracks when distributing a project to others.

3. Click Legacy Formats, and then select the Legacy Format option you want, as shown in Figure 3-10.

   Project automatically selects "Do not open/save file with legacy or non-default file formats in Project," but this option means that you can't work with existing files in older formats.

   If you have lots of files in legacy or non-default formats, then the most sensible option is "Allow loading files with legacy or non-default file formats," although this choice lowers your security level and increases the chance of your computer becoming infected by a virus embedded in a file. However, it lets you open and save legacy and non-default file formats without any interruptions. Otherwise, select the "Prompt when loading files with legacy or non-default file format" option so Project will ask if you want to open or save a file with an older or non-default format.

4. Click OK.

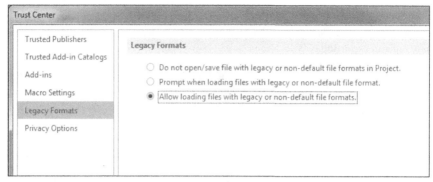

Figure 3-10. *If you select the "Prompt when loading files with legacy or non-default file format" option and then try to open an older file format or a file format that Project doesn't work with directly, a dialog box asks you whether you want to load the file. And when you save these types of files, Project asks whether you want to save them in the Project format (the most recent format).*

Protecting Your Project Files

At some point, you've probably been devastated by the disappearance of an important file. You can protect the work in your Project files from inadvertent changes by creating backup copies. Moreover, passwords can protect files from unauthorized editing.

Some security options don't appear in the Project Options dialog box. Instead, they're tucked away in the Save and Save As dialog boxes. If you choose File→Save while you're working on a Project file that you've already saved, the program immediately saves the file without opening a dialog box. So if you want to add security options to an existing file, choose File→Save As instead, and then select the location and folder in which you want to save the file. In the Save As dialog box, click Tools→General Options (to the left of the Save button); the Save Options dialog box opens. After you choose the security options you want (described below), click OK, and then click Save.

> **Tip:** Even if you open the Save As dialog box, you can save the file with the same name.

Here's what the settings in Project's Save Options dialog box can do for you:

- **Always create backup**: Creates a backup copy of a file when you first open it, so you can quickly eliminate all the changes from the current session. The file extension for a backup is .bak. To open a backup file, choose File→Open. In the Open dialog box, in the "Files of type" box, choose All Files. Select the backup file, which looks like *FileName.BAK*, and then click Open.

- **Protection password**: Sets a password that you have to type before Project will open the file. Without the password, the file can't be opened for editing or even to view as read-only. When you type a password in this text box and then click OK to close the Security Options dialog box, a Confirm Password dialog box opens, so you don't end up with a file you can't open due to a typo in the password. Retype the password, and then click OK.

When you open a file with a protection password, a Password dialog box opens. In the Password box, type the password, and then click OK. Project opens the file.

> **Note:** Suppose you want to remove the password from a file. To do that, open the file and fill in the password to open it. Then, when you save the file, open the Save Options dialog box and clear the password from the "Protection password" box before you click OK.

- **Write reservation password**: Sets a password that you have to type if you want to *edit* the file. (You can open the file as read-only without a password.) Type a password in this box and when you click OK to close the Security Options dialog box, a Confirm Password dialog box opens so you can retype the password.

  When you open a file with a write reservation password, a Password dialog box opens. To open the file for editing, in the Password box, type the password, and then click OK. If you want to open the file as read-only, click Read Only instead.

- **Read-only recommended**: When you open a file that has this check box turned on, a message box appears that tells you to open the file as read-only unless you need to write to it. To take Project's advice, click Yes; the file opens as read-only. To write to the file, click No.

More About Calendars

Earlier in this chapter, you learned how to modify project working and non-working times using Project's built-in Standard calendar as an example. In many cases, you'll need additional calendars than the ones that come with the program, for example, for specialized shifts. Within calendars, you may also need to create additional work weeks, for instance, to account for shorter work weeks during the summer or longer work weeks to meet a crucial deadline. This section explains creating Project calendars and workweeks, and provides a few tips for customizing them.

Creating New Calendars

Although you can modify the built-in Standard calendar, copying it to create a separate calendar for your organization's work and holiday schedule makes it easy to tell which calendar defines your organization's work time and days off. Then, if you use the Organizer to store that custom calendar in the Project global template (described in Chapter 23's "Sharing Custom Elements" section), and apply it as the project calendar for a new project (described earlier in this chapter), it'll know about your work weeks and time off.

Setting up work schedules for people and tasks is another reason to modify calendars. You could create a "Half time" calendar for the people who work the company's part-time schedule and specify the work times as 8 a.m. to 12 p.m. Then you apply that calendar to every resource who works mornings.

You can create as many calendars as you need. Whether you want to create a calendar for a project, resource, or task, the steps are the same: Create the new calendar, edit it to reflect the working and nonworking times, and then apply it. Here are the steps for creating a new calendar, using an evening shift as an example:

1. In the Project tab's Properties section, click Change Working Time.

    The Change Working Time dialog box opens. The "For calendar" box shows the calendar you've applied to this project. For example, "Standard (Project Calendar)" indicates that the Standard calendar is set as the project calendar for the current Project file.

2. Click Create New Calendar.

    The Create New Base Calendar dialog box appears, shown in Figure 3-11. **Base calendar** is Project's name for calendars that act as templates for other calendars. For example, the Standard calendar is a base calendar because you can use it as the foundation for other customized calendars.

Figure 3-11. *Project suggests that copying an existing calendar is the preferred way to create a new base calendar by automatically selecting the "Make a copy of" option.*

3. In the Name box, type a new name for the calendar, such as Evening Shift.

    If you copy an existing calendar, Project adds "Copy of" in front of the calendar's name, like "Copy of Standard" in Figure 3-11. If you create a new calendar, Project fills in the box with a name like Calendar 1. The best names are short but give you a good idea of the working time they represent, like Evening Shift.

> **Tip:** If your organization has many different work schedules, it's a good idea to use calendar names that indicate the work schedule they represent. For example, Standard 5d 8h is the standard work week with 5 8-hour workdays. Day 5d 10h would be a work week with 5 10-hour workdays.

4. Most of the time, it's easiest to keep the "Make a copy of ___ calendar" option selected.

    To use an existing calendar as your starting point, leave the "Make a copy of" option selected, and then, in the "Make a copy of _ calendar" drop-down list, choose the calendar you want.

    For a calendar that's very different from any you have already, you can create one from scratch by selecting the "Create new base calendar" option. If you do, you must specify all working and non-working days and times.

5. Click OK.

The Create New Base Calendar dialog box closes, and the new calendar's name appears in the "For calendar" box. Because this new calendar isn't assigned as the project calendar for the current project, only the calendar name appears in the box [it doesn't have "(Project Calendar)" after it]. (The section "Choosing a Project Calendar" earlier in this chapter explains how to make a calendar the project calendar.)

Now you're ready to set the calendar's working times, which is described in detail in the section "Defining a Work Week's Working and Nonworking Days and Times." For practice, edit the Evening Shift calendar so that work times are Monday through Friday from 3 PM to midnight with a meal break from 8 PM to 9 PM.

> **Tip:** You can copy calendars you create using the Organizer so they're available to other projects. The section "Sharing Customized Elements" in Chapter 23 tells you how.

Defining a New Work Week for a Calendar

Suppose you need to define an additional work week, for example, to reflect your organization's summer schedule. Every additional work week needs a name, start and stop dates, and the modified work schedule. Here are the steps for creating a new work week:

1. In the Change Working Time dialog box, in the "For calendar" drop-down list, select the calendar (in this example, Standard), and then click the Work Weeks tab.

   "[Default]" appears in the table's first row. If you've defined other work weeks, they appear in rows 2 and higher.

2. On the Work Weeks tab, click the first blank Name cell, and then type a meaningful name for the work week schedule, such as Summer 2021.

3. Click the Start cell in the same row, click the down arrow that appears in the cell, and then choose the first date to which the work week applies. Click the Finish cell in the same row, and then choose the last date to which the work week applies, as shown in Figure 3-12.

   When you click the down arrow in a Start or Finish cell, a calendar drop-down appears. Click the left arrow or right arrow to move one month into the past or future, respectively. To select a date, click the date in the monthly calendar. You can also type the date (like *6/7/2021*).

> **Tip:** If the date you enter is within the current month, you can type the day date and Project fills in the rest. For example, if the current date is 6/1/2021, you can type 7, and Project will fill in 6/7/2021.

4. To specify workdays and times, click Details. Then specify the workdays and times as described in the section "Defining a Work Week's Working and Nonworking Days and Times" earlier in this chapter.

For practice, define summer hours to be 8 AM to 7PM with an hour for lunch Monday through Thursday. Friday is a non-working day. When you set up additional work weeks with alternate work schedules, the calendar in the top half of the Change Working Time dialog box underlines the dates with non-standard workdays, as you can see for June 2017 in Figure 3-12.

5. When you're done, click OK to close the Details dialog box. Click OK to close the Change Working Time dialog box.

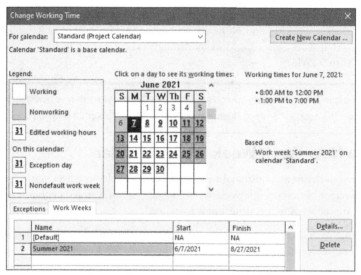

Figure 3-12. *If you click a day in the calendar at the top of the Change Working Time dialog box, Project displays the working times for that day, and the work week that applies to that day.*

Defining Recurring Exceptions

Sometimes, exceptions to the work week occur on a regular schedule—like the quarterly half-days of non-project working time for all-hands meetings or when your company takes every other Friday off. Recurring tasks and recurring exceptions have the same types of frequency settings. However, recurring tasks, which are explained in Chapter 4, represent project work that repeats, like a biweekly status meeting. Recurring exceptions represent work or nonwork schedules that repeat regularly.

The details for a calendar exception specify whether exception days are nonworking or working days (along with the work hours). The lower part of the "Details for <calendar name>" dialog box has options to set a frequency for the exception and when it starts or ends. Here are the steps for defining a recurring exception in a calendar, using a quarterly meeting as an example:

1. In the Change Working Time dialog box, select the calendar from the "For calendar" drop-down list, in this example, Standard, and then click the Exceptions tab.

2. In the table, enter the name, start date, and finish date as you would for a regular exception (described earlier in this chapter). In this example, say the "Quarterly meetings" exception starts on 1/1/2020 and finishes on 12/31/2025.

3. Click Details and specify the nonworking or working time settings for the days in the recurring exception, such as from 8:00 AM to 12:00 PM.

    The section "Defining a work week's working and nonworking days and times" earlier in this chapter describes how to specify nonworking and working times for days. With a Project calendar exception, every day of the exception must use the same settings. In this example, since the quarterly meetings are held in the morning, you can select the "Working times" radio button, and then click the second row in the table and press the Delete key to remove the afternoon work hours.

4. In the "Recurrence pattern" section, select the correct frequency option, as demonstrated in Figure 3-13.

    The options include Daily, Weekly, Monthly, and Yearly. The other settings that appear depend on which frequency option you select. For example, the Weekly option has a checkbox for specifying the number of weeks between occurrences (1 represents every week, 2 represents every other week, and so on) and checkboxes for the days of the week on which the event occurs. The Monthly option has one option for specifying the day of the month, and another for specifying the week and day of the week (like first Monday).

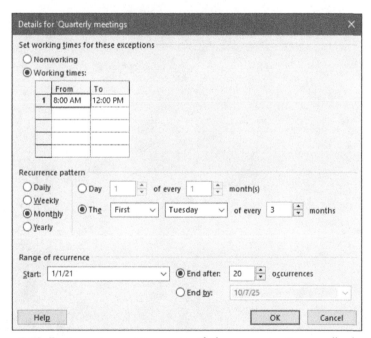

Figure 3-13. *For a recurring exception, you specify the recurrence pattern as well as how long the pattern lasts. Project initially sets the pattern to every day by selecting the Daily option and filling in the "Every _ days" box with 1. Project also fills in the Start and "End by" dates with the exception's start and end dates.*

5. In the "Range of recurrence" section, specify the date range or the number of occurrences.

    Project fills in the "Range of recurrence" Start box with the start date from the Exceptions tab—basically, the first date of the first exception. It also selects the "End after" option. Because the exception is initially set to Daily, it fills in the "End after" box with the number of days between the exception's start and finish date (from the Exceptions tab).

Suppose you want to carve out time from your project for a meeting every 3 months starting in January 2021 through the end of 2025. In the "Recurrence pattern" section, select the Monthly option and specify the frequency, such as the first Tuesday of every 3 months.

The other approach is to fill in the "occurrences" box with the number of occurrences you want. If the "End by" is too early to fit all the occurrences, Project automatically changes that date. For example, if you specify 30 occurrences, Project changes the "End by" date in this example to 4/2028.

6.   Click OK.

Whether you set dates or a number of occurrences, a recurring exception can repeat up to 999 times. If your recurrence pattern results in 1,000 occurrences or more, then Project displays a warning when you click OK.

4

Identifying the Work to Be Done

When you organize a simple endeavor like seeing a movie with friends, you probably don't bother writing out the steps. You call your friends, pick a movie, get tickets, and buy popcorn without a formal plan. But for more complex projects—like launching a new product—identifying the work involved is key to planning how and when to get it done. For example, you have to get all the prep work for the launch done *before* the big day, or your kickoff event will be a bust.

That's where a WBS (*work breakdown structure*) comes in. Carving up the project's work into a hierarchy of progressively smaller chunks (*summary tasks*, also called *work packages*) until you get to bite-sized pieces (individual tasks) is the first step toward figuring out how and when everything will get done. Once you identify the work to be done, you can move on to constructing a project schedule, covered in Chapter 5. In addition, the individual tasks at the bottom of the WBS are the small chunks of work that you assign to people as described in Chapter 7.

Before you create tasks in Project, it's a good idea to understand Microsoft Project's two task modes: Manually Scheduled and Automatically Scheduled. Manually Scheduled tasks wait for you to tell them when to start and finish. In contrast, with Auto Scheduled tasks, Project calculates your schedule using the task links, resource assignments, working calendars, and other details you specify. It's easy to set which task mode Project uses if you always use one or the other. But you can switch back and forth anytime you want or change a task's setting at any time.

This chapter helps you create and organize tasks. You might start by creating work tasks and milestones, and then adding summary tasks to wrangle low-level tasks into a WBS. Or you can change task outline levels to fine-tune your WBS hierarchy. In this chapter, you'll see the steps for building a WBS from the top down in Project. Then you'll learn how to rearrange your task list, whether you want to insert, copy, move, or delete tasks.

Finally, this chapter wraps up with a few additional task-related tricks. You'll see how to create recurring tasks, like team meetings that occur on a regular schedule. This chapter also explains how to document details about tasks and access that information from within Project.

Scheduling Manually or Automatically

Project *task modes* let you choose whether *you* want to control when tasks start and finish (Manually Scheduled) or whether you want *Project* to calculate start and finish dates automatically (Auto Scheduled). Although automatic scheduling is a huge help for projects with lots of tasks and resources, manual scheduling can help in several ways. This section describes what both task modes can do and how to decide which one you want.

Manually Scheduling Tasks

Out of the box, Project comes with Manually Scheduled mode turned on for all new tasks.

To seasoned project managers, manual scheduling sounds like heresy. After all, the point of using project-management software is to let a computer calculate the project schedule and adjust it automatically as you change tasks, resource assignments, and so on. But manually scheduled tasks come in handy for several common project-management situations, like at the beginning of a project when you have little info, or when you're planning from the top down with timeframes handed down from management. This section describes the different ways you can put manually scheduled tasks to work.

Setting the Start and Finish Date for a Task

Every so often, you run into a task that *must* occur on specific dates—for example, a training class for team members or a company-wide meeting. With a manually scheduled task, you can set the start or finish date, or both, to the calendar dates you want. (Project's date constraint feature is another method for setting either a task's start or finish date—but not both.) Chapter 5 describes how to set task dates using both these methods.

Creating Tasks with Incomplete Information

One challenge early in project planning is trying to define tasks and build a schedule when you don't have all the information you need. For example, you may not know how long some tasks will take. With manually scheduled tasks, you can fill in the information you *do* know and leave the rest blank without Project complaining. You can type notes in the date or duration fields to jog your memory when you fill in the missing information later.

Out of the box, Manually Scheduled task bars are teal with darker end-caps for dates that you specify. As shown in Figure 4-1, Manually scheduled summary tasks use black brackets to indicate the durations you enter. If the subtasks take longer than their summary task's duration, the rolled-up summary task bar that shows the duration of all the subtasks turns red.

Figure 4-1. *Project uses task-bar formats, end-caps, and colors on task bars to indicate what information a task includes.*

Here's what happens when you create manually scheduled tasks with different types of information:

- **Set task duration**: If you set the duration for a manually scheduled task without setting either the task's start or finish date, Project draws a task bar starting at the project's start date with the duration you specify. The task bar doesn't have end-caps because you haven't defined either date. In addition, the task bar is a light blue and faded at each end.

> **Tip:** You can filter your task list to display only tasks without dates. To do that, in the View tab's Data section, click the Filter down arrow and then choose More Filters. In the More Filters dialog box, double-click the Tasks Without Dates filter (or click the Tasks Without Dates filter and then click Apply).

- **Two of three values set**: If you specify two of the three values Project needs to schedule a task (Start, Finish, and Duration), it calculates the third value. For example, if you set the Start and Finish dates, Project calculates the duration. Or you can set one date and the duration and let Project calculate the other date. In this case, the task bar is teal with darker end-caps, as shown for Identify potential venues in Figure 4-1.

- **One date set**: When you specify a date (either Start or Finish) for a manually scheduled task, Project draws an end-cap at that end of the task bar, as you can see with Research venues in Figure 4-1.

- **Notes entered in a date or duration field**: If you don't know the value for a date or duration field but you have some information about the value, you can type placeholder notes in the field. For example, in Research venues in Figure 4-1, the start date is set, but the duration is uncertain, so there's a note about that. When you determine the task's duration or finish date, simply fill in the value, and Project adds end-caps or colors to the task bar to indicate that the value is now present.

Automatically Scheduling Tasks

Most of the time, you'll want to change Project's task mode to Auto Scheduled. That way, Project takes care of calculating when tasks start and finish. With auto-scheduled tasks, Project automatically makes the first task's start date the same as the project's start date. When you specify the task's duration, Project calculates its finish date. Then, as you link tasks, assign resources, and add the occasional date constraint, Project recalculates the schedule for you.

> **Tip:** You can specify whether auto-scheduled tasks start on the project's start date or the date on which you create the task. To do that, choose File Options. On the left side of the Project Options dialog box, choose Schedule. In the "Auto scheduled tasks scheduled on" drop-down list, choose Project Start Date or Current Date. It's best to use the project start date for new tasks. That way, Project calculates task dates based on their dependencies and other settings.

If you use Project's automatic scheduling, resist the temptation to specify start or finish dates for tasks, or you'll lose one of the advantages of using Project's scheduling engine in the first place. Project calculates dates for you based on the sequence and duration of tasks. If you enter dates for tasks, the resulting date constraints (see Chapter 5) make your schedule inflexible and difficult to maintain.

Setting the Task Mode

Depending on whether you usually work on small informal projects or monster schedules, you'll probably work primarily in one task mode or the other. But you can also mix and match manually scheduled tasks and auto-scheduled tasks to your heart's content. Here are ways to set the task mode you want to use:

- **Setting the Task Mode for new tasks**: By default, Project's task mode option for new tasks is set to Manually Scheduled. The fastest way to change the mode Project uses for new tasks is to head to the status bar at the bottom of the Project window, click New Tasks: [task mode] (where [task mode] is the task mode that's currently set), and then choose either Auto Scheduled or Manually Scheduled (see Figure 4-2). Project sets all new tasks to the mode you choose until you change the mode again. If you have other settings you want to change, you can change the mode Project uses for new tasks in the Project Options dialog box, as described in Chapter 3.

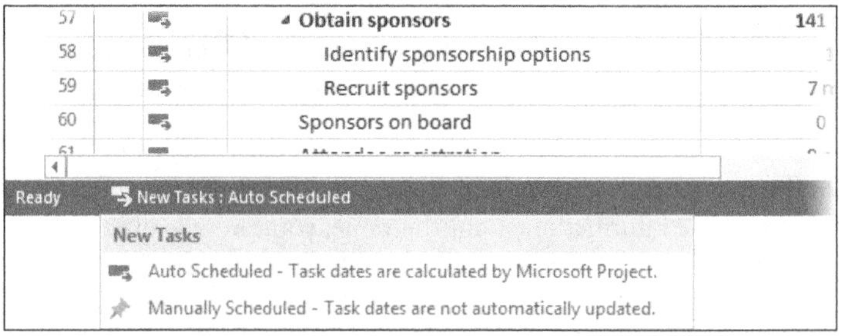

Figure 4-2. *Change the Task Mode at any time by clicking New Tasks in the status bar and then choosing the mode you want.*

- **Changing the mode of an existing task**: If you're in the early planning stages of a project, you may want tasks set to Manually Scheduled because you don't have all the info you need. As the project picture becomes clearer, many of those manually scheduled tasks will fall into place in your overall schedule, and you'll likely want them to be auto-scheduled. On the other hand, if you usually work with auto-scheduled tasks but have one task that occurs on a specific date, then you can switch it to Manually Scheduled mode. You can change a task's task mode anytime you want.

  The Entry, Schedule, and Summary tables automatically include the Task Mode column, so they're your ticket to switching modes. In the View tab's Data section, click Tables, and then choose Entry, Schedule, or Summary to display the corresponding table. To change a task's mode, click its Task Mode cell, click the down arrow that appears, and then choose Auto Scheduled or Manually Scheduled. The Manually Scheduled icon looks like a pushpin. The Auto Scheduled icon looks like a task bar with an arrow pointing to the right. In addition, the task bar style in the timescale changes to indicate whether the task is manually or automatically scheduled, as described earlier.

Adding Tasks to Your Project File

Don't worry about getting tasks in the right order or giving them the correct structure when you add them to your Project file. You can add tasks as you think of them or rearrange tasks any time after you create them. This section shows you how to create different types of tasks in Project.

> **Tip:** If you build a list of tasks in another program, like Word, Outlook, or Excel, you can paste or import task names and other info into Project. Head to Chapter 25 to learn how to bring data into Project from other programs.

Creating Tasks

Follow Along Practice

In Project, the table on the left side of Gantt Chart view is the place to be for fast task entry. To follow along, first create a blank Project file and save it with a name like Practice. Here's how to add tasks in this view:

1. Create a new blank file and save it as AddTasks.mpp.

    If you're not already in the Gantt Chart view, then on the ribbon's Task tab, click the bottom half of the Gantt Chart button, and then click Gantt Chart on the drop-down menu that appears.

    Alternatively, on the View tab, click the bottom half of the Gantt Chart button, and then choose Gantt Chart.

2. If the task mode isn't set to Auto Scheduled in the status bar, click New Tasks and then choose the task mode you want.

3. In the table on the left side of the view, click a blank Task Name cell, and then type the name of the task, in this example "Identify core event team" as shown in Figure 4-3. Press Enter to save the task and move to the Task Name cell in the next row.

    If the task is set to Auto Scheduled mode, when you save the task, Project fills in the Duration field with the value "1 day?" and sets the Start field to the project start date or the current date (depending on how you set the "Auto scheduled tasks scheduled on" option). If the task is set to Manually Scheduled mode, Project simply saves the task name.

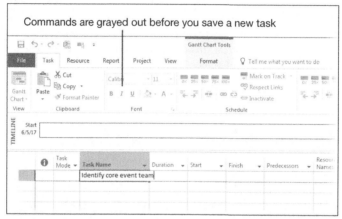

Figure 4-3. After you name your task but before you press Enter or the down-arrow key, the task name isn't saved and most commands on Project's menus are inactive. To make most commands available, simply press Enter or the down-arrow key to save the current task.

> **Tip:** Project lets you create blank lines in your task list. However, doing so can cause data integrity issues in your Project file.

4. Repeat step 3 to create as many tasks as you want.

    For practice, create the following tasks:

    - Define event goals and objectives

    - Identify event requirements

    - Determine budget

    - Prepare project definition

    - Obtain approval to proceed

> **Tip:** To edit a task's name, click its Task Name cell in the table area, and then click it again until the text-insertion point appears in the name. Then make your changes. You can also double-click the Task Name cell and edit the task name in the Task Information dialog box.

Creating Summary Tasks

Summary tasks help you schedule, track, and manage project work. If you entered all your WBS tasks into Project in one fell swoop, you can turn existing tasks into summary tasks by changing their outline level as described in the section "Reorganizing the Task List Outline" later in this chapter. But, if you want to create a new summary task (in any Gantt Chart view), you can choose from the following three methods:

Follow Along Practice

- **Create a new summary task for selected subtasks**: If you want to summarize several existing tasks, first, select tasks that you want as subtasks, in this example, the tasks you added in the previous section. Then, in the Task tab's Insert section, click Summary. Project selects the Task Name cell, which now contains the text "<New Summary Task>," as shown in Figure 4-4, so you can simply start typing to name the new summary task, in this example "Initial planning." When you press Enter to save the summary task with its new name, Project indents the selected tasks beneath the summary task.

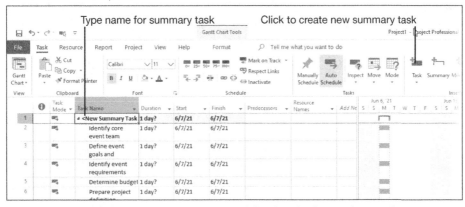

Figure 4-4. *After you create a new summary task for selected tasks, type the name for the task.*

Displaying the Project Summary Task

If you're new to Project, you might think about creating a summary task to summarize the entire project. No need! Project provides a built-in project summary task. All you have to do is turn it on:

On the Format tab, head to the Show/Hide section and turn on the Project Summary Task checkbox. Project adds a task row at the top of the task list with Task ID 0. Initially, the task name is the name of the Project file, but you can edit it to whatever you want.

You can also control the display of the project summary task with a Project option. (On the File tab, click Options. In the Project Options dialog box, click Advanced. Scroll to the "Display options for this project" section, and then turn on the "Show project summary task" checkbox.) However, toggling the checkbox on the Format tab is a lot quicker.

- **Create a new summary task with a new subtask**: This method is perfect if you want to add an entirely new batch of work, so you need to insert a new summary task and a new subtask. Click a blank Task Name cell, and then, in the Task tab's Insert section, click Summary. Start typing to name the new summary task, Prepare marketing messages, in this example. Press Enter to move to the new subtask's Task Name cell, as shown in Figure 4-5. Type the name for the subtask (Plan press releases, in this example) and press Enter.

> **Tip:** To insert a new summary task into the middle of your task list, first, insert a blank row. To do that, select the task above where you want to insert the blank row. In the Task tab's Insert section, click the down arrow below the Task icon, and then choose Blank Row. Then, insert a new summary task with a new subtask as described in the previous bullet point.

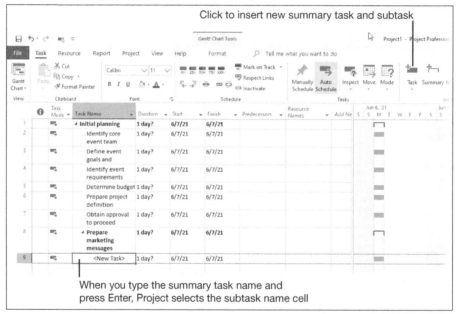

Figure 4-5. *When you type the summary task name and press Enter or the down arrow, Project selects the new subtask's Task Name cell so you can type its name.*

- **Create a new summary task as the parent of existing tasks**: Suppose you decide that several existing tasks should be organized within a new summary task. You can insert a new summary task and make existing tasks subordinate to it at the same time. First, select the tasks that you want to organize within the new summary task, such as all the tasks for initial planning and preparing marketing messages, task IDs 1 through 9, shown in Figure 4-5. In the Task tab's Insert section, click Summary. Project adds a new summary task above the first selected task and indents all the selected tasks in the task outline. Type the name for the summary task (in this case, Planning) and you're done!

- **Create a new task and make it a summary task**: If you want to insert new summary tasks in the middle of your task list, the easiest approach is to insert regular tasks and then change them into summary tasks. Select the row below the new task and then, in the Task tab's Insert section, click the Task icon (the blue bar with a green + sign). In the Task Name cell, type the new summary task's name, and then press Enter. Reselect the new task and then either press Alt+Shift+left arrow or, in the Task tab's Schedule section, click Outdent Task (the green, left-pointing arrow) until the summary task is at the level you want.

Displaying the Project Summary Task

If you're new to Project, you might think about creating a summary task to summarize the entire project. No need! Project provides a built-in project summary task. All you have to do is turn it on:

On the Format tab, head to the Show/Hide section and turn on the Project Summary Task checkbox. Project adds a task row at the top of the task list with Task ID 0. Initially, the task name is the name of the Project file, but you can edit it to whatever you want.

You can also control the display of the project summary task with a Project option. (On the File tab, click Options. In the Project Options dialog box, click Advanced. Scroll to the "Display options for this project" section, and then turn on the "Show project summary task" checkbox.) However, toggling the checkbox on the Format tab is a lot quicker.

Creating Milestones

In bygone days, a milestone was literally a stone that marked a distance of one mile from the last stone. In projects, milestones typically measure work progress, not distance. However, milestones can represent all kinds of progress: events (like receiving a payment), deliveries (like delivering a requirements document), or achievements (like completing a phase). And because milestones have no duration, you can add as many as you want without extending the project's finish date.

Follow Along Practice

Creating tasks for milestones couldn't be easier:

1. Select the task below where you want to insert a milestone by clicking anywhere in its row (in this example, Prepare marketing messages). In the Task tab's Insert section, click Milestone.

    Project inserts a new task with the name "<New Milestone>" and sets its Duration cell to "0 days."

2. Because the Task Name cell is selected automatically, go ahead and start typing the milestone's name, for example, "Initial planning complete," as shown in Figure 4-6.

3. Press Enter or the down arrow to save the milestone.

    In the Gantt Chart timescale, the task's task bar is a black diamond to indicate its milestone status.

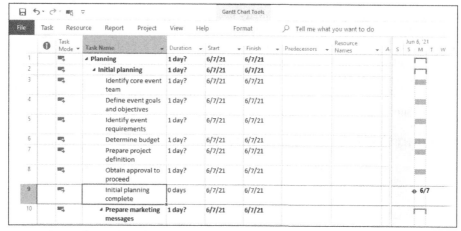

Figure 4-6. *Milestones have duration of 0 days. In the Gantt Chart timescale, a milestone appears as a black diamond.*

> **Tip:** You can designate tasks with durations as milestones. To appoint any task to milestone-hood, double-click the task in the task table to open the Task Information dialog box. (Or select the task and then, on the Task tab, click Information.) Then select the Advanced tab and turn on the "Mark task as milestone" checkbox.

Here are several ways to put milestones to use:

- **Project start or project phase**: Using a milestone as the first task in a project or phase makes it easy to reschedule an entire project or section. For example, if your customer doesn't send in the deposit payment you require to begin work, you can delay the entire schedule by changing the date for the deposit-payment milestone. Once a project is under way, you can delay a section of it by modifying the date of the section's starting milestone.

- **Project completion**: Quickly spot the current estimated project finish date by adding a milestone as the last task in a project schedule and linking the project's final tasks to it.

- **Decisions and approvals**: High-risk, big-budget projects often use feasibility studies to determine whether the project (and its funding) will continue. Milestone tasks are perfect for representing go/no-go decisions, approvals required before work can continue, or other decisions that affect the tasks that follow. For example, a go/no-go milestone might turn into the last milestone if the project is canceled, but it controls when work begins if the project gets the OK to continue. Milestones can also delay work that hinges on other types of decisions. For instance, the choice of programming language for your website determines who you hire, how the site is designed, and what code is written.

- **Progress**: Actual progress is stored within your project's work-package tasks, but you can gauge progress by adding milestones at significant points during the project, such as the completion of deliverables, be they documents, programs, booths, or cooked food. You can add a milestone after any summary task, for example, to show that all its work is complete.

- **Handoffs and deliveries**: A milestone can document when the responsibility for work transfers to a new group. Milestones also work for deliveries you expect from subcontractors or vendors. When you place an order for furniture for an event, you don't manage the rental company employees who load the delivery truck; you simply plan for the goods to arrive on the day they're promised. Thus, all you need is a milestone for that delivery date.

Rolling Up Milestones to Summary Tasks

When you use milestones to show key dates, you might want to display those milestones on Gantt Chart summary task bars. That way, you and the management team can easily spot important dates even when you collapse the task list to show only summary tasks. Here's how you roll milestones up to display on summary tasks:

1. Make sure summary tasks are configured to show rolled up task bars.

   To do that, double-click the summary task you want to check. In the Summary Task Information dialog box, click the General Tab, and then, if necessary, turn on the Rollup checkbox. If necessary, turn off the Hide Bar checkbox so the milestone task bars will display on the summary task.

2. Select the milestones that you want to roll up to summary tasks.

   To select multiple tasks, click the first milestone and then Ctrl-click all the remaining milestones that you want to display on summary tasks.

3. In the Task tab's Properties section, click the Information icon.

4. In the Multiple Task Information dialog box, click the General tab, and then, if necessary, turn on the Rollup checkbox. Click OK to close the dialog box.

   Milestone diamonds appear on all the summary tasks that the milestones are subordinate to, as shown in Figure 4-7.

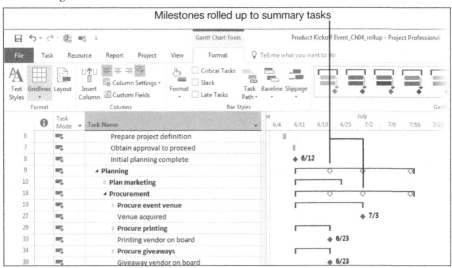

Figure 4-7. *When you configure milestones to roll up to summary tasks, they appear on summary tasks to which they are subordinate.*

> **Tip:** If you want to change the appearance of rolled up milestones, you can modify the format for that bar style. In the Format tab's Bar Styles section, click the down arrow beneath the Format button, and then choose Bar Styles. In the Bar Styles dialog box, in the Name column, select *Rolled Up Milestone. See the section "Changing the Way Types of Task Bars Look" in Chapter 20, to learn about bar style formatting techniques.

Organizing Tasks

Say you were in high gear churning out project tasks and now you want to reorganize your task list. You can insert, delete, and rearrange tasks as you work. The methods for adding, moving, and changing outline levels for tasks are the same whether you're creating or modifying your task list. This section covers all the options from adjusting the outline of tasks to adding, removing, and rearranging tasks.

Reorganizing the Task List Outline

Changing a task's level in the outline is easy, although the results depend on what type of task you modify and whether you move it lower or higher in the outline. You can use the following techniques to turn your task list into a WBS.

> **Tip:** When you're reorganizing your task list, the table in the Gantt Chart view helps you view your tasks' outline level in several ways, as shown in Figure 4-8. The outline symbol (a white or black triangle, depending on whether the subtasks are hidden or visible) precedes summary task names. If you click a white triangle, the summary task expands to show its subtasks, and the outline symbol changes to black. Clicking the outline symbol when it's a black triangle hides the subtasks and changes the triangle to white.

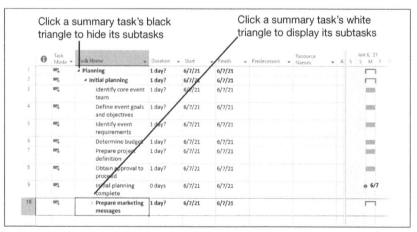

Figure 4-8. *Outline symbols identify which tasks are summary tasks. You can click them to expand and collapse summary tasks.*

You can use the following techniques to reorganize your task list:

- **Make a summary task into a non-summary task**: Select all the subtasks for the summary task, and then either press Alt+Shift+left arrow or, in the Task tab's Schedule section, click Outdent Task (the green, left-pointing arrow). You can also right-click a task and, on the formatting toolbar that appears, click the outdent icon (the green, left-pointing arrow). When you outdent the subtasks, the summary task turns into a regular task, and its summary-task triangle disappears.

- **Elevate a summary task to a higher level**: Select the summary task, and then either press Alt+Shift+left arrow or, in the Task tab's Schedule section, click Outdent Task (the green, left-pointing arrow).

- **Indent tasks to the next lower level**: If you add several tasks in a row, they all start out at the same level. To turn them into summary tasks and subtasks, you indent the subtasks. To do that, select the soon-to-be subtasks, and then press Alt+Shift+right arrow or, in the Task tab's Schedule section, click Indent Task (the green, right-pointing arrow). If the tasks were at the same level as the task above, then the tasks indent to the next-lower level in the outline, while the task above them turns into a summary task. If the tasks you indented were at a higher level than the task above, the task above doesn't become a summary task.

> **Tip:** To select several adjacent tasks, click the first task's ID cell and then Shift-click the last task's ID cell. You can also drag over the ID cells of the tasks you want to select. To select several nonadjacent tasks, Ctrl-click the ID cell of each task.

- **Elevate a subtask to the next higher level**: Moving a task higher in the outline comes in handy when you want to disconnect a task from its summary task (for example, when you want to delete a summary task without deleting its subtasks). Select the subtask(s), and then press Alt+-Shift+left arrow or, in the Task tab's Schedule section, click Outdent Task. If the outdented task was one of several at the same level, it turns into a summary task.

- **Indent or outdent several tasks at once**: If you want to indent or outdent several tasks, select them all, and then use the techniques in this section. To select adjoining tasks in the outline, drag across them. To select several separate tasks, Ctrl-click each one.

Hiding and Showing Tasks in the Outline

As you work on one part of the task list, tasks in other parts of the project might get in your way. Or your stakeholder team might be interested in only the first few levels of the WBS. Regardless of the reason, you can choose which tasks and subtasks to show or hide at any time. Here are several techniques for displaying only the tasks you want to see:

- **To display only non-summary tasks,** in the Gantt Chart Tools | Format tab's Show/Hide section, turn off the Summary Tasks checkbox. If you want to see the outline level for each task, then in that same section, turn on the Outline Number checkbox.

- **To display summary tasks**, in the Format tab's Show/Hide section, turn on the Summary Tasks checkbox.

- **To hide or show subtasks for a specific summary task**, click the outline symbol (the triangle icon) to the left of the summary task's name. You can also select the summary task in the outline and then, in the View tab's Data section, choose Outline→Hide Subtasks.

- **To show all tasks down to a specific outline level**, in the View tab's Data section, click Outline and then, from the drop-down list, choose the lowest level you want to display. For example, if you want to view the top three levels of the WBS, choose Level 3.

- **To display all the tasks in the project**, in the View tab's Data section, choose Outline→All Subtasks.

Building a WBS from the Top Down

Your WBS may not start out in Project—maybe you scribbled it on a whiteboard, scrawled it on sticky notes pasted to flip charts, or it's just rattling around in your head. Regardless of where your ideas are, you can make short work of getting them into Project. Now that you're familiar with outlining tasks (described earlier), you can quickly build your WBS in Project from the top down. Because Project creates each new task at the same outline level as the previous task, this approach keeps indenting and outdenting to a minimum.

The following steps show you exactly how to work your way down a WBS one level at a time:

1. Create a new blank file (see Chapter 3).

    The Gantt Chart view appears with the Entry table on the left and the Gantt Chart timescale on the right. (If you don't see the Gantt Chart view, in the Task tab's View section, click Gantt Chart.)

2. If you want to display a WBS column in the Entry table, right-click the Task Name heading and choose Insert Column from the shortcut menu.

    Project inserts a new column to the left of the Task Name column with "[Type Column Name]" in the heading cell.

3. Type **WBS**, and then press Enter.

    > **Note:** The WBS code format that Project uses out of the box is a number at each level, with levels separated by periods. If your organization has a custom WBS format, you can set up your own WBS code (see the section "Coding Tasks and Resources" in Chapter 21).

4. In the Entry table, click the first Task Name cell, type the name of the summary task, and then press Enter.

    Project selects the Task Name cell in the next row, so you're ready to enter the next task.

5. Repeat step 4 for each top-level task in the WBS. For practice, create the tasks shown in Figure 4-9.

Project creates the next task at the same level in the WBS outline as the previous task, so you're ready to enter the next top-level task. As you'll see shortly, this behavior makes it easy to add several tasks at the same level, no matter which level of the WBS you're creating. Once the top-level tasks are in place, you're ready to add tasks at the next level of the WBS.

6. To add subtasks to a summary task, click the Task Name cell immediately below the summary task you're fleshing out, and then press the Insert key on your keyboard as many times as there are subtasks, as demonstrated in Figure 4-9.

    This step is the secret to speedy outlining because it works in the same way at every level of the WBS: second-level, third-level, and lowest-level summary tasks. When you insert rows for a lowest-level summary task, insert as many rows as there are tasks for that summary task. Then you can type away and fill them all in quickly.

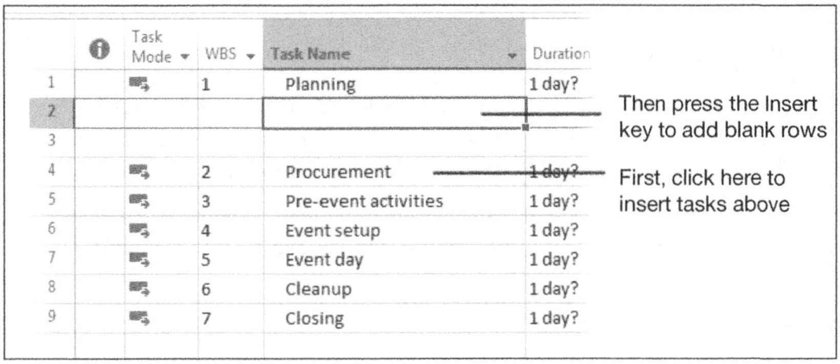

Figure 4-9. *Insert blank rows below a summary task for its subtasks.*

7. In the top blank Task Name cell, type the name of the subtask, and then press Enter to save the task.

    Pressing Enter moves the active cell to the next Task Name cell. However, the first subtask isn't at the right level—it's still at the same level as the summary task.

8. To indent the subtask, press the up-arrow key, and then press Alt+Shift+right arrow or, in the Task tab's Schedule section, click Indent Task (the green, right-pointing arrow).

9. Press the down-arrow key to move to the next Task Name cell, type the name, and then press Enter.

    Because the first subtask now is at the correct level, the remaining subtasks come in at the right level for their summary task.

10. Repeat steps 6–9 for every summary task in the WBS, ultimately filling in each level of the WBS. For practice, create the two planning subtasks shown in Figure 4-10.

		Task Mode	WBS	Task Name	Duration	
1			1	◢ **Planning**	**1 day?**	6
2			1.1	Initial planning	1 day?	6
3			1.2	Planning marketing	1 day?	6
4			2	Procurement	1 day?	6
5			3	Pre-event activities	1 day?	6
6			4	Event setup	1 day?	6
7			5	Event day	1 day?	6
8			6	Cleanup	1 day?	6

Figure 4-10. *The WBS code for the subtask includes an additional level of numbers. If the summary task's WBS number is 1, then its first subtask has the number 1.1, as shown here.*

Rearranging Tasks

You can organize tasks as you create them, or come back later and change their order. Summary tasks, work-package tasks, and milestones all respond to Project's organizational techniques. The following sections describe different ways you can arrange tasks in your Project file.

> **Note:** If you've downloaded the sample files, use the file Event_Ch04_start.mpp.

Inserting Additional Tasks

Sometimes your project planning uncovers more work than you originally estimated, and you need to add tasks to your existing list. Other times, you might decide to change the way you summarize work or to decompose work further, which means creating new summary tasks.

Follow Along Practice

Here's how to insert tasks in an existing list:

- **Insert a new summary task for several existing tasks**: First, select the soon-to-be subtasks. Then, in the Task tab's Insert section, click Summary. Project inserts the new summary task ***and*** transforms all the selected tasks into subtasks. For practice, drag over task IDs 14 through 19 (the tasks for procuring the venue). After you insert the summary task, name it "Procure event venue."

- **Insert a summary task**: Click the row below where you want the new summary task to go and then, in the Task tab's Insert section, click Summary. Project inserts the new summary task at the same outline level as the task above it, fills in the Task Name cell with the text "<New Summary Task>," and turns the task below it into its first subtask. Type the new summary task's name, and then press Enter to save it. In this example, click task 14 "Procure event venue." After you insert the summary task, name it "Procurement."

- **Insert a task at any level**: To insert a new task between two existing ones, click the lower of the two existing task rows, and then press the Insert key. In the Task Name cell of the blank task row that appears, type the new task's name, and then press Enter. If the task isn't at the correct outline level, press Alt+Shift+right arrow or Alt+Shift+left arrow to indent or outdent it, respectively. For practice, insert a task above task ID 21 "Sign venue contract and pay deposit," and fill in the task name "Define other venue services."

- **Insert a new subtask**: In the row below an existing subtask, click the Task Name cell, and then press the Insert key. A new, blank task row appears at the same outline level as the existing subtask.

Copying Tasks

If your project schedule includes similar tasks in several areas of the project, it's often easier to create a set of tasks and copy them to each place you use them. Or, if you have a task that already has values you want in a new task (such as hours and assigned resources), you can copy it so that the new task includes the same values. (You should rename the new, copied task to avoid confusion, as described in the section "Renaming Copied Task Names.") You can copy just task names or entire tasks.

Here are different methods for copying tasks and when to use each one:

- **Copy whole tasks**: When you copy and paste an *entire* task (or several tasks), Project inserts the tasks into new rows in the task list, so you don't need blank rows to paste into. First, select the entire task you want to copy by clicking its ID cell. (If you want to select more than one task, then drag the pointer across adjacent task ID cells. You can also Shift-click the first and last ID cells to select adjacent tasks, or Ctrl-click each task's ID cell to select nonadjacent tasks.) Then press Ctrl+C or, in the Task tab's Clipboard section, click Copy. Finally, click the ID cell of the task above which you want to insert the copied tasks, and then press Ctrl+V (or, on the Task tab, click Paste). For practice, select task IDs 23 through 28 (the tasks for Procure Printing) and Press Ctrl+C to copy them. Then click task 29 and press Ctrl+V to paste the copied tasks. To outdent the tasks, make sure the Procure printing task is selected, and then click Outdent on the Task tab.

- **Copy task names**: When you copy only task name cells, be sure to paste them only into *blank* rows, so you create new tasks. If you paste the task names into rows that contain values, you'll overwrite the current contents of the task name cells instead of creating new tasks. To copy one or more task names, select the Task Name cells you want to copy and then press Ctrl+C (or, in the Task tab's Clipboard section, click Copy). To paste the selected task names, click the first blank Task Name cell, and then press Ctrl+V (or, on the Task tab, click Paste).

> **Tip:** To select several adjacent Task Name cells, click the first one and then Shift-click the last one. (You can also drag over the Task Name cells you want to select.) To select several nonadjacent Task Name cells, Ctrl-click each one you want to select.

- **Repeat a set of task names**: Say you have a set of task names that you want to repeat several times, such as the steps for procuring several vendors for a project. In this case, Project's *fill handle* is just the ticket. The fill handle is the little green box at the lower right of a selected cell (or range of cells); it lets you copy the content of cells to adjacent cells in your task list.

First, select the Task Name cells you want to copy. Then position your mouse pointer over the lower-right corner of the last Task Name cell; you can tell when the pointer is over the fill handle because the pointer turns into a + sign, as shown in Figure 4-11.

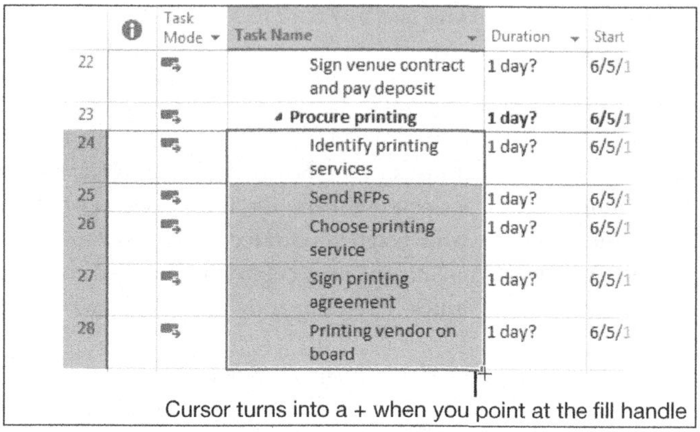

	ⓘ	Task Mode ▾	Task Name ▾	Duration ▾	Start
22		⬛	Sign venue contract and pay deposit	1 day?	6/5/1
23		⬛	◢ Procure printing	**1 day?**	**6/5/1**
24		⬛	Identify printing services	1 day?	6/5/1
25		⬛	Send RFPs	1 day?	6/5/1
26		⬛	Choose printing service	1 day?	6/5/1
27		⬛	Sign printing agreement	1 day?	6/5/1
28		⬛	Printing vendor on board	1 day?	6/5/1

Cursor turns into a + when you point at the fill handle

Figure 4-11. *When you position the cursor over the fill handle (which is at the bottom-right corner of the last selected cell), the cursor turns into a + sign.*

Then drag the fill handle over the Task Name cells into which you want to copy the selected names. When you let go of your mouse, Project repeats the set of selected values until it reaches the last cell you dragged over (so it might not repeat the entire set of names).

Renaming Copied Task Names

Follow Along Practice

If you work hard to keep task names unique, copying tasks raises an issue: The copied tasks have the same names as the originals. Don't despair—the Replace command can come to the rescue and replace the adjectives for each set of copied tasks. Here's how it works:

1. Select the tasks you want to rename that use the same adjectives or qualifiers. For example, select the copied tasks from the previous section called "Identify printing services," "Send RFPs," "Choose printing service," "Sign printing agreement," and "Printing vendor on board" for printing and you want to change the word "printing" to "music." In this example, select tasks 29 through 34, the copied Procure printing tasks.

2. To open the Replace dialog box, press Ctrl+H or, in the Task tab's Editing section, click the down arrow next to the Find button (it looks like a magnifying glass), and then choose Replace.

3. In the Replace dialog box, be sure that the Search box is set to Down, indicating that Project will begin at the first selected task and search in all subsequent tasks in the list.

4. In the "Find what" box, type the word(s) you want to replace—printing, in this example.

5. In the "Replace with" box, type the new term for the copied tasks, for instance, "music" to change the name "Identify printing services" to "Identify music services." Turn on the Match case checkbox.

6. Click Replace to replace the first occurrence of the term. Continue to click Replace once for each selected task. To skip an occurrence, click Find Next.

7. Click Close when you're done.

> **Tip:** It's tempting to click Replace All, but don't do it. Otherwise, Project will replace that word in all tasks in the schedule—including the ones you want to leave as is.

Moving Tasks

If you decide that tasks belong in another section of the WBS, you can move them in the Project task list. For example, you might move a subtask to a different summary task to change how you decompose work. Or you can move a subtask to a position before or after another subtask so the subtasks are in the sequence they'll occur.

Follow Along Practice

To move one or more tasks, do the following:

1. In the Gantt Chart view's table area, select the entire task you want to move by clicking its ***ID cell***, as shown in Figure 4-12.

    If you want to select more than one task, drag the pointer across adjacent task ID cells. If you want to select nonadjacent tasks, then Ctrl-click each task's ID cell. For practice, drag over task IDs 35 through 40 (the tasks to procure giveaways).

    When it's in the ID column, the pointer turns into a four-headed arrow to indicate that you can move the selected task(s).

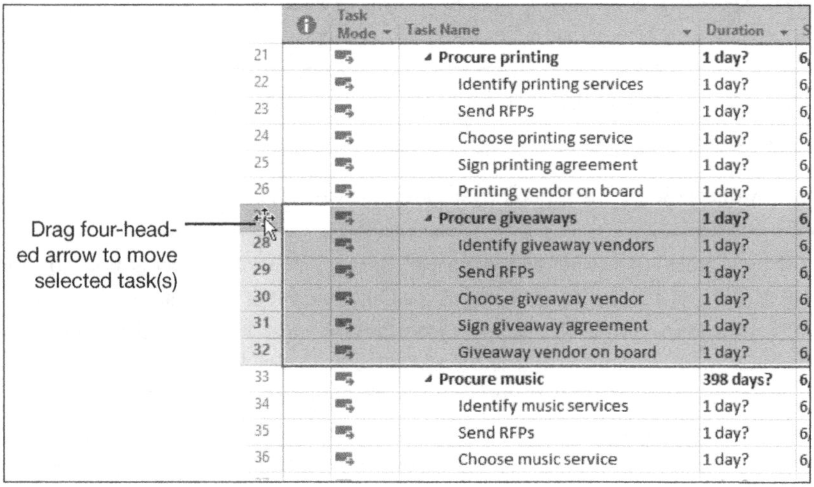

	ⓘ	Task Mode ▾	Task Name ▾	Duration ▾	S
21		🖪	⏴ **Procure printing**	**1 day?**	6,
22		🖪	Identify printing services	1 day?	6,
23		🖪	Send RFPs	1 day?	6,
24		🖪	Choose printing service	1 day?	6,
25		🖪	Sign printing agreement	1 day?	6,
26		🖪	Printing vendor on board	1 day?	6,
27		🖪	⏴ **Procure giveaways**	**1 day?**	6,
28		🖪	Identify giveaway vendors	1 day?	6,
29		🖪	Send RFPs	1 day?	6,
30		🖪	Choose giveaway vendor	1 day?	6,
31		🖪	Sign giveaway agreement	1 day?	6,
32		🖪	Giveaway vendor on board	1 day?	6,
33		🖪	⏴ **Procure music**	**398 days?**	6,
34		🖪	Identify music services	1 day?	6,
35		🖪	Send RFPs	1 day?	6,
36		🖪	Choose music service	1 day?	6,

Drag four-headed arrow to move selected task(s)

Figure 4-12. *Unlike other columns, the ID column doesn't have any text in its column heading; it's the first column in the table area.*

2. Position the pointer over any of the selected ID cells, which changes the pointer to a four-headed arrow.

3. When you see the four-headed arrow, drag the task(s) to the new location. For practice, drag the tasks so the gray line appears above the Procure music summary task.

    As you drag, a gray line appears in the border between rows, showing where the task(s) will end up when you release the mouse button.

4. If the task isn't at the correct outline level, press Alt+Shift+right arrow or Alt+Shift+left arrow to indent or outdent the task, respectively. In this example, press Alt+Shift+right arrow or click Outdent on the Task tab.

    You can also click Indent Task or Outdent Task in the Task tab's Schedule section (the icons with the green left and right arrows) to change the outline level.

> **Tip:** Project used to scroll like lightning, which made dragging tasks accurately beyond the visible rows all but impossible. Although Project's scrolling has slowed to a manageable pace, cutting and pasting tasks is still a more convenient way to move them when their new location is several pages away. To cut and paste tasks, select the tasks, and then press Ctrl+X. Then select the row below where you want to paste them, and then press Ctrl+V.

Deleting Tasks

Although work rarely disappears in real life, you may sometimes need to delete tasks in Project. Perhaps you've decided to decompose work differently, or the customer has chosen to reduce the project's scope to fit the budget.

> **Tip:** See Chapter 11 to learn how to inactivate tasks instead of deleting them. Inactivating tasks has several advantages: The tasks remain in your schedule for historical purposes, and they're easy to reactivate if the stakeholders change their mind about what they want.

Here are the various ways to delete tasks: To practice, you can delete any tasks you want and then press Ctrl+Z to undo the deletes.

*   **Delete a subtask**: Select the subtask by clicking the row's ID number, and then press Delete.

> **Tip:** If you press Delete when an automatically scheduled Task Name cell is selected, Project displays an indicator (a box containing an X) to the left of that cell. You can click the indicator's down arrow and select the "Delete the task name" option to delete the name or the "Delete the task" option to delete the whole task. To hide the delete indicator, choose File Options. On the left side of the Project Options dialog box, choose Display, and then turn off the "Deletions in the Name columns" checkbox.

- **Delete a summary task and all its subtasks**: To delete a summary task and all its subtasks, select the summary task's ID cell, and then press Delete, or right-click anywhere in the summary task's row and then choose Delete Task from the shortcut menu.

- **Delete a summary task but not its subtasks**: If you're moving subtasks to a different summary task, relocate the subtasks to their new home and then delete the summary task as described in the previous bullet point. If you're not sure where you want the orphaned subtasks to end up, simply change them to the same outline level as the summary task *before* deleting the summary task. To do that, select the subtasks and then press Alt+Shift+left arrow to move them to the same outline level as their summary task. Then select their former summary task by clicking its ID cell and press Delete.

> **Tip:** If you want to delete other aspects of a task, the Clear command is at your service. In the Task tab's Editing section, click the down arrow to the right of the Clear button (which looks like an eraser) and then choose what you want to delete from the drop-down menu: hyperlinks, notes, or formatting. Choose Clear All to clear all three types of elements. The Entire Row option clears all the cells in the row, including the task name, leaving you with a blank row.

More About Tasks

So far, this chapter has tackled basics like creating tasks and organizing them into a WBS. This section goes a little further by describing how to create tasks that recur on a regular schedule. In addition, task names are rarely enough to describe the work they represent. In this section, you'll see how to document task work in detail and how to access that information in Project.

Creating Recurring Tasks

Some tasks occur on a regular schedule—for example, monthly meetings of the change control board or biweekly status meetings. Fortunately, you don't have to create each occurrence separately in Project. Instead, you can create a *recurring task,* and Project then takes care of creating individual tasks for each occurrence and a *summary task* for all the occurrences.

Follow Along Practice

To create a recurring task, do the following:

1. Click anywhere in the row *below* where you want the new recurring task. In this example, click the first blank row at the bottom of the task list.

2. In the Task tab's Insert section, click the Task down arrow, and then choose Recurring Task.

3. In the Recurring Task Information dialog box's Task Name box, type the name for the recurring task, such as *Change Control Meeting*.

Project automatically sets the value in the Duration box to 1 day (abbreviated as 1d). This box sets the duration for one occurrence of this task—in this example, one change control meeting. If the occurrence takes less than a day, then in the Duration box, type the correct duration, such as *2h* to reflect a 2-hour meeting.

4. In the "Recurrence pattern" section, specify the frequency of the task. In this example, choose Monthly, and set the meeting for the second Monday of the month.

    Choose from Daily, Weekly, Monthly, or Yearly. For each option, you see additional settings that let you add more detail about the timing, as illustrated in Figure 4-13. To schedule occurrences for more than one day a week, you can turn on the checkbox for each day of the week on which occurrences are scheduled, such as Monday and Thursday. Occurrences for other periods have different frequency settings. For example, when you select the Monthly option, you can specify when the tasks occur each month, such as on the 15th or on the second Monday.

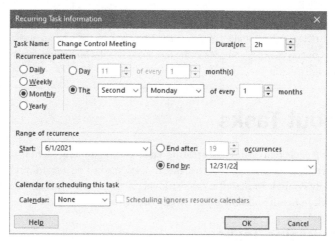

Figure 4-13. *If the occurrences don't happen every single period, choose the number of periods, like 2 to schedule a meeting every 2 weeks.*

5. In the "Range of recurrence" section's Start box, choose the date you want the occurrences to begin. In this example, use 6/1/2021.

    Project initially sets this box to the project's start date.

6. To specify when the occurrences end, select the "End after" option, and then type a number of occurrences. Alternatively, select the "End by" option if you want to set the end date. In this example, set the end date to 12/31/2022.

    Project initially selects the "End by" option and sets the date to the project's end date. With either option, you'll have to edit this recurring task later if the project runs longer than you anticipated—Project doesn't automatically extend recurring tasks to conform to a new end date.

7. Click OK to close the dialog box and add the recurring task to the project, shown in Figure 4-14.

In the Indicators column, a circular icon with arrows indicates that the task has multiple occurrences. To view the task's frequency and range, position your pointer over this icon.

Tip: To hide the individual occurrences, click the outline symbol to the left of the summary task's name. (The outline symbol is a black triangle when the subtasks are visible. It changes to a white right-pointing triangle when the occurrences are hidden.) To open the Recurring Task Information dialog box for a recurring task, double-click the summary task's name.

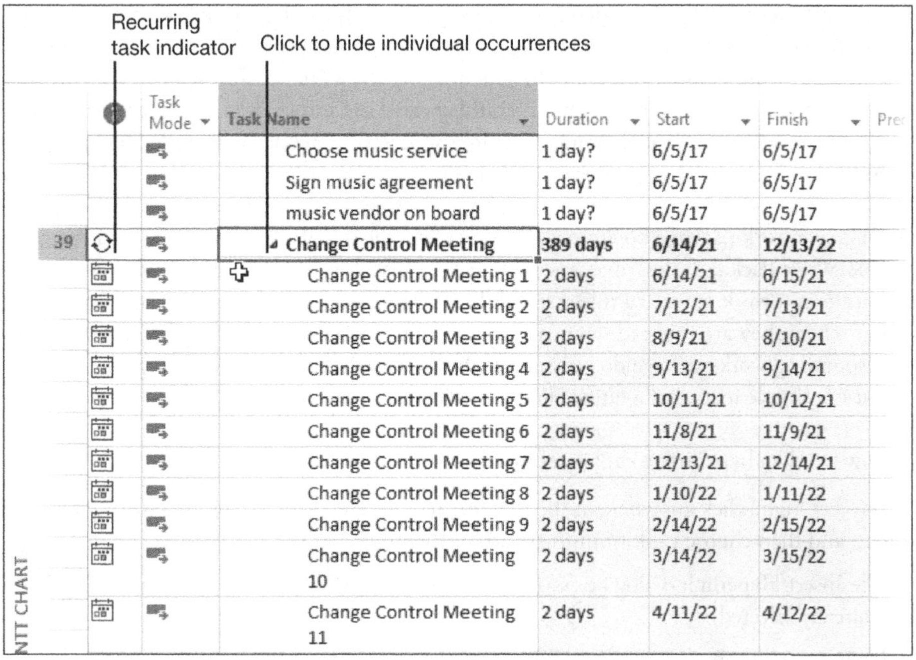

	Task Mode	Task Name	Duration	Start	Finish	Pre
		Choose music service	1 day?	6/5/17	6/5/17	
		Sign music agreement	1 day?	6/5/17	6/5/17	
		music vendor on board	1 day?	6/5/17	6/5/17	
39		**Change Control Meeting**	**389 days**	**6/14/21**	**12/13/22**	
		Change Control Meeting 1	2 days	6/14/21	6/15/21	
		Change Control Meeting 2	2 days	7/12/21	7/13/21	
		Change Control Meeting 3	2 days	8/9/21	8/10/21	
		Change Control Meeting 4	2 days	9/13/21	9/14/21	
		Change Control Meeting 5	2 days	10/11/21	10/12/21	
		Change Control Meeting 6	2 days	11/8/21	11/9/21	
		Change Control Meeting 7	2 days	12/13/21	12/14/21	
		Change Control Meeting 8	2 days	1/10/22	1/11/22	
		Change Control Meeting 9	2 days	2/14/22	2/15/22	
		Change Control Meeting 10	2 days	3/14/22	3/15/22	
		Change Control Meeting 11	2 days	4/11/22	4/12/22	

Figure 4-14. *A recurring task includes both individual occurrences and a summary task to shepherd all the occurrences into one spot.*

The summary task for a recurring task is always set to be automatically scheduled. That's because it calculates the total duration, work, and other values of all the occurrences. The subtasks for the individual occurrences use whichever task mode is currently selected. (The section "Setting the Task Mode" earlier in this chapter describes how to set the task mode.)

Note: Because recurring tasks are scheduled to take place on specific dates, occurrences that are automatically scheduled use Start No Earlier Than date constraints (see Chapter 5) to pin the occurrence dates. Whether an occurrence is auto-scheduled or manually scheduled, you can edit an occurrence if, for example, you need to reschedule one status meeting because of a scheduling conflict.

Documenting Task Details

Team members do better when you provide clear guidance about the work they need to perform and the results you expect, but task names aren't the place to get into detail. You need a place to store all the details that explain how to perform tasks completely and correctly. Fortunately, you don't have to worry about keeping track of lots of loose documents: You can link external documents to tasks or add details to notes attached to tasks. This section describes both options.

Documenting Work Details in Word

Ideally, a work-package document describes the work to perform, how to know when it's done, and how to tell whether it's done right. A work package for setting up publicity messages might include creating messages, importing the contact list, identifying the audience for each message and scheduling when messages are sent. The document could specify the information required for contacts and the best frequencies to use. The document could also describe the desired results, including logs for sent messages and reports of responses from recipients.

After you create work-package documents that spell out the details of tasks (the note titled "Creating a Reusable Work Package" describes one way to simplify this chore), you're likely to refer to those documents as you work on your Project schedule. There's no need to open them by hand or to try to remember where they are. Instead, you can insert a hyperlink from a task in the Project schedule to the corresponding work-package document. With the hyperlink in place, opening the work-package document is a simple matter of a quick click in Project.

Here's how to add a hyperlink to a Project task:

1. In Project, right-click anywhere in the row for the task you want to link to a work-package document, and then choose Link from the shortcut menu.

2. In the Insert Hyperlink dialog box's "Link to" column, click "Existing File or Web Page" (if it's not already selected).

   Selecting this option is how you tell Project that you want to link to a document that's already stored on your computer.

3. Use the options in the center of the dialog box to navigate to the folder that contains the work-package document, and then click the name of the work-package file.

   The "Look in" box shows the name of the current folder, and the Address box displays the current filename.

4. Click OK.

   In the Indicators column (its heading is an i in a blue circle), a hyperlink icon appears, as shown in Figure 4-15.

   If the Indicators column isn't visible, then right-click a column heading in the table and choose Insert Column on the shortcut menu. In the Field Name drop-down list that appears, choose Indicators.

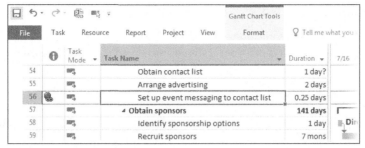

Figure 4-15. *The hyperlink icon looks like a globe with a link of chain, a not-so-subtle commentary that hyperlinks connect the world.*

5. To access a hyperlinked file, simply click the hyperlink icon in the Indicators cell.

    The program associated with the file launches and opens the file.

Creating a Reusable Work Package

Even small projects require a multitude of work-package documents. You can speed up your work by creating a Word template for work packages that's as basic or as fancy as your knowledge of Word. That way, you create a new document from the template and have everything labeled and ready for you to fill in. For example, you might set up a basic work-package template with the following information:

*   **WBS number**: This is the WBS number that Project assigned to the task in your project schedule. Chapter 21 describes out to set up a custom WBS numbering scheme.

*   **Work-package name**: The task name from the Project schedule.

*   **Description of work**: You can use paragraphs or bullet points and provide as much detail as you need to ensure success. If you know an experienced resource is going to do the work, the document can be brief. For trainees, on the other hand, you can provide detailed checklists of steps or the name of the person who can mentor them.

*   **Result**: Describe the final state when the work is done, as well as how to verify that it was done correctly. In a work package for recruiting sponsors, for example, you might include where to find potential sponsors and the sponsorship levels available.

*   **Reference materials**: Projects use many types of documents to specify deliverables: requirements, specifications, blueprints, and so on. If other detailed documentation exists, list where to find those documents, like the project notebook or the folder on the network drive.

Adding Details in Task Notes

Project can store additional information right with the tasks in your Project file in the form of *notes*. The downside to this approach is that your team members need to be able to open the Project file (or a copy of it) to view the notes.

To attach a note to a task, follow these steps:

1. In a task-oriented view (such as the Gantt Chart view or Task Usage view), right-click anywhere in the task's row and then choose Notes from the shortcut menu.

    The Task Information dialog box opens to the Notes tab.

2. In the Notes box, type the details of the task.

    The toolbar within the Notes box includes buttons for changing the font, setting the justification, creating bulleted lists, and inserting objects from another program (like an Excel spreadsheet, an email message, or a specifications document).

3. When you're done writing, click OK.

    A notepad icon appears in the task's Indicators cell. To see the beginning of the note (as in Figure 4-16), position your pointer over this icon. To see the entire note, double-click this icon; Project opens the Task Information dialog box to the Notes tab.

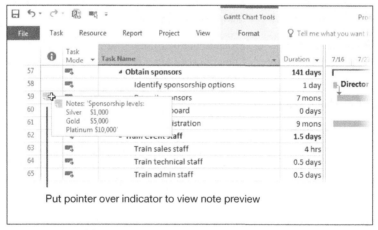

Figure 4-16. *Once you add a note to a task, the task's Indicators cell displays an icon that looks like a sticky note. To see a preview of the note (like the one shown here), put your pointer over the icon.*

5

Building a Schedule

In Project, as in life, building good relationships is a key to success. When you define relationships between tasks in a Project file—called **_task dependencies_** or **_task links_**—the program calculates task start and finish dates based on those relationships. Some tasks have to finish before others can start. For example, the law of gravity requires that you finish a building's foundation before you start pouring the concrete for the first floor's walls. Placing tasks in sequence is what turns a task list into a project schedule. This chapter describes the different types of task dependencies, the pros and cons of each one, and how to create and modify these links.

Once you've linked your tasks, the next step is specifying how many hours or days of work those tasks entail—and the length of time to allocate for that work. For example, you need to know how long it takes to repair and paint the front of a '67 Mustang Fastback to figure out whether you can hide the evidence before your parents get home from vacation. This chapter explains what work and duration represent. It then describes several ways to add duration to your tasks. (Work comes into play when you assign resources to tasks as you'll see in Chapter 7.) With task dependencies and duration values in place, you can finally see the entire project schedule from the start date for the first task to the finish date of the last task.

Also, although task dependencies let Project adjust task start and finish dates automatically, some situations call for specific dates for tasks. In this chapter, you'll learn two ways to specify when tasks can start or finish: manual scheduling and date constraints. More importantly, you'll find out how to use date constraints and deadlines to handle specific dates **_without_** limiting Project's ability to calculate the schedule.

> **Note:** The techniques for sequencing tasks in this chapter apply to both traditional and agile scheduling. To learn about Project's features for managing work via Scrum or Kanban (available only in the Project Online desktop client), head to Chapter 30.

> **Note:** *Before* you dig into defining the relationships between tasks, you should build a list of project tasks and milestones (and, ideally, organize those tasks into a work breakdown structure), as described in the previous chapter. Otherwise, you won't have all the information you need to put tasks into a logical sequence.

Linking Tasks

Task dependencies (a.k.a. *task links* or *task relationships*) are what transform a ragtag group of tasks into a well-mannered project schedule, so Project offers several ways to create and modify all types of task dependencies. This section describes your options and the pros and cons of each one, and then walks you through several methods for creating task dependencies, starting with the most common type—finish-to-start.

How Tasks Affect One Another

Clearly-defined task dependencies are essential to creating an easy-to-maintain schedule. Like a baton passed from one relay runner to the next, the start or finish date of one task (the *predecessor*) determines when the second task (the *successor*) starts or finishes. Although the tasks in a relationship are called predecessor and successor, a dependency isn't about which task starts first—it's about which task controls the timing of the other. For example, in a fnish-to-finish dependency, both tasks finish at the same time, but the finish of the predecessor task controls when the successor task finishes.

When you get your task dependencies in place (and use Project's automatic scheduling), project tasks fall into sequence, and the program can automatically calculate task start and finish dates—and from those, the end date of the entire project.

As Figure 5-1 illustrates, Project indicates task dependencies with small arrows showing how the start or end point of each task relates to the start or end of another.

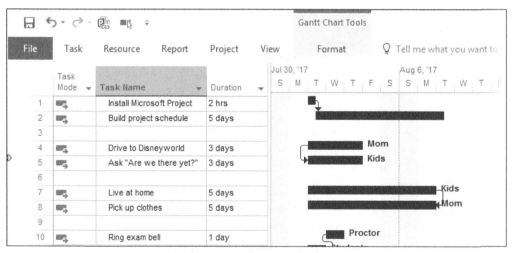

Figure 5-1. *Arrows show how the start or end of each task relates to the start or end of another.*

Task dependencies come in four flavors, listed here from the most to least common:

- **Finish-to-start (FS)** dependencies are the most common by far. In this relationship, the predecessor task comes first. When it finishes, the successor task begins—for example, when you finish installing a program on your computer, you can start using the program to do your real work.

- **Finish-to-finish (FF)** dependencies mean that the successor tasks continues only as long as the predecessor does. For instance, as long as your teenagers live at home (the predecessor), you ask them to pick up their clothes from the bathroom floor (the successor).

  These dependencies also tend to come with lag between the tasks. When a road crew inches along painting the lines on a highway, the folks who pick up the traffic cones finish a little while after the paint has dried.

- **Start-to-start (SS)** dependencies come in handy when the start of one task triggers the start of another. For instance, as soon as you start driving to your vacation destination (the predecessor task), your kids start asking, "Are we there yet?" (the successor task).

  Start-to-start dependencies often come with a delay (called *lag or lead*) between the predecessor and successor tasks (described later in this chapter). On that vacation drive, if your son starts poking his sister (the predecessor), she might not start crying (the successor) until 2 minutes have passed.

- **Start-to-finish (SF)** dependencies are rare, which is for the best, since this relationship can be confusing. To better grasp the relationship, avoid the terms "predecessor" and "successor," and simply remember that the start of one task controls the finish of another. For example, when an exam proctor rings the bell (the predecessor) to indicate that time is up, the students have to close their test booklets (the successor), whether or not they've answered all the questions.

All of these examples are pretty straightforward. In real life, it may not always be so clear what kind of dependency you're dealing with. See the next section for advice on figuring out which kind of dependency you should use.

Choosing the Right Relationship

For your project schedule to be accurate, you have to use the right type of dependency to link tasks. Simply put, if you don't connect tasks in the right way, the schedule won't reflect how work really proceeds once the project begins. Fortunately, the relationships between tasks are usually easy to identify. Most of the time, you're dealing with finish-to-start dependencies. But if you have trouble figuring out which relationship to use, ask yourself the following questions:

1. **Does the start or finish of one task control the other task?** When you answer this question, you know which task is the predecessor and which is the successor. You also know whether the dependency begins with "finish-to" or "start-to" in the list in the previous section.

2. **Does the predecessor control the start or finish of the successor?** The answer to this question settles the type of dependency. Simply add the answer to this question to the answer to question 1. For example, if the predecessor determines when the successor task *starts*, then "finish-to" becomes "finish-to-start."

Another way to sort out the relationship is to complete the following sentence: This predecessor must (start/finish) before I can (start/finish) that successor.

In addition to choosing the right type of dependency, it's important to identify *all* the dependencies between tasks. Several predecessors could drive a single successor or a single predecessor could affect several successors. Find relationships you missed by reviewing each task and asking yourself which other tasks affect it. Once you've identified all the predecessor tasks, you can identify the relationship between those tasks and the current task.

Creating Finish-to-Start Task Dependencies

Finish-to-start dependencies are so common that the Task tab's "Link the Selected Tasks" feature (it's in the Schedule section) is dedicated to creating them. When your tasks follow one another with the end of one task triggering the beginning of the next, this "Link the Selected Tasks" command is the fastest way to create those finish-to-start links. It's also the easiest way to link two tasks when you can't see both task bars in the Gantt Chart simultaneously.

> **Note:** If you've downloaded the sample files, use the file Event_Ch05_start.mpp.

Follow Along Practice

Here's how to create a finish-to-start task dependency using the "Link the Selected Tasks" feature:

1. Select the predecessor task, and then select the successor task you want to link it to.

    If the predecessor and successor aren't adjacent, click the predecessor first, and then Ctrl-click the successor. For this example, click the "Project start" milestone, and then Ctrl+click the "Identify core event team" task.

    If the predecessor and successor appear one after the other in the table area of the Gantt Chart, simply drag across the two tasks to select both. When you link the tasks, the one higher in the list will become the predecessor to the one immediately following it.

2. In the Task tab's Schedule section, click the "Link the Selected Tasks" icon (which looks like links of chain) to create the task dependency.

    Project creates finish-to-start dependencies between the selected tasks. The Gantt Chart timescale shows the link lines, as illustrated back in Figure 5-1, but you can also see predecessors and successors in the Task Form view, the table area of the Gantt Chart, and the Task Information dialog box, as you'll learn shortly.

> **Tip:** You can link more than two tasks at once. If several adjacent tasks link with finish-to-start dependencies, drag from the first to the last. If the order of the tasks in the table doesn't match their sequence, click the very first predecessor, and then Ctrl-click each task in the order you want Project to link them. Then click the "Link the Selected Tasks" icon.

When the task bars for two related tasks are visible in the Gantt Chart timescale, you can also create a finish-to-start link by dragging from the predecessor task bar to the successor task bar. This approach is advisable only if you pay close attention to what you're doing. If you don't select the first task correctly, you'll move the task instead of linking it, which creates an unintended date constraint. If the pointer turns into a one-headed or two-headed arrow as you drag, you're about to add a split into the middle of the task, or move it, instead of linking it to its successor. When you position the pointer over the first task, make sure you see a four-headed arrow. Then, as you drag the pointer to the second task, make sure the pointer changes to a link of a chain, as illustrated in Figure 5-2.

To practice this technique, drag from the "Identify core event team" task bar to the "Define event goals and objectives" task bar.

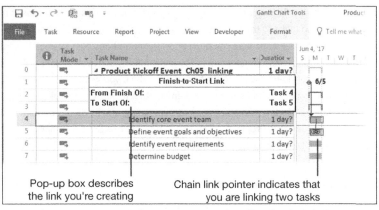

Figure 5-2. *In addition to the chain-link pointer, a pop-up box identifies the link that Project will create when you release the mouse button.*

Creating and Modifying All Types of Task Links

When you want to create, modify, or delete any kind of task dependency, you can take your pick from several locations in Project. This section is your guide to where you can define task links in Project, and the advantages or drawbacks of each.

> **Tip:** Sometimes, Project's attempts to be helpful are annoying. One way it may try to help is by automatically modifying task dependencies as you add, move, and delete tasks. For example, if you insert a new task between two existing linked tasks, Project removes the existing link and then creates finish-to-start dependencies between all three tasks. Likewise, if you delete a linked task, Project links the tasks above and below the deleted task.

> And if you move a task, Project deletes the links at the old spot and then links the task to the tasks above and below it in its new location.
>
> Project will Autolink inserted or moved tasks by default. If it is adjusting links automatically, here's how to regain control of linking: Choose File→Options, and then, on the left side of the Project Options dialog box, click Schedule.
>
> To change this setting for all new projects, in the box to the right of the "Scheduling options for this project" heading, choose All New Projects. Then, turn off the "Autolink inserted or moved tasks" checkbox.

Filling in Links in the Task Form

Project's Task Form includes fields for specifying predecessors, successors, types of links, and lag. It shows the values for the task that you select in the top view pane, so you can define, modify, or delete a task link.

> **Note:** Out of the box, Project turns on the "Update Manually Scheduled tasks when editing links" setting, which tells Project to change the dates for manually scheduled tasks if you link auto-scheduled tasks to them as predecessors. This setting is great when you create manually scheduled tasks because you don't know their durations but you want their dates scheduled based on their predecessors. (If you link manually scheduled tasks, Project creates the task link but doesn't change the task dates.) But if you want manually scheduled tasks to stay put, regardless of how you link them to other tasks (for example, for a training class that's scheduled for specific dates), turn this setting off. To do so, choose File Options. On the left side of the Project Options dialog box, choose Schedule, and then look in the "Scheduling options for this project" section.

Follow Along Practice

To link the selected task to its predecessor, do the following:

1. Display the Gantt Chart view in the top pane and the Task Form in the Details pane.

    In the View tab's Task Views section, click the top half of the Gantt Chart button. In the View tab's Split View section, turn on the Details checkbox. The Details box automatically chooses Task Form.

2. If you don't see the Predecessor or Successor tables in the Task Form, right-click within the form, and then choose Predecessors & Successors.

3. In the Gantt Chart view in the top pane, select the successor task, in this example, "Identify event requirements."

    The Task Form shows the values for the selected task.

4. In the Task Form, click a blank Predecessor Name cell and then, from the drop-down list, choose the predecessor task, "Define goals and objectives," as demonstrated in Figure 5-3. In

newer Project editions, the drop-down menu displays tasks in an outline, so it's easy to identify summary and subtasks.

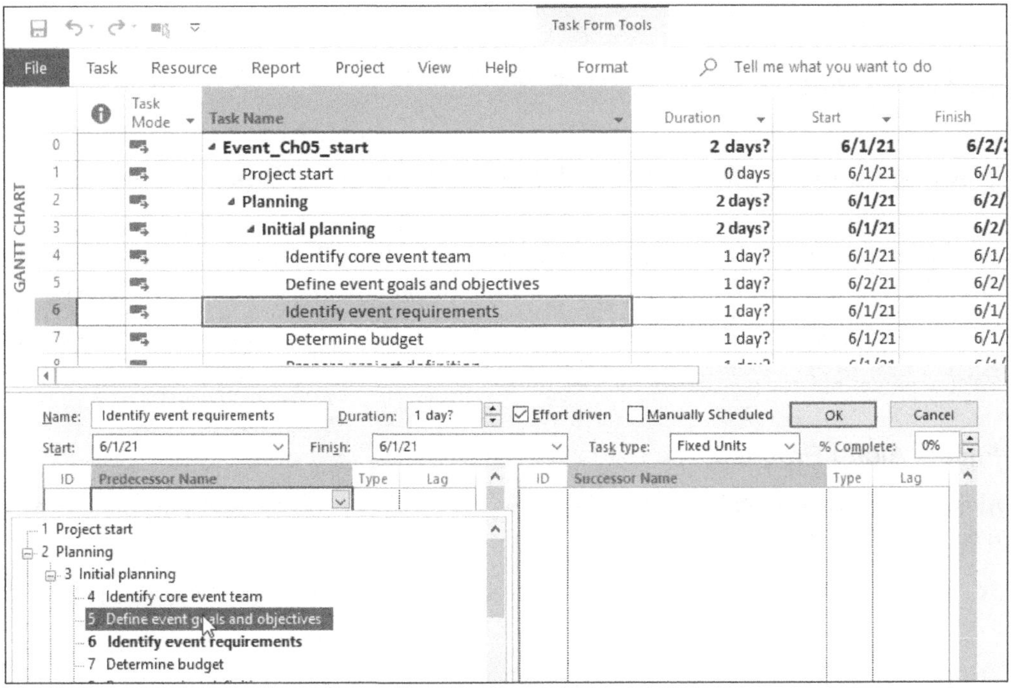

Figure 5-3. *If you're on a task-dependency tear, the Task Form can set both predecessors and successors at the same time. Right-click the Task Form and then, from the shortcut menu, choose Predecessors & Successors.*

5. In the Type cell's drop-down list, choose the task dependency, such as FS for finish-to-start.

    The names are abbreviated to initials: FS for finish-to-start, SS for start-to-start, FF for finish-to-finish, and SF for start-to-finish.

    > **Tip:** If you want to introduce a delay or overlap the tasks, then enter a time value or a percentage in the Lag box. (How lag time works is covered later in this chapter.)

6. Click OK to create the link. (If you don't want the link, press Esc or click Cancel.)

    The link lines for the dependency appear between the task bars in the Gantt Chart timescale.

The Task Form is a great timesaver, because you can use it to add, modify, or remove links with equal ease:

- **Add a link**: First, select a task in the table area of the top view pane. Then, in a blank predecessor row of the Task Form, specify the predecessor task's ID (or name), the type of dependency, and the lag duration (if any); then click OK.

- **Modify a link**: In the Task Form, click the cell you want to change, and then choose a different value. For example, if you created a task as start-to-start and it should be finish-to-finish, then click the link's Type cell and choose FF. You can modify the predecessor task and the lag, as well. When you're done, click OK.

- **Delete a link**: In the Task Form, click anywhere in the link's row, and then press Delete. Then click OK to confirm the deletion.

Working on Task Links in the Task Information Dialog Box

The Task Information dialog box is full of information about the currently selected task. To use it to create links, first select the successor task and then open the dialog box (by pressing Shift+F2; in the Task tab's Properties section, clicking Information; or simply double-clicking the successor task). In the dialog box, select the Predecessors tab to define links between the selected task and its predecessors, as shown in Figure 5-4. For practice, use the Task Information dialog box to make "Identify event requirements" the predecessor to "Determine budget."

Follow Along Practice

Although the Task Information dialog box is great when you want to see or edit everything about a task, it has a few limitations compared with setting dependencies in the Task Form:

- To work on links, you have to open the dialog box, as opposed to seeing the fields at all times in the Task Form.

- The Task Information dialog box lets you define only predecessors to the selected task, not successors.

- To work on links for another task, you have to close the dialog box, select the other task, and then reopen the Task Information dialog box.

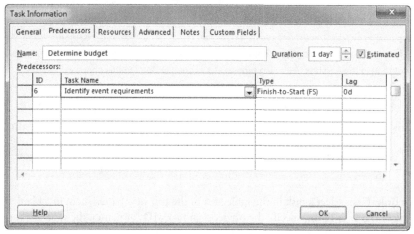

Figure 5-4. *Double-clicking a task opens the Task Information dialog box, displaying the values for that task.*

Defining Task Dependencies in the Table Area

The Entry table, which the Gantt Chart view displays out of the box, includes the Predecessors column, which is great if you prefer typing to mousing. You can specify everything about a link in a task's Predecessors cell—as long as you know the code:

- **Create a single finish-to-start link**: All you do is type the ID number (the first column in the table area) of the predecessor and then press Enter.

- **Create several finish-to-start links to the selected task**: Separate each ID number with a comma, like this: *1,2,5,10*. Then press Enter.

- **Create a link other than finish-to-start**: Type the dependency abbreviation immediately after the ID number. For instance, to create a start-to-start link with task number 3, type *3SS*. (The abbreviations for the dependency types are the first letters of each half of the relationship: FS, SS, FF, SF.)

- **Designate the lag or lead time**: Type a plus sign (+) followed by the length of the delay or a minus sign (–) followed by the length of the lead, such as *3SS+5days*.

Editing Links by Double-Clicking Them

Double-clicking a link line in the Gantt Chart timescale opens a small dialog box, shown in Figure 5-5, for modifying or deleting the link. Needless to say, you can't use the double-click method to *create* a task dependency, because you need a link to double-click.

Before you change any values, make sure that the From and To tasks represent the link you want to modify. Then, in the Type drop-down list, choose the new dependency. The Lag box is where you specify the lag or lead time. If you want to delete the link, click Delete.

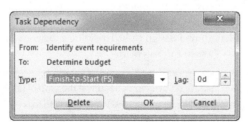

Figure 5-5. *Double-clicking a link is easy, unless you've got link lines splattered all over the Gantt Chart timescale, making finding the right link line a challenge.*

Removing Task Links

The Task tab's Unlink Tasks icon (which lives in the Schedule section and looks like a broken link of chain) does different things depending on what's selected when you click it:

- **Remove the link between two tasks**: If you select two linked tasks, then clicking Unlink Tasks removes the dependency between them.

- **Remove all links to a task**: If you select a single task and then click Unlink Tasks, then Project removes **all** the links to that task, not just the task link you probably had in mind.

You can also delete a link by double-clicking its link line in a Gantt Chart timescale and clicking Delete in the Task Dependency dialog box, removing a predecessor in the Task Information dialog box, or deleting the link in the Predecessors cell in the Entry table, as described in previous sections.

Delaying or Overlapping Tasks

Tasks don't always occur in rapid-fire succession. When a company submits an invoice, for example, it usually has to wait 30 days to receive payment. When you enter a positive number in Project's Lag field, the delay that creates between linked tasks is called "lag time," because the second task lags for a while before it starts (or finishes). If you enter a negative number in the Lag field, the tasks overlap, which is often called "lead time"—like giving someone a 30-minute head start because you're faster than they are. In Project, the Lag field handles both lags **and** leads.

> **Note:** Lag is a delay (or overlap) between tasks that comes about no matter what happens. Project also includes a field called Assignment Delay, which delays a task until an assigned resource is available to work on it.

In Project, you use the Lag field to specify delays and overlaps, which can be durations or percentages:

- **Add a time delay**: If you have to wait 30 minutes after eating to get in the pool, enter **30min** in the Lag field.

- **Add an overlap**: Enter a negative value, such as **–2d** to start testing publicity communication before the materials are complete.

- **Add a percentage delay or overlap**: Using a percentage tells Project to adjust the length of the delay or overlap if the duration of the predecessor changes—for instance, to increase the amount of overlap based on the length of a design task. To define a delay or overlap as a percentage, simply type a percentage like **75%** in the Lag field.

> **Tip:** Whether you use a delay or an overlap depends on the type of task dependency. If you link tasks with a start-to-start link, entering 75% in the Lag field tells Project to start the second task when 75 percent of the first one is complete. If you link the tasks as finish-to-start, you can obtain the same results by entering -25% in the Lag field. For example, consider a task for raking leaves and another for mowing the lawn. You can create a start-to-start link from raking leaves to mowing with a 75 percent delay so your spouse doesn't start mowing until you've raked three-quarters of the yard. If you create a finish-to-start link between these two tasks instead and enter –25% in the Lag field, the yard-mowing task still starts three-quarters through raking leaves. When choosing either relationship, focus on the first item in the relationship: Finish to Start where the Predecessor finishes and the Successor starts, or Start to Start where the Predecessor starts and the Successors starts.

All methods for creating and modifying task dependencies, except for the "Link the Selected Tasks" command, include a place to specify the delay or overlap. (If you link tasks with the "Link the Selected Tasks" command, you can edit those links later to add a delay or an overlap.) Here's how you set a delay or overlap using each method of defining task links:

- **Task Form**: When you display predecessors or successors in the Task Form, each link includes four fields: ID, Predecessor Name (or Successor Name), Type, and Lag. In the Lag cell, enter the delay (a positive number) or overlap (a negative number).

- **Task Information dialog box**: When you display the Predecessors tab in the Task Information dialog box, the last column is Lag. As in the Task Form, type the duration or percentage you want in the Lag cell.

- **Table area**: In the table area's Predecessor cells, you append the delay or overlap lead to the link information. If the successor task starts 3 days after the end of the predecessor task (whose task ID is 6), the Predecessor cell would read *6FS+3 days*.

- **Double-clicking a link line**: The Task Dependency dialog box includes a Lag box for the delay or overlap value (see Figure 5-5).

Entering Task Duration

You'll never predict project duration with total accuracy. However, estimating task duration and work time as closely as you can is the goal, because both high and low estimates can cause problems. Overestimate how long your project will take, and the project might get squelched before it begins. Underestimate, and you might run into disappointment, extensions, and financial consequences.

This section begins by explaining the difference between duration and work. After you link the tasks in your project, you usually add estimated durations to them. That's because you can add durations without figuring out how many resources you have available, who works on what, and assigning those resources to tasks. This chapter describes methods for entering task durations. (Chapter 7 explains how to enter work for tasks.)

Understanding Work and Duration

In Project, *work* and *duration* are both ways of measuring time, but each term has a specific meaning:

- **Work**: The number of person-hours (or equipment-hours) a task requires. For example, putting together presentations may take you (that is, one person) 40 hours.

- **Duration**: The span of work time from the start of a task to the finish. You can specify duration for a task, such as 5 days, without assigning resources to it. If you assign resources to the task, duration varies according to how many resources (people or equipment) you use, and when those resources are available, as you'll see in Chapter 7. For example, if you can't spend more than 4 hours each day on the presentations, you may need 10 workdays for that 40-hour task. On the other hand, if you convince three colleagues to help (and they share your skills), the duration decreases to a little more than one workday, but the four of you still devote a total of 40 hours of work to the task.

> **Tip:** Project team members spend time on a variety of administrative tasks, like preparing status reports, attending meetings, and so on. The easiest way to include admin work in a Project schedule is to include time spent on non-project tasks in your duration and work estimates. The hard part of this approach is figuring out how much time people typically spend on admin work each day. The amount depends on your organization, the amount of admin work in your project, where team members are located, and so on. A typical guideline is 20%.

Whether you enter duration, work, or both depends on whether you know how many people are available to work on tasks. If you don't know how many resources are available, then estimate the hours of work (or days of work for very large projects) and use that work estimate as the duration estimate. When one person is assigned to work full time on a task, the number of hours of work equals the hours of duration. However, if you have multiple resources in mind, you can estimate a duration that differs from hours of work. Either way, when you assign resources to a task, Project adjusts the task's work and duration accordingly (as Chapter 7 explains). In Project, the formula for calculating these values is:

$$\text{Assignment Work (hours)} = \text{Duration (days)} \times \text{Calendar} \left(\frac{\text{hours}}{\text{day}} \right) \times \text{Assignment Units (\%)}$$

For example, consider a task that has a 5-day duration and a resource who works 8 hours each day and is assigned at 100%. The assignment work is 5 x 8 x 1, or 40 hours.

> **Note:** If you create Auto Scheduled tasks without filling in their Duration fields, Project sets the duration to "1 day?" to indicate that it's an estimated duration. That question mark rolls up to summary tasks, so your project duration will contain a question mark if even one task has an estimated duration. (To quickly track down the tasks with estimated durations, in the View tab's Data section, click the Filter down arrow, and then choose Tasks With Estimated Durations. Then Project displays only tasks with question marks in their Duration fields.)
>
> You can tell Project to fill in regular durations instead of estimated ones when you create an Auto Scheduled task without a duration. (The downside to this setting is that you have to remember which tasks' durations you still need to fill in with your estimated values.) If you decide to change this setting, choose File→Options. On the left side of the Project Options dialog box, choose Schedule. In the "Scheduling options for this project" section, turn off the "New scheduled tasks have estimated durations" checkbox. With this setting, Project sets the duration to "1 day."

Filling in Task Duration

You can enter duration values for tasks in the table on the left side of any Gantt Chart view. Because Project calculates the duration for automatically-scheduled summary tasks, you only need to fill in duration for work tasks.

> **Note:** If you've downloaded the sample files from the book website, use the file Event_Ch05_addduration.mpp.

Here's how to set up a Gantt Chart view and enter durations quickly:

1. Display the Gantt Chart view by clicking the top half of the Gantt Chart button on the Task tab.

2. On the Format tab, in the Show/Hide section, turn off the Project Summary Task checkbox and the Summary Tasks checkbox.

    You can hide summary tasks because Project takes care of calculating their durations.

3. In the Gantt Chart table, click the down arrow to the right of the Duration heading. On the dropdown menu, turn off the "0 days" checkbox, and then click OK.

    Milestones are already set to "0 days," so you don't have to enter durations for them.

4. Now that the task list displays only activity tasks, click the first task's Duration cell, for example, the task "Identify core event team."

5. Type the duration, such as 3, which represents 3 days.

    Project's option for duration units, "Duration is entered in," (see Chapter 3) is set to days by default. If you change that option to another unit, such as weeks, then you need to type 3d in the Duration cell to specify three days.

    When you press the down arrow, Project replaces the abbreviated value you type with an expanded value. For example, 1w becomes "1 week," 2mo becomes "2 months," and so on.

6. Repeat steps 4 and 5 to fill in durations for the rest of the activity tasks in the project.

7. When you're done, redisplay the full task list.

    To do that, click the Filter icon to the right of the Duration heading, and choose Clear Filter from Duration. On the Format tab, turn on the Project Summary Task checkbox and Summary Task checkbox.

Copying Duration Estimates from Excel into Project

Although you **can** type duration estimates directly into task fields in Project, using an Excel spreadsheet to compile estimates instead has several advantages. First of all, many people who estimate tasks are familiar with Excel but not Project. (In fact, estimators may not even have Project on their computers, but they almost certainly have Excel.) And Excel makes it easier to adjust estimated values than Project; for instance, it can calculate the average of several estimates.

The first step in compiling estimates in Excel is to export activity tasks (tasks that aren't summary tasks or milestones) from Project to build a simple spreadsheet in Excel. You can divvy up the tasks for each estimator into a separate Excel workbook and then reassemble the results in one master spreadsheet that you use to get values into Project. This section guides you through the steps.

Creating a Task List in Excel

If you're estimating from the bottom up, the only tasks you estimate are the tasks that represent specific activities that need to be performed. You don't have to develop estimates for summary tasks because Project calculates their values from the tasks below them based on their dependencies and milestones have a duration of zero days.

Here are the steps for creating a spreadsheet with a list of activity tasks:

1. Open the Project file you want to estimate and, if necessary, display the Gantt Chart view (on the task tab, click the Gantt Chart button).

2. On the Format tab, in the Show/Hide section, turn off the Project Summary Task checkbox and the Summary Tasks checkbox.

3. In the Gantt Chart table, click the down arrow to the right of the Duration heading. On the dropdown menu, turn off the "0 days" checkbox, and then click OK.

4. Click the table's Task Name column heading to select the entire column of task names.

5. Press Ctrl+C to copy the task names to the clipboard.

6. Launch Excel and create a new blank workbook. (In the Excel Backstage, on the Templates page, click "Blank workbook.")

7. Click cell A1 at the top left of the worksheet.

8. Press Ctrl+V to paste the Task Name column heading and all the work task names into the first column of the worksheet.

> **Tip:** If the first column is too narrow to display full task names, point at the vertical divider between the first and second column headings. When the pointer changes to a two-headed arrow, drag to the right.

9. On the File tab, click Save, and then, on the Save As page, click the folder where you want to save the file. In the Save As dialog box's File name box, type the name for the worksheet, and then click Save.

10. Whether you send the file to someone else or fill in estimated durations yourself, fill in the second column in the worksheet with the estimated durations for each task, as shown in Figure 5-6.

    You can fill in abbreviated durations (like 3d) or expanded durations (like 3 days).

You can add additional columns in the Excel workbook for best- and worst-case estimates, or a column for the name of the person responsible for estimating the task. Add whatever columns you need to make your work in Excel easier: You don't have to copy those columns back into your Project file.

11. When all the durations are in place, save the file again.

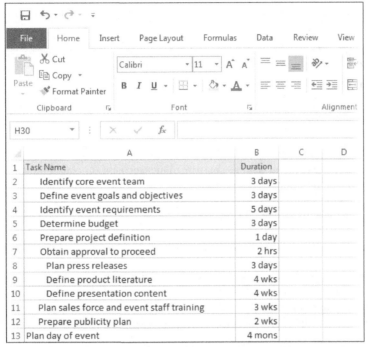

Figure 5-6. *Fill in the second column with task durations. The second column is the only one you need to copy back into your Project file.*

Copying Durations from Excel to Project

To copy estimated durations from a spreadsheet into Duration cells in a Project file, follow these steps:

1. In Project, be sure to hide summary tasks and milestones as described in the previous section.

2. Open the Excel spreadsheet and select the cells that contain your duration estimates. To follow along, open the file Ch05_copydurations.xlsx and copy the cells that contain duration values in the Duration column.

3. Press Ctrl+C to copy the cells to the Clipboard.

4. Switch to Project, and click the first cell in the Duration column in the table area.

5. Press Ctrl+V to paste the estimated values. Project copies each cell from the spreadsheet into the selected cell and the ones below it.

6. Redisplay summary tasks and milestones.

Comparing Estimated Durations to Management Timeframes

Executives and project customers have a habit of telling you how long you have to complete a project long before you know whether that length of time is sufficient. If you're scheduling a project based on timeframes you've been given by someone else, you can use manually scheduled tasks to compare target timeframes with the duration Project calculates. To do this, you create manually scheduled summary tasks with the duration and dates you're trying to meet. When you add subtasks to the summary tasks, you can see whether they fit within the summary-task duration or run over the allotted time (see Figure 5-7).

> **Note:** If you've downloaded the sample files, use the file Event_Ch05_ manualsummary.mpp.

Follow Along Practice

Here's how to compare durations in Project to management timeframes:

1. Select the summary task you want to compare to management timeframes, such as "Initial planning."

2. In the Task tab's Tasks section, click Manually Schedule.

3. In the summary task's Duration cell, type the duration you've been given for the summary task, for example, 15 days, and then press Enter.

Project keeps track of the duration you specified for the summary task and the total duration of all the subtasks, as you can see in Figure 5-7. The task bar immediately below the summary-task bracket shows the rolled-up duration of all the subtasks, which is drawn between the Scheduled Start and Scheduled Finish dates, although these fields don't appear in the view's table.

If the total duration of the subtask is shorter than the summary task's duration, the rolled-up task bar is blue to indicate that you have extra buffer time. If the total duration of the subtask is longer than the summary task's duration, the rolled-up task bar is red, as illustrated by the task in row 3. In addition, red squiggles under a finish date (see row 3) indicate a scheduling problem (in this case, the subtasks' total duration is longer than the summary task's duration).

> **Note:** For a manually scheduled task, the Scheduled Start and Scheduled Finish fields are read-only and contain the dates that Project recommends for the task's start and finish. Most of the time, the Scheduled Start and Scheduled Finish values are the same as the task's Start and Finish values.

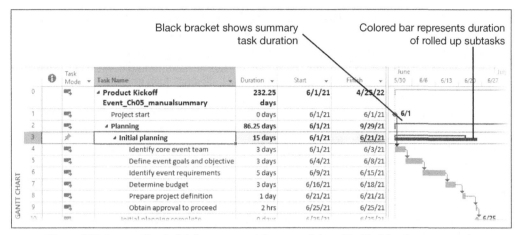

Figure 5-7. *A manually scheduled summary task has two task bars. The black brackets represent the summary task's duration. The colored bar represents the duration of all the rolled up subtasks.*

Scheduling Tasks to Accommodate Specific Dates

Anyone who's taken a project-management course knows the monumental tedium of manually calculating start dates, finish dates, slack time, and other schedule values. Letting Project calculate a schedule frees up your time for more important project-management activities, so normally you don't want to hobble the program's scheduling capabilities. From time to time, though, you need more control over task dates. Suppose the new database guru you just hired will start work on October 12 so she won't start her tasks before that date. Or the event your company is hosting takes place on April 10 whether you're ready or not.

To keep your schedule low maintenance, let Project calculate it as much as possible. That way, the program recalculates dates automatically when predecessors get delayed or take more (or less) time than planned. However, when you want tasks to occur on or around specific dates, you can make that happen in two ways:

- **Set a task's task mode to Manually Scheduled**: When tasks are set to Auto Scheduled mode, Project does what you expect project-management software to do: It calculates when tasks start and finish based on predecessors, resource availability, and so on. Setting a task to Manually Scheduled mode instead (which is the default setting unless you change it) means Project quietly steps aside as you change the task dates to your heart's content. Manually scheduling tasks is perfect when you want to specify both start and finish dates.

- **Add a date constraint to a task**: A *date constraint* (or simply *constraint*) limits when a task either starts or finishes. Every task has a constraint, even if it's the completely flexible As Soon As Possible constraint. On the other hand, completely inflexible constraints like Must Start

On make tasks behave a lot like manually scheduled tasks, except that you can specify a date constraint on only one of a task's dates. (A complete list of Project's date constraints is included in the section, "Types of Constraints.") One reason to use a date constraint instead of manual scheduling is if you want a constraint that's partially flexible—for example, when you want a task to start before a specific date, but you don't care how much before.

This section explains how to use manual scheduling and date constraints to set task dates. You'll learn about the types of date constraints at your disposal and how to use them without forfeiting schedule flexibility. In addition, you'll find out how to use deadlines to spotlight key dates without applying inflexible date constraints.

Manually Scheduling Task Dates

If a task occurs on specific dates—for example, the product kickoff event your company is throwing on April 10, 2018—Project's Manually Scheduled mode helps you set task dates in a jiffy. When a task is set to this mode, you're in the driver's seat date-wise. (To learn everything manual scheduling can do, see Chapter 4.)

> **Note:** If you've downloaded the sample files, continue to use the file Event_Ch05_manu-alsummary.mpp.

Follow Along Practice

Here's how to set task dates with manual scheduling:

1. Select the task whose dates you want to control (in this example, the task "Event day"). Then, in the Task tab's Tasks section, click Manually Schedule.

   You can also right-click the task and choose Manually Schedule from the shortcut menu. If you display the Entry, Schedule, or Summary table on the left side of the Gantt Chart view, click the task's Task Mode cell, click the down arrow that appears, and then choose Manually Scheduled.

2. In the task table, type the dates you want in the task's Start and Finish cells (in this example, 4/11/2022).

   In the Gantt Chart timescale, Project places brackets on each end of the task's bar, as shown in Figure 5-8, and changes the bar's color to teal to indicate that the task is manually scheduled (auto-scheduled tasks have blue bars). If the manually scheduled task's predecessors are delayed, then Project draws a red squiggle below the task's dates to flag that there's a problem. See Chapter 10 to learn what your options are when that happens.

	ⓘ	Task Mode ▾	Task Name ▾	Duration ▾	Start ▾	Finish ▾	Apr 10, '22 S M T W
78		🖩	Set up presentation area furniture	1 day	1/17/22	1/18/22	
79		🖩	Set up marketing and sales area	1 day	1/17/22	1/18/22	
80		🖩	IT setup	2 days	1/17/22	1/19/22	
81		🖩	Food setup (performed by venue sta	4 hrs	1/18/22	1/19/22	
82		🖩	Event setup complete	0 days	1/19/22	1/19/22	
83		🖩	◢ **Run event**	**1 day**	**4/11/22**	**4/11/22**	
84		📌	Event day	1 day	4/11/22	4/11/22	
85			◢ **Cleanup**	**3 days**	**4/12/22**	**4/14/22**	
86			Pack and remove supplies	1 day	4/12/22	4/12/22	
87			Take down marketing, sales, and de	1 day	4/13/22	4/13/22	
88			Send materials back to HQ	1 day	4/14/22	4/14/22	

Pushpin indicates task is
manually scheduled

Brackets indicate manually
scheduled dates

Figure 5-8. *Change a task to manually scheduled when you want to specify its start and finish dates.*

Types of Constraints

Date constraints run the gamut from totally flexible to totally firm, and each type has its place. Unless a task is associated with a specific date, stick to the most flexible constraints—As Soon As Possible or As Late As Possible. (Task constraints aren't available for tasks set to Manually Scheduled mode.) Here are all of Project's constraint types (from most flexible to least flexible) and when to use them:

- **As Soon As Possible**: When you schedule a project from its start date (see Chapter 3), Project automatically assigns the As Soon As Possible date constraint to tasks, because this constraint doesn't determine when a task occurs. The start and finish date for the task are scheduled as soon as possible given its task dependencies, duration, assigned resources, and work times.

- **As Late As Possible**: Project automatically applies this constraint to every task when you schedule a project from its finish date. It's just as flexible as As Soon As Possible. The one problem with As Late As Possible tasks is that they don't leave any wiggle room for delays if something goes wrong. So if you have to delay a task with this type of constraint, its successors (and in many cases, the project's finish date) get delayed as well.

- **Start No Earlier Than**: You use this partly flexible date constraint for tasks that can start only after a certain date. For example, you can't buy concert tickets until they go on sale, but you can buy them any time after that date (until they sell out, that is). If you type a date in a task's Start field in a project that's scheduled from its start date, then Project sets the task to this constraint type.

- **Finish No Earlier Than**: This is another date constraint with some built-in flexibility, and it's ideal for tasks that have to continue until a specific date—for instance, processing event registrations until the cutoff date. If you type a date in a task's Finish field in a project that's scheduled from its start date, Project changes the task's constraint type to this one.

- **Start No Later Than**: This date constraint sets the latest date that a task can begin. You might use this constraint to make sure that construction begins early enough to enclose a house before winter hits, for example. However, construction can begin earlier if everything goes smoothly. If you schedule a project from its finish date, Project uses this constraint type when you type a date in a task's Start field.

- **Finish No Later Than**: You can apply this date constraint to control the latest date for a task to finish. For example, if payments have to be recorded before a specific date, then you can schedule your registration task to finish a few days earlier than that to leave time for processing. If you schedule a project from its finish date, then Project uses this constraint type when you type a date in a task's Finish field.

- **Must Start On**: This date constraint is completely inflexible. It specifies when a task starts—no ifs, ands, or buts. Moreover, this constraint's inflexibility overrides any task dependencies you set, as explained in the note titled "When Constraints and Dependencies Clash." Because of that, avoid using this type of constraint unless it's absolutely necessary.

- **Must Finish On**: A control freak when it comes to the finish date, this date constraint specifies the exact date when a task ends. Like Must Start On, it also overrides task dependencies and is best left unused unless absolutely necessary.

When Constraints and Dependencies Clash

Setting a Must Finish On constraint sounds definite, but that constraint doesn't guarantee on-time completion. Moreover, inflexible constraints, such as Finish No Later Than or Must Start On, can generate subtle and dangerous behavior on Project's part. Suppose a predecessor task runs late and pushes a successor past its must-finish-on date. Project can't keep both the Must Finish On constraint and the finish-to-start task dependency, so it has to pick one. Out of the box, Project honors the date constraint, which seems fine until you notice that the two tasks now overlap instead of following each other, as shown in Figure 5-9a. When you execute the project, those tasks aren't likely to overlap, which will push the tasks' dates beyond the constraint you see in the Project schedule.

Most of the time, you want Project to warn you when your schedule might miss an important date. To get this type of warning, you have to tell Project to honor task dependencies, *not* date constraints. That way, predecessors and successors interact the way they should, but a task that blows past its constraint date displays a Missed Constraint indicator (shown in Figure 5-9b).

To honor task dependencies over date constraints, click File→Options. On the left side of the Project Options dialog box, click Schedule, and then turn off the "Tasks will always honor their constraint dates" checkbox. If you want this setting to apply to all future projects, then in the "Scheduling options for this project" drop-down list, choose All New Projects, and *then* turn off the checkbox.

Note: You can apply only one date constraint to a task at a time—for example, Must Start On or Must Finish On. If you change a task's mode to Manually Scheduled, you set both the start and finish date for the task, so it's like applying a Must Start On *and* a Must Finish On date constraint. If you *edit* task dependencies connected to manually scheduled tasks, Project recalculates the tasks' start and finish dates. However, you can tell Project to leave manually scheduled tasks' dates as they are, regardless of edits you make to task dependencies. To do so, choose File→Options. On the left side of the Project Options dialog box, choose Schedule. Scroll to the "Scheduling options for this project" section and turn off the "Update Manually Scheduled task when editing links" checkbox. Then click OK.

Project ignores this task link to honor the date constraint

Figure 5-9a. *Tasks that should follow each other can end up overlapping when Project ignores a task dependency in order to honor a date constraint. Project doesn't warn you about these overlaps, so you might not notice them.*

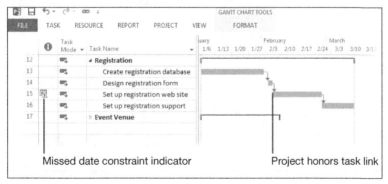

Missed date constraint indicator   Project honors task link

Figure 5-9b. *If you turn off the "Tasks will always honor their constraint dates" setting, Project keeps things in the correct sequence and warns you about missed date constraints by putting an icon in the Indicators column.*

Setting and Changing Constraints

Microsoft has been called a lot of things, but *minimalist* isn't one of them. As with most of its features, Project lets you work with constraints in several locations:

Follow Along Practice

- **Task Details Form**: Task Details includes a Constraint box and a Date box. To set or change a single task's constraint, select the task in the table area of a view like the Gantt Chart, in this example, "Train sales staff." Then, in the Task Details view in the Details pane, in the Constraint drop-down list, choose the type of constraint you want (in this example, Start No Earlier Than). If you select a constraint other than As Soon As Possible or As Late As Possible, choose a date in the Date box, too. In this example, type 3/21/22 in the Date box, and then click OK to save the task.

> **Note:** To display the Task Details Form in the Details pane, head to the View tab's Split View section and turn on the Details checkbox. Next, click the down arrow to the right of the Details box and choose More Views in the drop-down list. In the More Views dialog box, click Task Details Form, and then click Apply.

- **Task Information dialog box**: In this example, double-click the task "Monitor registrations." In the Task Information dialog box, click the Advanced tab. In the "Constraint type" and "Constraint date" boxes, choose the type and date for the constraint, in this example, choose Finish No Earlier Than and 4/10/22, respectively. (If you select a manually scheduled task, these two boxes are grayed out.)

- **Table area**: The table area is ideal when you want to change the constraints for many tasks at once. If you've just learned about the evils of inflexible constraints, you may want to change all tasks back to As Soon As Possible. To do so, right-click a column heading, and then choose Insert Column from the shortcut menu. In the drop-down list that appears for the new column, choose Constraint Type. In a Constraint Type cell, choose the new constraint type (As Soon As Possible, in this case). To copy that type to additional tasks, position the pointer over the cell's *fill handle* (the small square in the cell's bottom-right corner) until the pointer changes to a + sign. Then drag down through the Constraint Type cells you want to change.

Preventing Unwanted Date Constraints

Because Project automatically assigns the most flexible constraint to auto-scheduled tasks (As Soon As Possible if you schedule from the start date, As Late As Possible if you schedule from the finish date), the golden rule is to leave the constraint alone unless you have a very good reason to change it. But date constraints have an exasperating way of appearing when you're sure you didn't set them. It turns out that a few seemingly innocent actions on your part can create date constraints in Project.

Best Practices

To make sure your schedule doesn't gain date constraints you didn't intend, heed the following guidelines:

- **Don't type a specific date in a Start or Finish cell for an auto-scheduled task**: If you type a date in one of these cells, Project changes the date constraint to Start No Earlier Than in a project scheduled from its start date or Start No Later Than in a project scheduled from its finish date.

- **Don't set the finish date for a task just because that's the deadline**: The whole point of using Project is to find out ahead of time that a task won't finish on time, so you can adjust your schedule to bring the finish date back in line.

> **Tip:** For a better way to indicate deadlines without adding inappropriate date constraints, read the next section.

- **Don't drag a task bar horizontally in the Gantt Chart timeline**: This action tells Project to change the constraint to Start No Earlier Than or Start No Later Than, depending on whether you've scheduled the project from its start date or finish date. Dragging task bars incorrectly can also link tasks you don't want connected, or split a task into two pieces. Avoid editing tasks in the timescale unless you're completely fastidious and a maestro with the mouse.

> **Note:** If you set a task's mode to Manually Scheduled, you can safely drag its task bar horizontally to change when it occurs. Project doesn't change the Constraint Type field when tasks are set to Manually Scheduled mode.

Setting Deadline Reminders

As their name implies, deadlines are dates that usually have ghastly consequences if you miss them. However, they also usually represent dates that your project customer and stakeholders want your project to meet. Yet Project's date constraints don't guarantee that you'll meet your deadlines and, as explained in the previous section, setting constraints can have serious drawbacks. The best way to stay on top of deadlines in Project is to define the deadline date in a task's Deadline field. Meanwhile, schedule the project as you would normally. That way, with the deadlines set for various tasks, you keep on the lookout for Project indicators that a deadline is in jeopardy. If you spot a missed-deadline indicator, you can investigate the issue and develop a plan to pull the task dates in earlier.

> **Tip:** As you execute your project plan, remember to check the Indicators column regularly for missed date constraints and missed deadlines.

> **Note:** When you add deadlines, Project uses the deadline date to calculate the critical path, not the early start/finish and late start/finish dates. See Chapter 9 for more on deadlines.

Follow Along Practice

Here are the steps for setting and tracking a deadline for a task:

1. Double-click the task (in this example, "Sponsors on board") to open the Task Information dialog box.

    You can also select the task, and then, in the Task tab's Properties section, click Information.

2. In the Task Information dialog box, click the Advanced tab. In the Deadline box, click the arrow to display a calendar, and then choose the deadline date (in this example, 12/13/21). Then click OK to close the dialog box.

    In the Gantt Chart view's timescale, Project displays a green down-pointing arrow at the task's deadline date. If the task's bar ends before or at this arrow, the task is on or ahead of its deadline. If the task bar ends to the right of this arrow, as shown in Figure 5-10, the task is running late.

Figure 5-10. *The deadline for a task appears as a green down-pointing arrow in the Gantt Chart timescale. If the task is scheduled to finish after the deadline date, a missed-deadline icon appears in the Indicators column.*

3. To see whether any tasks have missed their deadlines, review the Indicators column for red diamonds with exclamation points inside.

    To make missed deadlines easier to see, you can filter the task list to show only tasks with Deadline dates assigned. To do that, in the View tab's Data section, click the Filter drop-down list (its icon looks like a funnel), and then choose More Filters. In the More Filters dialog box, double-click Tasks With Deadlines. Project displays tasks with deadlines assigned, along with the summary tasks to which those tasks belong. If you want to hide the summary tasks, in the Gantt Chart Tools | Format tab's Show/Hide section, turn off the Summary Tasks checkbox.

Scheduling Task Work Time with a Task Calendar

Sometimes tasks must run at specific times of the day or on certain days of the week. For example, scheduling computer maintenance during off-hours keeps complaints from information workers to a minimum. Calendars in Microsoft Project let you specify working and nonworking time to help schedule tasks on the days and times you want. By applying a calendar to a task, you can specify the hours when the task's work should occur. Because the Calendar box is set to None, by default, that means that the task uses the calendar assigned to the project. You don't have to apply a calendar to every task in the task list.

Follow Along Practice

You can easily assign a calendar to a task. Here are the steps:

1. In a view's table area, select the task(s) to which you want to assign a calendar (in this example, "Venue setup, performed by venue staff"), and then, in the Task tab's Properties section, click Information.

    If you select only one task, the Task Information dialog box opens. If you select more than one task, you see the Multiple Task Information dialog box, which is identical to the Task Information dialog box, except that fields unique to individual tasks are disabled.

2. Click the dialog box's Advanced tab and, in the Calendar drop-down list, choose the calendar you want to apply, Evening Shift as illustrated in Figure 5-11.

    Project comes with three built-in calendars: Standard for an 8-to-5 work schedule, Night Shift for the 11 p.m. to 8 a.m. grind, and 24 Hours for the gerbils on treadmills in your organization. If you want a different calendar, like Evening Shift, you have to create it (see Chapter 3) before opening the Task Information dialog box.

    After you select a calendar in the Calendar drop-down list, the "Scheduling ignores resource calendars" checkbox comes to life, but it's not turned on. With this checkbox turned off, Project schedules work for the working hours shared by the task calendar and calendars for the assigned resources. If the task calendar and resource calendars don't have any mutual work time, a message box warns you that the calendars don't jibe. You can then change the task calendar or the resource calendar to make them overlap. If you want Project to schedule work only by the task calendar (and ignore the resource calendar), turn on this checkbox. In this example, keep the checkbox turned off.

3. Click OK to close the dialog box and apply the calendar to the task.

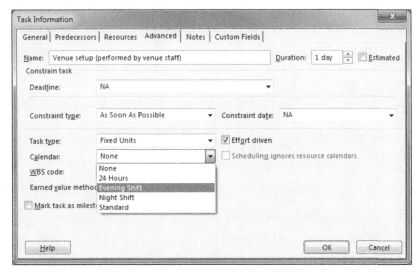

Figure 5-11. *When you apply a calendar to a task, Project schedules the task to occur during that calendars work days and times.*

6

Building a Team for Your Project

Without people, projects wouldn't start and certainly wouldn't finish. To keep projects running smoothly in between the start and finish, you need the right people, and *they* need to know the parts they play. Otherwise, collaboration and communication is like a rousing rendition of Abbott and Costello's "Who's On First?"

You can start building your project team once you've identified the project tasks. You analyze the work and identify the skills and other resources required. Then you're ready to look for resources that are both suitable and available. Whether you add generic resources or real people to your Project file, you can assign them to tasks so Project can calculate the schedule and the cost.

In this chapter, you'll learn the difference between Project's work, material, and cost resources, and when to use each one. People are almost always a project's most important resource, and when this book says "resource," that usually means "person." However, projects also rely on help from non-human resources, such as equipment, materials, and training. In Project, ***work resources*** represent anything you assign by time—people, a conference room you reserve by the hour, the event venue that you rent by the day, and so on. ***Material resources*** come in other units, like gallons of coffee or reams of paper—things that are consumed as part of the project. ***Cost resources*** cover expenses that aren't work or material, like travel or fees, where you're tracking financials.

This chapter gets down to the nitty-gritty of adding resources in Project and filling in fields for availability, costs, and so on. You'll learn how to set up generic resources if you don't know who your team members are just yet. In addition, you'll see how to add even more detail to your resources.

Understanding Project's Resource Types

Microsoft Project offers three types of resources for projects, each with its own purpose and idiosyncrasies. Here are the various types, what each one represents, and how it can affect your project:

- **Work**: Time is what distinguishes work resources from other resource types in Project. For example, people and equipment are work resources, because you track their participation by the amount of time they spend on the project. Whether you're assigning people to direct traffic or renting equipment for an event, your project's tasks depend on when those work resources are available, how much time they have, and how much they cost for a period of time.

> **Note:** Regardless of whether you know only the skills required for tasks or you have the specific names of warm bodies, you can create resources in Project to assign to tasks. Later in this chapter, you'll see how to use generic resources to act as placeholders until you identify real resources.

- **Material**: Materials are supplies that are consumed during the course of a project. Suppose you have a task to publicize an event. That task requires envelopes and printed materials, as well as people to stuff the envelopes. You assign the people based on the time it will take, but you assign material resources by the *quantity* you need: 10,000 brochures, for instance. Because materials aren't measured by time, they affect only the cost of your project (based on the quantities you need and the cost per unit). Materials affect dates or duration only when you have to wait for them to become available and you can create a task or milestone for that. For example, you can't begin setting up booths until they're delivered.

- **Cost**: Cost resources represent *only* costs—not time, not quantities. These resources are perfect for ancillary costs that aren't directly associated with the people, equipment, and materials you assign to tasks. For example, expenses such as training costs or permit fees increase the project's price tag, but they aren't associated with work or material resources.

The advantage of this resource type is that you can track different types of costs separately. For instance, you might set up cost resources for travel, building permits, rental expenses, and shipping. You can then assign those cost resources to each task they apply to, and then total what you spend on different types of costs for the entire project (see Chapter 7). A staff meeting might have, say, $10,000 in travel costs and $1,000 in communication costs for the people who attend in person and via videoconference. And the change control board might have $1,000 in travel costs and $2,000 for videoconferencing. When you see the $11,000 for travel vs. $3,000 for videoconferencing, you might consider changing your approach to meetings.

Note: If you look closely at the General tab of the Resource Information dialog box (double-click a resource in the Resource Sheet, Task Form, or Task Details Form to open it), you'll notice the Budget checkbox. With budget resources, you can record amounts budgeted for different categories of expenses and compare your project's cost performance to the budget. Chapter 15 describes how to use Project's budgeting features.

How Resources Affect Project Schedules

For a quick-and-dirty project schedule, all you need are tasks, dependencies between the tasks, and estimated task durations. Project shows a start date and a finish date for the project, but how do you know whether these dates are any good without resources assigned to do the work? And as you begin the work, how can you tell whether the project is proceeding according to schedule?

Assigning resources to tasks in Project provides the information you need to answer these questions. Resource assignments help you manage the project in several ways:

- **Defining the project's schedule**: Because you can specify when resources work and how much they're available, your project schedule is more accurate, since it calculates task durations based on when resources work.

- **Managing resources**: Resource assignments tell you whether resources have too much work, too little, or just enough. As you schedule the project, you can balance people's workloads to make the schedule more realistic (and make team members happier). In addition, you can play what-if games with time versus money. For example, you might decide to use less-expensive resources when the budget is more important than the finish date.

- **Preventing ownership problems**: Resource assignments also ensure that someone is working on every project task. At the same time, assignments can prevent overly enthusiastic team members from sticking their noses into someone else's work.

- **Tracking progress**: By updating your schedule with the actual progress people make, you can see whether or not the project is on track. This information is indispensable later on when you want to evaluate your estimating prowess and do better the next time.

- **Tracking spending**: When you track the costs of work, material, and cost resources, you can not only estimate the price tag for the project, but also see actual costs as the project progresses.

121

Adding Resources to Your Project File

Before you can play matchmaker between project tasks and resources, you have to tell Project about the resources you're using. You can get started by filling in a few basic fields, such as the resource names and types. As you identify detailed information, such as work schedules, availability, and costs, you can add that information to Project, as described in other sections in this chapter. In turn, Project uses that information to more accurately calculate your project schedule and price tag.

> **Note:** The section "Using Generic or Proposed Resources," later in this chapter, explains what you can do if you don't know resource names or whether they are available to your project.

Project offers two methods for entering resource data directly. The Resource Sheet is ideal for specifying values for every resource—you can copy and paste values, or simply drag values (even into several cells at once). This section explains how to use the Resource Sheet. If you have resource information stored in a company directory or other data source, importing information into Project makes short work of data entry, as described later in this chapter.

> **Note:** If you've downloaded files from the book website, you can follow along using the file Event_Ch06_start.mpp.

Adding Resources in the Resource Sheet

The Resource Sheet view is a quick way to get resources' names, ranks, and serial numbers into Project. (You'll learn how to add more resource details later in this chapter.)

Follow Along Practice

Adding resources in the Resource Sheet is similar to adding task information in the Gantt Chart's table area. Here's how to enter the essential information for resources:

1. In the View tab's Resource Views section, click Resource Sheet.

    The Resource Sheet displays the Entry table, which initially contains fields for work, material, and cost resources. To apply a table specific to work or material resources, in the View tab's Data section, click Tables, and then choose "Entry - Work Resources" or "Entry - Material Resources," respectively.

2. In the first Resource Name cell, type the name of a resource, for example, *Event PM*.

    To make resources easy to find later on, follow a standard naming convention. Commas and brackets are verboten in resource names, so consider something like "Smith J" for people. For generic resources, the job title (like Web Developer) works well. Similarly, a brief description is fine for equipment and materials.

3. To save the resource and move to the next row, press Enter.

Project saves the resource (and automatically assigns it the Work resource type, because that's the most common type) and moves to the Resource Name cell in the next row, so you can type the next resource name, as shown in Figure 6-1.

4. Repeat steps 2 and 3 until you've created and named all your resources. In this example, create the following resources:

Resource Name	Resource Type	Resource Name	Resource Type
Assistant PM	Work	Venue Team	Work
Admin Team	Work	Printer Vendor	Work
IT Team	Work	Giveaways Vendor	Work
Sales Lead	Work	Brochures	Material
Sales Team	Work	Giveaways	Material
Technical Sales Team	Work	Travel	Cost
Marketing Lead	Work	Permits	Cost
Marketing Assistant	Work	Music Vendor	Cost
Marketing Content Developer	Work		

Figure 6-1. *The Resource Sheet opens with the Entry table, which contains fields you fill in for work, material, and cost resources.*

5. For each material resource in the list, click its Type cell and type *m* for material. Or click the down arrow on the right side of the cell, and then, in the drop-down list, choose Material. In this example, Brochures and Giveaways are material resources.

When you choose Material, Project removes values in columns that don't apply to that type of resource, like Maximum Units (Max. Units in the table header), Overtime Rate (Ovt. Rate in the table header), and Base Calendar (Base in the table header). You can also fill in a Material label to specify the measurement units for the resource. The Material Label field is described in more detail later in this chapter.

6. For each cost resource in the list, click its Type cell and type *c* for cost. Or click the down arrow on the right side of the cell, and then, in the drop-down list, choose Cost. In this example, Travel, Permits, and Vendor Cost are cost resources.

When you choose Cost, Project removes values in columns that don't apply to that type of resource (like Maximum Units and Standard Rate).

> **Tip:** If all your material or cost resources are grouped together, you can change the Type cell for the first resource in the group. Then position the pointer over the fill handle (the small square in the cell's lower-right corner), and drag to copy that value to the other cells.

7. Change other values—such as Initials—by clicking a cell and then entering the value.

   You'll learn how to fill in other resource cells in the remaining sections of this chapter.

> **Tip:** Say you type a resource name that doesn't exist in the current project file into a Resource Name cell in the Resource Sheet or into an assignment in the Task Form. Project is happy to automatically add a new resource with default values for you. At times, this behavior is a tremendous timesaver, because you can simply type a resource name in the Task Form or in a Resource Name cell without having to detour to the Resource Sheet to create the resource. However, if a typo sneaks in, your project can acquire resources that don't actually exist.
>
> Fortunately, you can make Project notify you when it creates a new resource as it assigns the resource to a task: A message box opens and tells you the resource doesn't exist in the resource pool. If you want to add it, click Yes. If the resource represents a typo so you don't want to add it, click No. To tell Project to do this, choose File→Options. On the left side of the Project Options dialog box, click Advanced. In the "General options for this project" drop-down list, choose the project you want to work on (or select All New Projects), and then turn off the "Automatically add new resources and tasks" checkbox. Doing so also tells the program to notify you in a similar fashion when it creates a *task* if you type a *task name* that doesn't exist while assigning a resource to a task, for example, in a new row in the Resource Usage view.

Sorting Resources by Names and More

After an invigorating session of resource creation, your Resource Sheet might be a hodge-podge of resources in no particular order. An unsorted list not only makes it hard to see what resources you've got, but it also increases the likelihood of inadvertently duplicating them.

Removing duplicate resources prevents confusion and scheduling problems. If you accidentally create two or more resources with the same name, such as John Smith and john smith, Project considers those resources separate entities. So if you assign some tasks to one resource and other tasks to its twin, your schedule will be wrong. For example, tasks might look like they can run simultaneously and workloads might seem reasonable—but in reality, those tasks might have to run in sequence, or you might have double-booked a resource. Sorting your resource list by name places duplicate names next to each other, so you can delete the duplicates and assign the remaining ones to the correct tasks.

Follow Along Practice

Project makes it easy to sort your resource list by name: Simply click the down arrow to the right of the Resource Name column heading and then, in the drop-down menu, choose "Sort A to Z" or "Sort Z to A." If you want to sort the list by more than one field, here's what you do:

1. In the Resource Sheet (View→Resource Sheet), head to the View tab's Data section and click Sort→Sort By.

2. In the Sort dialog box's "Sort by" box, choose the field you want to use to sort the resources, and then select the Ascending or Descending option. For example, choose Type and Descending to separate each type of resource, starting with work resources.

3. In the "Then by" box, choose the next field to sort by, such as Name. Then pick the Ascending or Descending option, if necessary. (Project selects the Ascending option automatically, which is perfect for alphabetical order.)

4. If you want to sort by another field, then in the *second* "Then by" box, choose the final sort field. In this example, skip this step.

5. To make this order permanent, turn on the "Permanently renumber resources" checkbox. With this setting turned on, when you complete the sort, Project reassigns the ID numbers that uniquely identify the resources.

6. Click Sort to rearrange the resources.

7. If you chose to renumber the resources permanently (step 5), you should tell Project *not* to renumber resources the next time you sort (in case there is a next time), since that would mess up the numbering scheme for all the resources you've already assigned. To do that, simply reopen the Sort dialog box, click Reset to turn off the "Permanently renumber resources" checkbox, and then click Cancel to close the dialog box without resorting the list.

Defining When Work Resources Are Available

You may have already assigned a calendar for your project (see Chapter 3) to indicate when work usually takes place. Project automatically sets a resource's maximum units to 100 percent for full time and uses the calendar that applies to the entire project. But even if your office is open from 9:00 a.m. to 6:00 p.m., not everybody works the same hours. Resource calendars tell Project when people are available to work on their assigned tasks. The schedule is more accurate when Project knows about people's vacations, days off, and odd work hours. Project has two ways to specify when resources work, and each method addresses a different aspect of resource time:

- A **resource calendar** identifies work days and days off and spells out specific hours that a resource works—for example, Monday through Thursday from 8:00 a.m. to 7:00 p.m. with an hour at 12:00 p.m. for lunch. You can also use a resource calendar to specify part-time work schedules like Monday through Friday, 8:00 a.m. to 12:00 p.m.

- **Availability**, specified by resource *units*, tells Project what percentage of time the resource is available. For example, most resources work full time during normal working hours. You can alter a resource's units (in the Maximum Units field, which is usually abbreviated to Max. Units) to tell Project that someone works part time, or that a resource is really a three-person team. For example, the Max. Units for the three-person team that works on the project full time would be 300 percent. On the other hand, the folks who work part time could have Max. Units of 60 percent if they work 3 days a week. Alternatively, you can create a resource calendar to define a part-time schedule (the 3-day work week in this case). If you do that, then you set Max. Units to 100 percent for the resources who work that schedule.

Resource calendars and units apply only to work resources, because these are the only ones assigned by time. You can use a calendar and units separately or together to identify how much a resource works, as described in detail in the section "Specifying How Much Your Resources Are Available."

Specifying a Resource's Work Schedule

If someone doesn't work according to the overall project's calendar, then you can specify a special work schedule for that resource using a calendar. Resource calendars come in handy for a variety of special situations like the following:

- Your project spans multiple shifts, and you want to assign people to the shifts that they work.

- Your resources work in different time zones, and you want to assign working times according to their local times.

- A resource will be away from work for an extended period of time—for instance, your star developer is recuperating from carpal-tunnel surgery.

- Your company offers the option to work either 4-day or 5-day work weeks, and you want to assign the appropriate calendar to the people who choose each option.

- Equipment resources often require preventive maintenance, such as a computer server that's shut down for software patch installations once a month.

You can apply the same calendar to several resources or modify an individual resource's calendar. (To learn how to create and fine-tune calendars, see Chapter 3.) Here are the different methods for assigning a calendar to a resource:

Follow Along Practice

- **Apply a calendar in the Resource Sheet**: Click the resource's Base Calendar cell (if the column is narrow, then you may see only the word "Base") and then, in the drop-down list, choose the calendar you want to apply, as shown in Figure 6-2. In this example, apply the Evening Shift calendar to the IT Team resource and the Venue Team resource.

> **Tip:** The fastest way to apply a calendar to several resources is to apply the calendar to one resource and then copy and paste that value to other cells in the Resource Sheet. You can also drag the fill handle (the green square in the Base Calendar cell's bottom-right corner) to copy the value to several adjacent resources.

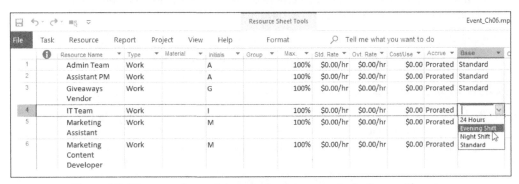

Figure 6-2. *You can apply an existing calendar to a resource in the Resource Sheet view.*

- **Apply an existing calendar using the Resource Information dialog box**: You can apply a calendar using the Resource Information dialog box. In the Resource Sheet view, double-click the resource to which you want to apply the calendar. In the Resource Information dialog box, on the General tab, click Change Working Time. In the Change Working Time dialog box's "Base calendar" field, choose the calendar you want to apply (for example, to make sure the event venue is ready, replace the Venue Team's Evening Calendar with the 24 Hours calendar that comes with Project), and then click OK.

- **Modify a resource's calendar**: Suppose a resource works according to the overall project calendar, but will be out on medical leave for part of the project. You can modify that resource's calendar to reflect the time off. In the Resource Sheet, double-click the resource with the custom work schedule, for example, the Marketing Content Developer. In the Resource Information dialog box, on the General tab, click Change Working Time. The label at the top of the Change

Working Time dialog box reads "Resource calendar for '[resource name].'" Define work weeks and exceptions for that resource (see Chapter 3). In this example, create an exception called Medical Leave with a Start date of 1/4/2022 and a finish date of 1/15/2022. Then click OK to save the resource calendar.

Specifying How Much Your Resources Are Available to Your Project

Availability is the percentage of time a resource is available during the resource's work schedule, whether it's the standard calendar or a special one. Here's how availability works:

- If the resource doesn't have a special calendar assigned, then Max. Units set to 100 percent represents full time during regular working hours according to the project's calendar.

- If the resource has a resource calendar with Monday through Thursday as 8-hour workdays, then Max. Units set to 100 percent represents all the time the resource works—that is, 32 hours a week.

- If the resource has a Monday through Friday 4-hour workday calendar (that's 20 work hours each week), then Max. Units of 50 percent means the resource is available half of the calendar's working time, or 10 hours a week.

- Units aren't limited to 100 percent or less. In fact, if you have a 5-person sales team, you can set up one work resource for the entire team and set the maximum units to 500 percent.

Follow Along Practice

The Resource Sheet view is the fastest way to specify maximum units. Simply click the Max. Units cell for a work resource, type the number for the maximum units, and then press Enter. Project adds "%" automatically. For this project, modify Max. Units as follows:

Resource Name	Max. Units
Admin Team	300%
IT Team	300%
Sales Team	500%
Technical Sales Team	500%
Venue Team	1000%

Tip: If you prefer to see resource maximum units as a decimal value instead of a percentage, choose File Options Schedule, and then, in the "Show Assignment Units as a" box, choose Decimal.

Plan for Downtime

No one is productive every minute of every day. Even workaholics spend some work time on tasks that aren't a part of your project. An alarming amount of time might be spent on unrelated meetings and administrative tasks like filling out health insurance forms. Moreover, the workdays just prior to holiday weekends are renowned for their low productivity. You can make your Project schedules reflect this downtime:

Change the working time for your project: For example, if experience tells you that 2 hours of every workday are spent on administrative tasks, you can shorten the workdays in your project calendar or resource calendars. This approach can also take into account corporate holidays and vacation time. One issue with this approach is that the working times you define don't match the start time and end time of your real-world workdays. If a meeting or other task should take place during a time that your project calendar considers nonworking time, you can assign a calendar with longer work days to the task.

Adjust Project's calendar options (Chapter 3) **to reflect shorter workdays:** After you change the working time in the project calendar, you need to adjust Project's calendar options to match. In the Project Options dialog box (File→Options→Schedule), you can tell Project that workdays are shorter by changing the values for "Hours per day," "Hours per week," and "Hours per month."

If you use Project Server or Project Online, assign nonproject work time to an administrative project: With Project Server or Project Online, people can associate non-project time to an administrative project or by using Administrative time categories.

Defining Costs for Resources

Unless money is no object (yeah, right), you need to keep a close eye on project costs. Labor and materials usually represent the bulk of the cost for a project. When you assign costs to work and material resources, Project calculates project costs as well as the schedule. The cost fields are available in both the Resource Sheet and the Resource Information dialog box, but the Resource Sheet is usually the quickest option. This section describes how to enter costs for all three types of resources.

Setting Up Work and Material Costs

Work and material resources use the same cost fields, although they don't always represent the same thing. The rate for a work resource is the cost per period of time, whereas a rate for materials is the cost per unit. Here are the cost fields for resources and what they do:

- **Std. Rate** (Standard Rate) is the typical pay rate for a work resource, the cost per time period for a piece of equipment, or the cost per unit for material. For example, a contractor's pay rate of $50 per hour shows up as $50.00/hr. Because work resources are assigned by time, Project

---

automatically adds "/hr" to the number you type. If you pay a contractor a flat rate per month, you can use a different unit of time, for instance, "$5000/mon."

> **Tip:** Because you usually don't want people's salaries in the public eye, you can fill in pay rates with the averaged burdened cost (an employee's hourly wages or salary, plus benefits, taxes, equipment, and so on, which you can get from your HR department) for someone in a given role.

Material resources are allocated by units other than time, such as gallons of sports drink, reams of paper, or rolls of shipping tape. For material resources, Std. Rate represents the price per unit. How do you enter the unit for a material resource? The unit is whatever you type into the Material Label cell (if the column is narrow, this column's heading just reads "Material"). For example, for brochures, the Material Label unit might be "each." When you type **$4.25** in the Std. Rate cell, Project calculates cost as $4.25 per brochure. On the other hand, you might purchase items to giveaway by the case. In that case, the Giveaways Material Label would be "Case." In reality, Project doesn't care what the unit is. The Material Label field is just there to remind *you* of the units you're using for a particular material so you assign the correct quantity to tasks. When you assign a material resource to a task, Project simply multiplies the quantity assigned by the material's Std. Rate to obtain the assignment cost for that material resource.

For a resource that represents a team of people, you still enter the Std. Rate as an amount per unit of time, such as $100 per hour. If you assign three people to a task and they work 24 hours in one work day, the cost is 24 hours multiplied by $100, that is, $2,400.

You can also keep a resource's Std. Rate set to $0.00/hour, so you can assign the resource to a task without incurring any cost. For example, the Printer Vendor and Giveaways Vendor have work to do on tasks, but your project pays only for the brochures and giveaways purchased.

Follow Along Practice

In this example, fill in the Std. Rate cells for work and material resources as follows:

Resource Name	Std. Rate	Resource Name	Std. Rate
Event PM	$150	Marketing Assistant	$100
Assistant PM	$100	Marketing Content Developer	$100
Admin Team	$80	Venue Team	$100
IT Team	$100	Printer Vendor	$0
Sales Lead	$150	Giveaways Vendor	$0
Sales Team	$120	Brochures	$4.25
Technical Sales Team	$100	Giveaways	$120.00
Marketing Lead	$150		

> **Tip:** Project includes options for setting the standard rate and overtime rate (discussed in a sec) for resources. Initially, these options are set to $0.00/hr ($0 per hour). However, if most of your resources cost the same amount per hour, you can save a few steps when you're creating resources by setting a default standard or overtime rate. Choose File Options and on the left side of the Project Options dialog box, click Advanced. In the "General options for this project" drop-down list, choose the project for which you want to set default resource rates, and then type values in the "Default standard rate" and "Default overtime rate" boxes.

- **Ovt. Rate** (Overtime Rate) applies only to work resources. You don't have to fill in this field unless the person earns a premium for overtime and you specifically assign overtime hours to the resource in Project (Chapter 14). People who work for a salary don't cost extra, so their Ovt. Rate is zero. If someone gets the same hourly rate regardless of how many hours he works, you don't have to bother with overtime. (In that situation, you could create an exception with long hours in the resource's calendar.) For this example, don't fill in overtime rates at this point.

> **Note:** When you assign resources to tasks, Project doesn't automatically use the overtime rate for hours assigned beyond the standard workday. To designate overtime hours, you have to modify the resource assignment (Chapter 14) to tell Project to apply the overtime rate.

- **Cost/Use** applies only when you pay an amount each time you use the resource. For example, if you pay a flat $50 each time the network technician comes on site, then enter *50* in the Cost/Use field. That way, every time you assign the network technician to a task, the task's cost includes the hourly rate for the technician *and* his $50 appearance fee. For this example project, don't fill in any Cost/Use fields.

- **Accrue At** is important only if someone cares *when* money is spent. For example, if cash flow is tight, knowing whether you pay up front, after the work is done, or spread out over time can make or break a budget. The Accrue At cell offers three settings: Start, Prorated, and End. Start means the cost occurs as soon as the task begins—like paying for a package delivered COD. End represents cost that occurs at the end of a task, such as paying your neighbor's kid when he finishes mowing your lawn. And Prorated spreads the cost over the duration of the task, such as the wages you pay to employees assigned to long tasks. For this example, keep Accrue At set to Prorated.

> **Note:** Project includes several options for specifying currency. To see them, choose File Options, and then, on the left side of the Project Options dialog box, choose Display. Below the "Currency options for this project" heading, you can specify the currency symbol you want to use, such as $ for dollars. Type the number of decimal digits you want to see (for example, 2 for cents) in the "Decimal digits" box. Choose the currency in the Currency drop-down list. The Placement setting specifies whether the currency symbol appears before or after the currency value with or without a space between the symbol and the value.

Specifying Cost for Cost Resources

The Cost resource type is perfect for costs that aren't based on time or any sort of material. (If you hire a subcontractor who provides a fixed-price, a cost resource is perfect for tracking that cost.) More than one cost resource can apply to a task, like travel, videoconferencing costs, and fees. If you look at cost resources in the Resource Usage view, you can review the total cost for each cost resource to see what those categories of costs add up to for the entire project.

To create a cost resource in the Resource Sheet view, all you have to do is type its name in the Resource Name cell (such as Travel, Permits, and Music Vendor created earlier in this chapter) and then choose Cost in the Type cell. When you press Enter, the standard values for a work resource disappear. The only other fields with values are Initials and Accrue At. To change either the resource's initials or when the cost occurs, click the appropriate cell and then type the new value.

Unlike work and material resources, you *don't* set a cost for a cost resource in the Resource Sheet. Instead, you specify its monetary value when you assign the cost resource to a task (Chapter 7), so the value can vary from task to task.

Adding Resource Information from Other Programs

If resource information is available in other programs, you can save time by importing or pasting that data into Project. This section describes a few methods for pulling resource info into your Project file.

Adding Resources from Excel

Getting resource information from an Excel workbook into Project is easy. For simple resource lists, you can copy and paste values from Excel into your Project file. Suppose the HR department sent you an Excel workbook containing a list of resources. You can paste values from that spreadsheet directly into the table in Project's Resource Sheet view. (For the example project, the resource list is complete. You don't have to perform these steps.) Here's how:

1. In the Excel workbook that contains resource information, select the cells that you want to paste into Project, and then press Ctrl+C (or, on the Home tab, click Copy).

    For example, if the resource names are in the first column, you can select just the cells in that column. If you want to copy several columns of data from Excel, such as names and standard pay rates, be sure that the data in the Excel worksheet is in the same columns as the columns in the Resource Sheet table. For example, in the Resource Sheet Entry table, the Standard Rate field is in the seventh column, so you want your pay-rate data in the seventh column in the Excel worksheet.

2. Switch over to Project and, if necessary, display the Resource Sheet by clicking View→Resource Sheet.

3. Click the first blank Resource Name cell where you want to paste the values, and then press Ctrl+V.

    Project inserts the values into the Resource Sheet table, filling in cells below and to the right of the cell you clicked.

Adding Work Resources from Your Email Address Book

Chances are you have resource information for people in Outlook or on a Microsoft Exchange Server. If so, you can import that information into a Project file. Project needs to be installed on the same computer as Outlook. (You don't have to add resource info from Outlook for the example project.)

To import resources from an address book, do the following:

1. With the Resource Sheet visible (View→Resource Sheet), on the Resource tab, click Add Resources.

    A drop-down menu appears with commands for creating and importing resources. (If you're using a view other than Resource Sheet, the Add Resources command is disabled.)

2. Choose Address Book.

    The Select Resources dialog box appears. If you see the Choose Profile dialog box instead, then choose the profile name for the email system you want to use. For example, if you have a profile for your business email and one for your personal email, choose the business profile.

    > **Note:** If your organization uses Active Directory to store information, then on the Add Resources drop-down menu, choose Active Directory to import resources from that data source. Then search through the Active Directory for resources instead of browsing as you do with an address book.

3. In the Select Resources dialog box, choose the resources you want to import, and then click Add at the bottom of the dialog box.

    Ctrl-click to select resources that aren't adjacent. For adjacent resources, simply click the first resource, and then Shift-click the last one. You can also select resources in batches and then click Add to append each batch to the import list.

4. When all the resources you want to import appear in the Add box, click OK.

Project adds the resources to the Resource Sheet. Any information you store in your address book that applies to Project fields transfers over. For example, Project imports email addresses into its own Email Address field.

Filling in Other Resource Fields

The most frequently-used resource fields appear in the table in Resource Sheet view, so you might never have to give up the convenience and familiarity of entering values in table cells. Besides, if you have other resource fields that you always fill in, you can insert those columns in the Resource Sheet's table (see Chapter 20). This section describes additional resource fields you might want to use and how to specify their values.

> **Tip:** If you don't want to change the Resource Sheet view's table, use the Resource Information dialog box instead. It contains all the resource fields you can set, and it's the only way to add a few of the more intricate resource settings.

Using the Resource Information Dialog Box

The Resource Sheet view shows the fields most project managers fill in: name, resource type, initials, and workgroup. In the Resource Information dialog box (Resource→Information), the General tab, shown in Figure 6-3, includes these fields and more.

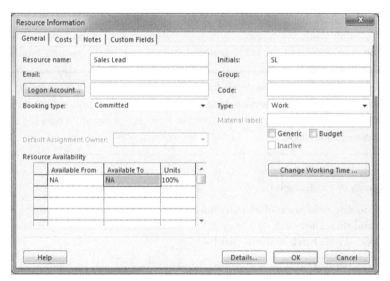

Figure 6-3. *The Resource Information dialog box includes most resource fields. If you don't work with costs, you might not have to venture beyond the General tab.*

Here are the additional resource fields (found on the Resource Information dialog box's General tab) that you might want to fill in, along with their uses:

- **Initials**: The usefulness of this field might not be obvious at first. When you view a schedule in the Gantt Chart timescale, displaying the resources assigned to tasks on the task bars is a quick way to see who does what or to spot tasks without resources. Full names take up too much room and cover up task link lines, especially when several resources work on the same tasks.

Fortunately, you can see who's assigned to tasks without the clutter by displaying resources' *initials* instead of names.

Project initially sets the Initials field to the first letter of the resource's name. With all but the tiniest teams, that approach doesn't help. You can change the value in this field to whatever you want, like a person's first and last initial or an abbreviated job description.

* **Group**: This field can represent any type of category you want—departments, subcontractors and vendors, or skillsets. In addition to grouping resources in the Resource Sheet view, you can also use the Group field to filter the task list to tasks performed by specific work groups, or group tasks by the type of resource required. In this example, assign the work resources down through the Marketing Content Developer to the Internal group. Assign the Venue Team, Printer Vendor, Giveaways Vendor, and Music Vendor to the Vendor group. The Group field is one of the few resource fields that can be displayed in a task-oriented view.

* **Code**: This field provides another way to categorize resources, which you can then use to sort, filter, or group resources. If your organization assigns job codes, you can enter them in this field and then filter for tasks that require a specific job code. (For more on job codes and what you can do with them, see the note titled "Categorizing Resources in Detail.")

* **Email**: If you distribute information via email directly from Project, then be sure to enter the person's email address here.

> **Note:** The Resource Information dialog box's Logon Account button applies only if you use Project Server to manage a portfolio of projects. Clicking this button tells Project to fill in the Logon Account box with the person's Windows account information. Then Project uses that info to log into Project Server.

Categorizing Resources in Detail

For a project with a cast of thousands, the Resource Information dialog box's Group and Code fields might not be enough to express all the categories you have. For excruciating detail, *resource outline codes* are a better approach. Similar to WBS codes, resource outline codes are hierarchical identifiers that can reflect the organizational structure of your company or employee skillsets. For example, you might change a custom outline field like Outline Code1 (Chapter 21) to something that represents the job levels within your organization, like "Eng. Net. Sr." for a senior-level network engineer.

To assign a custom outline code to a resource, in the Resource Information dialog box, select the Custom Fields tab. Any resource outline codes that you've set up appear in the list. In the Value cell, type the code for this resource.

Whether you use a resource outline code, the Group field, or the Code field to categorize resources, you can filter the list of resources in the Assign Resources dialog box to find resources that match your desired characteristics (Chapter 7).

Adding a Note to a Resource

If you want to enter additional information about a resource, head to the Resource Information dialog box. Project calls such additional info *notes*, which can include text, images, and documents. Keep in mind that the information you add to a note is available to *anyone* you share the file with, so don't include anything confidential.

To attach a note to a resource, follow these steps:

1. In the Resource Sheet view, right-click the resource (in this example, Venue Team), and then choose Notes from the shortcut menu.

   The Resource Information dialog box opens to the Notes tab.

2. In the Notes box, type or paste the text you want to add. In this example, type "Venue manager will provide team description and estimated cost."

   To format text, select it and then click the buttons on the toolbar above the Notes box, which let you change the font, set the justification, and create bulleted lists. Click the rightmost button (its icon looks like a landscape) to insert an object from another program (such as a document or a photo).

3. Click OK.

   A notepad icon appears in the resource's Indicators cell. To see the beginning of the note, position your pointer over this icon. To see the entire note, double-click the Notes icon, and Project opens the Resource Information dialog box to the Notes tab.

When Availability Varies

What do you do when availability changes over time? Suppose the number of people on the venue's setup team (and thus, the team resource's Max. Units) varies during the year: They have 10 team members most of the year but drop to only 7 during the winter. To help schedule tasks when availability changes like that, the Resource Information dialog box's General tab includes a table for setting varying availability levels.

> **Note:** When the work calendar changes over time—for example, a resource switches to 4-day work weeks in the summer—set up different work weeks in a resource calendar (Chapter 3).

Follow Along Practice

Here are the steps for setting up different levels of availability for different time periods:

1. In the Resource Sheet view, double-click the resource you want to edit (in this example, Venue Team).

   The Resource Information dialog box opens.

2. In the General tab's lower-left corner, look for the Resource Availability section (Figure 6-4).

In this dialog box's Resource Availability table, the Available From and Available To cells in the first row are initially set to NA, which indicates that the resource's maximum units apply to all time periods between the project start date and project finish date. The Units cell is initially set to the percentage that appears in the resource's Max. Units cell in the Resource Sheet view.

3. To specify a time period with different availability, in the Available To column's first cell, choose the date on which the default availability ends. In this example, choose 12/31/2021.

   The dates in the next row must be later than the first row's Available To date.

4. In the second row's Available From cell, choose the date on which the different availability begins, in this example, 1/1/2022.

5. In the Available To column's first cell, choose the end date for the different availability, in this example, 3/31/2022.

   The units you specify in the next step will apply to all assignments for the resource that occur between the Available From and Available To dates.

6. In the Units cell, type the percentage value for the maximum units (in this example, **700** for 700%), and then press Enter.

   If you omit the percentage sign, Project adds it.

7. To specify the availability for the remainder of the project, in the third row's Available From cell, choose the date immediately after the second row's Available To date, in this example, 4/1/2022.

8. In the third row's Available To cell, type NA. In this example, set the units in this row to 1000%.

   Typing NA in the last row's Available To cell indicates that the units you specify in the Units cell apply through the end of the project.

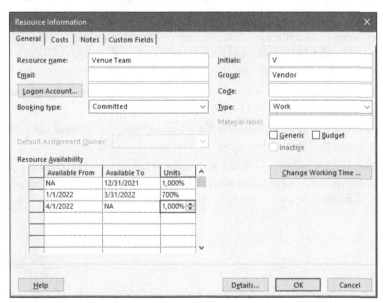

Figure 6-4. *The Resource Availability table is on the Resource Information dialog box's General tab.*

9. When you finish entering availability, click OK to close the dialog box.

   Now, when you look at the Resource Sheet, you'll see that the Max. Units for the resource are equal to the Max. Units you specified in the Resource Availability table for today's date.

From now on, when you assign this resource to tasks, Project uses the availability percentages that apply for the timeframe during which the task occurs.

When Pay Rates Vary

The Resource Information dialog box comes in handy for setting costs when a resource has different pay rates or when rates change over time, like if you hire a consultant who charges $100 per hour for work performed off-site, and $200 per hour for work performed onsite. Here's how you define different or variable pay rates:

Follow Along Practice

1. Double-click the resource you want to edit, in this example, Marketing Content Developer.

   The Resource Information dialog box opens.

   > **Tip:** If you want to make the same changes to *several* resources, select them all and then, on the Resource tab, click Information. The Multiple Resource Information dialog box opens. Any changes you make in the dialog box are applied to all the resources you selected.

2. In the Resource Information dialog box, select the Costs tab.

   The Costs tab contains a cost-rate table with five tabs of its own, labeled A through E (shown in Figure 6-5) so you can define up to five different pay rates for a resource. (If only Project let you assign names to each table so you could tell what each one is for...) Each tab of this table is a "cost-rate table." The "A (Default)" tab contains the original values that you entered for this resource.

3. To set a second pay rate for the resource, click tab B (shown in Figure 6-5) and then, in its first Standard Rate cell, type the second pay rate.

   To remind yourself what each pay rate is for, select the dialog box's Notes tab, and then type the kind of work and the pay rate that applies for that cost-rate table.

   You can also specify a rate change with a percentage. If a consultant tells you rates are going up 10 percent, then type 10% in the Standard Rate field. When you press Enter, Project calculates the new rate and replaces the percentage with the new dollar value.

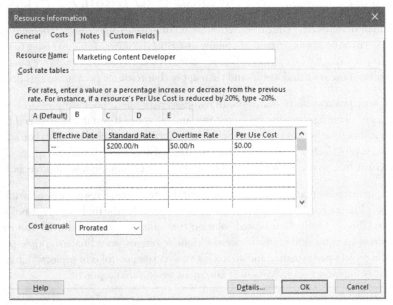

Figure 6-5. *Type the future rate in the appropriate cell (Standard Rate, Overtime Rate, or Per Use Cost cell).*

4. If the pay rate changes over time, select the second cell in a cost table's Effective Date column and then choose the starting date for the new rate. For this example, click the A tab to return to table A, and then type *2/1/2022* in the second row's Effective Date cell. In the Standard Rate cell, type *175*, and press Enter.

    The pay rate in the first row applies to any assignments that occur before the first effective date.

5. Repeat step 4 to define additional pay-rate changes and when they take effect. In this example, you don't have to make any other changes.

6. To set additional pay rates, select the C, D, or E tab, and then repeat steps 3–5.

    For each task that uses this resource and cost rate table, Project now applies the pay rate that's in effect when the task occurs.

> **Note:** After you define a cost-rate table, you can apply it to a resource assignment. Switch to the Task Usage or Resource Usage view, and then double-click an assignment (in the Task Usage view, that's a row containing a resource name; in the Resource Usage view, that's a row containing a task name) to open the Assignment Information dialog box. On the General tab, in the "Cost rate table" drop-down list, choose the letter that corresponds to the rate table you want to apply.

Making Resources Available to Multiple Projects

More often than not, the same resources work on more than one project, whether the projects all occur at once or conveniently follow one after the other. You don't have to recreate the same resources for every project file. It's more efficient to create a **resource pool** for the resources you use time and again, and then apply that resource pool to various projects.

When your projects don't occur simultaneously, a resource pool simply saves you the drudgery of defining the same resources over and over. But if you manage several projects at once without the benefit of Project Server, a Project resource pool can help you see who's available, who's already booked, or who's overloaded and needs some assistance. Chapter 24 describes how to use a resource pool to share resources among several projects.

If your organization manages lots of projects all the time, even a resource pool is unwieldy. Microsoft Project Portfolio Management Solution provides the tools for mega-project operations. (Project Online is a hosted solution that offers these capabilities.) You can categorize resources by skillsets to locate the right resources, coordinate multiple projects, and view project performance and status for your entire portfolio of projects. Chapter 29 provides an introduction to Microsoft enterprise project management.

Using Generic or Proposed Resources

Building a team for a project is often an iterative process. You might start by identifying the skills required and craft your initial schedule to determine how many people you need with different skillsets. Then, you find out what resources you can get and revise your schedule accordingly. Project can handle both resourcing steps.

Generic resources are easy to set up in Project. And if you use Project Professional, you can also **tentatively** add resources to your project, so you can determine whether you really need them without making waves in other projects. This section shows how to create generic resources and designate resources as proposed.

Using Generic Resources

The easiest way to create generic resources is to use job descriptions for resource names, such as Publicist or Web Developer. By creating work resources based on skillsets, you can assign those resources to tasks without worrying about overallocating them. If you need to assign a web developer at 300 percent to make the schedule work, you'll know you need at least three developers to finish on time.

Once you start building your real team, you replace the generic resources with real ones. (See Chapter 8 for the full scoop on replacing resources in assignments.) If you have a cast of thousands, finding assignments that are still using generic resources can take time. The Generic field in Project can simplify finding all your placeholder resources. All you do is filter your project (Chapter 17) for assignments that still have generic resources assigned to them and track down real people to fill those slots until your entire project is staffed.

The easiest way to flag resources as generic is by inserting the Generic column into the table in the Resource Sheet view. To do so, right-click a column heading and choose Insert Column; type ***g*** and then choose Generic from the drop-down list. Then, for each generic resource, change the Generic cell to Yes. (In this example, change the work resources through in the Internal group to generic resources.) When you do, the resource's Indicators column displays an icon of two heads to represent its generic status (Figure 6-6). The same icon appears in the rows for generic resources in the Resource Usage view so it's easy to see which assignments you need to edit to assign real people.

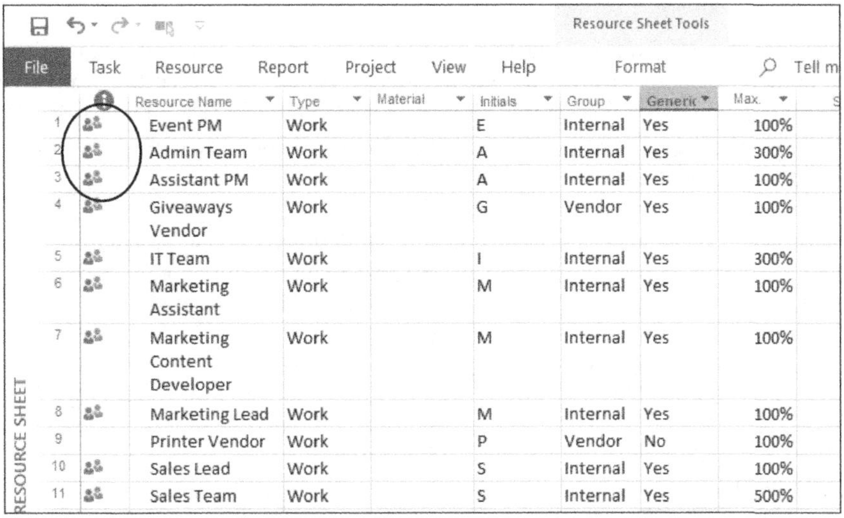

	Resource Name	Type	Material	Initials	Group	Generic	Max.
1	Event PM	Work		E	Internal	Yes	100%
2	Admin Team	Work		A	Internal	Yes	300%
3	Assistant PM	Work		A	Internal	Yes	100%
4	Giveaways Vendor	Work		G	Vendor	Yes	100%
5	IT Team	Work		I	Internal	Yes	300%
6	Marketing Assistant	Work		M	Internal	Yes	100%
7	Marketing Content Developer	Work		M	Internal	Yes	100%
8	Marketing Lead	Work		M	Internal	Yes	100%
9	Printer Vendor	Work		P	Vendor	No	100%
10	Sales Lead	Work		S	Internal	Yes	100%
11	Sales Team	Work		S	Internal	Yes	500%

Figure 6-6. *Resources with Generic fields set to Yes are easy to spot in the Resource Sheet, because the Indicators column displays a generic icon (circled).*

Working with Proposed Resources

Project Professional also includes the Booking Type field, which lets you designate resources as Committed or Proposed. If you don't share resources with other projects, you don't have to bother with this field at all. If you do, add this column in the Resource Sheet view by right-clicking a column heading, selecting Insert Column, and then choosing Booking Type in the drop-down menu.

This field offers two settings: Committed and Proposed. Project automatically sets new resources to Committed, which means any resource assignment you make reduces the resource's available hours so you can see the person's workload (Chapter 10). The Proposed value lets you ***tentatively*** assign resources to tasks without locking up their time. Suppose you want to work out a project schedule and budget based on resources that aren't yet officially assigned to your project. Creating them as Proposed means you can calculate dates and costs without taking away any of their available time. When a resource officially becomes yours, you can change its booking type to Committed.

Note: When you set a resource that's stored in a resource pool to Proposed, the resource shows up as Proposed in every project attached to the resource pool, which might not be what you want. So if you're using a resource pool, assign a generic resource instead, and then assign the real resource later.

Removing Resources from Your Project

If you've created duplicate resources or lost someone to another project, you might want to delete those resources in your Project file. However, deleting a resource in Project means any assignments you've made are gone as well. That's right—when you delete a resource, you run the risk of orphaning tasks without anyone to perform them. One way to prevent this issue is to replace the resource (Chapter 10) on task assignments before you delete it.

To simplify resource replacements, first filter the task list to show only the tasks to which the resource is assigned; then you can edit each task to replace that resource. (Because no resources have been assigned yet in the example project, you don't have to perform the following steps.)

To see the tasks to which a resource is assigned, do the following:

1. Select a task-oriented view like Gantt Chart and hide the summary tasks (in the Format tab's Show/Hide section, turn off the Summary Tasks checkbox).

    The task list shows only work tasks and milestones.

2. In the View tab's Data section, click the Filter drop-down list, and then choose Using Resource.

    The Using Resource dialog box opens with a "Show tasks using" drop-down list.

3. In the "Show tasks using" drop-down list, choose the resource you want to delete, and then click OK.

    Project displays any tasks that have that resource assigned.

4. To replace the resource with someone else, in the Resource tab's Assignments section, choose Assign Resources. In the table, select the task you want to reassign, and then, in the Assign Resources dialog box, select the resource you want to replace and click Replace. Then, choose the replacement resource. (Chapter 10 describes replacing resources in detail.)

5. After you finish editing resource assignments, click the Format tab and turn the "Show summary tasks" checkbox back on.

    The task list is back to its full complement of summary tasks, work tasks, and milestones.

6. In the View tab's Resource Views section, click Resource Sheet.

    Now you're ready to delete the resource.

To delete the resource, do the following:

- In the Resource Sheet, click the row number of the resource you want to delete, and then press Delete on the keyboard. Or right-click anywhere in the resource's row and choose Delete Resource from the shortcut menu.

7

Assigning Resources to Tasks

So far, you've created tasks in Project (Chapter 4), put them in the correct sequence (Chapter 5), and told Project about the resources you need (Chapter 6). Now all that hard work is about to pay off. You're ready to turn that Project file into a real schedule that shows when tasks should start and finish—and whether they're scheduled to finish on time.

Assigning resources isn't just picking a task team. You also specify how much time those lucky folks devote to their tasks. For example, once a giant construction crane is on a building site, it's available 100 percent of the time until you move it to another site. However, when you need a consultant for a few days to resolve a fiasco, you don't want 100 percent of her working time—or the monumental invoice that comes with it.

Although you may estimate task durations and work early on, you don't see the whole timing picture until you assign resources to tasks in your project. The number of resources you use, how much time those resources devote to their assignments, and when they're available to work all affect how long tasks take and when they occur. This chapter explains how duration, work, and units interact, which comes in handy as you create and modify resource assignments. And if you've set up your Project resources with costs and labor rates, resource assignments generate a price tag for the project, too.

Sometimes, finding the right resource for the job takes some research. In this chapter, you'll see how to search for resources that fit the criteria you're looking for, including resources with enough time to complete the tasks at hand.

If you manually schedule tasks, you're in complete control over when they start and finish. The Team Planner view (available in Project Professional) shows who's doing what and when, which tasks aren't assigned, or who's overallocated. With manually scheduled tasks, you can change any of these situations in Team Planner by dragging tasks to a resource or moving the tasks in the timescale.

Understanding Duration, Work, and Units

Whether you're assigning one resource to a task or modifying existing assignments to obtain specific results, understanding how duration, work, and units interact is crucial.

Project has built-in rules about which values it changes. To give you a fighting chance, it also offers features that let you control which variables hold steady and which ones change. Task duration, work (think person-hours), and assignment units (the proportion of time that resources work on a task) are like three people playing Twister—when one of these variables changes, the others must change to keep things balanced.

When you first assign resources to a task, the task's duration is inextricably connected to the work and units of those resource assignments. The formula is simple no matter which variable you want to calculate. The basic algebra you learned in high school is all you need:

Duration = Work ÷ Units, so Work = Duration x Units.

Project calculates one of these three variables when you set the other two, as you can see in Figure 7-1:

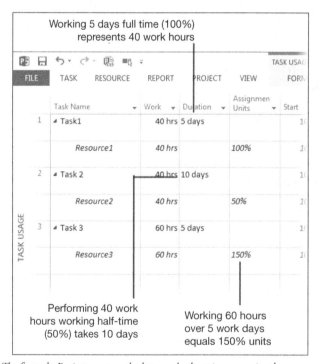

Figure 7-1. *The formula Project uses to calculate work, duration, or units always remains the same. Chapter 8 explains what's going on if Project seems to be shirking its calculation duties.*

- **Work = Duration x Units**: If you estimate task duration and specify the units that a resource devotes to that task, then Project calculates the hours of work the resource must perform. For example, a 5-day duration with a resource assigned at 100% (which, as a decimal, is 1) results in 40 hours of work for a typical workday: 40 hours = 5 days (x 8 hours/day) x 1.

- **Duration = Work ÷ Units**: If you estimate the amount of work a task requires, Project calculates the task's duration based on the resource units. For instance, 40 hours of work with a resource assigned at 50% (or .5) produces a 10-day duration based on 8-hour workdays: 10 days = (40 hours / .5) x 8 hours per day.

- **Units = Work ÷ Duration**: If you estimate the work involved and also know how long you want the task to take, Project calculates the units that a resource must spend on it. Sixty hours of work over 5 days is 12 hours a day, or a resource assigned 150% based on 8-hour workdays. Project would prefer to not calculate units, as Table 7-1 shows. If you specify work and duration, it might look like Project is ignoring your instructions. See the section "Assignment Units Versus Peak Units" in Chapter 8 to learn what's really going on with units in that situation.

> **Tip:** Project includes several calendar options for defining the standard number of work hours for different durations. See Chapter 3 for the full scoop on telling Project how to convert different units of time.

If you leave some of the assignment fields blank, Project plays favorites when it decides whether to calculate duration, work, or units. Unless you tell Project otherwise, it first tries to change duration, then work, and, as the last resort, units. So the only time Project calculates units is when you specify both task duration and the amount of work. Table 7-1 shows how this favoritism works depending on the values you enter.

Table 7-1. *Project calculates duration, work, or units depending on which values you enter for resource assignments.*

Duration	Work	Units
Project calculates	Your input	Your input
Project calculates	Your input	If blank, Project uses 100% or Max. Units.
Your input	*Project calculates*	Your input
Your input	*Project calculates*	If blank, Project uses 100% or Max. Units.
Your input	Your input	*Project calculates*
If blank, Project uses 1 day.	*Project calculates*	Your input

Assigning Work Resources to Tasks

Project lets you assign work resources in most of the usual places that you set up other task information. Once you've created resources as described in the previous chapter, all you have to do is match them up with the tasks they'll work on. The best way to do that depends on how much assignment detail you want to specify. Here are the methods and when to choose each one:

- **The Assign Resources dialog box**: This dialog box is the Swiss Army knife of resource-assignment tools, teeming with indispensable features. Assigning a resource to a task is as simple as clicking a resource's name, but you can also use it to search for specific types of resources, or for resources that have enough available time. This dialog box lets you assign several resources to a task, or assign a resource to several tasks at once. Moreover, you can use it to add, remove, or replace resources you've already assigned.

> **Note:** Project behaves differently depending on whether you are adding resources to a task initially or modifying resource assignments. See Chapter 8 for modifying assignments.

- **The Task Form:** When you already know the resource you want, the Task Form (or Task Details Form) has all the fields you need to craft precise resource assignments. It's easy to display this view in the Details pane as a companion to almost any view. The Task Form also helps when you want to make surgically precise modifications to existing assignments (Chapter 8).

- **A task table**: Choosing a resource in a table like the Entry table is good only for the simplest of resource-assigning chores—assigning one or two full-time resources to a task, for example. On the other hand, a table is ideal for dragging and copying resource assignments to several tasks.

- **The Task Information dialog box**: The Resource tab of this dialog box is another place you can assign resources. But since you have to open and close the dialog box for each task you want to edit, you may want to use it for assignments only when you've already opened the dialog box to make other changes to a task.

- **The Team Planner view**: Team Planner, available in Project Professional, helps you assign resources, whether you want to assign them to as-yet-unassigned tasks or you want to *reassign* them to get rid of overallocations. This view shows each resource in the project and the tasks they're working on in a timescale. Unassigned tasks appear at the bottom of the view. All you have to do to assign a resource is drag an unassigned task to the resource's row. To reassign a resource, simply drag a task from one resource to another. The section "Assigning Resources with Team Planner," later in this chapter, gives you the full scoop.

Assigning Resources with the Assign Resources Dialog Box

Whether you're assigning one resource to a task full time, assigning several resources to multiple tasks, or searching for the most qualified resources, the Assign Resources dialog box is the place to be. This dialog box can even remain open while you perform other actions in Project. For example, you can assign a few resources and then filter the schedule to evaluate what you've done. If you spot a problem, then you can jump right back to the dialog box to make the fix. It is one place where you can apply a single resource to multiple tasks at once. (You can also assign resources to multiple tasks in the Multiple Task Information dialog box.)

> **Note:** If you've downloaded files from the book website, you can follow along using the file Event_Ch07_start.mpp.

Follow Along Practice

To assign resources in the Assign Resources dialog box, follow these steps:

1. If necessary, switch to a task view like the Gantt Chart view (on the Task tab, click the top-half of the Gantt Chart button).

2. In the Resource tab's Assignments section, click Assign Resources.

    When the Assign Resources dialog box opens, drag it out of the way of what you're doing. It stays put and remains open until you move it or click its Close button.

3. In the Gantt Chart view (or any other task-oriented view), select the task to which you want to assign resources. In this example, select the task "Identify core event team."

    If any resources are already assigned to the task, they appear at the top of the list in the Assign Resources dialog box, preceded by a checkmark.

> **Warning:** Project doesn't stop you from assigning resources to summary tasks, but doing so is more confusing than it is helpful. If you assign resources to summary tasks, the rolled-up values (like cost and work) of summary tasks won't equal the totals from all the subtasks because the rolled-up values include values from the summary task's resource assignment. Moreover, summary-task bars in the timescale area of Gantt Chart view don't show assigned resource names at the right end of the bar by default, so unless you customize the view, you don't even see the resources assigned to summary tasks. (You can see the names in the Entry table, though.) If you use Project Server or Project Online, assignments on summary tasks won't be published to an assignee's timesheet or task grid.

4. In the dialog box's Resource Name column, click the name of the resource you want to assign, in this example, Event PM.

5. Click Assign.

    When you click Assign, Project provides several visual cues for the new resource assignment, as Figure 7-2 shows. The selected resource(s) shoots to the top of the list, above the unassigned resources. A checkmark appears to the left of the assigned resource's name and, in its Units cell, Project automatically enters either the resource's Maximum Units value or 100% if the maximum units are greater than 100% (as they are for a team). The cost of using the resource for the time involved appears in the Cost cell.

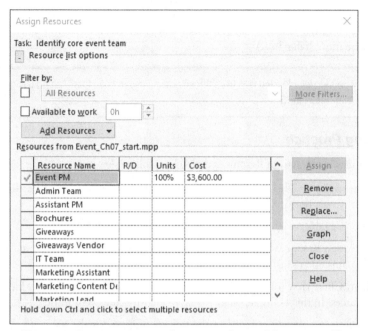

Figure 7-2. *Project moves assigned resources to the top of the resource table.*

If you want to assign more than one resource to a task, do the following:

1. Select the task you want to assign resources to. In this example, select the "Prepare project definition" task.

2. In the Assign Resources dialog box, click the first resource's name, and then Ctrl-click additional names (click Event PM, and then Ctrl-click Assistant PM). Then click Assign.

   If the resources you want are adjacent to one another in the list, click the first resource you want, and then Shift-click the last one.

3. To change the units for a resource, type the units percentage in the Units cell. In this example, click the Event PM's Units cell, and then type *75*. (Project adds the % sign for you.) Press Enter.

   You can type the percentage or click the up and down arrows that appear when you click the Units cell to jump to commonly used percentages. For example, if the Units value is 100%, clicking the down arrow once changes the Units to 50% and clicking it a second time changes the units to 0%.

> **Note:** Units can appear as percentages or decimal values (50% and .5 represent the same allocation), but you have to stick with one format or the other. To switch to decimal units, choose File Options. On the left side of the Project Options dialog box, click Schedule, and then, in the "Show assignments as a" drop-down list, choose Decimal.

You don't have to assign resources to only one task at a time. The Assign Resources dialog box can add assignments to several tasks, as you can see in Figure 7-3. To assign the same resources to several tasks, do the following:

1. Select the tasks you want to assign resources to. In this example, drag over the task ID cells for the tasks "Identify printing services," "Send RFPs," and "Choose printing service."

    When you select several tasks, the label at the top of the Assign Resources box changes to "Multiple tasks selected (x,y,z)," where x, y, and z are the ID numbers of the selected tasks.

2. In the Assign Resources dialog box, click the first resource's name, and then Ctrl-click additional names. (In this example, click Assistant PM.)

3. Click Assign.

    Gray checkmarks identify all the resources that are assigned to at least one of the selected tasks.

When you're finished assigning resources, click Close to close the Assign Resources dialog box.

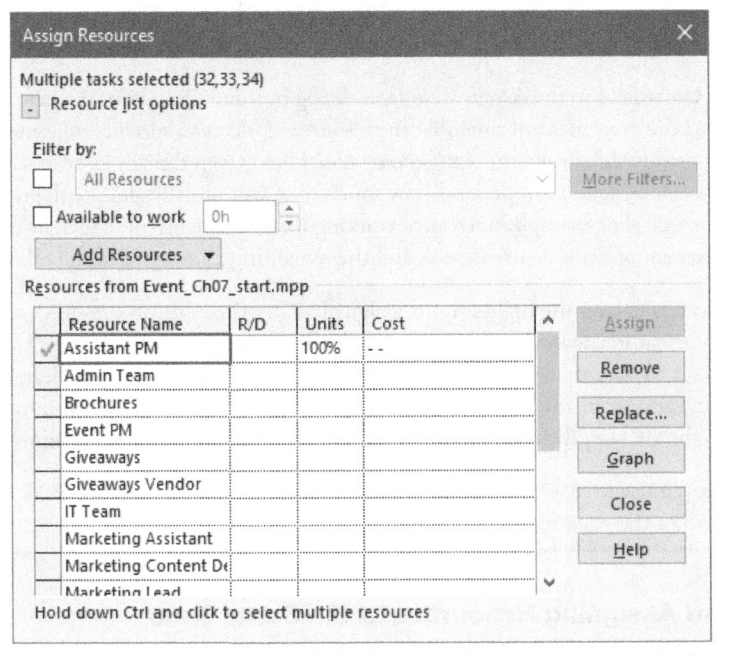

Figure 7-3. *The Assign Resources dialog box can add assignments to several tasks.*

What Project Calls a Unit

You'll see the term "units" in a couple of different places in Project: There's a Max. Units (Maximum Units) field in the Resource Sheet's Entry table, and a Units field that's located in the Assign Resources dialog box and the Task Form view. It's important to understand that Project uses the term loosely. These are a couple of different types of units in Project, though they're related. Each type is a percentage of time (or the equivalent decimal). The Max. Units field applies to resources, while the Units field (and the related Peak field, which you'll learn about later in this chapter) apply to the assignments you give those resources. Here's how to keep them straight:

- A resource's **Max. Units** field, which appears in the Resource Sheet view's Entry table and the Resource Information dialog box, is where you indicate the highest percentage of time that resource is available to work on your project. For example, 100 percent means all the resource's time is dedicated to your project; part-time availability can be any value between 1 percent and 99 percent. If you define a resource for a team of interchangeable workers, its Max. Units can even be a value like 300 percent, for three full-time workers.

- The **Units** field in the Assign Resources dialog box and Task Form is where you record the percentage of time that the resource works on a specific assignment. This field is technically the *Assignment Units* field (even though its label simply reads "Units"), and it represents how much time you initially allocate the resource to the task. For example, a resource working on two concurrent tasks may dedicate 75 percent of his time to one task and the remaining 25 percent to the other.

- Project calculates the highest units assigned at any time during a resource's assignment in the **Peak** field, while keeping the value in the Assignment Units field set to the original value you entered for Assignment Units. (The Peak field doesn't appear in any tables or forms out of the box. To see it, insert it into a table by right-clicking the table's header row, and then choosing Insert Column→Peak.)

Project flags a resource as overallocated if either the Assignment Units or Peak field value is greater than the resource's Max. Units value.

Creating and Assigning Resources at the Same Time

Suppose the resource you want to assign to a task is absent from the list of resources in the Assign Resources dialog box. This omission means that the resource doesn't exist in your Project file's Resource Sheet. Happily, you can create the resource *and* assign it to a task without leaving the Assign Resources dialog box. Here are the steps:

Follow Along Practice

1. In the task list, select the task you want to assign resources to, in this example, "Obtain approval to proceed."

2. In the dialog box's Resources table, click the first blank Resource Name cell (you may have to scroll down to see it), and then type the resource's name, in this example, *Sales VP*.

3. To save the new resource and select it, press Tab.

4. Click Assign. Project moves the resource to the top of the list, puts a checkmark next to it to indicate that it's been assigned, and changes its Units value to 100%.

5. If necessary, adjust the Units value. In this example, keep Units at 100%.

After you've completed your assignments, you can add the rest of the information about the resources you added on the fly. To do so, double-click a resource name in the Assign Resources dialog box to see its values in the Resource Information dialog box. Or work on resources in the Resource Sheet view. You can use any of the techniques described in Chapter 6 to edit or add to resource records.

> **Note:** The Assign Resources dialog box can also import resources from your email address book or Active Directory (if your computer is connected to an Active Directory domain). To do either, click Add Resources, and then choose either From Active Directory or From Address Book. (If you don't see the Add Resources button, click the + to the left of the "Resource list options" label to display it.)

Assigning Resources in the Task Form

The Task Form and its sibling, the Task Details Form, don't have the fancy features of the Assign Resources dialog box, but they make it easy to assign resources you've identified. The main limitation of these two views is that they let you work with only one task at a time—the one that's currently selected in the Gantt Chart or another task view. (But selecting another task is as easy as clicking it.)

Follow Along Practice

Here's how you assign resources in the Task Form or Task Details Form:

1. In the Task tab's View section, choose Gantt Chart or another task-related view.

   The Task Form is the standard view that appears in the Gantt Chart view's Details pane. If you don't see the Task Form there, in the View tab's Split View section, turn on the Details checkbox (if it's not already on) and choose Task Form from the drop-down list next to it.

2. In the table in the top pane, select the task that needs resources, in this example, "Plan press releases."

   The Task Form displays the information for the selected task.

3. If you don't see the Resource Name table in the Task Form, right-click within the Task Form, and then choose Resources and Predecessors.

4. In the Task Form's Resource Name table, click the first blank Resource Name cell, and then, from the drop-down list, choose the resource you want to assign (Marketing Lead, in this example).

   Clicking the down arrow on the right end of the Resource Name cell displays the drop-down list of resources. For large project teams, scrolling through this list can be tedious. When the list is open, you can begin typing a resource's name, and Project jumps to the closest matching name in the list. For example, to skip right to "Marketing Lead," type *M*. If Project hasn't located the exact resource, keep typing the resource's name until you see the one you want, and then click the resource's name in the list.

> **Note:** Out of the box, Project automatically adds new resources to your file when you type a resource name that doesn't already exist, so a typographical error may create a new—and nonexistent—resource. To prevent these phantom resources from joining your project team, choose File→Options. On the left side of the Project Options dialog box, choose Advanced. In the "General options for this project" drop-down list, make sure the project you want is selected, and then turn off the "Automatically add new resources and tasks" checkbox.

5. To specify the percentage of time the resource devotes to the task, click the Units cell in the same row and type the appropriate number—in this example, *75* for 75 percent, as shown in Figure 7-4.

If you want to assign the resource at 100 percent (or the resource's maximum units from the Resource Sheet), simply leave the Units cell blank. Project sets Units to 100% or the resource's maximum units automatically when you click OK. The only exception is group resources. If the group resource's maximum units are more than 100 percent, Project still fills in 100%.

The percentage in the Units cell is the percentage of the resource's work schedule, whether it's your organization's standard schedule or a special one. For example, for resources working typical full-time work schedules, 75 percent represents 30 hours a week for the typical 40-hour week.

> **Note:** To assign work instead of units, click the Work cell, and then type the hours, days, or other time units. Project calculates the units based on the work and the task's duration.

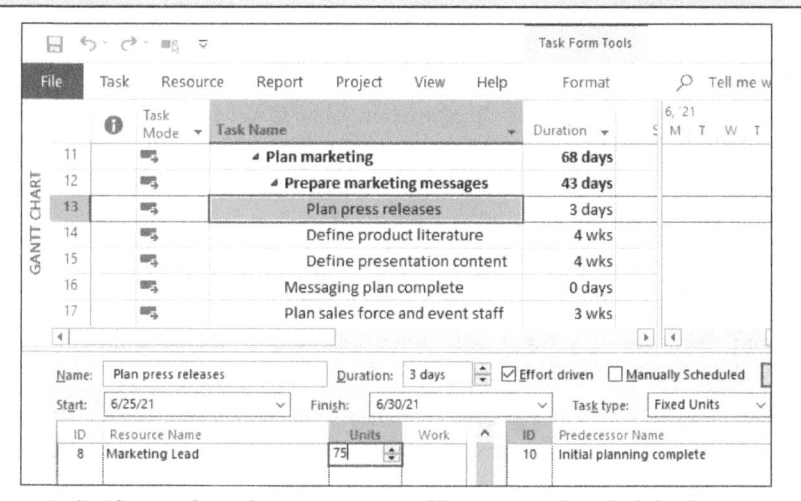

Figure 7-4. *After you choose the resource, you can fill in units, work, or both for the assignment.*

6. To assign another resource to the task, click the next blank Resource Name cell, and then repeat steps 4 and 5. In this example, add the Marketing Assistant at 100%.

7. After you assign all the resources, click OK.

    Project calculates the work hours for each resource based on the Units percentage and the task duration, as described earlier in this chapter.

Assigning Resources in a Gantt Chart Table

The Assign Resources dialog box and the Task Form described so far give you the power to enter varying percentages in the Units field, create new resources on the fly, and so on. But if all you need to do is assign all of a resource's available time to one task, then working directly in a table in the Gantt Chart view is fast and convenient.

Follow Along Practice

Here are the steps:

1. If necessary, display the Gantt Chart or other task-oriented view. (In the Task tab's View section, choose Gantt Chart.)

    The standard table applied to Gantt Chart view is the Entry table, which includes columns for the task's mode, name, duration, start and finish, predecessors, and resources. If you see different columns, right-click the Select All cell (the one in the table's upper-left corner) and then choose Entry.

    The Resource Names column is the last column in the Entry table, but it's typically out of sight (covered up by the timescale). Rather than scroll to display the column, make the table area wider so that it displays the columns for both task names and resource names. To do so, position the mouse pointer over the vertical bar between the table and the timescale. When the pointer changes to double arrows, drag the divider bar to the right until the Resource Names column is visible.

2. In the table, click the Resource Names cell for the task (in this example, "Define product literature").

    Project displays a down arrow for the resource drop-down list.

3. To assign a resource, click the down arrow, and then, in the list, turn on the checkboxes for the resource name(s) you want to assign (Marketing Content Developer, in this example).

4. After you turn on the checkboxes for all the resources you want to assign, press Enter.

    The name(s) you choose appear in the Resource Names cell. Project automatically assigns the resource at the resource's maximum units or 100% for a team resource. If the resource's Max. Units value is 100%, then the Resource Names cell shows only the resource name. However, if the resource's Max. Units value is something other than 100%, then the cell's contents look something like "Bob[50%]."

Copying a Resource to Multiple Tasks

Say that you want to copy the assignments you made on one task to another task in your project. A table makes copying assignments between tasks easy. When you want to apply the same resource and units to several tasks, follow these steps:

Follow Along Practice

1. Click the Resource Names cell that contains the resources and units you want (in this example, click the Resource Names cell for the "Plan press releases" task), and then press Ctrl+C (or in the Task tab's Clipboard section, click Copy).

    Project copies the values from the Resource Names cell to the Clipboard.

2. Select the other Resource Names cells into which you want to copy the assignment (in this example, "Prepare publicity plan"), and then press Ctrl+V (or in the Task tab's Clipboard section, click Paste).

    Project copies the resources and their corresponding assignment units to the second task.

Suppose your able assistant can handle all the tasks required to line up the vendor who will do all the printing for your event, so you want to assign all those tasks to her. If those tasks are consecutive, you can quickly copy the resources in the table. Here's how:

1. For this example, select the "Identify potential music options" task's Resource Names cell and turn on the checkbox for the Marketing Assistant. Press Enter.

2. Select the Resource Names cell with the value you want to copy, in this example, the cell you just filled in.

3. Position the pointer over the fill handle in the lower-right corner of that cell (it's a small green box).

4. When the pointer changes to a + symbol, drag over the rows that use the same resources (in this example, the Resource Names cells for "Send RFPs" and "Choose music vendor").

    Project copies the resource assignment(s) from the first cell to the ones you drag over.

Finding the Right Resources

When resources are plentiful, scrolling through a long list of names to find the resource you want to assign could take a while. You can reduce scrolling by telling the Assign Resources dialog box to list only the resources appropriate for the current assignment. All you have to do is tell it what you're looking for. You can apply a *resource filter* to find people who possess the right skills, belong to a specific group, or have the job code you're looking for. If you use resource outline codes (Chapter 21) to categorize resources, you can filter by those codes, too. But even the most qualified resources don't help at all if they aren't available. Fortunately, the Assign Resources dialog box also helps you find resources with enough available time.

These filtering features may not appear when you first open the Assign Resources dialog box. To coax the Resource list options into view, click the + sign to the left of the "Resource list options" label.

> **Tip:** When the filtering options are visible, the + button to the left of the "Resource list options" label changes to a –, which you can click when you want to hide the options once more. The Assign Resources dialog box remembers whether you had the filtering options expanded or hidden the last time you used it, and it reopens with that same setting the next time you use it.

Finding Resources by Criteria

You can use the Assign Resources dialog box's resource filters to restrict what appears in the Resources table. For example, you can filter the resource list with a built-in resource filter like Group to see only the resources that belong to a specific group. If you've created custom resource filters (Chapter 17), for instance to filter by the Code resource field, then you can filter the Resources table with those, too.

Follow Along Practice

To filter the resource list by criteria, follow these steps:

1. If necessary, display the Assign Resources dialog box (on the Resource tab, click Assign Resources).

2. In the task list, select the task that needs resources assigned (in this example, "Identify giveaway vendors").

3. If the "Resource list options" section is hidden, Click the + button to the left of that label.

4. Turn on the top "Filter by" checkbox.

   In the "Filter by" box, Project automatically selects the All Resources filter, so the Resources table continues to show all available resources. If the filter options are grayed out, make sure the first "Filter by" checkbox is turned on.

5. In the "Filter by" drop-down list, choose the filter you want to apply. (In this example, choose Group. In the Group dialog box, type Internal, and then click OK.)

   The Resources table displays only the resources that pass the filter, as illustrated in Figure 7-5.

   The "Filter by" drop-down list includes all existing resource filters. If none of these filters suit your needs, click More Filters to open the More Filters dialog box. There, you can create a new filter, edit an existing filter, or copy a filter to obtain exactly the resource filter you want—for example, to search for resources based on their Outline Code values, or to view only Confirmed resources.

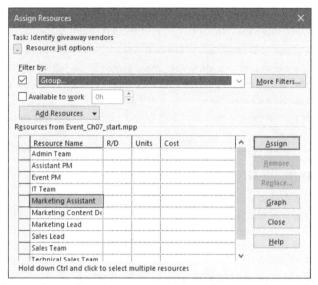

Figure 7-5. *When you choose a filter, the Resources table lists only resources that pass that filter's criteria.*

6.   Once the Resources table is filtered, assign resources as described earlier in this chapter. In this example, select the Assistant PM, and then click Assign.

To view the entire resource list again, in the "Filter by" drop-down list, either choose All Resources or turn off the "Filter by" checkbox.

Finding Resources with Available Time

Resources with the right skills aren't any help if they don't have enough time to complete an assignment. The Assign Resources dialog box's "Available to work" checkbox is just the ticket for finding folks who are available when the task is scheduled. When you turn it on, Project searches for the resources that have the amount of time you specify available between the task's start and finish dates.

Follow Along Practice

To find people who have enough hours available, do the following:

1.   Select the task to which you want to assign resources ("Identify potential music options," in this example).

If the Assign Resources dialog box isn't open, then, in the Resource tab's Assignments section, click Assign Resources.

2.   With the Assign Resources dialog box's "Resource list options" visible, turn on the "Available to work" checkbox. For this example, remove the Marketing Assistant from the music tasks. (Select the tasks in the Gantt Chart. In the Assign Resource dialog box, select the Marketing assistant, and then click Remove.)

The box to the right of the "Available to work" label becomes active.

3. In the "Available to work" box, type the amount of time the assignment requires, as illustrated in Figure 7-6. In this example, type 40h to match the work hours for the task's 5-day duration.

    Project updates the dialog box's Resources table to include only the resources who have that amount of time available between the task's start and finish dates. In this example, the Assistant PM doesn't appear on the list, because they are already assigned to other tasks at the same time.

    > **Note:** If you don't type a time unit, Project uses the standard units for work, which is one of the program's settings. (Choose File→Options, and then choose Schedule. The "Work is entered in" box specifies the standard time units for work.) For example, if work units are hours and you type 5, Project converts the value to 5h. If you type 5d, Project converts the "Available to work" value to 40h.

4. Choose and assign resources from the filtered list as you would normally. In this example, select the Event PM, and then click Assign.

    To view resources regardless of availability, turn off the "Available to work" checkbox.

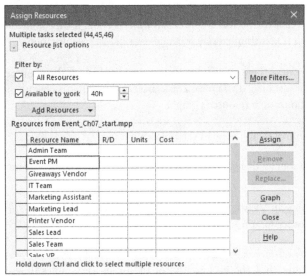

Figure 7-6. *Although you can filter the list of resources by available time alone, filtering by type of resource and available time (as shown here) shows you the resources that are both qualified and available.*

Building Teams with Project Server/Online

If you use Project Server or Project Online to manage your project portfolio, you can classify resources by skillsets with *enterprise resource outline codes* and *resource breakdown structure (RBS)*. These products also offer *multi-value resource outline codes*, which means you can assign more than one skillset to extraordinarily talented resources.

The Team Builder tool in Project Server/Online searches the enterprise resource pool for available resources with the skills you need. If you have to replace someone on a task, the Build Team feature helps you look for resources with the same skills as the resource you're replacing.

Reviewing Availability in Detail

The Assign Resources dialog box doesn't see shades of gray when it filters resources by availability: Resources either have enough time available or they don't. But you can use the Resource Graph view to get a better idea of whom to assign to a task. For example, if one resource is almost completely booked, then someone with more available time would give you more wiggle room should task dates slip. Or you may see that the perfect resource has *almost* enough time available and realize that the assignment may work if you simply delay it by a day or increase its duration.

The Resource Graph view (Figure 7-7) shows the number of hours the resource has available during each time period. For instance, if you have a task that requires 8 hours of work during a week, you can look for 8 available hours on a resource's graph.

You can display Resource Graph view in the following ways:

- In the Assign Resources dialog box, select the resource you want to evaluate, and then click Graph.

- In the View tab's Split View section, turn on the Details checkbox. Then, in the drop-down list, choose Resource Graph.

To see a graph of the resource's *available* time, which is usually what you want when you have an assignment to fill, right-click the background of the Resource Graph's timescale and then choose Remaining Availability on the shortcut menu. When you set the Resource Graph view to display Remaining Availability, the graph shows available work hours and proposed hours for the selected resource during each time period. Because the graph shows availability over time, it applies only to work resources, not material or cost resources. See Chapter 20 for other ways to customize the Resource Graph view.

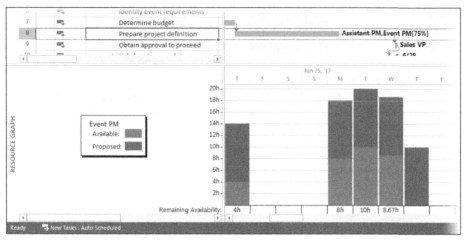

Figure 7-7. *Right-click the background of the Resource Graph's timescale and then choose the field you want to display in the view.*

Viewing Proposed Bookings

You can also use the Resource Graph to evaluate the work assigned to proposed resources to see how many more real resources you have to round up. As described in Chapter 6, when you add resources to your Project file, you can specify that they're either committed or proposed resources. Committed resources are those you know are in your roster, whereas proposed resources represent resources you'd *like* to get but don't have for sure. The Resource Graph shows work you've assigned to both committed *and* proposed resources—the only difference is that the vertical bars for proposed work are purple.

> **Note:** Be careful about changing the status if you use a resource pool (Chapter 24). Changing a resource to "Proposed" in a resource pool changes the resource's status to "Proposed" in every project to which the resource is assigned.

Assigning Resources with Team Planner

The Team Planner view (available in Project Professional) is perfect for more informal assignments, when you have several tasks (manually or automatically scheduled) that you want to fling resources at. (To display it, in the View tab's Resource Views section, click Team Planner.) Team Planner makes it easy to see which tasks are currently orphaned without resources. Then you can drag a task onto a resource's row and—poof!—you've got a resource assignment.

In addition to initial assignments, Team Planner also helps you spot unassigned tasks or overallocated resources. You can drag a task to a resource who doesn't have anything to do or move a task in the timeline to even out workloads—without messing with Project's fancier leveling features (described in Chapter 10).

> **Warning:** Moving tasks around in Team Planner is easy—maybe too easy. If you're working with manually scheduled tasks, dragging a task to a new date is often exactly what you want to do—for example, to nudge the task one day later so the assigned resource isn't overallocated. However, if your tasks are auto-scheduled, then dragging them around in the timeline creates date constraints (Chapter 5), which limit Project's ability to calculate start and finish dates. So if you use Team Planner to assign or swap resources on auto-scheduled tasks, make sure you don't drag auto-scheduled tasks to different dates.

Anatomy of the Team Planner View

The Team Planner view is divided into four quadrants, each with its own story to tell, as shown in Figure 7-8:

- **Resources**: The upper-left part of the view lists resources in the project, one resource per row.

  You don't have to assign dates to manually scheduled tasks. You can even type text like TBD (for "To be determined") in the tasks' Start and Finish fields, if you want. When you do that, in effect, you create unscheduled tasks—which appear right where you'd expect in Team Planner: the Unscheduled Tasks column.

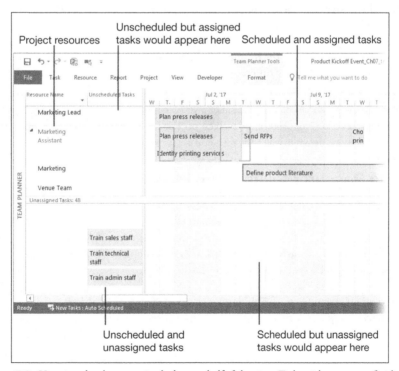

Figure 7-8. *Unassigned tasks appear in the bottom half of the view. Tasks without start or finish dates appear in the Unscheduled Tasks column.*

- **Assigned task timescale**: Similar to the timescale in a Gantt Chart view, the upper-right part of the view shows a timescale that positions bars based on tasks' start and finish dates. However, these bars are *assignment* bars, not task bars. If a task has more than one resource assigned to it, you see a bar for the task in the row for each assigned resource. The tasks in this quadrant are both assigned to resources and scheduled in time.

- **Unassigned but scheduled tasks**: The timescale in the bottom-right part of Team Planner view shows scheduled tasks that have no resources assigned. If you're trying to tie up the last loose unassigned tasks, look no further than this quadrant.

- **Unassigned and unscheduled tasks**: The lower-left quadrant is reserved for the least-defined tasks of all: ones that don't have start or finish dates, or assigned resources.

> **Tip:** You can format Team Planner to control the information you see or to change the size of the bars. For example, after you assign all the tasks to resources, you can hide the Unassigned Tasks pane. Simply head to the Team Planner Tools | Format tab and turn off the Unassigned Tasks checkbox. To hide the Unscheduled column, turn off the Unscheduled Tasks checkbox. Or, to display a single row for each resource, turn off the Expand Resource Rows checkbox.

Assigning Tasks with Team Planner

If a task sits forlornly unassigned in the bottom half of Team Planner, you can assign a resource to it in no time. Just drag the task from its place in the Unassigned Tasks portion of the view to the row for the resource you want to assign it to.

> **Note:** If you've downloaded files from the book website, you can experiment with Team Planner using the file Event_Ch07_teamplanner.mpp. You'll go back to using Event_Ch07_start.mpp in a bit, so don't close it.

This technique works just as well if you want to reassign a task from one resource to another. Simply drag the task's assignment bar from the assigned resource to the row for the resource you want to assign the task to. When you reassign a task in this way, be sure to drag the bar vertically in the timescale so you don't change the task's dates.

> **Note:** If you drag a manually scheduled task to different dates, the only things that change are the task's start and finish dates. However, if you drag an auto-scheduled task to different dates, you add a date constraint to the task, which limits Project's ability to calculate the schedule. See Chapter 5 to learn how to find and remove date constraints.

Scheduling Tasks with Team Planner

When you figure out when you want an unscheduled task to occur (whether or not it's assigned to a resource), you can drag it to the correct date in the timescale. If it's still unassigned, simply drag it to the date you want in the unassigned portion of the timescale. If you know who will perform the task, drag the bar to the row for the resource and to the date you want in the timescale.

Eliminating Overallocations with Team Planner

A resource can work on two tasks at the same time without a problem, as long as neither task is full time. Each task appears in its own row, as Figure 7-9 shows. However, if the concurrent tasks take up more time than the resource has available, a red box or bracket appears around the timeframe over which the resource is overallocated.

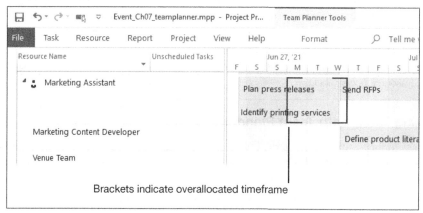

Figure 7-9. *In addition to red brackets around overallocated assignments, you can spot overallocated resources by looking in the Resource Name column for names in red text.*

Resolving overallocations in Team Planner is as simple as assigning resources in the first place. Here are the methods you can use:

- **Reassign a task to another resource**: To reassign a task to a resource who has time available, simply drag the assignment bar to the row for the new resource. Alternatively, right-click the assignment bar and point to Reassign To on the shortcut menu. Then, on the submenu, choose the appropriate resource.

- **Move the task to a different date**: If the resource has a short backlog, you can bump the task further into the future or move it earlier. You can reschedule a task by dragging its bar to a new date in the timescale, or you can use a Move Task Forward or Move Task Backward command. For example, to push the task ahead by a week, click the task's assignment bar to select it and then, on the Task tab, in the Tasks section, choose Move→1 Week.

- **Reschedule the task to when a resource is available**: If a resource works on a hodgepodge of short assignments, finding adjacent timeslots for a longer assignment is almost impossible. Instead, you can tell Project to chop the assignment up and slide it into a resource's open slots. To do so, select the assignment you want to reschedule. Then on the Task tab, in the Tasks section, choose Move→When Resources Are Available.

Don't Let Team Planner Resolve Overallocations

When Team Planner is visible and you click the Team Planner Tools | Format tab, you might have noticed the Prevent Overallocations button. Telling Project to prevent resource overallocations might sound like a free lunch. But, of course, it isn't.

If you click the Prevent Overallocations button to turn on that setting (you know it's on because "Prevent Overallocations: On" appears in the status bar at the bottom of the Project window) and then try to assign a task to an already-allocated resource, Project prevents the overallocation by delaying the assignment until the resource *is* available. However, delaying an assignment isn't the only way to eliminate an overallocation, and it might not be the one you would choose.

The other disadvantage to this feature is that Project could make changes when you aren't looking. Say you display Team Planner and turn on Prevent Overallocations. Then you switch to a different view and make schedule changes that overallocate some resources. If you switch back to Team Planner, the Prevent Overallocations feature immediately delays any overallocated assignments to remove the overallocations. But you might not notice that the program made the changes, which makes them tough to find and undo.

Assigning Material Resources to Tasks

Assigning material resources is similar to assigning work resources—with one exception: When you assign material resources, you fill in the quantity of material the task will consume instead of the time a work resource spends.

Work resources are always allocated by some unit of time, but you can dole out material resources by whatever unit of measurement makes sense: milligrams of medication, reams of paper, or gallons of water. Truth be told, Project couldn't care less about a material resource's unit of measurement. It calculates cost by multiplying the material resource's Standard Rate (Chapter 6) by the quantity you enter in the assignment. It's your responsibility to define the unit of measurement in the resource's Material Label cell and the Standard Rate as the cost of one unit of the material. Figure 7-10 shows how the material resource fields produce cost in an assignment.

> **Note:** If you've downloaded files from the book website, you can follow along by resuming with Event_Ch07_start.mpp.

Follow Along Practice

You can assign material resources using any of the methods described in this chapter. To assign a material resource to a task using the Assign Resources dialog box, do the following:

1. On Project's Resource tab, in the Assignments section, click Assign Resources.

    The Assign Resources dialog box opens.

2. In the Gantt Chart view or any other task-oriented view, select the task to which you want to assign a material resource, in this example, the "Create publicity materials" task.

    Any resources already assigned to the task appear at the top of the list, preceded by a checkmark.

3. In the dialog box's Resource Name column, click the name of the material resource (for example, "Brochures"), and then click Assign.

    The material resource moves to the top of the list (just like assigned work resources do).

4. In the Units cell, type the correct quantity (in this example, 2000). Press Enter or click another cell to complete the change.

    Project automatically recalculates the Cost field by multiplying the quantity by the material's Std. Rate. In the Assigned Resources dialog box, 2000 brochures are assigned to the "Create publicity materials" task. The Material Label for the Brochure resource is "Each" and the Std. Rate for each brochure is $4.25. When you enter the quantity "2,000" in the Units cell, Project then multiplies the Std. Rate ($4.25) by the quantity (2,000) to calculate the total brochure cost of $8,500.

Close the Assign Resources dialog box when you're done assigning resources.

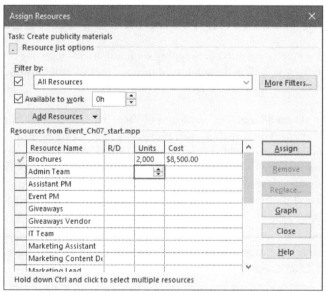

Figure 7-10. *When you assign a material resource to a task and fill in the quantity in its Units cell, Project calculates the total cost.*

When Material Quantity Depends on Time

With some material resources, the quantity assigned to a task is the same regardless of how long the task takes. In other words, that resource has a *fixed consumption rate*. If your task is to put up signs, the quantity of signs is 50, whether the task takes 2 hours or 8 hours. A *variable consumption rate*, by contrast, means the quantity of material varies based on the duration of the task. Say your car chugs 5 gallons of gas each hour you drive around putting up signs. If you complete the job in 2 hours, you use 10 gallons of gas, whereas an 8-hour escapade guzzles 40 gallons.

You specify the unit of measurement for a material resource in the Resource Sheet's Material Label field, and the cost per unit in the Std. Rate field. But after that, entering variable consumption rates in Project gets a little tricky. Typing *gallons/day* into the Material Label cell *doesn't* tell Project to calculate quantity based on task duration. The solution—and it's a bit obscure—is to type the quantity per unit of time in the Units field when you *assign* the material resource to a task. For example, assign your Gasoline resource to a task. Then, in the Units cell, type *5 gallons/h*. Project calculates the total cost of gasoline by multiplying the standard rate (the price per gallon) from the Resource Sheet's table by the duration in hours.

Assigning Cost Resources to Tasks

Cost resources differ from work and material resources in that you don't specify how much they cost until you assign them to tasks. Although you can use any of the methods described in this chapter to assign a cost resource, you have one additional step to perform. To assign a cost resource to a task using the Task Form, do the following:

Follow Along Practice

1. If necessary, in the View tab's Split View section, turn on the Details checkbox, and then in the drop down list, choose Task Form.

2. In the Gantt Chart view or any other task-oriented view, select the task to which you want to assign a cost resource ("Research venues," in this example).

3. In the Task Form's Resource Name column, click the name of the cost resource (Travel, in this example).

4. If you don't see cost fields in the Task Form, right-click it, and choose Cost on the shortcut menu.

5. In the Task Form's Cost cell, type the cost for this use of the cost resource (in this example, *800* for $800).

6. Click OK to complete the assignment, as shown in Figure 7-11.

   Unlike work and material resources, you specify the cost each time you assign a cost resource to a task, so its cost can differ for each assignment.

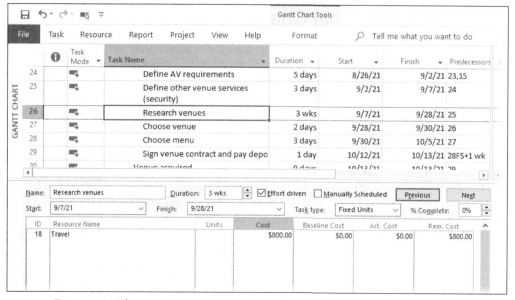

Figure 7-11. *When you assign a cost resource to a task, you specify the cost for that assignment.*

8

Modifying Resource Assignments

Sometimes you want to control how Project calculates resource assignments because the built-in calculations described in the previous chapter don't quite fit your situation. For example, if you assign two people to a 3-day task, Project initially assigns each person full time for all 3 days. Suppose you later decide that what you really need is the 3-day task collapsed into 1.5 12-hour days.

Before you start modifying resource assignments, it's important to understand the two types of assignment units that Project offers. When you first assign resources to tasks, Project remembers the units you specify and stores them in the Assignment Units field. As you change assignments and track progress, the program's Peak field stores the highest allocation for a resource on an assignment. This chapter begins with how these fields work.

Sometimes, you want to add more resources to get tasks done in a shorter duration. Other times, you might remove resources because they're needed elsewhere. In this chapter, you'll see how to add and remove resources from the tasks they're assigned to.

A factor to consider when modifying resource assignments is Project's ***effort-driven scheduling***, which means that the total amount of work required for a task drives the changes that Project makes. Effort-driven scheduling keeps a task's total amount of work the same when you add or remove resources to the task by reducing or increasing the work each resource performs. But effort-driven scheduling doesn't always hold true, particularly for tasks like project meetings that refuse to grow shorter no matter how many people attend. This chapter explains how to integrate task types and effort-driven scheduling with duration, work, and units to modify resource assignments exactly the way you want.

You can modify resource assignments in all manner of ways, as described in the rest of this chapter: add resources to a task or remove them, modify task duration or work time, or modify a resource's allocated units (the percentage of time devoted to a task).

Assignment Units vs. Peak

Project can keep track of the workload you originally assigned to a resource as well as any changes made to that workload. It does that by using two sets of units for assignments: the Assignment Units field and the Peak field. Although those two fields help Project do a better job of assigning resources the way you want, they won't win any awards for most-intuitive feature. For example, you may have noticed that Project doesn't seem to follow the formula Units = Work ÷ Duration when changing a resource assignment. This section explains how Assignment Units and Peak work together to handle resource assignments.

Here's what the Assignment Units and Peak fields do:

- The **Assignment Units** field represents the units you set when you first assign a resource to a task—and the units Project uses if you later reschedule the task. For example, say you assign an 8-hour-a-day resource to a task at 100%, so a 4-day task represents 32 hours of work. If you later increase the task's duration because there's more work to do, Project assigns the resource at 100% for those days as well.

- The **Peak** field, on the other hand, represents the maximum allocation for the resource on the assignment. For example, the third task in Figure 8-1 shows that the resource's maximum allocation to the assignment is only 25%, because the resource works 8 hours over 4 days, even though the initial assignment units were 100%.

> **Tip:** It's hard to follow the Assignment Units and Peak action with Project's built-in views and tables. To see what's going on with the Assignment Units and Peak values as you work on assignments, switch to the Task Usage view (in the View tab's Task Views section, click Task Usage) and insert an Assignment Unit column and a Peak column into the table, as shown in Figure 8-1.

Consider the task named Actual Work in Figure 8-1 (it's in row 4). Suppose you assign the resource to work 100% of the time on the task, but he works 10 hours the first day. If Project *didn't* have the Peak field, it would recalculate the resource's Assignment Units to be 125%, and use those units to recalculate the assignment duration. Then, suppose you add another 40 hours of work to the task. Project would divide the additional work by the 125% Assignment Units value and add another 4 days to the task's duration. Just because your team member was gung-ho his first day doesn't mean he wants to work 10-hour days for the rest of the project.

That's where the Peak field comes in. It records the 125% allocation for the modification you made, while the Assignment Units field value remains 100%. That way, if you increase the task work by 40 hours, Project divides the 40 hours by 100% units and adds 5 more days to the task—just as you intended and your team member expected.

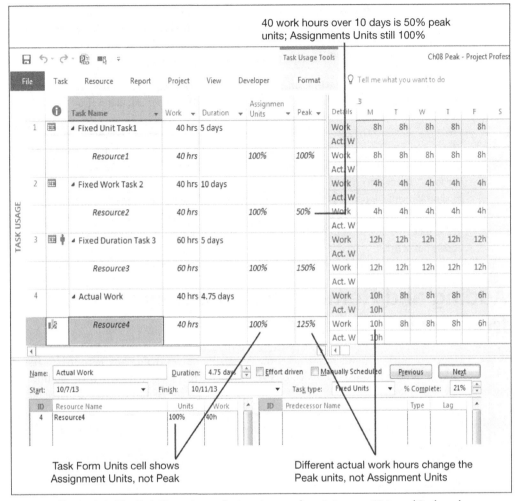

Figure 8-1. *The Task Usage view makes it easier to see how Assignment Units and Peak work.*

The Peak field also comes into play if you change assignments on tasks set to either the Fixed Duration or Fixed Work task type (which you'll learn about later in this chapter). Tasks set to the Fixed Units task type don't affect the Peak field. Figure 8-1 shows the result of changing tasks set to Fixed Units, Fixed Work, and Fixed Duration task types. They're named Fixed Unit Task 1, Fixed Work Task 2, and Fixed Duration Task 3, respectively. Here's what happens if you change each type of task:

- **Changing a Fixed Units task**: If a 5-day task is assigned full time (100%), the work hours equal 40 hours. If you increase the task's duration to 10 days, Project keeps 100% units and recalculates the work to be 80 hours. Assignment Units and Peak are still both equal to 100%.

- **Changing a Fixed Work task**: Suppose you start with the same 5-day task assigned at 100%. You set the task to Fixed Work so the amount of work doesn't change. If you change the task's duration to 10 days, the work is still 40 hours, as shown in Figure 8-1, so the resource works half time. Project changes the Peak value to 50%, but Assignment Units still equals 100%.

- **Changing a Fixed Duration task**: Using the same 5-day task assigned at 100%, you set the task to Fixed Duration. If you increase the work hours to 60, Project calculates the Peak value to be 150%.

> **Tip:** Project calculates an assignment's Peak values minute by minute, so a 1-minute over-allocation will flag the resource as overallocated (by displaying the red overallocation icon in a table's Indicators column). If an overallocation is short and you have your timescale set to show longer time periods like months, you won't see the overallocation—for example, in the Resource Graph view or the time-phased pane of the Task Usage view. However, if you expand the timescale to hours or minutes, the overallocated time period eventually comes out of hiding.

Adding and Removing Resources from Tasks

When it comes to quick assignment changes, the Assign Resources dialog box is your best friend. After you add or remove resources, Project asks you what you're trying to do and then modifies the appropriate values. Here's how to add and remove resources with the Assign Resources dialog box:

> **Note:** If you've downloaded files from the book website, you can follow along using the file Event_Ch08_start.mpp.

Follow Along Practice

1. On the Resource tab, click Assign Resources to open the Assign Resources dialog box.

2. In the Gantt Chart view or any other task-oriented view, select the task you want to modify (in this example, "Plan press releases").

   The resources already assigned to the task appear at the top of the dialog box's list, preceded by a checkmark.

3. To remove an existing resource from the task, click the name of the resource (in this example, Marketing Assistant), and then click Remove.

   The assigned checkmark disappears, and the resource takes its place back in the alphabetical list of unassigned resources. Project automatically clears the resource's Units cell.

4. To assign another resource to the task, in the dialog box's Resource Name column, click the name of the resource (in this example, Marketing Content Developer), and then click Assign.

In the Gantt Chart table, a green feedback triangle may appear in the upper-left corner of the Task Name cell to indicate that Project needs you to clarify what you're trying to accomplish so it can complete your change. If that happens, move the cursor over the indicator, and then click the Smart Tag indicator (a yellow diamond with an exclamation point) that appears, as shown in Figure 8-2. Then you can choose how you want Project to adjust work, duration, or units.

> **Tip:** Smart Tag indicators are so helpful, it's best to keep them turned on. See Chapter 2 to learn more about them, including how to turn them off.

5. In the Smart Tag menu, select the option for what you want Project to change.

    If you've added resources, the first option is "Reduce duration but keep the same amount of work," as shown in Figure 8-2. This option keeps the amount of work the same, and recalculates the task's duration based on the units you specified. (Project selects this option automatically, because shortening duration is the most common reason for adding resources.) Use this option in this example.

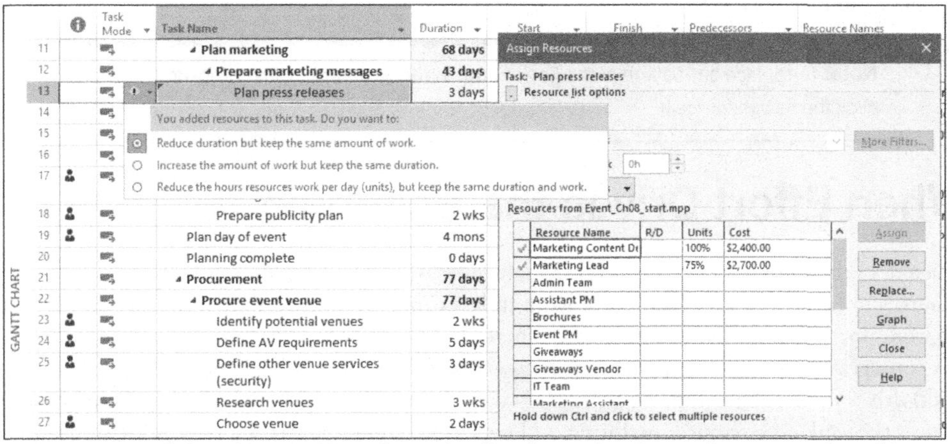

Figure 8-2. *Clicking the Smart Tag indicator (a yellow diamond with an exclamation mark inside) to the left of the task's name displays a list of the changes you're most likely to make.*

Selecting "Increase the amount of work but keep the same duration" keeps the same duration but recalculates the amount of work based on the units you specified. This option is perfect when you add resources to a task because the client asked for more features.

The "Reduce the hours that resources work per day (units), but keep the same duration and work" option calculates the units that resources work based on the duration and amount of work. This choice keeps the same duration and total work, while redistributing work to all the assigned resources.

If you remove resources, the three options are similar: The first option increases duration because you have fewer resources; the second option decreases the total amount of work; and the third option increases the units that the remaining resources work each day to compensate for the missing resources.

You can add or remove several resources before you close the dialog box or select another task. When you're done, either select another task in the Gantt Chart table or close the Assign Resources dialog box.

Replacing Resources

Sometimes you don't have to add or take away resources, just replace one assigned resource with another. Here's how:

Follow Along Practice

1. Select the task you want to swap resources in (in this example, "Plan sales force and event staff training").

2. In the Assign Resources dialog box, select the resource you want to replace (Assistant PM, in this example), and then click Replace.

3. In the Replace Resource dialog box, select the new resource (Marketing Assistant, in this example), and then click OK.

> **Note:** To replace a resource in the Task Form, in the Resource Name drop-down list, just click the new resource.

When Effort Drives the Schedule

When does the amount of work control the schedule? Almost always. Project managers typically add resources to finish the same amount of work in less time. If resources disappear, the sad fact is that the work doesn't. Tasks take longer as the remaining resources shoulder the work. Project's term for this conservation of total work is ***effort-driven scheduling***, because the effort (the total amount of work) drives the schedule (how long the task takes). With effort-driven scheduling, adding resources reduces the work each resource performs, and removing resources increases the work assigned to each remaining resource.

> **Note:** Effort-driven scheduling kicks in only when you add or remove resources from a task when there is more than one resource applied. Project doesn't apply effort-driven scheduling when you change resources already assigned to a task. If you modify the duration of a task, the task type determines whether the amount of work or the units change (explained in the next section).

Out of the box, Project's effort-driven setting is turned on. If it isn't turned on and you want it on, choose File→Options. On the left side of the Project Options dialog box, choose Schedule. In the "Scheduling options for this project" drop-down list, choose All New Projects, and then turn on the "New tasks are effort driven" checkbox. Then click OK to apply this setting.

Once effort-driven scheduling is turned on, Project automatically turns on the "Effort driven" checkbox for new tasks you create, but you don't have to leave it turned on. (The numbered list below explains how to turn it on and off.) Some tasks take the same amount of time no matter how many people you add. For example, adding attendees to a meeting doesn't shorten the meeting's duration—each attendee has to suffer through the same number of hours. For these uncompressible tasks, the total work *grows* with each resource you add. (As you watch the alarming increase in cost, you see why it's so important to keep meetings focused.) Consider a 2-hour status meeting. If you meet with two other people, the total amount of work is 6 hours—2 hours for each attendee. If you decide to invite the entire 10-person team, the total work expands to 20 hours.

Work can also increase because of things like change requests or unforeseen problems. For example, if you want to add resources to complete the change requests the client just delivered, turn off the "Effort driven" checkbox. That way, as you add resources, Project adds work based on the units you specify. Table 8-1 shows how Project adds resources with or without effort-driven scheduling.

Table 8-1. *How Project adds resources with the effort-driven scheduling setting on vs. off.*

Task Type	Effort-Driven Scheduling Turned On	Effort-Driven Scheduling Turned Off
Fixed units	Adding resources shortens duration.	Adding resources increases total work but keeps units and duration the same.
Fixed duration	Adding resources decreases units for each resource.	Adding resources increases total work but keeps the units and duration the same.
Fixed work	Adding resources shortens duration.	Doesn't apply. Fixed work is the same as effort-driven scheduling turned on.

Follow Along Practice

To turn off effort-driven scheduling for a task, do the following:

1. In the Gantt Chart view or another task-oriented view, select the task (in this example, "Obtain approval to proceed").

    The Task Form in the Details pane displays the values for the selected task. (If the Details pane isn't visible, in the View tab's Split View section, turn on the Details checkbox, and then choose Task Form in the drop-down menu.) Alternatively, you can double-click the task, and then, in the Task Information dialog box, click the Advanced tab.

2. In the Task Form (or the task Information dialog box), turn off the "Effort driven" checkbox.

3. Click OK.

4. When you add resources to the task, its duration remains the same and each new resource represents additional person-hours. In this example, add the Event PM, Sales Lead, and Marketing Lead to the task, and then click OK.

    In this example, the meeting duration remains 2 hours. However, the total work increases to 8 hours.

> **Note:** If you remove resources, the task's duration remains the same, but the task represents fewer total person-hours.

After you finish adding or removing resources, restore the task's "Effort driven" checkbox to its original setting.

Controlling Assignment Changes with Task Types

Depending on the assignment change you're trying to make, you may want a task's duration, work, or units to stay the same. Say you want to reduce a task's duration by adding another resource to take on some of the estimated work hours. Or perhaps you want to keep its units the same as you add more work. The Task Type field tells Project which variable you want to anchor.

You already know that duration, work, and units are inseparable, so you won't be surprised to learn that Project has three task types: Fixed Units, Fixed Work, and Fixed Duration. This section explains how to use all three.

> **Tip:** Although the Assign Resources dialog box is a powerful tool for initial resource assignments, the Task Form and the Task Usage view are better for changing assignments with precision.

Keeping Resources Assigned with the Same Units

The Fixed Units task type tells Project to keep the same units for each assigned resource regardless of the changes you make to the task's duration or work amount. Out of the box, Project automatically sets the Task Type field to Fixed Units (you can set it in the Task Form or in the Task Information dialog box), because a resource's availability is usually the limiting factor. For example, if you add work to a task, you shouldn't expect a resource assigned at 100 percent to work 200 percent to finish in the same timeframe.

The Fixed Units task type keeps units constant. Here's what Project does to a task assigned this type, depending on whether you change its duration, work, or units:

- **Duration**: If you change the task's duration, then Project adjusts the amount of work based on the set units.

- **Work**: If you change the amount of work, then Project adjusts the task's duration based on the set units.

- **Units**: If you change the units in a Fixed Units task, then Project adjusts the task's duration and keeps the amount of work the same, because of the program's built-in bias toward changing duration before work (explained in Chapter 5).

Maintaining Task Duration

Suppose you lose a resource assigned to a task, and you want the remaining resources to step up to complete the work without increasing the task's duration. The Fixed Duration task type helps you do just that. Here's how a fixed-duration task behaves:

- **Work**: If you change the task's amount of work, then Project adjusts the task's Peak units to keep the set duration.

- **Units**: If you change the task's units, then Project adjusts its amount of work to keep the same duration.

- **Duration**: If you change the duration in a fixed-duration task, then Project adjusts the amount of work, because of the program's bias toward changing work before units.

Follow Along Practice

Here's how to modify assignments without affecting task duration:

1. In the Gantt Chart view, select the task you want to modify ("Plan sales force and event staff training," in this example).

   If the Task Form is visible in the Details Pane, the values for the selected task appear there.

2. In the Task Form, in the "Task type" drop-down list, choose Fixed Duration, as shown in Figure 8-3.

   Project will keep the task's duration the same until you change the "Task type" to another value or type a new value in the task's Duration field.

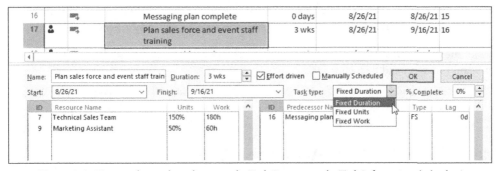

Figure 8-3. *You can change the task type in the Task Form or on the Task Information dialog box's Advanced tab.*

3. To remove a resource from the task, select the resource name (in this case, Marketing Assistant) in the Task Form and then press Delete.

If you want to reduce the percentage of time that a resource works on the task, select that resource's Units cell, and then type the new value, for example, changing units from 100% to 50%.

The values in the Work cells don't change just yet. The recalculations will occur when you click OK in the next step.

> **Tip:** If you add resources to the task, you can't specify their units. Project automatically fills in the Task Form's Units cell with 100% or the resource's Maximum Units. After you add the resources and click OK, *then* you can edit the assignments to modify the units.

4. After you've made the changes you want, click OK.

    The task's duration remains the same, and Project calculates the work assigned to each resource, as shown in Figure 8-4. In this example, the task's duration is still 3 weeks because the task is set to Fixed Duration. However, work assigned to the Technical Sales Team resource increased from 180 hours to 240 hours.

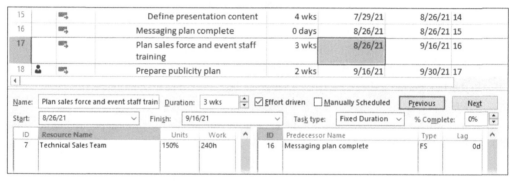

Figure 8-4. *Project doesn't recalculate assignments until you click OK.*

5. In the Task Form's "Task type" drop-down list, choose Fixed Units to reset the task to its standard task type, and then click OK.

    Restoring the task type to Fixed Units ensures that every task will behave consistently. Whenever you choose a different task type for a specific assignment change, remember to choose Fixed Units when the modification is complete.

Maintaining the Same Amount of Work

If you've estimated the amount of work that tasks involve, you don't want Project messing with tasks' work values. Using the Fixed Work task type means you can adjust a task's duration or units without modifying the amount of time a resource spends working on it. For example, if you discover that a resource is available only 50 percent of the time, then Project can keep the amount of work the same while changing the task's duration.

Here's how a fixed-work task behaves:

- **Duration**: If you change the task's duration, Project adjusts the task's Peak units to keep the amount of work the same. For example, if a resource is assigned 40 hours of work in a week, the initial Assignment Units are 100%. If you change the task's duration to 10 days, its Assignment Units are still 100% but its Peak units drop to 50% (see Figure 8-1).

- **Units**: If you change the task's units, then Project adjusts its duration. If a resource is assigned to work 40 hours in 5 days and you change the units to 50%, the task's duration increases to 10 days.

- **Work**: If you change the amount of work in a fixed-work task, Project adjusts the task's duration, because of the program's bias against changing units.

> **Note:** You can change the standard task type if you typically keep a different variable steady. Suppose you estimate the work for project tasks, and you don't want Project changing those values as you adjust resource units or change task durations. To change the standard task type, choose File→Options→Schedule. Below "Scheduling options for this project" in the "Default task type" box, choose Fixed Duration or Fixed Work.

Reviewing Resource Assignments

If assignments don't produce the schedule you want, you need to examine the assignments you've made to see what tweaks might be required. Here are several methods for looking at resource assignments:

- **View assignment details as you work on your task list**: The Task Form (shown earlier in this chapter) can show you who's assigned to a task, the units they're assigned, and the hours of work they're allocated. This view works equally well for creating, reviewing, and modifying resource assignments. To display this view below any task-oriented view, in the View tab's Split View section, turn on the Details checkbox, and then choose Task Form in the drop-down menu.

- **View assignments grouped by task or resource**: The Task Usage view displays a summary row for each task and additional rows for each assignment, which is helpful when you want to see assignment details for all the resources assigned to tasks. However, you might find the ***Resource Usage*** view handier when you're trying to smooth out the workload for an overworked resource. The Resource Usage view displays a summary row for each resource and additional rows for the resource's assignments, as shown in Figure 8-5. Another advantage to usage views is that the right side of the view is a time-phased grid that shows when work occurs over time. If a resource is overallocated during a time period, the total hours in the summary row appear as red text. You can look at the individual assignments with hours during that period to see how you might resolve the overallocation.

- **View assignment details**: The Assignment Information dialog box lets you dig even deeper into an assignment to, for example, see a work contour (Chapter 10) or a cost rate table (Chapter 6) that's applied. When you're in either the Task Usage or Resource Usage view, double-click an assignment's row to open the Assignment Information dialog box. (If you double-click a task-summary row instead, the Task Information dialog box appears. Similarly, double-clicking a resource-summary row displays the Resource Information dialog box.)

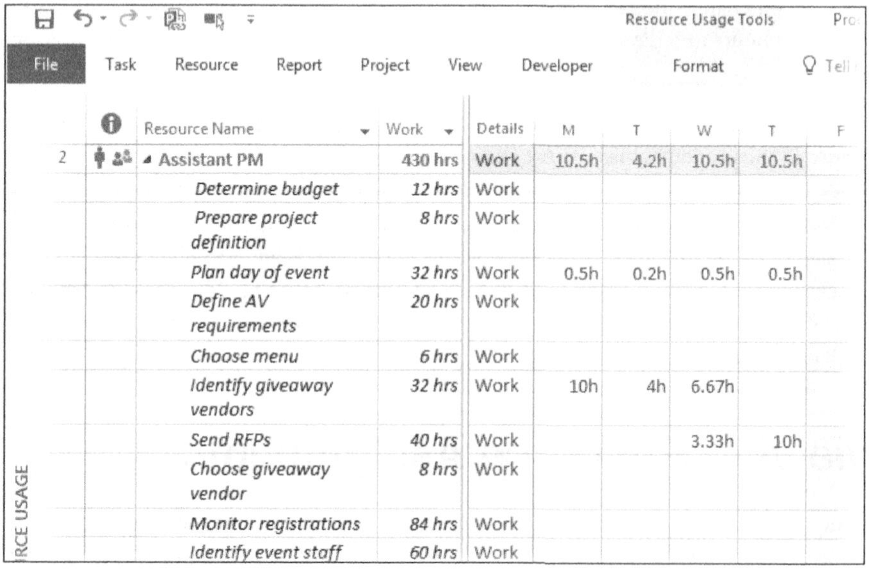

Figure 8-5. *The Resource Usage view is great for identifying the assignments that contribute to overallocations.*

Tip: The Resource Usage view is also helpful for seeing whether you're utilizing your resources fully. To do that, click the black triangle to the left of a resource's name to hide its assignments. That way, you see only the resource's summary row. Then, in the View tab's Zoom section, choose a time unit like Weeks or Months. If you choose Weeks, scan the columns in the time-scaled portion of the view. If the Work cells for most weeks are close to or equal to 40, you're all set. On the other hand, if the assigned work hours vary widely from week to week, you may want to see if you can modify your schedule to keep your resources' workloads more stable over time.

9

Reviewing Your Schedule

Balancing a project's scope, schedule, cost, and quality is a bit like juggling eggs: If you don't keep an eye on every element, you'll end up with egg on your face. Once you have resources assigned to tasks, it's time to see whether the project schedule and price are right.

Your review of the schedule starts with making sure your tasks are set up the way they should be. Missing or incorrect task dependencies affect when tasks begin and end, so the dates that Project calculates might be too early or too late. In addition, task date constraints and manually scheduled tasks go on the calendar where you tell them to. If those constraints or dates are wrong—or you accidentally create constraints you don't need—the schedule is both incorrect and less flexible. This chapter tells you how to find and correct task dependencies and inadvertent constraints.

This chapter then explains how to examine your project's schedule and cost. You'll learn how to find the best tasks to shorten if the schedule is too long and how to compare task finish dates to deadlines. This chapter also describes several methods for reviewing project costs.

Making Sure Tasks Are Set Up Correctly

Project can't read your mind. It can't point out missing task dependencies or dependencies that depend on the wrong things. Similarly, Project adds the task constraints you tell it to add. The problem is, seemingly innocuous actions can produce constraints you never intended. So, before you fine-tune your schedule, it's important to review tasks to make sure you have the dependencies and constraints you want—and *only* those.

What Project *can* do is make it easier to find task dependency and constraint problems, as this section explains.

> **Note:** If you've downloaded files from the book website, you can follow along using the file Event_Ch09_start.mpp.

Reviewing Task Dependencies

Following the link lines in a Gantt Chart is like trying to untangle a plate of spaghetti. It's hard to trace the lines to see if a task links to the right predecessors and successors, or if the dependencies you've set up are correct. After work gets rolling, you might end up with a task-related problem—the assigned programmer is out of commission while she heals from carpal tunnel surgery, say. In that case, you might want to see how that task affects the rest of the schedule. This section explains two ways to review task dependencies.

Highlighting Task Paths

Task path highlighting makes it easy to review both predecessors and successors to review task dependencies. This section provides a rundown on how it works.

Follow Along Practice

Task path highlighting emphasizes the predecessors and successors of the selected task. Although this feature is turned off initially, once you've built a schedule of linked tasks, it's easy to turn it on to review task dependencies. Here's how:

1. Display a Gantt Chart view, such as plain ol' Gantt Chart or Detailed Gantt.

    You can turn on task path highlighting for any view that includes a timescale with task bars.

2. Select a task whose dependencies you want to review ("Plan press releases," in this example).

3. Click the Gantt Chart Tools | Format tab. In the Bar Styles section, click Task Path, and then choose the items you want to highlight, as shown in Figure 9-1.

    When you choose Predecessors, the task bars for all predecessors are shown in yellow. If you also choose Driving Predecessors, then the task bars for the predecessors that control when the selected task occurs change to orange. For example, any linked tasks that finish sooner than the selected task are predecessors; the task that determines the selected task's start date is a *driving predecessor*.

    Similarly, choosing Successors highlights successors whose dates aren't directly controlled by the selected task. *Driven successors* are successors whose dates are directly controlled by the selected task.

4. Review the highlighted tasks to make sure that all those task dependencies should be there. If you find an unnecessary task dependency, delete it (Chapter 5).

5. Look for tasks that aren't highlighted that should be linked to the selected task. If any task dependencies are missing, link the tasks (Chapter 5).

6. To review the dependencies for a different task, select that task.

    The highlighting shows the predecessors and successors of the task you select.

When you get to the final task or milestone, you're done! When you don't need task path highlighting any more, click the Gantt Chart Tools | Format tab. In the Bar Styles section, click Task Path→Remove Highlighting.

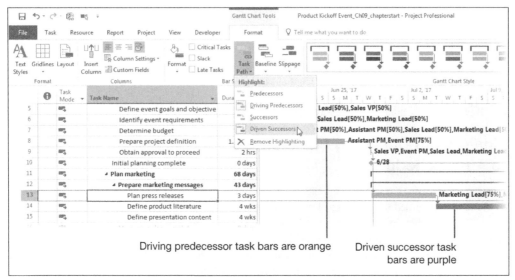

Driving predecessor task bars are orange   Driven successor task bars are purple

Figure 9-1. *Task path highlighting displays task bars in different colors depending on their roles in task dependencies.*

> **Note:** If you save your Project file while task path highlighting is turned on, the same highlights appear the next time you open the file.

Reviewing Dependencies in the Task Form

To check that you've added the right types of dependencies with the correct amount of lag, you can't beat the Task Form. Here are the steps for displaying predecessors and successors in the Task Form, and checking that your dependencies are correct:

1. With a Gantt Chart view in place, click the View tab, turn on the Details checkbox, and then, if necessary, choose Task Form in the Details drop-down menu.

   When you select a task in the top view pane, the Task Form view displays information about it in the Details pane.

2. Right-click anywhere in the Task Form and choose Predecessors & Successors.

   The predecessors to the selected task appear on the left side of the Task Form, and the successors appear on the right side.

3. Make sure that tasks in the Predecessor Name column are predecessors to the selected task and that the tasks in the Successor Name column are successors to the selected task.

If you find links that shouldn't be there, click the erroneous predecessor or successor's row, and then press the Delete key on your keyboard.

4.   Check whether other predecessor or successor tasks aren't listed.

If you find missing links, link the two tasks as you would normally (Chapter 5).

5.   Make sure the dependency type for each predecessor and successor is correct, and verify the lag or lead time.

Remember, lag time (a delay from one task to the other) is a positive number. If the second task gets an early start, the value in the Lag field is a negative number.

6.   If you find redundant links in your schedule, delete them.

Finding and Changing Manually Scheduled Tasks to Auto Scheduled

If some task information was unavailable when you started your project schedule, you may have created manually scheduled tasks to record the info you *did* have. Project changes the appearance of task bars to indicate what information is available or missing (see Chapter 4). As you get more information about tasks, you can fill in the missing fields and turn many of those manually scheduled tasks into auto-scheduled ones. (In some cases, you create manually scheduled tasks so you can pin the tasks' dates to the calendar. Those tasks remain manually scheduled for the duration of the project.) Be sure to review all your manually scheduled tasks to confirm that you've filled in missing task information.

Project's Tasks Without Dates filter (in the View tab's Data section, click the Filter down arrow, choose More Filters, and then double-click Tasks Without Dates) displays tasks without start and finish dates. However, incomplete task info comes in other forms—like tasks with start dates but no finish dates—so that filter doesn't show *all* the tasks you need to see. Filtering your task list to display all manually scheduled tasks is a better place to start. Here's how you can filter your task list and switch tasks to auto-scheduled as you fill in their missing info:

Follow Along Practice

1.   Display the Entry table by right-clicking the Select All cell at the table's top left, and then choosing Entry on the shortcut menu.

If you use a different table that doesn't include the Task Mode field, right-click the column heading to the right of where you want to insert that field, choose Insert Column, and then choose Task Mode.

2.   To filter your task list to show only manually scheduled tasks, click the down arrow in the Task Mode column heading; turn off the Auto Scheduled checkbox, as shown in Figure 9-2; and then click OK.

The task list includes all manually scheduled subtasks and the summary tasks to which they belong. A filter icon appears to the right of the Task Mode column heading to indicate that the list is filtered by that column (this icon is circled in Figure 9-2).

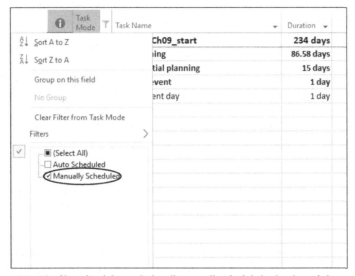

Figure 9-2. *The filtered task list includes all manually scheduled subtasks and the summary tasks to which they belong.*

3. Review each task in the list, and fill in any missing information (In this example, the manually scheduled tasks don't have any missing information.)

    A partially shaded task bar without end-caps means you haven't defined either a start or a finish date for that task. If a task bar has only one end-cap, then the duration or one of the task's dates is missing. To keep the task manually scheduled, fill in the task's Start or Finish fields. You can also switch the task to auto-scheduled, as described in step 4, so Project can use the task's predecessors and successors to calculate its dates.

4. To switch a task to auto-scheduled, right-click the task and then choose Auto Scheduled from the shortcut menu (or click Auto Schedule in the Task tab's Tasks section). In this example, keep the ID 84 "Event day" task manually scheduled, because the event will occur on 4/11/22 no matter what.

    The task bar style in the timescale changes to solid blue (or red if it's critical and the view differentiates critical tasks) to show that the task is auto-scheduled. The newly auto-scheduled task remains in the view. To reapply the Manually Scheduled filter and hide any tasks you've switched to auto-scheduled, simply press Shift+F3.

5. Repeat steps 3 and 4 until you've handled all manually scheduled tasks.

    When the task list shows only the manually scheduled tasks you created to control task dates, you're done!

6. To return to the full task list, click the down arrow in the Task Mode column heading and then choose Clear Filter from Task Mode on the dropdown menu.

    An even easier way to restore the full task list is by pressing F3, which removes the filter.

Freeing Tasks from Date Constraints

Most schedules originate from a start date, and the project's finish date is calculated from there. When you schedule a Project file from the start date (Chapter 3), Project automatically assigns the As Soon As Possible date constraint to new auto-scheduled tasks, so every task begins on the earliest possible date. (If you work backward from a finish date, Project assigns the As Late As Possible constraint instead.) Other less-flexible date constraints make sense now and then. For example, you can change the assignments for a key resource who's going on sabbatical to a Start No Earlier Than constraint to schedule assignments for when she returns.

Because less-flexible date constraints get in the way of Project doing its job, you're better off using as few of them as possible. Unfortunately, some Project actions create date constraints you don't intend. For example, typing (or copying) a specific date in a Start or Finish cell creates a new date constraint for that task. This section tells you how to find and eliminate unwanted date constraints.

The hunt for unwanted, unintended constraints is a must-do task on every project manager's checklist. Project offers two ways to examine your date constraints: the Constraint Indicator icons, and the Constraint Type field. Here are the steps for finding and fixing date constraints:

Follow Along Practice

1. Display the Gantt Chart view in the top pane (in the View tab's Task Views section, click Gantt Chart).

2. In the View tab's Split View section, turn on the Details checkbox, and then, choose Task Details Form. (If the Task Details Form doesn't appear on the drop-down menu, choose More Views in the Details drop-down list. In the More Views dialog box, select Task Details Form, and then click Apply.)

    The Task Details Form appears in the Details pane and includes the Constraint Type and Constraint Date fields.

3. To see what happens when you add an erroneous date constraint, select a task (in this example, task ID 7 "Determine budget"). In the task's Start cell in the table, type a date, such as 6/26/21, and then press Enter or click OK in the Task Details Form. If the Planning Wizard appears, choose the option "Move the task to start on <date> and keep the link" and then click OK.

    A date constraint indicator appears in the task's Indicators cell. In addition, when you select the task in the Entry table, in the Task Details Form, the Constraint type changes to Start No Earlier Than for a project scheduled from the start date, and the Constraint Date changes to the date you typed.

> **Note:** Project adds a date constraint if you drag a task bar in the timescale. When you put the pointer over a task bar, the cursor changes to a four-headed arrow. If you then drag the bar to the left or right, Project adds a Start No Earlier Than (or Start No Later Than if you schedule the project from the finish date) date constraint and changes the task's Start date.

4. To find tasks with date constraints, first display the Constraint Type column in the view table by right-clicking in the table heading area and then choosing Insert Column. In the drop-down list, choose Constraint Type.

5. Filter the task list for constraints other than As Soon As Possible by clicking the down arrow to the right of the Constraint Type column heading, turning off the As Soon As Possible checkbox, and then clicking OK.

    Project filters the task list to display only tasks that have a constraint type *other* than As Soon As Possible, as you see in Figure 9-3. To see tasks with date constraints more easily, hide summary tasks (on the Format tab, turn off the Summary Tasks checkbox).

6. In the task list, select a task with a date constraint (in this example, task ID 7 "Determine budget") so its information appears in the Task Details Form in the bottom pane.

    The Task Details Form shows both the constraint type and the date, which might jog your memory about why you set a constraint for this task.

7. If the constraint shouldn't be there, as in this example, then in Task Details Form view in the Details pane, choose As Soon As Possible from the Constraint Type drop-down list, and then click OK.

    In the Task Details Form, Project changes the constraint's Date field to NA, and in the Entry table, the Constraint icon disappears from the Indicators column.

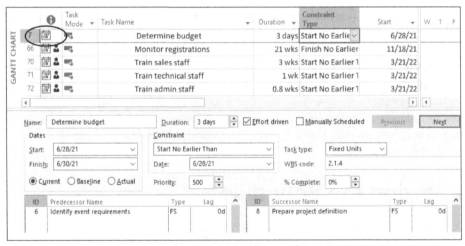

Figure 9-3. *Tasks that have a date constraint other than As Soon As Possible or As Late As Possible sport a date constraint icon in the Indicators column (circled).*

8. Repeat steps 6 and 7 to replace date constraints that shouldn't be there. To hide tasks whose constraints you've removed, press Shift+F3 to reapply the Constraint Type filter.

    When you're done, the only date constraints you should see are the ones that are supposed to be there.

9. Remove the filter by clicking the filter icon in the Constraint Type column heading, turning on the Select All checkbox, and then clicking OK.

10. To hide the Constraint Type column, right-click its column heading, and then choose Hide Column on the shortcut menu. If you hid summary tasks, on the Format tab, turn on the Summary Tasks checkbox.

Other Errors to Look For

In addition to issues with task dependencies, manually scheduled tasks, and date constraints, here are a few more items to check:

Recommendatons

- **Work or duration values that seem too low or too high:** You may have typed a value incorrectly. Check your original estimates to ensure that the values in Project are correct.

- **Work tasks without assigned resources:** If resource assignments are missing, the cost in your Project file will be lower than it should be. In addition, when you add the missing assignment, the assigned resource may become overallocated.

- **Summary tasks with assigned resources:** Best practice dictates that you assign resources only to work tasks, not summary tasks (see Chapter 7).

- **Resource calendars that don't represent people's actual availability:** If resources are available more or less than their calendars indicate, the schedule that Project calculates won't be accurate.

Follow Along Practice

- **Costs that haven't been entered:** In this example, the Music Vendor is a cost resource assigned to the "Sign music agreement" task, but no cost has been entered. To enter the cost for this resource, double-click the task, and then, in the task Information dialog box, click the Resources tab. In the Music Vendor's Cost cell, type 2000 to enter a $2,000 charge for the band. Click OK to close the dialog box.

Reviewing the Schedule

The fat lady won't sing until the finish dates in Project meet the project's deadlines **and** the project's cost is right. Your job is to keep fine-tuning the schedule until both the schedule and the cost are in line. In this section, you'll learn how to review dates in your Project file, and how to find the best tasks to change.

> **Note:** If you've downloaded files from the book website, you can follow along using the file Ch09_criticalpath.mpp.

Understanding the Critical Path and Slack Time

Stakeholders usually care deeply about when the project is going to finish. The ***critical path*** determines the project's finish date, which is why it gets a lot of attention during project planning and execution. This section explains why the critical path is critical and how slack time determines which tasks are on the critical path.

The critical path is the longest sequence of tasks in the project schedule. It starts on the project start date and runs to the project finish date. The tasks on the critical path are called ***critical tasks***. Why is the critical path critical? Because a delay in ***any*** of its tasks delays the project's finish date.

To understand where the critical path comes from, you need to understand ***slack time*** (also called float), which is the amount of time that a task can slip without delaying the tasks that follow it (see Figure 9-4). When you link tasks, predecessor tasks can push (or pull) their successors around. For instance, if a predecessor starts late enough or takes too long, it delays the tasks that follow it. Slack time is the amount of wiggle room a task has. (As you'll see in Chapter 10, you can use slack time to help balance people's workloads.)

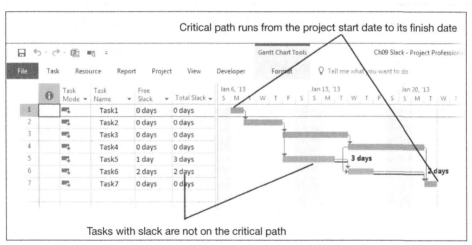

Figure 9-4. *When a task's Total Slack is zero, any delay in it will affect the project finish date, which makes that task part of the critical path.*

Driving somewhere is a simple example of a critical path and slack time. Suppose you and your brother are both heading to your elderly Aunt Thelma's for lunch, which starts at noon sharp. You're taking the highway, which takes 65 minutes. Your brother, on the other hand, is driving his sports car over the scenic route, which is 90 minutes of twists and turns. Your brother's drive is the critical path, because it takes the longest. That gives you 25 minutes of slack time before you have to start driving (or you can use the time to stop and pick flowers for your dear auntie).

Project has two fields for slack:

- **Free Slack** represents the amount of time a task can slip before it delays another *task*. For example, Task5 in Figure 9-4 can slip 1 day before it will delay Task6.

- **Total Slack** is the amount of time a task can slip before it delays the ***project finish date***. In Figure 9-4, Task6 has 2 days of total slack, because it can delay 2 days before it affects the last task in the schedule. Once a task uses up its total slack, it becomes critical and joins the critical path. (Later in this chapter, you'll see how tasks can end up with ***negative*** slack, which can lead to too many tasks on the critical path.)

To add either of these fields to a view's table pane, right-click the table's heading area, choose Insert Column, and then pick the field you want to add.

> **Note:** The Early Start, Early Finish, Late Start, and Late Finish fields show the earliest and latest dates that a task can start based on the slack of predecessor or successor tasks.

Adding Buffers Between Project Phases

Nothing ever runs according to plan, so the reality is that some tasks in your project are going to finish late. If your schedule is tighter than a Hollywood face-lift, the tiniest delay in one task could work its way through the schedule to delay the finish date.

A good way to protect your schedule from delays is to add wiggle room at key points. For example, you can create a task specifically as a buffer between the end of one phase and the beginning of another. Then, if a few tasks take longer in an earlier phase, they eat into the buffer instead of your due date.

You don't need buffers between *every* task. Breathing room for phases or key summary tasks is usually good enough. In many projects, tasks that end early may offset tasks that run late, and you don't need the buffer at all. But if a series of tasks adds up to a real delay, you can reduce the buffer by the time that's been lost, and the project finish date will hold fast unless the delay *completely* consumes the buffer.

- To add a buffer, simply create a buffer task at the end of a task sequence and link it as you normally would. For instance, add a project buffer task as a successor to the last task or project finish milestone.

- To use buffer time for a task, shorten the buffer duration to compensate for the increased task duration. If you set a project baseline (Chapter 12), you can check buffer status by comparing current and baseline durations using the Duration Variance field.

If you look closely at Figure 9-4, you'll notice that the tasks on the critical path (Task1–Task4 and Task7) have one thing in common: Their Total Slack values are **0**—meaning they have no slack whatsoever. When predecessors and successors are linked with no slack at all, then any delay propagates down the line, delaying the project finish date.

The critical path's tight coupling has an upside: If a critical task finishes early, its successors can start earlier, too (as long as their assigned resources are available)—which could mean an *earlier* project finish date. So the critical path is the key to success whether you're trying to keep your schedule on track or need to shorten it.

Reviewing the Critical Path

When a project schedule is too long, you want to rein it in with the least amount of disruption to your plan. Because tasks on the critical path directly affect a project's finish date, they're the best candidates for shortening. This section shows you how to see which tasks are on the critical path, so you can focus on the tasks that really make a difference to your schedule.

> **Note:** If you've downloaded files from the book website, you can continue with the file Event_Ch09_start.mpp.

Displaying the Critical Path in Project

The Gantt Chart view makes the critical path easy to see. Some built-in views show the critical path out of the box, but it's easy to display it in any Gantt Chart view:

- The standard **Gantt Chart view** doesn't show the critical path or slack time initially—all you see are blue task bars. However, in Project, you can easily format this view to display the critical path and slack time. In the Gantt Chart Tools | Format tab's Bar Styles section, turn on the Critical Tasks checkbox and the Slack checkbox. Once you do that, the view's timescale displays critical tasks in red and slack as thin black bars (they look like underscores) at the right end of task bars (as shown in Figure 9-4).

  In the example project, the day of the event is scheduled for 4/11/2022, which also happens to be the target date. However, as you can see by the people icon in the Indicators column in Figure 9-5, resources are overallocated on several tasks. Eliminating those overallocations could affect the event date, so you'll have to re-examine the critical path after you smooth out resource workloads (see Chapter 10).

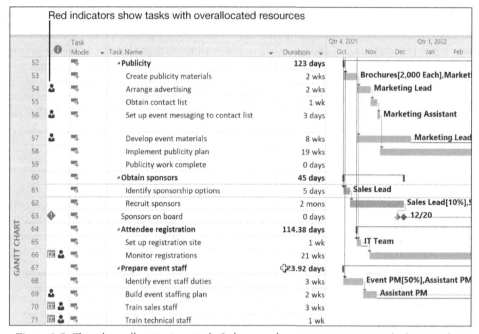

Figure 9-5. *The red overallocation icons in the Indicators column is one way to spot tasks that contribute to resource overallocations.*

- **The Tracking Gantt view** (in the Task tab's View section, click the down arrow, and then choose Tracking Gantt) shows the critical tasks' bars in red and noncritical tasks' bars in blue. The table area initially displays the Entry table. (If you've set a baseline for your project, as described in Chapter 12, gray task bars represent the baseline schedule.)

- **The Detail Gantt view** (in the Task tab's View section, click the down arrow, choose More Views, and then double-click Detail Gantt) also shows critical tasks in red and noncritical tasks in blue. It applies the Delay table so you can evaluate leveling delays.

Filtering the Task List to Show Critical Tasks

Filtering the task list to show only critical-path tasks helps you focus on the tasks that need to stay on schedule or, even better, finish early. To filter the task list to show only critical-path tasks, do the following:

Follow Along Practice

1. In the View tab's Data section, click the down arrow next to the filter box, and then choose Critical.

   Project shows critical path tasks and the summary tasks to which they belong.

2. To hide the summary tasks, in the Gantt Chart Tools | Format tab's Show/Hide section, turn off the Summary Tasks checkbox.

The summary tasks disappear, so you see only critical work tasks. In the example project, the critical path doesn't run from the project start to project finish. See the section "When the Critical Path is Incomplete" to learn how to handle this situation.

3. To return to the full task list, turn the Summary Tasks checkbox on, and in the View tab's Data section, click the down arrow next to the filter box, and then choose [No Filter].

> **Tip:** The critical path can be slippery. Sometimes shortening a critical task adds a different task to the critical path that wasn't there before. Conversely, since the critical path shows the longest path from start to finish, shortening a task may turn it into a *noncritical* task. To understand how this works, consider two tasks that start on the same day. The critical task takes 10 days, and the noncritical one takes 9 days. If you shorten the critical task to 8 days, it isn't the longest path anymore, so it becomes a noncritical task. In the meantime, the 9-day task is now the longest and, thus, is now on the critical path.
>
> Because the critical path changes, make sure you're using the *current* critical path to choose the tasks you want to work on. Although the Critical filter initially shows only critical tasks, it doesn't update itself as tasks' critical status changes. To quickly reapply the current filter, press Shift+F3.

Showing Critical Tasks in a Gantt Chart Table

Bright red task bars in the timescale make the critical path easy to see. But the tasks in the table area still look exactly the same. Project has formatting features to highlight the critical path in tables as well. If you want to see the critical path even in the Gantt Chart table area, do the following:

Follow Along Practice

1. To change the appearance of the text of critical tasks, in the Gantt Chart Tools | Format tab's Format section, click Text Styles.

    The Text Styles dialog box opens. The advantage to formatting text *styles* instead of individual textual elements is that Project then applies the style whenever it's appropriate. For example, if you modify the formatting for the critical-task text style, then Project applies or removes the formatting as tasks join or drop off the critical path, making it easier for you to spot these changes.

2. In the "Item to Change" drop-down list, choose Critical Tasks.

    Any changes you make to the font or colors will apply to all critical-path tasks.

3. Adjust the font, font style, and font size. In this example, change the font style to Italic.

    The Font list displays the fonts installed on your computer. The "Font style" list controls whether the text is bold or in italics. The Size list includes the standard font sizes (you can type a number in the box to specify a font size not in the list). Turn on the Underline checkbox if you want the text underlined as well.

> **Tip:** Colors other than black can make text hard to read. If you decide to change the text color, opt for dark hues. In addition, remember that colors may not reproduce well when you print in black and white. To change the font color, in the Color drop-down list, choose the one you want (for example, dark red to mimic the red task bar formatting).

4. To highlight cells that use this text style, in the Background Color drop-down list, choose the color you want (in this example, a pale pink).

   As you select options and settings, the Sample box previews the text's appearance.

> **Note:** Initially, the Text Styles dialog box's Background Pattern box is set to a solid color. If you prefer, you can change this setting to apply a hatch pattern or to stipple the background, for example, to emphasize critical tasks on a black-and-white printout.

5. Click OK.

   Cells that use the Critical Tasks text style immediately show the new formatting. The font, background color, and pattern, if you selected one, apply to all critical-task cells except for the Indicators and Task Mode columns. These changes appear every time you apply the current table.

   In this example, edit the text style again to remove the formatting. In the Text Styles dialog box, select Critical Tasks in the Item to Change box. In the "Font style" box, choose Regular. Change the Text color and Background Color to Automatic.

	ⓘ	Task Mode ▼	Task Name ▼	Duration ▼	Start ▼	Finish ▼
0		▦	◢ **Event_Ch09_start**	**234 days**	**6/1/21**	**4/26/22**
1		▦	Project start	0 days	6/1/21	6/1/21
2		▦	◢ **Planning**	86.58 days	6/1/21	9/30/21
3		📌	◢ **Initial planning**	15 days	6/1/21	6/21/21
4		▦	Identify core event team	3 days	6/1/21	6/3/21
5		▦	Define event goals and objectives	3 days	6/4/21	6/8/21
6		▦	Identify event requirements	5 days	6/9/21	6/15/21
7		▦	Determine budget	3 days	6/16/21	6/18/21
8		▦	Prepare project definition	1.33 days	6/21/21	6/22/21
9	👤	▦	Obtain approval to proceed	2 hrs	6/25/21	6/25/21
10		▦	Initial planning complete	0 days	6/25/21	6/25/21
11		▦	◢ **Plan marketing**	68 days	6/25/21	9/30/21
12		▦	◢ **Prepare marketing messages**	43 days	6/25/21	8/26/21

Figure 9-6. *Formatting the font and background of critical-path tasks makes them stand out in the table.*

Comparing Finish Dates to Deadlines

Finish dates are conspicuous in the Gantt Chart timescale because they're where task bars end. The Finish field appears in the Entry, Schedule, Summary, Usage, and Variance tables, to name a few. But what you really want to know is whether the finish dates come on or before the project's deadlines.

During planning, you can compare the finish dates of the project and key tasks with the deadlines requested by stakeholders. As you learned in Chapter 5, the Deadline field helps track important dates during project planning and execution. You can filter the task list to focus on tasks with deadlines and look for missed-deadline indicators to identify problem areas.

> **Tip:** Tasks that are scheduled to finish on time during planning may not stay that way when the work begins. Missed-deadline indicators appear as soon as estimated finish dates are later than their corresponding deadline dates, so it's a good idea to check for missed-deadline indicators regularly.

When you assign a date in a task's Deadline field, a deadline arrow appears at that date in the Gantt Chart timescale (the arrow may be solid green or outlined in black, depending on the view). The task's finish date is late if its task bar ends to the right of the arrow. However, these deadline arrows aren't especially eye-catching. Filtering the task list to show missed deadlines makes them easier to see. The missed-deadline indicator is another hint that the finish date isn't working. Here's how to compare finish dates with deadlines:

Follow Along Practice

1. To show only tasks with deadlines, in the View tab's Data section, click the down arrow next to the Filter box, and then choose More Filters. In the More Filters dialog box, double-click Tasks With Deadlines.

    Project shows tasks with deadlines but also shows the summary tasks to which they belong, as you can see in Figure 9-7.

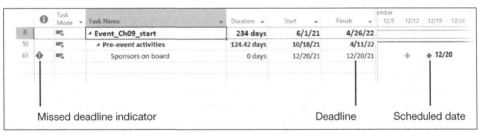

Figure 9-7. *The Tasks With Deadlines filter displays tasks with deadlines and the summary tasks to which they belong.*

2. To find tasks that miss their deadlines, look in the Entry table's Indicators column (the column's heading is an i in a blue circle) for red diamonds with exclamation points inside (see Figure 9-7).

If tasks miss their deadlines by a mile, the deadline arrows in the timescale may be a long way from the end of the task bar, so the two may not be visible in the timescale at the same time, depending on the timescale's units. Remember, you can drag the Zoom slider in the status bar to change the time periods that appear in the timescale.

By scanning the Indicators column for missed deadline indicators, you can identify the tasks to focus on. Of course, if you don't see any missed-deadline indicators, you can move on to checking whether the project's cost works.

In the example, the "Sponsors on board" task is scheduled to finish a few days past its deadline. Chapters 10 and 11 delve into methods for finishing tasks earlier.

3. After you review tasks with deadlines, in the View tab's Data section, click the down arrow next to the filter box, and then choose [No Filter] or simply press F3.

When Too Many Tasks are Critical

Project might show some tasks as critical that don't seem critical at all. To Project, any task with Total Slack equal to or less than zero is a critical task. When you apply a deadline or an inflexible date constraint to a task, Project uses that deadline or constraint to calculate slack instead of task finish dates. If the deadline or constraint date occurs earlier than the task's calculated finish date, the result is negative slack.

In Project, the Late Finish field is the latest date a task can end without affecting the project finish date, and the Finish field is a task's currently scheduled finish date. Project's Total Slack field is the length of time between a task's late finish and finish dates. For example, if the late finish date is 6/17/2021 and the finish date is 6/14/2021, then the task's total slack is 3 work days.

When you enter a date in a task's Deadline field, Project sets the late finish date to the deadline date. So, in the example above, if you set the deadline date to 6/10/2021, that's earlier than the task's finish date so you end up with negative slack.

If negative slack adds too many tasks to the critical path, the key is to fine-tune your schedule so it meets all the deadlines and date constraints you added. To find the tasks that are causing schedule problems, look for missed deadline and missed date constraint icons in the Indicators column. (See Chapter 11 to learn two methods for shortening project duration.)

> **Tip:** Negative slack makes it difficult to see which tasks are *really* critical. Because inflexible date constraints and deadlines can lead to negative slack, it's best to use them sparingly in your Project schedules. If a task finishes later than its deadline, you get a warning when your schedule doesn't meet the deadline, so you can see where the problem is and work to resolve it. Date constraints, in contrast, can overrule task dependencies, which prevents Project from calculating the project schedule for you. For that reason, you're better off applying *deadlines* to tasks instead of inflexible date constraints.

When the Critical Path is Incomplete

Every project schedule has a critical path that runs from the project's start date to its finish. But sometimes, the critical path in Project has chunks missing, like a garden hose after it's been run over by a lawnmower. You'll see a series of tasks with red task bars, then a bunch of noncritical tasks, then another set of critical tasks later in the schedule. An incomplete critical path can arise for several reasons. This section explains what can cause gaps in the critical path and what to do about them.

Some missing pieces of critical path are okay. For example, Project doesn't show completed tasks on the critical path, because they're complete and you can't do anything about them. Lag time on the dependencies between critical tasks or nonworking time on a calendar can also produce gaps in the critical path.

Gaps can also arise due to missing task dependencies, date constraints, resource or task calendars, external predecessors, and resource leveling. For example, if a date constraint prevents a critical task from starting right after its predecessor, it's still a critical task, but its Total Slack value is greater than zero.

To fill in the gaps in the critical path, you need to change how Project measures critical tasks. Out of the box, Project considers a task critical if it has Total Slack equal to or less than zero, but you can tell the program to use a different value (which is referred to as a near-critical path). First, you need to figure out what the slack value for critical tasks *should* be. Here are the steps to reuniting your project's critical path (you don't have to perform these steps in the example project):

1. With the Gantt Chart view applied, click the Gantt Chart Tools | Format tab. In the Bar Styles section, turn on the Critical Tasks checkbox.

    The task bars for critical tasks appear in red.

2. In the view's table pane, right-click the column heading area, choose Insert Column on the shortcut menu, and then choose Total Slack in the drop-down menu.

    Total Slack tells you which tasks are on the critical path.

3. Starting at the last task in the schedule (in Figure 9-8, that's Task7), work backward until you find a task that should be critical, but isn't.

    In Figure 9-8, Task2 is part of the longest path from start to finish, but its Total Slack is greater than zero, so Project doesn't consider it a critical task.

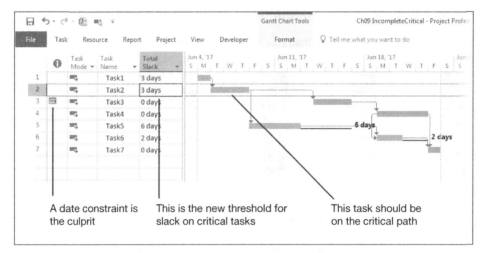

Figure 9-8. *Total Slack (3 days, in this example) is the value you use to judge whether a task is critical.*

4. To change the threshold for critical tasks, click File→Options. On the left side of the Project Options dialog box, choose Advanced and then scroll to the very bottom of the dialog box.

    The option that controls critical slack is in the "Calculation options for this project" section. Make sure that the project you want appears in the box to the right of the section's label.

> **Tip:** The "Calculate multiple critical paths" checkbox resides in the same section of the Project Options dialog box. This setting is turned off initially, which tells Project to display only one critical path—in this case, the overall critical path that affects the project's finish date. However, if you want to see more than one critical path (for example, the critical path for each subproject in a master project or for each project phase), then turn on this checkbox.

5. In the "Tasks are critical if slack is less than or equal to" box, type the value you want to use for critical slack. Then click OK to close the Project Options dialog box.

    In Figure 9-8, the task that should be critical has a Total Slack value of 3 days. So for this project, you'd type *3* in the box.

After you change the threshold value, Project adds tasks to the critical path if their Total Slack value is less than or equal to the new threshold you set.

Reviewing Project Costs

Suppose the sales VP makes it very clear that the maximum price tag for the event project is $450,000, and she hints more than once that less than $350,000 would be even better. Now that you've entered tasks, resources, and any associated costs in Project, it's time to see what the event is likely to cost.

In this section, you'll learn how to review total planned costs for all project tasks. By extension, you get a handy forecast of your overall project costs. You'll also learn how to review planned costs for tasks, resources, and assignments, so you can analyze costs at whatever level of granularity you need.

Seeing Overall Project Costs

When you first compare your project's performance against the budget, start with a quick bottom-line snapshot. A single number for your project's planned cost tells you whether you need to delve into cost containment or whether you can sit back and relax. This section shows a few ways to come up with that top-level number.

Remember the old garbage in/garbage out maxim? Your total project cost forecast is only as reliable as the information you provide. At this stage of the game, many costs and durations are merely estimates. Still, because these estimates affect project cost, it pays to be as accurate as possible. To forecast the project's total cost reliably, make sure you have the following information in your project schedule:

Recommendations

- Costs, including hourly rates and per-use costs, for all work resources assigned to tasks

- Costs for all material resources assigned to tasks

- Costs for all cost resources assigned to tasks

- Any additional fixed costs for tasks

- All resource assignments for tasks

Viewing the Total Project Cost in the Project Summary Task

The project summary task is a great place to spot the total planned project cost, because it rolls up the totals for all tasks and you can keep it visible in the first row of the project task list. To use the project summary task to see rolled-up cost values, follow these steps:

1. With a task-oriented view like the Gantt Chart visible, head to the Gantt Chart Tools | Format tab's Show/Hide section and turn on the Project Summary Task checkbox.

    A new row appears at the very top of the table in most views. A project summary node also appears in the Network Diagram view. The project summary task rolls up the column values in the current table. For example, in the Entry table (the typical table shown in the Gantt Chart view), you can see the total duration, the start date, and the finish date for the entire project.

For columns that don't roll up, like the Predecessor and Resource Names columns, the corresponding project summary cells remain blank.

2. Apply the Cost table by clicking the View tab. In the Data section, click the Tables button and then, from the drop-down list, choose Cost.

> **Tip:** If cells contain # characters, the column is too narrow to display cell values. Double-click the vertical divider to the right of the column heading to automatically resize that column so it is wide enough to display all its values or drag the vertical divider to the right.

The project summary task displays the total cost of the project in its Total Cost cell, as shown in Figure 9-9. It also shows rolled-up values for Baseline Cost, Cost Variance, Actual Cost, and Remaining Cost in other columns. In the example, the total project cost is greater than the target cost. Chapter 11 describes several methods for reducing cost.

Values in the Fixed Cost column don't roll up into the Fixed Cost field for outline summary tasks or the project summary task. There's a reason for this behavior: so you can enter a fixed cost for a project phase or the project as a whole. (The note titled "Fixed Costs or Cost Resources" tells you whether it makes sense to use Project's Fixed Cost field and, if so, where fixed costs you enter there show up in your overall project costs.)

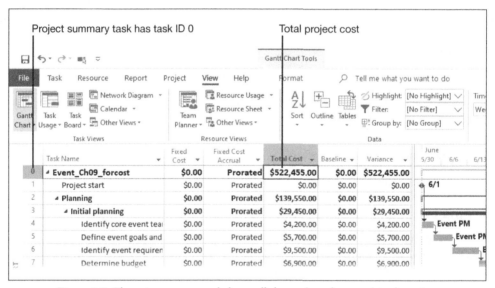

Figure 9-9. *The project summary task shows rolled-up values of every task in the project.*

Fixed Costs or Cost Resources

Cost resources have several advantages over the Fixed Cost field. You can assign multiple cost resources to a single task (Chapter 7), making different types of costs easier to see and track; and you can assign the same cost resource to multiple tasks, even if they have different cost amounts. In addition, if you use budget resources (Chapter 15) to compare budgeted and planned costs, budget resources take cost resources into account, but they *don't* take values in the Fixed Cost field into account.

On the other hand, costs for cost resources don't roll up into earned value fields, which makes sense for things like fees or training tuition. However, you might want the cost of a fixed-price contract to show up in your earned value calculations. (A fixed-price contract means someone commits to delivering a chunk of work for a set price, so you don't have to track work hours or assign resources to a task for such a contract.) That's one situation in which the Fixed Cost field might make sense. If you want to include that cost in your budget comparisons (Chapter 15) and don't use earned value, a Cost resource still makes sense: you create a cost resource for fixed-price contracts, assign the cost resource to the corresponding task, and fill in the contract cost.

However, if you don't use budget resources and you do use earned value, you can forgo cost resource assignments and simply fill in the Fixed Cost field with the contracted amount. For example, suppose the venue caterer provides a fixed price for food and service based on your attendance estimate. Here's how to record that cost in the Fixed Cost field:

1. To assign a value to the Fixed Cost field, display the Gantt Chart view or another task-oriented view. In the View tab's Data section, click the Tables button, and then choose Cost from the drop-down menu.

2. In the Fixed Cost cell for the task "Food setup (performed by venue staff)," fill in the value of the fixed-cost contract, ***30000***, in this example.

3. If necessary, select the Fixed Cost Accrual field for the task, and then select Prorated, Start, or End to indicate when the cost should be incurred during the task duration. The typical accrual for fixed costs is Prorated, which means the fixed cost is divided into equal portions across the task's duration—perfect if you make several payments over the course of the contract.

Project adds the value in the Fixed Cost field to the Total Cost field, so it represents work, material, cost-resource costs, and any fixed costs.

Entering a fixed cost for a summary task is helpful when a cost corresponds to a project *phase* rather than an individual task. You add fixed costs to a summary task the same way you add them to regular tasks. Project doesn't roll up the Fixed Cost field to summary tasks, so you can fill in a value in a summary task's Fixed Cost field.

> **Tip:** The Fixed Cost field is just a value; it doesn't describe what the cost is for. You can add a note to a task (Chapter 4) to identify the source of the fixed cost.

Viewing the Total Project Cost in Project Statistics

To get to the single number that indicates your project's total costs, use the Project Statistics dialog box as follows:

1. In the Project tab's Properties section, click Project Information.

    The Project Information dialog box appears.

2. At the bottom of the dialog box, click the Statistics button.

    The Project Statistics dialog box appears, as shown in Figure 9-10.

3. In the Cost column, review the value in the Current field, which is the forecasted cost for the project as currently planned.

    After you set a baseline (Chapter 12) the Baseline fields are also filled in. And when you start tracking status (Chapter 13), the Actual and Remaining fields have values, too.

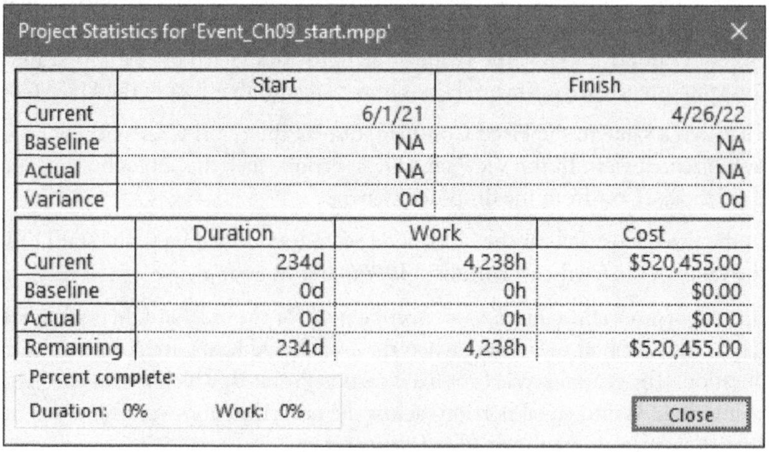

Project Statistics for 'Event_Ch09_start.mpp'				✕
	Start		Finish	
Current		6/1/21		4/26/22
Baseline		NA		NA
Actual		NA		NA
Variance		0d		0d
	Duration	Work		Cost
Current	234d	4,238h		$520,455.00
Baseline	0d	0h		$0.00
Actual	0d	0h		$0.00
Remaining	234d	4,238h		$520,455.00
Percent complete:				
Duration: 0%	Work: 0%			Close

Figure 9-10. *The Project Statistics dialog box includes high-level project information that lets you and others gauge the most important aspects of the project as a whole.*

Seeing Costs for Tasks, Resources, and Assignments

Now that you've seen the big picture of forecasted costs, you're probably champing at the bit to learn how to find task costs when all resources are assigned and where to look for the total cost of one resource's assignments. This section shows how to break costs down to individual assignments—that is, how much it costs for one particular resource working on one particular task. Use one of the following methods to drill down into costs:

- **Total cost for a task**: First apply the Cost table to a task view (View→Tables→Cost), and then, in the Total Cost column, check the value. Or insert the Cost column into any task view (right-click a column heading in the table and choose Insert Column), and then check the Cost value for the task. In both cases, the Cost value is the scheduled (planned) cost for the task, including all assigned resources (work, material, and cost) and any fixed costs. See Chapter 14 to learn the difference between baseline, scheduled, and actual values. Depending on the table you display, you may see the Total Cost or the Cost column. However, both columns show the same information. The Cost table simply uses "Total Cost" as the column heading.

    > **Tip:** If the total project cost is too high, you can sort tasks by cost to find the ones that cost the most. To do so, display the Gantt Chart view (in the View tab's Task Views section, click Gantt Chart). Then, in the Gantt Chart Tools I Format tab's Show/Hide section, turn off the Summary Tasks checkbox. Next, in the View tab's Data section, click Tables→Cost, and then click Sort→By Cost. In the example, several tasks cost more than $30,000 each. In Chapter 11, you can evaluate different ways to reduce the cost of these pricey tasks.
    >
    > After you make these changes, the most expensive task is at the top of the table. After you review high-cost tasks, resort the task list by clicking Sort→By ID. On the Format tab, turn on the Summary Tasks checkbox.

- **Total cost for a resource**: Display the Resource Sheet view (View→Resource Sheet), and then insert the Cost column somewhere in the table (right-click a column heading in the table and choose Insert Column). The Cost value for a given resource is the total cost for the resource for all its assigned tasks, based on the standard rate, overtime rate, cost/use, or other specified resource cost. This technique is perfect when you want to see how much you're spending for a specific work resource, such as a contractor, or a specific cost resource, such as travel or training. If you insert the Cost column in the Resource Usage view, you can see total cost for a resource in the resource's summary row, as shown in Figure 9-11.

    > **Tip:** If you insert the Cost column in the table in the Resource Sheet, you can sort resources by how much you pay for them over the life of the project. In the View tab's Data section, click Sort, and then choose "by Cost." To revert to the original order, click Sort→"by ID."

- **Cost for assignments**: If you want to see the cost of the assignments associated with a task or a resource, display the Task Usage view or Resource Usage view, respectively. As usual, you can either apply the Cost table or insert the Cost column in the Usage table (or whatever table you want to use), as shown in Figure 9-11.

	🛈	Resource Name	⌄	Work	⌄	Cost	⌄	Details	T	
1	👤👥	◢ Event PM		529 hrs		$92,575.00		Work	8h	
		Identify core event team		24 hrs		$4,200.00		Work	8h	
		Define event goals and objectives		12 hrs		$2,100.00		Work		
		Identify event requirements		20 hrs		$3,500.00		Work		
		Determine budget		12 hrs		$2,100.00		Work		
		Prepare project definition		8 hrs		$1,400.00		Work		
		Obtain approval to		2 hrs		$350.00		Work		

Figure 9-11. *In the Resource Usage view, the Cost field in a task-assignment row represents the cost for that individual assignment. The cost in a resource-name row represents all assignment costs rolled up to give you a total for all tasks assigned to that resource.*

In the Task Usage view, the cost in a resource-name row represents the cost for that individual assignment—what it costs to have that resource assigned to that task. The cost in a task-name row represents all assignment costs rolled up to give you a total for that task.

Using Project Cost Reports

Project includes several reports that show project costs—both graphical reports and visual reports (see Chapter 18). You can use the following reports to look at cost for tasks and assignments or to evaluate cash flow over time:

- **Cash Flow report**: The graphical Cash Flow report (on the Report tab, click Costs→Cash Flow) shows Total Cost by quarter. A line shows the cumulative cost over time, as you can see in Figure 9-12. The table below the graph shows cost values for the project's top-level tasks. You can change the report's time period or display lower-level tasks.

Figure 9-12. *You can modify the time periods or fields displayed in the graph. Chapter 19 provides the full scoop on customizing reports.*

- **Resource Cost Overview report**: The graphical Resource Cost Overview report (on the Report tab, click Costs→Resource Cost Overview) includes a graph that shows how much the project spends on each resource. If you need to cut costs, look at the resources that take a big bite of your budget to see if you can replace them with less expensive resources. This report also includes a pie chart that shows how much your project spends on work, material, and cost resources.

- **Task Cost Overview report**: The graphical Task Cost Overview report (on the Report tab, click Costs→Task Cost Overview) shows how much you spend on each top-level task. The table below the graph shows cost values for all top-level tasks.

- **Budget Cost Report visual report**: This report (on the Report tab, click Visual Reports and then choose Budget Cost Report in the "Visual Reports - Create Report" dialog box) displays costs in an Excel pivot table. The Chart1 worksheet contains a Microsoft Excel chart that initially shows cost by quarter. Display the Assignment Usage worksheet to view the data behind the chart and to use pivot table tools to modify the costs you see (Chapter 19).

- **Cash Flow Report visual report**: Project has one Excel-based cash flow visual report and two Microsoft Visio visual reports (one metric and one using U.S. dimensions). Cash Flow Report is an Excel pivot table rendition of project costs (it initially displays them by quarter). To run this report, on the Report tab, click Visual Reports and then choose Cash Flow Report in the "Visual Reports - Create Report" dialog box.

Adding Custom Cost Information

The Cost field is great for tracking what the project costs during planning and execution. What if you have specialized cost or budget information you'd like to see for your project, for example, targeted costs that management has approved for the project. In this section, you'll learn how to create your very own type of cost field.

Follow Along Practice

To create a custom cost field for these types of figures, follow these steps:

1. If necessary, display a task-oriented view, such as Gantt Chart (on the Task tab, click Gantt Chart).

2. Decide whether you want to add the custom field to the table in the current view, and then, depending on what you decide, use the appropriate method of opening the Custom Fields dialog box.

   The steps for opening the dialog box differ depending on whether you want to add the custom field to the current table:

   - To create a custom cost field *without* adding it to the table, in the Project tab's Properties section, click Custom Fields.

   - To insert a custom cost field into the table, right-click a heading in the table and choose Insert Column on the shortcut menu. In the field name drop-down list, choose a field name, such as Cost1. Then right-click the new column and, on the shortcut menu, choose Custom Fields. In this example, use the Cost1 field.

   Either way, the Custom Fields dialog box appears.

3. At the top of the dialog box, select the Task option if you want to create a custom cost field that you can use in task-oriented views, or select the Resource option if the new field is for resource-oriented views. In this example, the Task option is already selected.

   A task-cost field represents just task costs, while a resource-cost field works only with resource costs. If you opened the Custom Fields dialog box using the method described in step 1 for adding the custom field to the table, then Project automatically selects the Task or Resource option here, depending on whether a task or resource view is visible. If, on the other hand, you opened the Custom Fields dialog box via the Project tab, the program automatically selects the Task option, so you have to choose the Resource option if that's what you'd like to create.

4. In the Type box at the top of the Custom Fields dialog box, select Cost, and then in the Fields box below that, select one of the Cost fields that isn't already in use. In this example, Cost1 is already selected.

   The Field box lists all the custom cost fields—Cost1 through Cost10—along with any aliases you define for them (which you'll learn about in the next step), as shown in Figure 9-13.

5. Click the Rename button to give the custom field a new name so you can easily tell what it's for. In this example, type **Approved Cost Target**.

   You don't **have** to rename custom fields, but it's a good idea. The name you assign to a custom field (called an *alias*) appears as the column title when you insert the field into a table. The alias and built-in name both appear together in other places. For example, if you rename the Cost1 field, then the field appears in field name drop-down menus as "Approved Cost Target (Cost1)" as well as "Cost1 (Approved Cost Target)."

6. To roll up the values into summary tasks the way the built-in Cost field does, in the "Calculation for task and group summary rows" section, select the Rollup radio button, and then choose Sum in the drop-down menu.

   Chapter 21 provides more information on customizing fields.

7. In the Custom Fields dialog box, click OK.

   The cost field is ready for you to use in tables. If you haven't already added the custom cost field to the table, to insert it, simply right-click a column heading in the table, choose Insert Column, and then pick the name of your new custom field.

Figure 9-13. *Although Project doesn't force you to rename custom fields, in the Custom Fields dialog box, an alias is your only indication that a field is spoken for and it provides a hint what the field is used for.*

10

Fine-Tuning Your Schedule

Because your initial schedule is almost guaranteed to need fine-tuning, this chapter describes several Project features that can help you change the schedule. For example, Project's Task Inspector scans your file for scheduling problems and ways to improve the schedule—flagging scheduling problems with red squiggly lines and opportunities for improvement with green squiggly lines. When you make changes to the schedule, Project highlights all the fields affected by your edits (this feature is called *change highlighting*).

To get a schedule to work, you first have to make sure that all elements of your project are based in reality—like task duration, dependencies, and resource assignments. This chapter describes techniques for making a schedule more realistic, including how to handle part-time resources and to take productivity levels into account. Even when you plan with regard to your workers' schedules, you might find that some resources have crushing workloads. You can relieve the pressure by reassigning resources, contouring resource assignments, and leveling assignments to match the time resources have available. This chapter explains all your options.

> **Note:** If you've downloaded files from the book website, you can follow along by creating a copy of the file Event_Ch10_start.mpp. (Create a copy of this file because you also need the original file in the Leveling Assignments section.)

Project Tools for Change

As you start changing the schedule in search of steady workloads, shorter project duration, or lower cost, you can put a triumvirate of Project's change-oriented features through their paces:

- **Task Inspector** shows the elements that make tasks start when they do or last as long as they do, so you get some hints about how to fix them. In many cases, the task- or assignment-editing commands you need (Reschedule Task and Team Planner if resources are overallocated) are ready for you, right in the Task Inspector pane.

- **Change highlighting** shades all the cells whose values change in response to an edit you make. You can then review these highlighted cells to see whether the changes you make produce the results you had in mind.

- **Multilevel Undo** lets you undo as many changes as you want. So if you zip through several edits only to find that another strategy is in order, you can undo the changes you made and try a different tack.

This section covers each feature in detail.

See Why Tasks Occur When They Do

Whether you're trying to shorten a project schedule during planning or recover from delays during execution, a typical strategy is to make tasks start or end earlier. A schedule problem in one task often starts somewhere else in your project—in elements that control the task's start date, like predecessors, calendars, or date constraints, to name a few. Task Inspector lists all the factors that affect the task you select, so you can decide what to do. Task Inspector can also help *after* you've begun project execution. If an important task is delayed, you can look at the factors that affect the task to identify which items to change to get back on track. For instance, you might talk to the team leader for the task that's causing the delay, or the manager of a person who's unavailable.

Because Project doesn't calculate dates for manually scheduled tasks, those types of tasks are particularly prone to scheduling problems. In Project, red squiggly lines (just like the ones for typos in Microsoft Word) indicate potential schedule problems. When you right-click a cell that has a red squiggly line, you can open Task Inspector to see what the fuss is about or choose the action you want to perform from the shortcut menu.

> **Note:** Task Inspector also checks your schedule for potential improvements. For example, if it sees a task that could start earlier, it draws a green squiggly line under the Start Date value. Make decisions about schedule optimizations in the same way you use Task Inspector to correct problems.

To open the Task Inspector pane, click the Task tab. In the Tasks section, click Inspect. The Task Inspector pane appears on the left side of the view and shows the factors that affect the dates for whichever task you select, as shown in Figure 10-1. (To close the Task Inspector, click the x at the pane's top right.)

If resources are overallocated or task links are a problem, the Task Inspector pane includes repair options. For example, in Figure 10-1, Task Inspector includes Reschedule Task and Team Planner buttons in case you want to remove the overallocation on an overallocated resource. The factors that appear in the Task Inspector pane may change as you modify the schedule. For example, if you find another resource to replace the one that's overallocated, the overallocation issue disappears. However, you could then discover that the new resource's calendar or a predecessor task is now the controlling factor.

> **Note:** Team Planner is available in Project Professional. If you use Project Standard, you won't see the Team Planner button.

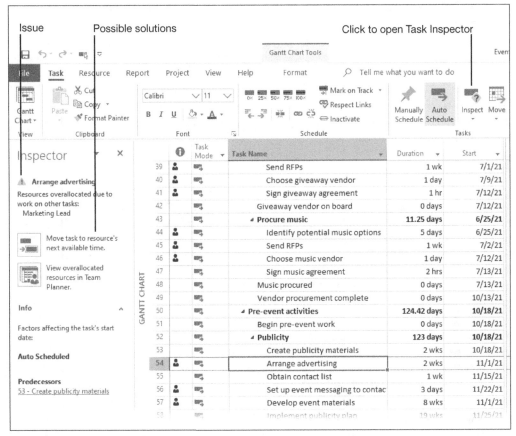

Figure 10-1. *The factors that appear in the Task Inspector pane may change as you modify the schedule.*

If you see a red or green squiggly line below a task's value, right-click that cell to display a shortcut menu, as shown in Figure 10-2. Here are some ways you can fix tasks using Task Inspector and the commands on the shortcut menu:

- **Switch to Auto Scheduled**: The solution to a problem may be to switch a task from Manually Scheduled to Auto Scheduled (see Chapter 3), so Project can take over calculating the task's dates.

- **Respect Links**: Because manually scheduled tasks start and finish when you specify, those dates may conflict with the task dependencies you've defined. Even with auto-scheduled tasks, date constraints you set can conflict with task dependencies. If you want Project to use task dependencies to determine when to schedule tasks, choose Respect Links on the shortcut menu.

- **Ignore Problems for This Task**: Sometimes a problem that Project finds isn't *really* a problem. Say you schedule a task to occur over a weekend, and the person you've assigned has agreed to that schedule. Sure, you can change the resource's calendar to show that they're available that weekend, but it's easier to simply ignore the problem. In this case, choose "Ignore Problems for This Task" from the shortcut menu, and Project turns off the red squiggly line.

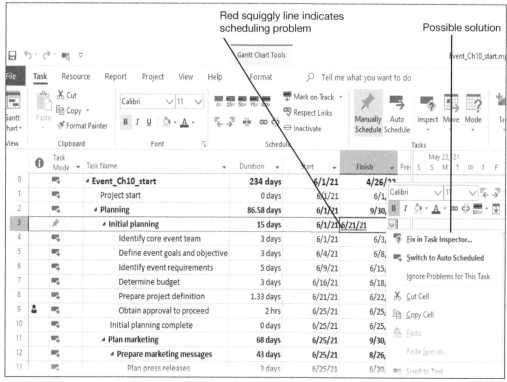

Figure 10-2. *Other commands may appear on the shortcut menu to help resolve other problems, such as Assign Resources to shorten the task or remove overallocations.*

- **Fix in Task Inspector**: If you aren't sure how to resolve a problem, choose "Fix in Task Inspector" to open the Task Inspector pane shown in Figure 10-1. The first section of the pane displays the name of the selected task and the problems Task Inspector identified, such as overallocations, resource calendar issues, predecessor conflicts, and so on. The second section provides commands you can use to correct the problem, like Respect Links and Auto Schedule for task scheduling problems, or Increase Duration and Assign Resources for resource overallocations.

- **Show ignored problems**: After you've fixed a slew of problems, you may decide to take another look at the problems you ignored. To restore problem indicators to the view, in the Task tab's Tasks section, click the down arrow below the Inspect icon and then, on the drop-down menu, choose Show Ignored Problems. The red squiggly lines reappear for problems you had previously ignored.

> **Tip:** Task Inspector is a good start, but it isn't the be-all and end-all for optimizing schedules. For example, Task Inspector shows task predecessors, but *you* have to dig deeper to discover that a predecessor's duration is caused by a resource who's scheduled for medical leave and that the resolution may be to reassign the predecessor task to someone else. Other sections in this chapter show you how to look at tasks and assignments from every angle.

Seeing What Changes Do

There's no guarantee your changes will correct the problems you're trying to fix. For example, you could assign more resources to shorten a critical path task, only to find out that another task prevents the finish date from changing as much as you need. Fortunately, Project's *change highlighting* feature shades table cells that have changed due to your last task edit, so you can easily see whether the results are what you want.

Suppose you have to remove a resource from a task, which lengthens its duration. Because the task finishes later, its successor tasks start and finish later, too. So change highlighting lights up the successor task's Start and Finish cells with background color, as Figure 10-3 demonstrates with the "Define presentation content" task. (In this example, the task units decreased from 300% to 200%.)

> **Tip:** Project considers all changes you make in a Task Form before you click OK as a single edit. So to get the most out of change highlighting, make all your changes in the Task Form at the same time. Then when you click OK, change highlighting shows the results.

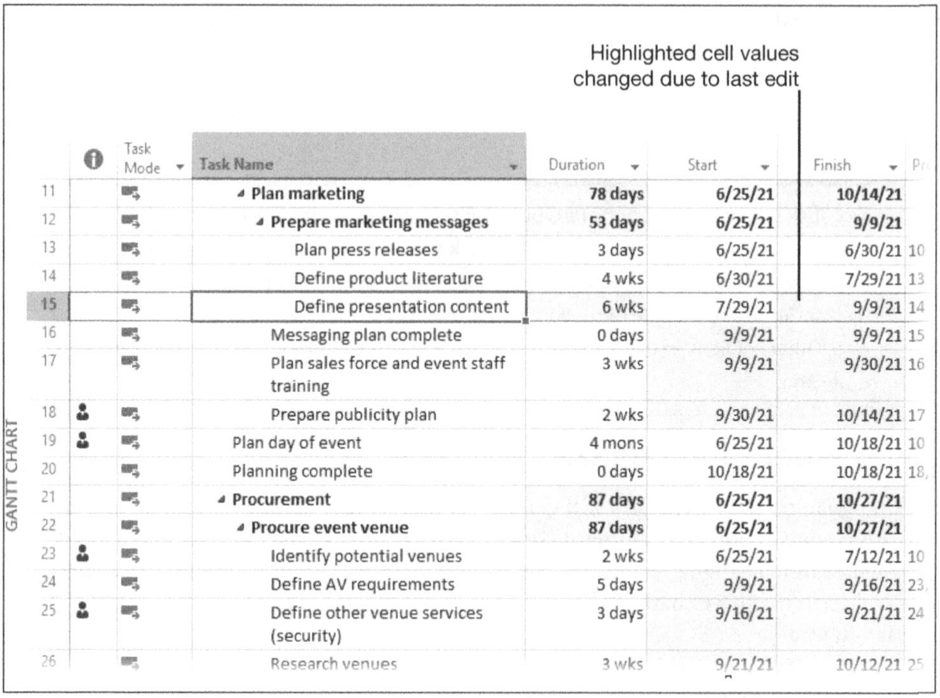

Figure 10-3. *Change highlighting shades cells affected by your last task edit.*

Happily, modifying your view doesn't wash away change highlighting. You can display a new table, filter the schedule, or group tasks, and *still* see highlighted cells from the last edit. For example, if the Summary table is visible, you can review the changes in dates, duration, and cost. Switching to the Cost table would highlight cost cells affected by the last edit.

When you make another edit, change highlighting shows the effect of this new change. And saving the Project file *erases* any current change highlighting.

> **Tip:** It's unlikely, but if you want to turn change highlighting off for some reason, you have to add the Change Highlighting command to a custom group on the ribbon. See Chapter 22 to learn how to customize the ribbon. The Change Highlighting command is in the All Commands group on the "Customize the Ribbon" screen.

Undoing Changes

Some adverse results are obvious, like a delay in a project finish date after you change the duration of a task. In many cases, though, as in a game of chess, you can't tell whether a strategy will pay off until you're a few moves in. Multilevel Undo lets you try short what-if games in your current Project file. It lets you backtrack through any number of actions if they don't pan out. (See Chapter 11 to learn how to work on more involved what-if scenarios.) Multilevel Undo can unravel everything a macro does, or reverse changes that other applications make to your Project file. Keep in mind, Project clears the Multilevel Undo list when you save your Project file.

> **Note:** You can specify how many actions Multilevel Undo remembers: Choose File→Options. In the Project Options dialog box, choose Advanced. Under General, change the "Undo levels" setting to the number of actions you want to be able to track (up to 99) and then click OK. Choosing higher numbers for Multilevel Undo can increase the size of your Project file.

Multilevel Undo keeps track of your actions and displays them on a cumulative menu so you can select the ones you want to undo (the most recent at the top of the list to the earliest at the bottom). Here's how to put Multilevel Undo to work:

1. On the Quick Access toolbar, click the tiny down arrow to the right of the Undo button (which looks like a curved arrow pointing to the left).

   A drop-down menu appears, listing your previous actions with the most recent at the top and the earliest at the bottom. (Project clears this list when you save your Project file or close and reopen it.)

2. Put your cursor over the earliest action you want to undo, such as, Entry 'Task Details Form'.

   Project highlights every action from the most recent to the one where the pointer is. The last entry in the drop-down menu changes to "Undo x Actions," where x is the number of actions you've selected, as in Figure 10-4.

   If you're a prolific editor, you may see a few recent actions and a scroll bar on the drop-down menu. Drag the slider until you can see the earliest command you want to undo.

> **Tip:** The entries in the Undo list aren't always as informative as you'd like. For example, if you make changes in the Task Form, the Undo menu simply says "Entry 'Task Form.'" If you can't remember which Task Form edit you want to undo, undo one entry at a time until the erroneous edit is gone.

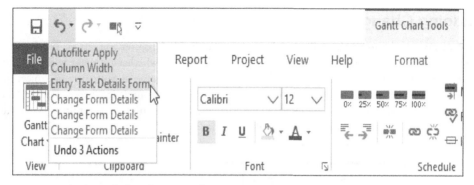

Figure 10-4. *The Undo drop-down menu lists your previous actions with the most recent at the top and the earliest at the bottom.*

3. Click the action your cursor is over to undo the recent commands up to and including the action you clicked.

Building Reality into Assignments

A first-draft schedule almost always represents the way projects would go in an ideal world. But you live in the real world, and just as the jeans you buy never look like they do on the catalog model, your real-world project will have a few bumps and wrinkles. Understanding resource units and calendars (Chapter 6) is only half the battle. You also have to figure out how to combine them to handle real-world resourcing situations. This section explains how to make Project's resource features model reality.

Replacing Generic Resources with Real Ones

Sometimes you know the skill set you need, but you don't know exactly who you'll get. In these situations, you may have assigned a resource that represents the role that resource plays, such as marketing content developer, event project manager, or sales lead. Once the powers that be have assigned a real person to your project, you can replace the generic resource with one that represents the flesh-and-blood team member. The Assign Resources dialog box makes it easy:

Follow Along Practice

1. If you haven't added your team members' names to the Resource Sheet yet, on the Task tab, click the bottom-half of the Gantt Chart button, and then choose Resource Sheet.

2. In the first blank Resource Name cell, type the name of the person you will replace the generic event project manager with, in this example "Jaye Smith," and then press Tab.

   Fill in the other resource fields, as needed. In this example, change the initials to JS and the Standard Rate to $150.

3. Repeat step 2 for each team member who has been committed to your project. For the example project, you don't have to add any other team members.

4. Switch to the Gantt Chart by clicking the top half of the Task tab's Gantt Chart button.

5. If necessary, apply the Entry table by heading to the View tab's Data section and clicking Tables→Entry.

   The Entry table includes the Resource Names field.

6. Turn off summary tasks by clicking the Gantt Chart Tools | Format tab and, in the Show/Hide section, turning off the Summary Tasks and Project Summary Task checkbox.

   Now only subtasks appear in the task list.

   > **Note:** You must turn off summary tasks in order for the following steps to work.

7. Filter the task list to show only tasks assigned to the generic resource you want to replace.

   To do that, click the down arrow to the right of the Resource Names column heading, and then turn off the Select All checkbox. Turn on the checkbox for the generic resource, in this example, Event PM, and then click OK.

8. Select all the tasks that appear in the table by clicking the Select All cell at the table's top left (above the task ID numbers and to the left of the column headings).

   The backgrounds of the selected tasks change to gray.

   > **Tip:** Another way to select all the tasks is to click the task ID for the first task in the table and then Shift+click the task ID for the last task.

9. In the Resource tab's Assignments section, click Assign Resources.

   The Assign Resources dialog box opens.

10. In the dialog box, select the generic resource you want to replace (Event PM, in this example), and then click Replace.

    The Replace Resource dialog box opens, as shown in Figure 10-5.

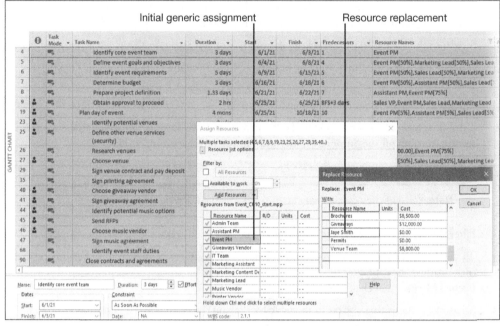

Figure 10-5. *You can select only one resource in the Replace Resource dialog box.*

11. In the Resource Name column, select the named resource you want to use (in this example, Jaye Smith), and then click OK.

Project replaces the generic resource with the named resource in every selected task.

Optionally, you can type the units for the assignment in the Units cell. If you do, the program uses that Units value for every assignment. If you leave the Units cell blank (as in this example), the program keeps the Units from the generic resource's assignment.

12. Repeat steps 7 through 11 for each generic resource in your project. In this example, there are no other resources to replace.

> **Tip:** To see whether you've reassigned all your generic resources, display the Resource Usage view (in the View tab's Resource Views section, click Resource Usage). The generic resources in the project shouldn't have any tasks listed below their names. To return to the Gantt Chart, click the View tab's Gantt Chart button.

13. When you're done replacing resources, close the Assign Resources dialog box, press F3 to remove the resource filter, and turn summary tasks back on.

> **Note:** Project Server includes the "Build Team from Enterprise" feature, which lets you replace a resource in a project with one from the Enterprise Resource list.

Assigning Part-Time Workers

Part-time workers don't work full weeks, so they take longer to finish tasks. For example, someone working half-days takes twice as long, because you get only 4 person-hours a day instead of 8. The best way to model a part-time schedule in Project is to edit the resource's calendar (or create a shift calendar for all the resources that work the same part-time schedule and apply it to the resources). Then, when you assign part-time resources to tasks, Project automatically doles out time based on the dates and times the people are available. This section provides an overview of the steps for setting up and assigning resources using a part-time calendar.

Using a part-time calendar works equally well whether part-timers work 5 short days a week, full time a few days a week, or a combination of full-time and part-time days. If you share the person with another project, the best approach is to use a resource pool (Chapter 24) to assign the person to tasks in multiple projects.

Don't Model Part-Time Work with Maximum Units

Changing resources' Maximum Units values might *seem* like a simple way to handle part-time work, but it has a couple of limitations:

- It applies only to people who work the same amount of time each standard workday—for example, 4 hours a day Monday through Friday.

- It doesn't reflect a resource's true allocation to an assignment. Suppose you set a part-time worker's Maximum Units to 50% and assign him to a meeting. Project assumes that resources are available every workday up to the percentage in their Maximum Units cells, so the program automatically assigns the person to the meeting at 50% units. If the meeting is one full day, Project assigns him to the meeting for only 4 hours, even though he will be at the meeting for 8 hours.

Because of these limitations, you're better off using the techniques described in this section instead.

Here's how you handle part-time workers in Project when several resources work the same schedule:

Follow Along Practice

1. Create a calendar for that part-time shift.

   a) In the Project tab's Properties section, click Change Working Time, and then, at the Change Working Time dialog box's top right, click Create New Calendar.

   b) In the Create New Base Calendar dialog box, type a name in the Name box that reflects the part-time work week, in this example, Halftime.

---

c)   Select the option to copy the Standard calendar you've applied to your project, and then click OK.

2.   Edit the work week to define the working and non-working times for a half-time schedule.

a)   In the lower half of the Change Working Time dialog box, click the Work Weeks tab.

b)   In this example, select the "[Default]" workweek (in row 1), and then click the Details button.

c)   In the "Details for <work week>" dialog box, specify the working days and working hours, and the nonworking days. In this example, drag over Monday through Friday.

d)   Make sure the "Set day(s) to these specific working times" option is selected.

e)   To remove the morning hours, click the first row (9:00 AM to 12:00 PM) in the table, and then press the Delete key. The second row (1:00 PM to 6:00 PM) moves up to the first row.

f)   To specify 4 work hours in the afternoon, in the To cell, change 6:00 PM to 5:00 PM.

g)   Click away from the To cell, and then click OK.

> **Note:** In this example, keep the Summer 2017 work week in the Halftime calendar.

3.   Click OK to close the Change Working Time dialog box.

4.   Assign the new calendar to each person who works that shift.

In this example, display the Resource Sheet. Click the resource's Base Calendar cell (Sales VP, in this example), click the down arrow that appears, and then choose the shift calendar (Halftime). Click away from the Base Calendar cell.

5.   Switch back to the Gantt Chart view by clicking the Task tab's Gantt Chart button.

6.   Assign the part-time worker as you would any resource. (In this example, the sales VP is already assigned to tasks.)

When you assign a resource to a task, Project automatically enters the resource's Maximum Units value in the assignment's Units field, whether the percentage is 20%, 50%, or 100%. For part-time workers, the assignment's Units should be 100% to include all the work hours defined in the part-time calendar. To assign the resource at a lower percentage, type the percentage in the assignment's Units field.

Project calculates the duration of a task based on the resource units assigned to the task and the resource's calendar. If the resource calendar includes a vacation the first week of June, for example, Project assigns the resource at the assignment units but skips the week that the resource is absent.

> **Note:** If people work part-time at *different* times, such as during the summer, you can set a date range for a work week, as described in Chapter 3.

Modeling Productivity in Project

People are usually optimistic about how much they can get done in a given amount of time. (Have you ever had a "5-minute" trip to the grocery store turn into 2 hours?) In the world of project management, a 40-hour work week does **not** necessarily mean people spend 40 hours on their project assignments. Filling out paperwork, attending meetings, and keeping up with gossip can eat into productive time by as much as 25 percent a day. Widely distributed teams—whether they're scattered around the world or throughout a skyscraper—often require more time because of time spent communicating, waiting for someone else to complete a task, or even riding elevators.

If you assign resources at 100 percent, one of two outcomes is likely:

- **People have to work longer days to stay on schedule**: Some folks work longer to finish their tasks according to the schedule, but this won't last. Eventually, low morale and exhaustion take their toll, and work starts to slip.

- **The project falls behind**: Expecting 100 percent productivity usually leads to late deliveries. People work the normal workday, but their project work gets only a portion of that day, and durations increase beyond what you estimated. For example, a task that requires 24 person-hours takes 3 days when resources work at 100 percent. Reduce the units to 75 percent, and the duration increases to 4 days.

You can tackle the productivity problem in a few ways in Project. If you use Microsoft Project Server, you can use administrative projects to schedule the time people work on non-project work. Otherwise, the following approaches provide a more realistic estimate of project duration. Here are the two ways to make a Project schedule reflect your project team's productivity and the pros and cons of each:

- **Assign resources at lower units**: To assign resources at their real percentage of productive time, in the Task Form view's Units field, fill in the lower percentage. This approach has a small disadvantage: because Project automatically fills in the assignment Units field with the resource's Maximum Units, you have to edit that value.

  a) In this example, select task 13, "Plan press releases."

  b) In the Task Details Form (on the View tab, turn on the Details checkbox, and then choose Task Details Form on the drop-down menu), change the Marketing Lead's units to 50% and the Marketing Content Developer's units to 75%, as shown in Figure 10-6.

  c) Click OK.

  If you change the Units field for part-time workers to 75%, Project assigns them at 75% of their available hours, such as 3 hours a day if they normally work 4 hours a day.) In this example, the duration changes from 3 days to 4.5 days.

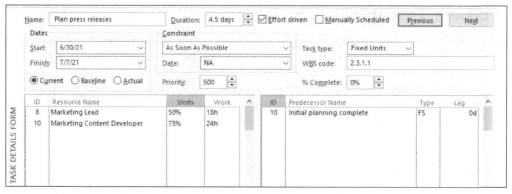

Figure 10-6. *The units represent a percentage of a resource's available hours.*

- **Shorten the standard Project workday**: If non-project work consumes 25 percent of each day, an 8-hour day contains only 6 productive hours, and a work week is 30 productive hours. You might think about resetting Project's standard 8-hour workday to fewer hours to reflect true productive hours. However, this approach has disadvantages that make it undesirable.

  Shortening the workday takes two steps. First, you change the "Hours per day" and "Hours per week" calendar options (Chapter 3), so Project translates the person-hours into the correct duration in days and weeks. For example, you may change "Hours per day" to 6 and "Hours per week" to 30. You also redefine the standard work week in the project calendar. For example, to snip 2 hours off each day, set each day's end time 2 hours earlier.

  Here are the two disadvantages to shortening the Project workday. First, the productivity problem is hidden within Project's calculations. Resources look like they're assigned 100%, but Project assigns them only 6 hours of work a day. Second, the work times that you set in Project don't accurately reflect the start and end time of each workday. With a shorter workday in place, the only way you can schedule a task at the end of the real workday is by applying a task calendar (Chapter 5).

  > **Note:** Because of these disadvantages, do not shorten the standard workday to reflect productivity.

Adjusting Tasks for Resource Capability

Occasionally, you get someone who polishes off work like a dog does an unguarded plate of hamburgers. Other times, you may use trainees who take longer and need more guidance. Most organizations don't reward fast workers by letting them go home early, and you can't make newbies work around the clock to keep up.

The only way to account for people's capability is by changing the person-hours you assign to people (the Work field for an assignment). When you change the task work, Project recalculates the assignment duration (and vice versa).

If you change work or duration due to people's above- or below-average capabilities, then keep track of your original estimate in case you switch resources again. And consider adding a note to the task to explain the adjustments you made. In a task-oriented view, like the Gantt Chart view, right-click the task and then, from the shortcut menu, choose Notes. When the Task Information dialog box opens, the Notes tab is visible. Type your comments, and then click OK.

> **Note:** In the example project, do not change any assigned work hours.

Balancing Workloads

Before you can call a schedule done, you have to balance workloads so your assigned resources (people and equipment) are busy, but not burning out. The first step is recognizing the problem, and Project makes it easy to find assignment peaks and valleys.

Then you have to correct the workload imbalances you find. Project offers several ways to even out workloads. Asking resources if a heavier schedule is OK with them might be an easy solution when overallocations are small and short-lived. The more practical options are adding more resources and replacing a resource with someone who has more time. Of course, in order to do that, you need to have other resources available with the right skills.

When longer hours or more resources aren't an option, delaying assignments may do the trick. For example, when a resource has two assignments that overlap by a day, delaying one of those assignments by 1 day solves the problem.

This section describes how to spot resource-allocation issues and offers several ways to fix them.

> **Note:** When you overload your resources, the project finish date may look good, but it's bogus, because your resources are *overallocated*. In other words, giving people 20 hours' worth of work a day doesn't mean they're going to *do* it. On the other hand, resources who don't have *enough* work cause a whole other set of problems. Besides distracting the people who are working all out, these resources could cost money without delivering results—like the networking consultant who sits idle while your IT staff puts out the fire in the server room. The ideal workload is to assign your resources as close as possible to the amount of time they have to give.

Finding Resource Over- and Under-Allocations

Assigning resources to tasks is like using a credit card. While you're assigning people's time, you don't see the deficit you're running up. The Gantt Chart and other task-oriented views that you use when assigning resources show the assignments for the current task but they aren't as helpful when you want to see all the other tasks a resource may work on. Project's resource- and assignment-oriented views help you see when you've assigned someone too much time overall. This section identifies the talents of different views and tools for finding overallocations.

Finding Overallocated Resources with the Resource Sheet View

For a sneak peek at the workload balancing ahead, take a look at the Resource Sheet view (if necessary, click the Gantt Chart in the primary pane; then, in the View tab's Resource Views section, click Resource Sheet). If a resource is overallocated at least once during the project, all the text in the resource's row is bold and red. Because of this, you can quickly spot the resources whose assignments you need to revise. For example, if you're following along in the example project, the Assistant PM, Marketing Lead, Marketing Assistant, Marketing Content Developer, and Jaye Smith (the event project manager) are overallocated. However, this view *doesn't* tell you exactly *when* the resource is overallocated, how much, or on which assignments.

> **Tip:** The Overallocated Resources filter is another helpful tool for finding resources with too much work, regardless of which resource view you use. This filter displays only resources that are overallocated at some point during a project. In the View tab's Data section, click the Filter down arrow, and then choose Overallocated Resources. You can apply this filter to any resource view: the Resource Sheet, the Resource Usage view, the Resource Graph, and so on. To display all resources again, in the Filter drop-down list, choose [No Filter].

Viewing Assignment Details with the Resource Usage View

The best way to see the assignments that contribute to resource workloads in detail is with the Resource Usage view (in the View tab's Resource Views section, click Resource Usage). This view groups all the assignments for each resource in the project, so you can see the hours assigned during any time period. If a resource is overallocated, you can examine the hours for each assignment to come up with ways to smooth out the workload.

The left pane of the Resource Usage view lists each resource in your project and displays the tasks to which the resource is assigned underneath the resource's name. The timescale on the right side of the view shows the assigned hours during each time period, as shown in Figure 10-7.

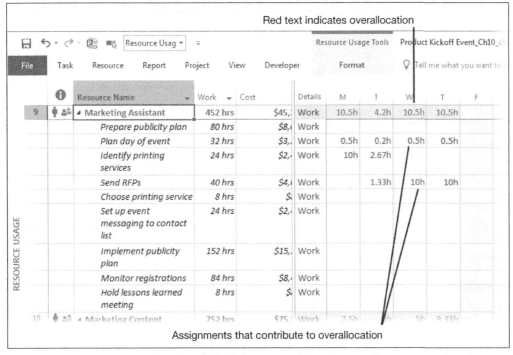

Figure 10-7. *Look for overallocated time periods by scanning the total hours in the resource row for red text.*

Like other views, the Resource Usage view highlights overallocated resources with bold, red text. In the time-phased grid on the right side of the view, hours that exceed the resource's maximum available time appear in red, too. For example, if a single task exceeds the resource's available time in one period, the hours in the cell are written in red. However, if several tasks contribute to the overallocation, the individual task hours may be black, but the total hours in the resource's summary row are red.

To see overallocations more easily, modify the Resource Usage view in the following ways:

- **Show only overallocated resources**: To the right of the Resource Name column heading, click the down arrow and then, in the shortcut menu that appears, choose Filters→Overallocated Resources. Only resources with overallocations appear in the left pane. Alternatively, in the View tab's Data section, click the Filter down arrow, and then choose Overallocated Resources.

- **Display other fields**: Other fields can help you figure out how to correct overallocations. On the right side of the Resource Usage view, right-click anywhere in the Details column. On the shortcut menu, choose the fields you want to see; you can select as many as you want. For example, the Overallocation field tells you exactly how many hours are beyond the resource's availability. And the Remaining Availability field helps you find resources who have enough time to take over the extra hours. (The Assign Resources dialog box also lets you look for resources with sufficient time and the right skills, as described in Chapter 7.)

Finding Overallocations with the Resource Graph View

The Resource Graph view plots allocation over time, resource by resource, which is helpful when you want to figure out how to resolve each resource's overallocations. To open the Resource Graph view, click the View tab, and then, in the Resource Views section, choose Other Views→Resource Graph. To display the fields you want to see, right-click within the graph, and then choose the field you want to display, in this example, Percent Allocation.

> **Tip:** You can also display the Resource Graph view in the Details pane. In the View tab's Split View section, turn on the Details checkbox, choose More Views, and then, in the More Views dialog box, double-click Resource Graph. When you do that, the Resource graph displays allocation for the resources assigned to the task(s) selected in the primary pane.

A vertical bar graphically indicates the selected resource's allocation in one time period. When the vertical bar is higher than the resource's availability, Project emphasizes the overallocation by coloring the overallocated portions bright red.

In the Resource Graph view (Figure 10-8), you don't see the assignments for the allocated time. But you can find the problem time periods and then look at the resource's assignments for those time periods in the Resource Usage or Resource Allocation view to correct the issue.

Here's how to use the Resource Graph view to find overallocations:

- **Choose a resource**: The Resource Graph view shows the allocations for just one resource at a time. The current resource appears in the view's left pane with a legend for the information that's displayed in the timescale. If you display the Resource Graph as the primary view (not in the Details pane), press Page Down to display the next resource, or Page Up to view the previous resource. You can also scroll through your various resources using the horizontal scroll bar below the legend.

- **Change the timescale**: Sometimes, resources are overallocated for 1 or 2 days but have enough time for assignments over the course of a week or so. Before you start rearranging short overallocations, increase the Resource Graph view's time period to see whether the overallocations work themselves out. To lengthen the time period when the Resource Graph view is displayed in the primary pane, in the status bar, drag the Zoom slider to the left to switch from days to weeks to months, and so on. To shorten the time period, drag the slider to the right. To specify the units for the timescale, in the View tab's Zoom section, click the Timescale down arrow, and then choose the period you want.

- **Graph other values**: Although percentage allocation values make overallocations stand out, the Resource Graph can show other values, such as Work (the hours of assigned work), Overallocation (only the hours beyond the resource's maximum units), Remaining Availability, and so on. For example, after you use the Resource Graph view to find an overallocation, you can switch it to display Remaining Availability to locate someone to take over the extra hours. To do so, right-click the Resource Graph view's timescale, and then, from the shortcut menu, choose the field you want to display in the graph.

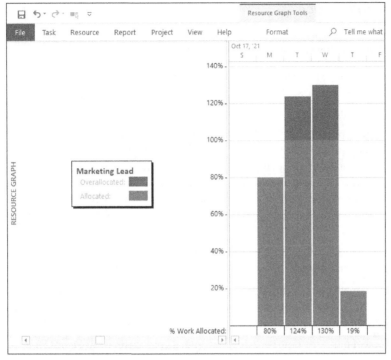

Figure 10-8. *The Resource Graph makes overallocations easy to see.*

Viewing Assignments in the Resource Allocation View

The Resource Allocation view displays the Resource Usage view in the top pane so you can see the assignments that overallocate a resource, and the Leveling Gantt view in the Details pane so you can manually add a leveling delay to resolve overallocations. To use this view, in the View tab's Resource Views section, click Other Views→More Views. In the More Views dialog box, double-click Resource Allocation.

The table in the Leveling Gantt view includes the Leveling Delay field, which you can use to delay tasks to remove overallocations. When you make these kinds of edits in the Leveling Gantt view, the leveling delay changes the start date for a task, not just the overallocated resource's assignment. See the section "Delaying Assignments" later in this chapter for instructions on delaying tasks and individual assignments.

Modifying the Schedule to Eliminate Overallocations

Sometimes, the way you build your schedule can lead to resource overallocations. You might not notice these issues until you assign resources to tasks. This section uses the example project to highlight some techniques for finding these schedule issues and modifying tasks and task dependencies to eliminate resource overallocations.

Follow Along Practice

The steps you take to track down problem tasks and resolve those issues will vary. The following steps represent an example of what you might do:

1. Display the Gantt Chart view to see the task list.

2. In the View tab's split View section, turn on the Details checkbox, and choose Task Form in the drop-down menu.

    In the example project, task 19 "Plan day of event" has a red overallocation indicator in its Indicators cell. This task starts on 6/30/2021, a few weeks after the project start date. The "Plan day of event" task is set up in a way that leads to resource issues. First, several resources are allocated to work on it 5 percent of their time, which means that those resources will be overallocated if they are assigned to work full time on other tasks scheduled at the same time. In addition, the task's duration is 4 months, so the task could overallocate resources during a substantial portion of the project.

3. To see which tasks contribute to overallocations, display the Resource Usage view (on the View tab, click Resource Usage).

4. Click the triangle twice to the left of an overallocated resource name (they're shown in red text) to display the resource's assignments. In this example, click the triangle to expand Jaye Smith's assignments.

    Overallocated hours for time periods appear in red text, as shown in Figure 10-9.

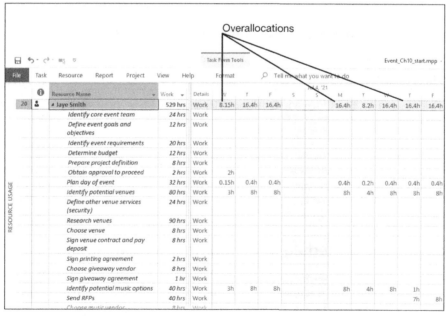

Figure 10-9. *Overallocated time periods display values in red text.*

5. Use the horizontal scrollbar to scroll through dates to find overallocations.

   In this example, Jaye Smith is overallocated beginning on June 30, 2021 due to "Plan day of event," "Identify potential venues," and "Identify potential music options" being scheduled at the same time.

   > **Note:** If you examine other resources and other date ranges, you'll find that "Plan day of event" contributes to numerous overallocations.

6. To determine how to reschedule tasks, return to the Gantt Chart view. Click the "Plan day of event" task to display its information in the Details pane.

7. Right-click the Task Form and choose Predecessors & Successors on the shortcut menu, so you can see how the task is linked to other tasks.

   In this example, the "Initial planning complete" milestone, which is the milestone that indicates that the project is approved, is a predecessor to the "Plan day of event" task. Suppose you decide that other tasks must be completed before work on the "Plan day of event" task can begin. For example, you might need sponsors lined up before you plan the details of event day.

8. Modify the task and its links (which will help you shorten this task).

   a) In this example, in the Task Form's Predecessors table, click in the first row, and then press Delete to remove the "Initial Planning complete" milestone. In the Successors table, click the "Planning complete" row, and then press Delete. Click OK to save the changes.

   b) Still in the Task Form, click the first blank Predecessor Name cell, and then choose "Sponsors on board" in the drop-down menu. Click OK to save the change.

   c) Right-click the Task Form and choose "Resources and Predecessors".

   d) Next, because the event day planning is more concentrated, in the Task Form, change each resource's assignment units to 10%. Click OK. Project shortens the task duration from 4 months to 2 months, as shown in Figure 10-10.

Now, when you scroll down the task list, red overallocation indicators no longer appear in the Indicators column for the "Plan day of event" task and several other tasks in the list.

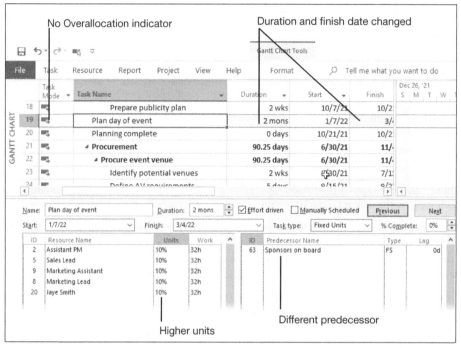

Figure 10-10. *When the Indicators cell for a task is empty, the assigned resources are not overallocated.*

Replacing Resources

Suppose a resource is swamped with work on two simultaneous tasks on the critical path. You can't delay either one without affecting the project finish date. In this situation, the Assign Resources dialog box (on the Resource tab, click Assign Resources) can help you find someone with similar skills who has more time available. If money is a bigger problem than time, you can replace the person with someone who costs less (assuming that the replacement can get the work done in the same amount of time). And if you have resources who can pinch hit, you can reassign only the overallocated hours or an entire assignment—Project doesn't care which method you choose. The Assign Resources dialog box can handle all three scenarios.

> **Note:** If you use a custom field like an outline code to identify resources' skills, the Assign Resources dialog box can help you find resources with similar skills (Chapter 7). Also, the Assign Resources dialog box's "Available to work" checkbox can help you find resources with enough time to complete the work. (Although the Team Planner view lets you drag an assignment from one resource to another, it *doesn't* help you find resources with similar skills or identify cost implications. (And if you also drag the assignment to another date, Project creates a date constraint, which reduces Project's ability to calculate the schedule for you.)

Follow Along Practice

Here's how you reassign a portion of work with the Assign Resources dialog box:

1. In the Resource tab's Assignments section, click Assign Resources.

    The Assign Resources dialog box opens.

2. In the Gantt Chart view (or any other task-oriented view), select the task(s) you want to modify, in this example, select task 69, "Build event staffing plan."

    The resource(s) already assigned to the task (Assistant PM, in this example) appear at the top of the dialog box's Resources table, preceded by a checkmark.

3. To switch a portion of the work to another resource, in the Assign Resources dialog box, click the assigned resource's Units cell, and then type the new percentage, in this example, type **50%**.

4. Click the Units cell for the resource you want to add to the task (in this case, Jaye Smith), and then type the percentage you're assigning (50, in this example).

5. Click Assign. If you see a scheduling tip icon to the left of the task name, click the down arrow and choose the "Reduce duration but keep the same amount of work" option.

    Project updates the existing assignment. The newly assigned resource moves up to the top of the list with the other assigned resource(s) and now has a checkmark to the left of its name.

Follow Along Practice

If you want to replace one resource with another, follow these steps:

1. With the Assign Resources dialog box open, in the task-oriented view's table, select the task you want to modify, in this case, task 56 "Set up event messaging to contact list," which has the Marketing Assistant assigned.

    The assigned resource(s) for the selected task appear at the top of the dialog box's Resources table, with checkmarks next to them.

2. In the Resources table, select the assigned resource you want to replace, in this example, Marketing Assistant. (You'll select the replacement resource in a sec.)

    In this example, click the resource's *name* (Marketing Assistant), not the check marked cell. You can replace only one resource at a time.

3. Click Replace.

    The Replace Resource dialog box appears (Figure 10-11). The Replace label at the top of the dialog box shows the resource you want to replace, and the table lists all the resources in your project. You can assign different units for a replacement resource than you used for the original resource if, for instance, the replacement is more or less productive as the person you're replacing.

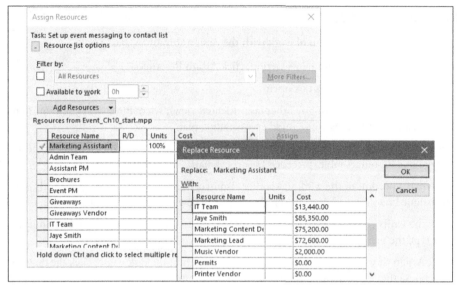

Figure 10-11. *Select the replacement resource and, if necessary, fill in the units you want to use.*

4.   Select the replacement resource, and then click OK. In this example, select IT Team.

Project swaps the replacement in for the original resource and assigns the units for the original resource (or the units you typed) to the replacement.

5.   When you're done with the Assign Resources dialog box, click the Close button or the X at the dialog box's top right.

Delaying Tasks and Assignments

When tasks overlap and overallocate their assigned resources, one solution is to delay some of the tasks so the people assigned can work on the tasks one after the other. If you have only a few overallocations to correct, you can manually add delays to tasks and assignments with the help of a few Project views.

> **Note:** Project has a leveling feature, which can eliminate overallocations for you. If your project schedule is rife with resource overallocations, this feature can be a real time-saver, as long as you set up your schedule so leveling can do its job. See the section "Leveling Assignments" later in this chapter for the full story.

Project offers two types of delays:

- **Leveling delay** applies to tasks; it pushes out the start date for a task and *all* its resource assignments. It's meant specifically for delaying tasks to remove resource overallocations. When you use the Leveling Delay field, you can remove all leveling delays in one fell swoop—for instance, if you decide that the leveling delays you add to assignments aren't doing what you want. If you want to remove leveling delays and start over, in the Resource tab's Level section, choose Clear Leveling.

> **Note:** A leveling delay isn't the same as lag time. Lag time is the real-world delay that occurs between the end of one task and the start of another—for example, the 3 weeks it takes a county to issue a construction permit after you apply for one. Lag time remains in place regardless of resource availability.

- **Assignment delay** applies to a single assignment within a task. Suppose you have a cyber security consultant coming in to help lock down your registration website. However, your employees have prep work to do before the consultant can get started. With an assignment delay, you can assign all your employees to the same "Try hacking into website" task, but delay the consultant's assignment by 2 days.

Follow Along Practice

To delay an entire task using leveling delay, do the following:

1. In the View tab's Resource Views section, click Other Views→More Views. In the More Views dialog box, double-click Resource Allocation.

    The Resource Usage view appears in the top pane, and the Leveling Gantt view appears in the Details pane.

    > **Tip:** You can drag the slider at the Project window's bottom right to zoom out to see when tasks occur. To view a specific task in the timescale, select it in the table, and then choose Task→"Scroll to Task."

    When you select a resource's summary row in the Resource Usage view, the Leveling Gantt view in the Details pane lists all the tasks that resource is assigned to. That way, you can quickly review tasks that might need to be delayed. For example, select Jaye Smith in the Resource Usage view. In the Leveling Gantt in the Details pane, you'll see that she is assigned to tasks for procuring the event venue and music, which are scheduled at the same time. In this example, it's more important to line up the venue, so a leveling delay can postpone the music procurement tasks until after the venue tasks are complete.

2. In the Leveling Gantt view's table, select the assignment that's causing a problem (click anywhere in the assignment's row). In this example, select the assignment for "Identify potential music options."

    > **Note:** If you select an assignment in the top pane, the Details pane displays only the task to which that assignment belongs.

3. In the Leveling Delay cell, type the length of time you want to delay the task.

    In this example, the task "Choose venue" finishes on 10/21/2021. The task "Identify potential music options" is scheduled to start on 6/30/2021. There are 114 calendar days between those two dates. To delay the task for 114 days, type *114* in the "Identify potential music options" task's Leveling Delay cell. Project replaces your entry with "114 edays," as shown in Figure 10-12. The

---

"e" at the beginning stands for "elapsed time," because the number of resources or the percentage they're assigned doesn't affect the delay. You want the task to start a specific amount of time later, and elapsed time does just that.

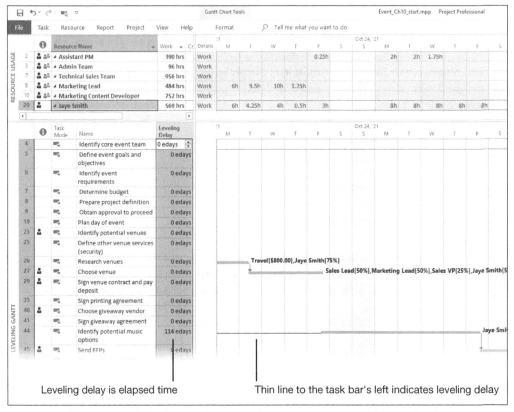

Leveling delay is elapsed time   Thin line to the task bar's left indicates leveling delay

Figure 10-12. *In the Leveling Gantt view, Project represents leveling delays with a thin line at the start of the task.*

To delay a single assignment within a task, add an assignment delay by doing the following:

1. In the View tab's Resource Views section, click Other Views→More Views. In the More Views dialog box, double-click Resource Allocation.

   The Resource Usage view appears in the top pane, and the Leveling Gantt view appears in the Details pane.

2. Add the Assignment Delay column to the Resource Usage table. (Right-click the table header, and then choose Insert Column→Assignment Delay.)

   The new column appears to the left of the column you right-clicked.

> **Note:** If you use the Task Form to work on assignments, you can see the Assignment Delay field by right-clicking the Task Form's table area and then choosing Schedule. The Delay column represents the Assignment Delay field.

3. In the Resource Usage view, click the Assignment Delay cell for the assignment you want to delay.

   In this example, remove the Overallocated filter from the Resource Usage view (on the View tab, in the Filter box, choose [No Filter]). If necessary, expand the Marketing Content Developer's summary row to show those assignments. Then click the Assignment Delay cell for the "Develop event materials" task.

4. In the Assignment Delay cell, type the length of delay.

   Suppose the Marketing Content Developer doesn't have to start working on the task for 2 days, while the Marketing Lead and Sales Lead discuss what's needed. To delay the assignment by 2 days, type *2d* and press Enter. Unlike a leveling delay, an assignment delay is in regular days, not elapsed days, so Project doesn't change the delay you enter to elapsed days. In the time-phased grid on the right, Project fills in the Work cells for the first two days with 0h and pushes the assigned work to the days after the assignment delay is over. In addition, because of the delay, the assignment continues after the other assignments end.

Splitting Longer Tasks to Work Around Shorter Tasks

Short but high-priority tasks might end up scheduled smack in the middle of longer, less important tasks. If the same resource works on both, you face a dilemma. Do you schedule the important task after the longer task finishes (and possibly delay the project finish date) or do you ask the assigned resource to knuckle down and work on both tasks simultaneously? Project offers a third solution. You can split the longer task into two pieces, creating a gap just long enough for the assigned resource to complete the short task.

> **Note:** When you insert a split into a task, you specify when the split starts and finishes. Be forewarned: you have to use your mouse to position the split, so chances are good that you won't select exactly the dates you want. In addition, if the short task's dates change, Project doesn't automatically reschedule the split. You have to edit the split to realign it with when the short task occurs. If these idiosyncrasies prove too frustrating, consider telling Project to add them for you as described in the section "Leveling Assignments" later in this chapter.

Here's how to split a task so someone can complete a short task:

1. If necessary, display the Gantt Chart view by clicking the Task tab's Gantt Chart button. To display more of the task list, hide the Details pane by double-clicking the horizontal divider between the top pane and the Details pane.

To restore the Details pane, double-click the small rectangle immediately below the down arrow in the vertical scroll bar.

2. If necessary, scroll in the task list until you see the task you want to split (in this example, task 45 "Send RFPs").

3. In the Task tab's Schedule section, click the Split icon (it looks like a task bar with a break in the middle).

When you click the Split icon, the pointer changes to two vertical lines with an arrow pointing to the right.

4. On the task bar that you want to split (in this example, task 45), click where you want the split to begin, and then drag to the date where you want work on the task to resume.

In this example, the split makes room for Jaye Smith to finish task 29 "Sign venue contract and pay deposit." To do that, click task 45's task bar to start the split on Thursday 11/3/21. Then drag the split so work resumes on Friday 11/5/21. When you click the task bar, a popup box displays the date you click and the task finish date. When you drag the task bar, the popup box displays the start and finish date for the work scheduled after the split, as shown in Figure 10-13.

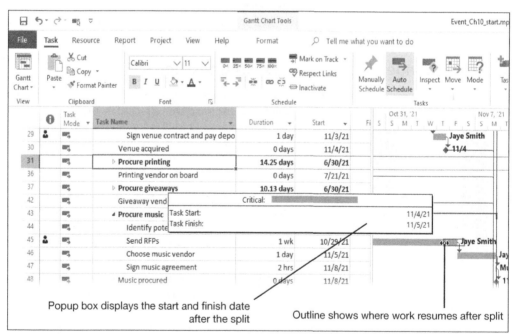

Figure 10-13. *In the Leveling Gantt view, Project represents leveling delays with a thin line at the start of the task.*

A dotted line within a task bar indicates where a split is scheduled.

5. If you need to split the task again, repeat steps 2, 3 and 4.

> **Tip:** To remove a split in a task, drag the section to the right of the split until it touches the section before the split. To move one section of a split task, put the pointer over the section you want to move (other than the first section in the task). When the pointer changes to a four-headed arrow, drag the section to the left or right to start it earlier or later, respectively. To change the duration of a split section, put the pointer over the right end of the section. When the pointer changes to a vertical line with a right-pointing arrow, drag to the left to shorten the section or to the right to lengthen it.

Reducing Resource Allocation to Tasks

When resources are assigned to more than one concurrent task, overallocations are almost sure to occur. Fortunately, many tasks don't need someone's full attention day after day. When that's the case, an easy way to eliminate overallocations is to decrease the units you've assigned on each of the tasks competing for the resource's time. Chapter 8 described how to adjust resource assignments. This section describes one way to find overallocations and eliminate them by decreasing assignment units:

Follow Along Practice

1. To evaluate overallocations, display the Resource Usage view (on the View tab, click Resource Usage).

    If necessary, display the Task Form in the Details pane by clicking the View tab, and then, in the Split View section, turning on the Details checkbox, and then choosing Task Form in the drop-down list. If necessary, right-click the Task Form table and then choose Resources & Predecessors on the shortcut menu.

2. If necessary, in the Resource Usage table, click the triangle (you might have to click twice to expand) to the left of the overallocated resource's name (Marketing Lead, in this example) until its assignments appear, shown in Figure 10-14.

    In this example, the Marketing Lead is assigned to two tasks that contribute to overallocations in October. The Marketing Lead is assigned to work 75% on "Prepare publicity plan" and 50% on "Choose venue."

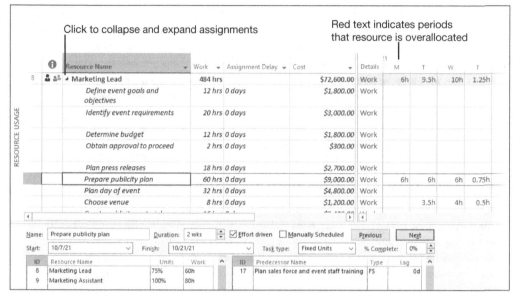

Figure 10-14. *The Resource Usage view helps you see assignments that contribute to overallocation.*

3. In the Resource Usage view, select the first task whose assignment you want to adjust. In this example, select the "Prepare publicity plan" task (see Figure 10-14).

4. In the Task Form, click the Units cell for the resource whose assignment you want to adjust and type the new value. In this example, click the Marketing Lead's Units cell, type 50, and press Enter.

    Project adjusts the task durations to accommodate the lower allocation. In this example, the duration increases from 2 weeks to 3 weeks, which eliminates the overallocation. (You can tell that the overallocation has been eliminated because the cells for the days where the tasks overlap in the Marketing Lead's summary row are no longer shown in red text.)

> **Note:** If the resource were still overallocated during this timeframe, reduce the units on any other tasks that occur at the same time.

Adjusting Work Contours

Most people don't leap out of bed in the morning raring to go, nor do they work full speed up until the moment they close their eyes at night. Yet Project assumes that resources work at an even pace from the start of every task to the finish—unless you tell it otherwise. To reflect how work *really* gets done, you can apply *work contours* to reshape assignments. Work contours alter the amount of work assigned over the entire duration of assignments. Like people's energy, tasks tend to start slowly, run at their peak in the middle, and then wind down at the end.

> **Note:** Work contours work only for auto-scheduled tasks, not manually scheduled ones.

Work contours reduce the hours for some time periods (for example, the hours assigned on the first and last days of an assignment), so they extend assignment duration and, in turn, task duration. The Flat contour, which is what Project applies automatically, schedules the same hours of work each day during an assignment, like 8 hours if a resource works 100 percent on the task. Every other contour type has high and low points. The highs schedule the same number of hours in a day as a Flat contour. But because the lows are less than a full schedule, the task ends up taking longer.

Table 10-1 describes Project's work contours and what they're good for. The great thing about work contours is that you can assign resources to work on other tasks when other assignments don't demand their full attention. Work contours may be all you need to eliminate some overallocations.

Table 10-1. *Work contours and their uses.*

Contour Name	Purpose
Flat	Project automatically assigns this constant contour to new tasks.
Back Loaded	This contour starts off slow and increases until the task is complete. If your work hours correspond to your adrenaline level, this contour is perfect.
Front Loaded	This contour starts at full effort and decreases, kind of like unpacking after a move: The first few days you spend all day unpacking boxes, but as time goes on, you unpack less and get back to your life.
Double Peak	This contour looks like the profile of a suspension bridge with a peak near each end and lower hours at the beginning, middle, and end. For example, a debugging task could have an early peak when hundreds of bugs need fixing and a second peak to fix the bugs that stand between you and project acceptance.
Early Peak	This contour starts slowly but quickly peaks and then drops off. This gives you some time to get oriented to a task before really digging in.
Late Peak	Late Peak ramps up to a peak, but has a drop-off at the end for tying up loose ends.
Bell	Bell is like a combination of a Back Loaded contour and a Front Loaded contour: The work continually increases to a peak and then gradually drops off.
Turtle	This contour has low levels at the beginning and the end with fully scheduled resources in the middle. It's probably the closest match to how tasks really proceed.

Follow Along Practice

Here are the steps for applying a work contour to a resource assignment:

1. Display the Task Usage or Resource Usage view (in the View tab's Task Views section, click Task Usage or Resource Usage).

   Because you apply contours to assignments, you have to open one of these views to see assignments.

2. In the view, double-click the assignment you want to contour, in this example, Jaye Smith's "Identify potential venues" assignment.

   In the Task Usage view, double-click the row for the resource assigned to the task. In the Resource Usage view, below the resource's name, double-click the task name for the assignment you want to contour. The Assignment Information dialog box appears.

3. In the Assignment Information dialog box's General tab, in the Work Contour list, choose a contour (in this example, Double Peak), and then click OK.

    Project calculates the new work hours for each day and then applies them to the assignment. The Task Usage view and Resource Usage view show the newly contoured hours.

4. If you can't see the time periods in which the assignment occurs in the time-phased grid on the right, in the Task tab's Editing section, click "Scroll to Task."

    The time-phased portion of the view jumps to the dates that have work for the selected assignment, shown in Figure 10-15. (To change the timescale to show weeks instead of days, on the View tab, in the Zoom section, click the down arrow in the Timescale box, and then choose Weeks.) In this example, the assignment was originally 2 weeks (10 workdays) duration. After applying the Double Peak contour, the duration spans 5 weeks in the time-phased grid.

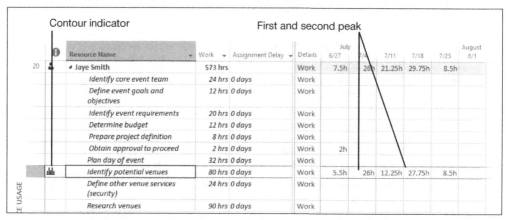

Figure 10-15. *Applying a contour extends an assignment, because it reduces the hours on some periods within the assignment.*

> **Tip:** Although you can't define custom contours, you can manually change the hours in the Task Usage view's time-phased grid. Simply click an assignment cell and then type the new hours for that period; continue changing cells until you've reassigned all the work hours. This method has a couple of disadvantages, however. First, you have to ensure that the hours you type add up to the original hours. Second, you inherit the responsibility of maintaining that assignment for the life of the project. When you manually edit work hours, you see the Edited Work icon (which looks like a bar chart with a pencil) in the assignment's Indicators cell.

Rescheduling a Task to Another Day

When tasks are manually scheduled, rescheduling them to new dates is often the easiest way to remove an overallocation. You can reschedule tasks to other days by using the Move feature on the Task tab or by dragging their taskbars in the Gantt Chart timescale. This section describes both techniques.

Follow Along Practice

- **Rescheduling with the Move feature**: Move reschedules tasks, not assignments, so you need to use a task view like the Gantt Chart view (on the Task tab, click the Gantt Chart button). To move a task into the past or future, in the Task tab's Tasks section, click Move. In the drop-down menu, choose a command for the amount of time you want to move it, as shown in Figure 10-16. In this example, the Marketing Lead is overallocated with work on task 54 "Arrange Advertising" (2 week duration) and task 57 "Develop event materials" (8.4 week duration). To reschedule "Develop event materials" after "Arrange advertising" is complete, select the "Develop event materials" task, and then click the Task Tab's Move icon. On the drop-down menu, in the Move Tasks Forward section, choose Custom. In the "Move tasks forward" dialog box, type *10* in the "Move selected tasks forward by __ working days" box, and then click OK. Notice that a date constraint indicator appears in the task's Indicators cell.

> **Tip:** Rescheduling auto-scheduled tasks in the timeline (by dragging or using the Move feature) creates date constraints, which limit Project's ability to calculate start and finish dates. For that reason, it's usually best to *not* reschedule auto-scheduled tasks using these techniques when you're initially building your schedule. However, if the project is underway and a task is due to start in the near future, you can reschedule it with these techniques. Date constraints aren't as problematic when tasks are about to start, because they don't affect Project's calculations as much. (If you accidentally reschedule a task, Chapter 9 explains how to find and fix date constraints.)

The Move drop-down menu also contains commands for moving tasks by one day, one week, or four weeks. This menu also includes commands for rescheduling incomplete work, which you'll learn how to do in Chapter 13.

If a resource works on a hodgepodge of short tasks, finding adjacent time for a longer assignment is almost impossible. Instead, you can tell Project to chop a task up and slide it into a resource's open slots. To do that, select the task you want to reschedule in a task-oriented view like the Gantt Chart. Then, in the Task tab's Tasks section, choose Move→When Resources Are Available.

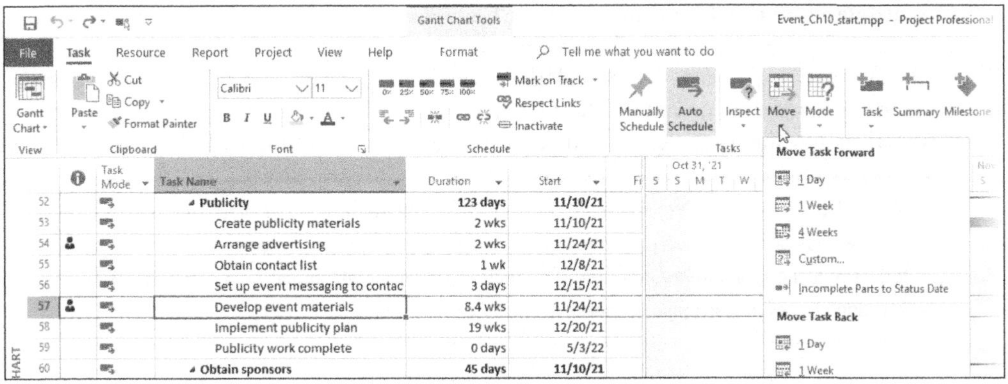

Figure 10-16. *The entries beneath Move Tasks Forward move tasks later in time. The Move Tasks Back entries reschedule tasks earlier.*

- **Dragging a task bar**: You can also reschedule a task by dragging its task bar to a new date in the timescale. This technique is helpful when you don't know how much you need to move a task—but you can see in the timescale where it needs to go to eliminate an overallocation. For example, tasks 70 and 71 "Train sales staff" and "Train technical staff" are scheduled to start at the same time and both use the Marketing Content Developer. (To see these task bars, select task 70 and then, in the Task tab's Editing section, click Scroll to Task.) To reschedule the "Train sales staff" task to start after the technical staff training is complete, put the pointer over the "Train sales staff" task bar. When it changes to a four-headed arrow, drag the task bar until the bar's left end lines up with the right end of the "Train technical staff" task. Release the mouse button to save the task with its new dates.

> **Note:** If you've followed the examples so far in this chapter, most of all the overallocation in-dicators have disappeared from the Indicators cells. However, the "Event setup complete" task is scheduled for 5/16/22, which is almost a month later than the planned event day (4/11/22). The Leveling feature described in the "Leveling Assignments" section can help eliminate resource overallocations without delaying event day.

Eliminating Overallocations with Team Planner (Available in Project Professional)

In the Team Planner view (in the Views tab's Resource Views section, click Team Planner), you can easily reassign or reschedule tasks to eliminate overallocations. In this view, if two or more concurrent tasks eat up too much of a resource's time, red brackets appear around the parts of assignment bars that contribute to the overallocation. Here's how to remove overallocations in Team Planner (you don't have to perform these steps in the example project):

- **Reassign a task to another resource**: To reassign a task to a resource with available time, right click the assignment bar and choose Reassign To on the shortcut menu (or drag the assignment bar to the row for the new resource). When you select the new resource, the task bar jumps into their swimlane and is scheduled on the same days as the original assignment.

- **Reschedule a task to a different date**: In the Team Planner view, you can drag each assignment independently. However, if more than one resource is assigned to a task, you usually want to reschedule both assignments. To select all the assignments for a task, right-click one of the task's assignment bars and then, from the shortcut menu, choose "Select All Assignments on This Task." Then drag the assignments to a date where the resources won't be overallocated.

> **Note:** If you work in a Project Server environment, the Team Planner view shows a re-source's assignments on *all* projects, not just the current project, if you opened the file with the default "Load summary resources" checkbox selected, which can be a reminder that you don't have exclusive use of that shared resource.

Leveling Assignments

As you learned in the previous section, you can resolve the occasional resource overallocation by delaying tasks and assignments so a resource can work on them in sequence. Project's resource-leveling feature can resolve resource overallocations *for* you by delaying tasks and assignments in the same way. It can also *split* tasks (introduce small gaps in assigned work) so resources can briefly stop what they're doing to crank out a short but more important task. You can use Project's resource leveling to level an entire project, a portion of a project, or the assignments for a resource that's in high demand. Just as with other methods of balancing resources' workloads, leveling tasks and assignments makes them finish later.

> **Tip:** Project's resource-leveling feature is a powerful tool in the quest for balanced workloads. However, it can wreak havoc on a schedule if you don't apply it properly. For example, leveling resources without choosing the appropriate settings could push your project finish date out by months. For this reason, it's a good idea to make a copy of your Project file before you level resources. That way, if the results aren't what you want, you can undo the changes or make another copy of the original for additional experiments.

Before you try your hand at automated resource leveling, it's helpful to understand what it can—and can't—do for you:

- **It can balance workloads for Project work resources**: Project's resource-leveling feature can even out workloads for people (generic roles or specific people), equipment, and other resources you've set up using the Work type in Project. But it doesn't do anything with material or cost resources, because those types of resources don't have any work to balance.

- **It can delay or split tasks and assignments**: During leveling, Project looks for resource overallocations. For each one it finds, it locates the offending tasks and decides whether to delay or split them to eliminate the overallocation. Resource leveling only delays or splits tasks (it doesn't assign different resources, adjust resource units, or contour work), but it can balance workloads for both manually and automatically scheduled tasks.

- **It doesn't change the amount of work assigned or who is assigned**: The work hours for tasks and assignments stay the same. Leveling simply reschedules when that work occurs to eliminate resource overallocations. Similarly, the resources assigned to the task stay the same. If you decide to reassign work to someone else, the section "Replacing Resources" earlier in this chapter tells you how to do that.

- **It doesn't change task dependencies**: The dependencies that you've added between tasks remain the same.

> **Note:** Are you wondering how you delay and split tasks in a project scheduled from the finish date? You can't push the finish date later, so Project adds *negative* delays to tasks and changes their *start* dates. The result of leveling a from-finish-date project is that the project's start date moves earlier.

Prepping Your Schedule for Leveling

Recommendations

There are a few best scheduling practices that help you get the most out of Project's resource-leveling feature.

> **Note:** If you've downloaded files from the book website, you can follow along by creating a second copy of the original file Event_Ch10_start.mpp.

Here's what you do to prep your schedule for leveling:

- **Don't link tasks to remove overallocations**: People new to project scheduling sometimes add links between tasks—not because the tasks depend on one another, but to schedule the tasks so the assigned resource can work on the tasks one after the other without being overloaded. If you want Project to level resources for you, remove these workload-related task dependencies from your schedule.

- **Set resources' Maximum Units to 100% (fully available)**: Although your project might get only half of someone's time, setting that resource's Maximum Units to 50% *isn't* the way to go, as explained in the section "Assigning Part-Time Workers." The better approach is to set resources' Maximum Units value to 100% and then define their working and non-working time in their resource calendars. That way, they're fully engaged in their project tasks when it counts. For example, if your financial expert Priscilla comes in one day a month to review the books, she's dedicated to that review for that day. If you set her Maximum Units value to 5% (one day out of the 20 workdays in a month), Project will assign her at 5% units, and her one day of work will be scheduled for 20 workdays. Instead, you can change her resource calendar to define her workdays on your project.

- **Add project admin time to work tasks**: You can handle administrative tasks in a couple of ways. For resource leveling, the best approach is to add time for project administration (5% or 10%, say) to each work task estimate. For example, if the task estimate is 40 hours, you would enter *44* in the task's Work field. That way, the assigned resource can record time spent on a status report against her work task.

> **Note:** Recurring tasks or long tasks for administrative work give Project's resource-leveling feature heartburn because it has trouble splitting or rescheduling these tasks to schedule project work and admin work. Recurring tasks are tough to manage in Project, and they produce lots of splits in your project work tasks when you use the resource-leveling feature. A long admin task could lead to a much longer project after Project levels resources. If leveling produces these types of issues, go back and add admin time into work estimates.

- **Use priorities to tell Project what's important**: Project's Priority field is your way of telling the resource-leveling feature which tasks you consider important, so that it places more emphasis on getting those tasks done first when it levels resources. The next section explains how priorities work and how to use them.

Prioritizing Projects and Tasks

In the real world, finish dates for some tasks and projects are more important than others—for example, lining up an event venue is more important than getting the musicians on board. But when you use resource leveling, Project has no way of knowing these priorities unless you tell it. The Priority field tells Project which tasks and projects should be completed first, and which ones it can delay to remove overallocations.

> **Note:** The Priority field comes into play only when you use Project's resource-leveling feature; this field has no effect on your regular scheduling activities. However, you can use the Priority field to focus on key tasks. For example, when you're trying to manage a schedule, you can filter or group the task list by priority to find the tasks to fast-track or *crash* (the project-management term for spending more money to shorten duration; see Chapter 11).

Priority values range from 0 to 1,000. Project automatically assigns new tasks and projects a Priority value of 500 (the middle-of-the-road value). 1,000 is the highest priority, which means that Project doesn't delay projects or tasks with that value. So if you don't want Project to level a task, set its priority to 1,000. You can also change a task's Can Level field to No (you have to insert this field into a table to see it), but that field doesn't appear in any tables automatically (which often produces mystifying leveling behavior, as the note titled "Leveling Skips Overallocations" later in this chapter explains).

To tell Project to give a task preferential treatment for leveling purposes, set the task's priority to a value greater than 500. That way, the program will delay and split lower-priority tasks so that the tasks with higher priority are completed first. For example, it gives tasks with priority of 800 precedence over tasks with priority of 700, and so on.

You're not likely to need all 1,000 of Project's priority levels, no matter how many projects and tasks you want to level. Whether you opt to use three, five, or 20 priority levels, keep 500 as the standard setting. For example, if you use only five levels, you can use 1,000 for high priority (tasks that don't level), 800 for above-average priority, 500 for most tasks, 300 for below-average, and 0 for low priority. (You can use 1000, 501, 500, 499, and 498 as well, as long as you don't have to reassign all the tasks with a priority of 500.)

Changing Task Priority

The Priority field appears on the Task Information dialog box's General tab, which is fine if you plan to change the priority for only the most important tasks. To assign a new Priority value to a task, in a task-oriented view like the Gantt Chart, select the task (click anywhere in its row), and then press Shift+F2. In the Task Information dialog box, select the General tab, and then, in the Priority field, type the number. (You can also double-click a task to open the dialog box.)

Follow Along Practice

However, if you prioritize many tasks, it's easier to add the Priority field to a Gantt Chart table so you can quickly type, copy, and paste priority values to every task, as shown in Figure 10-17. Here's how:

1. In the Gantt Chart view or another task-oriented view, add the Priority field to a table like Entry.

   If necessary, right-click the Select All Cells cell at the table's top left and then, on the shortcut menu, choose Entry. Right-click the column heading to the right of where you want to insert the field (in this example, Duration), and then, on the shortcut menu, choose Insert Column. In the drop-down list, choose Priority.

2. Click a Priority cell, and then type the new value.

   You can copy and paste values from one cell to another using Ctrl+C and Ctrl+V. If several adjacent tasks have the same priority, position the pointer over the first cell's fill handle (the green rectangle at the selected cell's bottom right). When the cursor changes to a + sign, drag over the other Priority cells.

   In this example, change the following priorities:

   Change the procure event venue tasks (IDs 22 through 30) to 800.

   Change task 58 "Implement publicity plan" to 700.

   Change task 62 "Recruit sponsors" to 800.

   Change task 71 "Train technical staff" to 400.

		Task Mode ▾	Task Name ▾	Priority ▾	Duration ▾	T
21		⬛	⊿ **Procurement**	**500**	**77 days**	
22		⬛	⊿ **Procure event venue**	**800**	**77 days**	
23	👤	⬛	Identify potential venues	800 ⬍	2 wks	
24		⬛	Define AV requirements	800	5 days	
25	👤	⬛	Define other venue services (security)	800	3 days	
26		⬛	Research venues	800	3 wks	
27	👤	⬛	Choose venue	800	2 days	
28		⬛	Choose menu	800	3 days	
29		⬛	Sign venue contract and pay depo	800	1 day	
30		⬛	Venue acquired	800	0 days	
31		⬛	⊿ **Procure printing**	**500**	**14.25 days**	
32	👤	⬛	Identify printing services	500	3 days	
33	👤	⬛	Send RFPs	500	1 wk	

Figure 10-17. *When you click a Priority cell, you can click the up and down arrows to change the value by 20-point increments; from 500 to 520, for example. However, typing or copying and pasting are usually faster.*

Changing Project Priority

If you have several subprojects in a master project, then entire projects may have a higher priority than the rest, like the presentations for a tradeshow that had better be ready when the show starts. That's why projects have a Priority field, too. Project priority is powerful, so use it sparingly. When you assign priorities to projects and then use resource leveling, Project levels all tasks in lower-priority projects before the lowest-priority tasks in high-priority projects. For example, suppose one project has a Priority value of 800 and another has a Priority value of 500. When you use Project's resource-leveling feature, the program levels a task with Priority 900 in the 500-priority project before it levels a task with Priority 0 in the 800-priority project. (The note titled "Leveling Multiple Projects" describes the steps for leveling multiple projects.)

Note: A priority of 1,000 is sacred, so Project doesn't level tasks set to Priority 1,000 regardless of any priorities their projects have.

To change a project's priority, follow these steps (you don't have to perform these steps for the sample project):

1. Open the project and then, in the Project tab's Properties section, click Project Information.

    The Project Information dialog box opens.

2. In the Priority field, type the new priority, and then click OK.

    The Project Information dialog box closes.

The next time you level projects, Project's resource-leveling feature takes this new priority into account.

Using the Leveling Gantt View

Switch to Leveling Gantt view before you level assignments. That way, once you apply resource leveling, you can see the results immediately—and undo them if they aren't what you want. To display this view, in the View tab's Task Views section, click Other Views→More Views, and then, in the More Views dialog box, double-click Leveling Gantt.

The upper set of task bars (which are tan in the built-in Leveling Gantt view) show your original schedule. The lower set of task bars (which are blue) show the leveled tasks with any added delays and splits. Leveling delays appear as thin lines at the beginning of task bars. Figure 10-20 shows the Leveling Gantt view after the project has been leveled.

Leveling Multiple Projects

When you share resources among projects, overallocations from other projects can create delays and splits. But you can change task and project priority and then relevel the assignments to try for better results. The trick is seeing which tasks are causing the problems.

To figure out which tasks are causing trouble, create a master project that contains **all** the projects that share the resources you use (Chapter 24). This master project contains all the tasks that compete for your resources' time, so you can see why the delays and splits are there. To view tasks that share resources with tasks in other projects, follow these steps:

1. Choose File→Open. Choose the location where you store Project files (Computer or Recent Projects, for example), and then open the Project file for your resource pool (Chapter 24).

2. In the Open Resource Pool dialog box, select the "Open resource pool read-write and all other sharer files into a new master project file..." option. Project creates a new master project, which contains the resource pool and all its sharer files.

3. In the View tab's Window section, click Switch Windows→Project 1 to view the new master project.

4. In the View tab's Task Views section, click Other Views→More Views and then, in the More Views dialog box, double-click Leveling Gantt.

5. If necessary, in the View tab's Split View section, turn on the Details checkbox and then, in the Details drop-down list, choose Resource Usage.

6. Select a task that has a questionable split or delay. In the Details pane, Project displays the resources assigned to the task and its assignments from all the sharer projects.

7. In the Task tab's Editing section, click "Scroll to Task."

8. In the Resource Usage pane, examine the competing assignments to see which split or delay should win, and adjust the assignments as necessary.

Setting Leveling Options

You can level an entire project, tasks you select, or a single resource. By leveling several tasks that are all vying for the resource—or, alternatively, leveling only the most in-demand resources—you can focus on the problematic portions of your project. Project automatically chooses initial settings in the Resource Leveling dialog box, shown in Figure 10-18, but a few tweaks to these settings might give you better results. You can try one set of settings and then, if you don't like the changes Project makes, undo the leveling and then try different settings. This section describes your leveling options and how to decide which ones to choose.

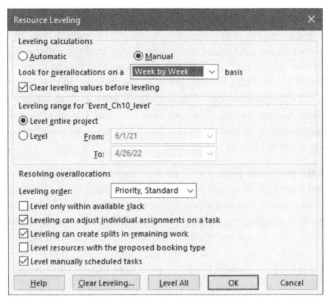

Figure 10-18. *Project remembers the leveling settings you choose until you change them.*

To choose leveling options, head to the Resource tab. In the Level section, click Leveling Options to open the Resource Leveling dialog box. When you change the settings in this dialog box, Project uses your settings until you change them. Here's a guide to the options in the Resource Leveling dialog box and how to use them:

- **Automatic or manual calculations**: At the top of the Resource Leveling dialog box, the Manual option is selected initially, and that's almost always what you want. With the Manual option selected, *you* control when Project relevels the schedule. When you want to relevel it, simply choose one of the leveling commands in the Resource tab's Level section. Then you can review the changes—and undo them if they aren't what you want.

  The Automatic option, on the other hand, tells Project to recalculate your schedule every time you make a change, which not only slows down the program, but also doesn't give you a chance to review the overallocations before making modifications. In addition, it's hard to see whether the leveling changes that Project makes are what you want.

- **The overallocation time period**: To Project, 1 minute beyond a person's available time is an overallocation. But you know that an overallocation one day often balances out with available time the next day, so longer time periods generally mean fewer overallocations to resolve. In the "Look for overallocations on a __ basis" box, choose "Week by Week" or "Day by Day." These choices usually eliminate overallocations without too much leveling. In this example, choose "Week by Week."

- **Remove previous leveling values**: Out of the box, the "Clear leveling values before leveling" checkbox is turned on, which tells Project to remove any previous delays (added by you or by Project) before starting the next round of leveling. If you level the entire project in one fell swoop, starting fresh each time is the best approach, because you can more clearly see the changes Project makes. If you've added leveling delays manually, turn off the "Clear leveling values before leveling" checkbox. Otherwise, Project removes *your* leveling delays as well as any it has added. If you want to clear leveling delays without releveling the schedule, you can click the dialog box's Clear Leveling button (or, in the Resource tab's Level section, click Clear Leveling). In this example, keep the checkbox turned on.

- **How much of the project to level**: The "Leveling range" section's heading includes the project's name to indicate that the option you select here applies only to the current project. Project automatically selects the "Level entire project" option, which means it looks at *every* task as a leveling candidate. By leveling the entire project, you'll be able to see how long the project will take given your team members' availability. To level only the tasks that occur during a specific date range, select the Level option instead and then, in the From and To boxes, choose the start and end dates to level. For example, if a phase runs from October 1 to March 1, level between those dates. (Of course, after leveling, the phase will finish later than March 1.) In this example, keep the "Level entire project" radio button selected.

- **How Project decides which tasks to level**: Initially, Project sets the "Leveling order" dropdown list to Standard, which uses predecessor dependencies, slack (how long a task can delay before it affects the end of the project), task dates, task constraints, and task priority to decide which tasks to level. However, the "Priority, Standard" leveling order is the one you want (as long as you assign priorities to tasks as described earlier in this chapter). With this leveling order selected, Project weights task priorities first and then the other criteria. In this example, use "Priority, Standard."

The reasoning behind Project's ordering of characteristics is that you can delay tasks that don't have successors without affecting other tasks, so they're the best candidates for leveling. When tasks have successors, the ones with the most slack can delay longer without delaying other tasks. Similarly, the later tasks start, the less they affect the project schedule. Task constraints make tasks less flexible schedule-wise, so Project leaves those tasks alone if possible.

The ID Only leveling order isn't very helpful, because it levels tasks with higher ID numbers *first*, and that's not what you typically want.

- **Level within slack**: Project initially turns off the "Level only within available slack" checkbox, which is usually what you want, because using only slack typically doesn't resolve many overallocations. If you don't want the project finish date to move later, you can turn on this checkbox to level resources as much as possible without changing the project finish date. Then you can use other techniques to shorten the schedule (Chapter 11).

- **Level individual assignments**: Project initially turns on the "Leveling can adjust individual assignments on a task" checkbox, which levels only assignments that overallocate resources. If you assign more than one person to a task, those people usually work together to get the job done. To tell Project to level entire tasks so assigned resources can work together, turn this checkbox off.

If leveling tasks doesn't resolve your overallocation issues, then turn this checkbox on and relevel the project. In this example, keep this checkbox turned on.

- **Split remaining work**: The "Leveling can create splits in remaining work" checkbox is turned on initially and that's the setting you want. When this checkbox is turned on, Project levels tasks that haven't started and adds splits to the remaining work for tasks in progress. With this checkbox turned *off*, Project delays assignments only until the resource can complete the work without stopping, which often pushes tasks out for exceedingly long periods of time.

- **Level proposed resources**: Proposed resources are resources you want to use but don't yet have permission for (Chapter 6). If you turn on the "Level resources with the proposed booking type" checkbox, Project levels both committed and proposed resources to show what the project schedule would look like if you get everyone you ask for.

- **Level manually scheduled tasks**: Project turns this checkbox on automatically, which is exactly what you want, because manually scheduled tasks are more prone to overallocating resources than auto-scheduled ones.

> **Tip:** Deadlines (Chapter 5) in Project aren't carved in stone. Leveling resources can push a task beyond its deadline, because Project's leveling doesn't pay any attention to task deadlines. To prevent Project from leveling a task with a deadline, change the task's priority to 1,000.

Applying and Clearing Leveling

The commands for applying and clearing leveling are all in the Resource tab's Level section. Here's how to level different parts of your project using these commands:

- **Level an entire project**: Click Level All.

  In the example project, leveling inserts splits and delays and successfully eliminates resource overallocations. As you review the schedule (see Figure 10-19) to make sure the results are what you want, you'll notice a few issues:

  First, task 63 "Sponsors on board" has a missed deadline indicator in its Indicators cell. This task has a deadline of 12/13/21 (see Chapter 5). After leveling, the task doesn't finish until 1/17/22. The task's only successor is the "Event preparation complete" milestone. You might go back to the project sponsor and stakeholders to verify the reason for the deadline. For example, the deadline could be set to complete before the sponsors 2021 budgets are finalized. Chapter 11 will examine ways to shorten the schedule to meet this deadline.

  Second, two tasks extend past event day: task 58 "Implement publicity plan" and task 66 "Monitor registrations." "Implement publicity plan" isn't an issue. Looking at the Resource Usage view, the Marketing Lead has available time when the task begins. In this example, you can increase the Marketing Lead's and Marketing Assistant's units to 30% for "Implement publicity plan" to complete the task before event day. (If the duration doesn't change when you change the resources' units, remove the Giveaways material resource from the task and save it, which recalculates the task duration. Then add the Giveaways resource back to the task.) "Monitor registrations" is also not an issue, because the task duration merely needs to run up until event day. For this task, you can change its duration to 16 weeks. When you change the duration, the Assistant PM becomes overallocated working on "Monitor registrations" and "Build event staffing plan." To eliminate this new issue, replace the Assistant PM with someone from the Admin Team (using 10% units to match the Assistant PM's units).

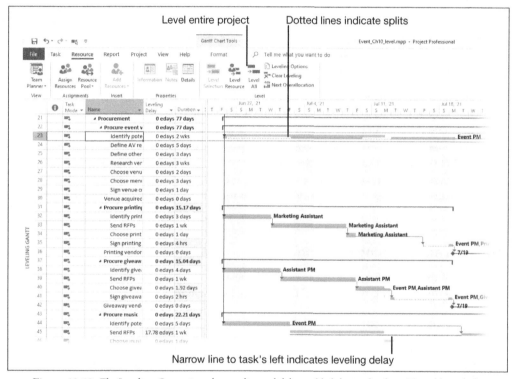

Figure 10-19. *The Leveling Gantt view shows splits and delays added during leveling. The table includes the Leveling Delay field.*

- **Level selected tasks**: Select the tasks you want to level, and then click Level Selection.

- **Level a resource**: Select the resource you want to level, and then click Level Resource.

If you don't like the results you get, the quickest way to remove the leveling is to press Ctrl+Z to undo the leveling command. However, if you've leveled a task here and a resource there, you can remove all delays and splits by heading to the Resource tab and, in the Level section, clicking Clear Leveling.

Leveling Skips Overallocations

After leveling, often times the overallocations you wanted to remove are still there. Project doesn't level tasks and resources for a number of reasons. Check for the following circumstances to see if they're preventing leveling:

- Project doesn't delay tasks that have Must Start On or Must Finish On date constraints. To level these tasks, first change their date constraints to a more flexible type, like As Soon As Possible (Chapter 5).

- When you've scheduled a project from the start date, As Late As Possible date constraints prevent leveling. For projects scheduled from the finish date, As Soon As Possible date constraints inhibit leveling.

- Project doesn't level tasks with a Priority value of 1,000. To level a task, change its priority to 999 or less. Conversely, if you manually add delays or splits to a task with a priority of 1,000, then the Clear Leveling command doesn't remove your manual changes.

- Project doesn't delay tasks that have already started, although it might split remaining work if the Resource Leveling dialog box's "Leveling can create splits in remaining work" checkbox is turned on.

- Setting a resource's Can Level field to No prevents Project from leveling that resource's overallocations. If you can't see any obvious reason why leveling isn't working, add the Can Level field to the Resource Sheet view, and then change the value to Yes.

- For tasks, the Level Assignments and Leveling Can Split fields control whether Project levels them. If these fields are set to No, then Project doesn't level the tasks no matter which settings you choose in the Resource Leveling dialog box. Change these values to Yes to allow leveling.

11

Shortening the Schedule and Reducing Costs

After you've worked all the kinks out of your tasks and resource assignments, the project's schedule and costs might not be what stakeholders want. This chapter describes the most common schedule-shortening techniques: *fast-tracking* (vigorously overlapping tasks), *crashing* (aggressively adding resources or spending more money to shorten duration), shortening lag time between tasks, and reducing scope. In addition, this chapter identifies methods that can help you reduce project cost.

Shortening the Schedule

After you rid your project schedule of omissions and resource overallocations, your next challenge could be that the project finishes later than the customer and other stakeholders want. In addition, once the project is under way, delays often creep in and push the finish date out further than you had planned. Either way, you have to dive back into the schedule to see if you can shorten it. This section starts with a quick overview of options for shortening a schedule. Because the critical path determines the project duration, it's a good idea to make sure the critical path is correct before shortening the schedule. Once that's done, this section describes the various shortening techniques in detail.

> **Note:** If you've downloaded files from the book website, you can follow along using the file Event_Ch11_start.mpp. At this point in scheduling the example project, task ID 82 "Event setup complete" (a milestone) is scheduled for 5/4/22. However, the kickoff event date is supposed to be 4/11/22, so you need to shave a few weeks off the schedule.

There are several shortening methods to choose from, each with its own set of pros and cons:

- **Splitting tasks into smaller pieces**: Something as simple as breaking long tasks into several shorter ones can sometimes shorten a schedule. You can assign the subtasks to different people, who work on them in tandem, or schedule around other work. Or you may be able to link successors to one of the earlier pieces. This technique also doesn't affect scope, quality, or cost.

- **Overlapping (a.k.a. *fast-tracking*) tasks**: With this approach, you overlap tasks a little instead of working on them in sequence. Fast-tracking works as long as the same resources don't work full-time on both of the fast-tracked tasks. If they do, they'll end up overallocated. The one downside to fast-tracking is that it increases risk, because changes that occur toward the end of the predecessor task could mess up work that's already complete in the successor (for example, changes in software design after code has been written).

- **Shortening lag time between tasks**: Some waiting periods between tasks can't be shortened: You can't speed up the time it takes for glue to dry, for instance. However, you might be able to shorten some lag times by, for example, paying for expedited processing or asking the customer to shorten their deliverable review times. Shortening lag time doesn't affect scope or quality, but it might cost more.

- **Crashing the schedule**: The term *crashing* refers to paying more to shorten the schedule, for example, by adding more resources or paying more to expedite shipping. This is one of the last techniques to consider, because it could reduce the quality of your deliverables and it increases the project cost.

- **Reducing scope**: Cutting project scope does shorten the schedule. However, stakeholders must agree to the reduction. And even if the customer and other stakeholders say yes to less scope, there's a risk that they might not be happy with the truncated end result. The section at the end of this chapter tells you how to handle this in Project.

Correcting the Critical Path

As described in Chapter 9, the critical path is the longest sequence of tasks in the project—and that means you can shorten the project schedule if you can find a way to shorten the critical path. In Project, a task is flagged as critical if its total slack is less than or equal to zero. Unfortunately, Project deadlines, date constraints, and manually scheduled tasks can cause problems with slack calculations (also described in Chapter 9), which make too many tasks appear to be critical. When that happens, it's tough to tell which tasks will actually shorten the project schedule. Before trying to shorten the critical path, it's important to make sure it's correct. This section shows you how.

Viewing the Critical Path

To make sure the critical path is correct, you need to look at task slack values. Here's how to view slack for tasks:

Follow Along Practice

1. Display the Tracking Gantt view (on the View tab, click the bottom half of the Gantt Chart button, and then choose Tracking Gantt on the drop-down menu).

    By default, in the Tracking Gantt view, task bars for tasks on the critical path are shaded red.

    > **Tip:** If you don't see task bars in the view timescale, select a task in the table, and then, at the right end of the Task tab, click "Scroll to Task."

2. In the Tracking Gantt view's table, insert the Total Slack field by right-clicking a column heading (Duration, say), choosing Insert Column on the shortcut menu, and then choosing Total Slack in the drop-down list.

3. In the Format tab's Bar Styles section, turn on the Slack checkbox.

    If you're following along using the example project, many Total Slack values are negative, as shown in Figure 11-1, which makes too many tasks critical. The next sections describe techniques for removing non-critical tasks from the critical path in Project.

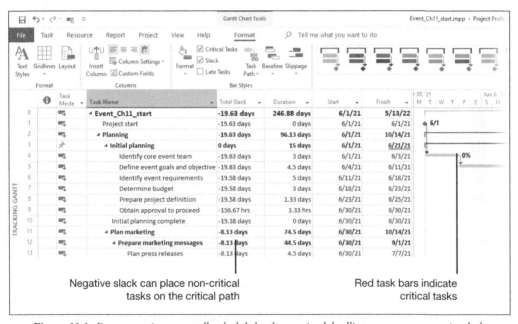

Negative slack can place non-critical tasks on the critical path

Red task bars indicate critical tasks

Figure 11-1. *Date constraints, manually scheduled tasks, or missed deadlines can generate negative slack.*

Correcting Manually Scheduled Task Problems

When manually-scheduled tasks are linked to other tasks, they might not obey their task dependencies, as demonstrated in Figure 11-2. Ignored dependencies are one source of negative total slack in Project. When a manually scheduled task produces negative slack, you can eliminate the problem either by changing the task to automatically scheduled or by telling Project to respect the task links.

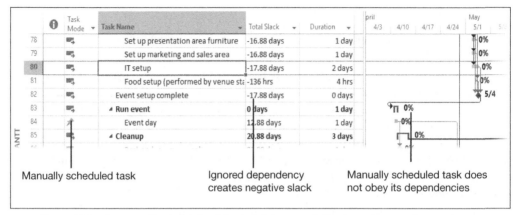

Figure 11-2. *If a manually scheduled task is scheduled to occur before its predecessors, those predecessors end up with negative slack.*

Follow Along Practice

To eliminate negative slack created by a manually-scheduled task, simply change the task to auto-scheduled:

1. In this example, make taskbars easier to see by changing the timescale period from days to weeks. (In the View tab's Zoom section, click the Timescale down arrow, and then choose Weeks.)

2. In the view's table, click the Task Mode cell for the manually-scheduled task, in this example, task ID 84 "Event day."

3. Click the down arrow that appears, and then choose Auto Scheduled.

   Project changes the task to auto-scheduled and recalculates its start and finish dates based on the task's dependencies. As shown in Figure 11-3, negative slack disappears for several tasks in the schedule.

> **Note:** When you change a task to auto-scheduled, the task may no longer be scheduled on the dates you want. For example, in Figure 11-3, the start date for task ID 84 "Event day" has changed from 4/11/22 to 5/4/22. You now must monitor the task to make sure that it remains scheduled on the correct dates as you make changes to the schedule.
>
> You can add a note to the task to remind yourself when the task is supposed to occur. Right-click the task's row in the table, and choose Notes on the shortcut menu. In the Task Information dialog box's Notes tab, add the date the task is supposed to occur, in this example, type "Event day is 4/11/22" Click OK.

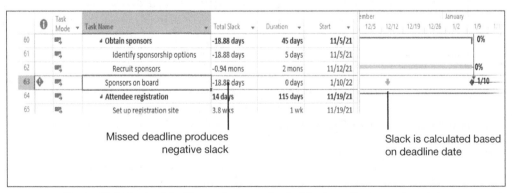

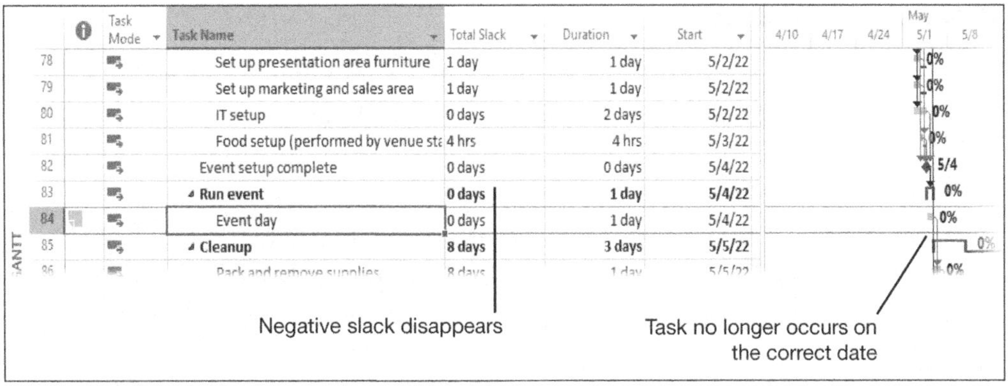

	ⓘ	Task Mode ▾	Task Name ▾	Total Slack ▾	Duration ▾	Start ▾				May	
							4/10	4/17	4/24	5/1	5/8
78		�	Set up presentation area furniture	1 day	1 day	5/2/22				0%	
79		▪	Set up marketing and sales area	1 day	1 day	5/2/22				0%	
80		▪	IT setup	0 days	2 days	5/2/22				0%	
81		▪	Food setup (performed by venue sta	4 hrs	4 hrs	5/3/22				0%	
82		▪	Event setup complete	0 days	0 days	5/4/22				5/4	
83		▪	▲ Run event	0 days	1 day	5/4/22				0%	
84		▪	Event day	0 days	1 day	5/4/22				0%	
85		▪	▲ Cleanup	8 days	3 days	5/5/22					0%
86		▪	Pack and remove supplies	8 days	1 day	5/5/22					0%

Negative slack disappears   Task no longer occurs on the correct date

Figure 11-3. *Changing a task to auto-scheduled eliminates negative slack due to ignored dependencies.*

> **Tip:** You can also eliminate negative slack by telling Project to respect the manual task's task dependencies. To do that, select the manually scheduled task and then, in the Task tab's Schedule section, click the Respect Links button. Keep in mind, if your schedule changes in the future, you may need to repeat this step. In the example project, you don't have to do this because you already changed the task to Auto Scheduled.

Eliminating Problems Due to Missed Deadlines

Another source of negative slack is a missed deadline in Project. When you add a deadline to a task, Project calculates total slack for linked tasks based on the deadline date, not the scheduled start or finish date. If the task misses its deadline, the result is negative slack, as shown in Figure 11-4. The easiest way to eliminate negative slack is to remove the deadline from the task.

	ⓘ	Task Mode ▾	Task Name ▾	Total Slack ▾	Duration ▾	Start ▾	ember				January		
							12/5	12/12	12/19	12/26	1/2	1/9	1/1
60		▪	▲ Obtain sponsors	-18.88 days	45 days	11/5/21							0%
61		▪	Identify sponsorship options	-18.88 days	5 days	11/5/21							
62		▪	Recruit sponsors	-0.94 mons	2 mons	11/12/21							0%
63	◆	▪	Sponsors on board	-18.88 days	0 days	1/10/22							1/10
64		▪	▲ Attendee registration	14 days	115 days	11/19/21							
65		▪	Set up registration site	3.8 wks	1 wk	11/19/21							

Missed deadline produces negative slack   Slack is calculated based on deadline date

Figure 11-4. *A missed deadline produces negative slack in the predecessors to the task that missed its deadline.*

Follow Along Practice

To eliminate negative slack created by a missed deadline, you can remove the deadline:

1. In the view's table, double-click the row for the task with a deadline, in this example, task ID 63 "Sponsors on board."

2. In the Task Information dialog box, click the Advanced tab.

   In this example, the deadline for getting sponsors on board is 12/13/21.

3. Click the Deadline box, and then press the Delete key on your keyboard.

   Project removes the deadline date from the task.

4. Click OK.

   The task's scheduled dates don't change. However, the missed deadline indicator disappears from the task's Indicators cell and negative slack disappears, as shown in Figure 11-5.

> **Note:** When you remove a deadline from a task in Project, the program won't be able to warn you when the task misses its deadline. You have to keep track of the deadline yourself. You can add a note to the task to document its deadline date. (Right-click the task's row in the table, and choose Notes on the shortcut menu. In the Task Information dialog box's Notes tab, add the deadline date, in this example, type "Deadline is 12/13/21." Click OK.)

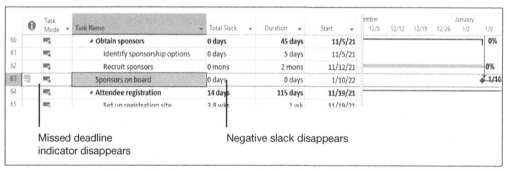

Figure 11-5. *Removing a Project deadline eliminates negative slack.*

Correcting Gaps in the Critical Path

Date constraints can cause critical path problems in two ways. If tasks miss their date constraints, they generate negative slack in predecessors, just like manually scheduled tasks and missed deadlines do. In addition, date constraints can create positive slack that creates gaps in the critical path. That happens when parts of a project can be completed before a date constraint is reached. Figure 11-6 shows a gap in the critical path due to date constraint (most of the tasks in the Procurement section of the Project are shown as non-critical). To close gaps in the critical path, you can change the value at which tasks are flagged as critical.

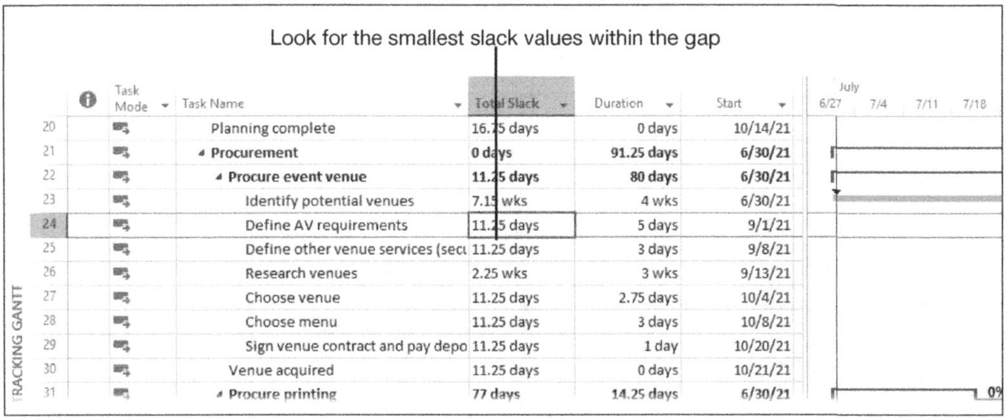

Figure 11-6. *Date constraints can create gaps in the critical path.*

Follow Along Practice

Determining the new threshold for critical tasks usually requires trial and error. Here's how to specify a new critical threshold:

1. Find a gap within the critical path.

    In this example (Figure 11-6), the entire procurement section is non-critical.

2. Review the values in the Total Slack column to look for the slack that created the gap.

    In this example, the summary task ID 43 "Procure music" has Total Slack of 0 days, which is the smallest value in the procurement section. However, that slack value comes from the milestone that follows procurement (task ID 51 "Begin pre-event work"). Therefore, you need to look for the next smallest slack value, which is 11.25 days in task ID 27 "Choose venue." For simplicity, you can round up that value to the next whole day, in this case, 12 days.

3. To change the critical threshold, on the File tab, choose Options. In the Project Options dialog box, click Advanced and scroll to the "Calculation options for this project" section at the bottom of the dialog box.

4. In the "Tasks are critical if slack is less than or equal to" box, type 12. Click OK to close the dialog box.

    After you click OK, Project shows tasks with Total Slack less than or equal to 12 days as critical, as shown in Figure 11-7. If you're following along in the example project, scroll through the timescale. Notice that the critical path no longer has gaps.

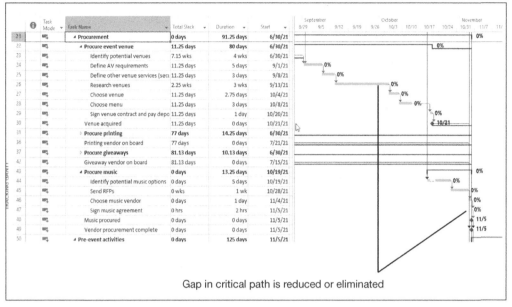

Gap in critical path is reduced or eliminated

Figure 11-7. *By increasing the critical threshold, you can reduce or close gaps in the critical path.*

Now that the critical path is correct, you can hide the Total Slack column if you wish. (Right-click the Total Slack heading in the table, and then choose Hide Column on the shortcut menu.)

Overlapping (Fast-Tracking) Tasks

Fast-tracking is about getting where you're going faster than usual. Unfortunately, just like applying makeup, drinking coffee, and dialing into conference calls *while* driving to work, fast-tracking projects can also increase risk considerably.

Fast-tracking a project means overlapping tasks that usually follow one another. At its best, fast-tracking shortens a project schedule without increasing cost or sacrificing quality. For example, if you're building a new website for event registrations and donations, you could ask the web team to start working on the site's basics before the planning tasks are complete.

The risk is that work done in a predecessor task won't mix with work that's already been done in an overlapping successor task. Backtracking to recover from these wrong turns can negatively affect your project's time, cost, quality, or scope. In the website example, for instance, change requests could require redesigning and recoding the site.

Finding Tasks to Fast-Track

Some tasks are more conducive to overlapping than others. For example, tasks that occur earlier in a project are riskier to overlap. Designs tend to change in the early stages, so if you're scheduling a construction project, you wouldn't want to pour concrete based on early sketches. But once the design is finished and approved, you can overlap plumbing and wiring without too much trouble. You may need to tell each contractor where to start working, but the systems shouldn't interfere as long as everything goes where the architectural plans say it should.

Critical tasks are the tasks to target for fast-tracking, because a shorter critical path means shorter project duration. In addition, long tasks on the critical path are the most effective choices for fast-tracking, because a small percentage of task overlap represents a significant cut in project duration. Moreover, overlapping the longest tasks may shorten the schedule with only a few changes, so you don't have as many risks to monitor. For example, overlapping a 3-month task by 10 percent shortens the critical path by 9 days. If that's the amount you need to shorten the schedule, you have to fast-track only that one task.

Filtering the task list for critical tasks is the easiest way to find tasks to evaluate for fast-tracking. You can then work backward from the finish date looking for critical-path tasks that you can overlap with acceptable risk.

Follow Along Practice

To focus on fast-track candidates, do the following:

1. Hide the summary tasks in the task list by choosing the Format tab, and then in the Show/Hide section, turning off the Summary Tasks checkbox and the Project Summary checkbox.

    If your project uses several WBS levels, summary tasks can outnumber critical tasks, so hiding summary tasks helps you focus on critical work tasks.

2. Apply the Critical filter to view only critical-path tasks.

    Click the down arrow to the right of the Task Name column heading, and then choose Filters→Critical.

3. Jump to the last task in the task list by pressing Ctrl+End, and then work backward, looking at every pair of linked critical tasks for tasks you can overlap.

    For example, in Figure 11-8, "Build event staffing plan" and "Train sales staff" (task IDs 69 and 70) are good candidates for fast-tracking. Both tasks are at least 2 weeks in duration. In this example, suppose you know that the entire sales staff will work at the kickoff. You can start training them before the staffing plan is complete with very little risk.

    In the example project, another pair of candidates are task ID 19 "Plan day of event" (2 months duration) and task ID 68 "Identify event staff duties" (3 weeks duration).

Figure 11-8. *Look for linked critical tasks with longer durations.*

Modifying Task Dependencies to Overlap Tasks

Fast-tracking means starting the next task before its predecessor is complete. When you identify partial overlaps like these, you create them in Project by adding negative lag (also called lead) to the link between the tasks.

Follow Along Practice

The Task Information dialog box is the easiest place to specify lag. The following steps show you how to adjust lag time in task dependencies using the example project:

1. In this example, start by removing the date constraint on task ID 70 "Train sales staff."

    Double-click the row for task 70 "Train sales staff." In the Task Information dialog box, click the Advanced tab. In the "Constraint type" drop-down list, choose As Soon As Possible.

2. While still in the Task Information dialog box, click the Predecessors tab.

3. To overlap tasks 69 and 70, in the Lag cell in the row for task 69, fill in *-8d* and then, click OK.

    Project overlaps the two tasks by 8 days.

4. To overlap tasks 19 and 68, double-click task ID 68 to open the Task Information dialog box. On the Predecessors tab, in the Lag cell for task 19, fill in *-5d*, and then click OK.

    Figure 11-9 shows the updated schedule. In this example, the date for task "Event day" (task ID 84) has moved from the delayed date, 5/4/22, to 4/18/22. The following sections will help bring the event day's date back to what it is supposed to be: 4/11/22.

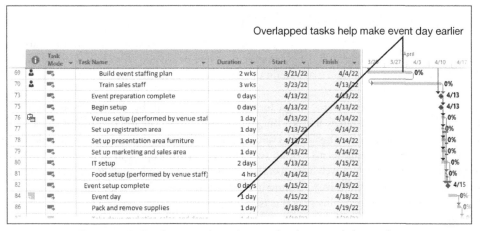

Figure 11-9. *Overlapping tasks on the critical path move task dates earlier.*

Shortening Lag Time Between Tasks

If critical-path tasks have lag time between them, shortening that lag time seems like a simple way to shorten the critical path, since you don't have to jockey resources around or pay more for faster results. But remember: Lag time is there for a reason, like the delay you add while you wait for paint to dry. However, sometimes you can streamline processes to cut lag time.

In projects, approvals can chew up time, especially if you have to wait until the next meeting of stakeholders or the change control board. When you need to shorten the schedule, you can see whether faster turnaround on approvals is feasible. For example, ask stakeholders if they can meet more often or request that people take 2 days to review documents instead of 5.

Just like with fast-tracking, changing lag time between tasks is easiest in the Task Information dialog box. Here's how you shorten lag time:

1. Double-click the task that is the successor in the task dependency you want to change.

   In this example, double-click the row for task 29 "Sign venue contract and pay deposit."

   > **Note:** You select the successor task because the Task Information dialog box displays only predecessors to the selected task.

2. Click the Predecessors tab.

3. To overlap the tasks, in the Lag cell in the row for the predecessor, fill in the new lag time. In this example, click the Lag cell for the task "Choose menu." Change the value to "2d."

4. Click OK.

   The successor task now finishes sooner (in this example, the finish date changes from 10/22/21 to 10/18/21).

Paying More for Faster Delivery

Spending more money to deliver in less time can make financial sense. If you've already sunk a lot of money into your product kickoff's date, changing the event date could cost a bundle more and lead to a lower turnout. Spending more to maintain the date could be worthwhile.

Crashing is the term project managers use for shortening a schedule by spending more money—usually by throwing more resources at tasks. But you can also investigate whether paying extra for faster deliveries from vendors is worthwhile or evaluate whether buying parts is faster than making them. To the uninitiated, crashing seems like an easy choice. If two people can build your website in 12 weeks, for example, then four web developers should be able to wrap it up in only 6 weeks. But reality doesn't always work out that way. And sometimes crashing doesn't work at all. The note titled "When Crashing Doesn't Work" explains several reasons why crashing might not be the best way to shorten a schedule.

It's easy to assume that crashing won't change cost—it looks like you're paying the same rate for the same number of hours. But in reality, there's always a trade-off between time and money. When you crash tasks, you have to choose the tasks that shorten the schedule the amount you need for the least amount of money. That's because every task has a magical duration that results in the minimum cost. If the task runs longer, you spend more money on things like office space, people's salaries and benefits, and keeping the freezer stocked with Cherry Garcia ice cream. Ironically, shorter tasks can cost more, too—for items like additional computers, higher-cost contractors, and managing the larger team it takes to expedite the work. This section explains how to evaluate whether crashing is the right approach for shortening your project.

Time Vs. Money

Stakeholders might open the checkbook to crash a project, but they don't want to spend more than they have to. So it's important to remember that shortening tasks that *aren't* on the critical path is a waste of money, because doing so doesn't change the project's duration one bit. Also, keep in mind that crashing doesn't mean shortening *every* task on the critical path. You crash only enough tasks to shorten the project by the amount you need. Like cars, some tasks cost more to crash than others. Your job is to choose the tasks that shorten the schedule for the least amount of money.

Crash tables can help you compare the cost and time you could save by crashing different tasks. For example, one task might cost an additional $50,000 to cut 2 weeks from the schedule, whereas another task may cut 2 weeks for only $25,000. To choose cost-effective tasks, you have to compare apples to apples—that is, how much it costs for each week of duration you eliminate.

> **Tip:** Long critical tasks are the best candidates for crashing, since you can eliminate longer durations in fewer tasks. Shortening a few long tasks may cost less—and save more time—than crashing a bunch of shorter tasks.

When Crashing Doesn't Work

Say your project's finish date is fast approaching and it's later than planned. The typical reaction to project delays is to throw people at the problem. But adding more people, especially later in the project, may not deliver the schedule-shortening results you seek. Here are some reasons why:

- If you round up additional resources on short notice, they might not be as good as the people already working on the project. They could be available because they're on the B-list, for example. Using second-string resources might reduce the quality of the work.

- In many cases, adding more resources *increases* duration instead of decreasing it. New people need time to get up to speed, so they run up the cost while they're less productive than the original team. The problem can be compounded because the original resources sacrifice productivity when they have to help the new people. And more bodies mean more costs for supervision and communication. To learn more about this phenomenon, read ***The Mythical Man-Month*** (Addison-Wesley, 1995) by Frederick Brooks.

- Sometimes, crashing simply won't work. Some tasks *can't* finish in less time, no matter how many resources you assign. For example, much to the dismay of most pregnant women, you can't assign nine women to have a baby in one month.

Calculating Crash Costs

Using custom fields in Project to calculate crash costs can help you identify which tasks to crash. Ideally, you want to crash the tasks with the lowest crash cost per week—and you also want to crash the fewest tasks to get the duration reduction you need. One task might offer several weeks' worth of low-cost crashing. However, if shortening that task by 1 day takes it off the critical path, then there's little point spending money to shorten it. The most effective approach is to crash one task at a time (by making the crash modifications in Project), and then evaluate the critical path again to see what the next step should be. (The LinkedIn Learning course, Managing Budget-Constrained Projects with Microsoft Project, also shows how to calculate crash cost in Project.)

To decide which tasks to crash, you need to see how much tasks cost per week of reduction in duration. That way, you can choose the most cost-effective tasks to crash. All you have to do is create a custom table with a few custom fields. Here's how:

Follow Along Practice

1. If necessary, with a task-oriented view (like Tracking Chart) displayed, click the down arrow to the right of the Task Name column heading, and then choose Filters→Critical.

   In the example project, summary tasks are already hidden. If you haven't hidden summary tasks, head to the Gantt Chart Tools | Format tab. In the Hide/Show section, turn off the Summary Tasks checkbox.

2. To create a custom table, in the View tab's Data section, click the Tables button, and then choose "Save Fields as a New Table" on the drop-down menu.

3. In the Save Table dialog box that appears, in the Name box, type a name for the new table, in this example, **_C_Crash Cost_**. Click OK.

    Beginning the name with a prefix like "C_" makes it easy to differentiate custom tables you've created from built-in tables.

4. To insert a column for duration reduction, right-click a column heading, such as Duration, and then choose Insert Column on the shortcut menu. In the drop-down menu, choose Duration10.

    Because duration reduction is a span of time, you use a Duration-type custom field. This example uses Duration10 in case you've already set up Duration1 through 9 for other purposes.

5. To edit the field, right-click its heading, and then choose Custom Fields on the shortcut menu.

    Project opens the Custom Fields dialog box and selects Duration10.

6. Click the Rename button. In the Rename Field dialog box, type **_Duration Reduction (Weeks)_** as shown in Figure 11-10, and then click OK. In the Custom Fields dialog box, click OK to close it.

    In the view table, Project fills in the fields with "0 days." You'll fill in these fields with values later.

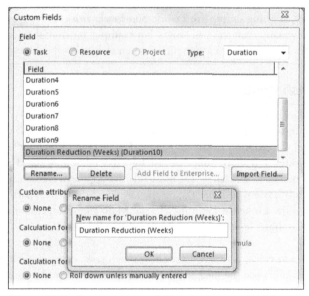

Figure 11-10. *Rename a custom field to give it a meaningful name.*

7. To insert a column for crash cost, repeat steps 4-6 with the following information. Insert the custom field Cost10 (because the crash cost is a monetary value). Open the Custom Fields dialog box and rename the field to "Crash Cost." Click OK.

8. To insert a column for crash cost per week, insert the custom field Cost9. Rename the field to "Crash Cost per Week."

The Crash Cost per Week field needs to calculate the result. In the following steps, you define the formula for this field.

9. While the Custom Fields dialog box is still open and Crash Cost per Week is selected, click the Formula button beneath the field list.

   The Formula for 'Crash Cost per Week' dialog box opens.

10. Click the Field button, point at Cost on the drop-down menu, point at Custom Cost on the submenu, and then choose Crash Cost.

11. Beneath the formula box, click the "/" button (for division).

12. Click the Field button, point at Duration on the drop-down menu, point at Custom Duration on the submenu, and then choose Duration Reduction (Weeks).

13. In the Formula dialog box, click at the beginning of the formula, and then click the "(" button to insert an open parenthesis.

14. Click at the end of the formula, and then click the ")" button to insert a closing parenthesis.

15. To convert the duration value to weeks, click the "*" button and then type **2400**. Figure 11-11 shows what the formula should look like.

   Project stores duration in minutes. To calculate the cost per week correctly, you need to multiply the result by the number of minutes in a work week: 60 minutes per hour multiplied by 8 hours per day multiplied by 5 days per week, or 2400.

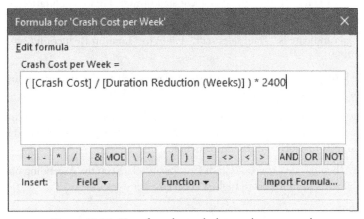

Figure 11-11. *Use a formula to calculate crash cost per week.*

16. Click OK to save the formula. In the message box that warns you about existing data being deleted, click OK. Click OK to close the Custom Fields dialog box.

   You might notice that "Crash Cost per Week" cells include the text "#ERROR." That's because the Crash Cost values are currently zero, so the formula is dividing by zero. As soon as you fill in values, the errors will disappear.

Choosing Tasks to Crash

Finally, you're ready to choose the tasks to crash. Here are the steps using the example project:

Follow Along Practice

1. To list the longest critical tasks first, click the down arrow to the right of the Duration column heading (you may need to widen the table portion of the view to see that field), and then choose "Sort Largest to Smallest."

    Since you evaluate the longest tasks and crash only a few, you sort the critical tasks by duration, so the longest tasks appear at the top of the task list.

2. Fill in each crash candidate's row with the total amount of time you can shorten the task, and how much it costs to do so.

    In the example project, the first task listed ("Implement publicity plan") has a long duration, but isn't a crash candidate. That's because it's an administrative task that continues until the event occurs. "Recruit sponsors" is another administrative task that isn't a crash candidate.

    a) The second task listed, task ID 19 "Plan day of event," is the first crash candidate. In this task's Duration Reduction (Weeks) cell, fill in 2w. Press the Tab key to move to the Crash Cost cell, and then type *1000*. Press Enter.

        Project calculates the Crash Cost per Week to be $500.00.

    b) The next candidate task is "Identify event staff duties." Fill in its Duration Reduction (1w) and its Crash Cost (2000).

    c) The final candidate is "Train sales staff." Fill in its Duration Reduction (2w) and its Crash Cost (2000).

3. To find the least expensive tasks to crash, sort the rows first by the amount of duration reduction and then by the crash cost per week.

    a) On the View tab, click the Sort down arrow, and then choose Sort By. In the "Sort by" box, choose Duration Reduction (Weeks). Keep the Descending option selected so the table sorts from longest to shortest duration reduction.

    b) In the "Then by" box choose "Crash Cost per Week. Keep the Ascending option selected, so the table sorts from lowest to highest crash cost per week.

    c) Click Sort.

    As shown in Figure 11-12, the task with a 2-week duration reduction and the lowest crash cost per week ($500) is listed first. Then the task with the 2-week reduction at $1,000 per week is listed before the task that only reduces the duration by 1 week.

    Figure 11-12 shows what the table should look like.

	❶	Task Mode ▾	Task Name	Duration Reduction ▾	Crash Cost ▾	Crash Cost per Week ▾	Duration ▾	
19		▪	Plan day of event	2 wks	$1,000.00	$500.00	2 mons	
70	👤	▪	Train sales staff	2 wks	$2,000.00	$1,000.00	3 wks	
68		▪	Identify event staff duties	1 wk	$2,000.00	$2,000.00	3 wks	
1		▪	Project start	0 days	$0.00	#ERROR	0 days	
4		▪	Identify core event team	0 days	$0.00	#ERROR	3 days	
5		▪	Define event goals and objectives	0 days	$0.00	#ERROR	4.5 days	

For same crash cost per week, longer duration reductions appear first

Lower crash costs are listed first

Figure 11-12. *The most cost effective candidates appear at the top of the list.*

Crashing Tasks

Finally, you're ready to modify crash candidates to shorten the schedule. Here are the steps using the example project:

1. In the "Plan day of event" task's Duration cell, fill in the shorter duration.

    In this example, Task ID 84 event day is currently scheduled for 4/18/22 and needs to move back 1 week to 4/11/22. "Plan day of event" has duration of 2 months. In the "Plan day of event" task's Duration cell, type *7w* and press Enter to change its duration to 7 weeks.

    > **Tip:** To keep track of which tasks you've crashed, you can add a note describing what you did. In this example, right-click the task and choose Notes on the shortcut menu. In the box on the Notes tab, type something like "Task crashed by hiring a consultant. Fixed price $500."

2. Scroll down to find Task ID 84 "Event day" and check its Start date.

    In this example, the task is now back to the correct date. That means you don't have to crash any additional tasks.

3. If necessary, add the crash cost you spent to the task.

    How you record the crash cost depends on what you do to shorten the task duration. For example, if you use more resources or more expensive resources, the resource assignment changes you make will automatically change the task cost.

    In this example, suppose you pay an event consultant $500 for an event template, which saves your team a week of planning. You can include that cost with a cost resource.

    a) On the View tab, click Resource Sheet.

    b) Click the first blank Resource Name cell, type ***Consultant***. Press Tab to jump to the Type cell, type ***C*** to choose Cost as the type, and then press Enter.

c) On the View tab, click the bottom half of the Gantt Chart button, and then choose Tracking Gantt. In the View tab Data section, set the Filter box to [No Filter].

d) Select the task (in this example, "Plan day of event"). If you don't see Task ID 19, remove the critical task filter. (The decrease in duration to 7w has removed it from the critical task list.)

e) If necessary, on the View tab, turn on the Details check box, and then choose Task Form in the drop-down list.

f) In the Task Form in the Details pane, click the first blank Resource Name cell, and then choose Consultant. Click OK.

g) To add the cost, right-click the Task Form, and choose Cost on the shortcut menu.

h) In the Consultant's Cost cell, type **500**. Click OK.

Figure 11-13 shows what the task looks like after it's been crashed.

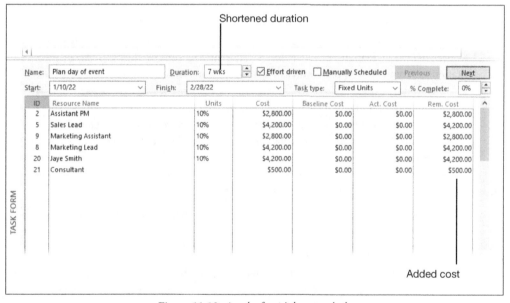

Figure 11-13. *A task after it's been crashed.*

Repeat these steps until the project's duration is the length you want—or the cost prohibits shortening it any further.

Cleaning Up the Example Schedule

If you've been following along in the example project, the schedule still needs some cleanup. This section describes the tweaks to make.

Follow Along Practice

First, restore the view to the way it was before crashing:

1. On the View tab, click the Tables button, and then choose Entry.

2. Display all tasks in the list (in the Filter box drop-down list, choose [No Filter] or Clear Filter).

3. To list the tasks in their original order, click the Sort button, and then choose "by ID."

4. Click the primary pane to make the Tracking Gantt view active. On the Format tab, turn on the "Project Summary Task" check box and the "Summary Tasks" check box. Change the table in the view to Entry.

Here are the changes you need to make in the schedule:

1. Adjust task ID 66 "Monitor registrations" so it finishes immediately before the event.

    This task should run from the time registration opens to when registration closes, which is known as a ***hammock task*** in project management lingo. (Chapter 25 describes one way to create a hammock task.) In this example, simply shorten the task duration so it ends the day of the event. To do this, click the task's Duration cell in the view table, type the shorter duration, in this example, "19w," and then press Enter.

    The task now ends on 4/11/22.

2. Remove the resource overallocations on task ID 70 "Train sales staff" and task ID 71 "Train technical staff."

    One of the schedule-shortening changes made earlier in this chapter was to schedule two of the training classes at the same time. That change overallocated the marketing content developer who teaches both classes. In this example, suppose you decide that you can train the sales team and the technical sales team at the same time. Here are the steps to make this change:

    a) In the Tracking Gantt view, right-click task ID 71 "Train technical staff" task, and then choose Delete Task on the shortcut menu.

    b) Select task ID 70 "Train sales staff."

    c) In the Task Form in the Details pane, turn off the "Effort driven" checkbox, so the duration and existing work assignments remain the same when you add a resource to the task.

    d) In the Task Form table, click the first blank Resource Name cell, click the down arrow that appears, and the choose Technical Sales Team in the drop-down menu.

> **Note:** In this example, the units for both the Sales Team and Technical Sales Team are set to 100% because each team is assigned to 120 hours of training during the task's 3 weeks. The Marketing Content Developer is responsible for scheduling when and how many people attend each training session.

3. Change the duration for the task "IT setup" (task ID 79) to one day.

> **Note:** Although the Venue Team appears to be overallocated in the schedule, you can ignore those overallocations. The manager for the venue is responsible for scheduling that team.

4. Add a Must Start On date constraint to the "Event day" task (task ID 83).

    Although date constraints have their disadvantages, the event in this example must occur on 4/11/22. By creating a Must Start On date constraint, Project will display a missed date constraint indicator in the task's Indicators cell to warn you when the task starts later than that. To add the constraint, double-click the task in the Tracking Gantt view. In the Task Information dialog box, click the Advanced tab. In the "Constraint type" box, choose Must Start On. In the "Constraint date" box, type 4/11/22. Click OK.

Now the schedule is the way it should be. The next section describes a few techniques for reducing cost.

Reducing Project Costs

You've diligently entered costs into your Project file and either looked at the resulting cost totals as described in Chapter 10 or compared your planned costs against your budget, as described in Chapter 15. If your target is $100,000 and your costs are coming out to $130,000, you have to figure out how to trim $30,000 from your planned project costs or heads will roll—most likely yours. How do you go about cutting thousands of dollars from a project? Answer: very carefully.

First, look at your cost assumptions to make sure mistakes haven't sent project costs into the stratosphere. If you're lucky, you can correct a misplaced zero and everything will be hunky-dory. The next line of defense is to examine resource assignments to look for ways to cut costs.

This section discusses each of these cost-cutting techniques. However, if these methods aren't enough to solve your budget crisis, it's time to take a hard look at the budget itself and propose a change to the project's budget, scope, or schedule.

Checking for Cost Errors

When your TV suddenly doesn't turn on or you can't get the channel that's showing world championship bass fishing, you probably don't schedule a technician service call right away. You poke around, hit buttons on the remote, turn things off and on, and see if the picture comes back. If you're really thinking straight, the very first thing you check is whether your dog accidentally unplugged the TV cables or power cord again.

The same troubleshooting principle applies when planned project costs don't jibe with your budget. Don't assume that the project is really $30,000 over budget just yet. Look for errors, starting with the simple, most obvious things first. In this section, you'll learn how to systematically scan your project schedule for mistakes in cost values or calculations.

To look at your schedule and associated costs, display the Gantt Chart view (on the View tab, click the Gantt Chart button) and then apply the Summary table (on the View tab, click the Tables button, and then choose Summary). In the example project, the total cost is $532,250.

> **Note:** The example project doesn't have any cost errors.

Here are cost-related items to check and where to look for them:

- **Task duration**: Review task durations for any that approach the length of geologic eras. An excessive duration could be a mistake, such as a typo in the Duration field or a resource assigned to work only a few minutes a day. Durations affect cost because Project calculates labor costs by multiplying labor rates by the work that contributes to the duration.

- **Cost per use**: In the Resource Sheet view, look for values in the Cost Per Use column (Chapter 6). Remember that a cost per use is levied for each task a resource is assigned to. For example, suppose a crane costs $5,000 to get it on site. If you apply the $5,000 as cost per use and then assign the crane to six tasks, your project cost includes $30,000 for crane setup instead of only $5,000. In this situation, a cost resource for getting the crane on site makes more sense than cost per use. On the other hand, a consultant may include a $100 travel fee each time she comes to your office. If a resource has a standard rate combined with a cost per use, make sure they're both legitimate.

- **Resource rate**: Also in the Resource Sheet view, review the rates you've assigned to human, equipment, and material resources. If you have a lot of resources, consider sorting the view by standard rate so that excessively high or low rates stand out. (For example, if a janitor comes out higher than an information architect, someone's standard rate is off.) To do so, click the down arrow to the right of the Std. Rate column heading and then, on the drop-down menu, choose Sort Descending. To return the view to its normal order, in the View tab's Data section, click Sort→"by ID."

- **Cost resource amount**: To easily review cost resource amounts, display the Resource Usage view (in the View tab's Resource Views section, click Resource Usage), apply the Cost table as explained in the previous bullet point, and then group the view by resource type (click the down arrow to the right of the Resource Name column heading and then, on the drop-down menu, choose "Group by"→Resource Type). Scroll down to the Type: Cost grouping, as shown in Figure 11-14. To return the view to its normal ungrouped arrangement, click the down arrow to the right of the Resource Name column heading and then, on the drop-down menu, choose No Group.

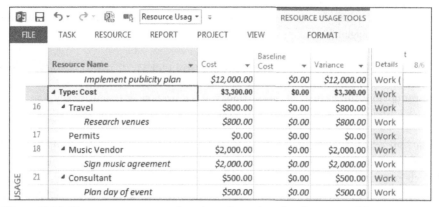

Resource Name	Cost	Baseline Cost	Variance	Details	t 8/6
Implement publicity plan	*$12,000.00*	*$0.00*	*$12,000.00*	Work (	
▲ **Type: Cost**	**$3,300.00**	**$0.00**	**$3,300.00**	Work	
16 ▲ Travel	$800.00	$0.00	$800.00	Work	
Research venues	*$800.00*	*$0.00*	*$800.00*	Work	
17 Permits	$0.00	$0.00	$0.00	Work	
18 ▲ Music Vendor	$2,000.00	$0.00	$2,000.00	Work	
Sign music agreement	*$2,000.00*	*$0.00*	*$2,000.00*	Work	
21 ▲ Consultant	$500.00	$0.00	$500.00	Work	
Plan day of event	*$500.00*	*$0.00*	*$500.00*	Work	

Figure 11-14. *The group summary row here shows the total cost for all resources of that resource type.*

- **Fixed cost for tasks**: If you used the Fixed Cost field, in the Gantt Chart view, check any fixed costs for tasks to see if they have one or two zeroes too many. Apply the Cost table to the view (in the View tab's Data section, click Tables→Cost), and then sort by the Fixed Cost field. (Click the down arrow to the right of the Fixed Cost column heading and then, on the drop-down menu, choose "Sort Largest to Smallest" to see the highest fixed costs at the top of the view.) Make sure you're not using a fixed cost *and* a cost resource for the same expense on the same task.

After you've thoroughly reviewed resource cost assumptions and task information that affects cost, be sure to take a closer look at the budget itself. Rather than being carved into stone by lightning bolts from on high, the budget is prepared by a human being like you. Check the assumptions in the budget, and make sure someone hasn't made any outlandish mistakes there.

Adjusting Assignments to Reduce Cost

If you've adjusted the schedule to optimize your costs but you still have more belt tightening to do, try adjusting resource assignments. Here are a couple of strategies to try:

- **Replace expensive resources with cheaper ones**: Consider having your more experienced (and probably more expensive) resources mentor your less costly resources on tasks for a short time, rather than working entire task durations. Or use cheaper in-house—perhaps borrowed—resources rather than more expensive outside consultants, as shown in Figure 11-15. On the other hand, sometimes hiring temporary contract labor is cheaper than using your in-house employees.

Follow Along Practice

Here's an example of using a less expensive resource:

a) Display the Resource Sheet view (on the View tab, click Resource Sheet), and then apply the Cost table (in the View tab's Data section, click Tables→Cost).

b) To see the resources with the highest costs, sort the view by the Cost field (click the down arrow to the right of the Cost column heading and then, on the drop-down menu, choose

"Sort Largest to Smallest"). In this example, the Marketing Content Developer is one of the resources that contributes significant cost to the project and you decide that a less expensive technical writer can help on those tasks.

c)   If necessary, create a new resource. (Display the Entry table. In the first blank Resource Name cell, type **Technical Writer**. In the Std. Rate cell in that row, type **75**, and then press Enter.)

d)   Switch to the Gantt Chart view (on the View tab, click the Gantt Chart button) and display the Summary table (on the View tab, click the Tables button, and then choose Summary).

e)   On the View tab, click the Filter down arrow, and then choose Using Resource on the drop-down menu. In the Using Resource dialog box, click the down arrow and then choose Marketing Content Developer and click OK.

f)   Select the "Develop event materials" task (task ID 57). It's cost is $51,200.

g)   In the Task Form, right-click and choose Resources & Predecessors, if necessary. Click the Work cell in the Marketing Content Developer's row. Type **120**.

h)   Before clicking OK, in the next blank Resource Name cell, choose Technical Writer. In the Work cell in that row, type **200**.

i)   Click OK. The task shortens to 8 weeks and the cost decreases to $46,200.

In this example, on the View tab, choose [No Filter] or Clear Filter in the Filter box to display the entire task list.

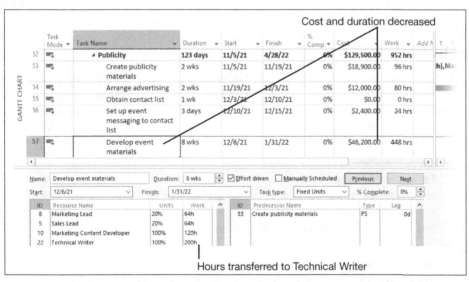

Figure 11-15. *By adding a less expensive resource, the task duration and cost decreased.*

- **Do away with overtime**: If your current schedule involves overtime (and your resources cost more when they work overtime), see if you can adjust assignments to eliminate overtime. Chapter 14 explains how to use overtime in Project.

Rethinking Your Budget

If your best efforts on project costs still don't line them up with the project's budget, then it's time for renegotiation. You've checked and rechecked that your costs reflect the project's reality—as you know it so far. The next step is talking to the customer, the project sponsor, or whichever head honcho holds the purse strings. There are two choices in this situation.

- **Increase the budget**: The first and usually most difficult option is trying to get more money appropriated for the project.

- **Cut back on project scope or quality**: Cutting the number of tasks (for example, axing a particular phase), or reducing quality objectives can cut costs—but only if all the stakeholders agree. If the stakeholders find more money and decide to add the scope back in, you can reactivate those tasks in no time.

Playing What-If Games

There's more than one way to skin a cat—or schedule a project. The project's stakeholders may ask for the moon—but when they see how much it costs to land on that hunk of rock, they might backpedal and ask for alternative plans. They'll have questions like, "How much less would it cost if we cut this portion of the scope?", "How much longer will it take if we add these change requests to the schedule?" and, invariably, "Why can't we do all this extra work in the same timeframe and for the same cost?" In Project, inactive tasks (available in Project Professional) and the Compare Project feature help you evaluate alternatives. This section shows you how to use both.

Inactivating Tasks

If nothing seems to shorten your project's schedule or reduce its budget, a reduction in scope may be in order. As project manager, you can't arbitrarily eliminate scope. Only the stakeholders can redefine the scope, and even then, only if the project's customer or sponsor approves. Decisions have a way of changing, so making tasks inactive is a great way to cut scope. Should the stakeholders decide to revert to the original schedule later on, you can reactivate the inactive tasks without skipping a beat.

> **Tip:** Inactive tasks also work well if you want to document nice-to-have work. Create tasks, assign resources to them, and fill in other fields; then make the tasks inactive. That way, their values are visible (and editable) but don't affect your project schedule. If you find that the project has the time and budget for the work, then you can make them active.

Making tasks inactive removes their values from your project's rolled-up schedule and cost. However, the tasks, their resource assignments, and field values remain in the schedule, as Figure 11-16 shows, so you have a record of what you cut out. You can edit inactive tasks just as you do active tasks. If you reactivate the tasks, you don't have to re-enter any information.

Follow Along Practice

Changing tasks to inactive is a snap in Project Professional:

1. Select one or more tasks in a task-oriented view. In this example, select all the "Procure music" tasks by dragging over task IDs 43 through 48.

2. In the Task tab's Schedule section, click Inactivate.

    The inactive tasks immediately change to gray with a line drawn through their values in the table area. Inactive task bars are white with a light gray outline. However, you can edit an inactive task's values by double-clicking it to open the Task Information dialog box or by editing values directly in the table cells.

3. If you're following along, save the file you've been working on and call it Event_Ch11_compare. mpp.

> **Note:** Inactivating tasks frees up time that was previously scheduled for assigned resources. If you inactivate tasks to reduce scope, then relevel the assigned resources to see the effect on the schedule. The resources have more time available so their other assignments may finish sooner.

To *reactivate* a task, select it and then, in the Task tab's Schedule section, click Inactivate again. In this example, select the music tasks, and then click Inactivate again.

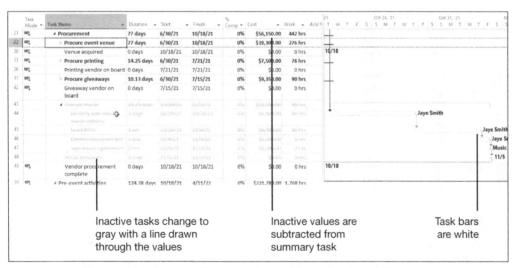

Inactive tasks change to gray with a line drawn through the values

Inactive values are subtracted from summary task

Task bars are white

Figure 11-16. *Inactive tasks are grayed out and have a line through their values.*

Comparing Projects

For more involved what-if games, it can be useful to make a second copy of your Project file. With a backup safely in place, you can edit to your heart's content while keeping both the original file and the new one. That way, you can examine both options in detail to see which is better. For example, you may save copies of a Project file at different stages of project execution or to compare changes in the critical path as you shorten it. Or perhaps a colleague sent you a revised copy of the project schedule and you want to identify what the differences are between it and the one that you prepared.

Happily, when you want to compare two Project files, you don't have to open the files side by side, planting your left and right index fingers on the computer screen as you scan through the corresponding fields in each file. Project's Compare Projects feature simplifies these types of comparisons. The Compare Projects feature produces a report that compares values from two files side by side along with a column showing the difference between the two. In addition, the timescale includes two sets of task bars, so you can visually compare when tasks start and finish.

> **Note:** In this section, you can compare Event_Ch11_compare.mpp with the original downloaded file Event_Ch11_start.mpp.

Follow Along Practice

Here's how to compare two versions of the same project:

1. Open the two Project files you want to compare (Event_Ch11_compare.mpp and Event_Ch11_ start.mpp).

2. Display the one that's your current version.

    To do that, on the View tab, in the Window section, click Switch Windows, and then choose the project, in this example, "Event_Ch11_compare."

3. Choose Report→Compare Projects.

    The Compare Project Versions dialog box opens with the "Compare the current project ([project_name]) to this previous version" label at the top, where [project name] is the name of the active project, in this example, "Event_Ch11_compare."

4. If Project hasn't filled in the filename box with the correct project name, in the drop-down list, choose the name of the file you want to compare with the current file (whether it's a previous version or an alternative schedule).

    In this example, Project automatically fills in Event_Ch11_start. If the other file isn't open, click Browse and then, in the Open dialog box, choose the file you want to compare.

> **Note:** The Compare Projects feature uses the word "current" to identify the values for the first file you selected and "previous" to identify the values for the file you selected in the Compare Project Versions dialog box. That's why it's easier to keep things straight if you select your current file first.

5. In the Task Table drop-down list, choose the table that contains the fields you want to compare, in this example, choose Summary.

    The comparison table that Compare Projects builds can become unwieldy because it includes three columns for each field in the original table you selected. To focus on the information you care about most, consider creating a custom table (Chapter 20) that contains only the fields you want to compare. For example, for tasks, you might include Task Name, Duration, Finish Date, and Cost.

    > **Tip:** To ensure that the comparison works correctly, be sure to apply the same tables (containing the same fields) in both files.

6. In the Resource Table drop-down list, choose the table that contains the resource fields you want to compare (in this example, keep Entry selected).

7. Click OK.

    A message box tells you that Project is creating a comparison report, and windows flicker on and off for a few seconds. Click OK to continue. If you have Project set up to display the Project Information dialog box when you create a new project, you'll see the Project Information box, because Project creates a new project file to contain the comparison. Click OK.

    When things calm down, you see a Comparison Report pane at the top and the two versions you're comparing at the bottom, as Figure 11-17 shows.

A legend on the left side of the Comparison Report window identifies the symbols it uses:

*   Tasks that appear only in the current project include a + sign.

*   Tasks that appear only in the previous version include a – sign to indicate that they've been removed in the current version.

*   The task bars for the current version are green.

*   The task bars for the previous version are blue.

*   For each column in the table you selected, the Comparison Report displays three columns. For example, the "Cost: Current" column shows the cost for the first file you selected; "Cost: Previous" shows the cost for the second file you selected; and "Cost: Diff" shows the difference between those two values.

Figure 11-17. *When you compare two versions of a project, the Comparison Report window appears at the top of the main Project window.*

While you're looking at the comparison between the two files, the Compare Projects tab sits between the File tab and the Task tab on the ribbon. On the Compare Projects tab, you can click Task Comparison or Resource Comparison to switch between the task table and resource table you specified. In the tab's Show section, you can choose a filter in the box to the right of the Filter icon to examine different aspects of the comparison. For example, in the drop-down list, choose "Changed items" to see only the tasks or resources that changed between the two versions. You can also view items that appear only in the current or previous version. If you want to view a task in each version, select the task in the Comparison Report window and then, in the Compare Projects tab's Compare section, click "Go to Item." Project highlights the task in the windows for each version.

12

Saving the Project Plan and Schedule

A plan is merely a ***proposed*** plan until the stakeholders accept it and commit their approval in writing. Once you obtain the stakeholders' approval, it's time to save an official, approved version of your project plan. This approved plan wears a lot of hats during the life of your project. It's documentation of the agreed-upon scope, schedule, budget, and so on; when questions arise later, you can turn to the approved plan to help sort them out. The project plan also acts as a reference for the project team as they do their work. Finally, the project plan contains the targets you've set for the project. As the team performs the project work, you compare actual performance to the plan to see whether you're on the right track.

A project plan isn't stored in a single file. Saving a project plan means saving an approved copy of ***every*** file that contributes to the plan. This chapter talks about setting up a storage system not only for the planning documents, but also for files generated during the rest of the project's life. You'll learn about different ways to store project files and how to structure project information so it's easy to find and manage.

For some types of files, saving a copy is as simple as appending ***v1.0*** to the end of the filename, but Project files require more attention. This chapter describes how to set a baseline in your Project schedule so you can compare your planned schedule and cost to what you actually achieve. You'll learn how to set baselines at several points during a project to watch for trends over time. Finally, you'll find out how to view baselines in Project, either alone or in comparison to actual performance.

Obtaining Approval for the Plan

With the convenience of email distribution lists and shared file storage, you may be tempted to email project stakeholders and ask them to review the plan and email their approvals back to you—without holding a sign-off meeting to make sure everyone understands what they're approving. Unfortunately, the attached plan is likely to sit unread in all those email inboxes. You may receive approvals, but they may get unapologetically revoked later when people realize that the plan doesn't meet their needs.

To obtain approvals that really stick, set up a sign-off meeting to review the plan and snag approvals then and there. Here are some tips for a successful sign-off:

1. Distribute the project plan in advance, and urge the stakeholders to read it before the meeting.

    You can hand out hard copies, send the plan as an email attachment, or place a copy of the plan online where everyone can access it. The sign-off meeting (described in the next step) provides some motivation for the stakeholders to read the plan beforehand.

2. At the sign-off meeting, don't assume that the stakeholders have read the plan.

    Your job as project manager is to present the plan at the meeting, covering its key aspects and pointing out potential conflicts, problems, and risks. Encourage questions and discussion—this is your last chance to hash out issues before changes have to go through your organization's change-control process. To jump-start the discussion, ask stakeholders pointed questions about the areas you see as potential problems.

3. A nod or a verbal "yes" doesn't constitute approval; circulate the sign-off page and ask everyone to actually sign it.

Storing Project Documents

Even small projects generate an astounding amount of information. Initially, the project plan is a collection of requirements and specification documents, budget spreadsheets, the schedule in Project, and so on. Don't forget the draft documents you generated before you obtained approval, and the emails and memos that flew around as planning progressed. When project execution starts, the amount of information expands exponentially because of project results like design documents, contracts for services, software that's been written, databases, and blueprints. Meanwhile, managing the project produces status reports, change request forms, and so on.

The container for project documentation is usually called a ***project notebook*** or Project Management Information System (PMIS). In the good old days it was a three-ring binder (or several) that held paper copies of every project-related document. These days, a PMIS tends to be electronic, with files stored somewhere on a computer or in the cloud. Either way, you need a filing system so everyone can find and access the information they need.

The best project filing system depends on the project: what sort of information it produces, who needs access to that info, any security issues, and the standards your organization follows. The choice boils down to structure and technology. You need a way to track various versions of documents and deliverables—for instance, things like contracts, designs, drawings, and so on. In addition, you may need a system to manage document access and changes. For example, all team members can read the project requirements to see what their tasks are supposed to deliver, but only a few authorized team members can ***modify*** those requirements.

Regardless of the storage technology you use, you need to structure the information so that finding it isn't an Easter egg hunt. Project information typically falls into a few high-level categories that you can use to build the basic storage structure (as illustrated in Figure 12-1):

- **Project deliverables**: Deliverables are the tangible results that a project produces. Because payment often hinges on these deliverables becoming reality, you want them to be easy to find and control. Having separate subfolders within this category for draft and final versions make it even easier to see whether a deliverable is complete.

Figure 12-1. *You can design an information hierarchy with different storage tools.*

- **Project-management deliverables**: Managing a project produces all kinds of intermediate deliverables, like the project plan, status reports, and change request logs. Separate folders for different types of info can forestall information overload. However, the best way to break down this information depends on what makes the most sense to you. For example, you might organize it by project-management phase with folders for planning, execution, control, and closure. Or you may prefer to organize it by project-management activities: planning, communication, finance, risk management, change control, and so on.

- **Reference**: Projects almost always include background information that can be essential. For example, you may need to refer to your organization's strategic plan, but that document isn't part of your product launch project.

- **Project work**: All the work products that team members produce have to go somewhere, but (happily) where to store them may not be your problem. For example, software-development projects often store and manage code in source-control systems. In other cases, teams may set up their own work areas and organize their files as they see fit, delivering their work to you when it's complete.

Document Management Options

How you store project documents depends on the technology available to you. If your organization uses Microsoft Enterprise Project Management Solutions, SharePoint provides document libraries and places for tracking issues and risks.

If you don't have power tools like this, don't despair. Your far-flung project teams can share documents in plenty of other ways:

- **Microsoft OneDrive**: With this cloud storage service, people can upload, access, and sync files between a OneDrive location and their computers and other devices, or through a web browser.

- **Other cloud storage services**: If you use a cloud storage service that's registered with Microsoft Office, the service appears in the Open and Save As screens of the Backstage view.

- **SharePoint**: You don't need Project Server or the cloud version, which is called Project Online, to set up a SharePoint server for sharing documents. For example, if you use Office 365 for midsize businesses, you can store files in an Office 365 SharePoint location or if you are using the SharePoint files location from within Microsoft Teams. A SharePoint website can carry out workflow processes, such as checking documents in and out, storing multiple versions of a document, or requiring approvals before documents proceed to the next step. You can also set SharePoint permissions to control who can read or write to different areas. Moreover, Project Professional lets you export project files to a SharePoint list (you need SharePoint 2010 Foundation or later), so you can share project information with anyone who's interested.

- **Directory structure**: Forgoing fancier tools, you can simply set up folders on a shared network disk drive and use file-naming conventions to track versions of documents. For example, track document versions by appending the date saved to filenames. When a file reaches a milestone, such as Approved, you can add that to the filename as well.

Preserving the Original Schedule in Project

After stakeholders approve a project plan and its schedule, they want the project team to follow that plan and schedule. If it *doesn't*, the stakeholders expect an explanation of the difference between planned and actual performance (called *variance*). A variance is the foundation of a variety of project performance measures (Chapter 14), like earned value and the schedule performance index. To calculate variance, you first have to save the original planned values in your Project schedule.

As you've seen in previous chapters, Project constantly updates fields like dates, duration, work, and cost as you make changes (as long as tasks are set up as automatically scheduled, that is). For example, if you increase the work hours for a task, Project recalculates the task's duration and finish date. When you begin to track progress, Project continues these recalculations; for example, as a delayed predecessor task pushes the start dates of its successors later.

Fortunately, Project has no problem keeping track of both your original schedule and the current one. When you *set a baseline* (explained in the next section), the program stores the original schedule in a *baseline*, which is a snapshot of schedule and cost information. At the same time, the schedule you see every time you open Project is the *current* schedule, which shows the schedule and cost based on any revisions you've made, as well as the effects of actual performance. Project uses baseline values and current values to calculate variances and other performance measures, as you'll learn in Chapter 14.

A baseline doesn't save *all* the info that resides in a Project file. From hundreds of Project fields, a baseline saves key schedule and cost values for each task, resource, and assignment in the Project file. The following fields show the information stored in Project's primary baseline, appropriately named *Baseline*, but the fields in other baselines (which are named Baseline1 through Baseline10) work the same way:

- **Baseline Start**: Shows the values that were in Start fields for tasks and assignments when you set the baseline. For automatically scheduled tasks, Project calculates these dates; for manually scheduled tasks, it uses the dates you specify.

- **Baseline Estimated Start**: In most cases, when you set a baseline, this field gets filled in with the Scheduled Start date that Project calculates. For automatically scheduled tasks, Baseline Start and Baseline Estimated Start are *always* identical. If you fill in a manually scheduled task's Start field with a date, Project copies that date to Baseline Estimated Start when you set a baseline. However, if you leave a manually scheduled task's Start field blank or type a note in that field, Project copies the Scheduled Start value (the start date that Project recommends for the task) to the Baseline Estimated Start field when you set a baseline.

- **Baseline Finish**: Shows the values that were in Finish fields for tasks and assignments when you set the baseline. For automatically scheduled tasks, Baseline Finish represents the dates Project calculates; for manually scheduled tasks, it represents the dates you specify.

- **Baseline Estimated Finish**: When you set a baseline, this field usually copies its values from the Scheduled Finish dates Project calculates. If you type a date in a manually scheduled task's Finish field, Project copies that date to this Baseline Estimated Finish field when you set a baseline. And if you leave a manually scheduled task's Finish field blank or type a note in that field, Project sets the Baseline Estimated Finish field to one day after the task's start date.

> **Note:** With manually scheduled tasks, Scheduled Start and Scheduled Finish fields may not contain values (Chapter 4). The Baseline Estimated Start and Baseline Estimated Finish fields are specifically for manually scheduled tasks *without* specified date values. Project sets these fields to the dates that most closely match where the tasks occur in the project schedule. For example, a top-level manually scheduled task without dates or duration has a Baseline Estimated Start date that's the same as the project start date. A manually scheduled subtask without dates has a Baseline Estimated Start date equal to its summary task's start date.

- **Baseline Duration**: Represents the planned duration of tasks based on the Baseline Start and Baseline Finish dates.

- **Baseline Estimated Duration**: Shows the duration based on the Baseline Estimated Start and Baseline Estimated Finish dates.

- **Baseline Work**: Contains the planned person-hours for tasks, resources, and assignments. For example, if you display the Baseline table in the Gantt Chart view, the Baseline Work field shows the total planned work for each task when the baseline was set. However, if you include the Baseline Work field in the Resource Sheet view, the field indicates the hours that were assigned to each resource when you set the baseline. In addition, the Baseline Work field in a time-phased view like Task Usage shows planned work for each time period.

- **Baseline Cost**: Represents the planned cost of tasks, resources, and assignments when the baseline was set. This field stores time-phased cost, so views like Task Usage and Resource Usage show baseline costs for each time period.

- **Baseline Budget Work**: Saves the budgeted person-hours (Chapter 15) for work resources and budgeted units for material resources. You can compare this field with the Budget Work field to see how actual (or scheduled) budgeted work compares with the baseline budget.

- **Baseline Budget Cost**: Shows the planned budget for project cost resources (Chapter 15).

> **Note:** If you use the Fixed Cost field to track costs like fixed-price contracts (Chapter 9), the Baseline Fixed Cost field holds your baseline fixed-cost value. The Baseline Fixed Cost Accrual field documents the accrual method you set for your fixed cost. If you're wondering about the Baseline Deliverable Start and Baseline Deliverable Finish fields, these correspond to the planned start and finish dates for the Deliverable feature in Project Server, which lets you publish project deliverables on which other projects may depend.

Setting the First Baseline

When stakeholders approve the project plan and schedule, one of your very next steps is to set a baseline in Project to save the targets you've committed to.

> **Note:** If you've downloaded the sample files, use the file Event_Ch12_start.mpp.

Follow Along Practice

To set the first baseline in Project, do the following:

1. Open the file you want to set a baseline for (in this example, Event_Ch12_start.mpp), head to the Project tab's Schedule section, choose Set Baseline, and then choose Set Baseline on the drop-down menu.

    The Set Baseline dialog box (Figure 12-2) opens.

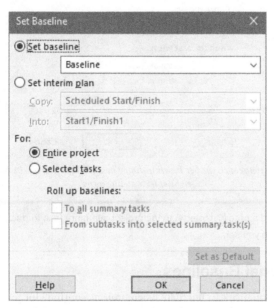

Figure 12-2. *The options that Project selects automatically are exactly what you want for the first baseline you set.*

2. For the first baseline for your project, make sure the "Set baseline" box is set to Baseline and that the "Entire project" option is selected.

    Whether you plan to set only one baseline or are setting the first of several, save your schedule to Baseline this time around. When you first set a baseline, you want to save the values for the entire project. Later on, you may want to save values for selected tasks, like when you add tasks to a project for a change request.

3.   Click OK.

Project stores the current values for start, finish, duration, work, and costs in the corresponding Baseline fields. The next time you open the Set Baseline dialog box, the "Set baseline" box shows the date you set the baseline (Figure 12-3).

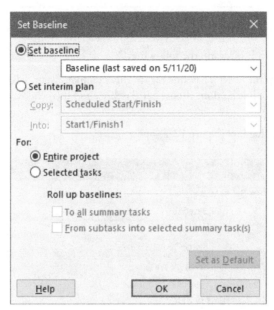

Figure 12-3. *When you reopen the Set Baseline dialog box, the date you set the baseline appears to the right of the baseline name.*

> **Tip:** You can add a note (Chapter 4) to the project summary task to document the reason for each baseline you set.

Setting Additional Baselines

Schedule and cost performance can fluctuate when projects continue for months or years. For example, suppose that after 3 months, a project is 2 weeks behind schedule; at the 6-month mark, it's 6 weeks behind schedule; then, at 1 year, your recovery strategy pays off and the project is back to only 2 weeks behind schedule. By setting additional baselines at key points in a project (at the end of each phase or at regular intervals), you can evaluate trends over time.

An additional baseline is also helpful when a project experiences a big change—an interruption to the schedule, a big scope increase, or a spike in the price of materials. Suppose your project is 20 percent complete when a different, high-priority project intervenes. When you resume your project, the original baseline start and finish dates are too old to produce meaningful variances, and costs may have changed significantly. When you recommence work on your project, you need a new baseline that reflects the updated targets. If you don't want to lose the original baseline values, you can save the new values to one of the additional 10 baselines that Project provides.

> **Note:** If you've downloaded sample files from the website, use the file Event_Ch12_add-baseline.mpp. This sample file includes planned values saved in Baseline fields along with actual values for part of the project.

Follow Along Practice

To set another baseline for a project, follow these steps:

1. In the Project tab's Schedule section, choose Set Baseline, and then choose Set Baseline from the drop-down menu.

    The Set Baseline dialog box opens with the "Set baseline" box set to Baseline, and the "Entire project" option selected.

2. In the "Set baseline" box, choose the baseline you want to set, in this example, Baseline1.

    Baselines that have already been set have "(last saved on mm/dd/yy)" appended to the end of their names (see Figure 12-3), where mm/dd/yy represents the most recent date you saved the baseline.

3. Make sure the "Entire project" option is selected.

    When you save any of the 11 baselines for the first time, you want to save the values for the entire project. Later on, you may want to save values only for selected tasks—for instance, when you add tasks to a project, as described in the next section.

4. Click OK.

    Project stores the current values for start, finish, duration, work, and costs in the corresponding Baseline1 fields, such as Baseline1 Start, Baseline1 Finish, Baseline1 Duration, Baseline1 Work, and Baseline1 Cost. The next time you open the Set Baseline dialog box, the "Set baseline" drop-down list shows the last saved date for the baseline.

> **Tip:** When you set more than one baseline, you can tell Project which baseline to use to calculate variances. On the Gantt Chart Tools | Format Tab, click Baseline, and then choose the baseline you want from the drop-down menu. Project not only uses that baseline to calculate variances, but also uses it to draw baseline task bars in the timescale.

Editing a Baseline

A baseline starts out representing your schedule, but you might need to edit the baseline later on. For example, a client may make change requests and agree to the extra cost and time. The new finish dates and cost aren't variances from the original schedule (because the client is agreeing to *amend* the original schedule), so you want the baseline to absorb these additions. Or perhaps one portion of the project is taking longer than planned. The client agrees to the new, later finish date for that portion, so you want to update the baseline for all the tasks going forward.

Editing a baseline before project execution begins

If project execution hasn't started, you can simply reset the entire baseline:

1. In the Project tab's Schedule section, choose Set Baseline, and then choose Set Baseline from the drop-down menu.

2. In the "Set baseline" box, choose the baseline you want to.

3. Make sure the "Entire project" option is selected and then click OK.

    A message box warns you that the baseline has already been used and asks if you want to overwrite it.

4. Click Yes to overwrite the existing values in the baseline.

Editing a baseline after actual values have been added

When your Project file already includes actual values, you don't want to overwrite baseline values for tasks with actual values. If you do, Project replaces the original baseline values with current ones, and any variances disappear. Instead, you want to set the baseline values for only new or specific revised tasks while leaving baseline values for tasks with actual values alone.

> **Note:** If you want to follow along, use the file Event_Ch12_editbaseline.mpp. This sample file includes several tasks that have not yet been added to the baseline.

Follow Along Practice

To edit a baseline that's already set, follow these steps:

1. Display the Gantt Chart view by clicking the Gantt Chart button on the Task tab.

2. Select the tasks you want to update in the baseline. In this example, select task IDs 49 through 54 (the Tasks for "Procure additional entertainment"), which are new tasks added to the project for an approved change request.

    You can select any kind of task, including non-summary tasks, milestones, or summary tasks.

> **Note:** You can also update the baseline to reflect changes in existing tasks (for example, tasks whose durations you increased) by selecting those tasks. You won't update any existing tasks in this example.

3. In the Project tab's Schedule section, choose Set Baseline, and then choose Set Baseline on the drop-down menu. In the "Set baseline" drop-down list, choose the baseline to which you want to add tasks (in this example, choose Baseline1).

4. Choose the "Selected tasks" option.

    The checkboxes underneath the "Roll up baselines" label become active, as shown in Figure 12-4. These checkboxes tell Project how you want the added baseline values rolled up into summary tasks. Project doesn't automatically update summary task baseline values when you add tasks to a baseline.

5. Turn on the "To all summary tasks" checkbox.

    Typically, you edit a baseline because new tasks or changes to existing tasks have been approved. In that case, you want those changes to roll up all the way to the project summary task, so the updated values don't show up as variances in your project—which is why you turn on the "To all summary tasks" checkbox, as shown in Figure 12-4. If the "To all summary tasks" checkbox is turned on, Project rolls up baseline values to all summary tasks, even if the "From subtasks into selected summary tasks(s)" checkbox is turned on.

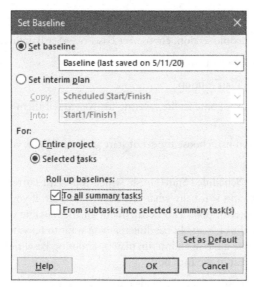

Figure 12-4. *You can select the tasks you want to add or update in a baseline.*

> **Tip:** The "From subtasks into selected summary tasks(s)" checkbox tells Project to update the baseline values for only the summary tasks you select *before* you open the Set Baseline dialog box. It's best to keep this checkbox turned off. Here's why: If you turn the "From sub-tasks into selected summary tasks(s)" checkbox on (and turn off the "To all summary tasks" checkbox), Project doesn't roll up the new baseline values to higher-level summary tasks. Those higher-level summary tasks will then have variances produced by the selected tasks you baselined. And you'll forever be explaining those variances to stakeholders.

6. Click OK. In the message box warning you that the baseline has already been used, click Yes to overwrite the data for the selected tasks.

    Project updates the tasks you specified. To change Project's standard baseline roll-up behavior to match the checkboxes you turned on, click "Set as Default" ***before*** you click OK.

Saving Sets of Start and Finish Dates

The second option in the Set Baseline dialog box is "Set interim plan." Unlike Project baselines, *interim plans* save only start and finish dates, not duration, cost, and work. If you don't need a full baseline, you can save an interim plan instead. The note titled "Baselines vs. Interim Plans" discusses various uses for interim plans.

Follow Along Practice

To save start and finish dates in an interim plan, follow these steps:

1. In the Project tab's Schedule section, choose Set Baseline→Set Baseline.

    The Set Baseline dialog box opens.

2. Select the "Set interim plan" option.

    The Copy and Into boxes come to life, waiting for you to tell them the start and finish fields to copy from and to.

3. In the Copy drop-down list, choose the set of start and finish dates you want to copy, in this example, Baseline1.

    Project initially selects Scheduled Start/Finish, which copies the current task start and finish dates that Project calculates and is usually what you want. However, if you want to copy dates from a baseline or another interim plan, choose the name of the baseline or interim plan instead. For example, suppose Baseline1 is an old baseline that you want to reuse for more recent information. You can save the baseline dates to an interim plan by choosing Baseline1 in the Copy box and then choosing an interim plan in the Into box.

4. In the Into drop-down list, choose the fields into which you want to copy the start and finish dates (in this example, keep Start1/Finish1).

    Project selects Start1/Finish1 here, which means it will copy dates to the first interim plan. However, if you want to save another interim plan, choose Start2/Finish2 for the second interim plan, up to Start10/Finish10 for the 10th interim plan.

    The Into drop-down list also includes the names of baselines. You might wonder why you would copy interim plan dates into a baseline, particularly if the baseline already has values. It turns out that copying from an interim plan to a baseline is how you bring interim plans saved in earlier versions of Project into your Project baselines. For example, you could choose Start3/Finish3 in the Copy drop-down list and Baseline3 in the Into drop-down list, and Project copies the interim plan dates into that baseline.

5. Select either the "Entire project" or "Selected tasks" option, and then click OK. In this example, select "Entire project."

    Saving values to interim plans works just like saving baselines. You can save the dates for the entire project or save dates for only some tasks, as described earlier in this chapter.

Baselines vs. Interim Plans

With up to 11 baselines available, you may wonder why Project offers interim plans as well. Interim plans popped up in Project several versions ago, when the program offered only one baseline and project managers clamored for more.

Even now, interim plans have some uses. First, if you import a project schedule from Project 2002 and earlier, any additional baseline information resides in interim plan fields (Start1/Finish1 through Start10/Finish10). You can copy that information from interim plan Start and Finish fields (Start2/Finish2, for example) into baseline fields like Baseline2 (as described above).

An interim plan is also a great way to review modeling results for the project before committing those changes. That way, you can compare your baseline, the current plan, and the interim plan all in a single view.

In addition, if you save additional baselines regularly, 11 baselines may not be enough. As a workaround, you can save interim plans to act as partial baselines in between the full baselines you save. Although interim plans can't track cost and work changes, you can track schedule performance by watching how interim plan task dates change over time.

Clearing a Baseline

When you run out of empty baselines, you can overwrite a previously saved baseline with current values, as described earlier in this chapter. But suppose that you set a baseline by accident or that a set baseline is so obsolete you want to completely eliminate it. Clearing a baseline removes all its values. Here's what you do:

Follow Along Practice

1. In the Project tab's Schedule section, choose Set Baseline→Clear Baseline.

   The Clear Baseline dialog box appears.

2. In the Clear Baseline dialog box, make sure the "Clear baseline plan" option is selected.

   If you want to clear an interim plan instead, select the "Clear interim plan" option, and then, in the "Clear interim plan" drop-down list, choose the plan's name. In this example, be sure to select "Clear baseline plan."

3. In the "Clear baseline plan" drop-down list, choose the baseline you want to clear, in this example, Baseline1.

   The "Clear baseline plan" drop-down list automatically chooses Project's primary baseline (Baseline), so you must take care to select the baseline you want to clear.

4. To clear the entire baseline, select the "Entire project" option.

   Although Project offers the "Selected tasks" option, there's no reason to clear values for only some tasks.

5. Click OK.

   Project clears the baseline's values.

6. In this example, head to the Quick Access toolbar and click the Undo arrow (a blue arrow curving to the left) to restore Baseline1.

   The next section shows how to view different baselines, so there has to be more than one saved baseline in the file.

Viewing Baselines

When you initially set a baseline, its values are exactly the same as the current Project-calculated field values. As the project team gets to work, the current values begin to stray from the baseline. Evaluating project performance (Chapter 14) involves reviewing the variances between current and baseline values. You can see baseline values in several places.

> **Note:** If you want to follow along, use the file Event_Ch12_view.mpp. This sample file includes actual values entered after the baseline was saved.

For a 30,000-foot view of baseline and current data, head to the Project tab's Properties section and click Project Information. In the Project Information dialog box, click Statistics to open the Project Statistics dialog box, which shows current, baseline, and actual values as well as the variance for the project's start date, finish date, duration, total work, and total cost, as shown in Figure 12-5.

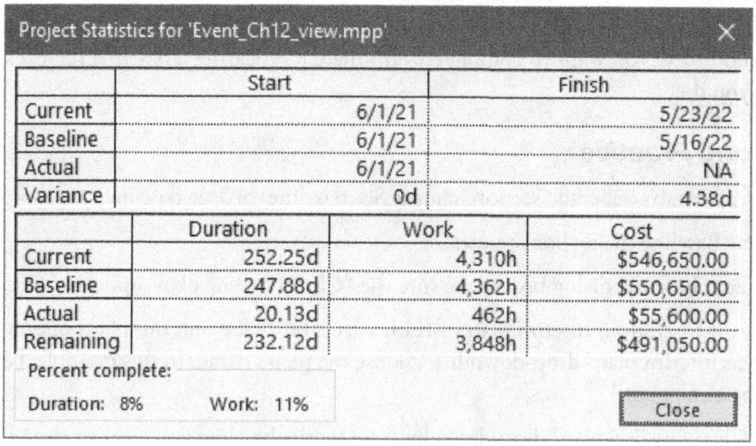

Project Statistics for 'Event_Ch12_view.mpp'			✕
	Start		Finish
Current	6/1/21		5/23/22
Baseline	6/1/21		5/16/22
Actual	6/1/21		NA
Variance	0d		4.38d

	Duration	Work	Cost
Current	252.25d	4,310h	$546,650.00
Baseline	247.88d	4,362h	$550,650.00
Actual	20.13d	462h	$55,600.00
Remaining	232.12d	3,848h	$491,050.00

Percent complete:

Duration: 8%   Work: 11%   [Close]

Figure 12-5. *The Project Statistics dialog box contains various values for the whole project.*

Viewing Baseline and Current Values in a Gantt Chart View

When you want to compare the baseline schedule with the current status, the Tracking Gantt view is perfect. It shows gray task bars for the baseline start and finish dates immediately below task bars for the current schedule.

To display the Tracking Gantt view, shown in Figure 12-6, do the following:

1. In the Task tab, click the bottom half of the Gantt Chart button, and then choose Tracking Gantt. (Or, in the View tab's Task Views section, click the bottom half of the Gantt Chart button, and then choose Tracking Gantt.)

   If you see only one task bar for each task in the view, you haven't saved a baseline yet.

2. To display a different baseline in the view, click the Gantt Chart Tools | Format tab. In the Bar Styles section, click the Baseline down arrow, and then choose the baseline you want to display.

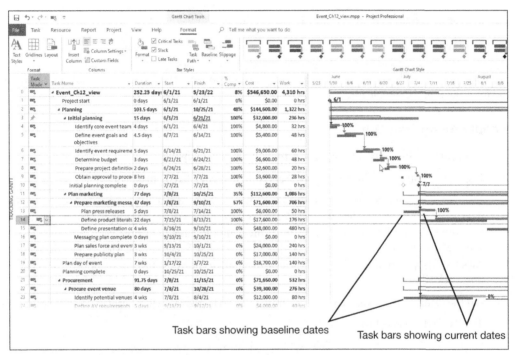

Figure 12-6. *The Tracking Gantt view displays task bars for the current schedule on top and baseline task bars below them.*

Viewing Multiple Baselines in a View

If you save more than one baseline, you may want to see them in the same Gantt Chart so you can compare performance from one to the next. The Multiple Baselines Gantt view displays different color task bars for Baseline, Baseline1, and Baseline2 (Figure 12-7 has bars for Baseline and Baseline1, because the file doesn't have Baseline 2 set). To display this view, in the View tab's Task Views section, choose Other Views→More Views. In the More Views dialog box's View list, double-click Multiple Baselines Gantt.

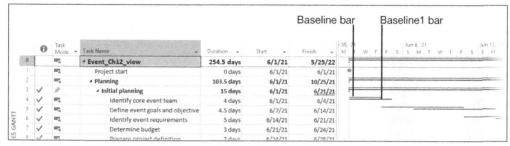

Figure 12-7. *Multiple Baselines Gantt shows task bars for only Baseline, Baseline1, and Baseline2.*

If you want to show more baselines or different baselines in the Multiple Baselines Gantt, you can modify the view to include task bars for other baselines. For example, you may want to see task bars for Baseline1 through Baseline4. The steps in this section are for information only. You don't have to perform them in the sample file.

Follow Along Practice

To change the baselines that the task bars represent, do the following:

1. Copy the Multiple Baselines Gantt view and give it a name like FourBaselines.

    Because swapping task bars requires several steps, it's a good idea to copy the view and then make the changes to the copy. Then you can copy the customized view to your global template and use it in other Project files (Chapter 23). With the Multiple Baselines Gantt view displayed, in the View tab's Task Views section, choose Other Views→More Views. In the More Views dialog box, click Copy, type a new name in the Name box, and then click OK. Back in the More Views dialog box, click Close.

2. On the Gantt Chart Tools | Format tab, in the Bar Styles section, click Format→Bar Styles.

    The Bar Styles dialog box opens.

3. Click the cell that contains the first task bar style name you want to replace.

    For example, click Baseline1 to edit the normal task bars for Baseline1.

4. Click the same cell a second time to make the name editable, and then type the new baseline number at the end of the name.

    For example, to change Baseline1 to Baseline4, replace the 1 at the end of the name with *4*.

5. In the From cell in the same row, choose the start date field for the new baseline.

    For example, to switch the view to show Baseline4, choose Baseline4 Start. This tells Project to draw the beginning of the task bars based on the Baseline4 Start field values.

6. In the To cell in the same row, choose the finish date field for the new baseline.

    To complete the task bar style that shows Baseline4, choose Baseline4 Finish. These From and To settings tell Project to draw the task bars for Baseline4 from Baseline4 Start to Baseline4 Finish in the timescale.

7. Repeat steps 3–6 to modify the Split, Milestone, and Summary task bars to use the same baseline.

    Simply editing the task bar's name isn't enough. The fields you choose for the task bar's start and finish dates are what really matter.

8. If you want to replace another baseline in the view, repeat steps 3–7.

    Click OK when you're done. Figure 12-8 shows what the bar style definitions look like when you're done.

Edit bar style name and fields used to draw task start and finish

Bar Styles

| Cut Row | Paste Row | Insert Row |

Name	Appearance	Show For ... Tasks	Row	From	To
Baseline4		Normal	1	Baseline4 Start	Baseline4 Finish
Baseline4 Split		Normal,Split	1	Baseline4 Start	Baseline4 Finish
Baseline4 Milestone	◆	Milestone	1	Baseline4 Finish	Baseline4 Finish
Baseline4 Summary		Summary	1	Baseline4 Start	Baseline4 Finish
Baseline		Normal	1	Baseline Start	Baseline Finish
Baseline Split		Normal,Split	1	Baseline Start	Baseline Finish
Baseline Milestone	◆	Milestone	1	Baseline Finish	Baseline Finish
Baseline Summary		Summary	1	Baseline Start	Baseline Finish
Baseline2		Normal	1	Baseline2 Start	Baseline2 Finish

Figure 12-8. *Edit the bar style name and the From and To fields used.*

Follow Along Practice

To include an *additional* baseline in the view, you have to insert task bar rows for the baseline's normal, split, milestone, and summary tasks. Here are the steps for inserting the rows:

1. Open the Multiple Baselines Gantt view or a copy you've created.

    Consider copying the Multiple Baselines Gantt view for your new multi-baseline Gantt Chart (step 1 in the previous section explains how). If you copy the customized view to your global template, you can use it in other Project files.

2. On the Gantt Chart Tools | Format tab, in the Bar Styles section, click Format→Bar Styles.

    The Bar Styles dialog box opens.

3. Select the row for the task bar you want to duplicate, and then click Cut Row.

    Project removes the row from the table.

4. Before you do anything else, click Paste Row.

    Project inserts the cut row back where it was originally.

5. Select the row below where you want to insert the new row, and then click Paste Row again.

    Project inserts another copy of the row immediately above the row you select.

6. Edit the new row's Name, From, and To cells to match the baseline you want to show.

    To display Baseline5, for example, change the name to include Baseline5, and then, in the From and To cells, choose Baseline5 Start and Baseline5 Finish, respectively.

7. On the Bars tab in the lower half of the Bar Styles dialog box, choose the shape and color you want for the bar.

    Baseline1, Baseline2, and Baseline3 already use red, blue, and green respectively, so choose a color like teal, orange, or purple. In the Shape box, choose a top, middle, or bottom narrow bar.

8. If you're including more than three baselines in the view, add a second task bar row to the view.

    In the Multiple Baselines Gantt view, Project uses narrow task bars so you can display up to three baselines on the same row of the Gantt Chart. But if you want to see more than three baselines, you have to tell Project to add another row to the view. To do that, in the Bar Styles dialog box, head to the new row you created in step 5 and, in that row's Row cell, type *2*, as illustrated in Figure 12-9. Doing this tells Project to place the baseline's task bar on a second row in the view timescale.

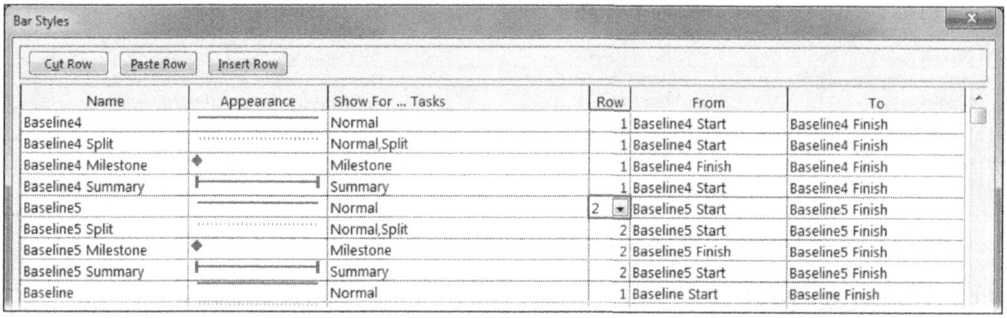

Figure 12-9. *The Multiple Baselines Gantt view includes task bar styles for Deliverable fields. Don't be misled: The Deliverable feature is available only when you use Project Server.*

9. Repeat steps 3–8 to create task bars for split, milestone, and summary tasks for the baseline.

    If you choose the narrow task bars that run at the top, middle, and bottom of a row, you can add three baselines to the second row of the view, just like the Multiple Baselines Gantt view does in the first row.

Viewing Baseline Values in a Table

Although the Multiple Baselines Gantt view's timescale shows different task bars for each baseline, you probably want to see baseline costs, duration, and work. The table area of one of the Gantt Chart views is the perfect place to see these values. You don't have to perform these steps in the example file.

Project includes the Baseline table, which displays columns for all the Baseline fields: Baseline Duration, Baseline Start, Baseline Finish, Baseline Work, and Baseline Cost. To display this table, in the View tab's Data section, click the Tables down arrow, and then choose More Tables on the shortcut menu. In the More Tables dialog box, select Baseline, and then click Apply.

> **Tip:** If you see values of "0" or "NA" in a baseline field, that's Project's way of telling you that you haven't saved a baseline for that task yet.

If you would rather add baseline fields to another table, you can simply insert columns in the table. To add the Baseline Cost and Baseline Work fields to the Variance table, for example, right-click the table heading area where you want to insert the column. On the shortcut menu, choose Insert Column and then, from the drop-down menu, choose the baseline field you want to add.

> **Note:** The Task Details Form can show baseline start and finish dates. Although the form opens initially with the Current option selected, select the Baseline option to see the baseline start and finish dates.

13

Tracking Status

After you finish planning a project and get approval from everyone necessary, you save a baseline of the project and give the signal for work to begin. You may then be tempted to sit back at this point and rest on your…ahem…laurels. The hardest part of your job as project manager is done, right?

Wrong. Now that you've stepped over the threshold from planning into execution, plenty of challenges await and you really earn your keep as a project manager: You monitor progress, evaluate performance, make adjustments as necessary, and manage the changes inevitable in projects.

Before you can evaluate project performance and make corrections, you need to know where the project stands. Project status is made up of two components: actual progress and forecasts of what remains to be done. Tracking status is all about information like tasks completed, when tasks actually start and finish, hours worked, and costs incurred. Just as important, you need to find out what's still left to do—that is, the duration or work that team members estimate that it will take to finish. This chapter begins by discussing the merits of different approaches to tracking status and the information you can collect. Then you'll learn about collecting that status data from your team—and several ways to do it.

The next step is updating your Project file with that status info. This chapter describes how to record status data, depending on the information you collect. If you opt for tracking status to a high level of detail, you'll also learn how to update progress at the assignment level, whether task by task or for the entire project.

Methods for Tracking Status

The approach you choose to track the progress of your project depends on your organization, the type of project, and the level of detail your stakeholders need. From a practical standpoint, it also depends on how much time you have to gather and incorporate progress data into the project plan. (Collecting detailed status data won't do any good if you don't have time to enter it into Project.) This section starts by describing the difference between updating tasks and updating assignments, and when it makes sense to use each one. Then you'll learn about the specific data you can collect.

Automated Methods for Updating Status

With more than a few tasks and resources, entering status updates manually becomes time-consuming and tedious. Other software can streamline the process of getting status info into your Project file. Even better, if you use automated methods, you can skip the rest of this chapter. Here are a few software solutions to consider:

- If your organization uses **Project Server/ Project Online**, then team members can submit their progress information through the Project Web App interface. That way, the
  data is automatically available for you to review and incorporate into your project plan.

- If your organization uses **SharePoint**, you can synchronize your Project file with a SharePoint tasks list so tasks are available on your SharePoint site. But this connection goes both ways. After team members update statuses in the SharePoint tasks list, you can re-synchronize to pull the updated values into your Project file. Then another synchronization pushes the updated schedule back to the SharePoint tasks list for the entire team to see. Chapter 28 describes more about SharePoint tasks lists and Project.

- Another option is to use a third-party application that let's your people fill out timesheets and then imports their hours into your Project file. **Standard Time Timesheets** (www.stdtime.com) and **Planbridge** (http://planbridge.ms/product/index) both help you import time data into Project.

Updating Assignments vs. Updating Tasks

The first decision you need to make about status is whether to update tasks or assignments. Updating assignments gives you a more accurate picture of status than updating tasks does, but it also demands more time from you and your team members. If your team members are too busy to submit status updates or you can't keep up with entering the data in your Project file, then your schedule won't reflect what's really happening in your project—and you won't have the information you need to make corrections. For that reason, updating tasks makes more sense for most projects. Don't worry: updating tasks can provide a reasonably accurate view of status.

> **Note:** In Project, you can update both assignments and tasks within the same project—but you can't update them both for the same task. If you update assignments on a task, the program rolls the assignment values up to the task level. If you update a task, you can tell Project to distribute the task's values to its assignments.

Here's the lowdown on both approaches:

- **Updating assignments**: With this approach, team members assigned to your project report actual hours for their assignments, as well as their estimates for each assignment's remaining hours. When you enter this data into your schedule, Project rolls up values for a task's assignments to calculate its overall duration, work, and percent complete. The downside is that the volume of data quickly adds up if you have more than a handful of tasks and people. Typically, you'll update at the assignment level if your stakeholders require the detail that updating assignments provides.

> **Note:** This method is usually feasible only if you have an electronic method for collecting status data from team members *and* an automated method for transferring that data into Project (for example, the task or timesheet system available in Project Server /Project Online). Without an automated system, team members might balk at the time it takes to report their statuses, you might not get timesheet data entered in a timely fashion, or errors could creep into your data as it's transcribed from a timesheet into a Project file.

- **Updating tasks**: This approach takes less time than updating assignments, yet it provides a reasonably accurate picture of schedule status. With this method, you typically collect and record actual and remaining durations and actual start and finish dates for project tasks. (You can also collect actual and remaining work hours if you want a more accurate status.) With this approach, the Project application takes care of allocating actual hours to assignments and time periods.

What Data to Collect

Microsoft Project offers a variety of fields for recording status information. The good news is that you can update your project accurately using as few as three fields. This section describes the alternatives and when it makes sense to use each one.

For a complete picture of status, you need four types of information about tasks or assignments:

- **Actual start date**: This is the date that a task or assignment actually starts. In Project, you record this info in the Actual Start field.

- **What's been completed**: Depending on the level of detail you choose to track, you can use the actual duration (Actual Duration field), actual work (Actual Work field), or percentage complete (% Complete or % Work Complete) to track what's been completed.

- **What work still remains**: If you track duration, you collect remaining duration (Remaining Duration field) or remaining work (Remaining Work field) information.

- **Actual Finish**: This is the date that a task or assignment actually finishes. When a task is complete, that is, its remaining duration or work equals zero, Project calculates this field. If Project doesn't calculate the actual finish date correctly, fill in the Actual Finish field with the correct actual finish date to get the most accurate picture of project status.

Because Project uses values that you enter to calculate other fields, these four types of status information translate into four main methods for collecting status data. (The note titled "Project's Status Calculations for Tasks" explains how Project calculates values for different fields using the data you enter.) Here are your options and the pros and cons of each:

- **Actual and remaining duration**: Asking team members for these two bits of information is the quickest and easiest way to get accurate task status. *Actual duration* is the number of work days someone has already worked on a task, so it's what's been completed. *Remaining duration* is the number of work days the person estimates they'll need to finish the task, so it's a forecast of what remains. You also need to ask for actual start dates, so you know whether tasks start early, late, or right on time. Although Project can calculate the actual finish date from other fields, it's still a good idea to ask people for the actual finish date, because it determines when successor tasks start or finish. (You can use these values at the task level or assignment level.)

- **Actual and remaining work at the task level**: For smaller projects and shorter tasks, getting statuses in terms of days (actual and remaining duration) might be too imprecise. In that case, it's better to ask team members for actual and remaining *work*, instead. *Actual work* is the number of hours someone has already worked on a task, and *remaining work* is the hours they estimate it will take them to finish the task. You also need actual start and finish dates, as you do when you collect actual and remaining duration, so Project knows when to schedule successor tasks.

> **Note:** In order to use work fields, you need to have work resources assigned to tasks (Chapter 7).

- **Actual and remaining work at the assignment level**: This method uses actual work and remaining work, just like the previous method. But in this case, you assign values at the individual *assignment* level, rather than for the entire task. For the highest level of detail and most accurate status, you can assign work day by day in the time-phased portion of the Task Usage or Resource Usage view, but be forewarned—it's a time-consuming endeavor.

- **Percent complete (% Complete) and remaining duration (or work)**: % Complete represents the duration that is complete, not the progress that's been made on the work to be done. Because of that, this is the least accurate approach for tracking status: Project copies the planned start (Start field) and finish (Finish field) values to the Actual Start and Actual Finish fields. Unless task status matches your plan, filling in % Complete is likely to result in an inaccurate forecast. One advantage to this approach is that updating a task's % Complete value is as easy as clicking one of the percent-complete buttons in the Task tab's Schedule section or on the mini-toolbar (described later in this chapter). In addition to % Complete data, you also need the task's actual start date and remaining duration (or remaining work).

> **Note:** If you use % Complete to collect task status, it's essential that you also get an estimate of remaining duration or work from your team members. Without remaining duration, percent complete could mean almost anything: the percentage team members think should be done, what they wish was done, or the percentage they think you want to hear so you'll leave them alone.

Project's Status Calculations for Tasks

Project calculates values for the status fields you don't update directly. That is, when you enter information into one field, Project calculates the values that belong in other associated fields. The following list gives you an "under the hood" look at the relationship between commonly used task-related status fields:

- Actual Start = Scheduled Start if you don't specify a value in the Actual Start field. If you fill in Actual Start, the Start and Scheduled Start fields both change to the Actual Start value you enter.

- Actual Finish = Scheduled Finish if you don't specify a value in the Actual Finish field. If you fill in Actual Finish, the Finish and Scheduled Finish fields both change to the Actual Finish value you enter.

- Duration = Actual Duration + Remaining Duration

- % Complete = (Actual Duration / Duration) x 100

- Work = Actual Work + Remaining Work

- % Work Complete= (Actual Work / Work) x 100

For example, say a team member reports a task's Actual Duration as 3 days and Remaining Duration as 9 days. When you enter that information, Project calculates the task's Duration value as 12 days, and the task's % Complete value as 25%.

In addition, you can rearrange any of these formulas so that Project calculates other fields. For example, Remaining Duration is equal to Duration minus Actual Duration. So if you enter a value in an Actual Duration field, Project calculates Remaining Duration by subtracting Actual Duration from the Duration value.

Preparing to Update Your Project

You may be raring to start adding status updates to your Project file, but you need to have a few things in place before you begin. Your file needs to be set up so Project can calculate the schedule and the variance between your plan and what actually occurs. You also need to tell Project how you want it to handle the updates you enter. In addition, you can make your updating job easier by setting up a customized view to go with your progress-tracking method. This section steps through each of these prerequisites.

> **Note:** If you want to follow along, use the file Event_Ch13_start.mpp.

Setting Tasks to Auto Scheduled Mode

If you've fine-tuned your schedule to make it realistic and to balance resource workloads (see Chapter 10), your project's tasks should already be set to Auto Scheduled mode. But if any tasks are set to Manually Scheduled mode and should be Auto Scheduled instead, switch them to Auto Scheduled mode before you start entering updates. (See Chapter 4 for reasons why you might create manually scheduled tasks and keep them that way, as well as how to change a task's mode.) That way, Project can recalculate your schedule based on the status updates you enter. For example, if an update shows that a task is going to take longer to complete, the program takes care of rescheduling the task's successors based on the revised finish date.

Follow Along Practice

In the example file, task ID 3 "Initial planning" is set to Manually Scheduled, but should be Auto Scheduled instead. To make this change, in the Gantt Chart view's table, click the task's Task Mode cell, click the down arrow that appears, and then click Auto Scheduled.

Baseline, Scheduled, and Actual Values

Now that you're about to enter actual values, you may wonder how baseline, scheduled, and actual fields differ. Here's how they work:

- **Baseline fields**: Also known as *planned* information, baseline fields are a snapshot of what your project's Start, Finish, Duration, Work, Cost, Budget Work, and Budget Cost values were when you saved the baseline. You should save a baseline immediately after the project plan has been approved. As you and your team work through the project, you can compare baseline values against scheduled or actual values to analyze variances and predict problems. For manually scheduled tasks without dates, the Baseline Estimated Start and Baseline Estimated Finish dates (Chapter 12) show the dates that most closely match where the tasks occur in the schedule.

- **Scheduled fields**: Also known as *current* information, scheduled information is constantly in flux. Before work begins, scheduled values and baseline values are the same. Whenever you enter actual progress information and forecasts of what remains, Project recalculates task schedules and costs to accommodate the new reality.

- **Actual fields**: Often referred to simply as *actuals*, these fields contain progress information for completed and in-progress tasks. You explicitly enter actuals into the fields you're most concerned about; Project calculates any other actual information based on the formulas defining the relationships between the fields. For example, if you enter dates in a task's Actual Start and Actual Finish fields, then Project calculates the task's Actual Duration as the span between the two dates.

Setting a Baseline

Another important step to perform before recording status updates is to set a baseline for your project (Chapter 12). When you have a baseline saved, Project keeps track of your original planned values as well as the current scheduled values. That way, you can see the variances between your plan and what actually occurs to identify issues that need your attention. If you're following along, the baseline is already set in the example file. (The note titled "Baseline, Scheduled, and Actual Values" explains the difference between baseline, scheduled, and actual values.)

Project Settings for Status Updates

Project has several settings related to updating tasks. Some of them are set the way you usually want them right out of the box, but you'll probably want to change others. This section identifies the settings you should choose for status updates and why.

Follow Along Practice

To get to the following settings, start by choosing File→Options to open the Project Options dialog box.

Settings in the Schedule Category

On the left side of the Project Options dialog box, click Schedule. Here are the relevant settings in that category and what they do:

- **Split in-progress tasks**: This setting (which lives in the "Scheduling options for this project" section) is turned on initially, which is what you want. With this setting turned on, Project can split tasks to reflect when work occurs—for example, to move the incomplete portion of the task to after the *status date* (the date through which you've collected status information).

- **Updating Task status updates resource status**: This setting is in the "Calculation options for this project" section. If you update tasks (rather than individual assignments), keep this setting turned on. That way, Project distributes task values you enter to the assignment level, calculating the actual and remaining work and cost for associated resource assignments. Project also rolls up assignment values to calculate the parent task's status. If you turn this checkbox off, you can enter different updates for tasks and resources. (In the example project, keep this setting turned on.)

Settings in the Advanced Category

On the left side of the Project Options dialog box, click Advanced and scroll down to the "Calculation options for this project" section, shown in Figure 13-1.

> **Note:** To see how the options in the Advanced category work, use the file Ch13_ updateoptions.mpp if you've downloaded the sample files. When you finish experimenting with updating that file, close it, and then resume your work in Event_Ch13_start.mpp by setting the following options.

Follow Along Practice

Here are the relevant settings in that category and what they do:

- **Move end of completed parts after status date back to status date**: This setting is turned off initially, but you want to turn it on. When you do, Project moves the completed work to before the status date. (The actual duration task bar moves to before the status date, and actual work is recorded in time periods before the status date.) In other words, the program records the completed work as occurring in the past, which is what actually happened.

  For example, say your status date is August 18 and a 4-day task has a start date of August 20. But the task starts early—on August 17. With this setting turned on, when you enter the task's status information (for example, entering actual start date, actual duration, and remaining duration), Project moves the actual start date to August 17 and sets the percent complete to 50 (because August 17 and 18 are two workdays). However, the remaining work is still scheduled to start on August 24—the date the remaining work was scheduled to occur based on the original start date. In this case, the task is split into two segments: The completed work runs from August 17 to 18 and the remaining work is scheduled for August 24 to 25.

- **And move start of remaining parts back to status date**: If you turn on the "Move end of completed parts after status date back to status date" setting, this setting's checkbox becomes active. It's turned off initially, which means that, when you enter status info for tasks, Project keeps the incomplete portions of tasks on the dates they were originally scheduled to occur. But if people finish some of their work early, chances are good that they're going to keep working on their assignments. That's why you usually want to turn this setting on—so Project moves the incomplete parts of tasks to start as of the status date. In the example project, turn this setting on.

  Using the example from the previous bullet point, if this setting is turned on, Project moves the start of the remaining work to August 19, the first workday after the status date, so the remaining work is scheduled to start immediately after the completed work.

Figure 13-1. *You can control how Project moves completed and remaining parts of tasks when you update status.*

- **Move start of remaining parts before status date forward to status date**: This setting is also turned off initially, but you should turn it on. (Turn it on in the example project.) That way, when you enter status info for tasks, Project moves the incomplete part of the task so that it's scheduled to occur in the future (after the status date). That makes sense, because unless you have a time machine, that's when it's going to get done.

  Consider a 4-day task with a status date of August 18 that has a scheduled start date of August 9. Suppose 2 days of work is complete. With this setting turned on, Project leaves that actual start date at August 9 so the completed work shows as occurring on August 9 and 10. However, Project schedules the remaining work to start on August 19, the first workday after the status date. Once again, the task is split in two segments, with the completed work recorded on the original dates and the incomplete work scheduled to start after the status date.

  > **Note:** This setting applies only to tasks that are in progress as of the status date. If a task should have started before the status date but *hasn't*, you'll have to reschedule it to occur in the future.

- **And move end of completed parts forward to status date**: If you turn on the "Move start of remaining parts before status date forward to status date" setting, the checkbox for this setting becomes active. It's turned off initially, which means that, when you enter status info for tasks, Project keeps the completed portions of tasks on their currently scheduled dates. (In the example project, keep this checkbox turned off.) If you turn this setting on, then the task's complete and incomplete portions are contiguous around the status date.

  Using the previous example, if this setting is turned on, Project moves the actual start of the completed work to August 17, so the completed work shows up right before the status date.

  > **Note:** The settings above come into play when you use % Complete to record progress. If you use track progress with other methods, these settings won't affect your updates.

- **Edits to total task % complete will be spread to the status date**: This setting is turned off initially, and there's no reason to turn it on unless you enter values in the % Complete field. In that case, turning this setting on spreads progress evenly up to the status date. For example, if you set a task's % Complete value to 50%, Project divides half the task's work hours evenly over each workday between the task's start date and the status date. (In the example project, keep this checkbox turned off.)

Setting Up a View to Make Updating Easy

As its name implies, the Tracking Gantt view helps you track your project's status. It's a good starting point when you're ready to update status values in Project. When you display this view, the timescale includes gray task bars for the project's baseline in the bottom half of each row, as shown in Figure 13-3. The top half of each row displays red and blue task bars for critical and noncritical tasks' current scheduled dates (respectively).

Follow Along Practice

The Tracking Gantt view initially displays the Entry table, which doesn't contain the fields that you update for status. The Tracking table contains the right fields, but it doesn't present them in the order that you usually fill them in (as you'll learn shortly). You can drag the columns to reorder them. Here's how to set up a view custom and table made for your updating work:

1. In the View tab's Task Views section, click the bottom half of the Gantt Chart button, and then choose Tracking Gantt.

2. In the View tab's Data section, click Tables→Tracking.

3. To create a custom view specifically for updating, on the View tab, click the bottom half of the Gantt Chart button, and then choose Save View. In the Save View dialog box, type a name for the view, in this example, **C_Status Updating**, and then click OK.

   Adding "C_" as a prefix to the view name makes it easy to differentiate a custom view from built-in views that come with Project.

4. To arrange the fields in a convenient order for updating, start by moving the Actual Duration field so it appears to the right of Actual Start.

   To do that, click the Actual Duration heading. When the pointer changes to a four-headed arrow, drag the column until the vertical gray line is between Actual Start and Actual Finish, and then drop it into place.

5. Drag and drop the Remaining Duration field so that it appears to the right of Actual Duration.

6. Drag and drop the Actual Work field so that it appears to the right of Remaining Duration.

7. To insert the Remaining Work field to the right of Actual Work, right-click the Actual Finish heading, and then choose Insert Field from the shortcut menu. In the field drop-down list that appears, choose Remaining Work.

8. To insert the % Work Complete field to the right of % Complete, right-click the Physical % Complete heading, and then choose Insert Field from the shortcut menu. In the field drop-down list that appears, choose % Work Complete.

   Note: Physical % Complete comes into play when you use earned value analysis to evaluate project performance, as described in Chapter 14. % Work Complete is described later in this chapter.

9. Filter the view to display tasks that might have updates.

   a. In the View tab's Data section, click the Filter box's down arrow, and then choose New Filter.

   b. In the Filter Definition dialog box, type a name in the Name box, in this example, C_Status Updating.

   c. In the first blank Field Name box, choose % Complete.

   d. In the Test box in the same row, choose "is less than."

   e. In the Value(s) box in the same row, type **100**. (This row filters for unstarted or incomplete tasks, because tasks that are already complete won't have updates.)

f. In the And/Or box in the second row, choose And.

g. In the Field Name box in the third row, choose Start.

h. In the Test box in the third row, choose "is less than or equal to."

i. In the Value(s) box in the third row, type *"Enter status date:"?* including the double quotes. (This row filters for tasks whose start dates are earlier or equal to the date you specify when Project prompts you to enter the status date.)

j. Click Apply to save the filter and apply it to the view. Figure 13-2 shows what the custom filter definition looks like. Figure 13-3 shows the filtered list.

10. If the "Enter status date:" prompt appears, type *7/7/21*, and then click OK.

> **Note:** The custom filter here asks you to enter the status date, because you can't choose a project-level field in the value box in the Filter Definition dialog box. Chapter 17 explains how to use additional customization to build a filter that automatically filters based on the status date that's currently set.

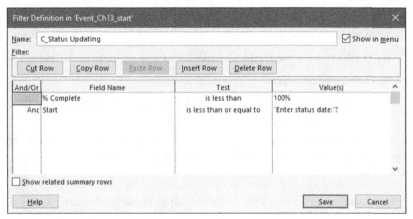

Figure 13-2. *This filter includes two tests. Because the filter includes the And operator, tasks must pass both tests to appear in the task list.*

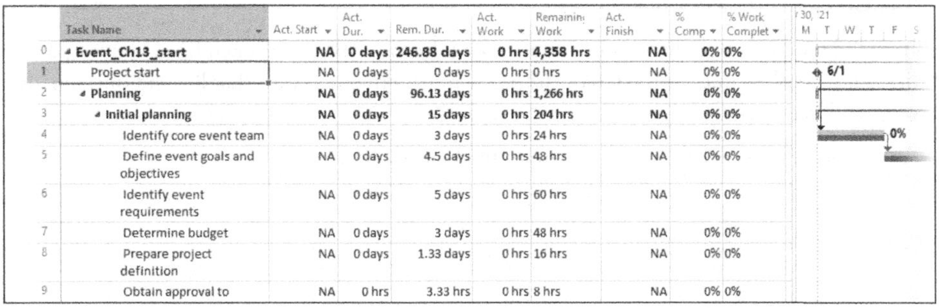

	Task Name	Act. Start	Act. Dur.	Rem. Dur.	Act. Work	Remaining Work	Act. Finish	% Comp	% Work Complet	M T W T F S
0	◢ Event_Ch13_start	NA	0 days	246.88 days	0 hrs	4,358 hrs	NA	0%	0%	
1	Project start	NA	0 days	0 days	0 hrs	0 hrs	NA	0%	0%	6/1
2	◢ Planning	NA	0 days	96.13 days	0 hrs	1,266 hrs	NA	0%	0%	
3	◢ Initial planning	NA	0 days	15 days	0 hrs	204 hrs	NA	0%	0%	
4	Identify core event team	NA	0 days	3 days	0 hrs	24 hrs	NA	0%	0%	0%
5	Define event goals and objectives	NA	0 days	4.5 days	0 hrs	48 hrs	NA	0%	0%	
6	Identify event requirements	NA	0 days	5 days	0 hrs	60 hrs	NA	0%	0%	
7	Determine budget	NA	0 days	3 days	0 hrs	48 hrs	NA	0%	0%	
8	Prepare project definition	NA	0 days	1.33 days	0 hrs	16 hrs	NA	0%	0%	
9	Obtain approval to	NA	0 hrs	3.33 hrs	0 hrs	8 hrs	NA	0%	0%	

Figure 13-3. *Because this custom view displays the fields in the order in which you enter values, when you record updates, you can type a value and then press Tab to move to the next cell in the row.*

Obtaining Status Data

Once you've chosen your preferred progress-tracking approach and prepped your Project file for up-dating, the battle has only begun. In this section, you'll learn ways to obtain the progress information you need without pulling team members' teeth. For instance, you'll see how to create an Excel spread-sheet with the tasks that might require updating.

Setting the Status Date

Before you begin updating status in Project, you need to set the ***status date***, that is, the date through which you want to collect status information. Setting the status date comes in handy if you receive status information from team members on one day, such as the last Friday of the reporting period, but update your schedule on a different day, like the following Monday. This section shows you how to set the status date and display it in the Gantt Chart timescale.

> **Note:** If you don't set a specific status date, Project uses your computer's current system date.

Here are the steps for setting and displaying the status date in a Gantt Chart-type view:

1. In the Project tab's Status section, click the calendar icon to the right of the Status Date label.

   The Status Date dialog box opens.

2. In the Select Date box, click the down arrow, and then choose the status date on the calendar (in this example, choose or type ***7/9/21***). Click OK.

   After you set the status date, it appears in the Project tab's Status section, circled in Figure 13-4. If you haven't set a status date, in the Project tab's Status section, you'll see "NA" to the right of the Status Date label.

To display the status date in the timescale (in this example, in the C_Status Updating view), do the following:

1. In the Gantt Chart Tools | Format tab's Format section, click Gridlines→Gridlines.

   The Gridlines dialog box opens.

2. In the "Line to change" list, choose Status Date. In the Type drop-down list, choose a pattern, like a long dashed line. In the Color drop-down list, choose a color that'll stand out, like orange or blue. Then click OK.

   A vertical line appears at the status date in the Gantt Chart timescale.

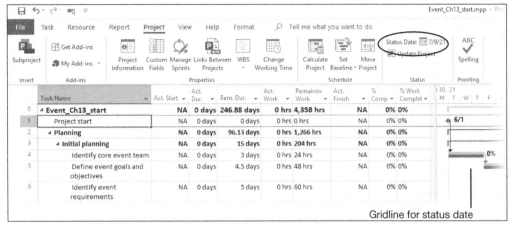

Figure 13-4. *After you set a status date, it appears to the label's right, as shown here.*

Collecting Task Status from Team Members

You can get most status information from your team members, although it's not always as easy as it sounds. This section describes how to extract reliable and consistent information from resources.

Whether you intend to ask people for updates in person, via email, or by using some other mechanism, you can simplify data collection by adding the tasks that are under way (or should be) to a form. An Excel spreadsheet is a great option: You can print it out and take it to your status meeting to fill in there or email it to team members. This section shows you how to quickly construct a task-update form.

Follow Along Practice

The first thing you need is a list of the tasks you need to update. It's easy to produce that list in Project and then copy it into an Excel spreadsheet. Here are the steps:

1. Display the status-update view you created in the previous section (in this example, C_Status Updating).

    To display the view, in the Task tab's Task Views section, click the bottom half of the Gantt Chart button, and then, on the drop-down menu, choose the view's name under the Custom heading.

2. In the C_Status Updating dialog box that opens, type the status date, in this example, *7/9/21*, and then click OK.

    When you click OK, the view's task list displays only the tasks that pass the filter tests, as shown in Figure 13-5.

	Task Name	Act. Start	Act. Dur.	Rem. Dur.	Act. Work	Remaining Work	Act. Finish	% Comp	% Work Complet
0	⊿ Event_Ch13_start	NA	0 days	246.88 days	0 hrs	4,358 hrs	NA	0%	0%
1	Project start	NA	0 days	0 days	0 hrs	0 hrs	NA	0%	0%
2	⊿ Planning	NA	0 days	96.13 days	0 hrs	1,266 hrs	NA	0%	0%
3	⊿ Initial planning	NA	0 days	15 days	0 hrs	204 hrs	NA	0%	0%
4	Identify core event team	NA	0 days	3 days	0 hrs	24 hrs	NA	0%	0%
5	Define event goals and objectives	NA	0 days	4.5 days	0 hrs	48 hrs	NA	0%	0%
6	Identify event requirements	NA	0 days	5 days	0 hrs	60 hrs	NA	0%	0%
7	Determine budget	NA	0 days	3 days	0 hrs	48 hrs	NA	0%	0%
8	Prepare project definition	NA	0 days	1.33 days	0 hrs	16 hrs	NA	0%	0%
9	Obtain approval to proceed	NA	0 hrs	3.33 hrs	0 hrs	8 hrs	NA	0%	0%
10	Initial planning complete	NA	0 days	0 days	0 hrs	0 hrs	NA	0%	0%
11	⊿ Plan marketing	NA	0 days	74.5 days	0 hrs	1,062 hrs	NA	0%	0%
12	⊿ Prepare marketing messages	NA	0 days	44.5 days	0 hrs	682 hrs	NA	0%	0%
13	Plan press releases	NA	0 days	4.5 days	0 hrs	42 hrs	NA	0%	0%
14	Define product literature	NA	0 wks	4 wks	0 hrs	160 hrs	NA	0%	0%
21	⊿ Procurement	NA	0 days	91.25 days	0 hrs	636 hrs	NA	0%	0%
22	⊿ Procure event venue	NA	0 days	77 days	0 hrs	276 hrs	NA	0%	0%
23	Identify potential venues	NA	0 wks	4 wks	0 hrs	80 hrs	NA	0%	0%
31	⊿ Procure printing	NA	0 days	14.25 days	0 hrs	76 hrs	NA	0%	0%
32	Identify printing services	NA	0 days	3 days	0 hrs	24 hrs	NA	0%	0%
33	Send RFPs	NA	0 wks	1 wk	0 hrs	40 hrs	NA	0%	0%
37	⊿ Procure giveaways	NA	0 days	10.13 days	0 hrs	90 hrs	NA	0%	0%
38	Identify giveaway vendors	NA	0 days	4 days	0 hrs	32 hrs	NA	0%	0%
39	Send RFPs	NA	0 wks	1 wk	0 hrs	40 hrs	NA	0%	0%

Figure 13-5. *The resulting list shows tasks that should have updates based on the status date you set.*

> **Note:** You can build a more customized filter that automatically sets the date in the filter to the status date. If you collect data from each person on the project, you can also customize the filter to prompt for the resource whose assignments you want to see. See Chapter 17 to learn more about customizing filters.

3. Click the Select All cell at the table's top left to select all the cells in the table, and then press Ctrl+C to copy the cells to the Clipboard.

   You can copy and paste task info from Project to cells in an Excel spreadsheet.

4. Open a blank or existing spreadsheet in Excel. Click the first cell in the spreadsheet, and then press Ctrl+V.

   Excel fills in the cells starting with the one you clicked and proceeding down and to the right.

5. Save the file (choose File→Save). Include the date range in the file's name, such as **Update_20210709.xlsx**.

Figure 13-6 shows what the spreadsheet looks like. Now you can print it out or email it to team members.

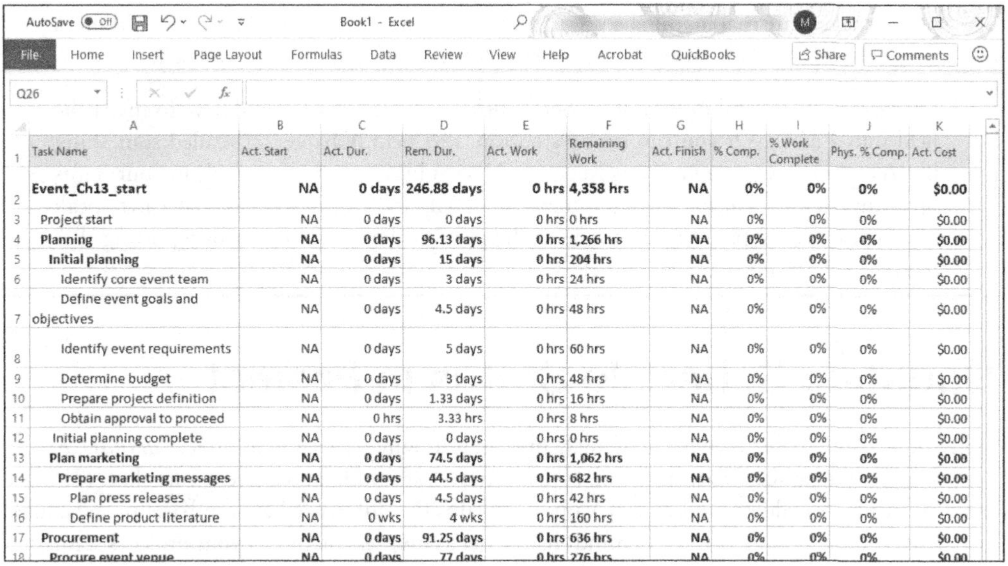

Figure 13-6. *Create an Excel spreadsheet to obtain updates from team members.*

Collecting Status Data about Other Resources

Some key resources may be inanimate objects. No, not like George in the corner cubicle, but rather equipment resources, material resources, and cost resources. But just because you can't chat up these types of resources at the water cooler doesn't mean you can ignore status information for them. They often represent significant project costs, and their progress is essential to accurately reflecting status and cost in your Project file.

One way to obtain this information is to have one of the ***human*** resources report on when equipment resources start working, how many pounds of goop were actually used, or the actual cost of the flight from headquarters to Timbuktu. The people who operate machinery, handle material, or spend money are the logical choices. Even if no one works directly with these inanimate resources, you can still assign status-reporting responsibility to someone or do it yourself. See the note titled "Designating an Assignment Owner" for a tip on documenting who owns this reporting responsibility.

Another idea is to check with the bean counters. The organization's general ledger or accounting system may contain time and costs incurred by equipment, material, and cost resources. If so, you may be able to obtain an Excel or Access file of the data to import into Project (Chapter 25).

Designating an Assignment Owner

Just as a designated driver gets inebriated partygoers home safely, a designated assignment owner makes sure that inanimate resources get their progress reported properly. Although Project doesn't include an assignment-owner feature, you can invent it yourself.

One approach is to fill in Project's Contact field with the owner (you'll have to insert the field into a table). Or you can create a custom text field (Chapter 21) called something like Assignment Owner or Status Reporter. Next, add this field to the table in your status updating view. Then, for the equipment, material, and cost resources that can't speak for themselves, simply type the name of the person who's responsible for reporting that resource's status into the custom field's cells.

Updating Schedule Status in Project

Status information based on what actually happened is usually referred to as project *actuals*. Actuals are made up of data like actual duration, actual start, actual work, and percent complete. (The note titled "Baseline, Scheduled, and Actual Values" explains the difference between baseline, scheduled, and actual values in Project.) Keep in mind that, to get a *complete* picture of your project's status, you also need estimates about the remaining duration or work.

In this section, you'll learn how to enter status information into your Project file, including the best methods for each situation. This section covers commonly used methods for tracking status in Project. Some techniques update status at the task level, and other techniques update resource assignments. You'll also learn how to quickly "catch up" to your project if it's gotten stalled for some reason. Finally, you'll learn about the best ways to update cost information in your project.

Updating Tasks That Run on Schedule

Follow Along Practice

Tasks don't run completely according to plan very often, but when they do you can update them with a single click whether they're complete or in progress. Here's how you update a task as on schedule:

1. Display the status-update view you created earlier in this chapter or a task view like the Gantt Chart.

2. Select the tasks that are on schedule by dragging over their Task Name cells or Ctrl-clicking individual Task Name cells. In this example, click task ID 1 "Project start" and then Ctrl-click task ID 4 "Identify core event team."

   You can simultaneously update several tasks that are complete or in progress, as long as they're all on schedule.

3. In the Task tab's Schedule section, click the "Mark on Track" button.

   Progress for the selected tasks is updated as running according to plan. Tasks that should have been completed by the status date are set to 100 percent complete, starting and finishing on their scheduled dates. For tasks scheduled to finish *after* the status date, the Actual Start field value is set to the task's Scheduled Start date, and % Complete is updated as complete through the status date.

Updating Task Duration

Recording task duration is a quick and reasonably accurate way to update status. All you need to know is the actual start date, actual duration, and, for incomplete tasks, remaining duration.

Updating Completed Tasks When Duration Doesn't Match the Schedule

Follow Along Practice

If a task didn't start or finish when it was supposed to but it's now complete, then the actual start and actual finish dates are the best values to enter. (You might think setting the % Complete field to 100% is easier, but if you do that, then Project assumes that the task started and finished on the *scheduled* dates.) Here's how to update completed tasks using actual start and actual finish dates:

1. If necessary, display your status-update view (created earlier in this chapter).

2. Select the Actual Start date cell for the task you want to update (in this example, task ID 5 "Define event goals and objectives").

    If the task started on its scheduled date, you can jump to step 4.

3. In the Actual Start date cell, type or select the date that the task actually started (in this example, *6/4/21*). Press Tab to move to the Actual Duration cell (or click the cell).

4. Fill in the actual duration for the task, in this example, type *2d*, and then press Tab.

    If the actual duration is greater than the scheduled duration, Project automatically changes the Remaining Duration value to 0 days, and you're done. If the actual duration is less than the scheduled duration, as it is in this example, Project subtracts the actual duration from the scheduled duration, resulting in remaining duration of 2.5 days.

    > **Tip:** The default units for work and duration are hours and days, respectively. (To set them, choose File→Options→Schedule, and then head to the "Scheduling options for this project" section.) With these default options set, you don't have to type a "d" in a duration field or an "h" in a work field.

5. If the value in the Remaining Duration cell is not 0 days, change the value to 0 days, and then press Tab.

    If you look at the fields in the table, you'll see that Project updates not only the task's actual start and finish fields, but also the percent complete field. If resources are assigned, then it updates the actual work and actual cost fields, as well. If you have change highlighting turned on (Chapter 10), then the ripple effect of delayed tasks appears immediately, as shown in Figure 13-7.

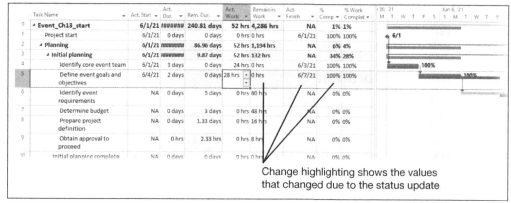

Change highlighting shows the values
that changed due to the status update

Figure 13-7. *When you make changes to a task's cells in a table, Project calculates other values like Actual Finish and % Complete.*

> **Tip:** The Update Tasks dialog box (to open it, in the Task tab's Schedule section, click the down arrow to the right of the "Mark on Track" button, and then choose Update Tasks) is another place to update duration. You can select a single task or multiple tasks before you open the dialog box, and then specify actual dates, % complete, or actual and remaining duration. However, if you're updating several tasks, entering values in a customized table is faster.

Updating Duration for Tasks That Are in Progress

When you update in-progress tasks, you can run into all kinds of statuses: on time, late starts, interruptions while work is under way, and so on. The techniques you use to update tasks depend on the status values you collect and the situation of the task in question. This section describes how to update in-progress tasks.

Follow Along Practice

To enter task status for an in-progress task, follow these steps:

1. If necessary, display your status-update view (created earlier in this chapter).

2. If the task started since your last update, select the Actual Start date cell for the task you want to update (in this example, task ID 23 "Identify potential venues").

   If the task started on its scheduled date, you can jump to step 4.

> **Note:** In this example, you select a task that is scheduled to finish after the status date.

3. In the Actual Start date cell, type or select the date that the task actually started (in this example, *6/28/21*). Press Tab to move to the Actual Duration cell (or click the cell).

4. Fill in the actual duration for the task, in this example, type *1w* (for 1 week), and then press Tab.

Project subtracts the actual duration from the scheduled duration, in this example, reducing the Remaining Duration value from 4 weeks to 3 weeks.

5. If the task is forecast to take more or less time than you planned, enter the remaining duration for the task. In this example, type **2.5w**, and then press Tab.

    If you expect the task to be completed in the scheduled duration, you don't have to change the Remaining Duration value.

    In your customized status-update table, you can see that Project updates the task's fields, like Actual Start, Actual Duration, Remaining Duration, and % Complete, based on your duration entries. If resources are assigned to the task, Project also updates its Actual Work field. Likewise, if you set up these resources with cost rates, then Project automatically updates the task's Actual Cost and Remaining Cost fields.

    As long as you turned on the settings for moving completed and remaining parts of tasks as described earlier in this chapter (Advanced options), Project takes care of recording completed work in the past and moving incomplete work to occur in the future, as shown in Figure 13-8.

    If you **didn't** turn on those settings, incomplete work still appears in the past, even though it isn't done yet. In that case, you have to manually reschedule incomplete work to occur after the status date. To do that, in the Task tab's Tasks section, choose Move→"Incomplete Parts to Status Date." If you need to record work that was completed early, choose Move→"Completed Parts to Status Date" instead.

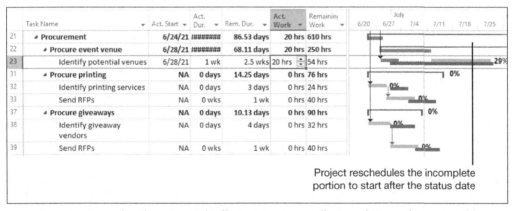

Figure 13-8. *Based on the settings in this file, Project automatically moves the incomplete portion of the task to start after the status date.*

Updating Task Work

Tracking work hours provides more accuracy than tracking duration. How much more depends on the level of work detail that you obtain from you team. This section describes several methods for recording task work.

Updating Actual and Remaining Work

Updating actual and remaining work provides a more accurate picture of project status because work is usually specified in hours, compared with duration's days. Similar to updating actual and remaining duration, you specify a start date if the task started since your last update, the actual work that's been completed, and a forecast of the work hours that remain.

Follow Along Practice

Here's how to update work using a table in a view:

1. Display your status-update view (created earlier in this chapter).

2. Click the Actual Start cell for the task you want to update (in this example, task ID 38 "Identify giveaway vendors"), and then fill in the task's actual start date (in this example, *6/25/21*).

    You can also type the date in the cell.

3. Click the Actual Work cell, and type the number of hours that have been worked so far, in this example, type *24h*.

    You can also click the up or down arrow in the cell to increment the value by 1 hour for each click. When you navigate away from the cell by pressing Tab or Enter or by clicking another cell, Project recalculates the value in the Remaining Work field. For example, if the task's Work value is 32 hrs and you type *24h* into the Actual Work cell, the Remaining Work value changes to 8 hrs.

4. If the estimated work needed to complete the task is more or less than you planned, in the task's Remaining Work cell, type the revised remaining work hours, in this example, type *20h*.

    When you navigate away from the cell (by pressing the Tab key or clicking another cell), Project recalculates the task's other status fields, such as % Complete, % Work Complete, and Remaining Duration. In this example, Project changes the task duration based on the increased total work hours, as shown in Figure 13-9. (If the task completed using fewer hours than planned, simply change the value in the Remaining Work cell to 0.)

    The note titled "Updating Work When Resources Work Longer Days" explains what to do when resources put in extra hours to keep task progress on time.

Note: If you turned on the settings for moving completed and remaining parts of tasks as described earlier in this chapter, then Project takes care of recording completed work in the past and moving incomplete work to occur in the future.

	Task Name	Act. Start	Act. Dur.	Rem. Dur.	Act. Work	Remaining Work	Act. Finish	% Comp	% Work Complet	July 6/20 6/27 7/4 7/11 7/18 7/25
31	⬧ Procure printing	NA	0 days	14.25 days	0 hrs	76 hrs	NA	0%	0%	0%
32	Identify printing services	NA	0 days	3 days	0 hrs	24 hrs	NA	0%	0%	0%
33	Send RFPs	NA	0 wks	1 wk	0 hrs	40 hrs	NA	0%	0%	0%
37	⬧ Procure giveaways	6/25/21	########	14.19 days	24 hrs	78 hrs	NA	26%	24%	26%
38	Identify giveaway vendors	6/25/21	3 days	2.5 days	24 hrs	20 hrs	NA	55%	55%	55%
39	Send RFPs	NA	0 wks	1 wk	0 hrs	40 hrs	NA	0%	0%	0%

Project increases duration due to increased total work

Figure 13-9. *If total work increases, Project increases the task duration.*

Updating Work When Resources Work Longer Days

Suppose actual work hours are **more than** the hours in the Work field. When you fill in the Actual Work field with that value (for example, actual work is 28 hours and the Work value is only 24 hours), the value in the task's Remaining Work field changes to zero without any action on your part. And the task's Actual Duration increases based on the number of hours, such as 3.5 days.

But what if the assigned resource worked longer days to help keep the task in its original duration, such as working those 28 hours in **3** days? In that case, you can change the person's units in the Task Details Form. Here's how:

Follow Along Practice

1. In the View tab's Split View section, turn on the Details checkbox. In the Details drop-down menu, choose Task Details Form in the Views list.

2. In the upper pane, click the Actual Start cell for the task you want to update, in this example, task ID 32 "Identify printing services."

3. Type the actual start date, in this example, **6/25/21**, and then press Tab.

4. In the Task Details Form, right-click the table, and then choose Work on the shortcut menu.

5. Select the Actual radio button.

6. In the "Task type" box, choose Fixed Duration, and then click OK.

7. In the Actual Work cell in the Task Details Form, type the actual hours (**28** in this example).

8. Click OK to save the task. In this example, Project keeps the task's Actual Duration set to 3 days even though the work increased to 28 hours.

9. Change the task's "Task type" back to Fixed Units, and then click OK.

Updating the Project Using Resource-Assignment Status

When resources are assigned to tasks, you can take status updates to a more detailed level. Instead of showing status for the task as a whole, you can update status for individual assignments *within* the task. Admittedly, for tasks that have only one resource assigned, you don't see much of a difference. But for tasks that have multiple resources assigned, entering updates at the assignment level provides more detailed status information.

You have to enter more data to update resource assignments this way, but it makes your status information more accurate. Plus, Project uses the values for individual assignments to determine status for the task as a whole. You don't have to resort to guesswork about a task's overall percent complete when, for example, one resource is 100 percent complete, another is 40 percent complete, and the third is 25 percent complete.

This section describes three effective methods for updating resource-assignment status: actual work complete and remaining work, percentage of work complete, and actual work complete by time period. You'll also learn how to create a specialized tracking view that simplifies entering progress information for resource assignments.

Entering Actual Work Complete and Remaining Work

While *duration* refers to the span of time from the beginning of a task until the end, *work* on an assignment refers to the person-hours a resource is assigned to work. Project can calculate work from duration and vice versa, but they don't measure the same thing (see Chapter 7 to get the full story about the difference between duration and work). If your resources report their hours worked, then entering the actual and remaining work for their assignments provides the most accurate picture of progress and the corresponding labor costs.

Follow Along Practice

Here's how to enter actual work complete and remaining work for assignments:

1. In the top pane of the window, display the Task Usage view. (Click the top pane if necessary, and then, on the View tab, in the Task Views section, click the Task Usage button.)

    If you receive status from a resource about his assignments, the Resource Usage view is better than the Task Usage view, because it groups all the assignments for each resource. That way, you can update all of a particular resource's assignments at once.

    > **Tip:** If you want to fill in fields in the Task Usage or Resource Usage view's table pane, you can create custom views and tables similar to the one created earlier in this chapter.

2. Filter the list to show tasks that might have updates. In this example, in the View tab's Filter box, choose C_Status Updating and type *7/9/21* in the "Enter status date:" box.

3. If necessary, display the Task Details Form in the Details pane (on the View tab, turn on the Details checkbox, and then choose Task Details Form in the drop-down list).

4. In the Task Details Form, select the Actual option if necessary.

   You can display current scheduled, baseline, or actual date values by selecting the Current, Baseline, or Actual radio buttons, respectively.

5. If necessary, right-click the Task Details Form and choose Work on the shortcut menu.

   The Work table includes fields for specifying actual work, remaining work, and overtime work.

6. In the table in the Task Usage view, select the task whose actual and remaining work you want to update. In this example, select task ID 6 "Identify event requirements."

   Info about the task appears in the Task Details Form in the Details pane, as shown in Figure 13-10.

7. If the task started since your last update, in the Task Detail Form's Start box, type the task actual start date (in this example, type *6/9/21*).

   The box displays NA until you enter a start date. If you don't enter the actual start date, then Project sets it to the scheduled start date. If you customize the Resource Usage view's table to include the Actual Start field, you can fill in actual start dates for individual assignments.

8. In the Task Details Form's table, in the first Actual Work cell, enter the actual amount of work that the resource has completed on his assignment. In this example, in the Sales Lead's Actual Work cell, type *16h*.

   Use the normal time-period abbreviations like 8h, 5d, or 2w.

9. In the Remaining Work cell, enter the remaining work hours needed to complete the selected assignment. In this example, type *0h* to indicate that the Sales Lead's assignment is complete.

10. If you want to fill in status for the other assignments, fill in the Actual Work and Remaining Work cells in the other rows in the Task Details Form's table.

    In this example, fill in the Actual Work cells for the Marketing Lead and Jaye Smith with 16h. Fill in the Remaining Work cells with 0h.

> **Tip:** You can fill in values for one assignment, and then click OK to save that update. Later, you can fill in values for other assignments for the same task.

11. In the Task Details Form, click OK to update the assignment.

Figure 13-10. *If total work increases, Project increases the task duration. If total work decreases, the duration decreases.*

Follow Along Practice

You can also update individual assignments in the Assignment Information dialog box. Here's how:

1. Double-click the assignment you want to update. In this example, double-click the Assistant PM row for task ID 7 "Determine budget."

    The Assignment Information dialog box opens.

2. Click the Tracking tab.

3. In the "Actual start" box, choose or type the actual start date for the assignment, in this example, *6/15/21*.

4. In the "Actual work" box, type the amount of work that's complete, in this example, *12h*.

5. In the "Remaining work" box, type the amount of work that remains, in this example, *0h*. Figure 13-11 shows the Assignment Information dialog box.

6. Click OK to update the assignment.

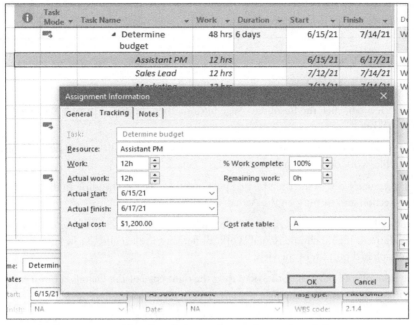

Figure 13-11. *If total work changes, Project changes the task duration.*

7. If several assignments share the same status, you can select them all by dragging over the assignments. In this example, drag over the cells in the task ID column for the Sales Lead's, Marketing Lead's, and Jaye Smith's assignments for the "Determine budget" task. Then, right-click anywhere within the selected rows and choose Information on the shortcut menu.

   The Multiple Assignment Information dialog box opens.

8. Click the Tracking tab.

9. In the "Actual start" box, choose or type the actual start date for the assignment, in this example, *6/16/21*.

10. In the "Actual work" box, type the amount of work that's complete, in this example, *6h*.

11. In the "Remaining work" box, type the amount of work that remains, in this example, *0h*.

12. Click OK to update the assignments.

Entering Actual Work by Time Period

For the ultimate in progress detail and accuracy, you can enter actual work by time period. But be forewarned that this is the most time-consuming method of tracking progress, for you ***and*** for your resources. Typically, if you need to track this level of detail, you'll use Project Server/Project Online and Project Web App to automate collecting and recording this information. However, you can enter actual work in the time-phased portion of a usage view, showing how much work was done on an assignment in each time period (day, week, or whatever). One way to streamline recording this type of detail is by copying and pasting values from an Excel spreadsheet.

Chapter 13: Tracking Status

> **Note:** If you want to follow along, use the file Ch13_statusupdate.xlsx.

Follow Along Practice

To copy and paste actual work by time period, follow these steps:

1. On the View tab, click the Resource Usage button. Then, in the View tab's Data section, click Tables→Work.

    Not only do the usage views show assignment information, but they also show time-phased information, like work or cost values over time.

2. Display Actual Work in the time-phased portion of the view by heading to the Format tab's Details section and turning on the Actual Work checkbox.

    Alternatively, you can simply right-click in the time-phased portion of the usage view and then, on the shortcut menu, choose Actual Work. Either way, Project adds a row labeled "Act. Work" to the time-phased portion of the view.

3. In the time-phased portion of the view, drag the right edge of the Details column to the right so you can see all the text it contains.

4. If you need to change the timescale time unit to match the one in the spreadsheet, in the View tab's Zoom section, choose the time unit you want in the Timescale drop-down list (Days, in this example).

5. Scroll to the summary row for the resource whose assignments you want to update, in this example, Marketing Content Developer.

6. In the table, select the assignment whose actual work you want to update, in this example, "Plan press releases."

7. To display the cells for the assignment in the time-phased portion of the view, in the Task tab's Editing section, click "Scroll to Task."

    Project scrolls the time-phased portion of the view to show when work is scheduled to begin on the selected assignment.

8. In the Task Details Form in the Details pane, in the Start box, fill in the actual start date for the assignment (*6/24/21*, in this example). Click OK.

    If you modify the table in the Resource Usage view to include the Actual Start field, you can fill in the actual start date in the table.

9. In Excel, open the spreadsheet with status data (Ch13_statusupdate.xlsx, in this example).

10. Drag over the cells that contain work hours for the assignment, in this example, drag over the cells containing work for 6/24/21 through 6/28/21, as shown in Figure 13-12. Press Ctrl+C to copy the values to the Clipboard.

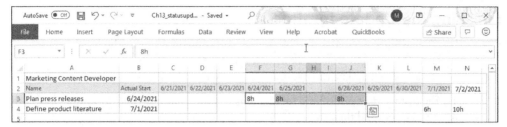

Figure 13-12. *Drag over the cells that you want to copy and paste into Project.*

11. Back in Project, in the time-phased portion of the view, click the cell in the assignment's Actual Work row that corresponds to the first date with actual work hours for the assignment in the spreadsheet (6/24/21, in this example).

12. Press Ctrl+V to paste the values.

Project copies the values from each selected cell in the Excel spreadsheet into the cells in the Resource Usage view's time-phased grid, as shown in Figure 13-13. In this example, the spreadsheet includes blank cells that represent non-working days, so you can paste values for more than one week at a time.

> **Tip:** If a resource tells you more time is needed, update the Remaining Work cell in the Task Details Form to the value they provide. If you don't explicitly enter a value for remaining work, then Project calculates it by subtracting the actual work you just entered from the scheduled amount of work.

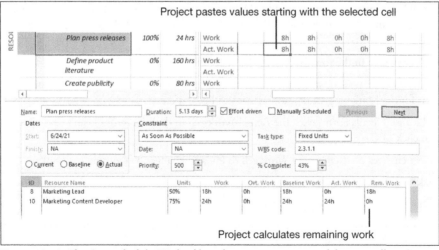

Figure 13-13. *If you've applied the Work table to the view, as you type work hours in cells in the time-phased portion of the view, Project updates the value in the table's Actual Work field.*

13. Repeat steps 6 through 12 to copy the actual work hours for the "Define product literature" assignment. For this assignment, fill in the Actual Start with *7/1/21*.

Finishing the Update for the Sample Project

If you've been following along in the example project, you've used various methods for updating tasks and assignments. The example project still has a few tasks that need to be update through the status date. In this section, you'll update those tasks while reviewing several of the update methods.

1. Display the custom view you created for updating (on the View tab, click the bottom half of the Gantt Chart button, and then choose C_Status Updating).

    The C_Status Updating filter box appears because the view is set up with an interactive filter.

2. In the C_Status Updating dialog box, choose or type the status date (in this example, *7/9/21*), and then click OK.

    The table lists tasks that are scheduled to start before the status date and are not yet complete.

3. In the custom view table, click the Actual Start cell for task ID 8 "Prepare project definition." Type the date *6/19/21*, and then press Enter.

4. In the Actual Duration cell, type *1.5d*, and then press Enter.

    Project calculates the actual work for the task and changes Remaining Duration to 0 days and % Complete to 100%.

5. Task ID 9 "Obtain approval to proceed" is now scheduled to start on 6/25/21. Suppose this task occurs and finishes on that date. The easiest way to update this task is to right-click in the task row and then click 100% on the icon bar that appears.

    Keep in mind, this technique only works when the task completes according to its current schedule.

6. Task ID 10 "Initial planning complete" is a milestone that indicates that the project has approval to proceed. In this example, right-click the task's row and then click 100% on the icon bar that appears.

7. Click anywhere in the row for task ID 13 "Plan press releases."

    Earlier, you updated the assignment for the Marketing Content Developer. However, the assignment for the Marketing Lead resource has not been updated.

8. In the Task Details Form, click the Actual Work cell in the Marketing Lead's row. Type *18h*, and then click OK.

    Project changes the Remaining Work cell to 0h, and changes % Complete to 100%.

9. Click the Actual Start cell for task ID 33 "Send RFPs." Type the date *7/2/21*, and then press Tab.

10. In the Actual Duration cell, type *2.5d*, and then press Tab.

    If a message box appears, click OK. Project inserts a split in the task and reschedules the incomplete duration to start on the status date, based on the options set earlier in this chapter.

11. Task ID 13 "Plan press releases," Task ID 23 "Identify potential venues" and Task ID 38 "Identify giveaway vendors" have incomplete work that is still scheduled to occur before the status date. To reschedule them to the status date, select these tasks. On the Task tab, in the Tasks section,

click the Move down arrow, and then, in the Move Tasks Forward section, choose "Incomplete Parts to Status Date."

12. If necessary, on the View tab, click the Timescale down arrow, and then choose Weeks. In the Filter drop-down list, choose [No Filter] or Clear Filter.

Figure 13-14 shows the updated tasks.

	Task Name	Act. Start	Act. Dur.	Rem. Dur.	Act. Work	Remaining Work	Act. Finish	% Comp	% Work Complet	June 5/30 6/6 6/13 6/20 6/27 Jul
0	▲ Event_Ch13_start	6/1/21	14.7 days	229.3 days	305 hrs	4,014 hrs	NA	6%	7%	
1	Project start	6/1/21	0 days	0 days	0 hrs	0 hrs	6/1/21	100%	100%	◆ 6/1
2	▲ Planning	6/1/21	23.59 days	72.91 days	213 hrs	1,004 hrs	NA	24%	18%	
3	▲ Initial planning	6/1/21	18.75 days	0 days	155 hrs	0 hrs	6/25/21	100%	100%	100%
4	Identify core event team	6/1/21	3 days	0 days	24 hrs	0 hrs	6/3/21	100%	100%	100%
5	Define event goals and objectives	6/4/21	2 days	0 days	28 hrs	0 hrs	6/7/21	100%	100%	100%
6	Identify event requirements	6/9/21	4 days	0 days	48 hrs	0 hrs	6/14/21	100%	100%	100%
7	Determine budget	6/15/21	3 days	0 days	30 hrs	0 hrs	6/17/21	100%	100%	100%
8	Prepare project definition	6/19/21	1.5 days	0 days	17 hrs	0 hrs	6/22/21	100%	100%	100%
9	Obtain approval to proceed	6/25/21	2 hrs	0 hrs	8 hrs	0 hrs	6/25/21	100%	100%	100%
10	Initial planning complete	6/25/21	0 days	0 days	0 hrs	0 hrs	6/25/21	100%	100%	◆ 6/25
11	▲ Plan marketing	6/24/21	8.6 days	70.9 days	58 hrs	1,004 hrs	NA	11%	5%	
12	▲ Prepare marketing messages	6/24/21	8.83 days	40.67 days	58 hrs	624 hrs	NA	18%	9%	
13	Plan press releases	6/24/21	6.25 days	0 days	42 hrs	0 hrs	7/2/21	100%	100%	
14	Define product literature	7/1/21	0.4 wks	3.6 wks	16 hrs	144 hrs	NA	10%	10%	
15	Define presentation cc	NA	0 wks	4 wks	0 hrs	480 hrs	NA	0%	0%	
16	Messaging plan complete	NA	0 days	0 days	0 hrs	0 hrs	NA	0%	0%	

Figure 13-14. *Completed task bars appear in dark blue. Completed portions of in-progress tasks are dark red if the tasks are critical.*

Updating Project Costs

Projects can have several different sources of costs: human resources, equipment, materials, cost resources, and fixed costs for tasks. Each type of cost that applies to your project needs actual cost information before you can see how the project's cost compares to its baseline cost. In this section, you'll learn how to update each of these cost sources. Project's Cost table is a great starting point, with fields for baseline, scheduled, actual, and remaining costs. You can apply this table to a usage view to see costs for individual assignments as well.

You can also insert cost-related fields like Actual Cost into any table. Just remember that, if you add these fields to a task-oriented table, their values represent *task* costs; if you add these fields to a resource-oriented table, their values relate to resources instead. And when you add these fields to a usage view, you can see values for the individual assignments.

Updating Actual Costs for Work Resources

If you set up work resources with standard rates, overtime rates, and costs per use (Chapter 6) and assign the resources to tasks, then Project calculates actual cost as soon as you enter actual work. That means you don't have to update actual labor and equipment costs yourself. The note titled "Manually Entering Resource Costs" below tells you what you have to do if you want to update resource costs manually.

With equipment resources, the challenge is making sure that actual work time is reported. To solve that problem, designate an assignment owner for equipment resource assignments, as described in the note titled "Designating an Assignment Owner."

Manually Entering Resource Costs

When you tell Project how much resources cost, assign those resources to tasks, and then enter actual work, Project automatically calculates their actual costs for you. What's not to like? However, Project lets you update resource costs manually—for example, when you want to enter the project costs provided by your accounting department. To tell the program you want to type actual costs into the fields that Project usually calculates, choose File→Options; on the left side of the Project Options dialog box, click Schedule; and then scroll down and turn off the "Actual costs are always calculated by Project" checkbox. (You don't have to do this in the example project.) With this setting turned off, Project still calculates actual costs, but you can enter total actual costs in tasks' Actual Cost fields.

To manually enter time-phased costs for tasks or resource assignments, display the Task Usage view. In the Task Usage Tools | Format tab's Details section, turn on the Actual Cost checkbox to add the Actual Cost row to the time-phased portion of the view. You can then enter actual costs by time period in the Actual Cost field either for the assignment or for the task as a whole.

Updating Actual Costs for Material Resources

With standard rates or costs per use in place for your material resources and the material resources assigned to tasks, Project calculates the actual cost for material resources based on the number of units used or the amount per time period, like 20 jugs of goop at $100 per jug or four jugs of goop per day times a 5-day task duration times $100 per jug (in that case, the actual cost for the material resource is based on the actual duration of the task).

To fill in the quantity of material used, type the quantity in the Actual Work field for the material resource. Remember, the Material Label field specifies the unit of measure for the material resource. If you specify a quantity consumed by time period (Chapter 7), Project calculates the quantity consumed based on the task duration. If the actual amount of material used that Project calculates isn't correct, you can change it in the Actual Work field for the material resource assignment. Use the Task Usage view or the Resource Usage view. In the example project, you don't have to update any material costs manually.

Updating Actual Costs for Cost Resources

When you assign a cost resource to a task, you enter the estimated cost (Chapter 7). However, if you assign a cost resource to a task that also has work and material resources, then when you enter actual progress, Project calculates actual work and material costs, but not cost-resource costs. Progress information is based on duration or work completed, and cost resources operate independently of time spent on a task. This disconnect means that you could try to set a task to 100 percent complete, but the cost resource would still show remaining cost, as illustrated in Figure 13-15 and % Complete would remain at 99%.

> **Note:** If cost resources are the only type of resource assigned to the task, then cost-resource costs become actual costs when you enter actual progress.

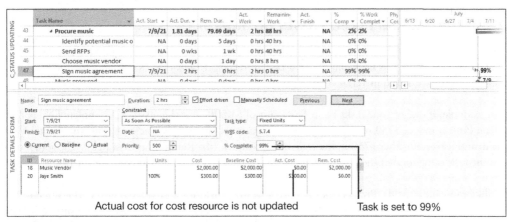

Actual cost for cost resource is not updated   Task is set to 99%

Figure 13-15. *When you enter actual work or duration, Project doesn't update cost resource actual values.*

Follow Along Practice

If a task has work and cost resources assigned to it, then you have to explicitly update the actual cost of the cost resources. To enter cost-resource costs as actual costs, follow these steps:

1. In the status updating view created earlier in this chapter (with the filter set to [No Filter]), select the task you want to update, in this example, task ID 47 "Sign music agreement."

   If the Task Details Form is not visible, on the View tab, turn on the Details checkbox, and then choose Task Details Form from the drop-down menu. If necessary, select the Actual radio button and display the Cost table by right-clicking the form and then choosing Cost on the shortcut menu.

2. In the Task Details Form, click the Actual Cost cell for the cost resource, in this example, Music Vendor.

3. Fill in the cost, in this example, type **2000**.

4. Click the Remaining Cost cell, and fill in the remaining cost for the cost resource, in this exam-

ple, type *0*.

5. Click OK to update the task.

> **Note:** You can update an assignment in the Task Usage or Resource Usage view, if you prefer. For example, double-click the cost resource assignment for the task, and then, in the Assignment Information dialog box, click the Tracking tab, which includes an "Actual cost" box.

At this point, the update for the example project is complete. If you're following along, save the project file with a new name. To do that, choose File→Save As. Navigate to the folder where you want to save the file. In the Save As dialog box's "File name" box, type the name for the file, in this example, *Event_Ch13_updatecomplete*. Click Save.

Updating Actual Fixed Costs on Tasks

Fixed costs are primarily used for fixed-cost contracts (Chapter 9). If you use fixed costs, then when you enter actual progress information on a task, Project calculates the actual cost for the fixed cost along with the work and material costs.

For example, if one of your tasks has a fixed cost of $1,500, and the task's % Complete field is now 50%, Project moves $750 of the fixed cost to the actual cost side of the equation (the Actual Cost field) and leaves the other $750 in the remaining cost side (the Remaining Cost field). The actual cost for the task is the total of these two fixed-cost values and any other actual costs on the task.

Unlike most other fields, Project doesn't have a separate field for actual fixed costs. The value in the Fixed Cost field is the total of your estimated fixed costs and actual fixed costs, so be sure to update the Fixed Cost field with the current fixed-cost value. The Cost table includes the Fixed Cost field.

Rescheduling the Whole Project

Sometimes, a project goes off kilter and you need a quick way to recover. For example, maybe several months of work was complete when you were told to stop work immediately. Now, a month later, the project is on again. Unfortunately, in the interim, the dates in your Project file are still set to the original schedule.

This section describes a quick-fix recovery method that lets you reschedule unfinished work by changing the start dates or resume dates of all tasks to today's date so you can continue from this point forward.

> **Note:** If you want to follow along, use Save As to save a copy of the file you saved in the previous section.

If your project was interrupted midstream and is now resuming, then you have a lot of schedule dates to adjust. Rather than adjust dates manually, it's simpler to have Project reschedule any uncompleted work. Here's how you get the program to do just that:

1. Display any task-oriented view.

    The Update Project command you'll use in the next step is available only for task-oriented views.

2. Apply the Entry table to the view so you can see the Indicators column.

3. To reschedule only certain tasks, select them. In this example, don't select any tasks.

    If a project has resumed after a delay, you'll typically want to reschedule all in-progress and unstarted tasks, which is why you don't need to select any tasks.

4. In the Project tab's Status section, click Update Project.

    The Update Project dialog box opens with "Update work as complete through" and "Entire project" selected automatically.

5. To reschedule the entire project, as in this example, keep the "Entire project" radio button selected.

6. Select the "Reschedule uncompleted work to start after" option shown in Figure 13-16, and then type the date when work should resume, in this example, **_8/16/21_**.

    The Update Project command adds a Start No Earlier Than date constraint to each task that is rescheduled. Any tasks that were in progress when the project was halted resume on that date. It also means that any unstarted tasks scheduled to start before that date now start on this new date instead, and any successors linked to those tasks are rescheduled to follow their predecessors as normal.

> **Note:** Any tasks that already have a date constraint set will not move to the new date. A message box warns you that those tasks will not be rescheduled to the new date.

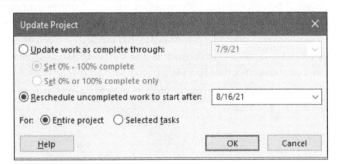

Figure 13-16. _Be sure to select the "Reschedule uncompleted work to start after" option._

7. Click OK.

All uncompleted work in the project now starts after the date you specified, as shown in Figure 13-17. Examine your schedule carefully for issues you need to address. If you created manually scheduled tasks or set date constraints, be sure to review those tasks. Check for conflicts between constraints and predecessors (see Chapter 5). Also, look at milestone dates and the project finish date to see if you need to shorten the remaining schedule because of the delay. Look at the project costs to see if anything is now going over budget.

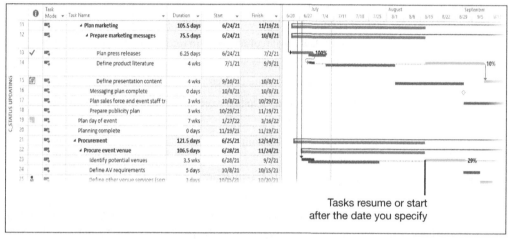

Figure 13-17. *When you reschedule uncompleted work, in-progress tasks show a stop/start split with dotted lines.*

If necessary, submit the new schedule to the stakeholders and get their approval again. Once that's done, you may want to save a new baseline. You can either overwrite your original baseline or save a second baseline (Chapter 12) and work with that as your primary benchmark from now on.

> **Tip:** The Update Project dialog box automatically selects the "Update work as complete through" option, which updates tasks as completed or in progress exactly as scheduled through a specified date. Updating a project in this way seriously compromises the accuracy of your project data, so using this option is a no-no. Bottom line: you simply have to gather the missing data and update your file.

14

Evaluating Project Performance

Small issues can blow up into project wildfires if you don't douse them early. A delay here, a cost over-run there, and suddenly the finish date, cost, and project objectives are at risk. Regular project performance reviews are a must if you want your daily jolt limited to your double espresso. Comparing the project's current status to baseline schedule and cost can give you early warning of trouble brewing.

Schedule, budget, and other project objectives are interdependent, so where you start your evaluation depends on what's most important. If the project's budget is crucial, you can start by evaluating costs. But in most cases, starting with the schedule makes sense, because delays can affect the finish date *and* the price tag.

This chapter starts by showing you how to evaluate schedule performance, whether you want a quick peek at overall progress or a heads-up about tasks in trouble. You'll learn how to use Project's views, reports, and filters to see high-level and task-by-task progress, as well as to uncover potential problems. You'll also discover ways to find overallocated resources and tasks that are exceeding their work budgets. Likewise, you'll learn about reports and filters for comparing project costs to the baseline cost or a budget. And no chapter on project performance would be complete without a section on earned value analysis. You'll find out how earned value and its related measures help you evaluate performance, and then learn how to use them in Project.

Once you know where your project stands, the next step is usually making adjustments to keep the project on time and within budget. Fortunately, most of the techniques you use during project execution are the same as the ones you use for fine-tuning a project during planning (see Chapters 10 and 11). This chapter describes one more option: assigning overtime.

> **Note:** Evaluating your project's schedule and costs means looking at the project from many directions. This chapter describes some of the ways you may want to customize elements to see performance. However, chapters later in this book (starting with Chapter 17) describe customizing Project elements in detail.

Scheduled, Baseline, and Actual Values

During project planning, there's only one set of values to watch—the dates, work amounts, and costs that Project calculates, which are known as *scheduled* or *planned* values. But once a project gets under way, additional types of values suddenly have roles in determining project performance. Before you dive into evaluating performance, it's a good idea to understand the differences among these values and how they contribute to measuring performance. Here are the different types of values that are important during the execution phase and where you find them:

- **Scheduled (also known as planned)** values are the forecast values at any point during the project, whether you're putting your plan together or already tracking progress. Scheduled fields like Start, Finish, Work, Cost, and Duration combine actual performance so far with the forecast values for the work that remains. For example, if you've worked 100 hours so far and you forecast another 200 hours to finish, then the Work field's value is the sum of the two: 300 hours. While you're planning, scheduled values are merely forecasts, because no *actual* values exist yet. At the end of the project, scheduled values equal actual values, because there's nothing left to forecast.

- **Baseline** values are what the scheduled dates, work, cost, and duration were when you saved your baseline (Chapter 12), usually after the stakeholders approved your project plan. When you set a baseline, Project copies the values from Start, Finish, Work, Cost, and Duration fields to Baseline Start, Baseline Finish, Baseline Work, Baseline Cost, and Baseline Duration, so you have a snapshot of your schedule's values before you begin tracking status. As you'll learn shortly, the difference between scheduled and baseline values is a *huge* part of evaluating project performance.

- **Actual** values are what actually happened: when tasks really started and finished, how long tasks took, how much work has been done, and how much tasks really cost. The fields for actual values are, unsurprisingly, Actual Start, Actual Finish, Actual Work, Actual Cost, and Actual Duration.

- **Remaining** values are simply the duration, work, and costs that remain. For example, suppose the original forecast work for a task was 120 hours. The assigned resource has completed 60 hours but estimates that it'll take 80 more hours to finish. In this example, the original estimate (120 hours) and actual work (60 hours) don't matter; the Remaining Work value is 80 hours. (If the resource is assigned full time to the task, the Remaining Duration is 2 weeks.)

- **Variances** are the difference between scheduled and baseline values. In Project, variance fields like Cost Variance and Finish Variance are calculated as scheduled value minus baseline value, like Cost – Baseline Cost. If the scheduled cost is greater than the baseline cost, the positive variance shows that the task is over budget. Likewise, if the scheduled finish date is later than the baseline finish date, the positive variance indicates that the task is behind schedule. In other words, positive variances are bad; negative variances are good. Later in this chapter you'll learn how earned value variances, CV (earned value cost variance), and SV (earned value schedule variance) differ from Project's basic variance fields.

> **Note:** A variance that's equal to zero (0) can mean one of two things: A task is exactly on track—or you forgot to set a baseline. During project execution, tasks that go exactly according to plan produce zero variance. But if *every* task has zero variance, the problem is the absence of a baseline.

Is the Project on Time?

Reviewing project dates is usually the first step in evaluating performance, because a project's duration has a way of affecting its price tag, too. This section explains ways to review the schedule, whether at the project level, for day-to-day task management, or to calculate schedule performance metrics. (The note titled "Risky Business" describes another way to evaluate performance that doesn't involve Project.)

> **Note:** If you've downloaded files from the website, use the file Event_Ch14_start.mpp.

Because actual progress affects the rest of the project, evaluating performance adds a few techniques to the ones you used to review a schedule during planning (Chapter 9). You keep tabs on the project schedule at several levels:

- **The project finish date**: The bottom line, of course, is whether the project is going to finish when it should, which is what a quick peek at the overall project finish date shows.

- **Tactical task management**: Keeping the overall schedule on track means keeping individual tasks on time. Most project managers check tasks each week to see if any are in trouble or heading that way. Because delays on the critical path mean a late project finish date, critical path tasks are the first ones to examine (Chapter 9). However, you also have to keep an eye on noncritical tasks, because they can *become* critical if they go on too long.

- **Overall schedule performance**: There's more to schedule performance than the finish date. Schedule performance measures like schedule variance (SV) and schedule performance index (SPI), described later in this chapter, tell you how well you're managing the project's schedule, or whether corrective actions are working. You can compare performance measures from week to week or month to month to look for trends.

The following sections explain how to check your project at each of these levels.

> **Tip:** If the Details pane is visible, hide it so you can use the entire Project window to review your project. To do that, double-click the horizontal divider between the primary pane and the Details pane. (Alternatively, in the View tab's Split View section, turn off the Details checkbox.)

Checking Status at the Project Level

Project-wide status for schedule, cost, and work comes as a package deal in several places within Project. Project-level variances are the first hint of problems. Here are three ways to see overall schedule, cost, and work statuses:

- **Project summary task**: The project summary task is a simple way to see high-level status. When you apply different tables to a view, you can see different values in the project summary task row. For example, the Cost table (in the View tab's Data section, click Tables→Cost) focuses on costs, including the planned, baseline, actual, and remaining cost, as well as the variance between the baseline cost and the current scheduled cost. As shown in Figure 14-1, the current project cost is $556,500, while the baseline cost is $550,050. The Variance field shows that the project is currently $6,450 over the baselined estimate. To see work variances, in the View tab's Data section, click Tables→Work.

> **Note:** Hash marks ("###") in table cells mean that the column isn't wide enough to display the values in those cells. The easiest way to view column values is to double-click the vertical line to the column heading's right.

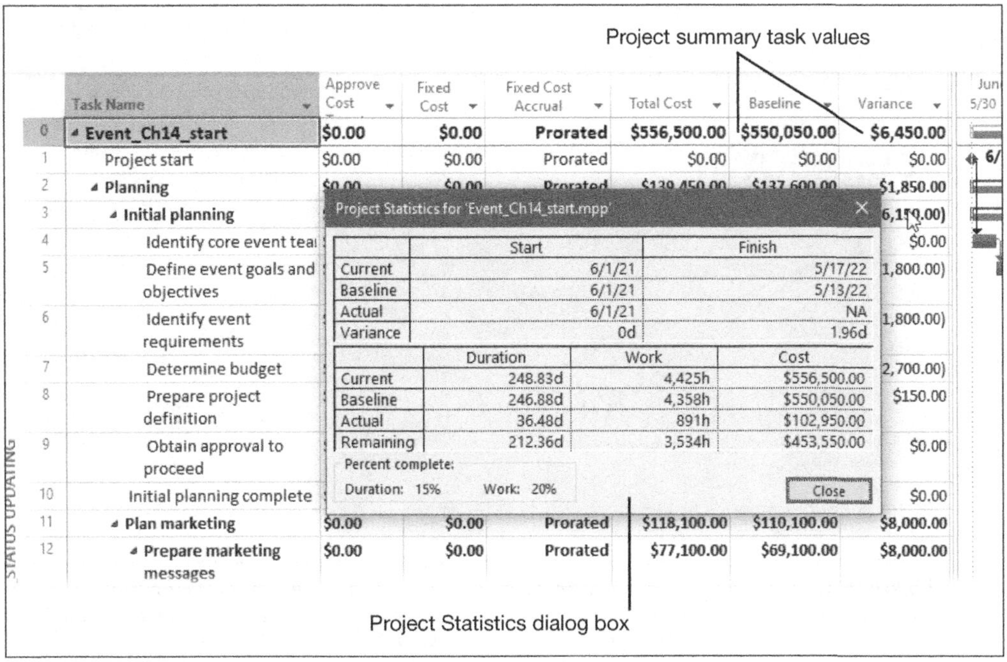

Figure 14-1. *The project summary task (background) and the Project Statistics dialog box (foreground) display project-level values.*

- **Project Statistics dialog box**: This dialog box (Figure 14-1, foreground) shows scheduled, baseline, actual, and remaining values at the project level for fields like start and finish dates, duration, work, and cost. To open it, head to the Project tab's Properties section and click Project Information; in the Project Information dialog box, click Project Statistics. It's easy to see that the current finish date is a few days later than the baseline finish date and that the current cost is higher than the baseline cost. To close the dialog box, click its Close button at the bottom right.

- **Burndown report**: This graphical report compares baseline, actual, and remaining work so you can see how much work has been completed (or "burned through," which is where the term "burndown" comes from), how much is left, and how that compares to what you planned (see Figure 14-2). To run it, in the Report tab's View Reports section, click Dashboards→Burndown. The chart on the right side of the report shows the number of remaining tasks. In this project, the Remaining Cumulative Work line is above the Baseline Remaining Cumulative Work line, which means that there is more work to complete at this point in the project than was originally planned.

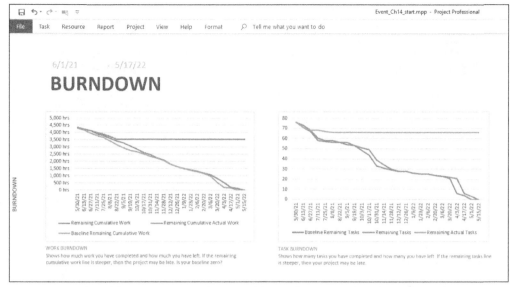

Figure 14-2. *If the Remaining Cumulative Work line in this report is above the Baseline Remaining Cumulative Work line (as shown here), then you have more work left to complete than you planned, a red flag that the project may finish late.*

Risky Business

When you plan a project, you put together a risk management plan, which identifies risks and what you'll do if they become reality. During the project's execution, you have to monitor risks.

Schedule delays and increasing costs can be a sign that a risk has turned into reality (at which point, it's called an issue), but talking to the team is a more proactive way to track risks. (A risk-management plan may identify events that foretell imminent risks, like a subcontractor who doesn't report status when progress is slow.) Ask team members if issues have come up—they may need help but are afraid to ask.

If risks ***do*** become reality, it's time to launch the response you laid out during planning. For example, you may replace a subcontractor, dip into the project's contingency funds, or reduce the project's scope to maintain its schedule and budget.

Although Project doesn't offer tools specifically to manage risk, you might consider several add-on tools, such as Barbecana's Full Monte and Palisade's @Risk.

- **Cost Overview report**: Another graphical report, this one summarizes the project's cost status. To run it, in the Report tab's View Reports section, click Dashboards→Cost Overview. One of the report's charts compares the percentage complete to the amount of money spent. If the chart's Cost line is above its % Complete line, then the percentage of the total project cost that you've spent is higher than the percentage of duration that's complete, which could indicate that the project might be over budget. This report also includes a table showing cost status for the project's top-level tasks. In this example, the Cumulative Cost line begins below the Cumulative Percent Complete line. By the end of the project, the two lines sync up because this project incurs more cost later in the project.

Keeping Your Eye on Critical Tasks

Tasks on the critical path affect a project's finish date, so it's a good idea to check on them frequently to make sure they aren't delayed. The Tracking Gantt view displays critical tasks as red task bars (Chapter 9). However, you can display critical tasks in any task-oriented view by heading to the Format tab's Bar Styles section and turning on the Critical Tasks checkbox. If you want to see *only* the tasks on the critical path, then in the View tab's Data section, click the Filter down arrow and then choose Critical.

Looking for Delayed Tasks

Finding tasks whose start dates are delayed can help you correct delays before they get any worse. Delays in noncritical tasks may not affect the project finish date *yet*, but they can if their duration increases. Part of your weekly tactical management routine should be looking for delayed tasks (critical and noncritical alike). Then you can evaluate each delayed task to try to prevent—or at least limit—further delays. This section describes several filters and reports that highlight delayed tasks.

The first step in a task checkup is looking for tasks that *should* have started but haven't. If you seem to have a lot of late starters, make sure you've entered status values into Project (Chapter 13). Once you've filled in any missing actuals, it's time to find out why the remaining tasks are delayed.

A good way to check for delayed tasks is to use the Should Start By filter. This filter shows tasks that should have started by the date you specify (say, your most recent status date) but haven't. This filter looks for tasks whose Start values are earlier than your Should Start By date but whose Actual Start cells are still empty. Once you've filtered your task list, you can then switch tables in the view to see different task values. Here's how to apply this filter:

1. Display a task-oriented view like the Tracking Gantt view (on the View tab, click the bottom half of the Gantt Chart button, and then choose Tracking Gantt on the drop-down menu).

2. In the View tab's Data section, click the Filter down arrow, and then choose More Filters.

   The More Filters dialog box opens.

3. Select Should Start By and then click Apply.

   The Should Start By dialog box opens.

4. Type your checkup date, in this example, type *7/10/21*, and then click OK.

The view changes to show only the tasks that should have started before the date you entered but haven't, as shown in Figure 14-3. If you can't see task bars in the timescale, select one of the tasks in the table, and then, in the Task tab's Editing section, click Scroll to Task.

5. Check in with the resources assigned to those tasks to find out why they haven't started yet.

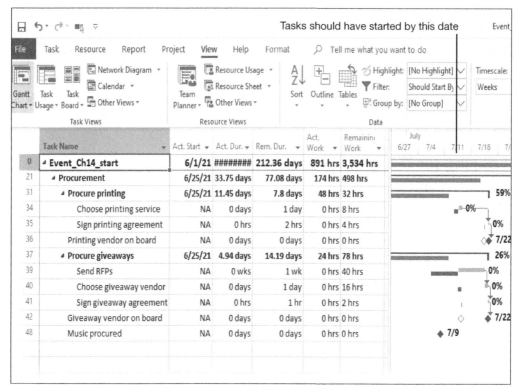

Figure 14-3. *When you apply the Should Start By filter to the Tracking Gantt view, red task bars are delayed critical tasks, and blue task bars are delayed noncritical tasks.*

Looking for Tasks Heading for Trouble

The next tactic is looking for tasks whose *finish* dates are late—later than their baseline finish dates, that is. These task delays can lead to a late project finish date *and* upset the resource workloads you so carefully balanced during planning, creating new resource overallocations you have to resolve.

Watching for ballooning work hours is another way to spot tasks that are in trouble. Just like time that slips away when attic cleaning turns into reminiscing over old pictures, the time it takes to perform tasks can expand beyond your estimates. These extra hours can produce longer task durations and higher resource costs, so it's especially important to nip these excesses in the bud.

This section shows you how to look for delayed tasks and tasks whose work hours exceed baseline work, even if they haven't yet delayed the finish date. Here are different ways to look for these at-risk tasks:

- **Tasks that are slipping**: The Slipping Tasks filter shows tasks whose finish dates are later than their baseline finish dates. These tasks may be scheduled to start late, have already started late, or are taking longer than planned. By looking for slipping tasks every week, you may have time to recover from the slip or to prevent it from getting worse. By applying different tables to the current view, you can see dates, variances, work amounts, or costs for the tasks in the filtered list. To apply this filter, in the View tab's Data section, click the Filter down arrow, and then choose More Filters. In the More Filters dialog box, select Slipping Tasks and then click Apply.

- **Tasks that are slipping or falling behind**: The Slipped/Late Progress filter (View→Filter→More Filters→Slipped/Late Progress) looks for slipping tasks **and** checks for tasks whose completed work is less than the amount that should be done (which could delay the finish date if that trend continues). In the example project, tasks in the planning and procurement portions of the project are slipping, which, in turn, are making tasks throughout the project slip.

> **Tip:** To look for schedule trends, sort the Variance table by finish date: On the View tab, click Tables→Variance, and then, in the table's header area, click the triangle next to the Finish heading and choose "Sort Earliest to Latest." That way, tasks appear from the earliest finish date to the latest. If the values in the Finish Variance field grow larger as the finish dates progress, the project is falling further behind over time. On the other hand, if the Finish Variance values are growing smaller, it may be a sign that your corrective actions are working. (The variances in the example project don't trend up or down.) To remove the sorting, on the View tab, click Sort, and then choose "by ID" on the drop-down menu.

- **Assignments that are slipping**: It makes sense that an assignment that slips can turn into a task that slips. The Slipping Assignments filter (View→Filter→More Filters→Slipping Assignments) is a resource filter that you can apply to the Resource Usage view to find assignments whose scheduled finish dates are later than their baseline finish dates. (You don't have to switch to the Resource Usage view with the Slipping Assignments filter in the example project.) One resource with several slipping assignments is a sure sign of someone who could use some help. The problem may be too many tasks at the same time, the wrong skillset, or too many distractions.

> **Tip:** Graphical indicators display images based on how late or over budget a task is. For example, you can set up a custom field with graphical indicators like a green happy face if Cost Variance is less than 10 percent of the baseline cost and a red *unhappy* face if Cost Variance is greater than 25 percent of the baseline cost. Chapter 21 describes how to set up custom fields with graphical indicators.

Work hours that exceed a task's baseline hours can increase your project's duration and cost. For completed tasks, of course, it's too late to make corrections. Still, it's a good idea to investigate the reason why such overruns occurred, particularly if the same resources are over budget on task after task. You can also check tasks in progress to see if the amount of work you expect is complete. To do that, use one or more of the following Project features:

- **Work table**: The Work table (on the View tab, click Tables→Work) shows several work fields: scheduled, baseline, actual and remaining work, and work variance. It also includes % Work Complete, which is the percentage of the current scheduled work that's done. Positive values in the Variance column show tasks whose scheduled work hours are greater than the baseline work hours.

  You can look for tasks that may be falling behind by inserting the % Complete field next to the % Work Complete column in this table (right-click the % Work Complete heading, choose Insert Column on the shortcut menu, and then choose % Complete on the drop-down list). If a task's % Work Complete value is less than its % Complete value, time is passing faster than work is being completed, which is often early warning for future delays.

- **Work Overbudget filter**: The Work Overbudget filter (View→Filter→More Filters→Work Overbudget) shows tasks whose actual work has already exceeded the baseline work (Figure 14-4), so it's already too late to recover from this overindulgence. However, if several tasks using the same resource are all completed over their work budget, you can try replacing that resource with one who's more productive. In the example project, remove the filter when you're done looking at overbudget tasks (click View→Filter and then choose [No Filter] or Clear Filter in the drop-down list).

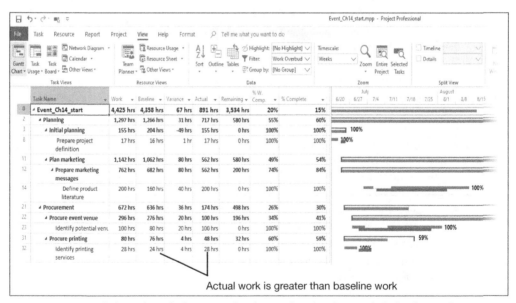

Actual work is greater than baseline work

Figure 14-4. *Work overbudget means that the actual work so far exceeds the baseline work.*

Is the Project Within Budget?

Checking cost status isn't as simple as seeing whether there's money in your wallet. When budgeted dollars run out in one place, accounting procedures sometimes grab money from another place. By tracking cost and budget resources in Project, you can follow project money *without* depending on your finance department. And if you work in a relatively simple financial environment, cost variance and other earned value measures may be enough. This section describes different ways to compare cost expenditures to the baseline costs you set.

As you learned earlier, the project summary task can show the cost variance for an entire project—that is, the difference between scheduled and baseline costs. If this variance is positive, then the project is forecasted to be over budget. Unless the project is almost over, you may still have time to reduce costs. (A negative cost variance means the project may come in under budget, although that outcome isn't assured until the project is complete.) This section explains how to dig deeper into your project's cost status if the project summary task shows that costs are over budget.

Comparing Costs Using Views and Filters

Similar to the way they help you look for over-budget work, Project's tables, filters, and reports can help you find expanding costs. Here are two of Project's built-in elements that show costs:

- **Cost table**: This table (in the View tab's Data section, click Tables→Cost) includes the project's scheduled, baseline, actual, and remaining costs. The Variance column is the Cost Variance field, so you can see whether tasks are forecasted to be over or under budget. (Positive variances mean over budget.) The Total Cost column is really the Cost field, which includes labor costs that Project calculates, cost resources you've assigned to tasks, and fixed costs you've set.

- **Cost Overbudget filter**: To display only tasks whose scheduled cost is greater than the baseline cost, apply this filter. In the View tab's Data section, click the Filter down arrow, and then choose More Filters. In the More Filters dialog box, double-click Cost Overbudget. In the example project, the Cost Overbudget filter displays the same tasks as the Work Overbudget filter does, because the overbudget amounts are due to labor costs for the overbudget work hours. When you're done filtering tasks, on the View tab, click the Filter down arrow, and the choose [No Filter].

Evaluating Costs with Reports

Project has several reports for studying costs. Chapter 18 describes working with Project's reports in detail. Here's a quick intro to reports that help you evaluate cost:

- **Cash Flow**: This graphical report (Report→Costs→Cash Flow) starts with a banner across the top that shows actual cost, baseline cost, remaining cost, and cost variance. A chart includes bars that represent how much is spent each quarter and a line indicating the cumulative cost over time. And at the bottom is a table with cost status for top-level tasks.

- **Cost Overruns**: This graphical report (Report→Costs→Cost Overruns) focuses on cost variance by task and resource. The two charts at the top show variance for top-level tasks and all work resources. As shown in Figure 14-5, a resource with a big cost variance could indicate someone who isn't as productive as you expected.

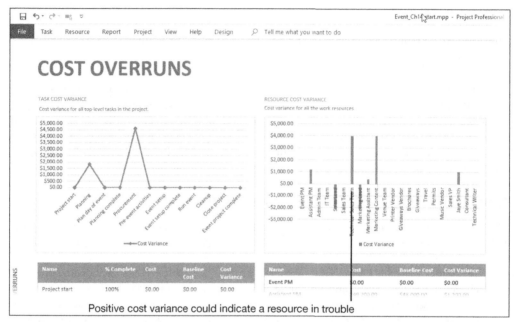

Positive cost variance could indicate a resource in trouble

Figure 14-5. *A resource with a large cost variance could indicate someone who doesn't have the right skill set or needs help.*

> **Note:** Earned value analysis is such an effective way to evaluate project costs that it gets its own section, which starts below. Project's earned value reports are described there.

- **Baseline Cost**: You can choose either the Excel or Visio Baseline Cost visual report (on the Report tab, click the Visual Reports icon, and then, in the Visual Reports dialog box, choose one of the Baseline Cost Report entries). The Excel Baseline Cost report is a bar graph that compares scheduled cost, baseline cost, and actual cost for top-level summary tasks. If the scheduled cost is greater than the baseline cost, then the summary task is over budget. You can alter the report to compare costs by fiscal quarter or drill down to compare costs task by task (or resource by resource). The Visio Baseline Cost visual report adds icons to task boxes that are over budget for cost or work.

> **Tip:** In order to see visual reports listed in the Visual Reports dialog box, you need to have Excel and/or Visio installed. Project exports data into the appropriate application either as a one-time transfer or as a refreshed template. See Chapter 19 to learn more about reporting.

Comparing Project Costs to a Budget

Budget resources can represent line items in a financial budget. You can allot budget dollars to budget resources in a Project file and then compare your project costs to the budgeted amounts. Setting up budget resources for this type of comparison takes several steps. If you use budget resources, then you can compare budgeted costs to scheduled costs by category. Using budget resources to evaluate project cost is explained in detail in Chapter 15.

Bringing the Project Back on Track

In the example project, you may notice that the day of the event has slipped due to slippage in tasks earlier in the project. This section guides you through finding ways to get the schedule back on track.

Follow Along Practice

First, find out how many days you need to shorten the schedule:

1. If necessary, apply the Tracking Gantt view to the example project. To examine task dates, apply the Variance table to the view (in the View tab's Data section, click Tables→Variance).

   The Variance table includes scheduled start and finish dates, baseline start and finish dates, and start and finish variances.

2. Scroll to task ID 89 "Event day."

   In the table, the Start Variance value is 9 days. That means you need to adjust predecessors to the task in some way to move the scheduled start date earlier by that many days.

The next step is to find a task or tasks that you can adjust that will get "Event day" back on track:

1. Suppose you want to adjust tasks as early in the project as possible. One way to look for candidates is to filter the task list to show only critical tasks. (In the View tab's Data section, choose Filters→Critical.)

2. Another way to shorten the list of candidates is to filter for tasks whose Finish Variance value is greater than or equal to how many days you need to cut. In this example, click the triangle to the right of the Finish Variance header, point at Filters, and then choose "Greater than" in the drop-down menu. In the Custom AutoFilter dialog box, type **9d** in the second box in the first test row, and then click OK.

   If you review the Finish Variance values shown in Figure 14-6, you'll see that task ID 18 "Prepare publicity plan" has a Finish Variance greater than the days to cut and it is a 3-week duration.

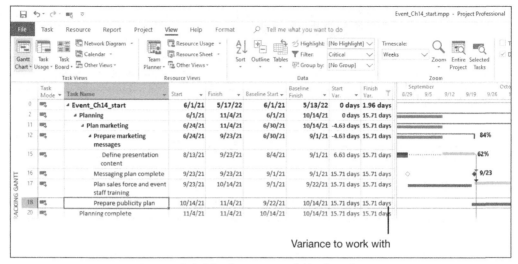

Figure 14-6. *Filter by variance to find tasks to shorten.*

3. Select the "Prepare publicity plan" task.

    If the Task Details Form is not displayed in the Details pane, in the View tab's Split View section, turn on the Details checkbox, and then choose Task Details Form on the drop-down menu.

4. In the Task Details Form, the task's duration is 3 weeks, which means there is a chance you can shorten it by the amount you need. In the Duration box, type **6d.**

    In this example, you would need to check with the assigned resources to make sure that shortening the task is feasible.

5. Click OK. The event day is back to the correct date.

Earned Value Analysis

Earned value analysis is like the idea behind that old Smith Barney slogan, "We make money the old fashioned way—we earn it." Earned value analysis measures progress according to how much of your project's value (its cost) you've earned so far by completing work.

Project customers, sponsors, and stakeholders want to know how far along a project is. Earned Value Analysis provides information about the status of your project budget and schedule. If a project has spent half its budget, consumed half its forecast duration, and completed half of its work, you're all set. However, if the budget and duration are half spent, but the work is only 25 percent complete, something is wrong. You have only 50 percent of the budget and duration left to complete 75 percent of the work.

This section explains how to use various earned-value measures to keep tabs on your project.

> **Note:** Earned value analysis requires a baseline and a status date in your Project file, so you have a plan to compare to. If you haven't set a baseline yet (Chapter 12), all the earned value fields are zero. You also have to set a status date and enter actual values as of that date (see Chapter 13) to show what you've accomplished and how much it cost.
>
> Earned value is typically reported at the project, summary, phase, or work package levels of a project, not for individual tasks. Because earned value analysis is performed at a higher level, it helps you review and manage trends.

Gauging Performance with Earned Value Measures

Earned value analysis uses several calculations to measure schedule and cost status. However, all earned value measures are based on three basic measurements:

- **Planned cost for scheduled work**: In project-management circles, you'll hear *planned value* (PV) described as the *budgeted cost of work scheduled* (or BCWS, which is also the name of the corresponding Project field). In English, planned value is the cost you expected to incur for the work scheduled through the status date—that is, the baseline cost for the work that should have been completed as of the status date.

  For example, suppose you're managing a project to build 10 micro-houses over 10 weeks for a total cost of $50,000—$5,000 per house. According to that plan, 5 houses should be built at the end of 5 weeks at a planned value of $25,000.

- **Planned cost for completed work**: This measure is called *earned value* (EV) because it represents the baseline cost you've earned by completing work as of the status date. It's also known as *budgeted cost of work performed* or BCWP (the name of the corresponding Project field). For example, if you've built 6 houses as of the status date (at the end of 5 weeks, say), then the earned value is $30,000.

- **Actual cost of completed work**: Actual cost (AC) is easy: it's how much you actually spent as of the status date. For example, if you've spent $20,000 through the first 5 weeks of homebuilding, that's your actual cost of completed work. This measure is sometimes called *actual cost of work performed* or ACWP (again, the name of the Project field).

> **Note:** In the Project Management Institute PMBOK®, planned cost for scheduled work is called PV (Planned Value), planned cost for completed work is called EV (Earned Value), and actual cost of completed work is called AC (Actual Cost).

Analyzing an Earned Value Graph

Because planned value, earned value, and actual cost are all monetary values, you can compare them to evaluate schedule and cost performance. In earned value graphs, the relative positions of the three lines for these measures show whether the project is on schedule and within budget.

Gleaning schedule and cost performance from an earned value graph is easy once you know how to compare planned value, earned value, and actual costs. The Earned Value Report, a graphical report shown in Figure 14-8, graphs all three measures over time. (Click Reports→Costs→Earned Value Report to display it.) Here's how you evaluate schedule and cost performance with these three measures:

- **Schedule performance**: The comparison between planned value and earned value is what provides you with a schedule status. Planned value is the baseline cost for the work you *expected* to complete, while earned value is the baseline cost of the work that's *actually* complete. If earned value is less than planned value, less work is complete than you expected—thus, the project is behind schedule. If earned value is greater than planned value (like $30,000 versus $25,000 in the homebuilding project), then more work is complete than you expected, and the project is ahead of schedule. In the example project, earned value is below the planned value (Figure 14-7), so the project is behind schedule. The formula for Schedule Variance is SV = EV - PV.

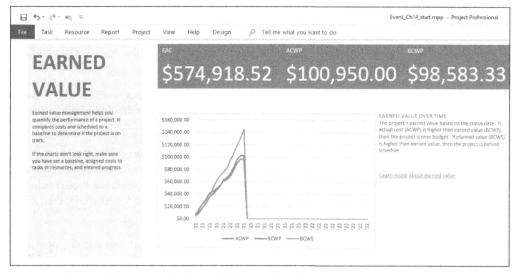

Figure 14-7. *An earned value graph shows cost along the y-axis and time along the x-axis.*

- **Cost performance**: This is the difference between earned value and actual cost. If the earned value is greater than the actual cost, then the work performed cost less than you planned—the project is under budget. For example, the earned value for the homebuilding project is $30,000, while the actual value is only $20,000, so it's $10,000 under budget. If earned value is less than the actual cost, then the project is over budget. In the graph in Figure 14-8, the actual value line is above the earned value line, so the project is over budget. (The formula for Cost Variance is CV = EV - AC.)

Viewing Earned Value in Project

You can examine earned value measures in several places in Project. To see earned value task by task, nothing beats the program's earned value tables. Project also has a graphical report that provides a visual status of earned value. And you can run the Earned Value Over Time visual report if you want to analyze earned value in more ways than the graphical Earned Value Report can (Chapter 18). Here's where you can find earned value in Project:

- **Earned Value table**: Apply this table, shown in Figure 14-9, to any task-oriented view (in the View tab's Data section, click Tables, and then choose More Tables. In the More Tables dialog box, double-click Earned Value). This table includes all the basic earned value fields: planned value (BCWS), earned value (BCWP), actual cost (ACWP), SV, CV, EAC, BAC, and VAC.

- **Earned Value Cost Indicators table**: This table focuses on cost performance. It includes basic earned value fields but adds CV% (CV as a percentage of the planned value), CPI, and TCPI.

- **Earned Value Schedule Indicators table**: This table focuses on schedule performance. It includes planned value (BCWS), earned value (BCWP), SV, CV, SV%, and SPI.

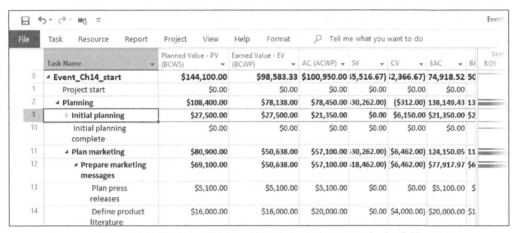

Figure 14-8. *The Earned Value table includes the basic earned value fields.*

- **Earned Value Report**: This report initially shows the graph of earned value over time (see Figure 14-8). To run this report, in the Report tab's View Report section, click Costs→Earned Value Report.

- **Earned Value Over Time visual report**: This report includes a graph of earned value over time like the graphical Earned Value Report does. As you'll learn in Chapter 19, you can modify this report to show earned value for specific time periods or specific tasks. You can also use this report to export earned value data to another program. To run this report, in the Report tab's Export section, click Visual Reports. In the "Visual Reports – Create Report" dialog box, select Earned Value Over Time Report, and then click View.

Using Additional Earned Value Measures

You can combine a project's planned value, earned value, and actual cost to view project performance from different perspectives. Additional measures show the efficiency of the project or estimated final costs based on performance so far. Here are the additional earned value measures and what they do:

- **Schedule variance** (the SV field in Project) is earned value minus planned value (BCWP – BCWS), the difference between how much work you've completed and how much you planned to complete. If SV is positive, more work is complete than you planned, so you're ahead of schedule. SV for the homebuilding project is $30,000 minus $25,000, which equals positive $5,000, so the project is ahead of schedule. In Figure 14-9, the SV value for the entire project is negative $45,516.67, which means the project is behind schedule.

- **Cost variance** (the CV field in Project) is earned value minus the actual cost—in other words, the difference between the baseline and actual cost of the work performed (BCWP – ACWP). If CV is positive, then the baseline cost is greater than the actual cost, so the project is under budget. CV for the homebuilding is $30,000 minus $20,000, or $10,000, so the project is under budget. (The note titled "Is Positive Variance Good or Bad?" explains the difference between Project's Cost Variance and CV fields.) In Figure 14-9, the CV value for the entire project is negative $2,366.67, which means the project is over budget so far.

Is Positive Variance Good or Bad?

You don't see the Cost Variance and CV fields side by side in any built-in Project tables, which is good because they seem to contradict one another. For example, if the Cost Variance field shows a variance of $1,000, then the CV field shows a variance of ($1,000)—that is, negative $1,000.

With one variance positive and the other negative, it's hard to figure out whether the cost variance is good or bad. The CV field is earned value minus actual cost, which is the **true** arbiter of cost performance. As you've already learned, if earned value is greater than the actual cost, then the project or task is under budget. To help you remember, CV is a positive value when the project or task is under budget, a desirable (that is, positive) result. Keep in mind that the CV field applies only to completed work, because tasks have earned value only for the portion of the task that's complete.

On the other hand, the Cost Variance field is the Cost field minus the Baseline Cost field, so it's a positive value when the result is **undesirable**—the project or task is over budget.

- **Schedule performance index** (SPI) is the ratio of earned value divided by the planned value (BCWP / BCWS). For example, when the project is on schedule, earned value and planned value are equal, and SPI equals 1.0. An SPI less than 1.0 means earned value is less than planned value, indicating that the project is behind schedule. SPI for the homebuilding project is $30,000 / $25,000 or 1.2—that is, it's ahead of schedule. If you apply the Earned Value Schedule Indicators table to the view in the example project, the SPI value for the project is .67, behind schedule.

Because it's a ratio, SPI tells you how good or bad schedule performance is, regardless of the dollars involved. For example, a small project may have SV equal to $5,000, while a large project SV may be $125,000. However, an SPI of 1.2 shows that both projects have earned value that's 120 percent of the planned value.

- **Cost performance index** (CPI) is the ratio of earned value to actual cost (BCWP / ACWP). If the ratio is greater than 1.0, then earned value is greater than actual cost, which means you spent less to complete the work performed than you'd planned—so the project is under budget. For example, CPI of 1.5 means earned value is 50 percent higher than the actual cost. CPI for the homebuilding project is $30,000 / $20,000 or 1.5. The project is under budget, but *not* by 50 percent! If you remember your algebra, the percentage this sample project is under budget is ($30,000 – $20,000) / $30,000. That's equal to $10,000 / $30,000, or 33 percent under budget. If you apply the Earned Value Cost Indicators table to the view in the example, project, the CPI value for the project is 1.09, that is, under budget.

> **Note:** You might wonder why earned value analysis calculates the cost performance index, instead of the percentage that the project is over or under budget. Because CPI is a simple ratio of earned value to actual cost, you can use it to forecast the cost of the project at completion, as described in the "Estimate at completion" measure described below.

- **Budget at completion** (BAC) is simply the baseline cost. If you look carefully, you'll see that the Baseline Cost and BAC fields are always equal.

- **Estimate at completion** (EAC) is an estimate of how much a task will cost when it's done, based on the performance so far. (PMI uses several formulas to calculate estimate at completion depending on the situation. You can create custom formulas in Project to calculate these (Chapter 21). Here's the formula for EAC as calculated in Project:

  ACWP + ((BAC - BCWP) / CPI)

EAC has two components. The first is the actual cost so far (ACWP). The second, (BAC – BCWP) / CPI, is a cost forecast based on the cost performance index. It's the remaining baseline cost (baseline cost minus the earned value) divided by the cost performance index. For example, here's the calculation for the homebuilding EAC:

  Actual cost = $25,000
  BAC - BCWP = $50,000 - $30,000 = $20,000
  (BAC - BCWP) / CPI = $20,000 / 1.5 = $13,333
  EAC = $38,333

Because the cost performance index shows that the project is under budget, EAC assumes that trend will continue. That's why project EAC is only $38,333 compared with project BAC of $50,000. In the Earned Value Cost Indicators table in the example project, the EAC value is $574,918.52, which is higher than the baseline cost of the project ($550,050).

> **Note:** Project's Cost and EAC fields are not the same. Cost combines actual costs, remaining labor costs (work multiplied to the resource rates), overtime, and other types of cost like those for materials and cost resources. EAC, on the other hand, assumes that the remaining cost will be inflated or decreased by the same amount as the cost so far; it doesn't take remaining work into consideration at all.

- **Variance at completion** (VAC) is the estimated variance when the task or project is done. It's the baseline cost at completion (BAC) minus the estimate at completion (EAC). For example, VAC for the homebuilding project is $50,000 – $38,333, or $11,667. In the example project, VAC is negative $24,868.52, which is the estimated amount that the project will be over budget.

- **To complete performance index** (TCPI) is the ratio of the work that remains (expressed in dollars) to remaining available dollars. Here's the formula:

  (BAC - BCWP) / (BAC - ACWP)

  The numerator of the ratio is the remaining baseline cost for the remaining work; the denominator is the remaining available dollars. If TCPI is greater than 1.0, then the remaining baseline cost is greater than the remaining dollars—in other words, you don't have enough money left to pay for the remaining work. If the baseline cost for the remaining work is less than the available dollars, then you have a surplus.

  TCPI for the homebuilding is $20,000 / $30,000 or 0.667, which means the project is under budget.

> **Tip:** When you're looking at Project tables and need a quick review of these fields and formulas, position your mouse pointer over the appropriate column's header. When the ScreenTip appears, click the link to the help topic for the column's Project field.

Controlling How Project Calculates Earned Value

Project has a couple of options for calculating earned values. You can specify which saved baseline Project uses as well as which field specifies how complete tasks are.

Initially, Project uses values in the Baseline fields. If you always store your current baseline in the Baseline fields, you don't have to change any settings. However, if you want to calculate earned values using Baseline1 through Baseline10 instead, choose File→Options. On the left side of the Project Options dialog box, click Advanced. Under the "Earned Value options for this project" heading, in the "Baseline for Earned Value Calculations" drop-down list, choose the baseline you want (in this example, choose Baseline1).

The PMI's Project Management Body of Knowledge (PMBOK®) recommends two possible definitions of "complete" for earned value calculations. But in Project you can choose among *three* ways to define complete:

- **All or nothing**: The conservative approach says a task is complete or it isn't, which means 100 percent complete is the only value that represents complete. Any less than that and the task is incomplete (and not included in earned value calculations).

- **Unstarted, started, or complete**: If a project has very long tasks, the all-or-nothing approach may be too harsh. Another approach is to leave unstarted tasks as 0%, set completed tasks to 100%, and set tasks in progress to 50%.

> **Tip:** Another approach is to mimic the values on the task mini-toolbar (right-click a task to see it): 0% for unstarted, 25% for started, 50% for halfway, 75% for almost complete, and 100% for complete.

- **Completed duration**: Project uses this approach unless you specifically set up your Project file to use one of the other options in this list. If a task's % Complete field is 50%, then Project calculates its earned value fields to be 50% of the baseline value.

If you want to use the first or second approach, you have to tell Project to use the Physical % Complete field to calculate earned value. Unlike % Complete, which Project calculates, Physical % Complete is a value *you* enter, so you can make it as accurate as you want. For example, you can set Physical % Complete to 0%, 50%, or 100% depending on whether tasks are unstarted, in progress, or complete. Or you can enter the value from the % Work Complete field into the Physical % Complete field.

> **Note:** Although Project lets you select different earned value methods for different tasks, it's best to use the same method for all tasks. If you use % Complete, then you know that Project calculates the values for you. If you use Physical % Complete, then you have to type in the values.

To use Physical % Complete, choose File→Options. On the left side of the Project Options dialog box, click Advanced. Under "Earned Value options for this project" in the "Default task Earned Value method" drop-down list, choose Physical % Complete. In the example project, keep the option set to % Complete.

> **Note:** Changing the "Default task Earned Value method" option has no effect on *existing* tasks, which are usually the ones you want to evaluate. (The new setting affects only tasks added to the project after the change.) Fortunately, there's an easy way to change the setting for existing tasks: Insert the Earned Value Method field into a table (right-click a table heading and then choose Insert Column→Earned Value Method). Change the value in the first Earned Value Method cell to Physical % Complete, and then drag that value over all the other cells in the column using the fill handle. You don't have to do this in the example project.

Assigning Overtime

Overtime has no place during project planning because it leaves you no room for maneuvering later on. For example, if you create a project plan that has resources working 12-hour days 7 days a week, it's unlikely you can fix a delayed schedule by having resources work *16*-hour days. However, when a project is under way and the schedule slips, overtime is another method for keeping task durations from increasing by, in effect, overallocating resources for short periods of time.

Project gives you several ways to represent overtime. You have to resort to the Overtime Work field *only* when resources cost more for overtime hours. Here are two ways to assign extra hours:

- **Increasing work time for a period**: For team members who aren't paid higher overtime rates, you can define longer hours through the resource calendar or the Resource Information dialog box. To specify work hours for a period of time, define a work week or an exception in a resource calendar (Chapter 3). You can set the start and end dates for the period and the start and end times for workdays. You don't have to do this in the example project.

  To change available units for a period of time, in the Resource Sheet view, double-click the resource. In the Resource Information dialog box, in the Resource Availability section, specify the start and end date for the extra hours and the units you want to assign during that time.

- **Overtime hours paid at an overtime rate**: When resources are paid more for overtime hours, you have to assign overtime hours in Project (you'll learn how shortly) or the labor costs won't be correct. The note titled "Overtime Costs" explains how Project tracks overtime and calculates overtime cost. You set a resource's overtime rate in the Resource Sheet view's aptly named Overtime Rate field.

Overtime Costs

In Project, work hours reside in the Work, Regular Work, and Overtime Work fields. Without overtime, all assigned work hours are regular work hours so the values in the Work and Regular Work fields are equal. If you enter hours in the Overtime Work field, Project subtracts those hours from the Regular Work field; the Work value stays the same. For example, if a task's Work value is 80 hours and you assign 20 hours of overtime, its Overtime Work value changes to 20 hours, while its Regular Work value shrinks to 60 hours.

Project calculates the labor cost for Regular Work hours by multiplying the regular work hours by the standard labor rate (Standard Rate in the Resource Sheet). Overtime labor cost is overtime work hours multiplied by the overtime rate. For example, consider the same 80-hour task. At $50 an hour for regular work, the labor cost is $4,000. If the overtime rate is $60 an hour, then the task's cost changes to $4,200 (60 hours x $50 and 20 hours x $60).

Follow Along Practice

To set up an overtime view to simplify working with overtime, follow these steps:

1. In the View tab's Task Views section, click the Task Usage button.

   In the example project, the C_Status Updating filter dialog box appears, because you applied it to the Task Usage view in an earlier chapter. Click Cancel to close the dialog box.

2. In the View tab's Data section, choose [No Filter] in the Filter box.

   Doing so removes the C_Status Updating filter from the Task Usage view.

3. In the View tab's Task Views section, click More Views, and then choose Save View.

---

4. In the Save View dialog box's Name field, type a new view name, like **C_Overtime Usage**, and then click OK.

5. In the table area, right-click the Duration column, choose Insert Column, and then choose Overtime Work in the drop-down list.

6. To display Overtime Work in the time-phased area, right-click anywhere in the time-phased grid, and then, on the shortcut menu, choose Detail Styles. In the Available fields list, click Overtime Work, and then click the Show button. Click OK to close the Detail Styles dialog box.

   Each assignment in the view now includes an additional row for Overtime Work (the label is "Ovt. Work").

Here are the steps for assigning overtime work:

1. In the table pane on the left side of the view, select the Overtime Work cell for the assignment you want to modify. In the example project, scroll to task ID 15 "Define presentation content," and then click the Technical Sales Team's assignment row.

2. In the Overtime Work cell, type the number of overtime hours (in the example project, **40h**). Press Enter to save the change.

   Project recalculates the task duration due to the extra hours and allocates the overtime hours to time periods, as shown in Figure 14-9.

3. To see overtime work in the Task Form, right-click the Details pane and then choose Work on the shortcut menu.

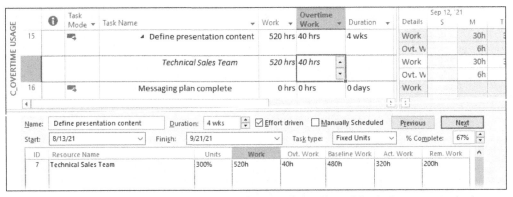

Figure 14-9. *Although the usage timescale shows overtime hours allocated day by day, you can't edit the hours in the individual time periods. You can, however, edit the Work hours.*

> **Tip:** You can also type overtime hours in the Task Form. Right-click the form, and then choose Work from the shortcut menu. Then, in the resource's Overtime Work cell, type the overtime hours.

15

Comparing Project Costs to a Budget

Projects cost money. Whether you're planning a small department retreat or building a new airport, the project's budget will be a key factor in the planning and managing decisions you make.

The budget is a benchmark—a line in the sand that project costs should not overstep. Initially, the cost of your project is the total of all your forecasted costs for scheduled tasks and their assigned resources. Once the project begins and you start tracking progress on tasks, Project adjusts these forecasts to reflect actual and remaining work and costs. One of your jobs as project manager is to make sure project costs don't exceed your allocated budget.

In this chapter, you'll learn how to compare project costs against your budget using the budget resource feature. If Project gives you bad (but realistic) news that costs are outrunning the budget, head back to Chapter 11 for cost-cutting strategies you can pull from your project manager's arsenal.

> **Note:** If you've downloaded files from the website, use the file Event_Ch15_start.mpp.

Setting the Project's Fiscal Year

You can set the fiscal year for a project to view performance over the same periods that your accounting department uses. Whether the fiscal year starts in January, July, or October, setting a project's fiscal year can help you communicate project costs to your accounting department in the format it wants.

> **Note:** You may have heard that Project lets you set up fiscal periods in the project, like 28-day periods, 13-week periods, and so on. This timesheet-related feature is available in the enterprise project-management features of Project Server and Project Online.

Project handles fiscal years in a rather limited way. While Project can show you the fiscal year in the timescale headings of Gantt Chart views and usage-oriented views, Project doesn't change any other dates in the project: The project's start and finish dates, working-time calendar, resource availability dates, and reports all still use the calendar year. If you want to see fiscal year dates in views, here's what you do:

Follow Along Practice

1. Choose File→Options, and then, on the left side of the Project Options dialog box, choose Schedule.

   Project displays all the schedule-related settings you can adjust, including fiscal calendar.

2. If you want this fiscal year setting to apply to the current project, keep the current project file name in the "Calendar options for this project" box. In this example, leave the project name in the box.

   To set the fiscal year for all new projects from this point forward, in the "Calendar options for this project" drop-down list at the top of the dialog box, choose All New Projects. This makes sense only if most of your projects work on this fiscal year.

3. In the "Fiscal year starts in" box, choose the month in which the fiscal year begins.

   In this example, suppose your fiscal year runs from June 1 through May 31. In the "Fiscal year starts in" box, choose June.

4. If your fiscal year is named by the calendar year in which it begins, turn on the "Use starting year for FY numbering" checkbox (use this setting in the example project).

   With this checkbox turned on, Project sets your fiscal year 2021 dates so they start in 2021: that is, from June 2021 through May 2022. Turn this checkbox off if your fiscal year is named by the calendar year in which it *ends*; for example, if your 2021 fiscal year runs from June 2020 through May 2021.

   > **Note:** The "Use starting year for FY numbering" checkbox is grayed out unless you choose a month other than January in the "Fiscal year starts in" box.

5. Click OK.

6. To see the fiscal year, display the Gantt Chart view (on the Task tab, click the Gantt Chart button).

7. To adjust the timescale so you can see fiscal years, right-click the timescale heading, and then choose Timescale on the shortcut menu.

    If you've set your fiscal year but the timescale headings haven't changed, first check the zoom level of your timescale. If it's zoomed way in to an hour-by-hour basis, Project typically doesn't list the year. If you want to change the year used in the middle tier, click that tab and then turn the "Use fiscal year" checkbox on or off. In this example, turn it off.

8. In this example, in the Show box, choose "Three tiers (Top, Middle, Bottom)." Click the Top Tier tab. In the Units box, choose Quarters. Turn on the "Use fiscal year" checkbox. Click OK.

    The fiscal year is reflected in the top timescale heading, as shown in Figure 15-1.

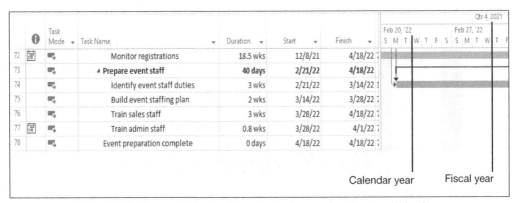

Figure 15-1. *You can display fiscal year or calendar year dates in timescale headings.*

Setting up a Budget in Project

Suppose your project plan has budget targets for different cost categories: $485,000 for labor costs, $43,000 for vendor expenses, $21,250 for materials, and $800 for miscellaneous costs. Using Project's ***budget resource*** feature, you can specify your budget for different cost categories. You can then group resources to compare your budgeted costs with your planned costs. That way, you can view your labor cost budget of $485,000 side by side with your planned costs of, say, $500,000, and immediately see that your next goal is to find a way to trim those labor costs. The note titled "Assigning Accounting Codes" describes another method for tracking project costs based on your organization's accounting system.

Budget resources are great for comparing budgeted costs against the planned costs for ***cost*** resources. Budgeted costs for ***work*** and ***material*** resources are a different story. For labor and equipment costs (work resources), you enter budgeted work amounts, not costs. So instead of a labor budget of $10,000, you have to enter an overall work amount like 200 hours. However, there is a way you can trick Project into comparing budgeted and planned labor costs, as you'll see shortly.

This section describes how to set up budget resources that you can compare with your planned costs and work. It's a five-step process:

1. Create and designate budget resources.

2. Assign those budget resources to the project summary task.

3. Associate work, material, and cost resources with their budget types.

4. Enter budgeted cost and work amounts for budget resources.

5. Group resources to compare budgeted costs and work alongside the planned values.

The whole process isn't quite as bad as it sounds. If your project is highly cost driven, then budget resources may give you the budget-performance information you need.

After you've done the first four steps, everything is in place for you to compare budget values and planned values (step 5) as you monitor and adjust your project plan to keep it in line with the budget. To make comparing values even easier, you can create a custom view with the columns and grouping you want. Then for step 5, all you have to do is display your custom view. This section also steps you through creating a custom view for entering budget data and comparing budget values to planned values.

Assigning Accounting Codes

Project data that maps to your organization's accounting codes may be just what you need to make the accountants and financial analysts happy. Fortunately, it's easy to include accounting codes in Project, whether it's a simple account number or a hierarchical structure of multilevel codes. Either way, you can enter accounting codes that map to resources, tasks, or project phases. For the full scoop on setting up a flat or multilevel list of codes, see Chapter 21. (You don't have to perform the steps in this sidebar for the example project.)

First, create a custom accounting-code field, and then add a column for it to the table of your choice (right-click a table heading and then choose Insert Column). Remember, you can add a task field only to task-oriented views and tables. Likewise, you can add a resource field only to resource-oriented views and tables. With the new column in place, enter the appropriate accounting codes for your tasks or resources.

After you've applied accounting codes, you can sort, group, and filter information by accounting code, as described in Chapter 17. You can also create reports that use the accounting codes. For more information about customizing reports, see Chapter 19.

Step 1: Create and Designate Budget Resources

Creating budget resources is the first step in the budget-resource process. These resources should correspond to the budget line items you want to track in your project (for example, line items that the accounting department uses). You can make them as broad or as detailed as you want, from labor, materials, and travel line items to employees, vendors, contractors, equipment, lodging, airfare, mileage, and meals.

Budget resources apply to a project as a whole—you can't assign them to tasks, as you do regular resources. Here's how to create budget resources:

1. In the Resource Sheet (View→Resource Sheet), double-click a blank Resource Name cell to open the Resource Information dialog box.

2. On the General tab, in the "Resource name" box, type the name of a budget resource. In this example, type **8020 Labor Budget**.

    It's a good idea to use names that differentiate budget resources from regular resources, as shown in Figure 15-2, so you can more easily pick the right fields for your budget comparisons. For example, you could start their names with the word "Budget" (such as Budget-Labor or start their names with the corresponding budget account number (8020 Labor Budget). One advantage to starting them with numbers is that budget resources appear together at the top of a resource list that's sorted alphabetically from A to Z, which is helpful because they're summary numbers.

3. In the Type field, choose Cost. Click OK to enable the Budget checkbox.

    Instead of setting up a budget resource that relates to work resources as a work resource itself (like you're supposed to), you can set it up as a ***cost*** resource instead. Then you can enter the budgeted labor cost and compare it with the rolled-up labor costs from tasks. This trick works equally well for material cost budgets. For that reason, it's easiest to set up all your budget resources as cost resources.

4. Double-click the 8020 Labor Budget resource you created. Turn on the Budget checkbox, and then click OK.

    Turning on this checkbox means you can assign this resource only to the project summary task, making it, in effect, a kind of project summary resource. Other fields that relate to work or material resources, like Email and "Material label," are grayed out.

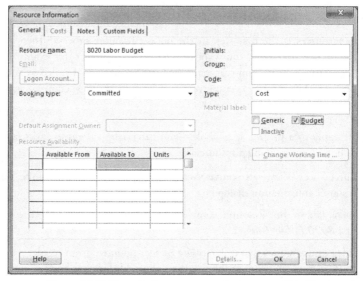

Figure 15-2. *Name budget resources so they're easy to identify.*

In this example, you're going to create a few additional budget resources. To simplify creating budget resources, add the Budget column to the Resource Sheet table:

Follow Along Practice

1. In the Resource Sheet (View→Resource Sheet), right-click the column heading next to where you want to add the Budget column (in this example, the Code column), and then choose Insert Column.

2. In the "Field name" drop-down list, choose Budget.

    Project inserts the Budget column to the left of the selected column.

3. In the first blank Resource Name cell, type the next budget resource name, in this example, *8080 Vendors Budget*. In the Type cell in the same row, choose Cost. In the Budget cell in the same row, choose Yes.

4. Repeat step 3 to create two additional budget resources named 9050 Materials Budget and 9070 Miscellaneous Budget.

    Figure 15-3 shows the budget resources created.

Figure 15-3. *You fill in only a few fields for budget resources.*

Step 2: Assign Budget Resources to the Project Summary Task

With your budget resources created, you're now ready to assign them to your project. A budget resource is meant to convey the total amount allocated to a budget category for an entire project, which is why you assign budget resources to the project summary task, not to individual tasks. In fact, a budget resource can't be assigned to anything *except* the project summary task.

Follow Along Practice

Assign budget resources to your project summary task by following these steps:

1. Display a task-oriented view, in this example, Gantt Chart.

    If you don't see the project summary task in row 0, in the Format tab's Show/Hide section, turn on the Project Summary Task checkbox.

2. Select the project summary task, and then in the Resource tab's Assignments section, click Assign Resources.

    The Assign Resources dialog box appears. If your resource list is long, your budget-resource naming convention comes in handy. For example, by starting all the budget-resource names with a number, budget resources are grouped together at the top of the resource list, as shown in Figure 15-4.

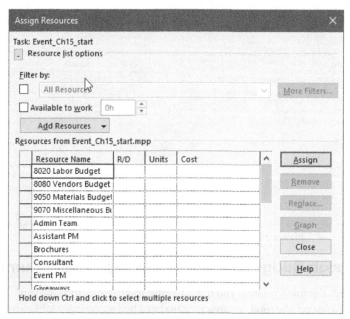

Figure 15-4. *If budget resources names start with numbers, they appear at the top of alphabetical resource name lists.*

3. Ctrl-click each of the budget resources you want to assign (in this example, all four budget resources), and then click Assign.

    Budget resources are the only kind of resource you can assign to the project summary task. So if you select one resource and the Assign button is grayed out, then the resource you selected isn't a budget resource. Perhaps you gave the resource a budget-resource name but forgot to turn on its Budget checkbox in the Resource Information dialog box.

    When you're done, you can close the Assign Resource dialog box if you want to see more of the screen.

Step 3: Associate Resources with Their Budget Types

Creating budget resources and entering target budget amounts for them in the project summary task is all well and good, but it's only one side of the equation. You also have to set up the other side: the resource costs you want to compare against the budget. This section explains how to connect work, material, and cost resources to budget categories, whether you want to track all resources against the budget or only a few. The trick is to use a text field to specify the budget categories you want to track.

Creating a Custom Resource Text Field

If you want to use a custom text field for budget categories, you first have to set it up for that purpose and then add it to the Entry table in the Resource Sheet view. Here are the steps:

Follow Along Practice

1. Display the Resource Sheet view (View→Resource Sheet), right-click a table heading (in this example, Group), and then choose Insert Column. In the drop-down list, choose the custom text field you want to use, in this example, Text25.

    Project inserts a new column for the text field to the left of the column you right-clicked.

2. Right-click the new column's heading and then, on the shortcut menu, choose Custom Fields.

    The Custom Fields dialog box opens with the Resource option selected at the top of the dialog box and the name of the text field selected in the list below that, which is exactly what you want.

3. Click Rename and then, in the Rename Field dialog box, type the name you want for this field, in this example, ***Budget Category***, and then click OK.

    When you rename custom fields you use, Project displays the field's original name in parentheses in the Custom Fields dialog box and in field drop-down lists, so it's easy to tell which fields you've already used.

4. To create a lookup table of values, click the Lookup button.

    The Edit Lookup Table dialog box opens.

5. In the Values column, create entries for the four budget categories, in this example, Labor Budget, Vendors Budget, Materials Budget, and Miscellaneous Budget. Then, click Close.

6. In the "Calculation for assignment rows" section, select the "Roll down unless manually entered" option. Then click OK.

    Selecting this option tells Project to distribute the custom field's values across assignments in usage-oriented views unless you manually type a value in a time-phased assignment cell.

Now that the text field is set up, you can designate budget categories for your project's work, material, and cost resources, as described in the next section.

Classifying Resources by Budget Category

Based on the lookup table you set up in the previous section, you have a different budget category name for each budget resource you've created—in this example, Labor Budget, Vendors Budget, Materials Budget, and Miscellaneous Budget. Here's how to classify resources by budget category:

Follow Along Practice

1. In the View tab's Data section, click Sort, and then choose "by ID."

   Project sorts the resources by their resource IDs.

2. For each work, material, and cost resource in the list, enter the appropriate budget category name for each one in the Budget Category column. Filter using the Group field on the resource sheet to assign the resources in the example project:

   a) For the first 10 resources (who all belong to the Internal Group), choose Labor Budget from the lookup table list.

   b) For the four resources who belong to the Vendor group, choose Vendors Budget.

   c) For the Brochures and Giveaways material resources, choose Materials Budget.

   d) For the Travel and Permits cost resources, choose Miscellaneous Budget.

   e) For the Sales VP, choose Labor Budget, and then set the Group field to Internal.

   f) For Jaye Smith, choose Labor Budget, and then set the Group field to Internal.

   g) For the Consultant resource, choose Vendors Budget, and then set the Group field to Internal.

   h) For the Technical Writer resource, choose Labor Budget, and then set the Group field to Internal.

3. Enter the corresponding budget category value in the Budget Category column for each budget resource.

   a) Labor Budget for the 8020 Labor Budget resource

   b) Vendors Budget for the 8080 Vendors Budget resource

   c) Materials Budget for the 9050 Materials Budget resource

   d) Miscellaneous Budget for the 9070 Miscellaneous Budget resource

   Figure 15-5 shows what the resource sheet looks like with the values filled in.

   That's how you connect resource costs and budget costs. For example, every resource whose Budget Category is Labor Budget is connected to the Labor Budget category.

		Resource Name	Type	Mater Label	Initials	Budget Category	Group	Gener
1	👥	Event PM	Work		EPM	Labor Budget	Internal	Yes
2	👥	Assistant PM	Work		APM	Labor Budget	Internal	Yes
3	👥	Admin Team	Work		Admin	Labor Budget	Internal	Yes
4	👥	IT Team	Work		IT	Labor Budget	Internal	Yes
5	👥	Sales Lead	Work		SL	Labor Budget	Internal	Yes
6	👥	Sales Team	Work		ST	Labor Budget	Internal	Yes
7	👥	Technical Sales Team	Work		TST	Labor Budget	Internal	Yes
8	👥	Marketing Lead	Work		ML	Labor Budget	Internal	Yes
9	👥	Marketing Assistant	Work		MA	Labor Budget	Internal	Yes
10	👥	Marketing Content Developer	Work		MCD	Labor Budget	Internal	Yes
11		Venue Team	Work		Venue	Vendors Budget	Vendor	No
12		Printer Vendor	Work		PrtV	Vendors Budget	Vendor	No
13		Giveaways Vendor	Work		GV	Vendors Budget	Vendor	No
14		Brochures	Material	Each	Broch	Materials Budget		No
15		Giveaways	Material	Case	Giv	Materials Budget		No
16		Travel	Cost		Trav	Miscellaneous Budget		No
17		Permits	Cost		Perm	Miscellaneous Budget		No
18		Music Vendor	Cost		MV	Vendors Budget	Vendor	No
19		Sales VP	Work		S	Labor Budget	Internal	No
20	👤	Jaye Smith	Work		JS	Labor Budget	Internal	No
21		Consultant	Cost		C	Vendors Budget	Internal	No
22		Technical Writer	Work		T	Labor Budget	Internal	No
23		8020 Labor Budget	Cost			Labor Budget		No
24		8080 Vendors Budget	Cost		8	Vendors Budget		No
25		9050 Materials Budget	Cost		9	Materials Budget		No
26		9070 Miscellaneous Budget	Cost		9	Miscellaneous Budget		No

Figure 15-5. *Choose a budget category for each work, material, cost, and budget resource in the Resource Sheet.*

> **Tip:** You can add new resources, create new budget resources, and create and assign additional budget categories at any time throughout your project. If you add a new resource, be sure to assign it a budget category if you plan to compare its cost or work values to your budgeted values. And if you create a new budget category, update any resources that belong in this new category. If you use enterprise resources in Project Server or Project Online, use an enterprise-level field for your budget categories.

Step 4: Enter Budget Cost and Work Values

With budget resources assigned to the project summary task, you're ready to add budgeted values to your budget resources. These budget values are the targets against which you'll compare project costs and work as you monitor project progress.

This section describes how to enter budget amounts either as a project total or as incremental totals by time period.

Entering Budget Totals for the Project

If time isn't a factor in your budget, you can add budget cost and work amounts to the entire project. Here are the steps:

Follow Along Practice

1. Display the Task Usage view (in the View tab's Task Views section, choose Task Usage). Apply the cost table to the view by clicking the Select All cell at the table's top left, and then choosing Cost from the dropdown menu.

    The Task Usage view is ideal for entering budget values because the project summary task sits at the very top with its assigned budget resources immediately below it, as shown in Figure 15-6.

2. Insert the Budget Cost and Budget Work columns into the table.

    Right-click the column heading next to where you want to insert the Budget Cost column (in this example, Fixed Cost), and then choose Insert Column; in the "Field name" drop-down list, choose Budget Cost. Repeat these steps for the Budget Work column.

3. Select the Budget Cost or Budget Work cell for an assigned budget resource, and then type the overall project budget value for that resource.

    For a budget resource that's a *cost* resource, type the budget value in dollars into the Budget Cost cell. Because all the budget resources in the example project are cost resources, fill in the budget values as follows:

8020 Labor Budget	$485,000
8080 Vendors Budget	$43,000
9050 Materials Budget	$21,250
9070 Miscellaneous Budget	$800

    If you set up a budget resource that's a *work* resource, type the budget value as work (hours or days) in the Budget Work cell. The Budget Work cell is also where you type the total number of units (cubic yards, tons, packages, each, and so on) for a budget resource that's a *material* resource.

> **Tip:** If necessary, widen a column (in this example, Budget Cost) to display its values by double-clicking the vertical divider to the right of the column heading. If you don't see the Baseline column in the table, put the pointer over the vertical divider between the table and timescale, and when you see a two-headed arrow drag to the right.

The Budget Cost value for the project summary task is $550,050, which equals the project's Baseline Cost for the project. If the budget resources cover the entire project, these values should be equal.

Compare the Budget Cost to the Baseline Cost

Task Name	Approve Cost	Budget Cost	Budget Work	Fixed Cost	Fixed Cost Accrual	Total Cost	Baseline	
◢ Event_Ch15_start	$0.00	$550,050.00	0 hrs	$0.00	Prorated	$543,900.00	$550,050.00	
8020 Labor Budget	$0.00	$485,000.00						
8080 Vendors Budget	$0.00	$43,000.00						
9050 Materials Budget	$0.00	$21,250.00						
9070 Miscellaneous Budget	$0.00	$800.00						
Project start	$0.00			$0.00	Prorated	$0.00	$0.00	
◢ Planning	$0.00			$0.00	Prorated	$126,850.00	$137,600.00	

Figure 15-6. *The Task Usage view shows the budget resources assigned to the project summary task.*

Entering Budget Totals by Time Period

The budget amounts you enter for a project summary task are the total project amounts for those budget items. Unless you tell it otherwise, Project spreads that budget amount equally over the duration of the project. To divvy up the overall budget amounts into the time periods when you expect them to be spent, you can easily edit budget amounts in the time-phased portion of a task-usage view.

Follow Along Practice

Follow these steps to add the Budget Cost and Budget Work rows to the time-phased portion of a usage view:

1. With the Task Usage view displayed (View→Task Usage), click the Task Usage Tools | Format tab. In the tab's Details section, click Add Details.

   The Detail Styles dialog box appears. Another way to open this dialog box is to right-click the time-phased portion of the view, and then, on the shortcut menu, choose Detail Styles.

2. In the "Available fields" box, Ctrl-click Budget Cost and Budget Work, and then click Show.

   Project moves the Budget Cost and Budget Work fields to the "Show these fields" box, as shown in Figure 15-7. The order of fields in the "Show these fields" box is the sequence in which Project displays the field's rows. To change this sequence, select a field's name in the "Show these fields" box, and then click the Move buttons until the order is what you want.

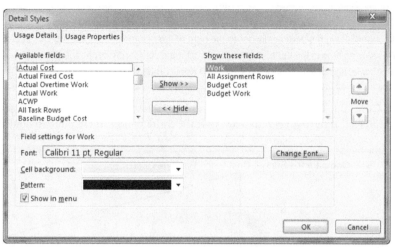

Figure 15-7. *Add fields you want to see in the time-phased grid to the "Show these fields" list.*

3. Click OK, and then resize the Details column so you can see the new fields.

   The two fields appear in the time-phased portion of the view, although you can see only part of their names in the Details column. To see their full field names, double-click the right edge of the Details column heading to automatically widen the column to display the longest field name. You can also drag the right edge of the Details column heading further to the right to increase its width.

4. To display the time period for which you want to enter time-phased budget values, in the View tab's Zoom section, choose the time period in the Timescale box, in this example, Quarters.

   If you see hash marks (###) in the time-phased grid columns, right-click the time-phased grid heading, and then choose Timescale on the shortcut menu. In the Timescale dialog box, type a larger number in the Size box in the "Timescale options" section. In this example, type **125**, and then click OK.

   If you've already entered budget amounts in the table, then those amounts are distributed equally across the project's timespan. You can edit them to the budget values you expect for each time period.

5. In the cell at the intersection of the row for a budget resource's Budget Cost or Budget Work field and the column for the time period you want, type the budget cost or work amount, as shown in Figure 15-8.

   In this example, fill in Budget Cost values for the 8080 Vendors Budget resource as follows:

Q1	$0
Q2	$2,500
Q3	$0
Q4	$40,500

You can't edit the Budget Cost and Budget Work cells for nonbudget resource assignments. The note titled "Entering Values in Budget Fields" tells you where you can enter budget amounts.

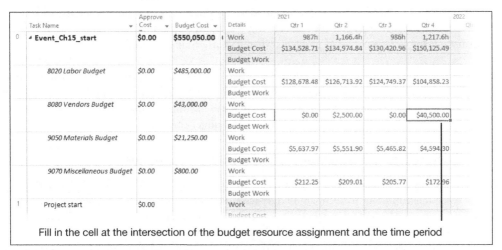

Fill in the cell at the intersection of the budget resource assignment and the time period

Figure 15-8. *Fill in Budget Cost and Budget Work values by time period.*

Tip: Even if you enter budget values in the time-phased portion of the view, it's good to keep the Budget Cost and Budget Work columns visible in the table. Those fields show you the overall project totals for each budget category you've created.

Entering Values in Budget Fields

When you add the Budget Cost and Budget Work fields to a usage view's table or time-phased portion, it's not always clear where you can actually ***enter*** your budget amounts. No visual cue like shading or hatching indicates areas that are off limits, so the fields seem to be available throughout the entire view. If you try to enter a value and nothing happens, that's your clue that the cell isn't editable.

Project is particular about where you can enter budget amounts. Here are the rules:

1.   Enter budget amounts in an assignment field (in the Task Usage view, the row with the budget resource's name; in the Resource Usage view, the row with the project summary task's name).

2.   In a project summary task's Budget Cost or Budget Work cell in the table portion of the view, enter project-wide budget totals.

3.   Enter time-specific amounts in the Budget Cost or Budget work cells in the time-phased portion of the view.

You can't enter budget amounts in assignments for regular resources to regular tasks.

Step 5: Compare Budget Resource Values

Finally, you're about to reap the harvest of the previous four steps: You're going to compare your project resource cost and work values against the budgeted values from your budget resources. You may find the occasional bad apple if your costs outrun your budgeted values. The good news is that this comparison helps you see potential problems when it's early enough to find solutions.

To compare budget values to planned values, you need a table that shows both budgeted and planned fields. Then you can group the contents of the view by your budget categories. The result is groups of budgeted and planned values for each budget category, and voilà—your budget situation becomes crystal clear. This section describes how to set up your budget-comparison view.

Setting Up a Custom View for Entering Budgeted Values

Budget resources are a special type of resource in Project, so you need a resource view like Resource Usage to see them in order to compare budget-resource costs to planned costs. When you group a Resource Usage view by budget category, Project creates a summary row for each budget category you track. The Budget Cost or Budget Work cells in group summary rows show the budgeted values for each budget category, allowing you to see all the work, material, and cost resources associated with that budget category.

Follow Along Practice

Here's how to set up a custom view and table for working with budgeted values:

1. In the View tab's Resource Views section, click Resource Usage.

    If the Details pane is open, close it by turning off the Details checkbox on the View tab.

2. To create a custom view, on the View tab, click the Other Views button, and then choose Save View. In the Save View dialog box, type a name for the view, in this example, ***C_Budget_Comparison***, and then click OK.

    Adding "C_" as a prefix to the view name makes it easy to differentiate a custom view from built-in views that come with Project.

3. To customize the fields in the view's table, in the View tab's Data section, click Tables, and then choose More Tables on the drop-down menu.

    The More Tables dialog box opens with the current table selected (in this example, C_Budget Comparison Table).

4. In the More Tables dialog box, click Edit.

    The Table Definition dialog box opens.

5. To delete fields from the table, select a field in the Field Name column, and then click the Delete Row button above the list.

    In this example, delete % Work Complete, Overtime Work, Baseline Work, Work Variance, Actual Work, and Remaining Work.

6. To insert a field, select the field that will be below the new field, in this example, click the Work row. Click the Insert Row button. Click the new blank cell in the Field Name column, and then choose the field, in this example, Budget Category (which is the custom field Text 25).

7. Repeat step 6 to insert the Budget Cost, Cost, and Budget Work fields. Click OK to close the Table Definition dialog box. Then click Apply.

    The table definition is shown in Figure 15-9. If the table doesn't change in the view, on the View tab, click Tables, and then choose C_Budget_Comparison Table.

> **Note:** Because all the budget resources are defined as Cost resources, you don't have to use the Budget Work field. However, the table contains the Budget Work and Work fields so you can compare budgeted and planned hours.

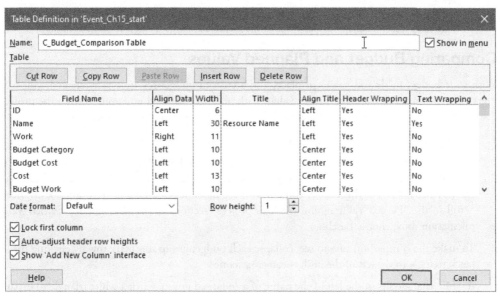

Figure 15-9. *You can remove, insert, and rearrange fields in a table in the Table Definition dialog box.*

8. Next, you want to group the assignments by the budget categories you've created. To do that, click the down arrow to the right of the Budget Category heading, and then choose "Group on this field" in the drop-down menu.

    When the Resource Usage view groups resources by budget category, each group includes one budget resource and all the work, material, and cost resources that apply to that budget category.

9. To hide entries with no Budget Category value, click the down arrow to the right of the Budget Category heading, turn off the (blank) checkbox in the Filters list, and then click OK.

    The first budget category summary row appears at the top of the table, as shown in Figure 15-10. If necessary, make columns wider. (Drag a column heading divider to the right to widen the column.)

Resource Name	Work	Budget Category	Budget Cost	Cost	De
⊿ Labor Budget	4,266 hrs	Labor Budget	$485,000.00	$481,300.00	Wc
					Act
1 Event PM	0 hrs	Labor Budget		$0.00	Wc
					Act
2 ⊿ Assistant PM	492 hrs	Labor Budget		$49,200.00	Wc
					Act
Determine budget	12 hrs	Labor Budget		$1,200.00	Wc
					Act
Prepare project definition	8 hrs	Labor Budget		$800.00	Wc
					Act
Plan day of event	28 hrs	Labor Budget		$2,800.00	Wc
					Act
Define AV requirements	20 hrs	Labor Budget		$2,000.00	Wc
					Act
Choose menu	6 hrs	Labor Budget		$600.00	Wc

Figure 15-10. *By grouping on budget categories, it's easy to compare budgeted and planned costs.*

Comparing Budget and Planned Values

With your budget fields and values in place, and a custom budget-resource view created, you have everything you need to compare budget values with planned values at any point during the project. See Chapter 14 for more information about monitoring costs during the execution phase.

1. In this example, start by specifying the baseline used to calculate earned value.

   If you've been following along, you set the "Baseline for Earned Value calculations" option to use Baseline1 in an earlier chapter. This option tells Project which baseline to use to calculate the variance fields. For this budget comparison, use Baseline. Choose File→Options→Advanced. Scroll to the "Earned Value options for this project" section. In the "Baseline for Earned Value calculation" box, choose Baseline.

2. To make the comparison easy to see, collapse each budget group summary row by clicking the black triangle to the left of the budget category name.

   A white triangle sits to the left of the name of a collapsed group. Click a white triangle to expand that group.

3. In the group summary rows (which have yellow shading), compare the Budget Cost or Budget Work values to the Cost or Work values, respectively. In this example, the budget resources are all cost resources, so you compare Budget Cost to Cost in all the summary rows (Figure 15-11).

   The Budget Cost or Budget Work cells in the group summary rows show the budget values for each budget resource. For each group, you see a value for Budget Cost or Budget Work, depending on whether the budget resource is a cost resource or a work (or material) resource.

   The Cost and Work cells in the group summary rows show the rolled-up cost and rolled-up work for the resources in that particular budgetary group. If the value in a group summary row's Cost cell is higher than the value in its Budget Cost cell, then you've exceeded your budget. If the value in the Work cell is higher than the Budget Work cell, then your work hours are over budget.

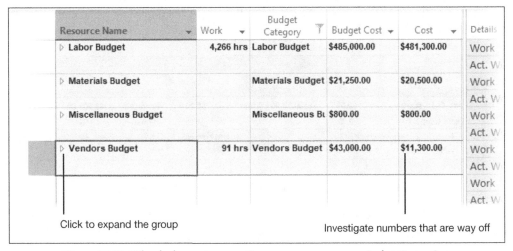

Resource Name	Work	Budget Category	Budget Cost	Cost	Details
▷ Labor Budget	4,266 hrs	Labor Budget	$485,000.00	$481,300.00	Work
					Act. W
▷ Materials Budget		Materials Budget	$21,250.00	$20,500.00	Work
					Act. W
▷ Miscellaneous Budget		Miscellaneous Bu	$800.00	$800.00	Work
					Act. W
▷ Vendors Budget	91 hrs	Vendors Budget	$43,000.00	$11,300.00	Work
					Act. W
					Work
					Act. W

Click to expand the group   Investigate numbers that are way off

Figure 15-11. *When budget resources are Cost resources, you compare Budget Cost to Cost.*

Follow Along Practice

In this example, the current cost for labor is $481,300, compared to the labor budget of $485,000. Labor is slightly below the budget. The materials budget is slightly below budget and the miscellaneous budget matches the current cost for miscellaneous expenses. The current cost for vendors, however, is $11,300, while the budget is $41,300. A discrepancy like that calls for research.

1. Compare the total Budget Cost value for all the budget resource groups to the baseline cost for the project, which is $550,050.

   You'll have to use a calculator to sum the values in the customized Resource Usage view. There's no way to see project-wide cost in this view, because it's grouped by Budget Category.

   The total Budget Cost for the budget resource groups is $550,050, which is equal to the baseline cost for the project. That's as it should be.

2. Add up the total Baseline Cost for the budget resource groups.

   The total Baseline Cost for the budget resource groups should equal the Baseline Cost for the entire project. However, that total is only $520,050. $30,000 from the project-level Baseline Cost is not showing up in the budget resource groups. The culprit in this situation is the Fixed Cost field, because the Fixed Cost field adds cost to the project that isn't associated with any resource.

3. To verify this hypothesis, switch to the Gantt Chart view (View→Gantt Chart).

   If necessary, apply the Cost table to the Gantt Chart view. The Cost table includes the Fixed Cost field.

4. To quickly find fixed costs applied to task, click the down arrow to the right of the Fixed Cost heading, turn off the "$0" checkbox, and then click OK.

One non-summary task appears (Figure 5-12): Food setup (performed by venue staff). $30,000 was added to the task as fixed cost for the cost of the catering.

	Task Name	Approve Cost Target	Budget Cost	Budget Work	Fixed Cost	Fixed Cost Accrual	Total Cost	Baseline
0	◢ Event_Ch15_start	$0.00	$550,050.00	0 hrs	$0.00	Prorated	$543,900.00	$550,050.00
79	◢ Event setup	$0.00			$0.00	Prorated	$47,440.00	$47,440.00
86	Food setup (performed by venue staff)	$0.00			$30,000.00	Prorated	$30,800.00	$30,800.00

Figure 15-12. *Fixed cost isn't associated with any resource.*

5. To include this food cost in the budget resource groups, remove the fixed cost and add a cost resource instead:

   a) Display the Resource Sheet (View→Resource Sheet).

   b) In the first blank Resource Name cell, type the name Catering. In the Type cell in that row, choose Cost. In the Budget Category cell, choose Vendors Budget.

   c) Display the Gantt Chart (View→Gantt Chart).

   d) Double-click task ID 86 "Food setup (performed by venue team)" to open the Task Information dialog box.

   e) On the Resources tab, click the first blank Resource Name cell, and then choose Catering.

   f) In the Cost cell in that row, type *30000*, and then click OK.

   g) Back in the Gantt Chart table in the Fixed Cost cell for the task, type *0*, and then press Enter.

   h) Click the down arrow to the right of the Fixed Cost heading, and then choose Clear Filter from Fixed Cost.

   i) Switch back to the custom resource usage view (on the View tab, click the down arrow to the right of Resource Usage, and then choose C_Budget_Comparison).

   j) Insert the Baseline Cost field to the right of the Cost column.

   The Baseline Cost for the Vendors Budget group is still $11,300. That's because the Baseline Cost values still reflect the $30,000 fixed cost on task ID 86.

6. To update the baseline for only task 86, follow these steps:

    a) Switch to the Gantt Chart view (View→Gantt Chart).

    b) Select task ID 86.

    c) On the Project tab, click Set Baseline→Set Baseline.

    d) In the "Set baseline" box, choose the baseline to update (Baseline, in this example).

    e) In the For section, select the "Selected tasks" radio button. Turn on the "To all summary tasks" checkbox.

    f) Click OK. In the message box that appears regarding the baseline already being in use, click Yes.

    g) Switch back to the C_Budget_Comparison view.

    h) The Baseline Cost cell in the Catering resource's summary row should be $30,000. If it isn't, type 30000 in the cell, and then press Enter.

    i) Collapse the Vendors budget group summary row by clicking the black triangle to the left of the budget category name.

Figure 15-13 shows the final comparison between budget category values and current planned values for the project. The labor budget is slightly under budget, while the other budget categories are right on track. This project is in great shape budget-wise.

Resource Name	Work	Budget Category	Budget Cost	Cost	Budget Work	Baseline Cost	Details
▷ Labor Budget	4,266 hrs	Labor Budget	$485,000.00	$481,300.00		$487,450.00	Work
							Act. Work
▷ Materials Budget		Materials Budget	$21,250.00	$20,500.00		$20,500.00	Work
							Act. Work
▷ Miscellaneous Budget		Miscellaneous Bt	$800.00	$800.00		$800.00	Work
							Act. Work
▷ Vendors Budget	91 hrs	Vendors Budget	$43,000.00	$41,300.00		$41,300.00	Work
							Act. Work
							Work
							Act. Work

Figure 15-13. *Compare Budget Cost and Cost values for each budget category.*

16

Managing Change

No matter how flawlessly or exhaustively you plan your project, you can't foresee *everything* that might bubble up. In addition to managing time, resources, and costs, you also have to manage change and a few other things (like risk and issues). Some people say that managing projects is essentially managing change. Chapter 1 provides a brief description of what goes into change management.

Project changes come in all shapes and sizes. A change can be as small as adding a single task you overlooked. Cost-cutting measures that eliminate your contract labor and part-time resources constitute major change. This chapter describes ways to incorporate changes into your project plan, whether the changes are small or large. You'll also see how to add tentative changes to a Project file, so you can determine the impact of a change request before presenting it to the change review board. Finally, you'll learn how to set a new baseline that includes change requests and how to track the progress of change requests.

Managing Changes in a Project Schedule

The work of the change review board and your work in Project are closely intertwined when the board is evaluating changes. The board typically compares the benefits of a proposed change with the costs (in dollars or days) and risk. To make that comparison, the board needs to know how a change request affects the project. In this section, you'll learn how to create simple or extensive what-if scenarios based on the level of information the change review board needs.

> **Note:** If you've downloaded files from the website, use the file Event_Ch16_start.mpp.

The change review board may want to know how long the finish date would be delayed or how much more the project would cost if it approves a sizable change request. Project does a great job of number-crunching to come up with this information. However, be sure to preserve the original Project schedule. If the board decides to nix the change, then you want to be able to remove the what-if changes quickly, and you don't want to accidentally leave a remnant of the change request in the project.

Creating a copy of your Project file is one way to play what-if games as much as you want. (Chapter 11 describes how to compare your original file with the one that contains your what-if scenario.) Another way to add change requests safely is to add the change-request tasks to your active Project file and then inactivate them until they're approved. This section describes both strategies.

Creating a What-If Copy of a Project

Copying your Project file is the safest way to explore the effects of a change request whether major or minor. Just be sure to clearly name the copy so you don't accidentally use it when you meant to work on the real thing. Suppose the Sales VP requests an additional area at the kickoff event for attendees to try products out for themselves. Planning for this additional area can be handled within existing project tasks with no additional time or cost. The effect on the project is simple: an additional setup task for the day of the event with additional cost to rent and set up extra furniture and additional cost for demo products.

In this example, copy the sample file, Event_Ch16_start.mpp and name it something like Event_Ch16_hands-on_cr001.mpp. (Including the change request number in the file name is a great idea for a substantial change request.)

> **Tip:** *Don't* name the what-if copy "Event2." Give the file a meaningful name, for example, one that includes the change order number.

Saving a Baseline Before Modifying Your Project

If your project is already in progress, you've probably set at least one baseline. If a change request is significant, saving a new pre-change request baseline makes the effects of the change request scenario stand out. You can compare the updated schedule with this new baseline you save to find changes to the schedule, cost, and resource workloads.

Follow Along Practice

Here are the basic steps for saving a pre-change request baseline:

1. Make sure your what-if change request copy (in this example, Event_Ch16_hands-on_cr001. mpp or the file you saved in the previous section) is the active Project file.

    If you have more than one Project file open, then make sure the what-if copy's filename appears in the main Project window's title bar.

2. In the Project tab's Schedule section, choose Set Baseline→Set Baseline.

The Set Baseline dialog box opens.

3. In the "Set baseline" drop-down list, choose the baseline you want to use (in this example, Base-line1), and then click OK.

    Baselines you've already saved include the date they were saved to the right of their names. In this example, Project will overwrite Baseline1.

> **Tip:** An alternative approach to baselines is to save each baseline you set to Baseline as well as to one of the numbered baselines (Baseline1 to Baseline10). That way, your most recent baseline values are stored in Baseline. With that approach, you don't have to change the baseline used in the "Baseline for Earned Value calculation" box (on the Project Options dialog box's Advanced tab) to tell Project which baseline to use for calculating variances.

Adding a Change Request to Your Live Project File

If a change request is simple—a single task or a summary task with a few subtasks, you can make those changes in your existing Project file.

Follow Along Practice

Here's how to add a change request to your Project schedule:

1. If necessary, switch to the Gantt Chart view (View→Gantt Chart). Apply the Entry table (View→Tables→Entry).

2. For the hands-on change request, you need a new task for setting up that area during event set-up. Select task ID 83 "Set up presentation area furniture" and then click Task→Scroll to Task.

    That way, you can see the task bars in the Gantt Chart timescale.

3. To insert a new task, in the Task tab's Insert section, click the Task button.

    Project inserts a new task row, fills in the Task Name cell with the text "<New Task>," and sets the tasks duration to 1 day?.

4. In the new Task Name cell, type **Set up hands-on area**, and then press Tab.

5. In the Duration cell, type 4h, and then press Tab.

6. To link the task so it follows the "Set up registration area" task, drag over task IDs 82 and 83 to select the two tasks. On the Task tab, click Link Tasks.

7. To link the task to the "Event setup complete" milestone, click task ID 83, Ctrl-click task ID 88, and then click Link Tasks on the Task tab.

Figure 16-1 shows the new task linked into the existing schedule.

ID	(i)	Task Mode	Task Name	Duration	Start	Finish	Predecessors	Gantt
79			⊿ Event setup	1.13 days	4/18/22	4/19/22		
80			Begin setup	0 days	4/18/22	4/18/22	78,63	◆4/18
81			Venue setup (performed by venue staff)	1 day	4/18/22	4/19/22	80	Venue Team[800%]
82			Set up registration area	1 day	4/18/22	4/19/22	80	Venue Team[200%]
83			Set up hands-on area	4 hrs	4/19/22	4/19/22	82	
84			Set up presentation area furniture	1 day	4/18/22	4/19/22	80	Technical Sales Team[300%]
85			Set up marketing and sales area	1 day	4/18/22	4/19/22	80	Sales Team,Technical Sales Team[300%]
86			IT setup	1 day	4/18/22	4/19/22	80	IT Team[300%]
87			Food setup (performed by venue staff)	4 hrs	4/19/22	4/19/22	81	Venue Team[200%],Catering[$30,000.00]
88			Event setup complete	0 days	4/19/22	4/19/22	87,82,84,85,86,83	◆ 4/19
89			⊿ Run event	1 day	4/20/22	4/20/22	88	

Change request task inserted
and linked to other tasks

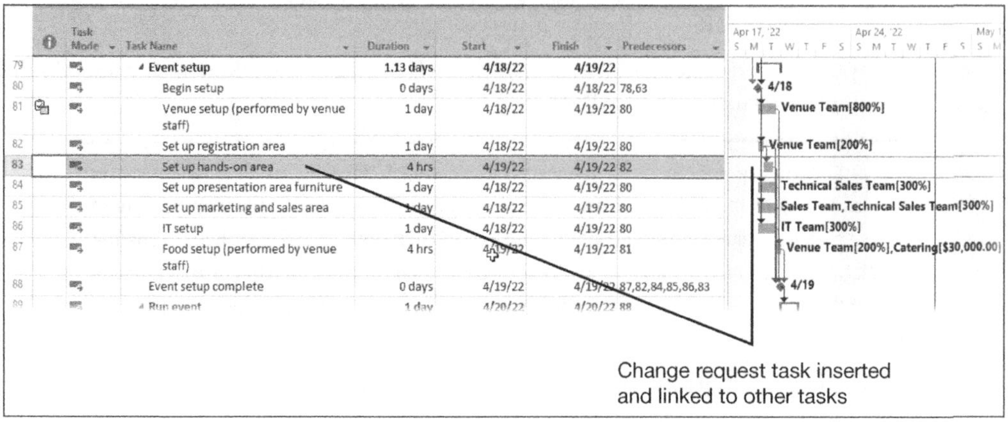

Figure 16-1. *The new task is linked into the existing schedule.*

8. Next, assign resources. Open the Assign Resources dialog box (Resource→Assign Resources). With the new task selected in the table, in the Assign Resources dialog box, click the Venue Team resource (at the end of the list), and then click Assign.

   Project assigns the resource at 100% with a cost of $400.

9. To add cost to the task for the demo products and the extra furniture, start by creating two additional cost resources. Switch to the Resource Sheet (View→Resource Sheet). In the first blank Resource Name cell, type **Rental Expense**. In the Type cell, choose Cost.

10. In the next blank Resource Name cell, type **Product Samples**. In the Type cell, choose Material. In the Std. Rate cell, type **200**, and then press Tab.

11. Switch back to the Gantt Chart view, and, if necessary, select task ID 83 again.

12. In the Assign Resources dialog box, click the row for the Rental Expense resource (near the bottom of the list). In the Cost cell in the same row, type **2000**. Click Assign.

13. In the Assign Resources dialog box, click the row for the Product Samples resource (near the bottom of the list). In the Units cell in the same row, type **25**. Click Assign. Close the Assign Resources dialog box.

14. To see the new task's information, apply the Summary table to the view (View→Tables→Summary).

   Now, the task has the Products Samples, Rental Expense, and Venue Team resources assigned. The total cost of the new task is $7,400, as shown in Figure 16-2.

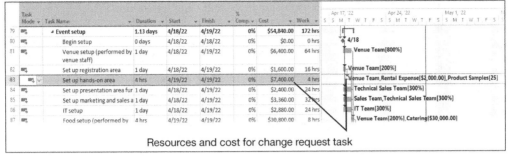

	Task Mode	Task Name	Duration	Start	Finish	% Comp.	Cost	Work
79		◢ Event setup	1.13 days	4/18/22	4/19/22	0%	$54,840.00	172 hrs
80		Begin setup	0 days	4/18/22	4/18/22	0%	$0.00	0 hrs
81		Venue setup (performed by venue staff)	1 day	4/18/22	4/19/22	0%	$6,400.00	64 hrs
82		Set up registration area	1 day	4/18/22	4/19/22	0%	$1,600.00	16 hrs
83		Set up hands-on area	4 hrs	4/19/22	4/19/22	0%	$7,400.00	4 hrs
84		Set up presentation area fur	1 day	4/18/22	4/19/22	0%	$2,400.00	24 hrs
85		Set up marketing and sales a	1 day	4/18/22	4/19/22	0%	$3,360.00	32 hrs
86		IT setup	1 day	4/18/22	4/19/22	0%	$2,880.00	24 hrs
87		Food setup (performed by	4 hrs	4/19/22	4/19/22	0%	$30,800.00	8 hrs

Resources and cost for change request task

Figure 16-2. *The Summary table shows the new task's basic info.*

> **Tip:** If you need to remove tasks from the project for a change request, consider inactivating them (Chapter 11). That way, you can easily reactivate them if the schedule and budget take a turn for the better.

Flagging Change Requests in Project

Change requests could spawn new or modified tasks scattered throughout your project. You need a way to identify change request tasks so you can track them. In addition, flagging them is particularly useful should the project sponsor or customer develop a severe case of amnesia about having approved this significant change. Keeping the change impacts visible during management status meetings can also be a gentle reminder of "This is what you asked for."

This section describes an effective way to identify all the tasks that represent work required to complete approved change requests in your project, so they're easy to find and review. The solution is to create a custom field to identify such tasks and then filter a view to see them all.

> **Tip:** In addition to flagging change requests, you can also use a task's Notes field (Chapter 4) to store information about how the change request affects that task.

Follow Along Practice

Here are the steps:

1. In a task-oriented view like the Gantt Chart view (View→Gantt Chart), right-click a column heading (in this example, Duration), choose Insert Column, and then choose a custom text field (in this example, Text 29).

2. Right-click the Text29 heading, and then choose Custom Fields.

    The Custom Fields dialog box opens with the Text29 field selected.

3. Click the Rename button. In the Rename dialog box, type a name (also known as an alias), in this example, *CR #*.

    A text or number field is great for flagging tasks by their corresponding change-request identifiers.

That way, you can type the change-request number or ID into the custom field.

4. Click OK to close the Custom Fields dialog box.

5. For every task that relates to a specific change request, type the change request number in the task's CR # cell. In this example, in the CR # cell for task ID 83 "Set up hands-on area," type *0001*.

   The value could be something like "Des-004" in a text field or "4" in a number field. Whatever helps you identify which change request this task is related to.

6. If other tasks are affected by the change request, fill in their CR # cells, too.

   In this example, type the CR number *0001* in the CR # cells for task ID 19 "Plan day of event" and task ID 74 "Identify event staff duties."

   To flag a second change request in this example, in the CR # cell for task ID 84 "Set up presentation area furniture," type *0002*.

	Task Mode ▾	Task Name ▾	CR # ▾	Duration ▾	St
79	▬	◢ **Event setup**		**1.13 days**	4/
80	▬	Begin setup		0 days	4/
81	▬	Venue setup (performed by venue staff)		1 day	4/
82	▬	Set up registration area		1 day	4/
83	▬	Set up hands-on area	0001	4 hrs	4/
84	▬	Set up presentation area fur	0002	1 day	4/
85	▬	Set up marketing and sales a		1 day	4/
86	▬	IT setup		1 day	4/
87	▬	Food setup (performed by venue staff)		4 hrs	4/
88	▬	Event setup complete		0 days	4/
89	▬	◢ Run event		1 day	4/

Change request identifiers in a custom field

Figure 16-3. *Add change request numbers to a custom field to identify tasks affected by change requests.*

7. If you want to describe the effect a change request has on a task, you can add a note to the task.

   In this example, right-click task ID 74 "Identify event staff duties," and then choose Notes on the shortcut menu. In the Task Information dialog box's Notes area, type *include schedule for people in hands-on area*. Click OK to close the dialog box. In the Indicators column, Project displays a Note icon. When you put the pointer over the icon, Project displays part of the note.

> **Tip:** If the table that's displayed doesn't include the Indicators column (as in this example), right-click the Task Mode heading, choose Insert Column on the shortcut menu, and then choose Indicators.

8. To filter the table to show only tasks associated with change requests, click the down arrow to the right of the custom-field column's heading. In the drop-down menu that appears, turn off the "(blank)" checkbox, and then click OK.

The task list hides all the tasks that don't have a change request number in their CR # cells, as shown in Figure 16-4.

Tip: If you want to filter for a specific change request, click the down arrow to the right of the change request field heading. In the drop-down menu that appears, turn off the "(Select All)" checkbox, and then turn on the checkbox for the CR number you want. In this example, you don't have to filter for a specific CR number.

	ⓘ	Task Mode ▾	Task Name ▾	CR # ▾	Duration ▾	Start
0		➡	◢ **Event_Ch16_handson_cr001**		**246.88 day:**	**6/1/**
19		➡	Plan day of event	0001	7 wks	1/10/
79		➡	◢ **Event setup**		**1.13 days**	**4/18/**
83		➡	Set up hands-on area	0001	4 hrs	4/19/
84		➡	Set up presentation area fur	0002	1 day	4/18/

Figure 16-4. *Filter shows tasks associated with change requests and the summary tasks to which they belong.*

Tracking Changes in a Project Schedule

After approval, the board wants to know how change requests are progressing. To track change request performance, you can save a baseline for approved change requests. You can compare your pre-change request baseline to the baseline for approved change requests to see how the change requests affect the project schedule. You can also compare your approved change request baseline to your current values to see whether change requests are performing according to plan. Updating progress on change request tasks is no different from updating original project tasks.

Updating Project with Approved Change Requests

You need to baseline approved project changes to your Project file for the same reasons you enter actual progress information: An up-to-date project lets you report quickly about what has already taken place and, more importantly, lets you accurately forecast what will happen in the future.

How you baseline the Project file depends on how you want to track the approved change requests you add. Each choice has its pros and cons, so choose the one that fits your needs the best. Here are two options you can use:

Follow Along Practice

- **Adding tasks to a baseline**: If you want to keep track of your original tasks from an older baseline and track new tasks going forward, the best approach is to add tasks to a baseline.

  a) Select the tasks you want to add (in this example, task IDs 19, 74, 83, and 84) and then, in the Project tab's Schedule section, choose Set Baseline→Set Baseline.

  b) In the "Set baseline" box, choose the Baseline you want to add to, in this example, Baseline1.

  c) In the Set Baseline dialog box, be sure to choose the "Selected tasks" option. Project keeps the existing baseline values for existing tasks and adds the current scheduled values for the added tasks to the baseline.

  d) In the "Roll up baselines" section, turn on the "To all summary tasks" checkbox and the "To selected summary tasks" checkbox. Project rolls up changes from the selected tasks all the way up to the project summary task.

  e) Click OK. Click Yes to overwrite the baseline.

- **Setting a new baseline**: For a significant change, you can save a new baseline for the entire project. This approach uses the project state *before* you implemented the change as the line in the sand for comparisons. (See Chapter 12 to save a baseline for the entire project.)

  The problem with this approach is that all the original tasks in the Project file have new baseline values. If you compare the current schedule with the baseline, the variances on original tasks represent variances from this more recent baseline. You lose the comparison to your original plan.

After you decide how you want to track change requests, the techniques you use to enter actual values are the same for original, modified, and new tasks (Chapter 13).

Comparing Your Original Baseline to the Change Request Baseline

The Multiple Baselines Gantt view makes it easy to compare your original baselined schedule to the baseline you save with change request modifications. However, you have to modify a table to compare baseline values in a table.

Follow Along Practice

Follow these steps:

1. Choose View→Other Views→More Views. In the More Views dialog box, double-click Multiple Baselines Gantt.

   If necessary, click the project summary task and then choose Task→Scroll to Task. In this example, you'll see two sets of thin task bars in the timescale: the blue bars represent Baseline and the red bars represent Baseline1. If you see green bars, they represent Baseline2.

2. To compare baseline values in the table, choose View→Tables→Save Fields As A New Table. In the Save Table dialog box's Name box, type *C_Multiple Baselines*, and then click OK.

3. Right-click the Duration heading in the table, choose Insert Column, and then choose Baseline Cost.

4. Right-click the Duration heading in the table, choose Insert Column, and then choose Baseline1 Cost.

    If necessary, widen the columns to see the values for the project summary task.

    Figure 16-5 shows a comparison between the original baseline and the change request baseline.

	❶	Task Mode ▾	Task Name ▾	Baseline Cost ▾	Baseline1 Cost ▾	Duration ▾
			Change request values rolled up to summary tasks			
0		▪⥐	⊿ **Event_Ch16_handson_cr001**	**$550,050.00**	**$551,300.00**	**246.88 days**
1	✓	▪⥐	Project start	$0.00	$0.00	0 days
2		▪⥐	▷ **Planning**	**$137,600.00**	**$126,850.00**	**101.17 days**
19	▪	▪⥐	Plan day of event	$18,700.00	$18,700.00	7 wks
20		▪⥐	Planning complete	$0.00	$0.00	0 days
21		▪⥐	▷ **Procurement**	**$82,050.00**	**$86,650.00**	**108.88 days**
56		▪⥐	▷ **Pre-event activities**	**$234,180.00**	**$234,180.00**	**123 days**
79		▪⥐	⊿ **Event setup**	**$47,440.00**	**$54,840.00**	**1.13 days**
80		▪⥐	Begin setup	$0.00	$0.00	0 days
81	📋	▪⥐	Venue setup (performed by venue s	$6,400.00	$6,400.00	1 day
82		▪⥐	Set up registration area	$1,600.00	$1,600.00	1 day
83		▪⥐	Set up hands-on area	$0.00	$7,400.00	4 hrs
84		▪⥐	Set up presentation area furniture	$2,400.00	$2,400.00	1 day
85		▪⥐	Set up marketing and sales area	$3,360.00	$3,360.00	1 day
86		▪⥐	IT setup	$2,880.00	$2,880.00	1 day

Figure 16-5. *See the overall effects of change requests by comparing the original baseline to the change request baseline.*

17

Filtering and Grouping Project Data

You can modify or create filters and groups to show particular types of information. In Project, filters screen out information you don't care about so you can easily see the info you do want. By filtering tasks and resources, you can display only what meets the conditions you set, such as tasks with duration longer than two months.

Alternatively, you can use groups to shuffle information into categories. Grouping tasks, resources, and assignments with similar characteristics makes it easy for you to scan and analyze your project information. Because groups can roll up the values of the items within them, it's easy to see how much you're spending on third-party vendors, for instance.

> **Note:** If you've downloaded files from the book website, you can follow along using the file Event_Ch17_start.mpp.
>
> Before starting to follow along in this chapter, display the Gantt Chart view (on the Task tab, click the bottom half of the Gantt Chart button). If the view is filtered for change requests, click the funnel icon to the right of the CR # heading, and then choose Clear Filter from CR #. Also, switch the option to track variances against the Baseline saved baseline. To do that, on the File tab, click Options. Click Advanced. In the Earned Value options for this project section, click the down arrow in the Baseline for Earned Value calculation box and choose Baseline.

Filtering Through Information

Project comes with quite a few built-in filters to get you started. For example, the Using Resource filter shows tasks that use resources you specify, and the "Tasks with Estimated Durations" filter shows tasks with question marks in their Duration fields, so you can fill in duration values. If built-in filters don't do what you want, you can copy one of them as a foundation for creating your own. You can also create ad hoc filters with AutoFilter. This section shows you how to build custom filters. You'll find several examples of custom and ad hoc filters throughout this book.

In this section, you'll learn how to build up a filter with several different types of tests. Suppose you want to filter your task list for tasks that are in trouble, so you can try to get them back on track.

Applying Filters

Follow Along Practice

To apply a filter to the current view, head to the View tab's Data section and pick an item in the Filter drop-down list, in this example, Critical. Project filters the task list to display only critical tasks (and the summary tasks to which they belong).

> **Tip:** Filters are a great way to confirm that you've made all the changes you need. For example, when you apply the "Tasks with Estimated Durations" filter, the task list displays only tasks with estimated durations. (The example project doesn't have any tasks with estimated durations, so you don't have to apply this filter if you're following along.) After you change the durations of those tasks, reapply the filter (by choosing it again in the Filter box drop-down list or, if you use Project Online, by pressing Ctrl+F3.) When the filtered list is empty, you know you're done.

> **Note:** The note titled "Summarizing a Project" describes another way you can filter tasks in a view.

After you apply a filter, changes you make to a project can affect what should appear in the filtered list—but you have to manually reapply the filter each time. For example, if you've applied the Critical filter (to display only critical tasks) and then you shorten a task so that it's no longer on the critical path, you'd expect it to disappear from view. But Project *doesn't* automatically update the filtered list as you make changes. So to make sure you're seeing the right items, reapply the current filter.

Creating and Editing Filters

Filters can be as simple as the Critical filter, which just checks whether a task's Critical field is equal to Yes. The AutoFilter feature described later in this chapter makes quick work of simple filters like these. But filters can also have several nested tests, like the Slipped/Late Progress filter. An existing filter makes a great template for creating your own, whether you want filter-building guidance or just a shortcut. This section describes how to create a new filter or to make a copy of an existing one.

> **Tip:** Built-in filters can act as a tutorial when you want to create your own. They provide examples of combining several tests in one filter, comparing the value of one field with another, and asking for input. For example, you could create a filter to find critical tasks

whose dates are slipping by starting with the built-in Slipping Tasks filter and adding a test on the Critical field.

Follow Along Practice

The methods for creating filters from scratch or from copies are almost identical. You create the new filter, change the name Project assigns, and then define the filter conditions. Here are the steps:

1. In the View tab's Data section, click the Filter down arrow and then, on the drop-down menu, choose More Filters.

   If a task-oriented view is visible, the More Filters dialog box opens with the Task option selected, and the Filters list includes all the task-oriented filters, like Completed Tasks and Milestones. If a resource-oriented view like the Resource Sheet is visible, the Resource option is selected automatically. If necessary, select the option for the kind of filter you want to work on (Task or Resource).

2. To start with an existing filter, in the Filters list, select the filter you want to copy (in this example, Critical), and then click Copy.

   To start with a blank slate, click New. To edit an existing filter, select the filter, and then click Edit. You can also start a new filter by going to the View tab's Data section, clicking the Filter down arrow, and then, on the drop-down menu, choosing New Filter.

   Whether you click Copy or New, the Filter Definition dialog box opens. Project fills in the Name box with something like "Filter 1" for new filters and "Copy of [filter name]" for copied filters.

3. In the Name box of the Filter Definition dialog box, type a new name for the filter, in this example, *C_Troubled Tasks*.

   With a prefix in their names, as shown in Figure 17-1, custom filters are easy to differentiate from built-in filters.

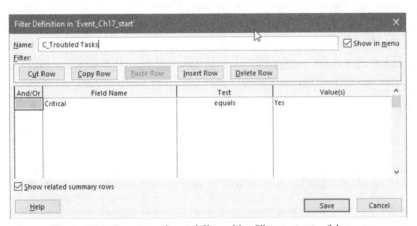

Figure 17-1. *For new and copied filters alike, fill in a meaningful name.*

4. Turn on the "Show in menu" checkbox to include a filter on the menu that appears when you click the View tab's Filter down arrow.

---

5. Add or modify the filter's tests (don't add any to the example filter), and then click Save to save the filter. Click Close to close the More Filters dialog box.

The next section explains how to set up filter tests.

Summarizing a Project

Most of the time, you want to see summary tasks **and** their subtasks. But when you're working only on subtasks—for instance, to find tasks without assigned resources—a task list without summary tasks is better. It's easy to filter out summary tasks in Project:

*   **Hide or show summary tasks**: If you want to hide summary tasks to focus on work tasks, choose a task view's Format tab (like Gantt Chart Tools | Format). In the tab's Show/Hide section, turn off the Summary Tasks checkbox. To bring the summary tasks back, turn the checkbox back on.

*   **Summarize the entire project**: Project can display a top-level task to summarize an entire project. In a task view's Format tab's Show/Hide section, turn on the Project Summary Task checkbox. Project adds a row with ID number 0, which rolls up all the values for **all** tasks in your project. To always show the project-summary tasks for new projects, in the Project Options dialog box, choose Advanced, and then, under "Display options for this project," turn on the "Show project summary task" checkbox.

Defining Filters

Filters represent a gauntlet of tests that tasks, resources, or assignments have to pass in order to appear in the current view. For example, the In Progress Tasks filter first tests whether a task has started, and then tests whether it is **not** finished. If a task has started but not finished (that is, it passes both tests), then it appears in the filtered task list because it's in progress. This section describes how to create different types of tests, including the following:

*   **Comparing a field with a value**: The simplest tests compare a field with a specific text string, number, or other value, like the Critical filter testing whether the Critical field equals Yes.

*   **Multiple tests**: Filters are often made up of several tests, like the built-in Should Start/Finish By filter. When you combine more than one test, you have to tell Project whether items must pass all the tests or some combination of them.

*   **Comparing two fields**: You can set up a filter to compare the values from two fields. For example, the Cost Overbudget filter tests whether Cost is greater than Baseline Cost.

*   **Interactive tests**: In some cases, you want to filter by a different value each time you apply the filter. For example, say you want to filter tasks by a specific assigned resource depending on whom you're trying to free up. An interactive filter is perfect for this situation because it asks for a value and then uses your answer to filter the list.

Comparing a Field with a Value

Comparing a field with a value is a good introduction to tests. Many basic filters need only one of these tests—like the perennial favorite Critical filter. In this example, suppose you want to filter for tasks that are both critical and not yet complete, so you still have a chance to correct them. Here are the steps to create a test that compares a field with a value, using the C_Troubled Tasks filter you created in the previous section:

Follow Along Practice

1. To resume work on a filter, in the View tab's Filters list, choose More Filters. In the More Filters dialog box, select the filter you want to edit (in this example, C_Troubled Tasks), and then click Edit.

   The Filter Definition dialog box opens to the selected filter definition.

2. To begin defining a test, select the first blank Field Name cell, click the down arrow that appears, and then, in the drop-down list, choose the field you want to test (in this example, % Complete).

   The field appears in the Field Name cell.

   > **Tip:** To quickly select a field in the drop-down list, start typing the first few letters of the field's name. When Project selects the field you want, press Enter, and Project inserts that field's name in the Field Name cell.

3. Select the Test cell, click the down arrow that appears, and then choose the type of test you want to apply, as illustrated in Figure 17-2. In this example, incomplete tasks have a % Complete value that's less than 100, so choose "is less than."

   Table 17-1 describes the tests that Project offers and gives an example of each one. For example, the Work Overbudget filter uses "is greater than" to see whether actual work hours are greater than baseline work hours.

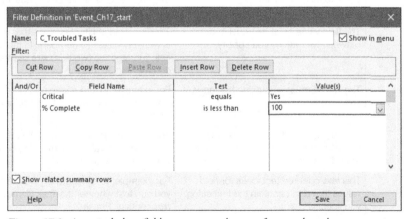

Figure 17-2. *A test includes a field name to test, the type of test, and a value to test against.*

---

4. In the Value(s) cell, type or choose the value to compare with the field. In this example, type *100*.

    If the field you're testing is a Yes/No field, you can type *Yes* or *No*, or choose the values from the drop-down list.

5. In this example, keep the "Show related summary rows" checkbox turned on to tell Project to include the summary rows for tasks that pass the filter's tests.

    If summary rows outnumber the tasks you're looking for, turn off this checkbox to see only the work tasks that pass the filter.

6. In this example, the filter isn't yet complete and you can't save it. Do not click Save yet. Instead, continue to the next section.

Table 17-1. *Project's filter tests*

Test	What It Does	Example
Does not equal	The field value does not equal the test value.	The Incomplete Tasks filter tests whether % Complete does not equal 100%.
Equals	The field and test values must be equal.	The Critical filter tests whether the Critical field equals Yes.
Is greater than	The field value must be greater than the test value.	The Slipping Tasks filter tests whether the Finish field is greater than the Baseline Finish field. (Later dates are greater than earlier dates.)
Is greater than or equal to	The field value must be greater than or equal to the test value.	The Date Range filter tests whether the start date is greater than or equal to the date you specify.
Is less than	The field value must be less than the test value.	The Should Start By filter tests whether the Start field is less than (earlier than) the date you specify.
Is less than or equal to	The field value must be less than or equal to the test value.	The Tasks Due This Week filter tests whether the Finish field is less than or equal to the date you specify for the end of the week.
Is within	The field value must be equal to or between two values you specify.	The Task Range filter tests whether the ID field is within two task ID numbers. In the Value(s) cell, you type the two numbers separated by a comma, like **50,100**.
Is not within	The values must be outside the range you specify.	For example, to find cheap and expensive resources, test whether Standard Rate is not within **25,300.**
Contains	This text-oriented test checks whether the field value contains the text string in the Value(s) cell.	For example, you can see whether the Task Name field contains "Payment" to find all the payment milestones.
Does not contain	This text-oriented test looks for field values that don't contain the text string you specify.	For example, to eliminate all phase two tasks, you can test whether the Task Name field does *not* contain "Phase 2."
Contains exactly	This test looks for exact matches between the field and the test value.	The Using Resource filter tests whether Resource Name contains the exact resource name you type.

Tip: The "equals" and "does not equal" tests can compare text field values against strings with wildcard characters; "*" is the wildcard for one or more characters, and "?" replaces just one character. For example, "* Design" finds all the tasks with "Design" at the end of their names. On the other hand, "Module?" finds the tasks with Module1 through Module9 in their names, but not tasks named something like Module10.

Creating Filters with Multiple Tests

In many cases, a filter needs more than one test to do what you want. In those situations, multiple-test filters are just the ticket. They let you combine tests in lots of different ways. You can set up filters in which items must pass every test or only some of the tests.

Initially, Project evaluates tests in the order they appear in the Filter Definition table, such as, "Is the task critical?", "Is the task not yet complete?", and only then, "Is the task in trouble?". The items that pass the first test move on to the next test. Project keeps testing until there are no more tests.

And and *Or* are called Boolean (logic) operators, which you use to specify whether an item has to pass both tests or only one. And and Or work just like they do in real life. If you want items to pass both tests, use And; for instance, "Is the task critical?" and "Is the task not yet complete?" Use Or if the items need to pass only one test, like "Is the task slipping past its baseline finish date?" or "Is the task's work behind schedule?"

You can use additional Ands or Ors to change the order of tests. For example, tasks have to be critical and incomplete; only then does it matter whether they're in trouble.

The following steps build onto the C_Trouble Tasks filter to first find tasks that are critical *and* are not yet complete. Then, it finds baselined tasks whose finish dates are delayed or whose work is behind schedule. If a task passes both sets of tests, then it appears in the filtered task list.

Each multiple-test filter is different, but the following steps demonstrate the concept. Because the following steps build on the filter started in the previous section, the filter already has two tests and you need to add a Boolean test to the second one:

Follow Along Practice

1. In the second row's And/Or cell, choose And.

    If you want the condition to become one of several that is evaluated as a set, add a Boolean operator to the row that contains the condition. When you do that, the operator (And or Or) appears on the right side of its cell in unbolded text, as shown in Figure 17-3. On the other hand, if you want to specify the Boolean operator to apply to the sets of tests, add a Boolean operator to a row that doesn't contain a condition, as described in the next step.

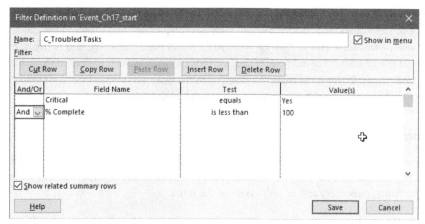

Figure 17-3. *Choosing And or Or in the same row as a test evaluates the tests as a set.*

2. To add another test to this group, in the third row's And/Or cell, choose And, and then add a test to check whether the task has a baselined finish date.

    Before you can test a task to see if it's slipping past its baselined finish date, you have to make sure the task has been baselined. To add this test, choose Baseline Finish in the third row's Field Name cell, choose "does not equal" in that row's Test cell, and type **NA** in that row's Value(s) cell. (A value of NA means that a field does not contain a value, so this test returns true if the field contains a value.)

3. To test the previous conditions as a group, in the fourth row's And/Or cell, choose And, and then click anywhere in the fifth row.

    As soon as you click any other row, several things happen. Project moves the And you just added to the left side of its cell, bolds the And, and shades its row. This formatting (shown in Figure 17-4) is Project's way of saying that the row acts like the parentheses in a mathematical equation before and after the empty row. For example, with And in the fourth row, Project evaluates the first three tests as a set and evaluates the tests after the fourth row as a set, as the following steps show.

    > **Tip:** If you forget to include a test in your filter, you don't have to start from scratch. The note titled "Inserting, Deleting, and Rearranging Rows" explains how to edit a filter to add, remove, and otherwise change condition order.

4. In this example, the filter still isn't complete. Do not click Save yet. Instead, continue to the next section.

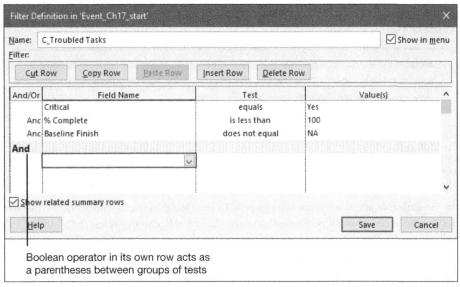

Figure 17-4. *Choosing And or Or in a row without a test acts like a parentheses in a mathematical equation.*

Comparing Two Fields

Many helpful tests compare two fields. For example, you can create a filter that checks whether the date in the Finish field is greater than the date in the Baseline Finish field to see if a task is slipping past its baselined finish date; if it is, then you know that the task is due to finish later than you originally planned.

Follow Along Practice

Setting up a test to compare two fields is similar to comparing a field with a value. Here are the steps:

1. Because the following steps build on the C_Troubled Tasks filter, this step starts by defining the first test in the second set of tests. In the fifth row, bypass the And/Or cell.

    You don't have to include an And or an Or, because this test is the first one of the second set.

2. In the fifth row's Field Name cell, choose Finish).

    The test for slipping tasks checks whether the Finish field is greater than the Baseline Finish field (that is, the finish date is later than the task's finish date according to the baselined schedule).

3. Press the right arrow key, click the Test cell's down arrow, and then choose the test you want to apply, "is greater than" in this example.

    The test you choose appears in the Test cell in the same row.

4. Press the right arrow key, click the Value(s) cell's down arrow, and then choose the comparison field (Baseline Finish, in this example).

In the Value(s) column, Project differentiates fields from text by enclosing the field's name in square brackets ([ ]), as shown in Figure 17-5.

> **Note:** In the Value(s) column, the drop-down list contains all Project fields, including custom fields like Number10. However, you see only task fields if you're building a task filter or only resource fields if you're building a resource filter.

5. To add a test for tasks whose work is behind schedule, in the sixth row, choose Or in the And/Or cell.

    The Or in front of this condition, shown in Figure 17-5, tells Project that a task has to pass either the slipped task test *or* the late progress test. Either situation means the task is in trouble.

6. In the sixth row, add the test for late progress. In the Field Name cell, choose BCWP, which is the baselined cost of work performed so far. In the Test cell, choose "is less than." In the Value(s) cell, choose BCWS.

    This test looks for tasks whose completed work is than the amount of work that was supposed to be completed as of the status date, in other words, tasks, whose work is behind schedule.

7. Click Save to save the filter. Figure 17-5 shows the completed filter.

8. To apply it to the current view, in the More Filters dialog box, click Apply.

    You can also apply a filter by choosing it in the View tab's Filter drop-down list.

When you apply the filter to your task list, Project runs tasks past the first three filter conditions. Tasks that pass all three tests in the first group are then checked to see whether they pass either of the two tests in the second set.

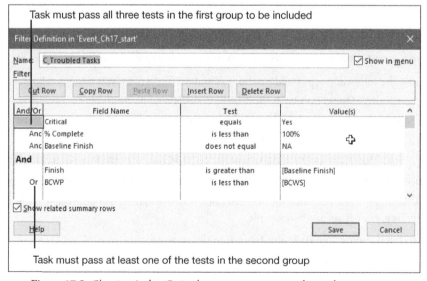

Figure 17-5. *Choosing And or Or in the same row as a test evaluates the tests as a set.*

Inserting, Deleting, and Rearranging Rows

Without planning ahead, chances are good that you'll forget one of your filter conditions. After testing a filter, you may realize that your logic isn't sound. If you find yourself in that situation, you'll find the Filter Definition Dialog box's buttons for inserting, deleting, copying, cutting, and pasting rows quite handy. Here's what each button does:

- **Cut Row**: Select a row, and then click Cut Row to place the row on the Clipboard. The Paste Row button then becomes active so you can paste the row in another location.

- **Copy Row**: Select a row, and then click Copy Row to place the row on the Clipboard. If one row is almost identical to the one you want to add, then copying and pasting an existing row may be easier than defining a condition.

- **Paste Row**: Select the row below where you want to paste the row on the Clipboard, and then click Paste Row. Project inserts the cut or copied row above the selected row.

- **Insert Row**: Select the row where you want to insert a new blank row, and then click Insert Row. The new row appears above the selected row.

- **Delete Row**: If a condition is wrong or unnecessary, select it and then click Delete Row.

Creating Interactive Filters

With some filters, you want to use different values each time you apply them, which is why Project offers *interactive filters*. An interactive filter is one that asks for values to use in tests. For example, the filter built in the previous sections still lists a lot of tasks. Suppose you want to specify a date by which tasks start, so the filter shows only tasks that are coming up soon. Each time you apply this filter, you tell it the date you're interested in. Values you enter in response to the filter's prompt act exactly as though you had placed them in the Filter Definition dialog box in Value(s) cells.

Follow Along Practice

Creating these inquisitive filters is easy once you learn how to define a prompt. Here are the steps:

1. To resume work on the filter created earlier in this chapter, in the View tab's Filters list, choose More Filters. Select the filter you want to edit (in this example, C_Troubled Tasks), and then click Edit.

2. In the first blank And/Or cell, choose And.

3. In the row for the interactive condition (in this example, the next blank row), choose the field you want (Start in this example).

4. Press the right arrow or click the Test cell in the same row, and then choose the test you want ("is less than," in this example).

This test will check for tasks that start earlier than the date you specify.

5.   In the Value(s) cell, type the prompt in quotation marks, in this example, "Enter the date that tasks should start by." After you add the closing double quote, type a question mark, as shown in Figure 17-6.

Make sure that the prompt text is enclosed in **double** quotes. The question mark after the quotes tells Project that the filter is interactive.

6.   Click Save. In the More Filters dialog box, click Close.

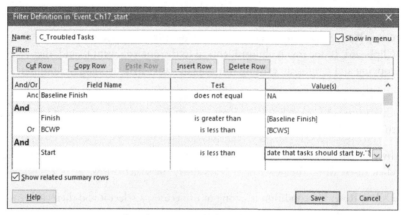

Figure 17-6. *Be sure to place the question mark at the very end of the string, outside the quotation marks.*

When you run the filter, Project displays your prompt as shown Figure 17-7. In this example, fill in *11/5/21*. When you click OK, Project runs through the filter's tests and displays the results that pass the tests.

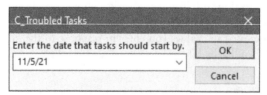

Figure 17-7. *When you apply an interactive filter, a dialog box opens with the prompt you typed. Project waits until you enter a value.*

To remove the filter from the view, in the View tab's Filter list, choose Clear Filter.

Quick and Dirty Filtering with AutoFilter

When you have a quick, one-time question, you don't have to go to all the trouble of creating and saving a filter. Instead, turn to Project's AutoFilter feature, which, like its relative in Excel, lets you pick filter fields and values for one field at a time. You can change the fields or the values at will, and combine filters on several fields at the same time.

Using AutoFilter

Follow Along Practice

Here's how to use AutoFilter:

1. Display the view and table you want to filter, in this example, keep the Gantt Chart view and Summary table in place.

    A table must be visible, because AutoFilter works on table columns.

2. If AutoFilter isn't turned on (down arrows aren't visible to the right of each column heading), then in the View tab's Data section, click the Filter down arrow, and then choose Display AutoFilter.

    Project comes with AutoFilter turned on. If you want to turn AutoFilter off for new projects for some reason, choose File→Options. In the Project Options dialog box, click Advanced, and then, under the General heading, turn off the "Set AutoFilter on for new projects" checkbox.

3. Click the down arrow in the column you want to filter—for instance, Duration.

    The AutoFilter drop-down menu includes several filter values based on the data in the column, as illustrated in Figure 17-8.

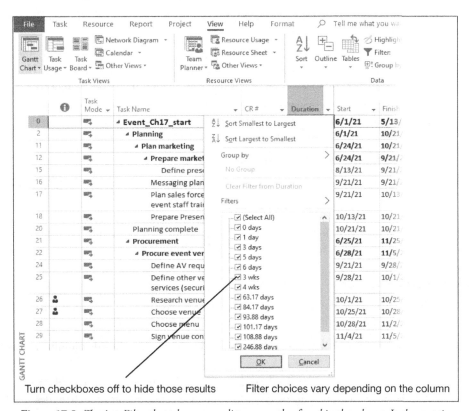

Figure 17-8. *The AutoFilter drop-down menu lists every value found in the column. It also contains likely choices based on the column.*

4. To filter by specific values, make sure the AutoFilter checkboxes for the values you want to use are turned on, and turn off all the other AutoFilter checkboxes. In this example, turn off the "0 days" checkbox. Click OK to apply the AutoFilter settings you've selected.

   By turning off the "0 days" checkbox, you hide all milestones in the project.

5. To apply a quick AutoFilter test, in the drop-down menu, choose Filters. Then, in the submenu, choose the test or condition you want, in this example, "1 week or longer."

   As soon as you apply an AutoFilter to a column, Project filters the list and displays the AutoFilter icon (which looks like a funnel) to the right of the column's heading.

   > **Tip:** If you choose a filter entry such as "Greater than," the Custom AutoFilter dialog box opens. The next section "Building Custom Filters with AutoFilter" shows you how to whip up a custom AutoFilter test.

6. To remove a filter in a column, click the AutoFilter icon (which looks like a funnel) in that column, and then choose "Clear Filter from [column name]."

   The filtered list updates to show items that pass the AutoFilters still in place.

7. To add an AutoFilter to another column, click the down arrow in that column's heading row, and then repeat steps in this section.

   AutoFilter doesn't have all the options the Filter Definition dialog box provides. Also, AutoFilters on each column act like they're joined with And operators: The results show items that pass **all** the tests. So you can't tell AutoFilter to show items that pass one AutoFilter test or another.

   > **Tip:** A funnel icon appears to the right of every column with an AutoFilter applied.

Building Custom Filters with AutoFilter

Quite often, the filter you have in mind goes a step or two beyond what the AutoFilter drop-down menu offers, but you don't need the full suite of tools from the Filter Definition dialog box. If that's the case, a custom AutoFilter may be the answer. Custom AutoFilters can have one or two conditions joined with an And or an Or. You can even save custom AutoFilters you want to use again and add them to the regular filter list. Here's how to build a custom AutoFilter:

Follow Along Practice

1. Click the down arrow in the column heading for the field you want to filter (in this example, Start), point at Filters, and then, on the AutoFilter submenu, choose Custom.

   The Custom AutoFilter dialog box opens. The field is set to the selected column, as shown in Figure 17-9.

2. For the first custom condition, in the drop-down list on the left, choose the test (the same ones you see in the Filter Definition dialog box when you define a filter from scratch, as described earlier in this chapter). In this example, choose "is greater than or equal to."

3. In the box on the right, choose or type the value, in this example, *10/31/21*.

4. If the custom filter includes a second condition, select the And option if results must pass both conditions, as in this example.

   Select the Or option if results must pass only one of the conditions.

5. If the custom filter includes a second condition, then define the second condition. In this example, choose "is less than" in the first box below the And radio button. In the second box, type *11/30/21*.

> **Tip:** To save the custom AutoFilter, click Save. The Filter Definition dialog box opens with all the tests in the test table. All you have to do is type a new name in the Name box and then click OK. If you want to make other changes—for example, to add the filter to the menu or to hide summary tasks—modify the settings in the dialog box before clicking OK. Do not save this custom filter.

6. To apply the custom AutoFilter, click OK.

   This custom AutoFilter filters the task list to show tasks that start on or after 10/31/21 and before 11/30/21.

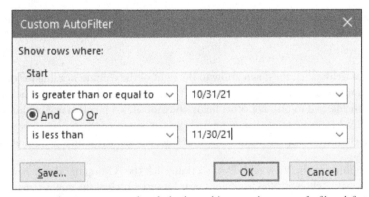

Figure 17-9. *The Custom AutoFilter dialog box is like a simple version of a filter definition.*

7. To remove the AutoFilter, click the funnel icon, and then choose "Clear Filter from [field]," which is Start in this example.

Grouping Project Elements

In Project, the Group feature lets you segregate tasks, resources, or assignments by field values (Figure 17-10). For example, if you group tasks by schedule variance, troubled tasks will jump out at you. Or you can group resources by availability to see who can jump in to help burned-out team members. This section explains how to use Project groups.

> **Tip:** If you're confused by the different uses of the word "group" in Project, see the note titled "Groups, Groups, and More Groups" for clarification.

Working with Groups

Like filtering, groups can work with several fields. For example, in the Resource Usage view, you can group assignments first by resource group, and then by whether the resource is overallocated. Here are a few methods for applying a group:

- **Choose a popular group**: In the View tab's Data section, click the "Group by" down arrow, and then, on the drop-down menu, choose the group you want, like Critical, Milestones, or "Complete and Incomplete Tasks."

- **Choose any group**: In the View tab's Data section, click the Group By down arrow, and then, on the drop-down menu, choose More Groups. In the More Groups dialog box, double-click the group you want.

- **Group by a field**: Click the down arrow to the right of the column heading for the field you want to group by, and then, on the drop-down menu, choose "Group on this field" (for Yes/No fields, text fields, and so on). For other fields, the drop-down menu may contain the "Group by" command. When you choose that command, a submenu of group options appears—for example, if you choose "Group by" in the Duration field, the submenu includes Duration and Weeks.

To remove groupings, in the View tab's Data section, click the "Group by" down arrow, and then, on the drop-down menu, choose [No Group] or Clear Group. Or click the down arrow to the right of a column heading and choose Clear Group on the drop-down menu.

Changes you make to a project can affect the group to which a task, resource, or assignment belongs. For example, if you add resources to shorten task duration, the task should appear in a different Duration subgroup. However, you don't see that happen until you reapply the group.

Figure 17-10. *When you group items, the group summary rows total the values in the group's numeric fields.*

Creating a Group

As with filters, the easiest way to create a group is to copy and edit an existing one. That way you keep the original group definition and customize the copy. For example, to set up a group that uses both the Critical and Duration fields, you can copy the built-in Critical group and then add the second condition to the copy. (Basic groups are so simple, though, that there's no problem starting from scratch.)

Project comes with several groups that apply to tasks and resources, but you can expand the list to analyze your projects in many ways. Here are a few examples:

- **Overallocated resources**: Group tasks by the Overallocated field to find tasks with overallocated resources.

- **Overbudget tasks**: Group tasks by Cost Variance to categorize tasks by how much they're over budget.

- **Critical tasks with overallocated resources**: Critical tasks that use overallocated resources are risking a late project finish date. Group tasks first by the Critical field, and then by the Overallocated field, to see the group of critical tasks broken into overallocated and not-overallocated resources.

- **Internal and external resources**: Group assignments by the Resource Group field to see how much work you've assigned to outside resources.

- **Long critical tasks with little or no work done**: If you're looking for tasks to crash (Chapter 11) to bring a project back on track, critical tasks with longer durations give you the most benefit. If the project is already in progress, tasks that are almost complete won't help. Filter first by Critical, then by % Complete (in ascending order), and finally by Duration (in descending order) so you can see the critical tasks with the least amount of work done and the longest duration.

Groups, Groups, and More Groups

The term "group" is used to describe several features in Project, each of which does something different. Here are the different kinds of groups Project uses, and advice on keeping them straight:

- **Group By command**: In the View tab's Data section, the drop-down list in the "Group by" box (the box initially contains the text *[No Group]*) lists groups that categorize tasks, resources, or assignments by field values. (You can also click the down arrow to the right of the column heading for the field you want to group by, and then, on the drop-down menu, choose "Group by" or "Group on this field," depending on the field.) For example, the built-in "Complete and Incomplete Tasks" group separates unstarted tasks from those that are in progress and completed tasks.

- **Resource group**: In the Resource Sheet view, the Group field specifies categories for resources. For example, you could set up group names to associate people with their departments: Sales, Marketing, and so on. Then you could use the Group field to find replacement resources from the same department.

- **Group resource**: A group resource represents several interchangeable resources. Suppose your technical sales team includes 5 people who can do any kind of salesy task. In that case, you could create one resource called Technical Sales Team (as in the example project). The Maximum Units for a group resource is the sum of each individual's maximum units, so this group resource may have maximum units of 500 percent, say. You can then assign the Technical Sales Team resource to tasks and let the team leader worry about who does what. As long as the assignments don't exceed 500 percent, your work is done.

- **Ribbon group**: If you customize the ribbon, one of the buttons on the "Customize the Ribbon" page is New Group. This command lets you add a new section to a tab on the ribbon.

The steps for creating and copying groups are almost identical. You create the new group (from scratch or by copying), name it, and then define the fields to group by. Here are the steps:

Follow Along Practice

1. In the View tab's Data section, click the "Group by" down arrow, and then, on the drop-down menu, choose More Groups.

   If a task-oriented view is active as in this example, the More Groups dialog box opens with the Task option selected and task-related groups displayed in the Groups list. To work on a resource-related group (for instance, to group resources by their Resource Group), select the Resource option instead.

---

2. To create a copy of an existing group, in the Groups list, select the group you want to copy (in this example, Critical), and then click Copy.

    The Group Definition dialog box opens. Copying a group, and then editing the copy, means you'll still have the original group definition in addition to the new one.

    > **Note:** To start a new group from scratch, simply click New. To make changes to an existing group, in the More Groups dialog box, select the group you want to edit, and then click Edit. The Group Definition dialog box opens with the settings for the existing group. Make the changes you want and then click Save.

3. In the Name box in the Group Definition dialog box, type a new name for the group, in this example, ***Critical/Duration***.

    New groups start with a name like "Group 1," whereas copied groups are named "Copy of [group name]." Replace Project's name with one that identifies what the group does.

    > **Tip:** To list a new group on Project's group drop-down menus, be sure to turn on the "Show in menu" checkbox.

4. If you copied a group and want to modify an existing entry, make the changes you want. In this example, in the Order cell in the Group By row, choose Descending.

    By doing so, the first group summary row will represent critical tasks, and the second group summary row will represent non-critical tasks.

5. To add a new field to group by, select the first blank Field Name cell, click the down arrow, and then choose the field you want to group by.

    For example, to add the Duration field to the Critical/Duration group, choose Duration in the first Then By row, as shown in Figure 17-11. If you create a group from scratch, start by choosing a field in the Group By row.

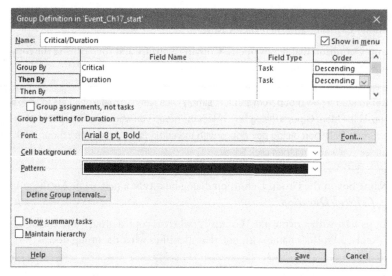

Figure 17-11. *Project fills in the Field Type cell with Task for a task-related group or Resource for a resource-related group.*

6. In the Order cell, choose Descending or Ascending. In this example, choose Descending to show tasks from the longest duration to the shortest.

    To show resources from lowest to highest hourly rate, choose Ascending. Ascending shows text fields grouped in alphabetical order. If you group by a Yes/No field like Critical, then choose Descending if you want the fields with Yes to appear first.

7. To group by assignment instead of by task, turn on the "Group assignments, not tasks" check-box. (In this example, keep the check box turned off.)

    In a Task Usage view, you can group by task or by assignment, which determines how Project rolls up values into summary tasks. For example, group by task to see which tasks have the highest schedule variance. If you want to find out which assignments produce those variances, then group by assignments. (For a Resource Usage view, the checkbox label is "Group assignments, not resources.") The note titled "Calculating Rolled-Up Group Values" explains how group roll-up and other calculations work.

8. To change the appearance of the group summary rows, change the values in the Font, "Cell background," and Pattern boxes. (In this example, click the Group By row. Then in the "Cell background" box in the middle of the dialog box, choose a medium blue.)

    When Project subtotals groups, it applies a different font to the summary rows and shades the cells. For example, the primary group rows use 8-point Arial, bolded, with a light yellow cell background. To print groups to a black-and-white printer, change the Pattern to cross-hatching, or choose colors that show up as different shades of gray.

> **Note:** If you want to see summary tasks in the groups, turn on the "Show summary tasks" checkbox. On the other hand, turning on the "Maintain hierarchy" checkbox shows all the levels of summary tasks for subtasks within groups. You can also maintain hierarchy from the ribbon by heading to the View tab's Data section, clicking the Group down arrow, and choosing "Maintain Hierarchy in Current Group."

9. Click Save.

    The Group Definition dialog box closes. In the More Groups dialog box, click Apply to see the results of your handiwork (Figure 17-12).

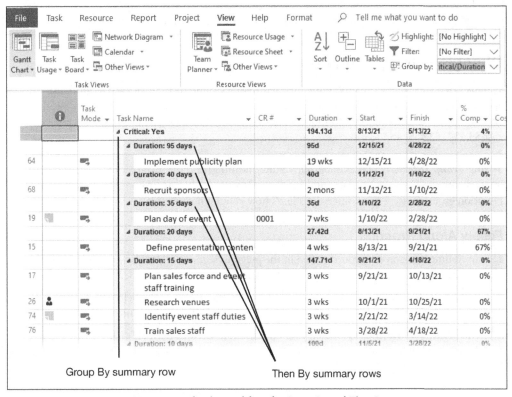

Group By summary row   Then By summary rows

Figure 17-12. *You can specify colors and fonts for Group By and Then By summary rows.*

Calculating Rolled-Up Group Values

Rolled-up values for built-in fields like Cost and Work are simply the sum of values in the group. Other calculations like Maximum, Minimum, and Average are available for group summary rows, but only if you use custom fields (Chapter 21), because you can't tell Project how to roll up built-in fields. If you want to see the average cost of a group of tasks or resources, set up a custom field like Cost1 that's equal to the built-in Cost field, and then set its Rollup value to the calculation you want (Average, in this example).

On the other hand, rolled-up Duration values may just look wrong. For example, a rolled-up Duration might be 63.5 days, while the four tasks in the group are each only 2 days long. That's because Project calculates the group's duration starting from the start date of the earliest task in the group to the finish date of the last task in the group.

Changing Group Intervals

Groups often start out with subgroups for each distinct value in the field you're grouping by. This approach is fine for Yes/No fields like Critical or Milestone. But when you group by cost, duration, and similar fields, the number of unique values could spawn **hundreds** of subgroups, for tasks that cost $3,450, $3,455, and so on.

Setting **group intervals** makes subgroups more meaningful. For example, on a short project, the intervals for the Duration group could be days. Or on a multiyear project, you might modify the Duration group to use 2-week intervals. Here's how you define intervals for a field in a group:

Follow Along Practice

1. To resume work on the group created in the previous section, in the View tab's Group By list, choose More Groups. Select the Critical/Duration group, and then click Edit.

2. In the Group Definition dialog box, click the Field Name cell for the field whose interval you want to set (in this example, Duration), and then click Define Group Intervals.

    The Define Group Interval dialog box opens, as shown in Figure 17-13. (If the selected field doesn't work with intervals—Yes/No fields are one example—then the Define Group Intervals button is grayed out.)

    The "Group on" field is set initially to Each Value, which creates a separate subgroup for each unique value.

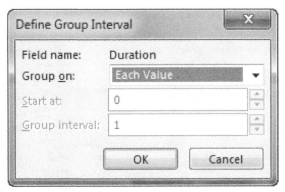

Figure 17-13. *The "Group on" field is set initially to Each Value, which creates a separate subgroup for each unique value.*

3. To reduce the number of subgroups, choose an interval measure. In the "Group on" box, click the down arrow, and then choose the units or type of interval you want, in this example, Weeks.

    The choices in the "Group on" drop-down list vary based on the field you selected. For example, for Duration, the "Group on" choices range from Minutes to Days to Months. % Complete lists typical percentage intervals like "0, 1-99, 100" which groups tasks into unstarted, in progress, and complete. On the other hand, for Cost, choose Interval in the drop-down list to set the interval size (1000 to group on every $1,000, for example).

4. To start the interval at a specific value, type the number in the "Start at" box (in this example, type *1*).

    You can group all the rows with tiny values by setting a "Start at" value. For example, if you're grouping on Duration and set the "Start at" value equal to 1 for a 1-week interval, then one group contains all tasks that last less than a week.

5. To define the interval size, type a number in the "Group interval" box, in this example, keep it set to 1.

    For example, if "Group on" is set to Weeks and "Group interval" is set to 1, then the subgroups come in 1-week increments, such as 1 week, 2 week, and so on.

6. Click OK.

    The Define Group Interval dialog box closes.

7. Click Save to save the edited group. In the More Groups dialog box, click Apply.

Figure 17-14 shows the results when grouped by weeklong intervals.

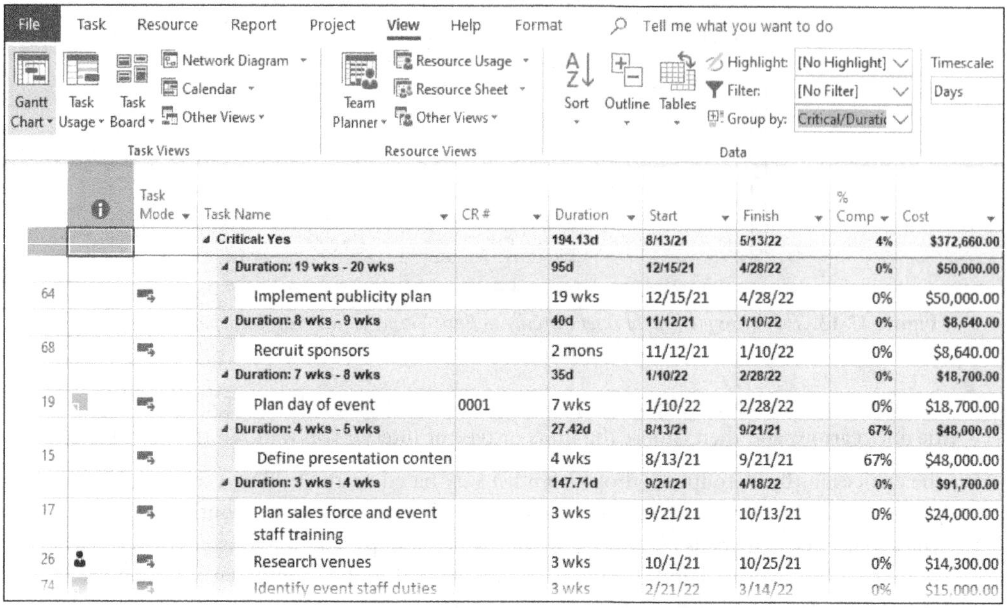
File
Task
Resource
Report
Project
View
Help
Format
Tell me what you want to do
Gantt Chart
Task Usage
Task Board
Network Diagram
Calendar
Other Views
Task Views
Team Planner
Resource Usage
Resource Sheet
Other Views
Resource Views
Sort
Outline
Tables
Highlight: [No Highlight]
Filter: [No Filter]
Group by: Critical/Duratic
Data
Timescale:
Days
Task Mode
Task Name
CR #
Duration
Start
Finish
% Comp
Cost
Critical: Yes 194.13d 8/13/21 5/13/22 4% $372,660.00
Duration: 19 wks - 20 wks 95d 12/15/21 4/28/22 0% $50,000.00
64 Implement publicity plan 19 wks 12/15/21 4/28/22 0% $50,000.00
Duration: 8 wks - 9 wks 40d 11/12/21 1/10/22 0% $8,640.00
68 Recruit sponsors 2 mons 11/12/21 1/10/22 0% $8,640.00
Duration: 7 wks - 8 wks 35d 1/10/22 2/28/22 0% $18,700.00
19 Plan day of event 0001 7 wks 1/10/22 2/28/22 0% $18,700.00
Duration: 4 wks - 5 wks 27.42d 8/13/21 9/21/21 67% $48,000.00
15 Define presentation conten 4 wks 8/13/21 9/21/21 67% $48,000.00
Duration: 3 wks - 4 wks 147.71d 9/21/21 4/18/22 0% $91,700.00
17 Plan sales force and event staff training 3 wks 9/21/21 10/13/21 0% $24,000.00
26 Research venues 3 wks 10/1/21 10/25/21 0% $14,300.00
74 Identify event staff duties 3 wks 2/21/22 3/14/22 0% $15,000.00

Figure 17-14. *You can define group intervals.*

18

Reporting on Projects

Because communication is such a large part of project management, reports are a mainstay for presenting project information to others. They're also handy when *you* want to see what's going on. During planning, reports show you what your schedule's dates, costs, and resource workloads look like. Once the project is under way, you can use high-level reports to see whether the project is on track. If it isn't, then more detailed reports help you find the problem spots.

Different audiences want different information. For example, teams like to know what tasks lie ahead. Executives, on the other hand, usually want a high-level view of the project's progress and how it compares with the plan. They get concerned if project-related red flags are flying. Coming prepared with reports that show your plan for correcting the project's course can keep status meetings on an even keel.

Microsoft Project's ***graphical reports*** present project information in ways that are easy to digest. Text boxes and fields can provide high-level project info. Charts can illustrate what's going on in your project graphically—like charts you can build from data in an Excel workbook. Tables present project values in rows and columns, like the tables in a view, but with formatting that makes values easier to see.

Project also offers ***visual reports***, which use Excel pivot tables and Visio pivot diagrams to turn heaps of data into meaningful information. Moreover, visual reports can twist data around to show information from different perspectives. For example, from one angle, you may see ***tasks*** that are in trouble; but by turning the data on its side, you can see whether specific ***resources*** are having problems. An added advantage of visual reports is that you can use them to export your Project data to other programs.

This chapter begins with an overview of the built-in reports Project offers. You'll learn what each report does, how you might use it, and where to find it. Then you'll learn how to run graphical and visual reports.

> **Note:** If you've downloaded files from the book website, you can follow along using the file Event_Ch18_start.mpp.

An Overview of Project's Reports

Although the information in graphical and visual reports overlaps a little, you use each type of report for different reasons. With the program's graphical reports, you can produce dashboard views of project data to make project status easy to see. Project information can appear in several formats within a single graphical report. For example, the Cost Overview report includes one chart comparing progress and cost, another chart showing actual and remaining cost for top-level tasks, and a table that displays numerical cost values for top-level tasks.

Visual reports, on the other hand, are ideal when you want to look at project performance from different angles. For example, you can run a visual report to check work status month by month, then flip the report to look at work hours by task, and then switch to evaluating work hours by resource. Visual reports can summarize results at the project level, and then drill down to details by task, resource, or time. (Chapter 19 explains how to get visual reports to perform all those tricks.) Visual report tools let you change the fields, resources, and timeframe you see. Visual reports are Excel pivot tables or Visio pivot diagrams that present project information. (To use an Excel or Visio visual report, you need to have Excel or Visio installed on your computer.)

How you run a report depends on which type it is:

- **To run a graphical report**, head to the Report tab's View Reports section, click a report category (explained below), and then choose the report.

- **To run a visual report**, in the Report tab's Export section, click Visual Reports, and then in the "Visual Reports - Create Report" dialog box, select the report you want. Then click View.

Project assigns reports to several categories. For example, visual reports are divided into summary and usage reports, and then into reports that cover tasks, resources, and assignments. Because visual reports can look at data in different ways, it's hard to know whether the Baseline Cost report is a task-summary visual report or a resource-usage report. This section gives some examples of when you might use different built-in graphical and visual reports, and where to find them within Project's report categories.

> **Note:** Confusingly, some visual reports and graphical reports have the same name, such as the Cash Flow graphical report and Cash Flow visual report.

Overall Status

Several Project reports provide a high-level view of projects. Here are a few reports you can use for a high-level status report:

- **Project Overview**: This graphical dashboard report (in the Report tab's View Reports section, click Dashboards→Project Overview) is great for a 30,000-foot project view you can attach to a status report. It shows the project's start and finish date, percentage of duration that's complete, percentage complete for top-level tasks, and milestones that are coming up. To help you spot problems that are brewing, it also includes a table of tasks that are late.

- **Burndown**: This graphical report (Report→Dashboards→Burndown) displays *burndown status* (in other words, how much of the project you've burned through or completed) in two ways: The Work Burndown chart shows the work that's completed and what's still left to do. The Task Burndown chart also focuses on what's done and what remains, except that it does so by showing the number of completed and remaining tasks. In either chart, your project might be behind schedule if the line for what remains is steeper than the baseline line.

- **Cost Overview**: This graphical dashboard report (Report→Dashboards→Cost Overview), shown in Figure 18-1, summarizes project costs in several ways. At the report's top left, you see the project's start and finish dates, the current scheduled and remaining cost, and % Complete. The Cost Status table displays cost values for top-level tasks, so you can see whether any portions of your project are overrunning their baseline costs. The Progress Versus Cost chart compares % Complete to cumulative cost. If the cumulative cost line is above the % Complete line, your project may be over budget. (However, a project that has high up-front costs will have a Progress Versus Cost chart that looks like that without being over budget.) In the example project, the cumulative cost line is below the cumulative percent complete line, which might mean the project is currently under-budget.

- **Work Overview**: Another graphical dashboard, this report (Report→Dashboards→Work Overview) presents work status from several perspectives. It starts with the Work Burndown chart, which compares baseline work with remaining work. The next chart shows baseline, actual, and remaining work for each top-level task. Two graphs at the bottom of the report show work and remaining availability by resource, so you can see who has a ton of work to complete and who has time available and might be able to help.

- **Task Status**: This Visio-based visual report initially shows work, cost, and the percentage complete for top-level tasks. As you'll learn shortly, you can include other fields like baseline cost or actual work in this report to see how your project is doing at the top level. If you want to examine parts of your project more closely, you can drill down to lower levels in the task list.

- **Milestone Report**: This graphical report (Report→In Progress→Milestone Report) starts with a list of late milestones, so you can quickly see which parts of the project you need to focus on. The next list is milestones that are coming up. The report also shows completed milestones and includes a chart of completed and remaining tasks.

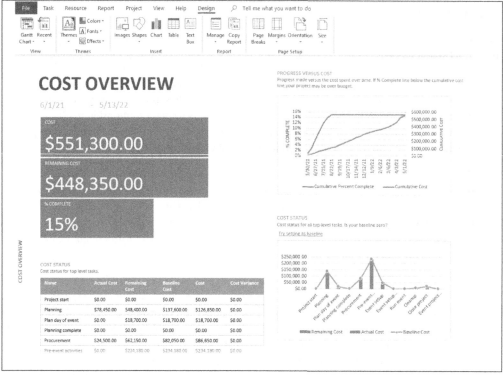

Figure 18-1. *The Cost Overview graphical report includes text boxes, fields, charts, and one table.*

> **Tip:** If you don't want to see decimal places in project cost values, in the Project Options dialog box's Display tab, change "Decimal digits" to 0.

Financial Performance

As you learned in Chapters 9 and 14, cost performance is an important part of overall project performance. Several of Project's visual reports and graphical reports cover different aspects of financial performance. Here are the reports that deal primarily with cost:

- **Cash Flow graphical report**: This report (Report→Costs→Cash Flow) starts with a bar chart of cost by quarter, though you can edit the chart to use different time units. The chart's orange line represents cumulative cost over time. The table at the bottom of the report presents cost and earned value measures for top-level tasks.

- **Cash Flow visual report**: The Excel Cash Flow report looks like the chart in the Cash Flow graphical report. You can expand the time periods to show weekly costs—for instance, to make sure your weekly allowance covers the expenses you incur. The Visio Cash Flow report displays orange exclamation points if the actual cost is over budget. The Cash Flow graphical report is easier to produce than either of these versions, so the Cash Flow visual report makes sense only if you need to look at cash flow from different angles or if you need to export cash flow information to another program.

- **Earned Value**: This graphical report (Report→Costs→Earned Value Report) includes the ever-popular earned value graph, which compares the project's planned value, earned value, and actual value, explained in Chapter 14. (You can see an example of this report in Figure 14-7.) This report also includes a chart that shows cost variance and schedule variance over time—perfect for seeing whether your course corrections are bringing the project back on track. The third chart in this report contains lines for schedule performance index (Chapter 14) and cost performance index over time.

- **Earned Value Over Time**: This Excel-based visual report looks like the chart in the graphical Earned Value Report.

- **Cost Overruns**: This graphical report (Report→Costs→Cost Overruns) shows cost variance by task and resource, so you can tell which portions of the project are over budget and which resources could be the culprits.

- **Resource Cost Overview**: This graphical report (Report→Costs→Resource Cost Overview) shows baseline, actual, and remaining cost by resource. If a resource's cost bar is higher than the baseline cost line, then you may spend more on that resource than you planned. The report's Cost Details table shows cost info about each resource.

- **Resource Cost Summary**: This Excel-based visual report is a pie chart that shows costs by resource type (work, material, and cost). It shows the same info as the Cost Distribution pie chart on the Resource Cost Overview graphical report.

- **Task Cost Overview**: This graphical report (Report→Costs→Task Cost Overview) is similar to the Resource Cost Overview report except that it shows cost by task.

- **Baseline**: You can use the Excel and Visio Baseline *Cost* visual reports to compare planned, actual, and baseline costs. With these reports, you can view costs for the entire project, drill down to analyze cost by phase, or switch the report to show cost by fiscal quarter. The Baseline *Work* visual report is a bar graph of baseline, planned, and actual work.

- **Budget**: The Budget Cost and Budget Work visual reports in Excel are graphs of cost or work by quarter. Initially, the bars in the graph show actual, baseline, and budget values, so you can see how actual values compare with the baseline by time period and also compare those values with accounting budget numbers (Chapter 15).

Task Management

Project includes several graphical reports that pinpoint tasks that may need help. For example, reports about critical tasks can help you identify what you need to do to keep your project on schedule. Here are the reports best suited for keeping tabs on task scheduling:

- **Critical Tasks**: This graphical report (Reports→In Progress→Critical Tasks) lists incomplete critical tasks with basic 411 like start and finish dates, percentage complete, remaining work, and assigned resources. If you see critical tasks that are just getting started, you might be able to takes steps to shorten their duration to correct a schedule delay.

- **Critical Tasks Status**: This Visio-based visual report shows scheduled work and remaining work for critical tasks. You can display additional fields, like baseline and actual costs, to see whether critical tasks are on track.

- **Upcoming Tasks**: This graphical report (Report→Dashboards→Upcoming Tasks) shows tasks that are due during the current week and tasks starting during the next week. It's great for identifying tasks that team members should report status on.

- **Late Tasks**: This graphical report (Reports→In Progress→Late Tasks) includes a table that shows tasks whose finish dates have passed or whose progress on work is behind schedule.

- **Slipping Tasks**: This graphical report (Reports→In Progress→Slipping Tasks) shows tasks that are due to finish after their baseline finish dates (so it works only when you've set a baseline).

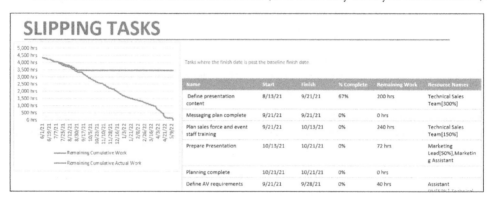

Figure 18-2. *The Slipping Tasks report shows the remaining cumulative work as well as tasks that are slipping past their baseline dates.*

Resource Management

Graphical and visual reports both help you manage project resources, whether you're first assigning them or trying to eliminate overallocations. Here are the reports that focus on resources and their assignments:

- **Resource Overview**: This graphical report (Report→Resources→Resource Overview) shows baseline, actual, and remaining work by resource. If a resource's work bar is higher than the baseline work line, then the resource may end up working more hours than you planned. The report's Work Status chart shows the percentage of assigned work that each resource has completed.

- **Overallocated Resources**: This graphical report (Report→Resources→Overallocated Resources) shows the number of remaining work hours for overallocated resources (see Figure 18-3). The report's Overallocation chart shows the work that unbalanced those resources' workloads and when it occurs. However, the Resource Usage view (Chapter 8) is more helpful for finding overallocations than this report.

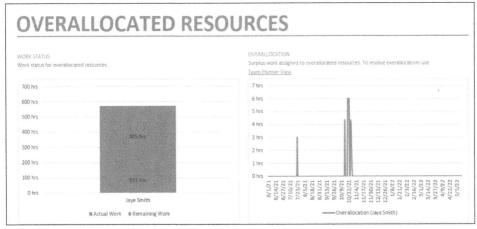

Figure 18-3. *This report shows work hours for overallocated resources. The Overallocation chart shows when overallocations occur.*

- **Resource Work Summary**: This Excel-based visual report shows everything you want to know about resources in work-unit percentages: total capacity, work, remaining availability, and actual work. You can see information for all resources side by side, filter the report to show specific resources, or view work for a specific timeframe.

- **Resource Status**: This Visio-based visual report shows work and cost for each resource. It shades bars darker as resources get closer to finishing their assignments.

- **Resource Work Availability**: This Excel-based visual report is like the Resource Graph on steroids. You can see total capacity, work, and remaining availability over time for work resources.

- **Resource Availability**: This Visio-based visual report shows remaining availability, along with a red flag for overallocated resources.

- **Resource Remaining Work**: This Excel-based visual report shows remaining and actual work for each work resource.

Working with Graphical Reports

Project's graphical reports make it easy to show the information you want. Generating a graphical report is easy, whether it's a built-in report or a custom report you created. This section explains how to run graphical reports.

Generating a graphical report takes just a couple of clicks on the Project ribbon. To generate a report, head to the Report tab's View Reports section, click the name of the category that contains the report you want (Resources, in this example), and then choose the report from the drop-down menu (Overallocated Resources, for example), as shown in Figure 18-4. If you run the same reports week after week, in the Report tab's View Reports section, click Recent, and then choose the report you want from the drop-down menu.

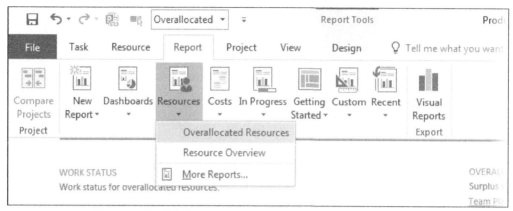

Figure 18-4. *Click the report category and then choose the report you want.*

Follow Along Practice

You can print graphical reports and copy parts of them into a Word document, PowerPoint slide, or other file. If you want to print the report, do the following:

1. Choose File→Print.

    The Print screen appears in the Backstage view. It includes print settings similar to the ones in other Microsoft programs.

2. Select the number of copies you want (next to the Print button) and, in the Settings section, choose the page range to print (Figure 18-5).

    You can also choose a different printer, the paper orientation, and the paper size. To change the page setup (such as margins, headers, and footers), click Page Setup below the Settings section.

    On the right side of the page, you can see a portion of your report. The toolbar at the bottom of the report preview has a few print-preview commands. The left, right, up, and down arrows move one page in the corresponding direction in a multipage report. To zoom in or out, simply click the report itself.

Figure 18-5. *Print settings for reports are similar to the print settings in other Microsoft programs.*

3. To print the report, click the Print button.

   That's it!

Suppose you want to include a graphical report in your status report or in a PowerPoint presentation. Here's how you copy and paste the report into another program:

1. Drag over the report elements that you want to copy and paste to select them.

   For example, you can select a single chart, a table, or the entire report. Selection handles appear at the corners and on the edges of the selected elements.

2. In the Task tab's Clipboard section, click Copy (or simply press Ctrl+C).

   Project adds the selected elements to the Clipboard.

3. Switch to the other program and click where you want to paste the report.

   For example, click in the PowerPoint slide into which you want to paste the report.

4. Press Ctrl+V.

   The report elements appear in the other file.

Generating Visual Reports

Although graphical reports are easy to edit and provide lots of options for displaying information, Project's *visual* reports use Excel pivot charts and Visio pivot diagrams so you can change them on the fly, whether to respond to questions or to drill down in several directions to unearth problems.

Project gets you started with several built-in visual reports (described earlier in this chapter), whose initial presentation is like the serving suggestions you see on cracker boxes. You can modify the report in real time until it's the way you want, which you'll learn about in Chapter 19.

This section starts with the easy part: generating a visual report.

Changing Your Perspective

Visual reports take advantage of the *pivot table* concept, so named because you can turn the data in different directions—pivoting it to gain a new perspective. For example, you may want to see your project phase by phase, and then twist it around to see overall performance quarter by quarter or by resource.

To make these contortions look easy, a visual report builds a specialized database called an OLAP (online analytical processing) cube on your computer, and then connects it to an Excel pivot table or Visio pivot diagram. A *data cube* (which has a *.cub* file extension) stores data in a format that makes it easy to retrieve data by different categories. For example, in a marketing department, you may want to find customers by household income, hobbies, or Zip code. Each OLAP cube category is like one dimension of a real-world cube, except that OLAP cubes can go beyond three dimensions. In Project visual reports, tasks, resources, and time are the most common dimensions.

After a visual report creates its data cube, it hooks the cube up to a pivot table or pivot diagram. At that point, it's your turn to use the tools in Excel and Visio to model the data into the presentation you want.

Generating a visual report is easy: Select the visual report template you want, and off you go. The template takes care of gathering the data for the report's cube (see the titled note above) and setting up the initial pivot table or pivot diagram. Here's how to generate a visual report from an existing template:

Follow Along Practice

1. In the Report tab's Export section, click Visual Reports.

   The "Visual Reports - Create Report" dialog box opens, as shown in Figure 18-6. Although the All tab is selected initially and displays every visual report that's available, you can click a tab to see specific types of visual reports. Summary reports show overall results and don't include time-phased data. For example, the Resource Summary visual report totals values for resources, such as actual work or remaining work. Usage visual reports, like their Usage view counterparts, *do*

---

include time-phased data. The Assignment visual reports are the most useful because they include time-phased data about both tasks and resources, so you can look at your project from every angle.

> **Note:** Project lists visual reports that correspond to the programs installed on your computer. For example, if you have Excel installed, but not Visio, you'll see only Excel-based visual reports.

When you start developing custom visual report templates, the All tab may fill up. You can look for more specific reports by selecting a tab like Task Summary. For example, the built-in Cash Flow Report is on the Task Usage tab because it focuses on task costs over time. The Critical Tasks Report is on the Task Summary tab because it looks at total results for critical tasks.

> **Tip:** Turn the checkboxes off or on to see only Excel- or Visio-based visual reports. (You can tell which program a report uses based on the icon next to its name.)

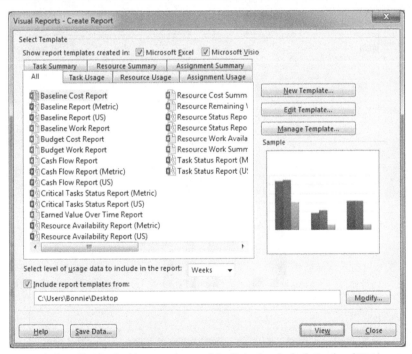

Figure 18-6. *Initially, the checkboxes at the top of the dialog box for both Excel and Visio reports are turned on, so every available visual report appears in the list.*

2. Click the name of the visual report you want to use, in this example, Baseline Cost Report.

    On the right side of the dialog box, check out the preview to see if the report's general format (bar graph, pie chart, or tree) is what you want. To *truly* tell whether a visual report is what you want, you need to generate the report.

3. Choose the time period for usage data, in this example, keep it set to Weeks.

   In the "Select level of usage data to include in the report" drop-down list, choose Days, Weeks, Months, Quarters, or Years. Days or Weeks are better for shorter projects. For longer projects, choose the shortest period you're likely to evaluate, like Weeks or Months. Keep in mind that collecting too much usage data can slow the visual report's performance to a crawl.

4. Click View.

   If you selected an Excel-based visual report, then Excel starts and then sets up an Excel file with the data cube attached to it (Figure 18-7). The Excel spreadsheet has two worksheets. The Chart1 worksheet is a *pivot chart*—a graph that displays the data. The second worksheet is a *pivot table*, which contains the data. As you expand, collapse, and reorient the pivot table, as described in Chapter 19, the pivot chart does the same.

   If you selected a Visio-based report, then Visio starts and creates a pivot diagram. The Visio file usually contains two drawing pages. The drawing page named "Page-1" is the diagram itself; if the VBackground-1 page is present, it's simply a Visio background page for adding graphics like your corporate logo.

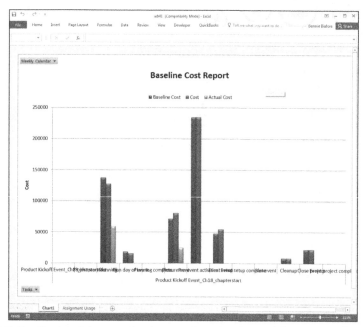

Figure 18-7. *One Excel worksheet contains the report data; the other worksheet contains the report graph.*

Printing Views to Report Project Information

A picture is worth a thousand words—and more than a thousand numbers in a view table. In Project, you can print views like the Gantt Chart, Task Usage, or Tracking Gantt to include in reports you produce for stakeholders, management, and other audiences. (The note titled "Creating a PDF or XPS Document" explains another way to create a document from a view.) Here's how you set up a view to print the way you want:

Follow Along Practice

1. Display the view you want and make sure the information is presented the way you want it when you print.

    In this example, apply the Gantt Chart view (Task→Gantt Chart). Apply the table you want (Summary, in this example) and, if necessary, insert, remove, or rearrange the columns in the table (keep the columns in the Summary table as they are). In this example, remove the Critical/Duration group by choosing View→Group→[No Group]. If necessary, to see task bars in the timescale, click a task, and then choose Task→Scroll to Task.

    For a view with a table and a timescale, drag the vertical divider so you see the amount of table and timescale you want. Adjust the timescale to show the time periods you want (in this example, in the View tab's Zoom section, choose Weeks in the Timescale box).

2. Choose File→Print.

    The Print page of the Backstage view appears. Printer settings are on the left side, and a preview of the view appears on the right side.

3. As you would for any other printout, choose the printer, number of copies, page range you want to print, paper orientation, and paper size.

    If you change the paper orientation or size, the preview changes to show what the printout looks like. For most Project views, landscape orientation is best.

4. For views that include a timescale, in the Dates boxes, choose the date range you want to display, in this example, change the "to" date to 12/31/21.

    Fill in the first box with the earliest date in the date range and the second box with the latest date in the range.

5. To set up the printed page, click the Page Setup link at the bottom of the Print page.

    The Page Setup dialog box opens with tabs similar to those in other programs. For example, on the Page tab, you can choose the paper orientation and size, adjust the scale of the view, or specify the number of pages to use to print the view. The Margins tab lets you adjust the margins on the page. The Header and Footer tabs are where you specify information to display in the printout's header and footer (for example, the project name).

6. To specify whether the printout includes a legend, in the Page Setup dialog box, click the Legend tab, and then select the option you want, in this example, None, as shown in Figure 18-8.

Project initially selects the "Every page" option, which means that a legend that identifies the bars appears on every page. To save some trees and show more of your project on each page, select the "Legend page" option instead, which includes one page with a legend. You can also specify the width of the legend by choosing a number of inches in the Width box. If you want to adjust the text formatting for the legend, click Legend Labels.

7. To fine-tune what appears on the printed page, in the Page Setup dialog box, click the View tab. Then turn on the checkboxes for the elements you want.

For example, to print all the columns in the table, turn on the "Print all sheet columns" checkbox. To print a specific number of columns on every page of the printout, turn on the "Print first __ columns on all pages" checkbox and then choose the number of columns. You can also choose to print notes, blank pages, or adjust the timescale to fill the page.

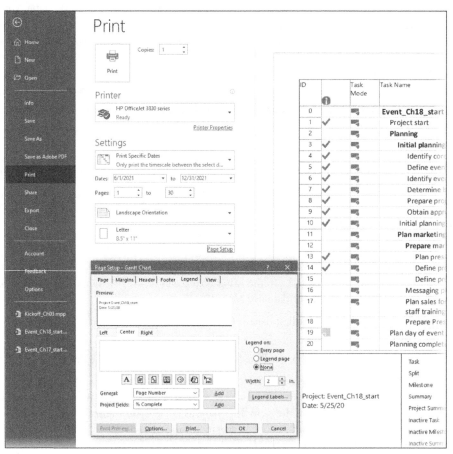

Figure 18-8. *Click OK in the Page Setup dialog box (not shown here) to update the print preview.*

8. Click OK in the Page Setup dialog box to update the print preview.

9. When the settings are the way you want, click Print.

    Project prints the view.

Creating a PDF or XPS Document

Rather than printing a Project view, you can create a copy of your project in PDF or XPS format. These two file formats contain the text data that you save, so you can index the files or copy information out of them. In addition, these formats keep all the formatting, fonts, and graphics that appear on your screen and spit them out looking the same on almost any computer. Anyone can view these documents using free viewers available for download. To create one of these documents, follow these steps:

1. Choose File→Export.

2. On the Export page of the Backstage view, choose Create PDF/XPS Document, and then click the Create PDF/XPS button.

3. In the Browse dialog box, navigate to the folder in which you want to save the file.

4. Name the file.

5. In the "Save as type" drop-down list, choose PDF Files or XPS Files.

6. Click OK.

7. In the Document Export Options dialog box that appears, specify the export options you want, and then click OK.

Tip: If you usually save reports and view outputs as PDF files, create a folder dedicated to those PDF files. The files you're looking for are easier to find when you use a standardized naming convention. For example, you might use a convention that starts with the project name followed by the output contents and the date, such as Event_Critical Path_20220304. By using a date format of yyyymmdd, files with the same names except for the date will appear in chronological order.

19

Customizing Reports

Although Microsoft Project comes with numerous built-in graphical and visual reports, chances are good that you want reports to show the info your company cares about, displayed in the way you want to show it. You can build a new report from the ground up with the data and layout your stakeholders are accustomed to. Or you can use Project's built-in reports as templates for custom reports. For example, the built-in Cash Flow graphical report shows cash flow by quarter, but you may want to see cash flow by month or see cash flow only for tasks in a specific project phase.

Visual reports are designed to be changed on the fly. Because they use Excel and Visio, you'll learn the key features for manipulating visual report data in both of those programs. In addition to changing the appearance of a visual report, you can also customize templates to modify or create your own visual reports.

Customizing Graphical Reports

Graphical report customization comes in two flavors. You can use the Field List task pane (which opens when you select a component in a report) to choose the information that component shows, like the fields that appear in a table or a chart. You can also apply a filter or group, choose the task outline level to include, or specify the field by which you want to sort results.

For more aesthetic changes, like using a different type of chart or formatting individual table elements, context-sensitive ribbon tabs come to the rescue. You simply click the element you want to customize—like a chart, a table, or a text box—and then head to the Design tab that appears, like the Chart Tools | Design tab, to make your adjustments. The Report Tools | Design tab includes commands for customizing the overall report.

This section describes how to create brand-new reports, copy existing reports, and customize report contents and formatting. Graphical reports come with an overabundance of features, so this section doesn't cover them all. However, if you read through this entire section, you'll see many examples of how to use these features.

> **Note:** If you've downloaded files from the book website, you can follow along using the file Event_Ch19_start.mpp.

Creating a Brand-New Graphical Report

If the graphical report you want isn't like any of Project's built-in reports or other custom reports you've created, you can start from scratch. Project helps you get started by adding a few elements to your creation. Here's how to create a new report:

Follow Along Practice

1. In the Report tab's View Reports section, click New Report, and then choose the type of report you want to create from the drop-down menu (in this example, choose Chart).

    Choosing Chart creates a report with a text box for the report's title and a basic chart. Table creates a report with a title box and a basic table. Comparison creates a report with a title box and two basic charts. And choosing Blank tells Project you want a report with nothing but a text box for the report's title.

2. In the Report Name dialog box, type a name (in this example, ***Project Performance***), and then click OK.

    Project creates the new report. The report name you typed appears in the title text box. If you chose a report type that inserts elements, they appear in the report, too, with a few fields and settings already in place, as shown in Figure 19-1.

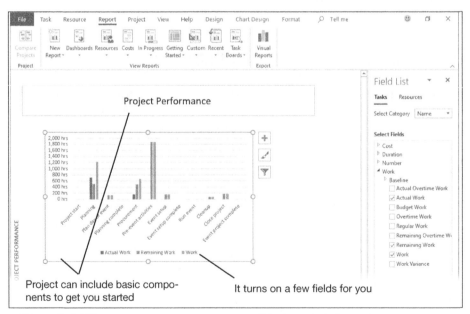

Figure 19-1. *When you create a new report, you can tell Project to include one or more components.*

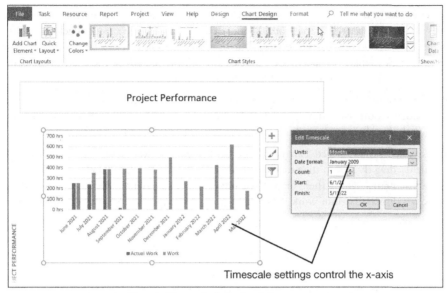

Figure 19-3. *The Edit Timescale dialog box helps you customize the x-axis.*

f) To specify the data range for the chart, choose dates in the Start and Finish boxes. Project initially sets the Start box to the project start date and the Finish box to the project finish date. In this example, keep these dates.

g) Click OK to close the Edit Timescale dialog box. The chart now includes data points for each month of the project (Figure 19-4).

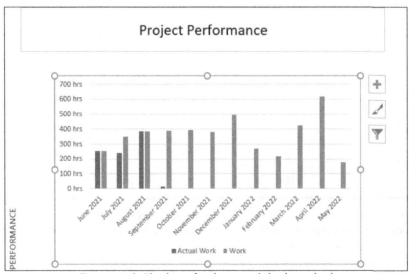

Figure 19-4. *The chart after the timescale has been edited.*

- **Select fields**: In the Field List task pane's Select Fields section, fields are grouped by data type, such as Cost, Number, Duration, and Work. To expand a data-type group, click the white triangle to the left of the data type's name. The triangle turns black. To collapse a data-type group, click its black triangle. To specify which fields you want to include in the chart or table, turn field checkboxes on or off to show or hide the fields, respectively:

  a) The inserted chart already has Work and Actual Work selected. To add the Baseline Work field, click the white triangle to the left of the Baseline label, and then turn on the Baseline Work checkbox. Project adds another set of bars to the chart for baseline work.

  b) The fields you've selected are listed in order below the Select Fields list. To rearrange the fields, drag them into the order you want. In this example, drag Baseline Work and drop it above Actual Work. Then, drag Work and drop it above Actual Work. Now, the bars in the chart display Baseline Work, Work, and Actual Work, in that order as shown in Figure 19-5.

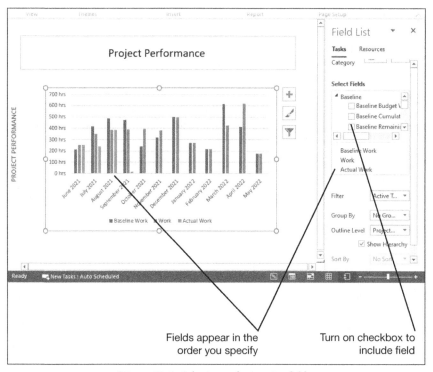

Figure 19-5. *Selecting and arranging fields.*

> **Note:** Although you can apply a filter or group to a chart, pick an outline level, or sort chart entries in some cases, this example keeps things simple by skipping these features. You'll see how to apply them, though, in the following sections.

- **Filter**: Similar to filtering a task list (Chapter 17), you can filter the tasks or resources that appear in the chart by choosing a filter in the Filter drop-down list. In this example, keep the filter set to Active Tasks, which includes all tasks in the project except those that have been inactivated (Chapter 11).

- **Group**: To group the results, choose a group in the Group By drop-down list. In this example, keep Group By set to No Group.

- **Pick an outline level**: For task-oriented charts or tables, the Outline Level box is active. To see project-wide results, choose Project Summary in this drop-down list, as in this example.

- **Sort**: To sort the entries in the chart or table, choose the field you want to sort by in the Sort By drop-down list. In this example, Sort By is grayed out, because you can't sort a chart that has time displayed along the x-axis.

In this example, insert another chart into the report to show cost for the resources working on the project. With this chart, you'll see how to group chart results.

1. Be sure to deselect any components in the report by clicking anywhere in the report background.

2. In the Design tab's Insert section, click Chart. The Clustered Column chart is selected by default, which is what you want in this example, Click OK to insert the chart.

3. Put the pointer over one of the chart edges. When the pointer changes to a four-headed arrow, drag the chart to position it to the right of the first chart in the report.

4. Below the Field List heading, click Resources to change the chart to a resource-oriented chart. The x-axis switches to show resources instead of tasks.

5. Change the fields that appear in the chart:

   a) In the Select Fields section, expand the Cost category by clicking the white triangle to the left of the Cost label. Turn on the Cost checkbox and the Actual Cost checkbox.

   b) Expand the Baseline category, and then turn on the Baseline Cost checkbox.

   c) Scroll down to the Work category and turn off the Actual Work, Remaining Work, and Work checkboxes.

   d) At the bottom of the Select Fields list, drag Baseline Cost and drop it above the Cost field.

6. To group the resources by the group they belong to (Internal or Vendor, in this example), in the Field List task pane, click the Group By down arrow, and then choose Resource Group.

The x-axis displays three sets of bars: one for resources that don't belong to a group, Internal for internal resources, and Vendor for resources associated with third-party vendors. Figure 19-6 shows what the chart looks like after completing the previous steps.

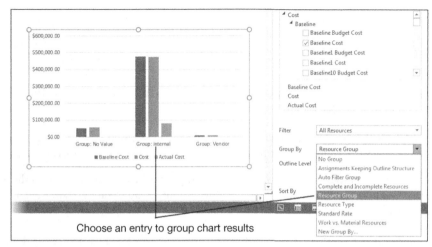

Choose an entry to group chart results

Figure 19-6. *When the chart x-axis displays resources or tasks, you can group the results.*

7. To filter a chart to show specific values, click the chart, and then click the funnel icon that appears at the chart's upper right. In the shortcut menu that appears (Figure 19-7), turn checkboxes on or off to filter what appears in the chart. In this example, turn off the Group: No Value checkbox, and then click Apply. (You can also filter a chart by selecting a filter in the Field List task pane.)

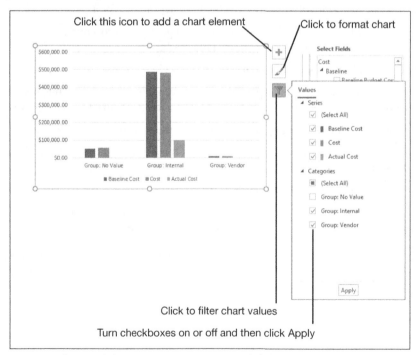

Figure 19-7. *When you click a report component, you can click the icons at its top right to add an element, format, or filter.*

Customizing a Chart

In addition to specifying the information you want to see, you can customize a chart to show that information in a specific way—for example, with a bar chart or a line graph. To customize the chart's type and layout, head to the Chart Design tab. Here are the types of changes you can make from this tab:

Follow Along Practice

- **Change the chart type**: Charts come in a variety of types, like bar charts, line charts, pie charts, and so on. In addition, each chart type has several variations, such as a side-by-side bar chart and a stacked bar chart (where the bars are stacked on top of one another).

  To change the type of chart, do the following:

  a) In this example, click the work by month chart on the left side of the report to select it.

  b) Before changing the chart type, in the Field List task pane's Select Fields section, scroll to the bottom of the list and turn on the Remaining Cumulative Work checkbox.

  The chart adds a fourth set of the bars to the chart.

  c) In the Chart Design tab's Type section (on the ribbon's right), click Change Chart Type.

  d) In the list on the left side of the Change Chart Type dialog box, choose the chart type you want, in this example, choose Combo. The Combo chart options appear along the top of the dialog box.

  e) Click the variation you want, in this example, keep Clustered Column – Line selected.

  The data series section at the bottom of the dialog box specifies how each field is charted. In this example, Baseline Work and Work are set to Clustered Column which includes a bar for each data point on the x-axis. Actual Work and Remaining Cumulative Work are set to Line which draws a continuous line.

  f) Click the down arrow in the Actual Work field's Chart Type box, and then click the Clustered Column icon at the top of the list.

  g) If the preview looks like what you want (Figure 19-8), click OK to close the dialog box and apply the new chart type.

Figure 19-8. *You can change the chart type and how different fields appear in the chart.*

- **Add a chart element**: Using the options in the Chart Design tab's Chart Layouts section, you can add individual chart elements or change their settings—for example, to add a legend or to change the location of data labels.

> **Tip:** You can also add a chart element by clicking a chart, and then clicking the green plus sign that appears to the chart's upper right. When you do that, a shortcut menu with chart elements appears. Turn on the checkboxes of the elements you want to add. Then, you can format those elements as described below.

To add a chart element, do the following:

a) Click Add Chart Element on the left side of the Chart Design tab.

b) In the drop-down menu that appears, point to the element you want to add (in this example, Chart Title), and then, on the submenu, choose the setting you want (Above Chart, in this case).

   If you add a legend, on the Legend submenu, you can choose None for no legend, or Right, Top, Left, or Bottom to specify where the legend appears.

> **Note:** To tweak the chart element even more, choose More [element] Options (where [element] represents something like Data Labels or Axes) at the bottom of the drop-down menu. If you do that, another task pane appears on the right side of the window with additional settings for things like text alignment (see Figure 19-9).

c) In this example, with the Chart Title element selected, type the title for the chart, ***Work over Time***.

- **Choose a ready-made chart layout**: Built-in chart layouts make quick work of setting up a chart. These layouts come with chart elements, like titles and legends, already in place. To choose one of these pre-built layouts, in the Chart Design tab's Chart Layout section, click Quick Layout. The drop-down menu that appears has thumbnails of the different layouts that are available. Click the one you want, and Project applies all the layout's settings to your chart. In this example, don't choose a different layout.

- **Apply/adjust chart styles**: Chart styles are similar to the Gantt Chart Styles on the Gantt Chart Format tab. These styles include chart settings like color schemes and background color. To choose one, in the Chart Design tab's Chart Styles section, click the style you want. Project applies the style's settings to the chart. In this example, don't choose a different chart style.

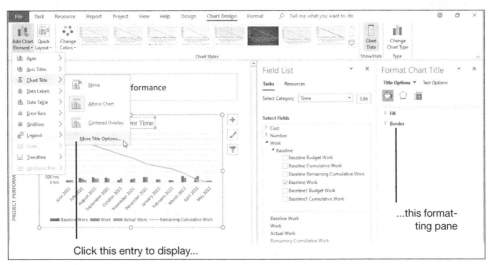

Figure 19-9. *In the Chart Design tab's Chart Layouts section, the Add Chart Element drop-down menu contains entries for different parts of a chart.*

Formatting a Chart

You can fine-tune your chart's appearance in various ways. The Format tab includes features for applying detailed formatting to different chart elements like the fill color for the plot area. If you want to dress up a report, you can insert shapes or use Word Art for text elements. If elements overlap, you can specify whether an element is in the foreground or the background. (To do that, select the element and then, in the tab's Arrange section, click Bring Forward or Send Backward.) In the tab's Size section, type dimensions to specify the size of the chart.

> **Tip:** When you click a chart, an icon with a paintbrush appears at the chart's upper right. Click that icon to display a shortcut menu with chart style and color options.

In many cases, you might want to format a specific element. The quickest approach is to click that element (in this example, click the Remaining Cumulative Work line). In the formatting pane that appears on the Project window's right (Format Data Series, in this case), make the changes you want. In this example, click the down arrow in the Color box, and then choose one of the green boxes.

> **Tip:** If the x-axis labels overlap, you can format them to change their orientation. To do that, right-click the labels beneath the x-axis, and then choose Format Axis. In the Format Axis pane that appears at the window's right, click Text Options. Click the Text Box icon (it looks like a sheet of paper with an A on it). In the "Text direction" box, choose the orientation you want. For example, to change to vertical labels that can be read from the right, choose Rotate All Text 270°.

Customizing Tables

If you've customized tables in Project views and reviewed how to customize graphical report charts in the previous section, you're already familiar with many of the features you can use to customize tables in graphical reports. This section provides examples of creating and customizing tables in graphical reports.

Choosing the Fields to Include in a Table

Similar to setting up a chart in a graphical report, the Field List task pane contains features for specifying the info you see in a table.

Follow Along Practice

In this example, start by adding a table to the Project Performance custom report created earlier in this chapter:

1. Click the Report Design tab on the ribbon.

    If the Table button in the Insert section is grayed out, click anywhere on the report background to deselect any selected components.

2. In the Insert section, click Table.

    The table appears in the report with selection handles at each corner and at the middle of each side. By default, the table is configured to show only the project summary task start date, finish date, and % complete.

3.   Put the pointer over one of the table edges. When the pointer changes to a four-headed arrow, drag the table to where you want it in the report, in this example, immediately below the work chart.

> **Note:** To select a table, click it. When you do that, Project displays the Field List task pane on the right side of the window and adds two additional tabs to the ribbon: Table Design and Table Format tabs.

In this example, suppose that you want a table that shows schedule performance for key tasks in your project. Here's how you can use the Field List task pane to customize the table you just inserted to do that:

- **Choose tasks or resources**: When you insert a new table, it's initially set to display tasks. (Immediately below the Field List heading, the word Tasks is bolded.) To switch a table to show resource data, below the Field List heading, click Resources. In this example, keep the table set to display tasks.

- **Select fields**: In the Select Fields section, fields are grouped by data type, such as Cost, Date, Duration, Number, and Work (the data types change depending on whether the table is task- or resource-oriented).

> **Tip:** To expand a data-type group, click the white triangle to the left of the data type's name. The triangle turns black. To collapse a data-type group, click its black triangle.

To choose the fields you want to include in the table, turn field checkboxes in the pane's Select Fields section on or off to show or hide the fields, respectively:

a)   With the table still selected, remove the % Complete field by turning off the % Complete checkbox (in the Number data-type group).

b)   To add a field to the table, turn on its checkbox. In this example, in the Date section, expand the Baseline category, and then turn on the Baseline Start and Baseline Finish checkboxes.

c)   Expand the Duration category, and then turn on the Finish Variance checkbox.

Before filtering, grouping, and sorting a task-oriented table, it's a good idea to specify the outline level you want to see.

- **Pick an outline level**: For task-oriented tables, the Outline Level box is active. When you first insert a table, the outline level is set to Project Summary, so you see only the project summary task. To display results down to a specific level of the task outline, choose the level you want, in this example, choose Level 2. The table displays tasks at the first two levels of the outline, as shown in Figure 19-10. (To see all levels, choose All Subtasks in the Outline Level drop-down list.)

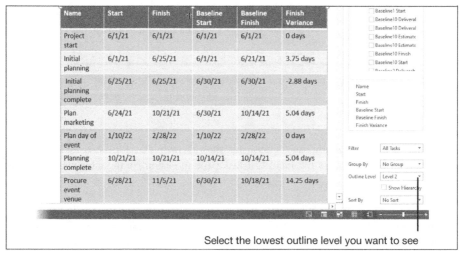

Name	Start	Finish	Baseline Start	Baseline Finish	Finish Variance
Project start	6/1/21	6/1/21	6/1/21	6/1/21	0 days
Initial planning	6/1/21	6/25/21	6/1/21	6/21/21	3.75 days
Initial planning complete	6/25/21	6/25/21	6/30/21	6/30/21	-2.88 days
Plan marketing	6/24/21	10/21/21	6/30/21	10/14/21	5.04 days
Plan day of event	1/10/22	2/28/22	1/10/22	2/28/22	0 days
Planning complete	10/21/21	10/21/21	10/14/21	10/14/21	5.04 days
Procure event venue	6/28/21	11/5/21	6/30/21	10/18/21	14.25 days

Select the lowest outline level you want to see

Figure 19-10. *For task-oriented tables, select the lowest outline level you want to see.*

- **Filter**: Similar to filtering a task list (Chapter 17), you can filter the tasks or resources that appear in a table by choosing a filter in the Filter drop-down list. In this example, suppose you want to display only critical tasks. Click the down arrow to the right of the Filter box, and then choose Critical in the drop-down list.

> **Note:** The filter drop-down list contains only filters present in your global template or in the active Project file. If you want to create a new filter to use in the report, you must display a view, and then create the new filter. Once the filter exists, jump back to the report, select the report chart or table, and then apply the filter.

- **Group**: To group the results, choose a group in the Group By drop-down list. In this example, keep the Group By box set to No Group.

- **Sort**: To sort the entries in the table, in the Sort By drop-down list, choose the field you want to sort by.

   a) In this example, in the Sort By drop-down list, choose Finish Variance. Initially, the table is sorted in ascending order. The button to the right of the Sort By box is labeled with an A above a Z to indicate that the sort order is ascending (from A to Z for letters and smallest to largest for numbers).

   b) To switch to descending order, click the A Z button to the right of the Sort By box. The table re-sorts to show largest values first. The button's label changes to a Z above an A to indicate that the sort order runs from Z to A for letters and largest to smallest for numbers (Figure 19-11).

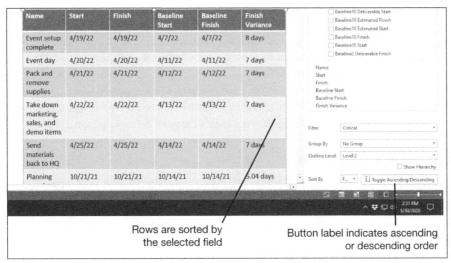

Name	Start	Finish	Baseline Start	Baseline Finish	Finish Variance
Event setup complete	4/19/22	4/19/22	4/7/22	4/7/22	8 days
Event day	4/20/22	4/20/22	4/11/22	4/11/22	7 days
Pack and remove supplies	4/21/22	4/21/22	4/12/22	4/12/22	7 days
Take down marketing, sales, and demo items	4/22/22	4/22/22	4/13/22	4/13/22	7 days
Send materials back to HQ	4/25/22	4/25/22	4/14/22	4/14/22	7 days
Planning	10/21/21	10/21/21	10/14/21	10/14/21	5.04 days

Rows are sorted by the selected field

Button label indicates ascending or descending order

Figure 19-11. *You can choose the field to sort by and whether to sort in ascending or descending order.*

Customizing a Table

To customize a table's layout, head to the Table Design tab. Here are the types of changes you can make on this tab:

- **Specify table style options**: The tab's Table Style Options section has checkboxes for controlling the appearance of table rows and columns. Initially, when you insert a table, the Header Row checkbox is turned on so the table includes a header row that shows the field names for each column in the table (see Figure 19-11). In addition, the Banded Rows checkbox is turned on so the tables rows appear in alternating colors.

   Although the example table doesn't require the following changes, you can turn on the First Column checkbox to emphasize the values in the first column. If the last row or last column represents totals, then turn on the Total Row or Last Column checkboxes to emphasize that information. To display columns in alternating colors, turn on the Banded Columns checkbox.

- **Apply/adjust table styles**: This section of the tab contains dozens of choices for table color schemes and basic layouts. Simply click the thumbnail for the style you want (in this example, choose the green table at the right end of the style gallery), and Project applies your choice's style settings to the table.

The Table Layout tab includes commands for fine-tuning the table's layout, such as the height and width of cells, the alignment of text in cells, and the overall width of the table.

> **Tip:** Tables also work for emphasizing a single project-wide value. To see how this works, choose Report→Dashboards→Cost Overview. Look at the boxes for project-wide cost, remaining cost, and % Complete at the top left. Each entry has the field name in a small font with the value in a large font below it. If you click one of these boxes, the Table Design and Layout tabs appear on the ribbon. That's because each of these project-wide values is in its own table with a header row. In addition, the Outline Level box in the Field List task pane is set to Project Summary, so the value represents a total for the entire project.

Customizing a Text Box

As you might expect, report text boxes don't have as many options for customization as charts and tables.

Follow Along Practice

To create a text box, do the following:

1. Switch to the Project Performance report (Report→Custom→Project Performance).

2. To insert a text box to describe what the cost chart does, in the Report Design tab's Insert section, click Text Box.

3. Drag to define a rectangle above the cost chart on the report's right.

4. Type the label or description, in this example, ***Cost for internal and external resources***.

When you select a text box in a report, the Shape Format tab appears in the ribbon. Here are a few things you can do to customize text boxes using this tab:

*   The tab's Insert Shapes section includes commands for inserting additional text boxes, inserting drawing shapes like circles and rectangles, and changing the shape of existing items.

*   The tab's Shape Styles section includes styles that boil down to the color of the text box's border, the fill color, and shape effects like shadows.

*   Like other elements in a report, you can apply WordArt settings to the text, specify whether the text box is in the foreground or background, or set its height and width. You can also rotate a text box to, for example, include a title that runs vertically along the side of the chart. In this example, select the text "Project Performance" at the top of the report. In the WordArt Styles section, click the blue A in the style gallery.

Organizing Report Elements

In a graphical report, you can position elements wherever you want. If you don't like a report's arrangement, you can move its elements to other locations. Rearranging elements is as simple as selecting the ones you want and then dragging them to their new positions.

Report elements respond to the same selection techniques you use elsewhere in Project and in other programs. Select a single element (like a chart) by clicking it. To select several elements near one another, drag over all the elements you want to select. (You have to drag so that the imaginary box you create *completely* encloses all the elements; elements that aren't completely enclosed won't be selected.) To select several elements that aren't adjacent to one another, Ctrl-click each one. In this example, Ctrl+click the Work over Time chart, the cost chart, and the text box above the cost chart.

After you select the elements you want to move, position your cursor within one of the selected elements. When the cursor changes to a four-headed arrow, drag the elements to a new location. In this example, drag to the left so the charts are closer to the left side of the window. (If you wish, click the schedule table and then drag it up and to the left so it's closer to the charts.)

Report-wide Customization

In addition to the customization you can apply to elements within a report, the Report Design tab offers a few tools for formatting the *entire* report. Here are your choices:

- **Color scheme**: In the tab's Themes section, click Themes and then select a color scheme for the report. Click Colors to change individual colors, click Fonts to specify the font for the whole report, and click Effects to change the effects applied to the objects in the report.

- **Adding elements to a report**: In the tab's Insert section, click a button to insert a new element. You can insert images, drawing shapes, charts, tables, and text boxes. After you insert an element, you can adjust it using the techniques described in the previous sections.

- **Specify page settings**: The tab's Page Setup section includes all the usual suspects for setting a report up for distribution. You can specify where page breaks occur, the width of page margins, page orientation, and size.

Creating a Custom Report from an Existing Report

If an existing report is close to what you need, you don't have to start from scratch. It's easier to copy the existing report and then edit the copy like you do with filters (Chapter 17), tables (Chapter 20), and other elements. The copy provides a foundation for your new report, and you still have the original built-in report if you need it. Here's how you copy an existing report:

Follow Along Practice

1. In the Report tab's View Reports section, click the report category, and then choose the report you want to copy from the drop-down menu. In this example, choose Report→Dashboards→Work Overview.

2. In the Report Design tab's Report section, click Manage→Rename Report.

    The Rename dialog box opens. The label for the box is "New name for report from [project name]:." Although the dialog box title and label imply that you're changing the current report's name, what you're really doing is creating a *copy* of the report in your Project file.

3. Type the name for the copy (in this example, ***Work Performance***), and then click OK.

    Project adds the report to your custom reports. For example, if you head to the Report tab's View Reports section and click Custom, the report appears on the drop-down menu (Figure 19-12).

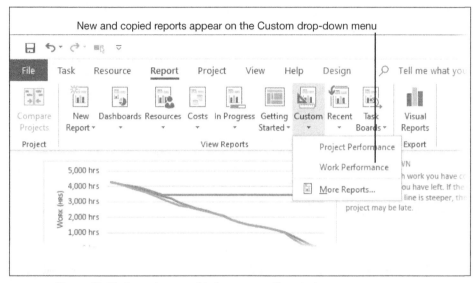

Figure 19-12. *Renaming a graphical report actually copies it as a new custom report.*

Customizing Visual Reports

The questions that stakeholders ask in status meetings shift like quicksand: When did costs start exceeding the budget?, How are employees doing compared with contractors?, Who's available to help bail out troubled tasks? Although graphical reports are easy to edit and provide lots of options for displaying information, Project's ***visual*** reports use Excel pivot charts and Visio pivot diagrams so you can change them on the fly, whether to respond to questions or to drill down in several directions to unearth problems.

The ability to slice and dice data in different ways sets these reports apart from other reports, whether you use the graphical reports in Project or you generate reports from a high-powered reporting tool. For example, you may start with a visual report that shows costs by fiscal quarter, but one quick change and the report can show costs by phase or resource instead. It's just as easy to change the report's graph from cost to work, examine a few time periods in detail while summarizing others, or look at specific tasks and resources. The note titled "Changing Your Perspective" in Chapter 18 explains what makes visual reports tick.

Project gets you started with several built-in visual reports (Chapter 18). You can modify the report in real time until it's the way you want.

Your options for massaging a visual report multiply once the report is open in Excel or Visio. The Pivot tools in Excel and Visio are a little different, so this chapter describes how to use both. You'll also learn how to modify or create visual report templates to produce custom visual reports.

> **Note:** Excel-based visual reports show information in bar graphs, pie charts, or line graphs. These reports work best when you want to compare values side by side or to look for trends. Visio-based visual reports break information down in a hierarchy, like a work breakdown structure. You can drill down level by level, and use icons to highlight good, bad, and indifferent values. (You see Excel-based or Visio-based reports listed in the "Visual Reports – Create Report" dialog box only if you have those programs installed on your machine.)

Rearranging and Formatting Excel Visual Reports

The real fun begins after you create an Excel-based visual report. Excel's pivot chart tools let you knead the report into the shape you want. This section describes the different ways you can configure an Excel-based visual report.

Follow Along Practice

For this example, open the Baseline Work Report. (Choose Report→Visual Reports. On the All tab, click the Baseline Work Report entry that has an Excel icon to its left. In the "Select the level of usage data to include in the report" box, keep Weeks selected. Finally, click View.)

When you open a visual report in Excel, you may see only the pivot chart. To display the pivot chart tools and the PivotChart Fields task pane, shown in Figure 19-13, click anywhere in the graph.

Adding the Measures You Want to See in the Graph

In the pivot chart, the fields you care about (like cost, hours of work, availability, and so on) usually show up as vertical bars in the chart. If you change the type of chart, the values may appear as a series of connected line segments, data points, 3-D bars, and so on. The fields you select also show up as the columns in the pivot table worksheet.

Although a visual report gathers data into its OLAP cube, the pivot chart doesn't display *every* field in the cube. When the visual report is open in Excel, you can add, remove, or change the fields that appear in the pivot chart.

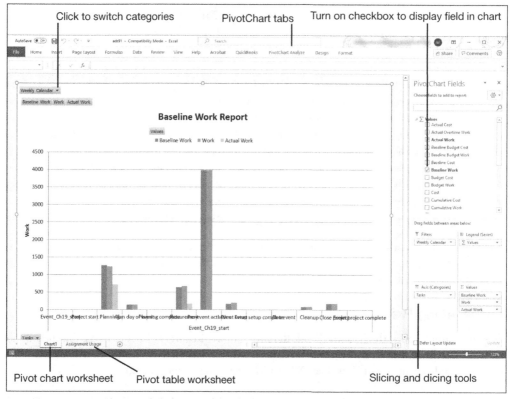

Figure 19-13. *When you click the pivot chart, the PivotChart Analyze, Design, and Format tabs appear on the ribbon.*

> **Note:** If the PivotChart Fields task pane isn't visible, then head to the PivotChart Analyze tab's Show/Hide section and click Field List.

The PivotChart Fields task pane to the right of the pivot chart, shown in Figure 19-13, lets you change what appears in the chart. Visual report templates start with a few fields turned on; in the task pane, they're identified by checkmarks in the checkboxes to the left of the names, which are also bolded. Use the following methods to add and rearrange the fields in the pivot chart:

- **Add or remove fields**: To include another field in the pivot chart, simply click its checkbox so the checkmark appears. (In this example, turn on the Cumulative Work checkbox. A fourth bar appears for each task shown along the x-axis.) To remove a field, click its checkbox, and the checkmark disappears. (Don't remove any fields for this example.)

  > **Tip:** You can also add a field by dragging the field's name from the Σ Values list at the top of the task pane into the Σ Values section (not on the section's heading) at the bottom of the task pane.

- **Reorder fields**: In the Σ Values section at the bottom of the task pane, drag a field to a new location in the list. Although the fields in the Σ Values section appear one below the other, they are ordered from left to right in the pivot chart. Suppose you want Actual Work to appear between Baseline Work and Work. To do that, drag Actual Work up; when a green horizontal line appears between the Baseline Work and Work fields, release the mouse button. When you reorder fields, the order of the bars in the pivot chart and the fields in the legend above the chart adjusts accordingly.

- **Change the field's calculation**: In the Σ Values section at the bottom of the task pane, click the field, and then choose Value Field Settings. In the Value Field Settings dialog box, click the Summarize Values By tab. In the "Summarize value field by" list, select the calculation you want. Depending on the field, you can choose calculations like Sum, Average, Minimum Value, Maximum Value, Count, and so on. For example, you might set the calculation to Count to see the number of complete tasks or the number of people in various resource roles. In this example, don't select a calculation.

Categorizing Information

The rows in a pivot table typically represent tasks, resources, or time. For example, the Baseline Work Report's pivot chart initially shows tasks along the x-axis. (If you click the Assignment Usage tab at the bottom of the window to view the pivot table, you'll see rows for tasks.) Changing the category is how you examine data from different perspectives—for example, to show work by resource or over time. You can also add categories to break down values further, to do things like evaluate work per phase broken down to each resource working on a phase.

These categories group information on the pivot chart's x-axis like the top-level tasks in the standard Baseline Work Report. Each top-level task has its own set of field bars. A pivot chart can slice up your project even further—just add another category to the Axis (Categories) section (called Rows if the pivot table is active).

Follow Along Practice

1. In this example, to break down the Baseline Work Report by resources, in the Σ Values section at the PivotChart Fields task pane's top, scroll until you see Resources (at the bottom of the field list). Put the pointer over the Resources checkbox. When the pointer changes to a four-headed arrow, drag Resources into the Axis (Categories) section.

   Resources appear above tasks in the pivot graph. The pivot graph displays sets of bars for each resource for each top-level task.

2. To remove tasks from the x-axis, drag Tasks from the Axis (Categories) section and drop it in the Σ Values section at the top of the PivotChart Fields task pane.

   Each resource along the x-axis has four sets of bars for baseline work, actual work, work, and cumulative work.

3. To analyze work by time period instead, drag Weekly Calendar from the Filters section into the Axis (Categories) section. Drag Resources from the Axis (Categories) section into the Filters section.

    By doing so, each time period has its own set of field bars (in this example, calendar years as shown in Figure 19-14).

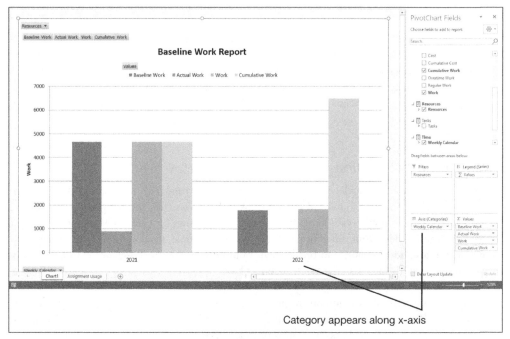

Category appears along x-axis

Figure 19-14. *You can drag entries between the Filters and Axis (Categories) sections to reconfigure the report.*

Filtering the Data that Appears

You can filter the information that appears in a visual report. For example, if overruns and delays have cropped up recently, you can filter the report to show data for only the current fiscal quarter. Likewise, you could filter a report to show only specific resources.

Follow Along Practice

To filter a report by a category, such as time, follow these steps:

1. If necessary, display the PivotChart Fields task pane by clicking the pivot chart.

    If the pivot table's tab is selected, you can click the table to make it active and display the Pivot Chart Fields task pane. (The pivot table tab's name is based on the visual report category to which it belongs, such as Assignment Usage for the Baseline Work Report. You can tell you're looking at the pivot table because the task pane's label reads "Pivot*Table* Fields" instead of "Pivot*Chart* Fields.")

2. In this example, Resources is in the task pane's Filters section, so you can filter by resources. To filter the report by tasks as well, in the task pane, drag Tasks from the Σ Values section into the Filters section.

    Now the report is set up to filter by tasks but still shows all tasks. When you drag fields into the Filters section, a button for that field appears at the pivot chart's top left (Figure 19-15).

    > **Tip:** If you have trouble reading any of the labels in the PivotTable Fields task pane, you can make the task pane wider by putting your cursor over the dividing line between it and the pivot chart; when the cursor turns into a double-headed arrow, drag the dividing line to the left.

3. To select specific tasks to display, at the pivot chart's top left, click the Tasks down arrow.

    Initially, this drop-down list shows only the top-level category. When the pivot chart is filtered by tasks, you see the name of the project. If you filter by time instead, you see All listed in this drop-down menu.

4. To select specific tasks as the filter, like a few phases of the project, turn on the Select Multiple Items checkbox. Then click the + signs in the drop-down menu to expand the tasks.

5. To remove specific tasks from the filter, turn off their checkboxes (in this example, the checkboxes from the end of the project through "Event setup"). Click OK.

    When a filter is in place, a filter icon (a funnel with a down arrow below it) appears to the right of the button.

    > **Tip:** If you're looking at the pivot *table* worksheet tab, you can apply filters by clicking down arrows to the right of fields in the pivot table. For example, to filter by tasks, click the down arrow to the right of the Tasks button at the top of the chart. To filter by resources, too, click the down arrow to the right of the resources cell. You can filter within those categories by clicking the down arrow and then choosing a filter to apply. See Figure 19-15.

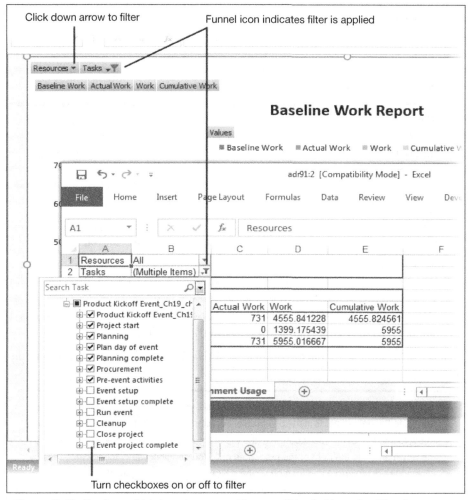

Figure 19-15. *To select multiple items in a pivot table, turn off the checkboxes for all but the items you want, and then click OK.*

Summarizing and Drilling Down

Drilling down into details or soaring up to summary views is almost effortless in visual reports. Simply click expand buttons (+) or collapse buttons (–) on the pivot table worksheet. Whatever you can see in the pivot table is what you see in the pivot chart, as Figure 19-16 illustrates.

In this example, the Baseline Work Report is set up to show work over time. To expand the chart to show quarters in 2021, click the + sign to the left of 2021. Then, if you want to expand that quarter to show work by week, click the + button to the left of the quarter's name (Q2, in this example). Note that the entire report doesn't have to be expanded or collapsed to the same level. One section of the report can show weeks while the rest of the report stays summarized.

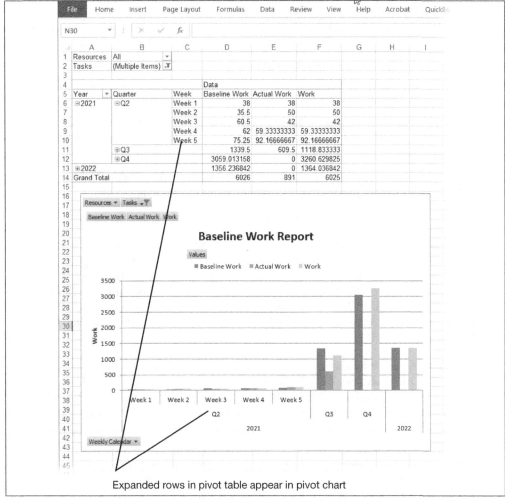

Expanded rows in pivot table appear in pivot chart

Figure 19-16. *Click + signs in the pivot table to expand portions of a category. Click a – sign to collapse a category.*

Formatting the Chart

Pivot charts are more muscular than most Excel charts, but you use the same methods for making them look good. For example, you can change the chart type, use a different bar style, and format the labels. Here are a few common formatting tasks:

- **Choose a chart type**: Sometimes, a different type of chart shows information more clearly. For instance, cumulative work is easier to understand when you draw it as a single line. Here's how to change the chart type:

a) To switch to a different type of chart, on the Chart1 worksheet, right-click the pivot chart and then choose Change Chart Type. (You can also open the Change Chart Type dialog box from the ribbon: In the Design tab's Type section, click Change the Chart Type.)

b) In the Change Chart Type dialog box, select the kind you want, in this example, Combo.

c) Then select the specific configuration you want, in this example, the first one: Clustered Column - Line.

d) In the Series Name table at the bottom of the dialog box, click the down arrow for the Work field, and then choose Clustered Column. By doing that, the Work field values appear as columns.

e) In the Series Name table, make sure the Cumulative Work field is set to Line, so Cumulative Work is drawn as a continuous line over the project duration.

f) Click OK to apply the changes. Figure 19-17 shows the pivot chart with its new chart type.

- **Format component**: To change the appearance of the chart's components, in the Format tab's Current Selection section, click the down arrow, and then choose Chart Title, Axis Titles, Legend, Data Labels, Series, and so on. You can also format portions of the chart by right-clicking what you want to format and then, on the shortcut menu, choosing a command like Format Chart Title. In this example, right-click one of the Baseline Work columns in the chart. On the shortcut toolbar that appears, click the Fill down arrow, and then choose dark red.

- **Rotate text to remove overlaps**: If the pivot chart contains more than a few resources, tasks, or time periods, the labels along the x-axis are likely to overlap. To fix this, realign the text vertically or at an angle. Right-click the labels on the x-axis, and then choose Format Axis. In the Format Axis task pane that appears, click the Size & Properties icon (a square with arrows inside it and dimension marks outside it). In the "Text direction" box, click the down arrow, and then choose "Rotate all text 270°."

> **Tip:** When you right-click the pivot chart, a mini-toolbar and a shortcut menu appear. The last command on the shortcut menu is "Format [pivot chart section]," where [pivot chart section] is the part of the pivot chart you right-clicked. Choose that command to format the selected part of the pivot chart. Then, on the mini-toolbar, choose the formatting you want to apply, like a fill color, outline color, or text style.

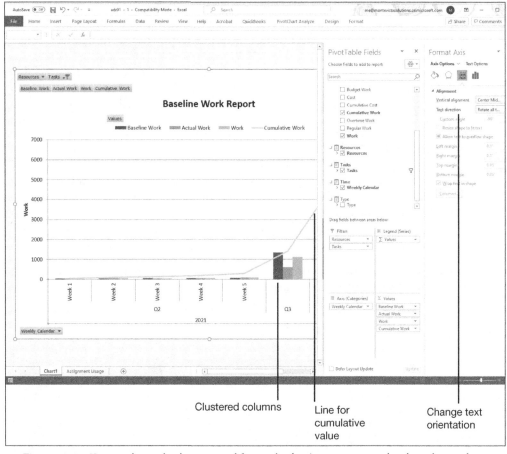

Clustered columns

Line for
cumulative
value

Change text
orientation

Figure 19-17. *You can change the chart type and format the chart's components, such as bar colors, and text.*

Rearranging and Formatting Visio Visual Reports

Visio-based visual reports use Visio pivot diagrams. The top box (called a ***node***) in a pivot diagram represents your entire project. You can break the diagram down to additional levels by adding categories. The nodes in a pivot diagram typically show field values, but a Visio visual report is best when you want to display icons to indicate status.

Follow Along Practice

In this example, in Project, choose Report→Visual Reports; in the Visual Reports – Create Report dialog box, choose Task Status Report (US). Keep the usage level box set to Weeks, and then click View. This report shows work, cost, and % Complete for the entire project in the top node, and then values for Outline Level 1 tasks in the second row of nodes.

> **Note:** You must have Visio 2010 or later installed on your computer to work with Visio Visual Reports.

When you open a pivot diagram, tools and settings appear in the PivotDiagram task pane. Similar to their Excel counterparts, Visio pivot diagrams accept additional fields and several levels of categories. The following are several of the more common changes you may want to make to pivot diagrams:

- **Add a new breakdown**: To break down a node into more detail, you add a category to that node. Click the node, and then, in the PivotDiagram task pane to the diagram's left, below the Add Category heading, click the category you want to add: Resources:Resources, Type:Type, or Tasks:Tasks. You can add Tasks as the second level to build the equivalent of a work breakdown structure diagram. If you add Resources instead, then you can see how resources contribute to task values. In this example, click the Planning node in the pivot diagram, and then choose Tasks: Tasks in the Pivot Diagram – Task pane to show Outline Level 2 planning tasks (Figure 19-18).

  To remove a level, right-click the node to which the level is attached (for example, right-click a task node in the work breakdown structure diagram), and then, on the shortcut menu, choose Collapse. In this example, keep the lower level you just added.

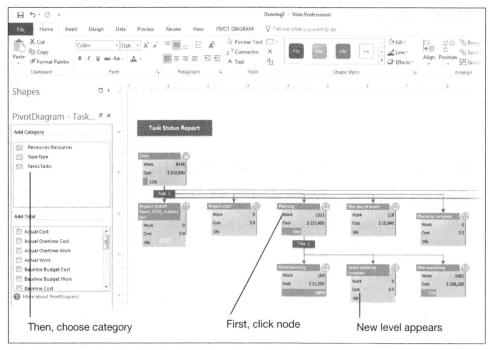

Figure 19-18. *You can also apply a category by right-clicking a node and then choosing Add Category from the shortcut menu.*

- **Change fields in nodes**: Visual report nodes contain some fields, but you can add or remove fields to show exactly what you want. In the PivotDiagram task pane, in the Add Total section, turn on the checkboxes for the fields you want to see. Turn checkboxes off to remove those fields from the nodes. In this example, turn on the Work Variance checkbox to add that field to the bottom of each node.

- **Filter data**: A level in a pivot diagram initially includes OLAP cube data for your entire project, but you can filter a level to show information for just *part* of the project. To do so, right-click the small shape between levels, in this example, the one labeled Task 1, and then, on the shortcut menu, choose Configure Level. In the Configure Level dialog box, you can define conditions that nodes have to meet. In this example, in the first (Select Operation) box, choose "contains," and then in the second box in that row, type *plan*. When you click OK, the diagram shows only the project tasks with "plan" in their names.

- **Combine nodes**: You can combine nodes in several ways with the Merge, Promote, and Collapse commands. In the Pivot Diagram tab's Arrange section, click the command you want. For example, to combine two tasks, select them, and then click Merge. The values in the merged node show the total for both tasks. In this example, click the Planning node and then Ctrl-click the "Plan day of event" node. On the ribbon's Pivot Diagram tab, click Merge.

- **Change the diagram's background**: Background pages are the place to add your corporate logo or a watermark of some kind. Most Visio visual reports include a Vbackground-1 page for just this purpose (if one exists, you'll see a drawing page tab, labeled "Vbackground-1," at the bottom of the window). If a diagram *doesn't* include a background page, then in the Insert tab's Pages section, click New Page→Background Page. In the Page Setup dialog box, on the Page Properties tab, the Background option is selected automatically. In the Name box, type a name for the page (Logo, in this example). Turn on the "Open page in new window" checkbox, and then click OK. You can insert the graphic file for your corporate logo by heading to the Insert tab's Illustrations section and clicking Pictures. In this example, insert any graphic file you have available.

- **Quickly format the diagram**: In Visio, *themes* are color-coordinated packages of formatting that help you make your diagrams look good (even if you wear plaids with stripes). To change the appearance of your diagram, in the Design tab's Themes section, click the theme you want; the diagram changes automatically. In this example, click the Page-1 tab at the bottom of the Visio window to display the pivot diagram. Then, click the Design tab, and choose a different theme.

Figure 19-19 shows the pivot diagram after making all the changes in this section.

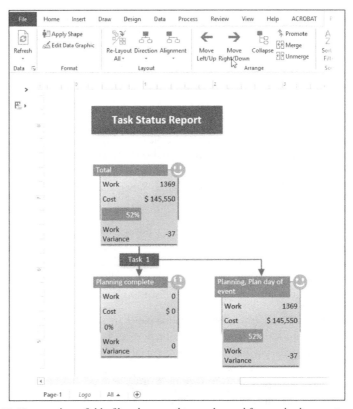

Figure 19-19. *You can choose fields, filter data, combine nodes, and format the diagram in various ways.*

Customizing Visual Report Templates

Visual reports are so flexible that customizing them may not even occur to you. But once you realize that you're frequently making the same field, category, and filter changes, you can eliminate this busywork by saving the modified pivot chart or pivot diagram as a ***visual report template***. A template saves the visual report's ***definition*** (that is, the report's layout and the fields it includes), not its actual data. When you use the new report template, it generates a pivot chart or a pivot diagram according to your preferred report settings.

At a lower level, you can also customize the data in a visual report's cube. Cubes come with plenty of fields, but you can add fields you want or remove fields you don't need.

Because visual reports are really Excel pivot charts or Visio pivot diagrams, visual report templates are simply Excel or Visio template files. Whether you copy a built-in template or create one from scratch, you pick the fields to include and the type of cube, and then set up the pivot chart or pivot diagram to look the way you want. Here are the details:

Follow Along Practice

1. In Project, if the Visual Reports – Create Report dialog box isn't open, in the Report tab's Export section, click Visual Reports.

2. Select the built-in visual report whose template is closest to what you want, in this example, the Excel Cash Flow Report, and then click Edit Template.

    The "Visual Reports - Field Picker" dialog box appears. Although you're editing an existing template, later on, when you save the template with a new name, you'll have a brand-new template.

    > **Tip:** To create a new template from *scratch*, click New Template instead. In the "Visual Reports - New Template" dialog box, select the Excel, Visio (Metric), or Visio (US Units) option to specify the type of visual report. Under Select Data Type, choose the type of cube (Task Summary, Resource Summary, or Assignment Summary for total information; Task Usage, Resource Usage, or Assignment Usage for time-phased data). Click Field Picker, and you're ready for step 3.

3. In the Available Fields list, select the fields you want in the data cube, in this example, Baseline Start and Baseline Finish, and then click Add.

    The Selected Fields list shows fields already tagged for inclusion in the data cube. When you click Add, the fields you picked jump to the Selected Fields list. To remove fields, select them in the Selected Fields list, and then click Remove. As with other list boxes, Ctrl-clicking and Shift-clicking work for selecting several fields. In this example, don't make any other changes.

    > **Tip:** A few fields have "(dimension)" after their names, which means they're the categories that the cube uses to organize data—the same categories you use to create additional levels in a Visio pivot diagram or to group and filter data in a pivot chart. Most visual reports use up to three dimension fields. For your own reports, keep the dimension fields to fewer than six, or the report's performance may slow down significantly. You can create a dimension for a custom field by using a lookup table.

4. At the bottom-right of the "Visual Reports - Field Picker" dialog box (Figure 19-20), click Edit Template.

    Project builds the OLAP cube with the fields you selected and then starts Excel or Visio (depending on the type of report).

5. Modify the report so it looks the way you want.

    Use the techniques described earlier in this chapter to customize the arrangement and formatting of the pivot chart or pivot diagram. In this example, turn on the Actual Cost checkbox.

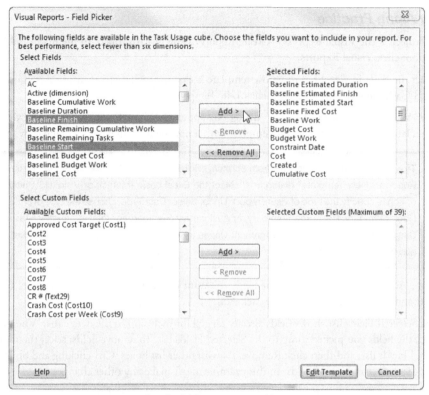

Figure 19-20. *Select the fields you want to add, and then click Add.*

6. Save the report as a template.

Choose File→Save As. Choose the location and folder where you want to save the template. (In this example, save the template to the desktop.) The Save As dialog box opens.

7. In the Save As dialog box, in the "Save as type" drop-down list, choose Excel Template for an Excel template, or Template for a Visio template. In the "File name" box, type a new name for the template, and then click Save. In this example, choose Excel Template, and then, in the "File name" box, type *Cash Flow Detail*. Click Save.

8. If a message box opens and asks if you want to clear the data before saving the template, click Yes.

Managing Visual Report Templates

Project stores its templates in the *C:\Users\[user name]\AppData\Roaming\Microsoft\Templates\1033* folder where 1033 represents English. You can save your templates in this folder or create a folder dedicated to your templates. If you save your templates in the default folder, they will appear automatically in Project's "Visual Reports - Create Report" dialog box. If you use your own folder, you have to tell Project where to look for them. Here's how:

1. Below the list of visual reports, turn on the "Include report templates from" checkbox.

2. Click Modify to set the path to your templates folder. (For example, you might set the path to a folder like Documents\Templates.)

3. Close and reopen the "Visual Reports - Create Report" dialog box, and your templates will appear in the list.

Saving Report Data

When you generate a visual report, Project chugs along for a few seconds (or minutes) as it gathers data into an OLAP cube, like a chipmunk gathering acorns in its cheeks. In addition to providing the shape-shifting capabilities for visual reports, that data can work beyond the report you're generating at the moment. For example, the data cube is a snapshot of project status. And unlike the 11 Project baselines you can save, the number of data cubes is limited only by your disk space. If you wanted to, you could save a data cube every month and open them to look for trends. You can open a cube directly in Excel or Visio, and then use the built-in pivot chart and pivot diagram tools to view the information.

Here are the steps for saving project data:

1. In the "Visual Reports - Create Report" dialog box (Report→Visual Reports), click Save Data.

   The "Visual Reports - Save Reporting Data" dialog box opens.

2. In the drop-down list, choose the type of OLAP cube you want to save (in this example, Task Summary).

   Task Summary, Resource Summary, and Assignment Summary cubes contain total work and cost data. Task Usage, Resource Usage, and Assignment Usage cubes include time-phased data like the data in usage views. These options correspond to the tabs at the top of the "Visual Reports - Create Report" dialog box. The data that they represent are described in Chapter 18.

3. To choose fields other than the ones the cube contains, click Field Picker.

   Select fields as described in the previous section, and then click OK. (In this example, you don't have to pick any fields.)

4. In this example, click Save Cube.

   Saving a cube creates a larger database file but makes data based on the cube's dimensions easier to find. If you click Save Database instead, Project creates a regular Access database with all the project's data. Then you can open that file using Microsoft Access.

5. In the Save As dialog box, select the Desktop, type a name for the file (*savecube*, in this example) and click Save.

   Back in the "Visual Reports - Save Reporting Data" dialog box, click Close. Close the Visual Reports – Create Report dialog box.

To open saved report data directly in Excel, do the following:

1. In Excel, create a new workbook. Select cell A1 in the worksheet.

2. In the Insert tab's Charts section, click PivotChart, and then choose "PivotChart & PivotTable."

   The Create PivotTable or Create PivotChart dialog box opens. Both dialog boxes have the same settings, but the Create PivotTable one creates only a pivot table. The Create PivotChart one creates **both** a pivot chart and the pivot table that contains the chart's data.

3. Select the "Use an external data source" option, and then click Choose Connection.

   In the Existing Connections dialog box, click "Browse for More." In the Select Data Source dialog box, navigate to the folder where you saved the data cube (Desktop, in this example), select the file (savecube.cub, in this example), and then click Open.

4. Back in the Create PivotTable or Create PivotChart dialog box, click OK.

   A new pivot table or pivot chart appears. The PivotTable Field or PivotChart Field task pane displays the fields from the cube or database, and you're ready to use the same pivot tools you've already met.

20

Customizing Views

Just as the tie-dyed T-shirts you wore in school no longer work in a buttoned-down office, what works for one organization may not be right for another. Even if you stay at the same job or on the same project, what you need to see in Project may change as you go along.

Fortunately, Project gives you lots of control over what you view in its window. Most views include a table of information, and these tables are customizable to show the data you want. You can add, remove, or rearrange columns and tweak tables in other ways. You can customize or create various types of views to present the right project information in the right way. For example, you can set up Gantt Chart task bars to emphasize the critical path, progress, or at-risk tasks. Of course, text is omnipresent, and its formatting is at your command—whether you want to accommodate the reading-glasses crowd or make key information stand out. Project can apply formatting to text that falls into a specific category, like critical tasks, or to individual elements like a crucial task bar.

> **Note:** When you create a new element like a table or view, Project automatically copies it to the global template. If you don't want to add new elements that you create to your global template, choose File→Options. On the left side of the Project Options dialog box, click Advanced. Under the Display heading, turn off the "Automatically add new views, tables, filters, and groups to the global" checkbox. Then you have to use the Organizer to manually copy your new elements to the *global.mpt* file. Chapter 23 gives the full scoop on reusing customized elements.

Changing Tables

Views like the Gantt Chart and Task Usage view come with a table of information on the left—each column displaying values for a Project field. (Sometimes, the table is the *only* thing in the view, like in the Resource Sheet view.) Project comes with several built-in tables, like Entry and Cost, that contain frequently used collections of fields. Like most elements in Project, you can change which table you see, what the table contains, and how data is displayed to suit your needs.

> **Note:** If you've downloaded files from the book website, you can follow along using the file Event_Ch20_start.mpp. If necessary, display the Gantt chart view, remove the applied group, and, in the View tab's Data section, click Outline and then choose All Subtasks.

You can easily swap the table you see in a view—for instance, to switch from a summary to a table that shows performance compared with the baseline. But you can also change the columns in a table by temporarily adding columns, or permanently adding, removing, and rearranging columns to reflect how you work. Going a step further, the table's column width, row height, and a few other options are customizable so you can make a table look exactly the way you want.

> **Note:** If you modify a built-in table, Project dutifully records every change you make to it, so the table shows those changes every time you apply it. Project stores the customized table in your Project file, although it has the same name as the original, built-in table. To use both the original and your custom version, make a copy of the built-in table *first*, and then modify it as described in the section "Creating a New Table by Copying an Existing One."

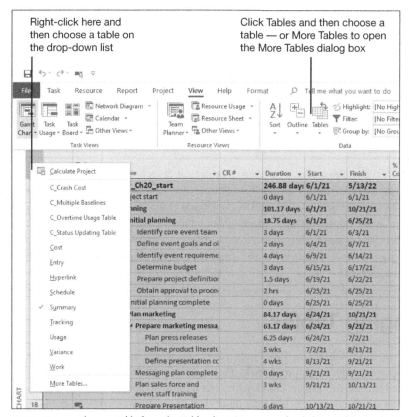

Figure 20-1. *You can choose a table from the Tables shortcut menu or by clicking Tables on the View tab to display a table drop-down list.*

Switching the Table in a View

Project offers two ways to swap out a table in a view. To choose *any* existing table, the More Views dialog box is the place to go. To choose from just the tables on the Tables menu, there's a shortcut. After you choose the view you want (in this example, display the Gantt Chart), here are your options (Figure 20-1):

- **Never-fails method**: In the View tab's Data section, click Tables→More Tables. In the More Tables dialog box, double-click a table's name (in this example, Earned Value Schedule Indicators). This dialog box lists every table that exists in your global template *and* the current Project file.

- **Fast method**: Right-click the Select All box at the intersection of the row and column headings (above the first ID cell), and then, on the shortcut menu, choose the table you want. You can also head to the View tab's Data section, click Tables, and then choose the table you want. The only difference between these two options is that the Tables drop-down list segregates custom and built-in tables.

Creating a New Table

You can create a new table from scratch or by copying one that's close to what you want. This section describes the methods at your disposal.

Creating a New Table from the Current Table

If you've already modified the current table to look the way you want, you can quickly turn it into a new table by heading to the View tab's Data section and clicking Tables→"Save Fields as a New Table." In the Save Table dialog box, type the name for the table and then click OK. Project saves the table and applies it to the current view.

> **Tip:** If you decide that you want to go back to a built-in table's original definition, display the table in a view, and then, in the View tab's Data section, click Tables→"Reset to Default."

Creating a New Table by Copying an Existing One

Suppose an existing table is close but not exactly what you want. The quickest way to get a new table that is what you want is to copy the existing table, give it a new name, and then make your changes. Here's how to copy an existing table:

Follow Along Practice

1. In the View tab's Data section, click Tables, and then choose More Tables.

   The More Views dialog box opens. Its table list includes all the tables in your global template and the active Project file.

2. In the list, select the table you want to copy (in this example, Summary), and then click the Copy button.

   The Table Definition dialog box opens.

3. In the Name box, replace the name that Project fills in (in this example, it's Copy of &Summary) by typing a name for the view, as shown in Figure 20-2. In this example, type **C_ExecSummary**.

Project initially fills in names like "Copy of [selected table]" for a copied table.

> **Tip:** If you want to use keyboard shortcuts to select a table from a drop-down menu, type & before the letter you want as the shortcut. For example, if you name the table *C_Exec-Summ&ary,* you can apply the table by pressing Alt to display keyboard shortcuts. Then, press W to display the View tab, press TA to display the table drop-down menu, and finally press A (the letter after the ampersand) to display the table. (If another entry uses the same letter for its keyboard shortcut, then you need to press the letter a *second* time to access your table.)

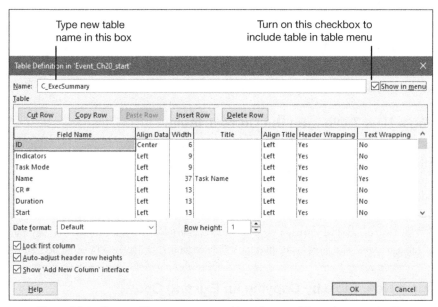

Figure 20-2. *Copy a table to create a new table without modifying the original table.*

4. To display the view in the menu, turn on the "Show in menu" checkbox to the right of the Name box.

When you turn on the "Show in menu" checkbox, the table will appear in the drop-down list that appears when you click Tables on the View tab. It also appears in the table shortcut menu that appears when you right-click the Select All cell at the top left of the table pane.

5. Click OK to save the table and close the Table Definition dialog box.

Project saves the table in your global template and/or active Project file depending on the Project options you set (see Chapter 23).

> **Tip:** Adding "C_" as a prefix to the view name makes it easy to differentiate a custom view from built-in views that come with Project.

6.   If you want to apply the new table to the current view, in the More Tables dialog box, click Apply. (Click Apply in this example.)

7.   Click Close to close the More Tables dialog box.

Now that the table exists, you can jump to the section "Changing a Table's Contents" or "Modifying a Table Definition" to modify the table.

Creating a Table from Scratch

If you want to start from scratch or choose other settings, the More Tables dialog box is the place to start. To create a new table in this way, follow these steps:

Follow Along Practice

1.   In the View tab's Data section, click Tables→More Tables.

      The More Tables dialog box opens.

2.   To create a table from scratch, select the Task or Resource option to specify the type of table (Task in this example), and then click New.

      The Table Definition dialog box opens.

3.   In the Name box, type the name for the table, in this example, *C_ScheduleStatus*.

      Project initially fills in names like "Table 1" for a new table. Replace Project's name with one that describes the table's contents.

4.   To include the table in table menus (for instance, when you click Tables in the View tab's Data section), turn on the "Show in menu" checkbox.

      With this setting turned on, the table also appears when you right-click the Select All box at the intersection of the column headings and row IDs.

5.   Add a column to the table, in this example, in the first Field Name cell, choose Name.

      When you create a table from scratch, you have to add at least one field in order to save the table.

6.   Click OK to save the table.

7.   If you want to apply the new table to the current view, in the More Tables dialog box, click Apply. In this example, click Close to close the More Tables dialog box without applying the table to the view.

Changing a Table's Contents

The easiest way to make changes to a table is to work on it directly in a view. That way, you can see the results immediately and try again until you get it right. Project records your changes in the table's definition, so working in a view changes the table just as working in the Table Definition dialog box does (see the next section).

> **Tip:** Chapters 13 and 15 include examples of modifying table contents.

Once you've applied the table to the current view (if you're following along, the C_ExecSummary table is already applied to the Gantt Chart view), here are the techniques for editing tables in a view:

Follow Along Practice

- **Add a column**: Right-click the heading of the column to the right of where you want to add the new column (in this example, % Comp), and then choose Insert Column. In the "Field name" drop-down list, choose the field (in this example, Baseline Finish).

  To add another field to the table, right-click % Comp again and choose Insert Column. To quickly scroll to the field you want, start typing the field's name (for example, type *fin*), and Project selects the first field that matches the letters you've typed, in this example, Finish. Click the field you want to insert, in this example, Finish Variance.

  You can also click the Add New Column heading in the last column of the table (Figure 20-3) and then choose the field you want from the drop-down list. In this example, click this heading to add Baseline Cost and Cost Variance to the table. (If you don't want to see the Add New Column column in the table, on the Format tab, click Column Settings, and then click Display Add New Column to toggle it off.)

> **Note:** If you start to type values into the Add New Column cells, Project identifies the type of information you're entering and automatically changes the column to an appropriate custom field. For example, if you type a value like 6/17/2021, Project changes the column to a custom Date field like Date1. In this example, don't fill in any values in the Add New Column column.

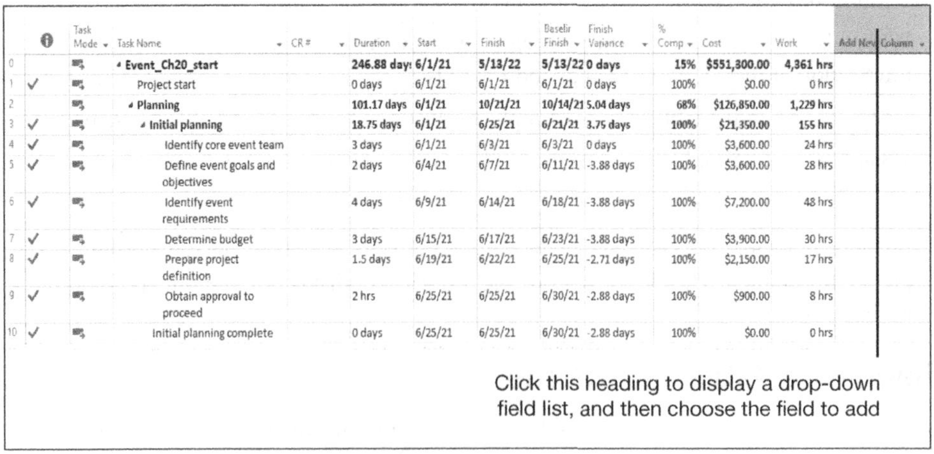

	Task Mode	Task Name	CR #	Duration	Start	Finish	Baselir Finish	Finish Variance	% Comp	Cost	Work	Add New Column
0		◢ Event_Ch20_start		246.88 days	6/1/21	5/13/22	5/13/22	0 days	15%	$551,300.00	4,361 hrs	
1	✓	Project start		0 days	6/1/21	6/1/21	6/1/21	0 days	100%	$0.00	0 hrs	
2		◢ Planning		101.17 days	6/1/21	10/21/21	10/14/21	5.04 days	68%	$126,850.00	1,229 hrs	
3	✓	◢ Initial planning		18.75 days	6/1/21	6/25/21	6/21/21	3.75 days	100%	$21,350.00	155 hrs	
4	✓	Identify core event team		3 days	6/1/21	6/3/21	6/3/21	0 days	100%	$3,600.00	24 hrs	
5	✓	Define event goals and objectives		2 days	6/4/21	6/7/21	6/11/21	-3.88 days	100%	$3,600.00	28 hrs	
6	✓	Identify event requirements		4 days	6/9/21	6/14/21	6/18/21	-3.88 days	100%	$7,200.00	48 hrs	
7	✓	Determine budget		3 days	6/15/21	6/17/21	6/23/21	-3.88 days	100%	$3,900.00	30 hrs	
8	✓	Prepare project definition		1.5 days	6/19/21	6/22/21	6/25/21	-2.71 days	100%	$2,150.00	17 hrs	
9	✓	Obtain approval to proceed		2 hrs	6/25/21	6/25/21	6/30/21	-2.88 days	100%	$900.00	8 hrs	
10	✓	Initial planning complete		0 days	6/25/21	6/25/21	6/30/21	-2.88 days	100%	$0.00	0 hrs	

Click this heading to display a drop-down field list, and then choose the field to add

Figure 20-3. *Click the Add New Column heading to insert a new column.*

- **Remove a column**: Right-click the heading of the column you want to remove (in this example, Work), and then choose Hide Column. Project removes the column from view *and* from the table's definition. See the note titled "Where's That Column?" for another way to hide columns.

- **Rearrange columns**: If the table has the right columns in the wrong order, you can drag columns into other positions. Simply click the heading of the column you want to move (% Comp, in this example). When the pointer turns into a four-headed arrow, drag the column to its new location (to the right of Cost Variance). A dark gray vertical line jumps from column edge to edge to show you where the column will settle when you release the mouse button.

- **Edit a column**: Right-click a column's heading (Finish Variance, in this example) and then, on the shortcut menu, choose Field Settings. The Field Settings dialog box (Figure 20-4) opens with the "Field name" box set to the selected field. You can change the column's title, width, and text alignment, and control whether its header text wraps, as described in the following bullet points.

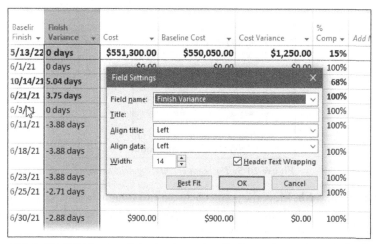

Figure 20-4. *The Field Settings dialog box has settings for fine-tuning a column and its heading.*

- **Fine-tune the column heading**: If you want the column heading to be something besides the field name, open the Field Settings dialog box (see the previous bullet) and in the Title box, type the heading you want (in this example, type ***Fin. Var.***). You can align this heading to the Left, Center, or Right using the "Align title" setting. In this example, in the "Align title" box, choose Center. As shown in Figure 20-4, turn on the Header Text Wrapping checkbox to wrap the words in the title over several lines when the column is narrow.

> **Tip:** If you change a column title, you might forget what field that column represents. Right-click the column heading and choose Field Settings in the shortcut menu. The field name appears in the "Field name" box. If the column represents a custom field, you'll see the built-in field name (such as Text1) as well as the field alias if you set one (see Chapter 21).

- **Align data**: In the Field Settings dialog box (see above), the "Align data" setting positions values in the column. In this example, choose Center in the "Align data" box.

To close the Field Settings box, click OK. Figure 20-5 shows what the Finish Variance column looks like after making the changes specified above.

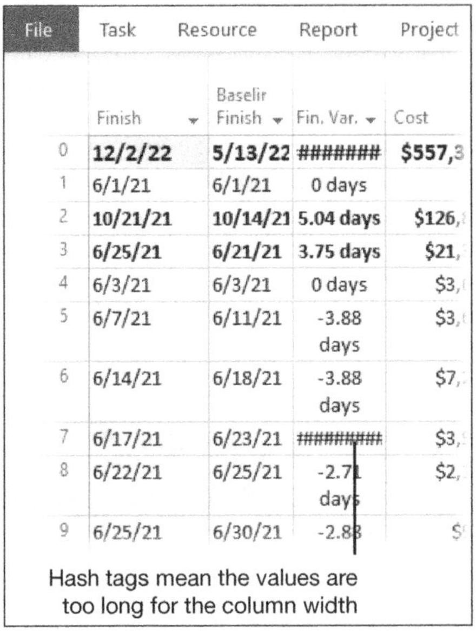

	File	Task	Resource	Report	Project
		Finish ▼	Baselir Finish ▼	Fin. Var. ▼	Cost
0		**12/2/22**	**5/13/22**	**######**	**$557,3**
1		6/1/21	6/1/21	0 days	
2		**10/21/21**	**10/14/21**	**5.04 days**	**$126,**
3		**6/25/21**	**6/21/21**	**3.75 days**	**$21,**
4		6/3/21	6/3/21	0 days	$3,
5		6/7/21	6/11/21	-3.88 days	$3,
6		6/14/21	6/18/21	-3.88 days	$7,
7		6/17/21	6/23/21	########	$3,
8		6/22/21	6/25/21	-2.7 days	$2,
9		6/25/21	6/30/21	-2.8	$

Hash tags mean the values are too long for the column width

Figure 20-5. *The result of changing field settings.*

- **Change column width**: Move the pointer between two column headings with the column you want to resize on the left. When the pointer changes into a two-headed arrow, drag to the left or right until the column is the width you want.

> **Tip:** When values don't fit in a column, Project replaces them with a series of hash signs (#) as you can see in Figure 20-5, which aren't very informative. Here's a quick way to resize a column to show all its values: Move the pointer to the right edge of the column's heading. When the pointer changes to a two-headed arrow, double-click. Alternatively, in the Field Settings dialog box, click Best Fit to do the same thing.

- **Wrap text in column cells**: Project initially sets some columns like Task Name to wrap text, which means that the program wraps long task names over several lines as you change the column's width. To wrap text in a column, right-click in the column's heading, and then, on the shortcut menu, choose Wrap Text. In this example, you don't have to apply this setting to any other columns.

- **Change row height**: You can change the height of specific rows in a table. First, select the rows whose height you want to change, in this example, drag over task IDs 3 through 10. Then place the two-headed arrow over the lower border of one of the selected row's ID numbers, and then drag up or down until the rows are the height you want.

Where's That Column?

You can conceal a column without it losing its place in a table, but finding the column again is another matter. To conceal a column without removing it from the table, move the pointer to the right edge of the column's heading cell. When the pointer changes to a two-headed arrow, drag past the column's *left* border. The column disappears, but a look at the table's definition explained below shows the column still there, just with a width of zero. If you have the Table Definition dialog box open as explained below, simply type a value greater than zero for the column's width.

In a table, Project doesn't give you any visual clues that the column is there. Truth be told, a column concealed like this may stay that way forever—you may even insert the column a second time without realizing that it's already there.

If you're smart enough to remember where the column was before you concealed it, move the pointer between the two column headings where the column is located, making sure the pointer is slightly to the right of the border line. When the pointer changes into a two-headed arrow, drag to the right until the concealed column stretches into view.

Modifying a Table Definition

If you prefer to do all your table editing in one dialog box, the Table Definition dialog box is for you. You can add, move, remove, rearrange, and modify columns for any table. To edit a table in the Table Definition dialog box, do the following:

1. In the View tab's Data section, click Tables, and then, in the drop-down list, choose More Tables.

    The More Tables dialog box opens.

2. In the More Tables dialog box, select the table you want to work on. If you're following along, select C_ScheduleStatus, which you created earlier in the chapter.

    If you don't see the name of the table you want, try clicking the Task or Resource option at the top of the dialog box.

3. Click Edit.

    The Table Definition dialog box opens, with all the customization features you can apply to a table directly when it appears in a view—and a few more besides. The note titled "Navigating the Table Definition Dialog Box" describes the various sections of this dialog box and how to move around in it.

Navigating the Table Definition Dialog Box

The Table Definition dialog box contains a table of its own, so terminology is a challenge. Project doesn't have official names for these elements, so here are the terms used in this section of this chapter:

Figure 20-6 identifies elements in the Table Definition dialog box and a view's table. The Table Definition dialog box's table is called the *grid*. A column in the Table Definition grid is a *property*, while a column in the table you're working on is called the *table column*. A row in the Table Definition grid is called a *row* and represents a Project field within the table you're working on. A row in the table you're working on is called a *table row* and represents a task, resource, or assignment.

Knowing which keys to press in the Table Definition dialog box helps you get to the elements you want to edit. Here's how you move around in the dialog box:

- To move to the next cell in the grid, press the right arrow. (Pressing Enter *doesn't* move to the next cell; it closes the dialog box as if you clicked OK.)

- Tab jumps from one section of the dialog box to the next. For example, if you're in the grid area and you press Tab, Project fills in the rest of the row you were in with standard choices and then jumps to the "Date format" box below the grid.

- To move to the end of a row, press Ctrl+right arrow. To move to the beginning of a row, press Ctrl+left arrow.

Here's how you make changes to a table in the Table Definition dialog box:

- **Display the table in table drop-down menus**: Turn on the "Show in menu" checkbox to tell Project to list the table in table drop-down menus. (In this example, turn on this checkbox.) If you use a table only occasionally, turn *off* this checkbox. Even with this setting turned off, you can still display the table by applying it from within the More Tables dialog box described earlier in this chapter.

- **Add a table column**: You can insert a table column in any row in the Table Definition grid. To insert a table column at the end of the grid, click the first blank Field Name cell, click the down arrow to the cell's right, and then choose the field you want. Keep in mind that the top row in the grid represents the leftmost table column; the bottom row in the grid is the rightmost table column. In this example, use this technique to add ID, Start, Finish, Finish Variance, SV%, and Actual Finish to the table.

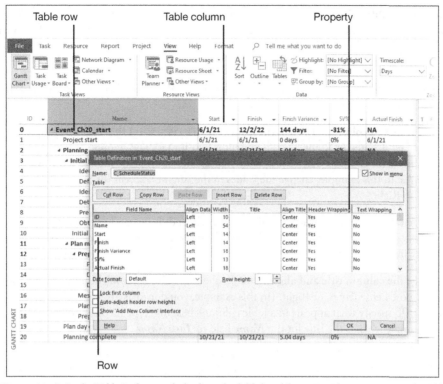

Figure 20-6. *In the Table Definition dialog box, the fields listed from top to bottom represent the table columns from left to right in a view's table.*

To add a table column in the middle of the grid, select the row above which you want to add a new row (in this example, Start), and then click Insert Row to insert a blank row, as illustrated in Figure 20-7. In the Field Name cell, choose the field you want to use (in this example, Duration).

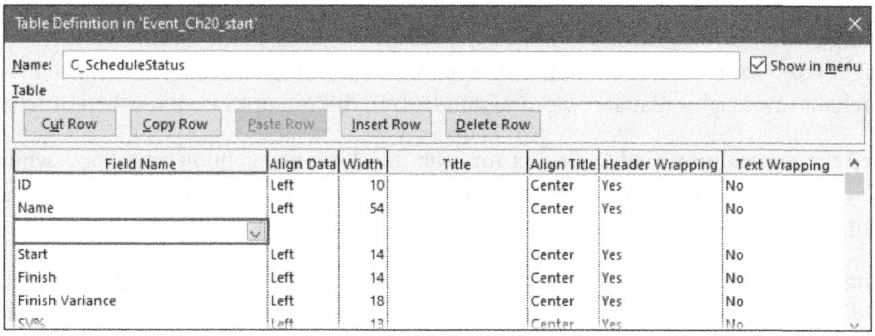

Figure 20-7. *The fields that appear in Field Name drop-down lists depend on whether you are working on a task-, resource-, or assignment-oriented table.*

- **Remove a table column**: Select the row containing the field name you want to remove (in this example, SV%), and then click Delete Row.

- **Rearrange table columns**: Select the field name you want to move (Actual Finish, in this example), and then click Cut Row. Project places the cut row on the Clipboard. Select the row below where you want to insert the cut field (Finish Variance, in this example), and then click Paste Row. The cut row slides into its new location.

  In this example, select the ID field, and then click Cut Row. Select the Name row, and then click Paste Row.

- **Align values in columns**: To align the values in table cells, select the Align Data cell, and then choose Left, Center, or Right. Left alignment is best for task and resource names. Center is a good choice for columns that include short values like Yes and No. Choose Right for numbers and dates. In this example, change the values in the Align Data cells for Start, Finish, and Actual Finish to Right.

- **Change table column width**: Select the Width cell, and then type a number. Although you can specify column width in the Table Definition dialog box, it's much easier to adjust column width directly in a table, as described in the previous section.

- **Change the column title and alignment**: To align the table column's heading, in the Align Title cell, choose Left, Center, or Right. (In this example, you don't have to change any Align Title values.) To specify what appears in a table column's heading, type the heading in the Title cell. In this example, change the title for the *Name* field to *Task Name*.

- **Wrap text in data cells**: Change the Text Wrapping property to Yes if you want Project to automatically wrap the text in table cells as you change the table column's width. In this example, change Text Wrapping for the Name row to Yes.

- **Specify date format**: Below the Table Definition dialog box's grid, in the "Date format" drop-down list, choose the date format you want for date fields in the table. In this example, in the "Date format" box, choose "Wed 1/28/09." Choosing a table date format here overrides the project-wide date format. (To set the project-wide date format, choose File→Options, click General, and then choose an option in the "Date format" box.)

- **Change table row height**: If you want to adjust the height of all the table rows, then in the Row Height box, type or choose a number. The number is a multiple of the standard height; that is, 2 represents row heights that are twice the standard. In this example, keep row height set to 1.

- **Keep the first column visible**: Project turns on the "Lock first column" checkbox, which means the ID column remains visible even if you scroll all the way to the right in the table. In this example, turn this checkbox on.

- **Adjust heading row height**: In this example, turn on the "Auto-adjust header row heights" checkbox. When this setting is turned on, Project adjusts the row height of the table column heading to show the entire heading, increasing the height for narrow columns and decreasing the height as the column widens. With the checkbox turned off, the column heading still wraps, but some of the text disappears at the bottom of the cell.

- **Show "Add New Column":** In this example, turn on the "Show 'Add New Column' interface" checkbox, which means the rightmost column in the table is Add New Column. The section "Changing a Table's Contents" describes how to use this column to add new fields to a table.

Click OK to save the changes to the view and close the Table Definition dialog box. To see what the table looks like, in the More Tables dialog box, click Apply. Figure 20-8 shows what the new table looks like.

> **Tip:** To widen the columns, drag column dividers to the right, as described earlier in this chapter.

Task Name	Duration	Start	Finish	Actual Finish	Finish Variance
▲ Event_Ch20_start	390.88 d ⬍	Tue 6/1/21	Fri 12/2/22	NA	144 days
Project start	0 days	Tue 6/1/21	Tue 6/1/21	Tue 6/1/21	0 days
▲ Planning	101.17 days	Tue 6/1/21	Thu 10/21/21	NA	5.04 days
▲ Initial planning	18.75 days	Tue 6/1/21	Fri 6/25/21	Fri 6/25/21	3.75 days
Identify core event team	3 days	Tue 6/1/21	Thu 6/3/21	Thu 6/3/21	0 days
Define event goals and objectives	2 days	Fri 6/4/21	Mon 6/7/21	Mon 6/7/21	-3.88 days
Identify event requirements	4 days	Wed 6/9/21	Mon 6/14/21	###########	-3.88 days
Determine budget	3 days	Tue 6/15/21	Thu 6/17/21	Thu 6/17/21	-3.88 days
Prepare project definition	1.5 days	Sat 6/19/21	Tue 6/22/21	Tue 6/22/21	-2.71 days
Obtain approval to proceed	2 hrs	Fri 6/25/21	Fri 6/25/21	Fri 6/25/21	-2.88 days

Figure 20-8. *This is what the table created in this section looks like before widening the columns.*

Creating Your Own Views

When you don't have the information you need, making decisions becomes a matter of luck (just ask someone sitting at a blackjack table in Vegas). Yet too much data can obscure the information you need (as anyone trying to choose an insurance policy can tell you). But the right data shown in the right light exposes flaws, highlights solutions, and generally makes managing projects easier.

Modifying Basic View Contents

In Project, a view is nothing more than a compilation of many elements: fields, tables, filters, groups, and layouts (Microsoft calls these layouts *screens*, as you'll see shortly). To make big, sweeping changes, you can create a new view and choose the screen and other elements you want. For example, you may prefer to have a Gantt Chart in the primary (top) pane and the Task Details Form in the Details pane.

Modifying views gets a lot easier when you understand the difference between ***single*** and ***combination*** views. As its name implies, a single view is like a picture window that shows one thing, like the Resource Sheet or Task Sheet view. A combination view is like a window in which the top and bottom panes slide up and down; it can have one single view on the top and a different single view on the bottom, like the Resource Allocation view, which shows the Resource Usage view on top and the

Leveling Gantt view on the bottom. Figure 20-9 shows the components of the Resource Allocation view (click View→Other Views→More Views, and then, in the More Views dialog box, double-click Resource Allocation).

> **Tip:** If you decide that you want to go back to a built-in view's original definition, display the view. Then, in the View tab, click one of the view down arrows, and then choose "Reset to Default."

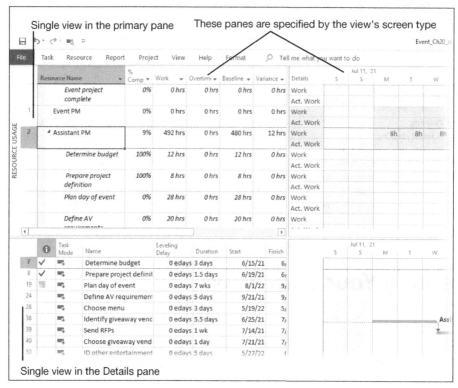

Figure 20-9. *View components.*

> **Note:** Some single views (like the Gantt Chart view) include two side-by-side panes: a table on the left and a timescale on the right. These side-by-side panes are features of the screens (described shortly) that the views use, which is why a Gantt Chart is still a single view. Combination views are ones that have a top pane and a bottom pane.

Most of Project's built-in views are single views. Gantt Chart, Task Usage, and Network Diagram views are all single views; you can display them in Project's primary pane or Details pane. For example, you often use the Gantt Chart view in the primary pane and the Task Form view in the Details pane while you're building your schedule (in fact, the built-in Task Entry combination view provides this very combination).

You get to modify different things in single and combination views. Here's what each one contains:

- **Single views**: In this kind of view, the *screen* is a basic layout of the view's elements (described in a sec). For example, all Gantt Chart views use a Gantt Chart screen with a table on the left and a timescale on the right. You can specify the screen you want to use *only* when you create a *new* view. In other words, you can't change the screen for an existing single view—built-in or custom, although you can change its other settings, including a table, group, and filter to apply to the single view.

- **Combination views**: A combination view is just a pairing of two single views, so you simply pick the views you want to see in the primary (top) and Details panes.

Screen Types

Project comes with many views that present project information in different ways, but they boil down to a few basic screen types. Each single view uses one of these screen types. (This chapter describes how to customize each type.) Here are the most common types and what they do:

- **Gantt Chart**: The charts project managers ogle every day are called Gantt Charts because Charles Gantt created a winner. This screen type lists project tasks and information about them in a table on the left side of the Project window. In the timescale on the right side, task bars visually indicate when tasks occur and how they relate to one another. With additional task bars to show slack time, progress, or delays, Gantt Chart views present a lot of what project managers need to know.

- **Usage**: Gantt Chart views don't show specific assignments or values for each time period, which is why you need usage views like Task Usage or Resource Usage. The usage screen has a table on the left like Gantt Chart views do, showing values and totals for tasks, resources, and their assignments. But instead of task bars on the right, the usage screen has another table, where the columns represent time periods. The rows show assignments with summary rows for each task or resource. Each cell in the timescale contains assignment (or summary) values for that period—for instance, work, baseline work, or cost for a day, week, or month.

- **Timeline**: The Timeline view (described in more detail later in this chapter) distills a project to a simple linear diagram. Out of the box, vertical lines in this view indicate the timeframe that's displayed in the timescale of a Gantt Chart or usage view. Point at either bar and the cursor changes to a two-headed arrow. At that point, you can drag that line to control the dates you see in the timescale. You can also add tasks to the timeline—for example, to keep project phases, key milestones, or ultra-critical tasks in view at all times.

- **Team Planner**: Team Planner view (available only in Project Professional /Project Online desktop client and described later in this chapter) includes a row for each project resource and the tasks to which it's assigned, like competitive swimmers lined up in a swimming pool. That's why these rows are referred to as *swim lanes*.

- **Resource Graph**: This screen type shows values for work, cost, and so on in a bar graph. Although the Resource *Usage* view shows resource allocation, the colored bars in the Resource Graph let you easily see when resources are overallocated or have time to spare.

- **Network Diagram**: Many project managers use network diagrams to define relationships between tasks and to evaluate the critical path. A network diagram includes a box (or node) for each task and lines for the relationships between them. However, because the diagram isn't drawn to a timescale, each task is the same size, which makes it easier for the eye to focus on task dependencies. In Project, you can build your schedule in the view you prefer and then let Project translate that info into a network diagram.

- **Calendar**: Gantt Charts take getting used to, but everyone understands calendars. This screen type lets you show tasks as bars spanning the days or weeks the way you mark off your much-needed vacation. The Calendar view is great for showing teams what their upcoming schedule looks like.

> **Tip:** The Task Sheet screen type is a view with only a table, which comes in handy if you want to enter data for a very large project. That's because Project doesn't have to spend time updating task bars in a timescale.

Depending on the work at hand, you can switch to the view that's most helpful. Within that view, you can change the information you see and how it's displayed. For example, when you're monitoring the critical path, red task bars let you more easily see critical tasks, and variance fields tell you whether progress compared with your plan is good or bad. And if none of the existing views are close to what you want, you can create a view from scratch. The following sections have all the details.

> **Tip:** Project is set up initially to display the Gantt Chart view with the timeline above it, which makes it easy to see your project schedule and adjust the date range. However, if you prefer to work with another view—for example, the Task Entry view, which includes the Gantt Chart in the top pane and the Task Form in the Details pane, or a custom view you create with the Gantt Chart on top and the Task Details Form on the bottom—you can change Project's default view. Choose File→Options. In the Project Options dialog box, click General. In the "Default view" drop-down list, choose the view you want Project to apply when you create a new project, and then click OK.

Modifying a Single View

The View Definition dialog box is command central for choosing settings for a view. It displays different settings depending on whether the view in question is a single view or a combination view. For a single view, you can choose the view's table, group, or filter. When you choose a table, group, or filter in the View Definition dialog box, the view opens every time with those choices in place, unless you then choose different elements in the View tab's Data section, which changes the view's definition.

Suppose you want to create a custom view based on the built-in Gantt Chart. Here's how to copy and then customize an existing single view:

Follow Along Practice

1. If you plan to use a table, group, or filter that doesn't exist, then create it **before** you open the View Definitions dialog box. In this example, you don't need to create any of these elements.

   You can't create elements on the fly in the View Definition dialog box. Creating a new table is described earlier in this chapter. For creating filters and groups, see Chapter 17.

2. In the View tab's Task Views or Resource Views section, click the down arrow next to any view's name (in this example, click the Gantt Chart down arrow), and then, on the drop-down menu, choose More Views.

   The More Views dialog box opens. It lists task-oriented or resource-oriented views depending on whether you clicked a down arrow in the Task Views or Resource Views section, respectively.

3. In the Views list, select the single view you want to use as a foundation, Gantt Chart, in this example, and then click Copy. (If you want to modify the view, select it, and then click Edit.)

   The View Definition dialog box opens with the single view settings (Figure 20-10). (If the View Definition dialog box opens with combination view settings instead, head to the next section of this chapter.) It lists the view's screen, but you can't edit it. To choose a different screen, you have to create a view from scratch (described later) or start with a view that uses the screen you want.

> **Note:** If you copy a view, Project opens the View Definition dialog box and automatically fills in the Name box with "Copy of [copied view name]."

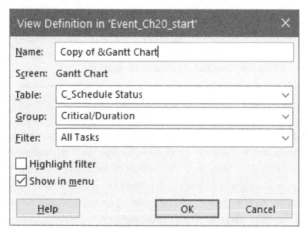

Figure 20-10. *The View Definition dialog box's heading ends with "in 'Project xyz,'" which tells you that Project stores the modified view in that particular project file.*

4. If you've copied a view, as in this example, type a new name for the view (in this example, replace the name in the Name box with **C_TroubledTasks**).

5. In the Table drop-down list, choose the table you want the view to display, in this example, Work.

    The tables you see in the drop-down list depend on whether you're editing a task or resource view. For example, if you edit the Gantt Chart or Task Usage view, the drop-down list contains task tables; if you edit views like the Resource Sheet and Resource Usage, then you see resource tables instead.

6. In the Group drop-down list, choose the group you want, in this example, Critical.

    Chapter 17 explains all about groups in Project. To forgo grouping, simply choose No Group.

7. In the Filter drop-down list, choose the filter you want to apply, in this example, C_Troubled-Tasks, if you created that filter in Chapter 17. Otherwise, choose the built-in Incomplete Tasks filter.

    Initially, a filter hides any items that don't pass its tests. But suppose you want a view that shows all tasks or resources but *emphasizes* the ones that pass the tests. In that case, turn on the "Highlight filter" checkbox, which uses blue text in rows that make the cut. To leave the view *unfiltered*, choose All Tasks or All Resources.

8. To list the view on drop-down menus for faster access, make sure the "Show in menu" checkbox is turned on.

    A single click on a view drop-down menu is all it takes to apply a view, including the ones you create yourself, as you can see in Figure 20-11. Because this is so handy, the "Show in menu" checkbox is turned on automatically, so you have to turn it off if for some reason you *don't* want the view in the drop-down menus. If you want to hide built-in views you never use, edit them and then turn off their "Show in menu" checkboxes.

9. Click OK.

    The View Definition dialog box closes. To apply the modified view, in the More Views dialog box, click Apply. (If you applied an interactive group or filter to the view, you'll see a dialog box that prompts you to enter a value. Fill in a value and click OK. If you applied the C_TroubledTasks filter, fill in *12/31/21* for the date that tasks should start by.)

    > **Tip:** If you make changes to a view as you work—for example, switching the table it uses, applying a group, or filtering the task list—you can quickly save the custom view as a new view or update the current view to include your edits. On the ribbon, click a view button's down arrow (for example, the Gantt Chart button on the Task tab), and then, on the drop-down menu, choose Save View. In the Save View dialog box, make sure the "Save as a New View" option is selected. (If you haven't made any changes to the current view, you won't see this option.) In the Name box, type a name for the view, and then click OK. Project saves the view with the table, fields, filters, and groups you've applied. To update the current view's definition with the changes you've made, select the Update Current View option, and then click OK. (If you haven't made any changes to the current view, you won't see this option.)

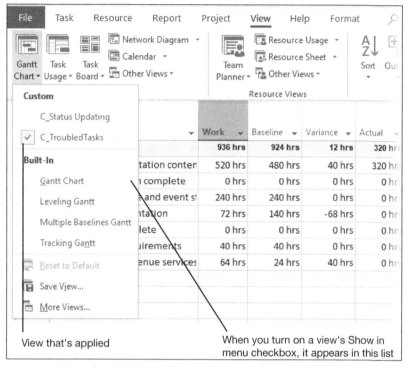

View that's applied

When you turn on a view's Show in menu checkbox, it appears in this list

Figure 20-11. *Views that you've created appear at the top of the menu under the Custom heading. Built-in views are listed under the Built-In heading, even if you've customized those views in some way. A checkmark to the left of a view's name tells you that view is currently applied.*

Modifying a Combination View

Project has only a few built-in combination views, such as Task Entry and Resource Allocation. Combination views are great because they display the single views you want in both the top and Detail panes. If you create your own combination views (described later), you can set them up to include the single views you want. (The note titled "One Pane or Two?" explains how to change the size of each pane or to hide the Details pane.)

Suppose you want to create a combination view that has the Gantt Chart on the top and the Task Details form on the bottom. Here are the steps for modifying a combination view:

Follow Along Practice

1. If you plan to use a single view that doesn't exist yet, create it first (as described in the next section).

    You can't create a new single view from within the View Definition dialog box.

2. In the View tab's Task Views or Resource Views section, click the down arrow next to any view button, and then, on the drop-down menu, choose More Views. In this example, click the Gantt Chart down arrow, and then choose More Views.

485

The More Views dialog box opens.

3. In the Views list, select the combination view you want to modify, in this example, Task Entry, and then click Copy.

    The View Definition dialog box opens with combination view settings.

4. If you copy an existing view, in the Name box, type the new name (*C_TaskEntryDetails*, in this example).

5. In the Primary View box, choose the view you want in the top pane (keep Gantt Chart, in this example).

6. In the Details Pane box, choose the view for the bottom Details pane (Task Details Form, in this example) shown in Figure 20-12.

7. Click OK.

    The View Definition dialog box closes, and the view is ready to use. To apply it, in the More Views dialog box, click Apply.

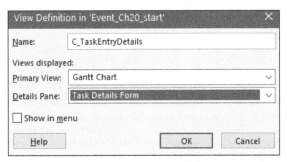

Figure 20-12. *When you modify a combination view, the only things you can change are the name of the view, which single views appear in the top and Details panes, and whether the combination view appears on view drop-down menus.*

Creating a New View

Most often, you create a new single view to choose the screen you want, because that's the one element you *can't* change when you edit a view. New combination views come in handy when you prefer a specific combination of views but don't want to touch the ones that Project provides. You've already seen how to create new views by copying existing views. You can also create new views from scratch.

Follow Along Practice

Here's how:

1. Click the down arrow on a view button, and then, on the drop-down menu, choose More Views. In the More Views dialog box, click New.

    The Define New View dialog box opens.

2. Select the "Single view" or "Combination view" option to create a single or combination view, respectively. In this example, select "Combination view." Click OK.

The View Definition dialog box opens and displays fields based on whether you are creating a single view or combination view.

3. In the Name box, type a name for the view, in this example, *C_TrackingDetails*.

4. Fill in the settings for the view.

    In this example, in the Primary View drop-down list, choose Gantt Chart. In the Details Pane drop-down list, choose Task Details Form.

    If you create a single view, you specify the screen, table, group, and filter to use.

5. Click OK. To apply the view, in the More Views dialog box, click Apply.

    Project saves the view and adds it to the list of custom views in your project. The note titled "Using New Views in Other Projects" explains how Project saves the views you create.

Using New Views in Other Projects

Suppose you modify a built-in view. Project stores this *modified* view in your Project file, so it shows the customized view each time you open it. If you want to use this modified view in *other* Project files, you have to use the Organizer to copy it into your global template or into another Project file. Chapter 23 describes how to simplify sharing customized elements with everyone in your organization.

If you want to keep Project's original views in addition to your custom versions, create a new view by copying an existing one *before* you modify it. Then you can use the original or your customized version. Bear in mind that changes in one view don't spill over into other views, which can be good or bad. The advantage to this barrier between views is that you can make scads of changes to a view without worrying about how those changes affect other views. The drawback is that you must repeat formatting in another view if you want to alter it in the same way.

In contrast to how it saves *modified* views, Project comes set up to automatically copy *new* views you create to the global template (whether you create them from existing views or create them from scratch), which is perfect when you work solo and don't have to worry about other people sharing your global template. However, if you and dozens of other project managers use the same global template, you may want to keep the new views you create in your file, to keep them from affecting other Project users. To change this setting, choose File→Options. In the Project Options dialog box, click Advanced. Under Display, turn off the "Automatically add new views, tables, filters, and groups to the global" checkbox. Then you have to use the Organizer to manually copy your new views to the *global.mpt* file.

Modifying a Gantt Chart View

A Gantt Chart view is a fertile field for customization. In the table area, you can apply various tables, which include columns of Project fields. The timescale displays task bars to show when tasks occur and how they relate to one another. Every component of a Gantt Chart view has its own customizing and formatting features:

- **Table**: The most obvious change is choosing a different table on the left side of the view. Within a table, you can add, remove, or rearrange columns; moreover, the columns' widths, titles, and alignments are at your command. The section "Changing Tables" is your guide to all these customizations.

- **Timescale**: The timescale on the right side of the view chops the project up into time periods, which you can change to fit the length of your project or what you want to focus on. Short projects may use days, whereas months may be better for multiyear projects. You can change the timescale's units, labels, and how many different units the timescale heading holds. If you want to change a Gantt Chart view's timescale and Timeline view is also open (in the View tab's Split View section, turn on the Timeline checkbox), you can simply drag one of the vertical bars in the Timeline view to change the date range or timescale units. See the section "Customizing the Timescale" for instructions. Dragging the Zoom slider when a view with a timescale is active also changes the timescale's date range and units.

- **Text**: Text is everywhere. You can modify text's appearance to highlight different information, like summary tasks or task bar text. You can also format only selected text. See the section "Formatting Text" to learn how.

- **Task bars**: Changing formatting on different types of task bars emphasizes information. For example, you can show critical task bars in red and noncritical task bars in blue. Or perhaps you want to display different types of task bars for each baseline you've set. You can modify the appearance of a whole category of task bars or just the task bars you select. Link lines and gridlines are customizable, too. The following sections explain how to change the appearance of task bars and other lines in the timescale.

Changing the Way Types of Task Bars Look

Task bars' color, fill pattern, and shape are all customizable, like the solid red fill for critical tasks, the dotted lines you see for splits in tasks, and the narrow bars that indicate progress. Task bars can also have marks at one or both ends, like the diamond for milestone tasks and the brackets at the ends of a manually scheduled task with defined dates.

Project has two categories of task bar formatting. You can specify bar styles to format *all* task bars in a specific category, like external tasks from other projects; this section describes the steps for formatting categories of task bars. On the other hand, you might want to highlight individual tasks that have special importance, like tasks whose completion trigger payments. In that situation, you can apply formatting only to the bars you select; the next section explains how to do that.

> **Tip:** When a Gantt Chart view is displayed, several changes to task bar appearance are available right on the ribbon. Head to the Gantt Chart Tools | Format tab's Bar Styles section, and then turn on a checkbox like Critical Tasks, Slack, or Late Tasks.
>
> With the Gantt Chart Style gallery, you can quickly change the colors of tasks set to Auto Scheduled and Manually Scheduled mode. When a Gantt Chart view is active, head to the Gantt Chart Tools | Format tab's Gantt Chart Style section and click one of the color combination buttons. The top task bar on the button represents manually scheduled tasks; the bottom task bar on the button shows the color for auto-scheduled tasks. The Gantt Chart Style section displays only a few buttons at a time (the exact number depends on the size of your monitor), but you can scroll to see additional color options.

Formatting a category of task bars is efficient because Project keeps track of the categories tasks fall into and changes their formatting if their category status changes. For example, when you're trying to shorten the schedule, you may want critical tasks' bars to appear in bright red with orange circles at the end. If a task falls off the critical path, the circles disappear and the color changes to that of a noncritical task. To change the look of a category of task bars, do the following:

Follow Along Practice

1. Display the Gantt Chart view whose task bars you want to format. In this example, display the built-in Gantt Chart.

    Bar style changes apply only to the active view in the active project. If you want task bars in another view to use the same formatting, then you have to repeat these steps for that view.

2. In the Format tab's Bar Styles section, click Format→Bar Styles. (Or double-click any working time period in the background of the Gantt Chart timescale—that is, anywhere in the timescale except on a task bar or a link line.)

    The Bar Styles dialog box opens.

    > **Note:** If you double-click nonworking time in the timescale—for example, the gray vertical bars that represent weekend days when the timescale shows individual days—the Timescale dialog box opens to the "Non-working time" tab, so you can format the appearance of nonworking time.

3. In the table, select the type of task bar you want to modify (in this example, Critical near the bottom of the list), and then, in the bottom half of the dialog box, click the Bars tab, shown in Figure 20-13.

    The Bars tab has three sections: Start, Middle, and End. The Start and End sections define the marks that appear at the beginning and end of a task bar. You can choose a shape, color, and whether the mark is solid or outlined. The Middle section sets the appearance of the bar itself.

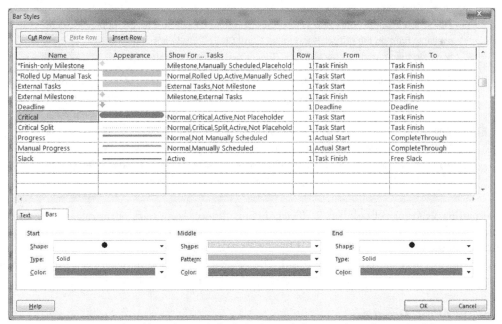

Figure 20-13. *The table in the Bar Styles dialog box includes a row for each type of task bar in the active view.*

4. To format the mark at one of the task bar's ends, in the Shape drop-down list (in either the Start or End section), select a shape. In this example, change the shape for both the start and end to a solid circle.

   Your choices include several geometric shapes: the familiar milestone diamond, various arrows, and even a star. The Shape drop-down list includes shapes for manually scheduled tasks, like the brackets that indicate that a task has a start or a finish date and the shaded ends that depict missing dates. Task bars don't *have* to have marks at the ends, so you can leave the Start and End boxes empty. To remove a mark, at the top of the Shape drop-down list, select the empty entry.

   If you choose a mark, Project initially fills in the Type box with Solid, which is usually the best choice, because it makes small marks more visible. You can also choose Dashed or Framed.

5. To change the color of a mark, you can choose it from the Color drop-down list. In this example, set the circles at the start and end to a dark orange.

   Try several colors until you find one that looks good. Darker colors are better, because bright colors like lime and yellow disappear into the white background.

6. To format the bar, in the Middle section, choose the bar shape you want. In this example, keep the bar shape set to the wide setting that's already selected.

   Bars can be wide, medium, or narrow, just like men's ties. When bars aren't full height, you can choose a position at the top, middle, or bottom of the task bar row. For example, regular and critical tasks are usually full height, progress bars are narrow bars in the middle, and slack is a narrow bar at the bottom.

Because narrow task bars take up less space, you can display more than one in the same task row. That's how the Multiple Baselines Gantt view (see Chapter 12) shows three baselines in the same row.

7. To apply a pattern and/or color to a bar, in the Middle section, choose the options you want. In this example, keep the Pattern set to solid. In the Color box, click the down arrow and choose bright red.

    Most task bars start with a solid pattern, although some tasks bar styles use other patterns, like the vertical hatching for splits in tasks. To emphasize task bars or to print a schedule on a black-and-white printer, use crosshatch patterns. Test colors to see how they look in the timescale. In the dialog box's table, the Appearance cell to the right of the task bar's name (Figure 20-13) previews your masterpiece.

8. To format a different type of task bar, select it in the table, and then repeat steps 4–7. In this example, don't format other bar styles.

9. When you're done, click OK.

    The dialog box closes, and the new formatting appears in the view.

Changing the Way Selected Task Bars Look

To change the look of individual task bars (for example, to change several sign-off meetings to purple bars), you format the *bars themselves*, not bar *styles*. Here's how:

Follow Along Practice

1. Select the tasks whose bars you want to format. In this example, select task ID 35 "Sign printing agreement," and task ID 41 "Sign giveaway agreement."

2. In the Format tab's Bar Styles section, choose Format→Bar. To format a single bar, double-click it in the timescale.

    The Format Bar dialog box opens to the Bar Shape tab, which has the familiar Start, Middle, and End sections with the same options that are available for bar styles (described in the previous section).

3. Pick the shapes, styles, pattern, and colors you want. In this example, don't choose marks for the start and end. In the Middle section, select a wide shape and set the pattern to solid. In the Color box in the Middle section, choose the purple box in the Standard Colors section of the drop-down menu.

    The preview appears at the bottom of the dialog box. (The background isn't white, though, so you can't accurately judge colors until you see them in the view.)

4. Click OK.

    The dialog box closes, and the selected bars sport their new look.

> **Tip:** If all you want to change about a task bar is its color, you can do that from the task bar mini-toolbar. Right-click the task bar you want to change. On the mini-toolbar that appears above the task bar, click the Bar Color down arrow, and then choose the color you want. Color-coordinated shades appear under the Theme Colors heading; basic colors appear in a row under the Standard Colors heading—or click More Colors to pick the exact hue you want.

Changing the Values that Appear on Task Bars

Project lets you attach fields to task bars so you can see key information right in the timescale. For example, displaying the initials of people assigned to tasks lets you see resources without checking the form in the Details pane or the finish date for a task.

Working with text on task bars is similar to working with the task bars themselves. You can specify the fields to display for a whole category of task bars, or assign fields to selected task bars. Actually, you can customize a task bar *and* its text at the same time, because the two tabs in the Bar Styles (and Format Bar) dialog box offer bar and text formatting options.

Follow Along Practice

To display fields as text for a category of task bars, follow these steps:

1. Display the Gantt Chart view whose task bars you want to format. In this example, display the Gantt Chart.

    Bar styles that you customize or create apply only to the active view in the active project. If you want task bars in another view to use the same formatting, then you have to repeat these steps for that view.

2. Go to the Format tab's Bar Styles section, and choose Format→Bar Styles or double-click any working time period in the background of the Gantt Chart timescale (that is, anywhere in the timescale *except* on a task bar or a link line).

    The Bar Styles dialog box opens.

3. In the Bar Styles dialog box's table, click anywhere in the row for the type of task bar you want to work on, in this example, select Task at the top of the list, and then click the Text tab.

    The Text tab displays fields already associated with the selected task bar type. Task bars have five places for text (although using them all makes the bars almost unreadable): left, right, top, bottom, and inside the bar.

4. Click the cell to the right of a position label, in this example, the cell next to the Right label. Click the cell's down arrow, and then choose the field to display at that position (in this example, Finish), as shown in Figure 20-14.

    Repeat this step to add fields at other positions. To remove a field, select the position box (Left, Right, or whatever), and then press Backspace. In this example, don't make any other changes.

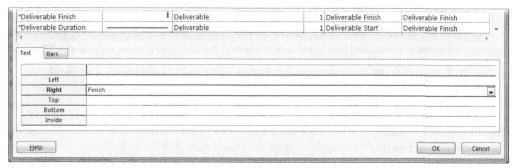

Figure 20-14. *The Start field obviously belongs on the left end of a task bar, and the Finish field belongs on the right.*

5. To add fields to another type of task bar, repeat steps 3 and 4. (Don't make other changes in this example). When you're done, click OK.

The Bar Styles dialog box closes, and task bars that fall in the categories you changed now show values.

> **Tip:** You may want to add fields to *individual* task bars—for example, to show the finish dates for a few key tasks. To do that, select the tasks you want to format (Ctrl-click anywhere in their rows in the view's table), and then in the Format tab's Bar Styles section, click Format→Bar. On the Text tab, choose the fields you want, and then click OK.

Designing Your Own Task Bar Style

Project views usually have several different task bar styles already defined. For example, the Detail Gantt view includes task bars for regular tasks, critical tasks, progress, milestones, slack, slippage, summary tasks, and more. But suppose you want a new type of task bar—for example, to highlight tasks added for change requests and flagged with the Flag1 field.

Designing a new task bar style involves more choices than modifying existing ones. You have to tell Project when to use the style and the dates to start and end the bar. To show off your creativity with a custom task bar, follow these steps:

Follow Along Practice

1. Display the Gantt Chart view whose task bars you want to format. In this example, display the Gantt Chart view, and, if necessary, apply the Summary table.

   Your task bar work of art applies *only* to the active view in the active project—unless you copy the view to the global template or another file (Chapter 23).

In this example, click the Add New Column heading, and choose the Flag1 column. For task ID 19 "Plan day of event," task ID 83 "Set up hands-on area," and task ID 84 "Set up presentation area furniture," change the Flag1 value to Yes. The task bar style you'll create will use this Flag field.

2. In the Format tab's Bar Styles section, click Format→Bar Styles or double-click any working time period in the background of the Gantt Chart timescale.

   The Bar Styles dialog box opens.

3. To insert the new task bar style in the middle of the list, select the row below where you want to insert the new row (in this example, Critical Split), and then click Insert Row.

   Project adds a blank row above the selected row. (The note titled "Task Bars Are Missing" explains why you might want to insert a row in a specific place in the list.)

Tip: If you want to base a new style on an existing one, you might be disappointed when you notice there's no Copy Row button. But you can fake it. Select the task bar style you want to copy, and then click Cut Row. The task bar style disappears from the table, but don't worry. Before you do anything else, click Paste Row to insert the row back into the table. Now click anywhere in the row below where you want the copy, and then click Paste Row again. The copied row appears above the row you selected, and you can modify it.

---

4. In the Name field, type a name for your task bar style, in this example, type **_CRTask_**.

   Make the name meaningful.

5. To tell Project which tasks it should apply the style to, select the style's Show For…Tasks cell. Click the cell's down arrow, and then choose the category of task to which this style applies, in this example, choose Flag1, as illustrated in Figure 20-15.

   The Show For…Tasks drop-down menu includes useful choices like Critical, Noncritical, In Progress, Not Started, Not Finished, and so on.

Note: Sometimes, a style applies to more than one condition in the drop-down list, like active tasks with the change-request flag turned on. To combine multiple conditions, choose the first one in the drop-down list. Without closing the list, type a comma, and then choose the second condition. Rinse and repeat to add more conditions. In this example, don't add other conditions.

A bar style can also apply when a condition _isn't_ true. Suppose you create a task bar style for active change requests. The combination "Active, Flag1" tells Project to use the style for active tasks with Flag1 set to Yes; the style wouldn't be applied to inactive tasks with Flag1 set to Yes. For change-request tasks that have been inactivated (Chapter 11), choose "Not Active, Flag1." (You have to type the _Not_ for these combinations.)

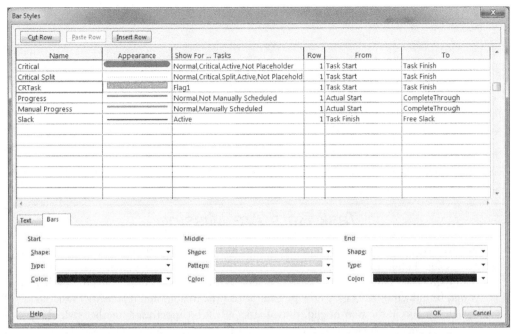

Figure 20-15. *You specify the conditions a task must meet for Project to apply the bar style.*

6. In the From and To columns, choose the date fields that specify when the task bar starts and ends. In this example, keep the From and To fields set to Task Start and Task Finish.

   For many task bars, the choices are easy: Choose Start in the From cell and Finish in the To cell to draw the task bar from the task's start date to its finish date. But other types of task bars use different dates. For example, a progress bar goes from the task's Start date to its Complete Through date. And slippage runs from the task's Baseline Start date to its Start date, to show how far the start has slipped.

7. On the Bars tab and Text tab, select the settings for the bar style and any fields you want to attach to the task bar. In this example, in the Middle section, change the color to a dark green.

   Formatting bars and text are described in earlier sections in this chapter.

8. To add more bar styles, repeat steps 3–7. (Don't add additional bar styles in this example.) When you're done, click OK. Figure 20-16 shows what the change request bar style looks like.

   Custom bar styles have a way of multiplying. For example, if you create a bar style for flagged tasks, you usually want another style for flagged milestones, and possibly flagged critical tasks. Simply repeat the steps in this list to create additional styles.

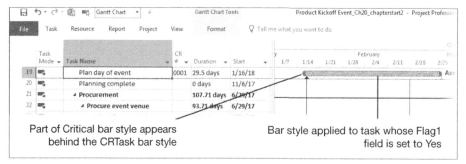

Part of Critical bar style appears
behind the CRTask bar style

Bar style applied to task whose Flag1
field is set to Yes

Figure 20-16. *The note titled "Task Bars Are Missing" explains why part of the Critical bar style appears behind the new bar style.*

Task Bars Are Missing

Project draws task bars in the timescale in the order they appear in the Bar Styles dialog box's table. Full-height task bars obscure narrow task bars drawn earlier, so that's why the Progress task bar style follows the Task style in the table. Otherwise, the progress bar would be hidden by the task whose progress it reports. In addition, if an earlier task bar style has marks at the start or end, those marks might be underneath another style that has no end marks, which is why the orange circles from the customized Critical bar style show up in Figure 20-16.

To make sure you can see all your task bars, you have to order task bar styles in the Bar Styles table with the same amount of care you use for the seating arrangements at a dysfunctional family reunion. To move a task bar style to another location, do the following:

1. Click anywhere in the row you want to move, and then click Cut Row. The row disappears from the table.

2. Select the row below where you want to place the cut row.

3. Click Paste Row. The new row appears above the selected row.

Stacking More than One Task Bar in the Same Space

While defining a new task bar style, you may have noticed the Bar Styles dialog box's Row column, which usually contains the number 1. This setting is the key to displaying more than one row in the timescale for each task. For example, the Tracking Gantt view uses narrow bars to show the baseline and current task bars in the same row, but if you'd rather use *full-height* task bars for each, then you can include current task bars on the first row and baseline task bars on the second row. Here's how it's done:

Follow Along Practice

1. Open the Gantt Chart view that you want to modify.

    In this example, apply the Tracking Gantt view. Then, on the View tab, click the bottom half of the Gantt Chart button, and choose Save View. In the Save View dialog box's Name box, type **C_FullBarBaseline**.

2. In the Format tab's Bar Styles section, click Format→Bar Styles.

    The Bar Styles dialog box opens.

3. In this example, select the Baseline row. In the Middle section of the Bars tab, in the Shape drop-down list, choose the wide task bar. Keep the Row cell in that row set to 1.

    By doing so, Project will display Baseline task bars with full height bars in the first row for a task. Use the Bars tab and Text tab to define the bar's appearance and text that surrounds it. For example, you might use a full-height task bar with blue diagonal lines for the baseline.

4. In this example, select the Task row at the top of the list. In the Middle section of the Bars tab, in the Shape drop-down list, choose the wide task bar. Set the Row cell in that row to 2.

5. In this example, select the Critical row at the top of the list. In the Middle section of the Bars tab, in the Shape drop-down list, choose the wide task bar. Set the Row cell in that row to 2.

    Project adds a second row to the timescale for each non-critical and critical task, as shown in Figure 20-17.

6. Repeat steps 3–5 to add other rows (up to four). In this example, simply click OK to close the dialog box.

    The rows in the table double (or triple, or **quadruple**, depending on your settings) their height, and the new bars appear for the tasks that meet the new task bar style's conditions.

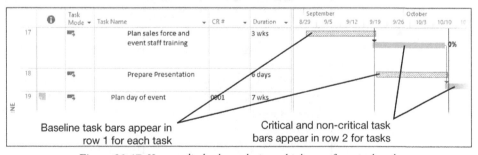

Figure 20-17. *You can display bar styles in multiple rows for a single task.*

Changing the Layout of Task Bars

You've probably struggled to follow link lines between predecessor and successor tasks. Even simple projects can look like a bowl of tangled spaghetti. You can modify the layout of task bars in the timescale to clear up clutter or improve readability. In addition to tweaking the appearance of link lines, you can change the height of task bars, roll up task bars from subtasks to summary tasks, and change the date format.

> **Note:** To follow along with this example, continue with the C_FullTaskBar custom view from the previous section.

To reach these layout options, in the Format tab's Format section, click Layout. Then adjust any or all of the Layout dialog box's settings:

Follow Along Practice

- **Link lines**: The Links section has three link-line options: completely hidden, an S, or an L. The S shape is best for visually separating link lines, and the L shape doesn't clutter the diagram as much. For the cleanest look, hide the link lines. In this example, select the L option (see Figure 20-18). To see what your settings looks like, click OK to apply the settings and close the Layout dialog box.

- **Task bar date format**: In the Layout dialog box, the "Date format" box sets the date format only for task bars. It's best to choose an abbreviated format (like 1/28), and leave the full dates to table columns. In this example, keep the date format as it is.

- **Task bar height**: With bar styles and bar formatting, you can choose task bars that are thin, medium, or full height. "Bar height" defines what that full height is; 12 is the standard. You can vary the height from 6 to 24. In this example, open the Layout dialog box if necessary, change the bar height to 8, and then click OK.

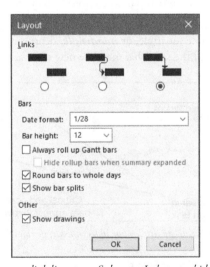

Figure 20-18. *You can set link lines to an S shape or L shape, or hide the links completely.*

- **Roll up task bars to summary tasks**: You know that summary tasks roll up field values like cost and work. The "Always roll up Gantt bars" checkbox is different; turning it on shows subtasks and milestones on summary task bars. But these roll-ups get messy fast. That's why, when the "Always roll up Gantt bars" checkbox is turned on, you can also turn on the "Hide rollup bars when summary expanded" checkbox. This hides the roll-up bars whenever the subtasks are visible and shows roll-up bars only when subtasks are hidden. In this example, open the Layout dialog box. Turn on the "Always roll up Gantt bars" checkbox and the "Hide rollup bars when summary expanded" checkbox. Click OK. Then, click the black triangle to the left of task ID 11 "Plan marketing" to collapse it to see what rolled-up Gantt bars look like.

- **Round bars to whole days**: Initially, Project draws task bars that represent the task's *exact* duration, so very short tasks practically disappear when the timescale is set to weeks or months. Turn on the "Round bars to whole days" checkbox to round out durations in the timescale to whole days. (Project still keeps durations in the *table area* exact.) In this example, don't change this setting.

- **Show splits**: Project chops up task bars into pieces if they contain *splits* (small delays between working times). Most of the time, you want to see splits (in this example, keep this checkbox turned on). But if they become too distracting, then turn off the "Show bar splits" checkbox, and Project draws the task bars as solid lines.

- **Show drawing shapes**: If you use Drawing commands (click the down arrow in the Format tab's Drawing section) to add shapes or text to the timescale, you can hide those shapes by turning off the "Show drawings" checkbox. In this example, keep this checkbox turned on.

Changing How Gridlines Look

Even the gridlines that separate table, timescale, and column-heading elements are customizable. For example, you can change the color of the lines that show the project's start date and the current date. And although the timescale doesn't draw lines between task bar rows initially, you can add them to make it easier to correlate bars to rows in the table.

> **Note:** To follow along with this example, you can continue with the C_FullTaskBar custom view from the previous section.

To format gridlines, follow these steps:

Follow Along Practice

1. Display the Gantt Chart view you want to modify, and then in the Format tab's Format section, click Gridlines→Gridlines.

   The Gridlines dialog box opens.

2. In the "Line to change" list, choose a type of line, in this example, choose Project Start at the bottom of the list.

   The "Line to change" list includes categories like Sheet Rows and Sheet Columns for the table, and categories like Gantt Rows and Current Date for the timescale.

3. In the Type drop-down list, choose the line style and the color you want. In this example, change the line style in the Type box to a solid line. Change the color to a medium blue, and then click OK. (Scroll in the timescale until you can see 6/1/21, which is the project start date.)

   You can choose from solid, dotted, short-dashed, and long-dashed lines. To remove a line, choose the white entry at the top of the list.

4. To draw lines at intervals—for instance, after every third row in the table—in the "At interval" section, select the option you want. In this example, reopen the Gridlines dialog box and select Gantt Rows in the "Line to change" list. In the Type box, select a dashed line style. In the "At interval" section, select the "4" radio button. Click OK.

   If the interval is larger than 4, select the Other option, and then type the number in the box. When you use intervals, select the line style and color for the intervals.

5. If you want to format another gridline, repeat steps 2–4. You don't have to change other gridlines in this example.

   When you're done making changes, click OK to close the Gridlines dialog box.

Customizing the Timescale

Views like the Gantt Chart view and Task Usage view have a timescale on the right side, which shows information over time. Because of this timescale, Gantt Chart task bars lengthen or shorten depending on their duration. In a usage view, each column of the grid is a time period, so you can see work or cost per day, per week, and so on.

> **Note:** Like other view customizations, timescale modifications apply only to the active view. They appear every time you use the view, but you have to repeat the changes to see them in other views.

Time units are the part of the timescale you change most frequently. For long projects, units like weeks or months squeeze more onto the screen. For short projects, units like days are better so the task bars don't look scrawny. And sometimes you might switch from months to weeks to focus on issues in part of a long project. You can customize other aspects of the timescale—for example, choosing the time period labels and their alignment, or shrinking or expanding columns to specific dimensions. A view can show up to three tiers of units in the heading area—for instance, to show the year on the top, then months, and finally weeks; or to show the fiscal year, and then fiscal quarters.

> **Tip:** To change time units quickly, drag the Zoom slider on the status bar at the bottom right of the window. Or, in the View tab's Zoom section, click the down arrow to the right of the Timescale box, and then choose the time units you want to display, which range from hours up to years.

To format the timescale, follow these steps:

Follow Along Practice

1. Display a view like a Gantt Chart view, usage view, or Resource Graph view. In this example, select the C_FullTaskBar custom view (or the Gantt Chart view if you didn't create the custom view).

    The view displays a timescale on the right side.

2. Double-click the timescale heading (or right-click the timescale heading, and then, on the shortcut menu, choose Timescale).

    Either way, the Timescale dialog box opens, as shown in Figure 20-19. The Middle Tier tab is selected initially.

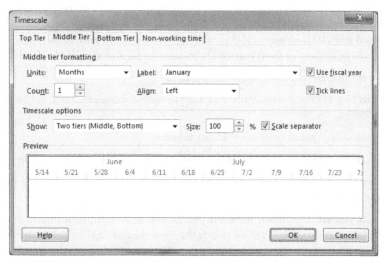

Figure 20-19. *The Timescale dialog box has four tabs: one for each tier of units that can be displayed at the top of the timescale, and the fourth for nonworking time.*

3. To change the number of tiers, under "Timescale options," choose a number in the Show dropdown list (in this example, "Three tiers (Top, Middle, Bottom).")

    When you choose two tiers, the timescale shows the middle and bottom tier; if you choose one tier, it shows only the middle tier.

4. Select the tab for the tier you want to format, in this example, Top Tier.

    The top, middle, and bottom tiers have the same settings: units, unit label, alignment, and so on.

5. In the Units box, choose the time unit you want to use for the selected tier, in this example, choose Years.

    Units for a lower tier must be equal to or shorter than the units of the tier above it. So if the bottom tier is days, for example, the middle tier can be days, weeks, or longer. In this example, the top tier is years, the middle tier is months, and the bottom tier is weeks.

6. Change how the tier label looks by choosing one of the formats in the Label box, in this example, keep the label set to "2009, 2010, …"

    The formats you see depend on the units you choose.

7. To position the label within its tier, in the Align drop-down list, choose Left, Center, or Right. In this example, choose Center.

    When the "Tick lines" checkbox is turned on, vertical lines appear between each period in a timescale tier.

8. To display the *fiscal year* instead of the calendar year, turn on the "Use fiscal year" checkbox. In this example, turn this checkbox off.

    You set the fiscal year in the Project Options dialog box (Chapter 15). For example, if the starting month is June and the calendar year in which the fiscal year *starts* denotes the fiscal year, then June 2021 is fiscal year 2021. However, if the fiscal year is based on the *ending* calendar year, June 2021 represents the beginning of fiscal year 2022, because the fiscal year ends in calendar year 2022.

9. To format the middle tier, select the Middle Tier tab.

10. In the Units box, choose the time unit you want to use for the selected tier, in this example, keep it set to Months.

    For the middle tier, typical units are weeks or months.

    After you save the timescale settings, the timescale will display 1-month intervals in the middle tier.

11. Change how the tier label looks by choosing one of the formats in the Label box, in this example, choose "Jan, Feb, ..."

    The formats you see depend on the units you choose. For example, formats for weeks include the robust "Sun January 23, 2009" as well as the most concise "23" (which is the first day of that week). Don't worry about the sample format showing a year in the past; the actual timescale labels show the correct year. Quarter formats include "1st Quarter," "Q1," and "Q1, Q2, Q3, Q4,… (From Start)," which numbers quarters sequentially from the project's start date.

12. To position the label within its tier, in the Align drop-down list, choose Left, Center, or Right. In this example, keep the Align setting equal to Left. Keep the "Tick lines" checkbox turned on.

13. Turn off the "Use fiscal year" checkbox.

14. To format the bottom tier, select the Bottom Tier tab.

    In this example, keep the Units, Label, and Align settings as they are. However, turn off the "Use fiscal year" checkbox.

15. To display an interval other than a single time unit, choose the number in the Count box. In this example, set Count equal to 2.

    The bottom tier will display 2-week intervals as shown in the preview in Figure 20-20.

16. If necessary, adjust the settings in the "Timescale options" section.

    Although the "Timescale options" section is below the tier-formatting section, the timescale options apply to all tiers, so you have to adjust them on only one tab.

If the headings in the Preview section are scrunched up, then increase the percentage in the Size box. The Size box is like zooming: Increasing the percentage from 75% to 100% stretches each time unit out, which is helpful when task bars are too skinny. If you see pound symbols (#) instead of values in a usage view, increase the percentage until the values appear. Decreasing the percentage squeezes the periods together to fit more duration on the screen. In this example, change the Size value to 75.

Keep the "Scale separator" checkbox turned on to draw horizontal lines between each tier.

17. To control how nonworking time *looks* on the timescale, select the "Non-working time" tab.

These settings don't change the nonworking time itself. (See Chapter 3 to learn about defining working and nonworking time in Project calendars.) Nonworking time starts as gray shading behind task bars. You can change that color and pattern, which calendar the nonworking time comes from, and whether to hide nonworking time or to draw it in front of task bars. In this example, don't change the settings.

18. When you're finished, click OK.

The dialog box closes, and your changes appear in the timescale.

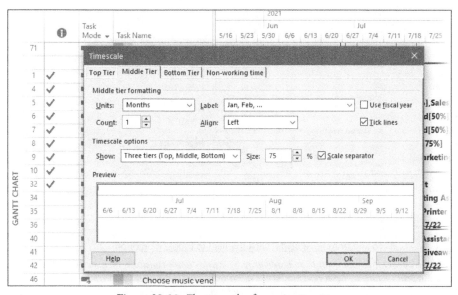

Figure 20-20. *The timescale after saving its settings.*

Changing a Usage View's Appearance

Usage views like Task Usage and Resource Usage have a table on the left and a timescale on the right, both of which you can customize. Unlike the timescale in a Gantt Chart view, the usage timescale is a grid in which each column represents one time unit, like a day or week, and each row represents an assignment or a summary row. This presentation is known as *time-phased data*. Chapter 15 includes an example of customizing a usage view to compare budget values to actual values.

> **Note:** This section describes how to choose which fields appear in a usage view's times-cale and how to format their values. The note titled "Quickly Change Column Widths" describes a shortcut for changing the width of columns in the usage timescale. See other sections in this chapter for info on customizing tables, text, and timescale settings.

To choose fields to show in a usage view, follow these steps:

Follow Along Practice

1. Display a usage view like Task Usage or Resource Usage. In this example, display the Task Usage view. (If a filter prompt appears, click Cancel to close it.) Then, on the View tab, click the Task Usage down arrow, choose Save View, and name the view **C_CustomUsage**.

2. In the time-phased grid, right-click any cell, and then, on the shortcut menu, choose Detail Styles, as shown in Figure 20-21.

    The Detail Styles dialog box opens. (If you right-click the timescale *heading* instead of the grid, then you see a shortcut menu for formatting the timescale heading and changing working time.)

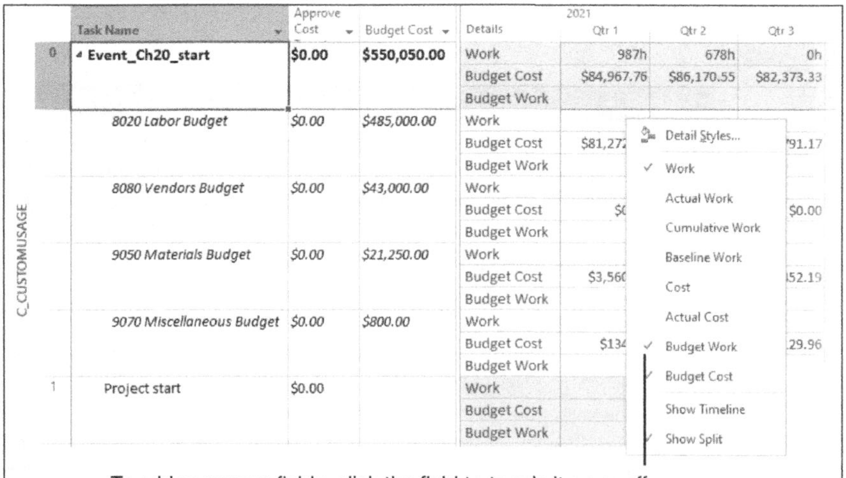

Figure 20-21. *If all you want to do is add or remove fields in the timescale, then on the shortcut menu, click a field's name, which toggles between displaying and hiding the field. A checkmark appears to the left of the field name when the field is displayed.*

3. In the Detail Styles dialog box, select the Usage Details tab, if necessary.

    This tab includes a list of fields you can add to the timescale: work fields, cost fields, allocation, performance measures like CV, and so on.

4. To add a field to the timescale, in the "Available fields" list, click the field's name, and then click Show. In this example, add Actual Work, and then click OK to save the change.

    The field jumps to the "Show these fields" list, as illustrated in Figure 20-22, and Project adds a new row for the field to each assignment.

504

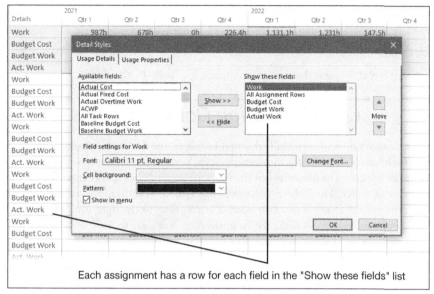

Each assignment has a row for each field in the "Show these fields" list

Figure 20-22. *Adding, removing, or rearranging the fields in the "Show these fields" list changes the rows displayed in the usage view timescale.*

> **Tip:** To add more than one field, in the "Available fields" list, Ctrl-click each field's name, and then click Show. You can rearrange the order of the fields by selecting a field in the "Show these fields" list, and then clicking the Move up or down arrows.

5.   Remove a field by selecting it in the "Show these fields" list and then clicking Hide. In this example, hide Budget Cost and Budget Work.

6.   To format the timescale cells for a field, click the field name in the "Show these fields" list, and then change the settings in the dialog box's bottom half. In this example, don't change any settings.

The built-in views use a light-gray background for the task or resource summary rows. The assignment rows have a white background. You can choose a different font, background color, or background pattern. If you want the field to be listed on the shortcut menu that appears when you right-click a cell in the timescale grid, turn on the "Show in menu" checkbox. That way, you can easily turn the field on or off simply by choosing it on the shortcut menu.

7.   If you want to format the view's column headers and detail data, select the Usage Properties tab, and then choose the settings you want. In this example, don't change any settings.

Typically, these settings are fine as they are. The "Align details data" box controls whether values in cells are aligned to the left, center, or right. When "Display details header column" is set to Yes, the timescale starts with a column that shows the field names for each row. (Changing this box to No isn't a good idea, because it means you have to remember which row is which when you type or review values.) The "Repeat details header on all assignment rows" checkbox is turned on initially

---

so that each row has a header. The "Display short detail header names" checkbox is turned on to abbreviate field names so that the first column is as narrow as possible.

8. Click OK.

The dialog box closes, and the changes you made appear in the timescale.

Quickly Change Column Widths

Because usage values often include decimal numbers, the timescale columns may display pound symbols (#) because the numbers don't fit. You can format the timescale to increase the size of the columns (described in the previous section), but it's faster to drag to make the columns wider. Move the pointer between two column headings in the timescale. When the pointer changes to a two-headed arrow, drag to the right until the column is wide enough for values. To make the columns narrower, drag to the left.

If a combination view has timescales in the top and bottom panes, then changing the column width in one pane changes the column width in the other pane, too. For example, if you display Task Usage view in the top pane and Resource Graph view in the Details pane, dragging a column's edge in either pane adjusts the column's width in both so the views stay in sync.

Customizing the Timeline

The Timeline view is a great way to summarize what's going on in a project, whether you want to sum up when project phases start and finish, highlight crucial milestones, or keep an eye on an important task that's delayed. In addition, the Timeline view makes it easy to share high-level project information with others, because you can copy what you see in this view to an email message or to another program. And the Timeline view can control the timeframe shown in a Gantt Chart view's timescale. In Project, you can even display multiple timelines at the same time, for example, to show project phases and milestones in one timeline and crucial tasks in another.

Like other Project views, the Timeline view has its own set of customization tools. You can drag its vertical bars to change the timescale dates and scale. By adding tasks to the timeline, you can emphasize key tasks—such as payment milestones or critical tasks—in a simple linear diagram. This section describes how to add tasks to the view's timeline, change how tasks look on it, and adjust the information that appears in them.

Note: In this example, display the Gantt Chart view before starting to work on the Timeline view.

Follow Along Practice

To display the Timeline view, head to the View tab's Split View section and turn on the Timeline checkbox. To work with or customize the timeline, click the Timeline pane and then click the Format tab, shown in Figure 20-23.

When the Timeline view and a Gantt Chart view are displayed at the same time, the Timeline view is initially set so you can drag its vertical bars to change the dates that appear in Gantt Chart view's timescale. The secret to this behavior sits on the Format tab. In the Show/Hide section, the Pan & Zoom checkbox is turned on by default (in this example, keep it that way). To keep the Timeline view set to the full project date range instead, turn off the Pan & Zoom checkbox.

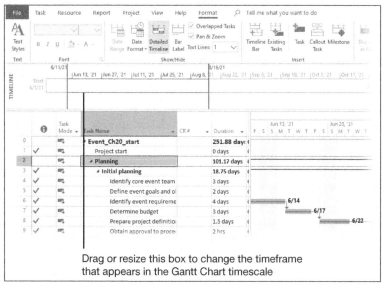

Drag or resize this box to change the timeframe
that appears in the Gantt Chart timescale

Figure 20-23. *The box in the Timeline represents the visible timeframe in the Gantt Chart view. You can drag or resize that box to change the timeframe in the Gantt Chart.*

> **Note:** You have to choose between displaying the Timeline view *or* the Details pane (the bottom view pane in the Project window). To display the Timeline view, in the View tab's Split View section, turn on the Timeline checkbox. If you turn on the Details checkbox there, Project automatically turns *off* the Timeline checkbox, and vice versa.

Adding Tasks to the Timeline

Work tasks, summary tasks, and milestones are all fair game for Timeline view. When you add tasks to the Timeline view, it indicates progress with different colors. For example, the portion that's complete appears in a darker color, while the incomplete portion is a light gray. You can add tasks to the timeline in several ways:

Follow Along Practice

- **Right-click a task**: In any task-oriented view, like Gantt Chart or Task Usage, right-click a task's Name cell, and then choose "Add to Timeline" on the shortcut menu that appears. In this example, right-click task ID 3 "Initial planning" and then click "Add to Timeline."

- **Drag a task to the timeline**: In any task-oriented view, click a task's ID cell (in the leftmost column of the table). When the pointer changes to a four-headed arrow, drag it to the timeline. In this example, drag task ID 11 "Plan marketing" to the timeline.

- **Add existing tasks**: If necessary, click the Timeline view to make it the active view. In the Format tab's Insert section, click Existing Tasks. In the "Add Tasks to Timeline" dialog box that appears, turn on the checkboxes for the tasks you want to add to the timeline. In this example, turn on the checkboxes for the Procurement summary task, the "Pre-event activities" summary task, and the "Event setup" summary task. Then, click OK.

- **Insert a new task**: In the Format tab's Insert section, click Task to insert a new task as a task bar in the Timeline view; click Callout Task to insert a new task as a *callout* (explained in the next section); or click Milestone to insert a new milestone. When you click any of these buttons, the Task Information dialog box opens so you can name the task, set its start and finish dates, or specify other task information. In this example, click Callout Task. In the Name box, type *Make final payment*. In the Duration box, type *1d*. Type *5/12/22* in the Start box and Finish box. Then, click OK.

See Figure 20-24 to see what these tasks look like.

> **Note:** Although you can add a manually scheduled task to the timeline, the task appears only if it has at least one specified date. If it has only one date (start or finish), it appears as a milestone; if it has both a start *and* a finish date, it appears as a task bar.

Displaying More Than One Timeline Bar

If your management team doesn't care for Gantt Chart presentations, you can set up a Timeline view with several timeline bars, each showing a different aspect of the project. For instance, you can start with a high-level timeline bar that shows project phases and key milestones, while a second timeline bar show key tasks in progress.

Follow Along Practice

In Project, the Format tab includes the Timeline Bar button in its Insert section. To add another timeline bar, just click that button. Figure 20-24 includes two timeline bars.

In this example, click the new timeline bar. In the Format tab's Insert section, click Existing Tasks. Turn on the checkboxes for the tasks starting with "Procure event venue" and ending with "Venue acquired." Each timeline bar can have its own date range. To set a timeline bar's date range, right-click the bar and choose Date Range on the shortcut menu. In the Set Timeline Dates dialog box, select the "Set custom dates" option, and then fill in the start and finish dates for the bar. In this exmapl,e set the start to 6/20/21 and finish to 12/31/21.

You can also label each timeline bar to identify what it represents. To label timeline bars, on the Format tab, click Bar Label in the Show/Hide section. In the Update Bar Names dialog box, fill in the labels for each bar and then click OK. In this example, label Bar 1 as "Whole project" and Bar 2 as "Venue."

Changing the Appearance of Tasks on the Timeline

The Timeline view can display tasks as task bars or as callouts (Figure 20-24 shows examples of each). Task bars are useful for displaying tasks with long durations, like the summary tasks for project phases. Callouts make it easier to see tasks with short durations like milestones, and are also helpful for displaying several tasks that occur at the same time.

In addition to choosing between task bars and callouts, you can also customize the appearance of text and dates in the timeline. Here's how to format the appearance of tasks on the timeline:

Follow Along Practice

- **Display a task as a bar or callout**: When you select a task in the timeline, the Format tab's Current Selection section highlights the button that represents the task's current appearance: "Display as Bar" or "Display as Callout." To change the task from a bar to a callout, click "Display as Callout." In this example, click the "Define AV requirements" bar, and then click "Display as Callout." Click the "Choose venue" bar, and change it to a callout. To change a callout to a bar, click "Display as Bar." You don't have to change any callouts into bars in this example.

- **Remove a task from the timeline**: To remove a task, select it, and then choose "Remove from Timeline." In this example, select the "Procure event venue" bar, and choose "Remove from Timeline."

- **Format text styles**: You can modify the appearance of different categories of timeline text just as you can in other views. In the Format tab's Text section, click Text Styles. The section "Formatting Text" at the end of this chapter provides the full scoop on formatting text styles.

- **Format text**: Any text in the timeline is fair game for unique formatting. For example, you may want deliverable milestones to stand out. Right-click the text you want to format (in this example, the "Make final payment" callout in the top timeline bar), and then choose formatting commands from the mini-toolbar that appears (change the font to size 10 and the font color to blue). Or select the text, and then in the Format tab's Font section, click the settings you want to adjust. Either way, you can change the text's font size, color, formatting (bold or italic), and background color.

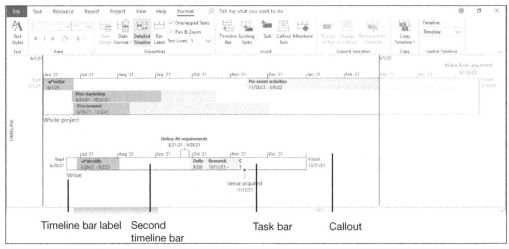

Figure 20-24. *Here is an example of two timeline bars showing different information about the same project.*

Customizing the Info on the Timeline

You can also control the *amount* of information you see in the Timeline view. For example, you might opt to keep the date format short and sweet, or to hide task names and dates. If you add lots of tasks to the timeline, you can choose how many lines of text appear in task bars and whether you want to see tasks that overlap. (You don't have to change any of these settings in this example.) Your options all reside in the Format tab's Show/Hide section:

- **Format dates**: Click the Date Format down arrow, and then choose a date format for the timeline. The choices are the same ones you can choose in Project Options (choose File→Options; in the Project Options dialog box, click General, and then click the "Date format" down arrow). When space is at a premium, use abbreviated formats like 1/28. For more detail, choose a format like Wed Jan 28, '09 (that's right—the format example in Project is based on the year 2009). At the bottom of the Date Format drop-down menu, you can turn the checkmarks on or off to show or hide task dates, today's date, and timescale dates.

- **Show timeline details**: For tasks you add to the timeline, click Detailed Timeline to toggle between showing only bars and showing bars that contain the tasks' names and dates.

- **Show tasks that overlap**: Turn on the Overlapped Tasks checkbox if you want to see *all* the tasks added to the timeline, even if they overlap date-wise (Project adds rows to the timeline to show more tasks on the same dates). If you turn this checkbox off, the timeline shows only the first task for a set of dates.

- **Set the number of text lines in task bars**: In the Text Lines drop-down list, choose the number of lines of text you want to see in tasks you add to the timeline. Initially, only one line of text appears. For longer task names, choose 2 or 3. Although you can choose up to 10 lines of text, keep in mind that larger values mean the timeline takes up more room on the screen.

Sharing the Timeline

After you get the timeline just so, you can copy it to share with others. In the Format tab's Copy section, click Copy Timeline, and then choose how you want to share the timeline—for example, by email or pasting it into another program. Project places the timeline on the Clipboard, so you can paste it into an email message, Word document, PowerPoint slide, or another program file.

In this example, hide the Timeline view (in the View tab's Split View section, turn off the Timeline checkbox).

Customizing the Team Planner View

The Team Planner view (Chapter 7) is resource-centric: It contains a row (also known as a *swim lane*) for each resource and, in that same row, shows the tasks to which the resource is assigned. To change the appearance of the Team Planner view, display the view (on the View tab, click the Team Planner button) and then click the Format tab. Many of the formatting options should be familiar: You can format text styles and change the appearance of different types of tasks.

The Team Planner view has a few unique formatting options. Here are your choices on the Team Planner view's Format tab:

Follow Along Practice

- **Show parent tasks**: The Team Planner view starts out showing *all* subtasks, which means that each bar in the view shows the name of the actual task. To see a summary of your project, in the tab's Format section, click Roll-Up, and then choose the outline level you want to see. That way, instead of the subtask names, bars show the parent task names for the outline level you specify. In this example, click Rollup, and then choose Level 1. Review the bars in the swimlanes, which now represent only Level 1 tasks. Then, click Rollup again, and choose All Subtasks.

- **Format gridlines and text**: In the tab's Format section, click Gridlines, Text Styles, or enter the number of lines of text you want the view to display in task bars. (See the "Formatting Text" section for the lowdown on text styles and the "Changing How Gridlines Look" section for info on formatting gridlines.)

- **Format task bars**: The Styles section of the tab has commands for formatting categories of tasks. You can change the border color and fill color for auto-scheduled, manually scheduled, external, and late tasks. You can also specify how to display the actual work that's been done. In this example, you don't have to change any settings.

- **Prevent Overallocations**: This setting is turned off by default and you should keep it that way. If you turn on Prevent Overallocations and assign a task to a resource whose time is already fully allocated for those days, Project automatically moves the task to the resource's next available time. If you turn this setting off and assign a task to a resource who's already fully allocated for those days, Project leaves the task where you placed it and draws red brackets around the overallocated sections of task bars. See the Chapter 7 section "Don't Let Team Planner Resolve Overallocations" to get the full scoop on the Prevent Overallocations command.

- **Expand resource rows**: This checkbox is turned on initially, which tells Project to expand a resource's row if you assign multiple tasks to the resource during the same timeframe. You should keep it set that way. If you turn the checkbox off, you see only the first assigned task for those days.

- **Show unassigned tasks**: This checkbox is turned on initially, which is what you want. That way, the view's bottom pane shows tasks that aren't assigned to specific resources, so it's easy to see which tasks still need resources.

- **Show unscheduled tasks**: This checkbox is also turned on initially, so that manually scheduled tasks without dates appear in the Unscheduled Tasks column, which is also what you want. That makes it easy to see which tasks need additional information.

Customizing the Resource Graph View

The Resource Graph view is a bar graph of resource data by time period. Although the bars in the Resource Graph view are vertical, the right side of the view is still a timescale with values indicated by the height of the bars. Choosing fields to include in Resource Graph view, shown in Figure 20-25, is similar to choosing fields in a usage view. As in a Gantt Chart view, you can change the appearance of bars and categories of text. The following sections explain your options.

Follow Along Practice

In this example, display the Gantt Chart. Then, in the View tab's Split View section, turn on the Details checkbox, and then choose Resource Graph in the drop-down list. In the Gantt Chart view, select task ID 19 "Plan day of event." In the Resource Graph, scroll in the left panel until Jaye Smith appears.

Choosing Fields to Display

To choose fields in the Resource Graph view, right-click the background of the view's timescale, and then, on the shortcut menu, choose the field name. In this example, keep Work displayed. (You can also head to the Resource Graph view's Format tab and choose the fields in the Graph drop-down list.) Here's what each field represents (listed here in the order they appear in the shortcut menu):

- **Peak Units**: The highest percentage of units assigned to a resource during a period on the graph. Units higher than the resource's maximum units appear as an overallocation (in red by default). See Chapter 7 to learn more about how the Peak field works.

- **Work**: The hours assigned to a resource during a period. If the assigned hours are more than the resource's total available hours (based on maximum units ***and*** the resource calendar), the excess hours show up as overallocated.

- **Cumulative Work**: The total work assigned to the resource since the beginning of the project.

- **Overallocation**: The hours that the resource is overallocated during the period.

- **Percent Allocation**: The work assigned as a percentage of the resource's available time.

- **Remaining Availability**: The resource's available hours that haven't been assigned. This field is helpful for finding someone with available time who can pitch in on assignments.

- **Cost**: The total of the labor cost and per-use cost for the resource during the period.

- **Cumulative Cost**: The total cost for the resource since the beginning of the project.

- **Work Availability**: A resource's total available hours based on its maximum units and resource calendar. (Unlike Remaining Availability, this field *doesn't* subtract hours for existing assignments.)

- **Unit Availability**: This field is Work Availability as a percentage.

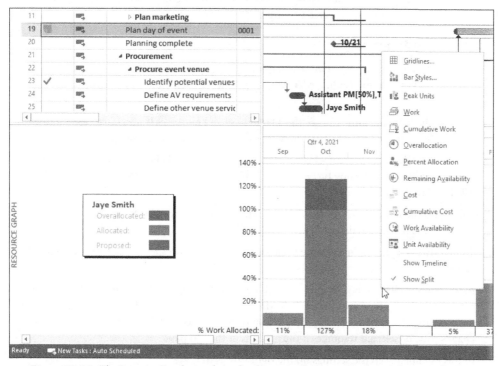

Figure 20-25. *The Resource Graph view has a few formatting limitations: you can't format individual bars and text, and you can pick fields only from the fixed list that the view offers.*

Changing the Way Resource Graph Bars Look

The Bar Styles dialog box for the Resource Graph view contains boxes for formatting each type of bar, but the information that the bars represent changes depending on the information you choose to display in the Resource Graph view itself. For example, if the graph shows a work-related field (like Work), then you can format bar styles for overallocated work, allocated work, and proposed bookings. If the Resource Graph view displays cost, the bar styles include resource cost and proposed bookings.

> **Note:** The Resource Graph view displays different information depending on whether it's in the top pane or the Details pane of a combination view. For example, if the Gantt Chart view is in the top pane, the Resource Graph view in the Details pane shows data for one resource at a time for the resources assigned to the selected task (you can scroll in the Resource Graph view's left pane to see values for other resources). On the other hand, if the Resource Graph view is in the top pane, you can tell it to show values for all resources or for a filtered list of resources.

The Resource Graph view draws separate bars for the selected resource and the group of filtered resources so you can compare values. Here's how to modify the Resource Graph view to show bars for both filtered resources and the selected resource:

Follow Along Practice

1. In this example, display the Resource Graph in the top pane. (On the View tab, turn off the Details checkbox. In the Resource Views section, click Other Views, and then choose Resource Graph.)

2. Scroll in the left pane until you see the Marketing Lead resource. If necessary, scroll in the timescale on the right until you see bars showing the work assigned to the resource.

3. In the View tab's Data section, click the Filter down arrow and choose Resource Range in the drop-down list. In the dialog box that opens, fill in the first box with **8** and the second box with **10**. Then, click OK.

    This filters the resource list to show the resources with resource IDs 8 through 10, which are the people in the marketing department.

4. To modify bar styles, right-click the background, and then, on the shortcut menu, choose Bar Styles.

    In the Bar Styles dialog box, the settings on the left side relate to a larger group of tasks or resources: all tasks, if the Resource Graph is in the Details pane, or filtered resources if the graph is in the top pane. The settings on the right side apply to selected tasks if the Resource Graph is in the Details pane or selected resources if the graph is in the top pane.

5. In this example, keep the settings on the right side as they are.

    These settings display allocated work up to the resource's maximum availability as blue bars and overallocated work as red bars, as shown in Figure 20-27.

6. To display work allocated to the filtered resources, on the Bar Styles dialog box's left, in the "Allocated work" section, choose Area in the "Show as" drop-down list. In the Color drop-down list, choose a medium green.

    You can have Project draw values in different ways by choosing one of the following from the "Show as" drop-down list:

    *   **Bar**: Displays a separate bar for each time period.

- **Area**: Fills in a triangular or trapezoidal area equal to the value, which can span one or more periods.

- **Step**: Instead of separate bars for each period, all adjacent bars are drawn as one filled-in area.

- **Line**: Draws only the boundary of the area you see when you choose the Area option.

- **Step Line**: Draws just the border of the Step filled-in area.

- **Don't Show**: Doesn't show the value on the graph.

7. In the Bar Styles dialog box, turn on the "Show availability line" checkbox to see a separate line for resource availability, as shown in Figure 20-26.

   The availability line compared with the height of bars is a great way to see how much work you can still assign. If you include filtered resources, the availability line shows total availability for the filtered resources. If the graph shows bars only for the selected resource, the availability line is availability for that resource.

   The "Show values" checkbox is turned on by default, and that's usually what you want. With this setting turned on, the graph displays the numerical values that the bars represent below each bar.

If you don't want to see something in the graph, choose Don't Show in the "Show as" menus.

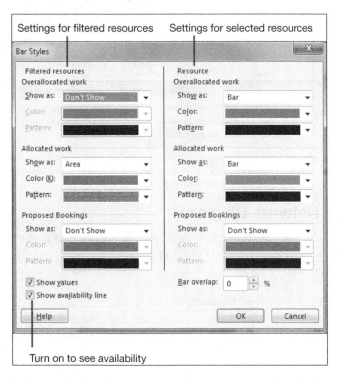

Figure 20-26. *You can display information about filtered resources as well as the selected resources.*

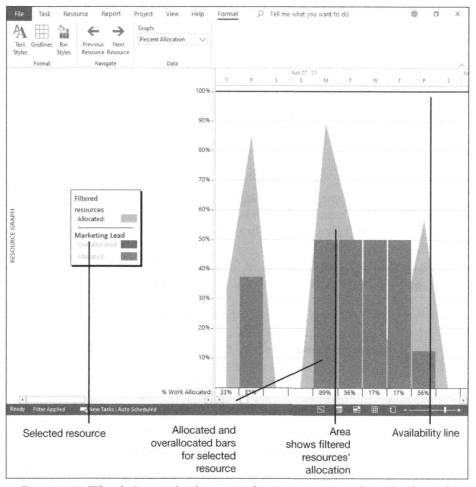

Figure 20-27. *When the Resource Graph appears in the primary pane, it can show values for specific resources as well as for filtered resources.*

Modifying a Network Diagram

A project-management network diagram is a latticework of boxes (called *nodes*) with link lines connecting them. The boxes represent project tasks, and the link lines are the same task dependencies you see in a Gantt Chart view.

Before the dawn of computers and Microsoft Project, a network diagram was where you manually calculated the early start, early finish, late start, and late finish dates that identify the critical path. Happily, you no longer need a network diagram and an abacus to calculate the critical path, because Project does it for you.

The Network Diagram view helps you work on task dependencies, because it doesn't show time at all. Whether a task takes 1 day or 6 months, its box in the network diagram is the same size, and its successor task is right next door. Because this view doesn't have a table area, task fields appear within each network diagram box. Choosing fields to display in boxes is the most common way to customize this view, but you can also change the appearance of boxes and how Project lays them out. The following sections explain your options.

Choosing Fields and Formatting for Network Diagram Boxes

Project's views are simply different ways of looking at the same information. In the Network Diagram view, boxes replace the task bars you see in a Gantt Chart view. And just as you can attach fields to each side of a task bar, network diagram boxes can contain several task fields. You can pick any fields you want to see and change what the boxes look like.

Like bar styles for a Gantt Chart view, box styles for a network diagram set the content and appearance of boxes within a category, like Critical, Critical Summary, or Noncritical External. To format a category of boxes, follow these steps:

Follow Along Practice

1. In the Task tab's View section, click the down arrow on the Gantt Chart button, and then, on the drop-down menu, choose Network Diagram.

    The Network Diagram view appears, showing each task in its own box. Every box is the same size, regardless of the duration of the task.

2. On the Format tab, click Box Styles (or double-click the background of the network diagram).

    The Box Styles dialog box opens and lists the box styles for the active view, as shown in Figure 20-28.

> **Tip:** To format individual boxes instead of categories, select the boxes you want to format, and then, on the Format tab, click Box (or double-click the border of a box in the diagram). In this example, you don't have to format any individual boxes.

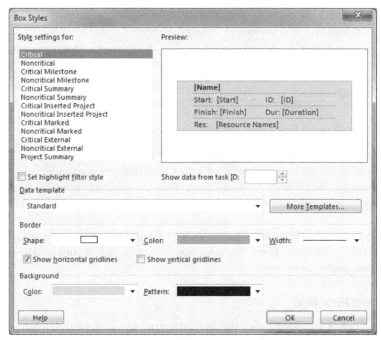

Figure 20-28. *In the "Data template" field, you can choose a template that specifies which task fields appear in each network diagram box and other settings like font and alignment.*

3. In the "Style settings for" list, select the category of box you want to format, in this example, choose Critical.

    The categories for network diagrams focus on critical and noncritical tasks. Most of the categories are a combination of critical or noncritical and another condition like milestone, summary, marked, or external.

4. To choose the fields that appear in a box, in the "Data template" drop-down list, choose the template you want to apply. In this example, choose Cost.

    Data templates define a set of fields and their position in a box. To see which fields a template includes, select it in the drop-down list, and then look at the box in the Preview area. To see what a box looks like with real data, in the "Show data from task ID" box, choose a task ID number, in this example, type *19*.

    To choose exactly the fields you want—for instance, to include a custom field, to create a new data template, or to modify an existing one—click More Templates. In the Data Templates dialog box, choose a template (in this example, Standard), and then click Edit or Copy. (Or click New to start one from scratch.) The Data Template Definition dialog box opens, as shown in Figure 20-29.

    To pick a field in the data template, in the "Choose cell(s)" section, select a cell. Click the down arrow that appears in the cell, and then, in the drop-down list, choose the field's name. If you want to change the number of rows and columns in a box, click Cell Layout. When you're done with the template, click OK to close the dialog box.

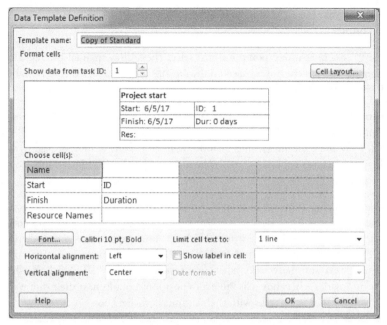

Figure 20-29. *You can modify a data template to include the fields you want.*

5. In the Box Styles dialog box's Border section, select the shape, color, and width of the box border. In this example, don't make any changes.

    Turn on the "Show horizontal gridlines" checkbox or "Show vertical gridlines" checkbox to add horizontal or vertical lines between the fields inside a box. To choose a different background color or pattern for the box, use the Background drop-down lists. Check the preview when you choose colors and patterns to make sure the fields are still legible.

6. To change the formatting for another category, repeat steps 3–5.

    When you're done, click OK to close the Box Styles dialog box.

Laying Out Boxes

The Network Diagram view lays out tasks like a flowchart, with link lines flowing from predecessor tasks to successor tasks. You can change the arrangement of boxes, including the alignment between rows and columns, the spacing between boxes, row height, and column width. You can also draw link lines straight from one box to the next, or use a combination of horizontal and vertical line segments. Your layout choices also include color selections and a host of other options. To make these kinds of changes, on the Network Diagram view's Format tab, click Layout to open the Layout dialog box, and then adjust the following settings:

*   **Manual or automatic layout**: In the Layout Mode section, the "Automatically position all boxes" is selected initially, which means you entrust positioning to Project, and that's usually what you want. The program uses the "Box layout" settings to arrange and space boxes. When this option is selected, make sure that the "Adjust for page breaks" checkbox is also turned on, so

Creating Your Own Views

Project doesn't place boxes on top of a page break (which means the box appears on two pages when you print).

If you can't resist fine-tuning box positions, select the "Allow manual box positioning" option. Project initially lays out the boxes based on the settings in the Box Layout section, but you can also move the boxes by dragging them to new positions.

- **Box layout**: The Box Layout section controls where boxes are and which boxes you see. The Arrangement drop-down list includes layouts like Top Down From Left and "Top Down - Critical First." The Row and Column settings include alignment (Left, Center, or Right), spacing (in pixels) between rows and columns, and box width and height. In this example, you don't have to make any changes.

Unlike the organizing influence of summary tasks in a Gantt Chart, summary tasks tend to muddle the Network Diagram view, which is why turning off the "Show summary tasks" checkbox is a good idea (in this example, turn it off). Without summary tasks, you can see the relationships among work tasks more clearly. On the other hand, if you link summary tasks to other tasks, then keeping the "Show summary tasks" checkbox turned on shows all your links. The "Keep tasks with their summaries" checkbox tells Project to position subtasks near their summary tasks. In this example, turn off the "Keep tasks with their summaries" checkbox.

> **Tip:** It's easy to change a few network diagram display settings right from the Format tab. For example, to turn off summary tasks, simply turn off the Summary Tasks and Project Summary Task checkboxes. And to display link lines as straight lines, turn on the Straight Links checkbox.

- **Link line look**: The Link Style section lets you switch link lines from rectilinear (horizontal and vertical segments) to straight from one box to another. The "Show arrows" checkbox is turned on initially, and that's usually what you want. You can also add task dependency text (like "FS" for finish-to-start) on link lines by turning on the "Show link labels" checkbox. In this example, select the Straight option.

- **Color**: The Link Color section starts with critical links set to red and noncritical links set to blue. If you use other colors for critical and noncritical, choose them in this section. In this example, don't change any colors.

- **Other options**: The Diagram Options section is a hodgepodge of settings: background color, background pattern, whether page break lines appear in the diagram, whether to show in-progress and completed tasks, and whether to hide all the fields except the ID (perfect when you're concerned only with task dependencies). In this example, don't change any of these settings.

When you're done changing settings, click OK to close the Layout dialog box and apply the new settings to the Network Diagram view.

Customizing the Calendar View

The Calendar view is great for showing teams what they're doing during a particular period, as Figure 20-30 shows. The bar styles, text styles, and gridlines are all within your aesthetic control. You can also customize the timescale for bars and change the calendar to show 1 week, several weeks, or whole months. In the Calendar view, move to the next or previous period by clicking the left or right arrows just below the Month, Week, and Custom buttons. For example, when the calendar shows an entire month, the left arrow switches to the previous month.

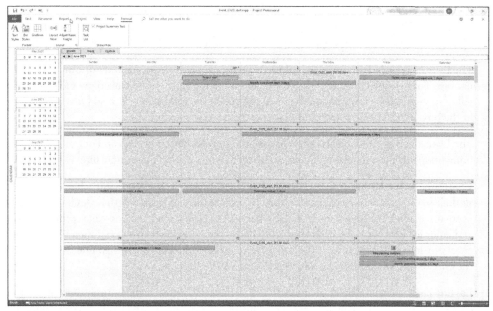

Figure 20-30. *To display the Calendar view, on the View tab, click Other Views, and then choose More Views. In the More Views dialog box, double-click Calendar.*

> **Note:** The Calendar view is different from a project, resource, or task calendar (Chapter 3). It's like the electronic version of an appointment book filled in with project tasks and assignments. Project, resource, and task calendars, on the other hand, are like the shift schedules that workers receive, telling them which days they work or have off, and which shifts they work, but not what work they do during that time.

Here's an overview of the Calendar view's settings (you don't have to modify the calendar view in this example):

- **Choose a time period**: The Calendar view displays 1 month at a time initially, but changing the time period is easy. Above the calendar, click Month, Week, or Custom. If you click Custom, the Zoom dialog box opens so you can set a number of weeks or the specific dates you want to see. Alternatively, you can drag the status bar's Zoom slider to see shorter or longer periods.

- **Add a monthly preview**: Out of the box, the Calendar view displays a preview of the previous, current, and next month like many paper calendars do. If you don't want to see these previews, right-click the calendar's background and then, on the shortcut menu, choose Timescale (or simply double-click anywhere in the calendar). In the Timescale dialog box, click the Week Headings tab, and then turn off the "Display month pane" checkbox.

- **Format the timescale**: Right-click the calendar's background, and then choose Timescale (or double-click anywhere in the calendar) to open the Timescale dialog box. Click the Week Headings tab and, in the Monthly, Daily, and Weekly titles drop-down lists, choose titles for months (for instance, January 2009 or 1/09—yes, Project uses examples based on the year 2009), weeks (1/28 or M 28), and days (Monday, Mon, or M). To focus on weekdays, select the "5 days" option. For round-the-clock operations, "7 days" shows every day of the week.

  The Date Boxes tab determines the information that appears at the top and bottom of each calendar box. For example, the day of the month sits at the top right, and the overflow indicator (which tells you there's more information than you can see) at the top left. You can add text at each corner of the box.

  The Date Shading tab controls how working and nonworking time appear. For example, initially, nonworking days on the base calendar are shaded, while working days are white.

- **Customize calendar bar styles**: Calendar bars are different from their Gantt Chart siblings, so their bar style options are different, too. To change the way calendar bar styles look, in the Format tab, click Bar Styles. You can use a bar, a line, or just text, and you can set the pattern and color for each type of bar. In the Field(s) box, click the down arrow, and then turn on the checkbox for the field you want to display inside bars. To include more than one field, turn on the checkboxes for additional fields, and then press the Enter key.

- **Layout tasks**: Head to the Format tab and click the small arrow at the bottom right of the Layout section to open the Layout dialog box. Initially, the calendar displays tasks based on the sort order that's applied (ID, initially). If you select the "Attempt to fit as many tasks as possible" option, then the calendar sorts tasks by Total Slack and then by Duration. Turn on the "Automatic layout" checkbox to tell Project to reapply the layout options as you add, remove, or sort tasks.

Formatting Text

Different Gantt Chart views may show the critical path in red or slack time as narrow green lines, but text appears in the same old 8-point Arial font. Project's ***text styles*** make it easy to format text for different categories of information, like row and column headings, text for critical tasks, or text at the same position on task bars.

Whether you want to emphasize critical tasks with bold red letters or your tired eyes beg for larger text, you can use text styles to change formatting quickly and keep formatting consistent. Simply choose the type of information to format (headings, milestones, and so on) and the text formatting you want (font, size, style, color, and background color). Or you can reformat a single string of text for special emphasis, like the "Manager of the Year" caption under your boss's picture. This section explains how to do both.

Changing Categories of Text

Project text styles are watered-down versions of their Word cousins: Project doesn't let you change as many text characteristics. Just as a heading style in Word changes all the headings in a document, a text style drapes itself over every occurrence of text in its category. Set the text style for milestone tasks to bold green Verdana font, for example, and the text for every milestone task follows suit. When a task's or resource's values change and it no longer fits the category, Project takes care of changing the text formatting to the style for the task's or resource's new category. Here's how to format text using text styles:

Follow Along Practice

1. Open the view in which you want to format text, in this example, Gantt Chart.

   You can use text styles in any kind of view.

   > **Tip:** When you modify text styles, the changes appear only in the active view in the active project. You can't copy these text styles to other views; you have to repeat the text style formatting in each view you want to use it in. On a brighter note, once you modify a view to use attractively formatted text styles, you can use the Organizer (Chapter 23) to copy that view to your global template or to another Project file.

2. Go to the view's contextual Format tab. In the tab's Format section, click Text Styles.

   The Text Styles dialog box opens.

3. In the "Item to Change" drop-down list, choose the category you want to reformat, in this example, Milestone Tasks, as shown in Figure 20-31.

   The categories you can format are built in, so you can't add your own. The last two items in the "Item to Change" drop-down list (which is closed in Figure 20-31) are Changed Cells and Inactive Tasks. Changed Cells corresponds to Project's change highlighting feature. Choosing Inactive Tasks lets you change the appearance of tasks that you set to inactive.

   If you want to format *all* the text in a view—for instance, to enlarge text for your aging stakeholders—select All in the "Item to Change" drop-down list. The formatting changes you make will apply to all text in the active view, including table headings, table text, and task bar text.

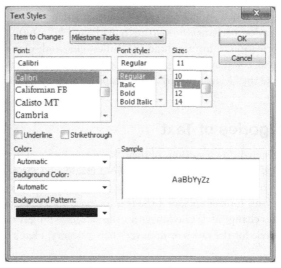

Figure 20-31. *You choose the category of text you want to format, and then specify how you want the text to appear.*

4. Choose the font, font style, and font size you want for the category. In this example, keep the Font set to Calibri. Change the font style to Italic. Change the Size to 12.

   The Font list displays the fonts installed on your computer. Font Style represents formatting like bold and italic. The Size list includes standard font sizes, but you can type a number in the Size box to pick a size that's not listed. You can also turn on the Underline checkbox to underline text, although underlining gets lost in view tables.

5. In the Color drop-down list, choose the color you want. In this example, keep the color set to Automatic.

   Colors other than black can be hard to read, although dark colors are better than light shades. Look at the text after you've formatted it, and maybe print samples in both color and black and white to make sure the colors work.

   > **Tip:** If you want Project to take care of choosing text color, background color, and background pattern, then in the Color, Background Color, and Background Pattern drop-down lists, choose Automatic.

6. To highlight cells that use the text style, in the Background Color drop-down list, choose the color you want, in this example, choose a light gray.

   Similar to the shading Project applies to changed cells, you can change the background color for critical tasks, summary tasks, and so on. If you tend to print to black-and-white printers, then it's a good idea to choose a background pattern in the Background Pattern drop-down list instead, because these patterns show up even in black and white. The Sample box shows you what your formatting choices look like.

7. Click OK.

    The Text Styles dialog box closes. Any text in your selected category displays the new formatting, as shown in Figure 20-32.

> **Tip:** A clever extension of background color makes change highlighting possible. In the Text Styles dialog box, the "Item to Change" drop-down list has a Changed Cells entry. If you select this entry, then the Preview area shows the light-blue highlighting that appears when cell values change. If you can't see the light blue due to color blindness, or if you simply prefer a different color, then in the Background Color drop-down list, choose the color you want instead. Once you click OK, cells burst into your favorite color whenever an edit you make changes their values.

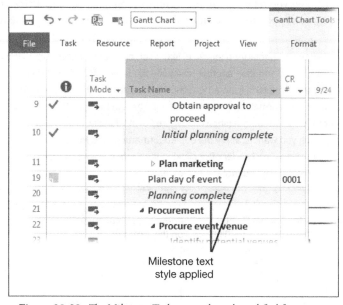

Figure 20-32. *The Milestone Tasks text style with modified formatting.*

Changing Selected Text

Suppose a couple of tasks are on a significant duration-cutting diet, so you want them to stand out from everything else. You can format text that you select down to an individual cell in a table. Formatting selected text is a snap with the mini-toolbar that appears when you right-click a cell, shown in Figure 20-33. You can apply the same kinds of formatting as with text styles, but the basic steps are a little different:

Follow Along Practice

1. Select all the cells with the text you want to format (in this example, the Task Name cell for task ID 29 "Sign venue contract and pay deposit"), and then right-click one of the selected cells.

   Select a single cell, several cells, a row, or several rows. The formatting commands format whatever text is selected.

2. On the mini-toolbar that appears above the shortcut menu selection, click the formatting commands you want. In this example, click the Bold button and change the color to blue.

   The first line of the toolbar has drop-down lists for fonts and font sizes. The second line has buttons for changing text to bold or italic, choosing a cell background color, and choosing text color. The selected text immediately displays its new formatting.

If you get the bloated tasks you reformatted under control, you have to select their text again to remove the special formatting you applied—there's no way to automatically undo the formatting you added.

> **Tip:** Say you apply a special font, font size, text color, and background color to the troubled tasks in your project, and then another task joins the ranks of troubled tasks. Fortunately, you can copy the formatting from an existing troubled task to the new one. To do this, select the text with the formatting you want to copy. Then, in the Task tab's Clipboard Group, click the Format Painter button (shown in Figure 20-33). Finally, click the cell that contains the text to which you want to apply the copied formatting, and Project formats it the same way. If you click a column *header* after clicking the Format Painter button, Project formats all the text in that column, but not the header itself.

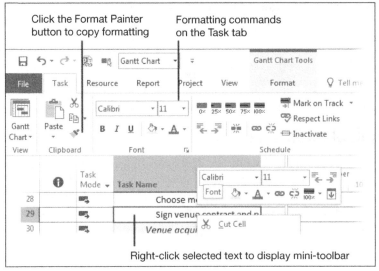

Figure 20-33. *Use the mini-toolbar that appears when you right-click something to change the font, font size, font color, bold, italic, or cell background color.*

21

Customizing Fields

Project comes with hundreds of built-in fields that track all sorts of information about projects. Although you can't mess with many of Project's built-in fields, like Duration, Start, and Cost, the program offers dozens of fields that you *can* customize. If you want to track values that Project's built-in fields don't cover, you can modify settings for custom fields and then add those fields to tables in Project views (Chapter 20) just as you would any built-in field. For example, you can customize fields to keep track of change requests and the effect they have on your project. In an IT project, you could customize fields for lines of code written or agile story points to track programming progress and productivity.

You can create custom fields that accept only the values you want by defining ***lookup tables***. That way, you or anyone else can pick a valid value from a drop-down list. Custom fields can also contain formulas to calculate results. The usual arithmetic suspects like addition, subtraction, division, and multiplication show up as buttons in the Formula dialog box. But Project offers all sorts of fancy functions that you can combine with any Project field to spit out the answers you're looking for.

Graphical indicators make it easy to see whether a project is on track, going better than expected, or headed for trouble. By customizing fields, you can tell Project to display icons instead of numbers or text.

Outline code fields work like the WBS values that project managers know and love. You can set up outline codes to categorize tasks and resources, and each level of the outline can have its own rules for values and what those values represent. Outline codes can be flexible and let people fill in whatever values they desire, or they can use lookup tables, if you have a specific set of values you allow.

This chapter explains how to customize fields in all these ways.

> **Note:** If you've downloaded files from the book website, you can follow along using the file Event_Ch21_start.mpp.

Understanding Custom Fields

The field drop-down list that appears when you insert a column into a Project table is proof of how many fields Project has. For built-in fields, your customization options are limited. You can change the title that appears in a table column's heading, its width, and the alignment of its text. But the field's behind-the-scenes calculations and data are set in stone.

Custom fields come in the same data types as Project's built-in fields. Project has one set of customizable fields for tasks and a similarly named set for resources. (To see the custom fields for a specific data type, click the down arrow to the right of the Type box, and then choose the custom field data type you want.) Here are the different types of customizable Project fields:

- **Cost**: Cost1 through Cost10 are currency fields for tracking anything that represents money. For example, you can set up a custom cost field to track the cost that change requests have added to the project. You could use a resource custom cost field to store resources' billing rates.

- **Date**: Date1 through Date10 are date fields—for instance, you can set up a custom Date field with a formula to calculate the date halfway between a task's start and finish date.

- **Duration**: Duration1 through Duration10 contain units of time. For example, you could use custom duration fields to store your optimistic and pessimistic estimated durations for tasks.

- **Finish**: Finish1 through Finish10 are date fields. Although these are custom fields, Project stores finish dates for interim plans in Finish1 through Finish10. So if you save interim plans, then leave Finish1 through Finish10 alone and use Date1 through Date10 for your custom dates instead.

- **Flag**: Perfect for tagging tasks or resources, Flag1 through Flag20 are fields that contain either Yes or No. What they say yes or no *to* is up to you. For example, you can use a flag field to designate the tasks for change requests. In addition, you can define a bar style when a custom flag field value is Yes, for example, to display a special task bar for all the tasks whose change request flag field is Yes.

> **Tip:** The Marked built-in field works similarly to a flag field. You can define text styles or bar styles (see Chapter 20) for records whose Marked values are Yes. For example, you could change Marked cells for new tasks to Yes. That way, Project would display the table text with the text style for Marked tasks and display the task bars for new tasks with the bar style for Marked Tasks. (Once the tasks no longer count as new, you have to change the Marked cells to No.)

- **Number**: Because number fields are so versatile—lines of code, lines of code per day, defects reported, and so on—Project provides 20 number fields: Number1 through Number20.

- **Start**: Like their finish date counterparts, Start1 through Start10 are date fields, which Project uses to store start dates for interim plans. If you save interim plans, use Date1 through Date10 for your custom dates instead.

- **Text**: Each of the 30 text fields, Text1 through Text30, can hold up to 255 characters. For short notes, a custom Text field can go right in a table next to another custom field to which it relates—for example, identifying the status of a change request. Notes (Chapter 4) are another way to annotate tasks and resources, especially when the notes are long or you want to insert pictures or objects.

- **Outline Code**: Outline Code1 through Outline Code10 represent a hierarchy of values, which you set up with a code mask (described later in this chapter). For example, you can use an outline code for skill sets, departments within an organization, and so on.

Customizing a Field

Custom fields let you specify how they look and behave. You can change the name of a custom field from, say, Text1 to something more meaningful, like Risk_Owner. You can use a formula to calculate a field's values or create a lookup table to help others pick valid values. How values roll up to summary rows is customizable, too, whether you want a total like other Project fields or another calculation like minimum, maximum, or average. Initially, fields display values, but you can define graphical indicators instead. For example, you can use stoplight colors to indicate whether a measure is on track, on thin ice, or in need of resuscitation.

This section begins with the basics: choosing a field's data type, whether it applies to tasks or resources, and picking the specific custom field you want to work on. From there, you can jump to other sections to learn how to work with lookup tables, formulas, calculations, graphical indicators, and the other available settings. (Because outline codes work a little differently, they warrant their own section "Coding Tasks and Resources.")

No matter which type of custom field you choose, what you can customize remains the same. Here are the basic steps for defining a custom field:

Follow Along Practice

1. In the Project tab's Properties section, click Custom Fields.

    The Custom Fields dialog box opens.

2. Select either the Task option or the Resource option.

    Project has two sets of custom fields: one for tasks and another for resources. The field *names* are the same, but the *fields* are different. For example, you can customize a Number1 task field to store percentage cost increase and a Number1 resource field to store a person's performance rating. When you insert a field into a table, the custom field you get depends on the table. For example, in the Resource Sheet, the Number1 field is the resource field. In a Gantt Chart view, the Number1 field is the task field.

> **Note:** If you use Project Professional with Project Online/ Server, the Custom Fields dialog box's Project option is also available, so you can define project-level custom fields (known as Enterprise Custom Fields).

3. In the Type drop-down list, choose the type of field, as shown in Figure 21-1.

Once you choose a Type option, the Field list displays the fields for the selected data type. (If you've renamed a field, you see the field's name *and* its updated name [a.k.a. alias] in the list.)

Figure 21-1. *Select the Task option or Resource option and then select the type of custom field you want to customize.*

4. In the Field list, select the field you want to customize, in this example, choose Cost7.

You can choose any field in the list. If you decide to customize a field you've already used—for example, to calculate values with a formula—you may see a warning that the calculated values will overwrite any existing data.

5. To give the custom field a more meaningful name, click Rename.

Custom field names start as a combination of the data type and a numeric ID; for instance, Cost3 is the third custom cost field.

> **Tip:** Although you can change the title in a column heading cell in a table (Chapter 20), the edited title applies only to the current table. (If you hide the column in the table, the edited title won't appear if you re-insert the column later on.) Renaming a custom field is the best approach because it displays the alias in drop-down lists and every time you insert the field in a table.

6. In the Rename Field dialog box, type a new name for your custom field (in this example, **CR Cost Delta**), and then click OK.

   Whenever you customize a field, rename it so its alias describes what the custom field is for. The alias and the original field name both appear in the field list, as shown in Figure 21-1. If you try to rename a custom field using an alias that you've already applied to another custom field, Project warns you that the name is already in use.

7. If you don't want to do any other kind of customization, then click OK. In this example, click OK. (You'll make other changes to the field later in this chapter.)

   The Custom Field dialog box closes, and you can insert the renamed field in a table.

At this point, the custom field accepts any value you enter as long as it's the right data type. For example, if you use a custom number field in a table, Project complains only if you try to type a date, some text, or any other value that isn't a number.

Creating Lists of Valid Values

Some custom fields are cut and dried. Flag fields accept Yes or No; those values appear in a drop-down list in a Flag cell. On the other hand, although Text fields expect text, they don't care what that text is. So if you want people to enter correct or at least **consistent** values, it's a good idea to provide some hints about valid values. For example, if the Text25 field is supposed to contain change request status, you don't want people typing anything they please. Likewise, you wouldn't want one person to type "Submitted" to indicate the change request has been submitted to the review board and someone else to type "Sbm." You can control the values that a custom field accepts with a **lookup table**—a list of valid values.

You can set up a lookup table to enforce a fixed list of values or to accept additional values not on the list. When a lookup table allows other values, the choices already there act as examples of what's expected. To build a lookup table for a custom field, in this case, a text field for tracking change requests status, follow these steps:

Follow Along Practice

1. In the Project tab's Properties section, click Custom Fields.

   The Custom Fields dialog box opens with the Task option selected.

2. In the Type drop-down list, choose Text. In the Field list, select the field you want to customize, in this example, choose Text25. Click Rename and name the field **CR Status**.

3. In the "Custom attributes" section, click Lookup.

   The "Edit Lookup Table for [field name]" dialog box opens. Project adds the name of the field or its alias to the title bar.

4. In the Value column, select a blank cell, and then type a value, in this example, **Submitted**. In the Description cell, type a description of the value, such as "CR submitted."

If you enter a value that doesn't match the type of field, Project turns the value red and bolds it. As soon as you correct the discrepancy, the value turns black and unbolded.

Descriptions are optional, but they can be useful to people filling in values. If you include a description, then the value and the description both appear in a table cell's drop-down list. For example, the description cell can spell out an abbreviation. That way, people know that "Sub" means Submitted, not Subcontractor.

5. Repeat step 4 to add more values to the list. In this example, add Evaluation, Pending, Approved, and Denied.

   If the lookup table values are available elsewhere, such as Excel or cells in the Resource Sheet view, you can also copy and paste lookup table values. The note titled "Reusing Lookup Tables" describes another shortcut to building a lookup table.

   The Edit Lookup Table dialog box has buttons for inserting, removing, copying, and rearranging the values in the lookup table, as Figure 21-2 shows. The first two row buttons, Cut Row and Copy Row, both place the row on the Clipboard so you can then relocate it by clicking Paste Row. To insert or remove rows, click either cell in the row, and then click Insert Row or Delete Row. Another way to rearrange rows is to click either cell in the row and then click the Move up and down arrows to the right of the lookup table

Figure 21-2. *Use the buttons above the lookup table to rearrange the entries.*

6. If you want the custom field to automatically fill in a value, click the cell that contains the default value (in this example, Submitted), and then click Set Default.

When you do, Project automatically turns on the "Use a value from the table as the default entry for the field" checkbox and changes the font for the default value to blue and bolded.

> **Note:** If you're wondering why the "Display indenting in lookup table" checkbox is grayed out, it's reserved for outline codes (described later in this chapter).

7. To display lookup values in a drop-down list in the order they appear in the Edit Lookup Table dialog box, expand the "Display order for lookup table" section (click the + button to the left of the label) and be sure to keep the "By row number" option selected. In this example, use this option.

    This option is ideal when you want to show the more frequently used values at the top of the drop-down list.

    If you want to sort the entries, in the "Display order for lookup table" section, select either the "Sort ascending" or "Sort descending" option, and then click Sort. When you select a sort order and then click Sort, Project re-sorts the list.

8. If it's OK for someone to type a value that's not in the lookup table, expand the "Data entry options" section, and then turn on the "Allow additional items to be entered into the fields" checkbox. In this example, keep the checkbox turned off.

    Project turns off this checkbox initially so the field accepts only values in the lookup table. By not allowing other values, you can prevent duplicate values or misspellings. If you *do* allow other values and someone enters a unique value not in the lookup table, then Project automatically adds that value to the lookup table. The other checkbox in this section, "Allow only codes that have no subordinate values," is grayed out because it applies to outline codes.

> **Tip:** Suppose you have a custom field column in a table that's already populated with values. You can tell Project to populate the custom field's lookup table with the values you've entered. Set up the custom field with a blank lookup table and turn on the "Allow additional items to be entered into the fields" checkbox. Click Close to close the Edit Lookup Table dialog box and click OK to close the Custom Fields dialog box. The lookup table is now populated with the values you've entered in the table.

9. Click Close.

    The Edit Lookup Table dialog box closes, and you're back in the Custom Fields dialog box. If you're finished making customizations, then click OK.

Selecting values from a lookup table is easy. Here's an example, using the CR Status field:

1. If necessary, display the Gantt Chart view (View→Gantt Chart).

2. To save the view as a new view for looking at change requests, click the down arrow on the Gantt Chart button, and then choose Save View. In the Name box, type *C_CR_View.*

3. In the table, right-click the Duration column, choose Insert Column on the drop-down menu, and then choose CR Status.

4. To insert a value for this field in a task row, click the task's CR Status cell (in this example, use task ID 19 "Plan day of event").

5. Click the down arrow that appears, and then choose the value you want, in this example, Submitted, as shown in Figure 21-3.

Reusing Lookup Tables

Building lookup tables can take time, especially if the list and descriptions are long. Fortunately, you can bypass this data-entry chore if another custom field already has what you want.

If you know that an existing custom field has everything you want—lookup tables, formulas, and so on—then open the Custom Fields dialog box (Project→Custom Fields) and click Import Field. You choose the Project file, the Task or Resource option, and the field name. Project imports the entire field with *all* of its customizations, not just the lookup table.

But if you want to import *only* the lookup table (a list of departments in your company, for example) into a custom field, here are the steps (you don't have to perform these steps in the example project):

1. If the lookup table belongs to a custom field in another project, open that Project file first.

2. Return to the Project file that you want to import a lookup table into.

3. In the Project tab's Properties section, click Custom Fields.

4. In the Custom Fields dialog box, select the field you want to edit, and then click Lookup.

5. In the Edit Lookup Table dialog box, click Import Lookup Table.

6. If the lookup table is in another project, then in the Project drop-down list, select the filename.

7. Select the option for the type of field (Task, Resource, or Project).

8. In the Field drop-down list, choose the custom field with the lookup table, and then click OK. All the lookup table values appear in the current custom field's table.

Importing a lookup table is the perfect solution if you defined a ginormous lookup table for a custom outline code and then realized that you customized a *task* outline code instead of a *resource* outline code. You can import the lookup table from the task outline code in the same file.

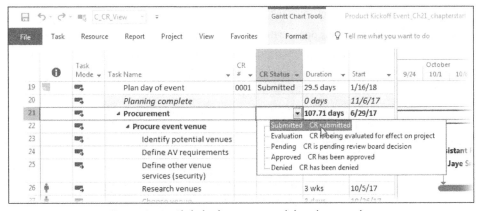

Figure 21-3. *Click the down arrow and then choose a value.*

Calculating Field Values

Another way to fill in custom field values is to calculate them. Don't reach for your calculator—Project can do the calculating as long as you give it the formula. A formula can use every Project field, along with typical numeric and logical functions. For example, suppose you want to calculate work variance in days instead of hours. You could set up a custom number field for this.

Tip: If the formula you want already exists in another custom field, then you can import it. First, open the Project file that contains the custom field with the formula you want. Then, back in the Project file with the field you're customizing, in the Project tab's Properties section, click Custom Fields. Select the custom field to which you want to add the formula, and then click Formula. In the Formula dialog box, click Import Formula. In the Import Formula dialog box, fill in the boxes as you do when importing a lookup table (see the note titled "Reusing Lookup Tables"). Unlike most other Project elements, you can't use the Organizer to copy formulas from project to project.

Don't copy custom fields with formulas into your global template. If you do and you receive Project files from others that have data in those fields, your custom field's formula will delete that data and fill in the field using your custom field's formula.

Follow Along Practice

To define a formula to calculate field values, follow these steps:

1. Open the Custom Fields dialog box, right-click anywhere in the table column heading area and choose Custom Fields on the shortcut menu.

   In this example, because a task-oriented view is displayed, the Custom Fields dialog box opens with the Task option selected automatically.

2. In this example, in the Type drop-down list, choose Number15. Rename the field ***Work Var in Days***. Click OK to close the Rename dialog box.

---

3.   In the "Custom attributes" section, click Formula.

The "Formula for" dialog box opens with the custom field's name or alias in the title bar.

4.   To add a field to the formula, click Field. In the drop-down list, choose the category and then the field you want to add, in this example, point at the Work category, and then choose Work on the submenu, as shown in Figure 21-4.

The categories are similar to different field data types. IDs and outline codes share a spot in the list, and the Project category contains properties related to the Project file, like the date it was created. When you select a field, Project inserts it into your formula and puts square brackets ([ ]) around the field's name.

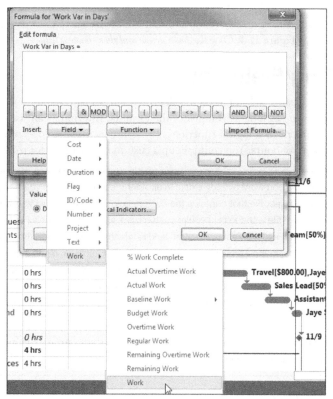

Figure 21-4. *Within a Field category, Project includes both built-in and customized fields. When the list entry represents several fields (for example, the main Work entry, shown here), a right arrow indicates it has a submenu.*

5.   To insert a function, click where you want the function in the formula, and then click the appropriate function button, in this example, click the – (minus) button.

The most commonly used functions have their own buttons, including addition, subtraction, multiplication, and division; equals, parentheses, greater than and less than; and the logical operators AND, OR, and NOT.

To find other functions, click Function, choose the category, and then choose the function. Take a few minutes to look at the functions in each category, because you have plenty to choose from. For example, in the Date/Time category, the Weekday function figures out the day of the week based on the date and the first day of the work week. The General category has functions for If-statements (IIf), case statements (Switch), and functions that check for null or numeric values (IsNull and IsNumeric). The Text category has a host of string functions, like Len, Left, and Trim, which are familiar to geeks who've written Visual Basic code.

6. In this example, insert the field [Baseline Work] after the minus sign. Click Field, point at the Work category, then point at Baseline Work on the submenu, and then choose Baseline Work on the next submenu.

> **Note:** To insert a value in the formula, click where you want to insert the value, and then type the number or text. You can also drag to select part of the formula—if you want to delete a field, for example.

7. To tell Project the order in which to calculate functions, add parentheses to the formula. In this example, enter parentheses at the beginning and end of the formula as it is so far.

   Click where you want to insert a parenthesis, and then type it (or click the button for the left or right parenthesis character).

8. When you've finished the formula, click OK.

   A message box warns you that any data in the field will be replaced by the formula's calculations. If you want to overwrite existing data or the field doesn't contain and data yet, click OK. Otherwise click Cancel and use a different field.

9. If you're done customizing, click OK to close the Custom Fields dialog box.

   In this example, close the Custom Fields dialog box. Then, insert the custom field into the table in the view. (Right-click the CRFlag heading at the right side of the table, choose Insert Column, and then choose "Work Var in Days.")

> **Tip:** When you include work fields in formulas, you have a few extra steps to perform. Project converts any time value into minutes. For example, the "Work Var in Days" value for task ID 38 "Identify giveaway vendors" is 960. That task is not 960 days off track. To get the correct answer in days, in the formula, you have to divide work by 1440 (60 minutes multiplied by 24 hours). In Project formula format, the calculation looks like this:
>
> ([Work] – [Baseline Work])/(1440)
>
> Once you make that change in this example and click OK to close the Formula dialog box and the Custom Fields dialog box, task 38's "Work Var in Days" value changes to .67.

Including Error Checking in Formulas

Suppose you define a formula only to see the custom field cells in a table awash with the dreaded value #ERROR. Dividing by zero is one cause of #ERROR; it's a no-no in Project formulas, as it is in any programming language. To prevent Project from squawking, you can set up formulas to perform calculations only if fields have values, which is where the IIf function comes in.

The IIf function works like an If statement in other programming languages. The function tests a condition, and then does one thing if the condition is true and another if the condition is false. For example, you could create a custom number field with the basic formula [Number1] / [Actual Work]. You don't want to calculate the formula unless the Actual Work field has a value other than zero. (Notice that formulas use *actual* field names, not the aliases you use to rename custom fields.) In this situation, the formula should calculate the result if Actual Work is not equal to zero, and otherwise return zero. Here's what the formula looks like with that error checking in place:

IIf([Actual Work]<>0,[Number1]/[ActualWork],0)

The less than sign followed by the greater than sign (<>) translates to "is not equal to."

> **Tip:** When you use a formula, be sure to set up several test cases to make sure the formula does what you want.

Calculating Values in Summary Rows

Custom fields don't automatically come with roll-up calculations, but you can control the calculation a custom field uses. The calculation options are in the Custom Fields dialog box's "Calculation for task and group summary rows" section. The simplest option is "Use formula," which calculates roll-ups using the same formula the field uses. You can also tell the program how to distribute values to assignments, as described in the note titled "Distributing Task Values to Assignments."

> **Tip:** For *built-in* fields, Project rolls up values into summary tasks and group summary rows—you don't have a choice in the matter. One way to work around this limitation is to create a custom field equal to the built-in field you want to roll up in a different way. Then simply choose the roll-up calculation you want for the custom field.

In the Custom Fields dialog box, when you select the Rollup option for a numerical field like a cost, date, duration, or number field, the Rollup drop-down list comes to life with several built-in calculations. (You don't have to apply these to custom fields for the example project.) Here are your choices:

- **And**: For custom flag fields, this choice sets the summary flag to No if at least one lower-level item is No. The value is Yes only if all lower-level values are Yes.

- **Or**: For custom flag fields, this choice sets the summary flag to No only if *all* lower-level values are No. The value is Yes if at least one lower-level item is Yes, like the built-in Critical field does with summary tasks.

- **Average**: For cost, duration, and number fields, this calculation determines the average of all nonsummary values belonging to a summary task or within a set of grouped tasks or resources. For example, you could calculate the average productivity for all work tasks assigned to a specific group.

- **Average First Sublevel**: For cost, duration, and number fields, this choice calculates the average of task values one level below the summary task (including summary and nonsummary tasks) or group.

- **Count All**: For number fields, Count All counts the number of items below a summary task or group (including summary and nonsummary tasks or resources).

- **Count First Sublevel**: For number fields, this choice counts the number of items one level below the summary task or group.

- **Count Nonsummaries**: For number fields, this calculation counts the number of nonsummary items below the summary task or group—for example, to count the number of resources that are overallocated.

- **Maximum**: For all types of fields *except* Flag, Text, and Outline Code, this option sets the summary value to the largest value underneath the summary or group.

- **Minimum**: For all types of fields *except* Flag, Text, and Outline Code, this option sets the summary value to the smallest value underneath the summary or group.

- **Sum**: For cost, duration, and number fields, this totals the nonsummary values below the summary task or group.

Distributing Task Values to Assignments

In the Custom Fields dialog box, the "Calculation for assignment rows" section is where you tell Project how to distribute the value of a custom field to a task's or resource's assignments. For example, suppose you set up a custom field to track the number of event registrations recorded. If you want to divvy up the total number of registrations among each registration resource's assignment, select the "Roll down unless manually entered" option. If you type values into the custom field for each assignment, then you can use those values to calculate individuals' productivity. Otherwise, Project divides the registrations evenly across all assignments.

If you don't want the value distributed to assignments, select None. Project selects this option initially for all custom fields.

Displaying Values Graphically

Displaying icons instead of values makes it easier to see what's going on. For example, many project managers use traffic-light icons to present project performance: A green light means variance from the plan is within an acceptable threshold, a yellow light means it's slightly beyond the threshold (for example, greater than 5 days), and a red light indicates the variance means trouble (15 days, say). Suppose you want to use graphical indicators to view schedule variance. You can set up a custom field to display a graphic instead of a number and specify the conditions under which each graphic should appear.

Follow Along Practice

In the "Values to display" section of the Custom Fields dialog box, Project initially selects the Data option, which simply shows field values. To use graphical indicators instead, follow these steps:

1. In this example, keep the customized view C_CR_View displayed. Open the Custom Fields dialog box, click Duration in the Type drop-down list, and then choose Duration9. Rename the field to *Schedule Var Graphic*.

2. To set the field equal to the built-in field Finish Variance, click Formula. In the Edit Formula dialog box, click Field, point at Date, and then choose Finish Variance on the submenu. Click OK to close the Formula box and then click OK to dismiss the message box.

    You can't define graphical indicators for built-in fields. By setting the custom field equal to the built-in Finish Variance field, you can display graphical indicators for the finish variance.

3. In the "Values to display" section, click the Graphical Indicators button.

    The Graphical Indicators dialog box opens. The custom field's name or alias appears in the title bar so you know which field you're working on.

4. In the "Indicator criteria for" section, select an option to tell Project whether you're defining graphical indicators for summary tasks or nonsummary tasks. In this example, keep "Nonsummary rows" selected.

    Project selects the "Nonsummary rows" option initially.

5. To set up a graphical indicator, select the first empty "Test for" cell, click the down arrow that appears, and then choose the test you want, in this example, "is less than."

    The tests are almost identical to the ones for filters (Chapter 17). The only additional test is "is any value," which displays the indicator as long as the field isn't empty. You can use the "is any value" test as the last condition to ensure that the field always shows a graphical indicator.

6. In the Values(s) cell in the same row, type the value, in this example, *2d*.

    Similar to filters, you can type a number or text, or choose a field in the drop-down list to compare the custom field to another field. Say you want to define an indicator for productivity and a value of 1 or less is poor. In the Test cell, choose "is less than or equal to," and then, in the Value(s) cell, type *1*. Or you could compare a custom Finish field to the Baseline Finish field and display a red light when Finish is greater than Baseline Finish.

7. In the Image cell, click the down arrow, and then choose the graphic you want Project to display when the condition is true, a green circle in this example.

8. Repeat steps 4–6 to define other conditions and graphical indicators. In this example, set the second test to "is less than," the value to **5d**, and the indicator to a yellow circle. Set the third test to "is greater than or equal to," the value to **5d**, and the indicator to a red circle, as shown in Figure 21-5.

    If you're testing for less than or greater than, be sure to include at least one test containing "equal to" to make sure you cover every value. For example, if you test for values less than 2 and 5, include a test for values greater than or equal to 5. Otherwise, the test doesn't cover the value 5.

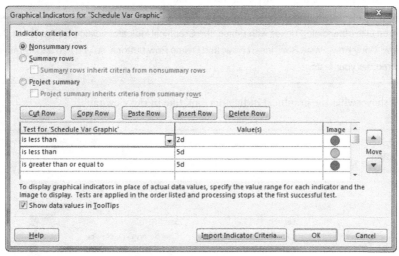

Figure 21-5. *The order of tests is important, because Project test conditions in order until the field value satisfies a condition.*

9. To specify the test for summary rows, select the Summary option. In this example, turn on the "Summary rows inherit criteria from nonsummary rows" checkbox.

    When you do that, summary rows use those same conditions to determine the indicator to display. In the traffic-light example, the summary tasks would show red lights if they were delayed by more than 5 days.

    You may want to use different conditions for summary rows—for example, to decrease the delay thresholds because you hope that delays and early deliveries will balance each other out (it could happen). In that case, select the "Summary rows" option and then turn off the "Summary rows inherit criteria from nonsummary rows" checkbox. That way, you can define a separate set of conditions and indicators—for example, to display a red light if summary tasks are delayed by 2 days.

10. To specify the test for the project-summary row, select the "Project summary" option. In this example, turn on the "Project summary inherit criteria from summary rows" checkbox.

To define different criteria for the project-summary row, select the "Project summary" option, turn off the "Project summary inherits criteria from summary rows" checkbox, and then define the conditions for the project-summary row.

11. When you're done, click OK to close the Graphical Indicators dialog box. Click OK in the Custom Fields dialog box if you're finished customizing fields.

    Project steps through the conditions in order until the field value satisfies a condition, and then it displays the corresponding graphical indicator. The order of tests is important. For example, for "less than or equal to" tests, test for the smaller value first—less than or equal to 2 before less than or equal to 5, say. If you test for less than or equal to 5 first, 0 passes that test and displays its indicator instead of the indicator for values less than 2.

> **Note:** Like other dialog boxes with tables, the Graphical Indicators dialog box includes Cut Row, Copy Row, Paste Row, Insert Row, and Delete Row buttons, so you can add, remove, or reorder your tests.

Figure 21-6 shows what the graphical indicators look like in the view table.

Figure 21-6. *Graphical indicators make it easy to see results.*

Coding Tasks and Resources

In Project, an ***outline code*** represents a hierarchy of values. The most obvious example of an outline code is the WBS field (Chapter 4), which includes values that correspond to each level in a work breakdown structure. Sometimes you work with other categorization schemes that are examples of outline codes, such as expense codes for the accounting department, job codes that define people's skills, or part numbers for material resources.

You can create up to 10 sets of custom outline codes to categorize tasks and *another* 10 sets to categorize resources. Assigning custom outline codes to tasks and resources is the same as for any other kind of field: You type a value or choose from a drop-down list. And you can use outline codes to filter, group, or sort, just like other types of fields.

The difference between an outline code and any other kind of custom field is its multiple levels of values, each separated by a symbol. Each level can be uppercase or lowercase letters, numbers, or characters. For example, if your organization's accounting codes are a hierarchical structure of levels within levels, create a custom outline code rather than a number or a text field. Then the drop-down list that appears in the custom field cell in a table shows this multilevel outline code, which makes it easier to find the code you need.

Because categorization schemes usually follow rules (similar to the Dewey Decimal System at the library), outline codes typically use a *code mask*, a set of rules that specify the type of characters and the length of each level.

Other than the code mask, customizing an outline code is similar to customizing a text field. For example, you can create a lookup table to help people choose the right values. (You can limit values to what's on the list or let folks add new ones.) And you can sort the values or leave them in the order you placed them in the lookup table.

This section describes how to create a new outline code, set up the format for the code, and create the outline code's lookup table.

Selecting and Naming a New Outline Code

Suppose you want to create an outline code to identify where resources are located. Follow these steps to begin creating an outline code:

Follow Along Practice

1. In the Project tab's Properties section, click Custom Fields.

2. At the top of the Custom Fields dialog box, select either the Task or Resource option as appropriate. In this example, select Resource.

   If some codes apply to tasks and others apply to resources, you'll have to create two sets of outline codes: one for tasks and the other for resources—you can't combine them.

3. In the Type drop-down list, choose Outline Code.

   Although almost all the custom fields let you create a lookup table for them, outline codes are the only type of custom field for which you can create a *multilevel* lookup table.

4. In the list of fields, select the outline code you want (in this example, Outline Code10).

5. Click Rename, type the name you want for this field (in this example, *Location*), and then click OK.

The renamed field appears in the list of outline codes with the new name followed by the original outline code field name in parentheses, such as "Location (Outline Code10)."

6. Keep the Custom Fields dialog box open, and continue with step 3 in the next section to set the format for your accounting code.

Setting Up a Template for Outline Code Values

A code mask spells out the characters and length for each level of the outline code, as well as the character that separates each level. The Edit Lookup Table dialog box contains an extra section for the code mask. If you create a lookup table with the complete list of valid values, you may think you can skip the code mask entirely. However, when you create a code mask, Project can flag lookup table values you enter that don't match the code mask's specifications.

Follow Along Practice

To set up the code mask, follow these steps:

1. To customize a custom outline code, in the Project tab's Properties section, click Custom Fields. In this example, you can skip to step 3.

   The Custom Fields dialog box opens.

2. Select either the Task option or Resource option, and then, in the Type drop-down list, choose Outline Code. In the Field list, select the outline code you want to work on (Outline Code1 through Outline Code10).

   Any settings you've specified for the outline code appear in the Custom Fields dialog box.

3. Click Lookup.

   The Edit Lookup Table dialog box opens. The dialog box's title bar includes the outline-code field's name or the alias you assigned to the outline code. In this example, the title bar is "Edit Lookup Table for Location."

4. Expand the "Code mask" section by clicking the + sign to the left of the label, and then click Edit Mask.

   The Code Mask Definition dialog box opens.

5. In the first Sequence cell, choose the type of characters you want for the top level of the hierarchy, in this example, Characters, as shown in Figure 21-7.

   Your choices are Numbers, Uppercase Letters, Lowercase Letters, and the no-holds-barred option, Characters, which accepts all three types.

6. In the first Length cell, choose Any or a number from 1 to 10 for the length of the top level. In this example, choose 4.

   Project initially selects Any, which means any number of characters is valid. Choosing a specific length means the value is fixed at that length. For example, if you choose 4, entries must have four characters or digits.

7. In the Separator cell, choose the character that separates the top level from the next level.

    The separator can be a period (.), a hyphen (-), a plus sign (+), or a slash (/). Project automatically fills in the Separator cell with a period (.). (The separator in the last row of the code mask never appears, since it doesn't need to separate anything.)

8. In this example, in the second Sequence cell, choose Characters. In the second Length cell, choose 6.

9. Repeat steps 5–7 to add additional levels to the mask. In this example, you don't have to add more levels.

    The code mask accepts dozens of levels, but outline code values can be no longer than 255 characters.

10. When you're done, click OK to close the Code Mask Definition dialog box.

    Keep the Edit Lookup Table dialog box open and go on to the next section to create the multilevel lookup table for your accounting code.

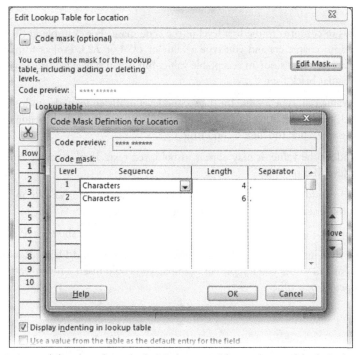

Figure 21-7. *As you define the code mask, the "Code preview" box at the top of the dialog box shows what an outline code value would look like with the code mask you've defined.*

Setting Up an Outline-Code Lookup Table

Like other fields, outline codes work best when people know the values that are legit. If you set up a code mask and stop there, then *any* value that follows the code mask is valid. If you don't create a lookup table for your outline code, you have to type a value and hope for the best. If the value doesn't match the code mask, an error message with the correct format appears. To provide examples or to restrict values to a predefined list, build an outline-code lookup table. The steps are the same as the ones for creating a regular lookup table, except that you have to tell Project how to handle the multiple levels. Here are the steps:

1. In the Edit Lookup Table dialog box, below the lookup table itself, if necessary, turn on the "Display indenting in lookup table" checkbox.

   This setting indents values in the lookup table based on their level in the outline, as illustrated in Figure 21-8.

2. Type a value in the first blank Value cell and a description in the Description cell in the same row. In this example, type *Amer* in the Value cell, and type *North and South America* in the description cell.

   The value has to conform to the first level of the code mask. For example, if the first level is supposed to be four characters and you type a value of *USA* or *123*, Project formats it in bold red text to indicate that that's not an acceptable value. But if you type a legitimate value like *Amer*, it appears in regular black font.

3. In the next Value cell, type a value for the second level of the code mask, in this example, type *Boston*. Click the Indent button (the dark-green right arrow) to push the value to the second level. (If necessary, click Indent a second time.)

   Until you indent the value, it may appear in bold, red text. That's because Project validates the value at the level you place it.

4. Repeat step 3 to add more outline code values. In this example, add *NYCity* and *Denver* (remember, in this example, the second level must have 6 characters).

5. In this example, continue adding entries to create the lookup table shown in Figure 21-8.

   You can use the Cut Row, Copy Row, Paste Row, Insert Row, and Delete Row buttons to rearrange values or add values you forgot. For example, you could insert a row to add a city when your company opens a new office.

Figure 21-8. *Fill in values and entries to build the lookup table. Click Indent to move to the next level.*

> **Tip:** As you work, you can hide or show outline levels by clicking the triangles to the left of higher-level values. (A black triangle indicates that the higher level is expanded to show lower-level values. A white triangle indicates that lower levels are hidden.) To indent or outdent values to the correct level, click the Indent button (the dark-green right arrow) or the Outdent button (the dark-green left arrow). Click the Show All Subcodes button (the one with two + signs) to display every value in the table for your final quality-control review.

6. If an outline code value should include every level of the code (for example, to correctly assign locations), expand the "Data entry options" section, and then turn on the "Allow only codes that have no subordinate values" checkbox. In this example, turn on the checkbox.

    Project initially turns off this checkbox, which means you can enter an outline code with only some of the levels, just like the WBS field works.

---

7. When you're done, click Close.

If the other settings are the way you want, then in the Custom Fields dialog box, click OK to save the changes.

> **Note:** You can import a custom outline code field or its lookup table just as you can with other types of fields (described earlier in this chapter). To import an outline code, in the Custom Fields dialog box, click Import Field. To import only the lookup table from another custom outline code, in the Edit Lookup Table dialog box, click Import Lookup Table.

After the outline code is set up, assigning values should be familiar. You can type values or choose them from a lookup table drop-down list, as shown in Figure 21-9.

Figure 21-9. With a lookup table like the one shown here, you simply click the down arrow in the cell and then choose the value you want.

Setting Up a Custom WBS Code

The WBS codes built into Project are simple outline codes with a number for each level in the outline hierarchy. For instance, a WBS code of 2.1.3 might represent the second phase of the project, the first summary task in that phase, and the third work package for that summary task. If your organization uses custom codes, you can build a tailored numbering system—called a ***code mask***—to specify each level of your WBS code. For example, if you use abbreviations for phases, numbers for summary tasks, and letters for work packages, a customized WBS for the design phase of a project might look like this: Dsn.1.a.

Follow Along Practice

To define a custom WBS code, follow these steps:

1. Display a task-oriented view like the Gantt Chart. If necessary, insert the WBS field into the view's table.

2. On the Project tab, click WBS→Define Code.

    The WBS Code Definition dialog box appears. Without a custom WBS code, Project automatically assigns WBS codes using numbers for each outline level with a period as a separator. (The fields in this dialog box don't show this out-of-the-box format. The fields remain empty unless you specify a custom scheme for your WBS codes.)

    > **Note:** If you assemble several projects into a single master project (Chapter 24), you can make WBS codes unique for each project, even if they use the same code mask. If you work with multiple projects, set up the code mask for a new project before you get too deep into defining the project's tasks. That way you don't have to renumber all the tasks later. In the WBS Code Definition dialog box's Project Code Prefix field, type a prefix for the current project, like "Launch-". Project then inserts this prefix at the beginning of the WBS codes for all the tasks in that project; for instance, Launch-1.4.1.

3. In the dialog box's "Code mask" section, in the first Sequence cell, choose the type of characters you want to use for the top level of the hierarchy, as shown in Figure 21-10. In this example, choose Characters (unordered).

    You can choose from Numbers (ordered), Uppercase Letters (ordered), Lowercase Letters (ordered), and—for the most flexible coding—Characters (unordered). The choices for characters, length, and separators are limited. If you use unordered characters, you have to type the characters you want for each code, such as Reg.1, Pub.3, or Acc.7, in each summary task's WBS cell. With ordered numbers and letters, Project automatically increments the numbers or letters as you add tasks to the WBS, proceeding, for example, from 1.1 to 1.2. to 1.3.

4. In the first Length cell, choose a number (from 1 to 10) for the length of the top level's mask. In this example, choose 3.

    Project initially selects Any here, which means the entry for the level can be of any length. If the level uses a number, then Project increments the number beginning at 1 and continuing to 10, 100, or 1,000, if necessary. If the level uses letters, then you can type a code of any number of characters at that level.

    Choosing a number limits the entry to the length you specify. For example, if you limit a numeric entry to one character, Project cycles through the numbers 1 through 9, moves to 0, and then repeats.

5. In the first Separator cell, choose the character that separates the top level from the next level.

    Your only choices for separators are periods (.), minus signs (–), plus signs (+), or slashes (/).

6. Repeat steps 2–4 for each additional level of the code mask. In this example, set levels 2, 3, and 4 to Numbers (ordered) and set the length to Any.

A WBS code can be as long as 255 characters, so you can specify dozens of levels in a code mask. However, limiting the number of WBS levels makes the schedule (and WBS codes) easier to comprehend.

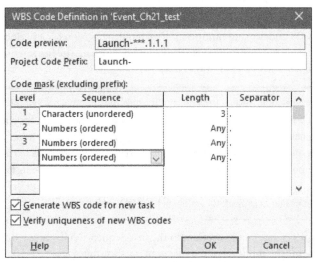

Figure 21-10. *As you specify the code mask for each level, the "Code preview" field at the top of the dialog box displays a sample of your new WBS code.*

7. After you've defined all the levels in the code mask, be sure that the "Generate WBS code for new task" checkbox is turned on so Project will automatically assign a WBS code to new tasks you create.

The only time you might want to turn this checkbox off is when you plan to renumber all the WBS codes after you've organized your tasks and don't want to be distracted by the interim codes that Project assigns.

8. To ensure that you don't create any duplicate WBS codes, keep the "Verify uniqueness of new WBS codes" checkbox turned on, too.

Although Project adds WBS codes to tasks when the "Generate WBS code for new task" checkbox is turned on, you might type some WBS codes manually, and that can lead to duplicate values. The only time you might turn off the "Verify uniqueness of new WBS codes" checkbox is if you're planning to renumber tasks later and you get tired of the warnings Project displays. As the note titled "Renumbering Task WBS Codes" explains, you can renumber the WBS codes for tasks to correct or reorder your project.

9. Click OK.

10. If you use unordered characters in your WBS, you must fill in the characters for that level of the WBS. In this example, select the WBS cell for task ID 2 "Planning." Replace the three asterisks with *Pln*.

Project replaces that level of the WBS for the subtasks beneath the Planning Summary task.

Congratulations! You've customized your WBS codes. The WBS codes in the task list should look like the ones in Figure 21-11.

	ⓘ	Task Mode ▼	WBS ▼	Task Name ▼	CR #
0		⬛	**Launch-**	◢ **Event_Ch21_test**	
1	✓	⬛	Launch-***	Project start	
2		⬛	**Launch-Pln**	◢ **Planning**	
3	✓	⬛	**Launch-Pln.1**	◢ **Initial planning**	
4	✓	⬛	Launch-Pln.1.1	Identify core event team	
5	✓	⬛	Launch-Pln.1.2	Define event goals and objectives	
6	✓	⬛	Launch-Pln.1.3	Identify event requirements	
7	✓	⬛	Launch-Pln.1.4	Determine budget	
8	✓	⬛	Launch-Pln.1.5	Prepare project definition	
9	✓	⬛	Launch-Pln.1.6	Obtain approval to proceed	
10	✓	⬛	Launch-Pln.2	Initial planning complete	
11		⬛	**Launch-Pln.3**	▷ **Plan marketing**	
19		⬛	Launch-***	Plan day of event	000

Figure 21-11. *If you use unordered characters in your WBS, then you need to edit the WBS value for each task using unordered characters to specify the code for that part of the WBS, such as "Pln" in this example.*

Renumbering Task WBS Codes

When you customize WBS codes, the WBS Code Definition dialog box's "Generate WBS code for new task" checkbox tells Project to automatically assign WBS codes to new tasks you create, whether you insert tasks within the outline or add tasks at the end. With this checkbox turned on, as soon as you press Enter to save a new task, the WBS code pops into the WBS cell, maintaining the sequence you've defined. If you rearrange and re-outline your tasks, your WBS sequence can turn into a mess.

The alternative is to turn *off* this checkbox, and then, after a heated session of adding or modifying the task order, renumber the WBS codes all at once. Fortunately, that's pretty easy to do. (In this example, you don't have to perform these steps.) When your tasks are organized the way you want them, do the following to renumber the tasks' WBS codes:

1. If you want to renumber only some of the tasks in the Project file, select them.

2. On the Project tab, click WBS→Renumber.

3. If you selected tasks, in the WBS Renumber dialog box, keep the "Selected tasks" option selected. To renumber the whole project, select the "Entire project" option instead. (If you didn't select tasks, Project automatically selects the "Entire project" option.)

4. Click OK. Project reapplies the WBS code scheme to the tasks, alphabetizing ordered letters and incrementing ordered numbers.

When you start to build other documents that reference your WBS codes (like work-package Word files), you don't want Project to change the existing codes. That's another time to turn off the "Generate WBS code for new task" checkbox. Before you type in new WBS codes manually, make sure the WBS Code Definition dialog box's "Verify uniqueness of new WBS codes" checkbox is turned on so Project will warn you if you've duplicated an existing WBS code.

22

Customizing the Ribbon and Quick Access Toolbar

Project's ribbon comes with built-in tabs, each organized in a way that makes project-management tasks easier for most people. After using the program for a while, you may discover that some commands get a lot of exercise, that some starve for attention, and that a few of your favorites are nowhere to be found. For example, you may never click any of the Gantt Chart Style buttons to change the color scheme of your task bars. Or you frequently use the Edit Links command to update the connections to files you link to your Project schedule, but it's not available as a button on the ribbon. Fortunately, you can customize which commands you see and where they're located.

The Quick Access Toolbar sits above the left side of the ribbon. It's always visible and doesn't take up much room, so it's an ideal home for your all-time favorite commands. As the following section explains, adding commands to it is simple.

You can also customize the ribbon to suit your needs. You can turn tabs on or off, create your own tabs and groups, add commands to groups, and rearrange the order of elements on the ribbon (tabs, groups, and commands). This chapter shows you how to do all these things. After you get the Quick Access Toolbar and the ribbon the way you want, why keep them to yourself? This chapter wraps up by showing you how to share your customizing with your colleagues.

Note: Project refers to the various sections within tabs as *groups*. The instructions throughout this book may refer to ribbon groups as *sections* to differentiate them from other Project features with the word "group" in their names, such as the Group field and the Group By command. In this chapter, the terms "section" and "group" are interchangeable.

Note: If you've downloaded files from the book website, you can follow along using the file Event_Ch22_start.mpp.

Customizing the Quick Access Toolbar

The Quick Access Toolbar perches conveniently above the File and Task tabs. Initially, this toolbar contains only buttons for the Save, Undo, and Redo commands, but you can add any commands you want to it. The Quick Access Toolbar doesn't have tabs or groups, so customizing it is fast and easy. You can also move it below the ribbon so it's within easy reach. Here's what you can do:

Follow Along Practice

- **Add a command to the toolbar**: Click the down arrow to the right of the Quick Access Toolbar and then choose the command you want to add, in this example, View. (Project adds a box with a down arrow that you can click to display a drop-down list of views. Click a view to apply it.) A checkmark appears to the left of the commands that are currently on the toolbar, as shown in Figure 22-1. Several popular commands, like New, Open, and Print Preview, are on the drop-down menu, so a quick click is all it takes to add them to the toolbar.

Figure 22-1. *To add other commands to the toolbar, choose More Commands to open the Project Options dialog box to its "Customize the Quick Access Toolbar" page.*

> **Tip:** When you customize the Quick Access Toolbar, you can specify whether your changes apply to *all* files you open in Project or just the active one. (Project applies your changes to all documents unless you say otherwise.) To customize the Quick Access Toolbar for just the active file, choose File→Options. On the left side of the Project Options dialog box, choose Quick Access Toolbar. In the Customize Quick Access Toolbar box, Project automatically chooses "For all documents (default)," which means the changes you make to the toolbar appear in every file you open. To apply the customized toolbar to only the active file, choose "For <filename>" where <filename> is the name of the active Project file.

- **Quickly add any Project command to the toolbar**: The quickest way to add a command to the Quick Access Toolbar is by right-clicking the command on the ribbon and then choosing "Add to Quick Access Toolbar." When you do that, the command's icon takes its place as the right-most item on the toolbar. In this example, in the Task tab's Properties section, right-click the "Notes" button, and then choose "Add to Quick Access Toolbar."

- **Add and organize commands on the toolbar**: Click the down arrow to the right of the Quick Access Toolbar and choose More Commands. The Project Options dialog box opens to the "Customize the Quick Access Toolbar" page. You can add or remove commands from the toolbar, and reorder them, using the same steps as for the ribbon. In this example, select the "Scroll to Task" entry in the list on the right side of the Customize the Quick Access Toolbar page. Then, click the down arrow to move the entry below the View entry.

> **Tip:** To quickly remove an item from the Quick Access Toolbar, right-click its icon in the toolbar and then choose "Remove from Quick Access Toolbar."

- **Add a ribbon group to the toolbar**: If a group on one of the ribbon's tabs contains commands you use all the time, you can add that group to the Quick Access Toolbar. Simply right-click the name of the group you want to add to the toolbar, and then choose "Add to Quick Access Toolbar." In this example, you don't have to add a group to the toolbar. (Depending on where you right-click, the command that appears on the shortcut menu is either "Add to Quick Access Toolbar" or "Add Group to Quick Access Toolbar.") An icon appears on the toolbar. (The icon's ToolTip is the name of the group.) When you click the icon, the group appears immediately below it.

- **Show the Quick Access Toolbar below the ribbon**: If you put your top commands on the Quick Access Toolbar, you can reduce the distance you have to move your mouse by putting the toolbar below the ribbon. Click the down arrow to the right of the Quick Access Toolbar and then choose "Show Below the Ribbon." The toolbar appears between the ribbon and your Project view. To move it back to the top of the Project window, click the down arrow to the right of the Quick Access Toolbar and then choose "Show Above the Ribbon."

> **Tip:** Suppose you overdid your Quick Access Toolbar customizations and want to revert to the short and sweet version you started with. Restoring the toolbar to its original settings is easy: Click the down arrow to the right of the toolbar, and then choose More Commands on the drop-down menu. In the lower-right part of the Project Options dialog box, click the Reset down arrow and then choose "Reset only Quick Access Toolbar." In the message box that appears, click Yes. The Quick Access Toolbar switches back to having only Save, Undo, and Redo icons.

Customizing the Ribbon

As you've seen throughout this book, the ribbon is made up of several tabs, like Task, Resource, Report, Project, View, and numerous contextual Format tabs. Within each tab, related commands are kept close to one another. For example, the Insert group (which this chapter also refers to as a section) of the Task tab contains commands for inserting tasks, summary tasks, milestones, and deliverables. Some commands reside in a group of one, like the lonely Subproject command in the Project tab's Insert group. The groups are visually separated from one another by vertical lines.

You can customize the ribbon to match how you work, whether you want to create your own tabs and groups; add groups you create to the program's built-in tabs; add commands to groups; reorder tabs, groups, and commands; or remove tabs, groups, and commands you don't use.

You customize the ribbon via the "Customize the Ribbon" page of the Project Options dialog box. The fastest way to reach this page is to right-click the ribbon and then choose "Customize the Ribbon." The long way around is to choose File→Options and then, on the left side of the Project Options dialog box, click Customize Ribbon.

Turning Tabs On and Off

The ribbon comes with several ready-made tabs, most of which are visible when you first launch Project. Whether you use the built-in tabs or build your own, you can turn tabs on when you need them and then turn them off to keep the ribbon tidy the rest of the time. For example, if you're having fun developing macros, you can turn on the built-in Developer tab, which is turned off initially. Then, when your macros are ready for prime time, you can turn off the Developer tab and run your macros from the View tab or a custom tab you create (described shortly). Here's how to turn tabs on and off:

Follow Along Practice

1. Right-click the ribbon, and then choose "Customize the Ribbon."

    The "Customize the Ribbon" page opens in the Project Options dialog box, as shown in Figure 22-2.

2. On the right side of the page, make sure the "Customize the Ribbon" box is set to Main Tabs.

    This drop-down list is initially set to Main Tabs, so the list below it shows the built-in tabs (Task, Resource, Report, Project, View, and so on) and any custom tabs you create. If you choose Tool Tabs in the drop-down list, you see the context-sensitive Format tabs for each type of view, such as the Gantt Chart Tools | Format tab and the Resource Usage Tools | Format tab.

3. In the Main Tabs list, turn on a tab's checkbox to make it visible on the ribbon. In this example, turn on the Developer checkbox.

    To hide a tab, turn off its checkbox. In this example, you can turn the Developer checkbox off if you wish.

4. When you're done, click OK to close the Project Options dialog box.

    The ribbon displays only the tabs whose checkboxes are turned on.

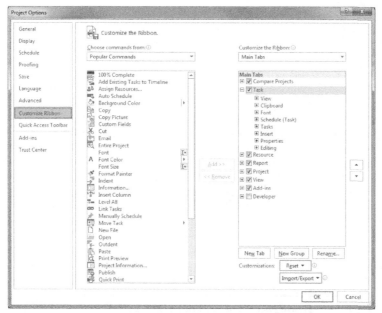

Figure 22-2. *Turn checkboxes on or off in the Main Tabs list to display or hide tabs, respectively.*

> **Note:** In the Project Options dialog box, you can choose to customize the ribbon or the Quick Access Toolbar. On the left side of the dialog box, click Customize Ribbon to open the "Customize the Ribbon" page. If you click Quick Access Toolbar instead, you see the "Customize the Quick Access Toolbar" page, which is like a simplified version of the "Customize the Ribbon" page, because the Quick Access Toolbar doesn't have tabs or groups.

Creating Custom Tabs

When existing tabs won't do, you can blaze a new trail by creating a tab from scratch. Completely new tabs are great when you constantly turn to the same set of commands. To create a new tab, open the "Customize the Ribbon" page, and then follow these steps:

Follow Along Practice

1. In the tab list on the right side of the page, select the tab below where you want to add your custom tab, in this example, select View.

    If you forget to select a position in the list before you create the tab, you can move the custom tab to another location later (described later in this chapter).

2. Below the tab list, click New Tab.

    Project inserts a new custom tab named New Tab (Custom) containing one custom group named New Group (Custom), as shown in Figure 22-3. Project saves you a step by automatically adding a custom group to your new tab. You can add commands only to custom groups, so a custom tab must have at least one custom group.

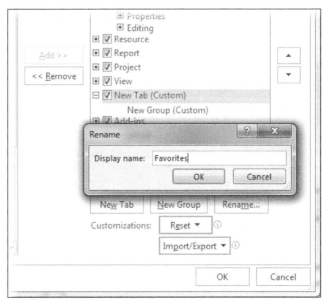

Figure 22-3. *To create a new custom tab, click New Tab.*

3. Click the new custom tab's name in the list to select it, and then click Rename. In the Rename dialog box, type a short but meaningful name, like *Favorites*, and then click OK.

    The new name appears in the tab list.

4. Click the new custom group to select it, and then click Rename. In this example, in the "Display name" box, change the group name to *Tasks*.

    The Rename dialog box opens with dozens of icons to choose from and a box for entering the new name. You don't *have* to choose an icon. (If you don't select an icon, Project uses a green circle.) In this example, don't choose an icon. But if you do, the icon you select appears if you add the group to the Quick Access Toolbar.

5. Click OK to close the Rename dialog box. Click OK to close the Project Options dialog box.

    Your custom tab and group are ready for you to add commands (described later in this chapter). The next section describes how to add more groups to a tab.

Creating Custom Groups

If you want to add commands to the ribbon, you have to create custom groups to hold them. (In other words, you can't add commands to Project's built-in groups.) Whether you want to add commands to a built-in tab or a custom tab, you must first create a custom group and then add it to the tab you want. To do so, first open the "Customize the Ribbon" page, and then do this:

Follow Along Practice

1. In the tab list on the right side of the page, click the + sign to the left of the tab (built-in or custom) where you want to add a new group, in this example, Favorites, the custom tab you created in the previous section.

    If the tab isn't already expanded, it expands to show the groups it currently includes.

2. Click the group below where you want to add the new group, in this example, the Tasks group.

    If you forget to select a position before you create the group, you can move the custom tab to another location later.

3. Below the tab list, click New Group.

    Project inserts a new custom group named New Group (Custom).

4. Click the new custom group to select it, and then click Rename. To display an icon for the group, choose one in the Symbol list. In the "Display name" box, type a short but meaningful name, like ***Resources***. Then click OK.

5. Click OK to close the Project Options dialog box.

    Your custom group takes its place in the tab, with vertical lines separating it from its neighboring groups.

Adding Commands to Custom Groups

All of Project's commands, as well as the macros you develop (see Chapter 27), are fair game for the ribbon. The "Customize the Ribbon" page (Figure 22-2) includes categories of commands to help you find the ones you want to add to a custom group you've created. You can choose a category like "Commands Not in the Ribbon" to add a command that isn't available in any of Project's built-in tabs.

Follow Along Practice

The steps for adding commands to the ribbon are easy:

1. Right-click the ribbon and choose "Customize the Ribbon."

    The "Customize the Ribbon" page opens in the Project Options dialog box.

2. In the "Choose commands from" drop-down list, select one of the command categories, in this example, keep Popular Commands selected.

    The categories, shown in Figure 22-4, represent different collections of commands. This drop-down list is set initially to Popular Commands, but you can also choose from all commands, commands on the File tab, and so on. When you select a category, the command list shows the choices within that category. Unless you know the built-in tabs inside and out, your best bets are the first three categories in this list. Popular Commands are the most frequently used commands. To add a command that isn't on the ribbon, choose "Commands Not in the Ribbon." If you don't know which category to choose, select All Commands.

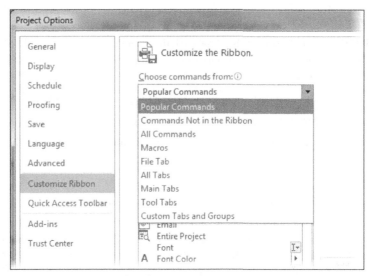

Figure 22-4. *To make sure you can find the command you want, choose All Commands and then scroll through the list.*

3.   In the list of commands below the "Choose commands from" box, select the command you want to add to the ribbon, in this example, choose Indent.

When you select a command in the list, the Add button becomes active, indicating that you can add it to the ribbon. But don't click Add just yet.

4.   On the right side of the page, expand the tab you want (Favorites) and then select the custom group for the command (Tasks). If other commands are in the group already, select the command below where you want to add the new command.

Although you can *select* a built-in group, if you click the + sign next to the group's name, you'll see that all the commands within it are grayed out to indicate that you can't add a new command to that group. If you try to add a command to a built-in group, a message box tells you that you can add commands only to custom groups.

5.   Click Add.

The command takes its place in the custom group.

6.   Repeat steps 3–5 to add other commands to the group. In this example, add Outdent and Link Tasks to the Tasks custom group.

7.   In this example, add commands to the Resources custom group.

In the "Choose commands from" drop-down list, choose Main Tabs. Expand the Resource tab and its Assignments section. On the right side of the dialog box, click the Resources (Custom) group. On the left side of the dialog box, select Assign Resources, and then click Add.

When you're done, click OK to close the Project Options dialog box.

Rearranging Tabs and Groups

Although Project is fussy about where you can put commands (only in custom groups), it's happy to let you rearrange tabs and groups in any way you want, regardless of whether the tabs and groups are built-in or custom. For example, if you prefer the View tab to appear to the left of the Task tab, simply open the "Customize the Ribbon" page and then, in the Main Tabs list, drag the tab's name where you want it. You can use the same techniques to rearrange groups (built-in and custom) and commands within custom groups (you can't modify the commands within built-in groups).

With the "Customize the Ribbon" page open, simply drag elements (or click the up and down arrows) to move them to another location. Here's how:

Follow Along Practice

1. Right-click the ribbon and choose "Customize the Ribbon."

    The "Customize the Ribbon" page opens in the Project Options dialog box.

2. In the right-hand list, select the tab, group, or command (only commands within custom groups) you want to relocate, in this example, expand the Favorites tab and then select the Tasks (Custom) group.

    You can move only one element at a time.

3. Drag the element to its new location, or click the up or down arrows to move the element higher or lower in the list. In this example, drag the Tasks (Custom) group beneath the Resources (Custom) group.

    If you drag the element, position the horizontal bar that appears where you want the element to go, as shown in Figure 22-5, and then release the mouse button. If you click the up or down arrow, the element moves up or down one position. Moving an element up in the list moves it to the left in the Project ribbon; moving an element down moves it to the right in the ribbon.

    > **Note:** Because you can add commands only to custom groups, you might see the up or down arrow grayed out or a No icon (a circle with a diagonal bar through it) indicating you can't relocate the element to the current location (for example, to a built-in group).

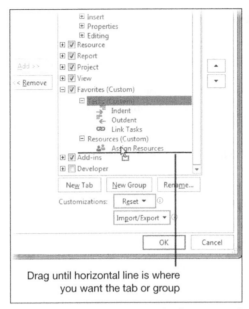

Drag until horizontal line is where
you want the tab or group

Figure 22-5. A horizontal bar shows you where the element goes when you drag it.

Renaming Tabs and Groups

You can also rename any tab or group—built-in or custom. Simply right-click the ribbon and then choose "Customize the Ribbon." In the list on the right side of the page that appears, select the tab or group you want to rename, and then click Rename below the list. In the Rename box, type the new name and then click OK. In this example, you don't have to rename any tabs or groups.

> **Note:** You can rename commands only in the custom groups you create, as described earlier in this chapter.

Removing Ribbon Elements

The obvious result of removing elements from the ribbon is that the elements you remove no longer appear on the ribbon. What happens behind the scenes depends on what you remove. Built-in tabs and groups that you remove disappear from the ribbon, but they're still available in the "Choose commands from" list on the left side of the "Customize the Ribbon" page, so you can easily restore them (the next section explains how). On the other hand, removing a custom tab or a custom group from the ribbon deletes that element from Project.

You can remove built-in and custom tabs, built-in and custom groups, and commands you add to custom groups. For example, you can remove the Insert group from the Task tab and replace it with a custom group that has the insert commands you want in the order you want. However, you can't remove commands from built-in groups, like Cut, Copy, and Paste in the Task tab's Clipboard group. The secret to removing elements is the Remove button on the "Customize the Ribbon" page.

Follow Along Practice

Here's how to remove elements from the ribbon:

1. Right-click the Ribbon and choose "Customize the Ribbon."

2. In the list on the right side of the "Customize the Ribbon" page, select the element you want to remove by clicking it, in this example, expand the Report tab and select its Project group.

    You can remove a custom tab, a built-in group, a custom group, or a command in a custom group. You can tell whether you're allowed to remove the selected element by glancing at the Remove button in the middle of the page: If it's grayed out, you can't remove that element; if it's active, you can.

3. Click the Remove button.

    When you click Remove, the selected item disappears from the list, which means it disappears from the ribbon when you click OK to close the Project Options dialog box.

Restoring a Built-in Group

Suppose you removed a built-in group from the ribbon and then realize that you want it back. No worries. Built-in groups stay in the "Customize the Ribbon" page's "Choose commands from" list, so you can add them back to the ribbon at any time. Here are the steps:

Follow Along Practice

1. On the "Customize the Ribbon" page, click the down arrow to the right of the "Choose commands from" box, and then choose All Tabs or Main Tabs, in this example, choose Main Tabs.

    The built-in tabs in that category appear in the list box.

2. To restore a built-in group, click the + next to the tab that contains the group, in this example, Report.

    The tab expands to show the groups within it.

3. Click the group you want to restore to the ribbon, in this example, the Project group beneath the Report tab.

    If you select a tab in the list box, the Add button in the middle of the page is active even if the tab is already in the "Customize the Ribbon" list on the right side of the page. That means you could add a *second* copy of the tab to the ribbon if you wanted to for some reason.

4. In the list on the right side of the page, click the item above where you want to restore the tab or group, in this example, the View Reports group.

    If you selected a group to restore, the Add button in the middle of the page becomes active as long as the group isn't already in the selected tab or group in the "Customize the Ribbon" list on the right side of the page. If the group *is* in the selected tab or group on the right side of the page, the Add button is grayed out, because the item is already added.

5. Click the Add button. If necessary, drag the restored group to the correct position. In this example, drag it above the View Reports group.

    When you click Add, the item you selected appears in the list on the right.

Resetting Ribbon Customizations

After you tweak the ribbon, you may decide you want some or all of the tabs back to the way they were when you first installed Project. Rather than finding each change you made and manually changing it back, it's easier to reset them. You can reset the customizations on a single tab or remove all the customizations you've made. Here are the steps (you don't have to perform these steps for the example):

1. Right-click the ribbon and choose "Customize the Ribbon."

2. If you want to reset a single tab, in the list on the right side of the page, select the tab.

    You can reset only built-in tabs, because custom tabs don't have an original state: the original state is it wasn't there at all.

3. Click Reset and then choose either "Reset only selected Ribbon tab" or "Reset all customizations."

    The "Reset only selected Ribbon tab" option is available only if you select a built-in tab in the list. It removes any customizations you made to that built-in tab. If you select "Reset all customizations," Project removes customizations you made to built-tabs *and* the Quick Access Toolbar, *and* deletes all custom tabs.

> **Tip:** Before you remove all customizations, export your customizations to a file as explained in the next section. That way, it you want the customizations back, you can import the file.

Sharing a Custom Ribbon and Quick Access Toolbar

You may wonder how you can copy your ribbon customization handiwork to other computers, because the ribbon isn't one of the elements you can copy with the Organizer (Chapter 23). To use your ribbon on another computer (or to share it with a fellow project manager), you have to export it to a file. Then you or your compatriot can import that file into Project on another computer. (You don't have to perform these steps for the example.) Here's how:

1. Right-click the ribbon and choose "Customize the Ribbon."

2. At the bottom right of the Project Options dialog box, click Import/Export and then choose "Export all customizations."

    The File Save dialog box appears, with its "Save as type" box set to "Exported Office UI file."

3. In the File Save dialog box, navigate to the folder where you want to save the file and type a descriptive name in the "File name" box (something like *MyProjectRibbon*).

    Initially, Project names the file Project Customizations.

4. Click Save.

    Project saves the UI customization file in the folder you specified.

To import a custom ribbon or Quick Access Toolbar, first copy the UI customization file to your computer. Then follow these steps:

1. In Project, right-click the ribbon and choose "Customize the Ribbon."

2. At the bottom right of the Project Options dialog box, click Import/Export and then choose "Import customization file."

    The File Open dialog box appears.

3. In the File Open dialog box, navigate to the folder that contains the file, and then double-click it.

    The drop-down menu to the right of the "File name" box is set to "Exported Office UI file" so the ribbon customization file will appear in the list of files.

4. A message box asks if you want to replace all existing Ribbon and Quick Access Toolbar customizations for Project. Click Yes to load the new customizations, or click No to cancel.

    After the customizations are in place, you can use the techniques described in this chapter to tweak the ribbon or Quick Access toolbar.

23

Reusing Project Information

As you use Project, you're bound to make changes to features like views, tables, filters, reports, to name a few, to help you do your job more effectively. Perhaps you prefer to work with the Gantt Chart view in the top pane and the Task Details Form in the Details pane. Or you insert the % Work Complete field into the Summary table. If you go to the trouble of customizing Project, as described in the previous chapters, you probably want to use those customizations in most, if not all, of your projects—or at least show them off to your friends. When you want to reuse your customized elements, you can store them in a special file called the *global template*, so every new project you create can use them. Copying customized elements into a Project file dedicated to customization makes it easy to share your handiwork with others—or transfer it to another one of your computers.

With each project you manage, you also add to your project-management toolbox. For instance, you might develop a task list and basic schedule for running an event that you can reuse for next year's affair or share with colleagues across the country who are hosting their own events. Part of the closing process for every project is archiving the work you've done, documenting what you learned, and recording that information so others can benefit from it. Saving the Project file to an archive location at the end of the project accomplishes much of this work. However, if you want to reuse what you learned, you can turn your completed Project file into a *project template* so it's ready to jump-start your next project. These templates are Project files that hold different types of project information, from customized elements to typical tasks with typical durations to Project settings you prefer. Because project templates can hold both customized Project elements and reusable project information, they're ideal for sharing your effort with anyone who needs it for future projects.

This chapter begins by explaining the difference between the global template and individual project templates you can use to create new projects. Once you understand that, you'll see where Project stores elements and settings and how you can keep your customized items in the same place. (You can tell Project to save new customized elements in your current Project file or to automatically copy them to the global template.) You'll also learn to transport and share customized elements using Project's Organizer (a dialog box that helps you manage Project elements like views, tables, calendars, and filters, and copy them between the global template and your Project files). This chapter concludes with an explanation of how to create and use project templates to jump-start your future project endeavors.

> **Note:** If you've downloaded files from the book website, you can follow along using the file Event_Ch23_start.mpp.

Understanding the Types of Templates

Project has two types of templates. Here's what each one does:

- **Global template**: This template acts as a storage facility for built-in and customized Project elements, such as views, tables, groups, filters, and calendars. It also contains the settings for Project options that determine how the program behaves, such as which task mode it uses when you create new tasks. If you customize the ribbon and Quick Access Toolbar (Chapter 22), those changes are kept in the global template, too. Project attaches the global template to every new Project file you create. That way, built-in elements, customizations, and settings are available whenever you work on a Project file.

> **Note:** If you use Microsoft Project Portfolio Management tools (Project Server, Project Online, and the Project desktop app), you'll also have an *enterprise global template*. This template is like the mother of all global templates—a *global* global template. This template attaches to every Project file that someone checks out, so they get the standards setup by your organization as well as the most up-to-date, enterprise-wide customized Project elements. Once a project is published to the server, you use the elements from the enterprise global template (along with your local global). When you're connected to the server, in the Organizer's "Views available in" box, you'll see "Global (+ non-cached Enterprise)."
>
> When you work in an environment like this, modifying an existing table or view might conflict with an enterprise table or view. If you want to customize an element for your own use, first rename the item (Chapter 20) you want to customize to prevent conflicts with the enterprise global template.

- **Project template**: This type of template does double-duty. You can store customized elements in a project template, just like you do in the global template. You can also save some settings, like scheduling options or calculation options, in this type of template. However, a project template can also contain task and resource information—a task list, task links, typical durations, generic resources, and more. For example, once you hold your first product kickoff and find out what it really takes, you can save a project template with all that information. Then, when it's time to start working on next year's event, you don't have to reinvent the wheel.

If you're just getting started with projects, you don't have to create your own templates. Project offers dozens of templates covering an array of project types. In addition, many companies offer specialized project templates that you can download. Or your colleagues may have templates they're willing to share.

Storing Project Settings and Elements

Project has to keep its settings and built-in elements somewhere, and that somewhere is called the *global template*. It stores settings that tell Project how to behave—like whether you use the Gregorian calendar or want to automatically turn on AutoFilter. All the built-in elements that Project provides are in this file, too—like the standard Gantt Chart view, the Standard calendar, and the Entry table. If you customize elements, you can copy them to the global template so they're available to other projects. This section explains what the global template has to offer.

> **Note:** Ribbon and Quick Access Toolbar customizations also reside in the global template. Changes you make to the ribbon apply to Project itself, not just to a particular file (unless you tell the program to do that), so you see them regardless of which project you work on. See Chapter 22 to learn how to apply Quick Access Toolbar customizations to a specific Project file.

The global template is so special that the program attaches it to every Project file you create so your program-wide settings and elements are available. Under the hood, though, the global template is really just a regular project template file called *global.mpt*. If you create a copy of this file, you can open it in Project like any other file. The note titled "Locating the Global Template" tells you where to find your global template file after you install Project. The global template stores the following elements:

- Views
- Reports
- Modules

> **Note:** Modules relate to macros and Visual Basic. See Chapter 27.

- Tables
- Filters
- Calendars
- Maps

> **Note:** Maps define the correlation between fields in Project and data in other programs when you import or export data, as described in Chapter 25.

- Fields
- Groups

> **Note:** Beginning with Project 2010, the program stopped supporting custom forms or toolbars, so you won't find them in the Organizer.

Storing Customized Project Options

If you change a ***program-wide*** setting in the Project Options dialog box (choose File→Options), then the global template memorizes that setting and applies that setting to every new Project file you create. In other words, when you create a Project file, it takes on the settings that are in place in the global template at that time. You can tell which settings in the Project Options dialog box apply program-wide because their section headings don't have a box for choosing a project, like the General heading shown in Figure 23-1.

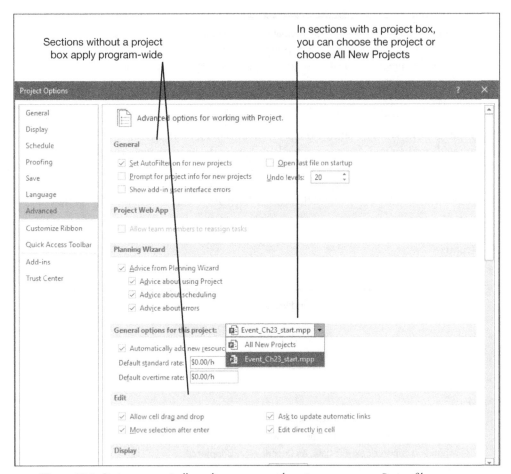

Figure 23-1. *Project automatically applies program-wide settings to every new Project file you create.*

Project also includes ***project-specific*** options. When a heading is something like "Display options for this project" and includes a box for choosing a project, you know that the settings in that section are project-specific. Those settings reside in the Project file, not the global template. Although they start out matching what's set in the global template, any changes you make to them remain in your Project file and don't affect other projects.

If you want to change a project-specific setting for **all** new projects, then in the "Display options for this project" box, choose All New Projects in the drop-down list (Figure 23-1).

> **Tip:** You can also use project-specific settings in certain types of new projects by creating a project template (see the section "Building Templates for Projects" later in this chapter) with those settings in place. Then, when you create a new project based on that template, the settings you want are already there.

Locating the Global Template

If you want to share your global template with a colleague, you may have trouble tracking it down on your computer. The Organizer dialog box isn't any help, because the label for the "<element> available in" box at the bottom left says only "Global.MPT." You have no way of knowing where that file resides.

When you install Project on a computer running Windows 7, 8 or 10 Project places a copy of **global.mpt** in **C:\Users\<username>\AppData\Roaming\Microsoft\MS Project\16\en-US**, where <username> is the name of the person who installed Project on the computer and en-US is the language code for English. (If you install Project using a different language, the name for the folder is set to the code for the installed language. In some cases, the language code folder might be named using the language tag, which is en-US for English.) If you want to use a global template that someone else sends you, replace the **global.mpt** file in this folder.

You may search for **global.mpt** files from the Start menu by choosing Search and never see the one in the AppData folder. Windows initially hides this folder, so it doesn't show up as you browse folders in Windows or use the Windows Search box. To see hidden folders and files in any folder window, in Windows Explorer for Windows 10, click the View tab. At the right end of the ribbon, click Options and then choose "Change folder and search options." In the Folder Options dialog box, click the View tab, select the "Show hidden files and folders" option, and then click OK. After that, you can see **global.mpt** and replace it with another copy.

If you have more than one version of Project installed, you may have more than one global.mpt file. Each global.mpt file resides in a folder based on the version of MS Project (such as 16 for Project 2016 and 19 for Project 2019).

> **Tip:** It's a good idea to make a backup copy of your global template before you add or remove elements in it. If you want to get rid of elements you added, or retrieve elements you deleted, then you can replace the active global template with the backup copy. The note titled "Locating the Global Template" above tells you where to find the global template on your computer.

Sharing Custom Elements

Project comes with dozens of built-in elements like views, tables, filters, and groups, which you can use as is or customize to suit your needs. When you customize any of these elements, a customized copy is saved in the Project file you're working on, so it initially shows up only when you open that file. (Same goes for project-specific Project Options settings, shown in Figure 23-1.) Other customized elements like maps go directly into the global template, because Project assumes that you want to use them for every project. Fortunately, the Organizer dialog box makes it easy to propagate customized elements to other Project files or to share them with colleagues. This section tells you how.

> **Note:** If you create *new* elements like views, tables, filters, and groups, regardless of whether you create them from scratch or by customizing an existing element and saving it with a new name, Project automatically copies them to the global template, which is a great timesaver if you're the only person who uses your copy of Project. Copying new elements to the global template means they're available for every new project you create. However, if you don't want to fill up the global template with lots of your customizations, you can control whether new elements attain global-templatehood. To set this behavior, choose File→Options and, on the left side of the Project Options dialog box, choose Advanced. Under the Display heading, turn off the "Automatically add new views, tables, filters, and groups to the global" checkbox. That way, if you create a new view called AwesomeView, which uses a new table called KitchenSink, Project keeps copies of those elements only in the active Project file. However, even when this checkbox is turned off, you can still *manually* copy customized elements to the global template (described later in this chapter).

The Organizer helps you copy customized elements from the global template to a Project file, from a Project file to the global template, or between two Project files. Here's how the Organizer can help:

- **Using customized elements in new projects**: In many instances, customized elements like views belong to the Project file in which you create them. After you've created customized elements, you can make them available to every new project you create by copying them to the global template.

- **Sharing customized elements**: Having customized elements in your global template is great when you're working on your computer. But if you're in a colleague's office and fire up Project there, your customized elements aren't available, because they're back in the global template on your computer. Likewise, folks in other offices are out of luck unless you share what you've done. To share customized elements, you can copy them to a Project file whose main purpose is to hold all your customizations, and then send that file to someone else (or copy it to a different computer). Then they can copy those elements into their global template.

- **Copying customized elements between Project files**: Sometimes a customized element is important for a specific type of project but not spectacular enough to copy to the global template. The Organizer lets you copy elements from one Project file to another (when both files are open).

- **Creating copies and renaming elements**: You can create copies of elements in the Organizer and rename them without opening them in Project.

- **Removing elements from a Project file or template**: The Organizer simplifies file cleanup, too. You can select one or more elements and then delete them at one time.

As you can see in Figure 23-2, the Organizer bristles with tabs, one for every type of element you can customize. (There's no tab for custom formulas, because they belong to custom fields. Chapter 21 describes how to copy custom fields and formulas.) When you select a tab, the Organizer displays the elements available in two different Project files: initially, the global template on the left side, and the active Project file on the right. However, on either side of the Organizer, you can select any Project file that's open, which is how you copy elements between files.

To open the Organizer, simply choose File→Info and then click Organizer in the Backstage view. Some dialog boxes, like More Views, More Tables, and More Filters, also include an Organizer button that opens the Organizer window.

Copying Elements Between Files

The steps for copying elements between files using the Organizer are the same regardless of which type of element you copy and which two files you use. You choose the file with the element that you want to copy, and the file you want to copy it to, and then copy the element.

Making Customized Elements Available to New Projects

To use a custom element in new projects you create, copy the element from the Project file to the global template. That way, when you create a new Project file, the program grabs the built-in and custom elements from your global template. (Remember, Project stores import/export maps directly in the global template, so you don't have to copy them to make them available to other files.)

Follow Along Practice

Here are the steps for copying elements to the global template:

1. Open the Project file that contains the customized element, in this example, use the sample file for this chapter. Choose File→Info, and then click the Organizer button on the Info page.

    The Organizer dialog box opens. It contains several tabs to cover all the elements it handles, as illustrated in Figure 23-2.

    > **Tip:** If you forgot to make the project with the customized element active before you opened the Organizer window, don't worry. In the "[element] available in" drop-down list on the right, simply choose the file (it must already be open in Project), where [element] is the name of the tab you've selected. For example, if the Groups tab is selected, then the label is "Groups available in."

2. Select the tab for the type of element you want to copy, like Calendars.

The elements stored in the global template appear in the list on the left. The elements in the active project appear in the list on the right.

3. In the list on the right, select the element you want to copy to the global template, in this example, the Halftime calendar shown in Figure 23-2, and then click Copy.

If the global template contains the same type of element with the same name, Project asks if you want to replace what's in the global template. Click Yes if you want to overwrite the one in the global template.

To keep the one that's in the global template, click No. Then, with the element on the right side selected, click Rename, type a new name, and then click OK. Now you can copy the element without a conflict.

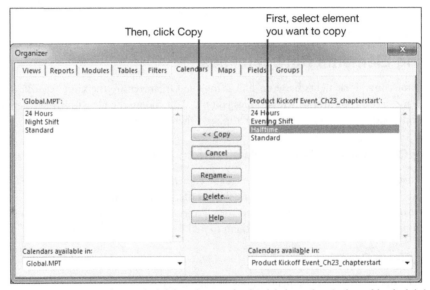

Figure 23-2. *Here the box on the left lists elements for the global template (indicated by the label "Global.MPT" at the bottom left of the window). The box on the right lists elements in the active project (the one you're currently working on).*

4. To copy other customizations in the sample file to your global template, repeat steps 2 and 3 to copy the customization you want to use in your copy of Project.

If you have the "Automatically add new views, tables, filters, and groups to the global" checkbox turned on in the Project Options Advanced category, your global template already has new views, tables, filters, and groups that you've created. However, you can copy custom reports, for example.

5. If you don't want to copy anything else, click the X button at the dialog box's top right.

The custom element you copied (the Halftime calendar, in this example) is now available to all your Project files.

Sharing a Customized Element with Someone Else

For most types of elements, you can share customizations simply by sending someone the Project file in which you created them, because that's where customized elements are stored. However, maps don't work the same way. Project stores them directly in the global template, so you have to copy them to another file to share them. Then you or the colleague with whom you share the file can copy elements directly from one Project file to another. If you share customizations frequently or like to carry a file with your customizations on a flash drive so they're always by your side, the best approach is to create a Project file specifically for customizations and copy your customized elements into it.

Follow Along Practice

Here are the steps:

1. If customized elements are in a Project file rather than the global template, open that file.

    In this example, use Event_Ch23_start.mpp.

2. Create and save a Project file to use to transfer customized elements.

    Choose File→New. On the New page, click Blank Project. Then, choose File→Save and save it to the folder where you want to store it (for example, in your templates folder). In this example, save it as MyCustomization.mpp.

3. Choose File→Info, click the Organizer button, and then select the tab for the type of element you want to copy, in this example, Views.

    The list on the right side of the Organizer dialog box is either empty or contains a few basic elements, unless you've used this transfer file before, as you can see in Figure 23-3. The list on the left shows elements in the global template.

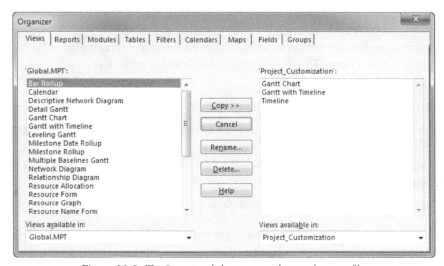

Figure 23-3. *The Organizer helps you copy elements between files.*

4. In the "[element] available in" box on the left (which is set to Global.MPT), click the down arrow and choose the Project file that contains your customizations, in this example, Event_ Ch23_start.mpp.

    After you choose a project, the list box on the left shows customized elements stored in that file (Figure 23-4).

5. In the list on the left, select the element you want to share. (In this example, click the first view that begins with "C_," and then Shift-click the last view that begins with "C_.")

    If you're feeling generous, you can select several elements in the left-hand list (Ctrl-click to select individual items or Shift-click to select several adjacent items).

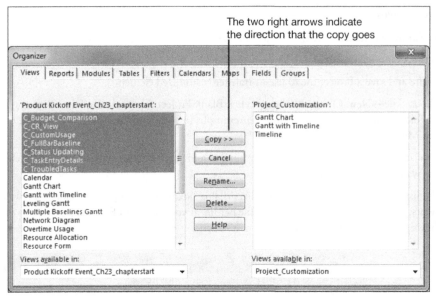

Figure 23-4. *You can select several elements to copy or delete.*

6. Click Copy.

    When you click Copy, Project copies the selected elements to the right at the same time.

7. If you want to copy other types of elements, select the corresponding tab, and then repeat steps 5 and 6.

    For example, copy tables, reports, filters, calendars, fields, and groups from the sample project to the MyCustomization.mpp file.

8. When you're done, click the X button at the dialog box's top right to close it.

The elements are now stored in the Project file, so you can share those customizations with colleagues by sending them the file.

Removing Customized Elements from Files

Customized elements can be tremendous timesavers, but sometimes you want to get rid of them. For example, after you copy a customized element to the global template, you don't need it in the Project file in which you created it.

Another reason to delete customized elements is to restore what Project came with. For example, suppose you made a dozen formatting changes to the Gantt Chart, and now you want the original version back. When you modify a built-in element, Project creates a customized copy in your Project file. (You can tell because the element shows up in the Organizer, in the box on the right for the active Project file.) To get the original back in the Organizer, simply delete the customized one.

> **Tip:** You can also reset a built-in element outside of the Organizer. Suppose you have the Gantt Chart view displayed and you want to reset it to its default definition. On the View tab, click the bottom half of the Gantt Chart button, and then choose "Reset to Default" on the drop-down menu.

Follow Along Practice

Deleting customized elements in the Organizer is easy. Just follow these steps:

1. In this example, make Event_Ch23_start.mpp the active project.

    If you have more than one file open, in the View tab's Window section, choose Switch Windows, and then choose the project you want to make active.

2. If you plan to delete a view or a table in the Organizer, first apply a different view or table, in this example, display the Gantt Chart view.

    You can't delete or copy tables and views when they're visible. In the View tab's Task Views section, choose a different view. In the View tab's Data section, click Tables and choose a different table.

3. Choose File→Info, click the Organizer button, and then select the tab for the type of element you want to delete, in this example, choose Views.

    The customized elements appear in the box on the right.

4. In the box on the right, select the element you want to delete (in this example, select the C_CR_ View view), and then click Delete.

    In the confirmation dialog box, click Yes to delete the element, or click No if you've had second thoughts. The element disappears from the list when you click Yes.

5. When you're done, click the X button at the dialog box's top right to close it.

> **Warning:** Be careful about deleting elements from the global template, because you can delete some built-in elements: views, groups, filters, tables, and so on. If you make a habit of deleting elements in the global template, it's a good idea to keep a backup copy in case you want to get something back.

Renaming Customized Elements

The Organizer also lets you rename customized elements, which is helpful if you're trying to copy elements with the same names between files. For example, if you want to copy a customized Gantt Chart view to the global template without overwriting the original Gantt Chart view that comes with Project, rename your version before you copy it.

> **Note:** Some built-in elements are willing to go by a different name, while others aren't. For example, you can rename built-in groups, except for the built-in No Group. And you can't rename custom fields using the Organizer; instead, you have to use the Custom Fields dialog box to do that.

Follow Along Practice

To rename an element, follow these steps:

1. Open the Project file with the customized elements, in this example, Event_Ch23_start.mpp.

2. Open the Organizer window (choose File→Info→Organizer), and then select the tab for the type of element you want to rename, in this example, Tables.

    The customized elements appear in the box on the right.

3. In the right-hand box, select the element you want to rename (in this example, Entry), and then click Rename.

    The Rename dialog box is simple, with a "New name" box and an OK button.

4. In the "New name" box, type the name, in this example, type ***MyCustomEntry***, and then click OK.

    The newly renamed element appears in the list.

5. When you're done working in the Organizer, click the X button to close the dialog box.

Building Templates for Projects

Despite the differences that make every project unique, many projects have a lot in common. Project gives you several ways to reuse work you've done before. Here are just a few examples:

*   **Save time**: Past projects make great starting points for new projects. You've already figured out many of the tasks you need, so why not them to jump-start new projects? A project template can contain tasks with task dependencies, typical durations, and even resource assignments. Keep anything that stays the same, and change only what's different.

*   **Standardize**: Quite often, you learn the hard way what works and what doesn't. You can improve your results by basing new projects on your previous successes, not your past mistakes. By creating templates that reflect your organization's project-management knowledge, everyone

can benefit from the lessons learned on each and every project. You can use project templates to define the standards your organization follows. (If your organization uses Microsoft Project On-line/Server, the enterprise global template is the repository for your organization's project-man-agement standards.) A template can act like a checklist, with project-management tasks that are part of every project. Or it can contain the views, reports, and customized performance measures that your organization uses to evaluate project status.

As you've learned earlier in this chapter, the global template stores program-wide settings that apply to every project. You can also make customized elements available to every new project you create by storing them in the global template.

- **Learn from others**: You don't have to learn everything from the school of hard knocks. Taking advantage of others' expertise can save time and improve your results. Starting with a template built by experts gets a project off on the right foot. You can use templates built by others in your organization or download templates that are available online (Chapter 3).

Creating a Project Template

Whether you want to use a completed project as a basis for new projects or build a standard project that shows off your best project-management practices, a project template can help. Project templates can contain tasks, resources, resource assignments, settings, views, calendars, and more. When you create a new Project file from a project template, the new file inherits everything the template has to offer.

Follow Along Practice

You can save any Project file as a project template. When you save a file as a template, the Save As Template dialog box lets you pick the information you want to throw away (and thus the information you want to keep). Here's how to save an existing Project file as a template:

1. Open the existing project (in this example, Event_Ch23_start.mpp), and then choose File→Save As.

   The Save As page appears in the Backstage view.

2. Navigate to the location or folder where you want to save your template.

   If you want the template to show up on the New page in the Backstage view, save the template in your personal templates folder (described shortly). This folder can be anywhere on your computer, but you have to tell Project where this folder is. For example, if your template folder is on your computer, in the Save As list, click Browse. Then, in the Save as dialog box, navigate to the folder.

3. In the Save As dialog box that appears, in the "Save as type" drop-down list, choose "Project Template." (If you've set up Windows Explorer to display file extensions for all files, the file type appears as "Project Template (*.mpt)" instead.)

   Choosing this option creates a file with the .mpt file extension. (If you forget to change the "Save as type" to Project Template, all you'll do is save the file to a regular .mpp Project file with a dif-ferent filename.)

> **Note:** If you've already told Project where you store your personal templates, the program automatically jumps to that folder as soon as you choose Project Template in the "Save as type" box.

4. In the "File name" box, type a name for the template, in this example, ***Event_Template***, and then click Save.

    The Save As Template dialog box (Figure 23-5) opens with checkboxes for specifying the data you ***don't*** want in the template.

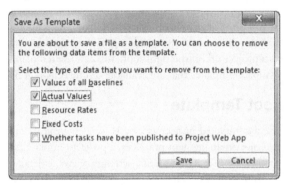

Figure 23-5. *You can specify the data you want to remove from the file before saving it as a template.*

5. Turn on the checkboxes for the items you want to ***remove*** from the project.

    Typically, you want to turn on the "Values of all baselines" checkbox, Actual Values checkbox, and Fixed Costs checkbox, because those values usually change from project to project. If resource rates change (for example, if you use different subcontractors in different projects), turn on the Resource Rates checkbox. Turn on the "Whether tasks have been published to Project Web App" checkbox, if you work in a Project Server or Project Online environment.

6. Click Save.

    Project creates a file with an .mpt file extension with only the information you want and opens it in Project.

Making Your Templates Easy to Find

After you set up a template with exactly what you want, using it to create a new file is painless—***if*** you tell Project where to find the template. Once you tell Project where you store your templates, they're waiting for you each time you go to create a new file. Here's how to tell Project where you store your templates:

Follow Along Practice

1. Choose File→Options.

    The Project Options dialog box opens.

2. On the left side of the Project Options dialog box, click Save.

The "Default personal templates location" box is initially empty. If you want to see your templates in the Backstage view, you must fill in this box so it points to the folder where you store your templates. You'll do that in the next step.

3. To change the location of your templates, to the right of the "Default personal templates location" box, click Browse.

The Modify Location dialog box appears.

4. Select the folder that holds your templates, and then click OK.

When you select a folder in the Modify Location dialog box, the "Folder name" field shows the name of the folder. When you click OK, the Modify Location dialog box closes, and the path to the template folder appears in the "Default user template location" box, as shown in Figure 23-6.

5. Click OK to close the Project Options dialog box.

Your templates appear in the New page of the Backstage view, described in detail later in this chapter.

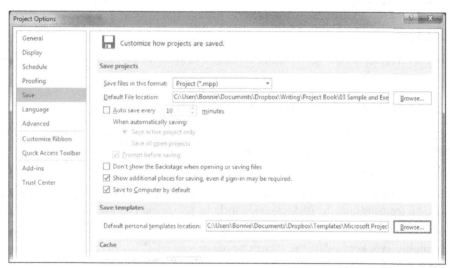

Figure 23-6. *You can tell Project which folder contains your personal templates.*

Editing a Template

If you want to make changes to a project template, you can't open and save it the way you do with regular Project files. If you do, Project saves a copy of the file as a regular Project file with an *.mpp* file extension. That's because Project assumes that you're using the template to start a new Project file—not opening the template in order to edit it. To save template changes in the template file, follow these steps (you don't have to perform these steps for the example):

1. Choose File→Open.

The Open page of the Backstage view appears.

2. Click Browse, and then navigate to the location that contains your templates.

3. In the Open dialog box, in the drop-down list to the right of the "File name" box, choose Project Templates. (If you've set up Windows Explorer to display file extensions for all files, the file type appears as "Project Template (*.mpt)" instead.)

   Choosing this setting displays only Project templates as you navigate through folders.

4. Click the template you want to tweak, and then click Open.

   Project opens the template for editing. Make the changes you want.

5. Choose File→Save as if you were creating a new Project file.

   The Save As page appears.

6. Choose your templates folder, and then in the Save As dialog box's "Save as type" box, choose Project Template (or "Project Template (*.mpt)" if you have file extensions turned on in Windows Explorer). Click Save.

   Because you're trying to save changes to an existing template, a warning appears asking if you want to replace the original file.

7. Click Yes.

   The Save As Template dialog box opens. Click Save to overwrite the existing template file with the changes you made.

Creating a Project File from a Template

Creating a project file from a template is easy regardless of where you get your template. Here are the steps (you don't have to perform these steps for the example):

1. Choose File→New.

   The New page appears in the Backstage view. If you've set the option that tells Project where you store our template files, the Backstage view includes Office and Personal headings.

   To look for more templates online, click Office to see popular templates. To find a particular type of template, type keywords in the "Search for online templates" box and then click the magnifying glass icon to the right of the box

   > **Note:** If you share templates with other project managers, you want the files in a location that everyone can get to, like a shared network drive. You can create a new Project file from a template simply by double-clicking the template's filename in Windows Explorer.

2. To use a template you created and stored in your personal templates folder (described earlier), click Personal.

   The New page displays the templates in your personal templates folder, as shown in Figure 23-7.

> **Note:** If your organization uses Project Server or Project Online, you'll see "Enterprise" instead of "Personal." However, any templates you save in your personal folder show up when you click the Enterprise heading.

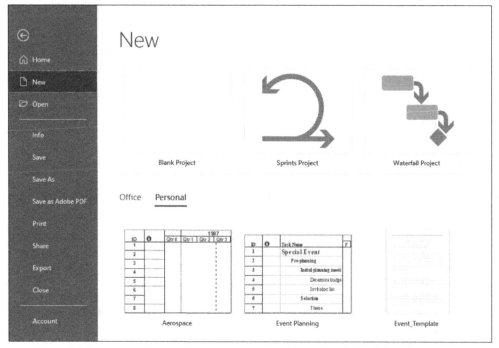

Figure 23-7. *If you told Project where to find your personal template folder, click Personal to see the templates in that folder.*

3. Double-click the icon for the template you want to use.

   Project creates a new file based on the template. The file looks and acts like a regular file.

4. Before you save the new file, make any changes you need, such as the project start date, and remove any data you don't want.

   The note titled "Adjusting Your New Project File" describes several things you should review and possibly change before you save your new Project file.

5. After you make the changes you want, choose File→Save.

   Even though you choose File→Save, Project displays the Save As page since this is the first time you've saved this new file. Once you choose where you want to save the file, the Save As dialog box opens with the "Save as type" box set to "Project" (or "Project (*.mpp)" if Windows Explorer shows files extensions for all files). These settings automatically save a copy of the template as a regular .mpp file, so you don't overwrite the template file.

Adjusting Your New Project File

A template can go a long way toward a new project schedule, but it won't be perfect. Things like the project's start date, resource list, and date constraints are guaranteed to need changing. To change dates and date constraints, in the Project tab's Schedule section, click Move Project. You specify the new start date and this feature changes the task dates and deadlines accordingly.

Here are other parts of the file to look at for adjustments you might need to make:

- **Task list**: In the Gantt Chart view or another task-oriented view, look over the list of tasks. Add tasks that are missing and remove ones you don't need.

- **Task mode**: In the Gantt Chart view, display the Entry table. If necessary, switch Manually Scheduled tasks to Auto Scheduled or vice versa.

- **Task estimates**: Durations that end with question marks represent estimated values. Replace these values with your planned values for the new project. It doesn't hurt to look over all durations and work values to see if they need to be revised.

- **Task dependencies**: Review the links between tasks to see if they still apply for your new project. Modify any task links that need changing.

- **Date constraints**: If you set dates for Manually Scheduled tasks or add date constraints (Chapters 4 and 5) to Auto Scheduled tasks, those dates are likely to be obsolete when you create your new project. Modify the dates to reflect your best guess of when those tasks should occur. You can adjust those dates again as you plan the new project.

- **Resources**: Display the Resource Sheet view. If you know the people assigned to your new project, add them to the resource list or replace the generic resources on the list with the people who will play those roles.

24

Working on More Than
One Project

If you're like most project managers, you juggle several projects at the same time. You may have several smaller projects that are part of a larger effort—like the subprojects for building the different parts of a new airplane. Or you may simply manage several separate projects at once, like several events that your company is hosting. In almost every case, you have to share resources with others. For organizations with oodles of projects, Microsoft's enterprise project-management software (Project Server or Project Online) provides tools for managing entire portfolios of projects (Chapter 29). However, the Project desktop app also has features for managing smaller numbers of projects.

In Project, *a master project* lets you work with several projects at the same time. You create a new Project file and then insert other Project files into it to consolidate them into one file. (Although you insert the files into a master project, they still exist as separate Project files.) A master project is great for assembling multiple subprojects in one place, but it works equally well if you're managing a bunch of unrelated projects and want an easy way to keep an eye on all of them at once. This chapter describes how to build a master project from related subprojects and how to consolidate several unrelated projects into one Project file.

Master projects aren't your only option when working with multiple projects, though. Sometimes all you need is a link between a task in one project and a task in another project. Suppose one project in your company has magnanimously funded a new database-management system. One of your projects can use the system, but you don't want to start your database work until the stakeholders have approved the other project's database design. In cases like that, you can create what's called an *external task dependency* (a.k.a. *cross-project dependency*) between the database-design milestone and the start of your project's database work. In this chapter, you'll learn how to create external task dependencies.

Whether you fight over resources with yourself or with other project managers, you eventually have to share the resources you use. Project Online/Server have the handiest tools for finding and sharing resources, but plain-Jane Project can share resources, too—the program lets you create a file called a *resource pool* to hold information about available resources. In this chapter, you'll learn how to create a resource pool and apply it to your projects. You'll also learn different ways of opening a resource pool and when to use each one.

Understanding Master Projects and Subprojects

If you don't have the option of using Project Server or Project Online to manage multiple projects, you can insert subprojects into a master project instead, no matter how much or how little the projects have in common. Here are a few situations in which inserting subprojects into a master project can help you manage multiple projects:

- **A large project with subprojects**: Suppose you're managing a project that requires several project managers to handle different parts. For example, a project to build a new airplane may have subprojects for the fuselage, engines, electronics, wiring, and so on. The separate systems progress individually, but they have to come together before the rubber can hit the tarmac. When you set up a master project that contains the separate subprojects, the project managers for the subprojects (whether they're subcontractors or part of your organization) each work on their own Project files. But you can see the big picture of all the subprojects simply by opening the master project.

> **Tip:** In reality, a project to develop an airplane would overwhelm the capabilities of Project's master projects. Master projects and subprojects aren't appropriate for managing humongous projects with casts of thousands, budgets in the millions, hordes of risks and issues, and project interdependencies galore. For a portfolio of big projects like those, Project Server, Project Online, and other enterprise project management tools are what you need to stay on top of everything.

- **Several projects share the same resources**: Say you and another project manager in your company work on different projects, but you both pull your resources from the same pool of employees. After a few hallway tussles over popular resources, you decide to try a better way. The two of you create a resource pool that contains the resources you both share. Then you both link your projects to that resource pool so you can check resources' availability.

- **Several unrelated projects**: If you spend each day juggling several small projects, you'd probably like to keep track of them all within Project. By creating a master project and inserting all your Project files into it, you can open all your projects simply by opening the master file. Even better, you can work on the projects without switching Project windows and create links between tasks in different projects. Similarly, you can produce consolidated views or reports for all your projects.

Tip: When you add subprojects to a master project file, Project calculates a single critical path for all the subprojects. However, if you're using a master project to track *unrelated* projects, you want each project to have its own critical path. To tell the program to calculate separate critical paths for each project, choose File→Options, and then choose Schedule on the left side of the Project Options dialog box. Scroll to the bottom of the dialog box and, in the "Calculation options for this project" section, turn off the "Inserted projects are calculated like summary tasks" checkbox. Then click OK.

- **Reporting on overall progress**: You can insert projects into a master project temporarily to produce consolidated views or reports for several projects.

Although you can insert a Project file into any ***other*** Project file (see the section "Linking Tasks in Different Projects"), the best way to keep track of multiple projects is to create a master project—a Project file that contains other projects. Here's how a master project works when you insert Project files into it:

- All the inserted subprojects appear in one Project window, so you can work on and save them all as if they were a single file, even though the individual projects remain separate files.

- The inserted projects look like summary tasks, which you can expand to show all the subtasks, or collapse to see the big picture.

- You can work on subproject tasks as if they belong to the master project—modifying, sorting, filtering, and grouping the aggregated tasks.

- Because a master project is a regular Project file, you can add tasks to it—for example, for the work you do supervising the other project managers.

- A master project maintains continuous contact with its inserted subprojects. If someone modifies and then saves a subproject, those saved changes are immediately visible in the master file. Conversely, if you make a change to a subproject in the master project, those changes are immediately visible to anyone looking at the original Project file for that inserted subproject.

Head to the section "Creating a Master Project" to learn how to create a master project that contains several subprojects.

Linking Tasks in Different Projects

Maybe only a few tasks in one project link to tasks in another project. For example, suppose that part of planning your product kickoff depends on reaching a key milestone in product development. In order to indicate this connection in Project, you need to link tasks in different projects to create an ***external task dependency***. The easiest way to do this is to insert both projects into a temporary master project and then link them the way you would two tasks in the same Project file.

> **Note:** If you've downloaded files from the book website, you can follow along using the file Event_Ch24_start.mpp, Ch24 Product Development.mpp, and Ch24 ProductDev2.mpp.

Follow Along Practice

To create an external task dependency, follow these steps:

1. Choose File→New, and then, on the New screen, click Blank Project.

    Project creates a new, blank file that's ready to accept your subprojects.

2. Select the first blank row, and then, in the Project tab's Insert section, click Subproject.

    The Insert Project dialog box appears. Navigate to the folder that contains the first project you want to insert.

3. Select the project you want to insert (in this example, Ch24 Product Development), make sure the "Link to project" checkbox is turned on, and then click Insert.

4. Repeat steps 2 and 3 to insert the second project, in this example, Event_Ch24_start.mpp.

    The two projects look like summary tasks, except that a Project file icon appears in the indicator column, as shown in Figure 24-1. Click the white triangle next to each project's name to expand the project to display all the subtasks.

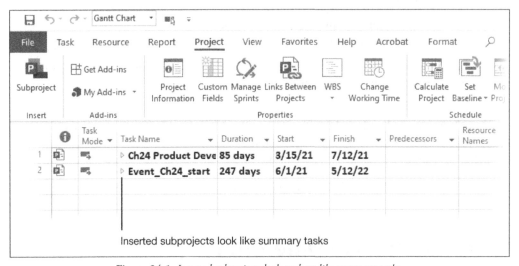

Figure 24-1. *Inserted subprojects look and act like summary tasks.*

5. Select the task that acts as the predecessor by clicking anywhere in its row.

    In this example, in the Ch24 Product Development subproject, select task ID 10 "Design phase complete."

6. Ctrl-click the successor task.

In this example, in the Event_Ch24_start subproject, select task ID 59 "Create publicity materials."

7. In the Task tab's Schedule section, click the "Link the Selected Tasks" icon (it looks like two links of chain).

Project draws link lines between the two tasks as if they were in the same project.

8. To see the link, insert the Predecessors field into the table (right-click the Duration column heading, choose Insert Column, and then choose Predecessors on the drop-down menu).

The Predecessors field for the successor task includes the full path to the file that contains the successor task with the task's ID appended at the end, as shown in Figure 24-2. Although you can see the external link in the Predecessor field and other places that show predecessors and successors, you don't see the external tasks in the master project. External predecessors and successors appear only when you open the Project file that includes those external links.

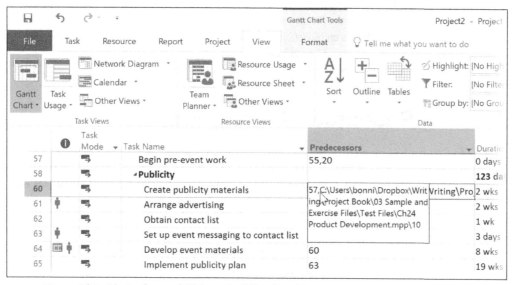

Figure 24-2. *The Predecessor field shows the full path and filename for the project that contains the predecessor, a backslash (\), and then the task ID of the predecessor.*

9. If you want to create other external links, repeat the steps in this section to insert another subproject, if necessary, and then link the tasks.

10. When you're done, choose File→Close. In the first dialog box that asks if you want to save your changes (for the master project), click No. In the second and third dialog boxes that ask if you want to save your changes (for the subprojects), click Yes.

By clicking No in the first dialog box, you discard the master project you created. However, the link between the tasks in the two projects is still in place. If you open the file that contains the successor task, the external predecessor appears in the row immediately above the successor task (the text in its row is gray). In the file that contains the predecessor task, the external successor appears in the row immediately below the predecessor task.

If you suspect that you'll have to add more external links in the future, you can save the master project and reopen whenever you have to create new links.

> **Note:** When you open a Project file that contains external task dependencies, the Links Between Projects dialog box might open, which shows all the file's external predecessors and external successors. If you don't see the dialog box or want to open it later on, in the Project tab's Properties section, click Links Between Projects. You can also control the appearance of cross-project links. Choose File→Options. On the left side of the Project Options dialog box, choose Advanced. In the "Cross project linking options for this project" section, you can turn off the "Show external successors" and "Show external predecessors" checkboxes (they're on by default) to hide external tasks. And if you don't want the Links Between Project dialog box to open automatically, then turn off the "Show 'Links Between Project' dialog box on open" checkbox.

Sharing Resources Among Projects

People often work on more than one project for more than one project manager. If each project manager creates a resource to represent the same worker in each Project file, then overallocated resources and resource squabbles will soon follow. The solution in the Project desktop app is a ***resource pool***, which is a Project file dedicated to resource information—the pool of resources who work on projects, their cost, availability, and most importantly, how much time they're already allocated to tasks. (A resource pool in Project is based on the same idea as the enterprise resource pool in Project Online/Server, although that pool includes a few more tools for managing resources, like security for who can create and edit resources.)

The beauty of a resource pool is that resource information is in one place. Project managers who use those resources simply link their projects to the resource pool. Assigning resources works exactly as it does when resources are contained in the Project file. The only difference is that you can see how much of the resources' time is allocated to tasks from all linked projects.

> **Note:** When you link projects to a resource pool, store the Project files and the resource pool in the same folder. By doing so, you can move that folder to another location (for example, if you reorganize your folder structure or move the folder to a new hard drive) without breaking the links between the resource pool and sharer files. Otherwise, you'll have to recreate the links, as described later in this chapter.

Creating a Resource Pool

The simplest way to set up a resource pool is to create a new Project file that does nothing but act as a resource pool. Although you *can* use a Project file with tasks in it as the resource pool, you may run into problems if you want to work on the tasks and someone else wants to work on resource information. A resource pool file does not work if you store it in a SharePoint directory folder.

Follow Along Practice

To create a standalone resource pool from scratch, do the following:

1. Choose File→New→Blank Project.

    Project opens a blank file.

2. In the View tab's Resource Views section, click Resource Sheet.

    The Resource Sheet is home to all the data about your resources.

3. Fill in information about your shared resources. (In this example, create four work resources named Business Analyst, Designer, Sponsor, and Mfg Lead. You don't have to fill in any other fields.)

    Typically, you fill in resource names, their standard charge rates or cost, and the maximum availability for work resources. If you want to include other information like work group, overtime rate, or cost per use, fill in those fields, too. See Chapter 6 for details on creating resources.

4. Choose File→Save.

    In the Save As page, choose where you want to save the file, in this example, the folder where you stored the book's sample files. In the Save As dialog box, name the project, in this example, *Ch24 Resource Pool*.

    Be sure to save the resource pool in a location that all project managers can access. Saving it to your laptop, for example, won't help other project managers who need to link to the file. So go with a network drive or another shared location instead.

> **Tip:** If you have resource information in Microsoft Outlook, Active Directory, or an HR database, then you can import that information into Project, as described in Chapter 25. Or you can copy resources from one Project file and paste them into the resource pool file. (See the note titled "Copying Data Between Project Files" in Chapter 25 for copy and paste steps.)

If an existing project contains all the shared resources in your organization, you don't have to build a resource pool from scratch. Here's how to turn an existing Project file into a resource pool Project file (you don't have to perform these steps for the example):

1. Open the existing project.

2. Choose File→Save As to save a copy of the project.

3. With the copy still open, delete all the tasks in it.

To quickly delete all tasks, display the Gantt Chart view. If necessary, turn off the project summary task (in the Format tab's Show/Hide section, turn off the Project Summary Tasks checkbox). To select all tasks, click the Select All cell immediately above the first ID cell. Then press Delete. If a message warns that progress has been reported on the selected item and asks if you still want to delete it, click Yes.

4. Save the Project file.

Voilà—you have a Project file with resources and no tasks that can serve as a resource pool.

Connecting a Project to a Resource Pool

Before you can assign resources from a resource pool to project tasks, you have to link the file that contains the tasks to the resource pool. Any Project file that uses a resource pool is known as a *sharer file*. With the project–resource pool connection in place, the resource pool resources act as if they're part of the project file.

Follow Along Practice

To connect a project to the resource pool, do the following:

1. In Project, open the resource pool file, in this example, Ch24 ResourcePool, created in the previous section.

   Since many project managers may share the resource pool, open the resource pool file as read-only so you don't lock anyone out of the file. To do that, in the Open dialog box, select the resource pool file, and then, on the Open button, click the down arrow, and then choose Open Read-Only.

2. Open the project files that need to access the resource pool, in this example, "Ch24 Product Development" and "Ch24 Product Dev2."

   If you have several projects to share with the resource pool, you can open them all at the same time and then cycle through to connect each one to the resource pool. When you open the "Ch 24 Product Development" file, if the Links Between Projects dialog box opens, click Close.

3. With the "Ch24 Product Development" Project file active, in the Resource tab's Assignments section, choose Resource Pool→Share Resources.

   The Share Resources dialog box opens (Figure 24-3).

4. Select the "Use resources (requires at least one open resource pool)" option and then, if necessary, in the From drop-down list, choose the resource pool file.

   If you have several projects open, the From drop-down list shows all open projects that aren't already sharer files.

5. Under "On conflict with calendar or resource information," select the "Pool takes precedence" option.

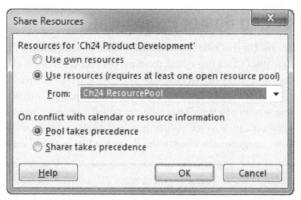

Figure 24-3. *The Share Resources dialog box includes options to tell Project whether to use resources from the project file itself or from the resource pool.*

The best choice is to let the resource pool take precedence (select "Pool takes precedence"), because then the resource pool has the final say about resource information. In that situation, changes made in the resource pool overwrite resource information in the sharer file. For example, suppose someone else opens the resource pool file and updates everyone's standard and overtime rates. When you open a sharer file, the project automatically uses the updated rates. In turn, if you change resource information in your project file, the resource pool is immune to those changes.

If you select "Sharer takes precedence" instead, then resource information you change in your project overwrites information in the resource pool. This approach is fine *if* you use a resource pool for resources dedicated to only your projects. With this option selected, you can change resource information in a project and Project automatically updates the resource pool when you save the project. But if you share the resource pool with several other project managers, the "Sharer takes precedence" option usually leads to unwanted resource changes, as each project manager tries to modify resources.

6. Click OK.

The project now obtains its resource information from the resource pool.

> **Note:** A Project file can only be linked to one resource pool at a time.

7. Repeat steps 3 through 6 to connect others projects (in this example, "Ch24 Product Dev2") to the resource pool.

8. Choose File→Save.

If the resource pool is opened read-only, Project displays a message asking if you want to update the resource pool to reflect changes for all open sharer projects. To update the resource pool, click OK. To save the sharer files without updating the resource pool file, click Cancel. In this example, click OK.

9. Close all the open files.

Opening and Saving Sharer Projects

When you open a sharer file (in this example, Ch24 Product Development), Project asks whether you want to open the resource pool (if it's not open), as shown in Figure 24-4. In almost every case, you do indeed want to open the resource pool, because that way you'll see all the resources from the resource pool in your project's Resource Sheet view. All resource assignments (from all sharer files) appear in the Resource Usage view, so you can see all the tasks on which a resource works. To open the resource pool, select the "Open resource pool to see assignments across all sharer files" option (see Figure 24-4) and then click OK. To see assignments, display the Resource Usage view (View→Resource Usage).

> **Tip:** If you level resources to remove overallocations (Chapter 10), be sure to open the resource pool. When you level resources in one sharer file, the resource pool hears about the modified assignments and passes them on to all sharer files.

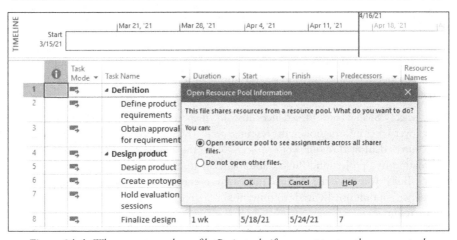

Figure 24-4. *When you open a sharer file, Project asks if you want to open the resource pool.*

> **Tip:** Because an open resource pool shows all assignments for a resource, your Resource Usage view is likely to have a lot more tasks than you remember. The problem is you can't tell which assignments are from *your* project and which come from *other* projects. To identify the project an assignment belongs to, right-click the heading row in the Resource Usage table area, and then choose Insert Column→Project. The Project cell for each assignment then shows the sharer file that made the resource assignment.

Opening the resource pool file also means that the resource assignments you make in your project file affect the resource's availability in the resource pool. When you **save** a sharer file while you have the resource pool file open, Project asks if you want to update the resource pool, as shown in Figure 24-5. To save the resource changes to the resource pool, click OK. (Click Cancel to save the sharer file without updating the resource pool, for example when you're testing what-if scenarios and haven't decided which one you're going to use.)

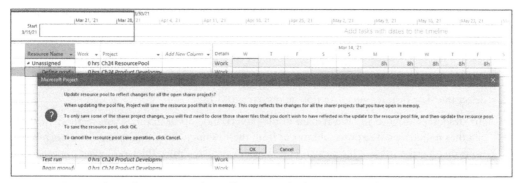

Figure 24-5. *When you save a sharer file, Project asks if you want to update the resource pool.*

Note: If other sharer projects are open, updating the resource pool saves the resource changes from *all* open sharer projects. So before you update the resource pool, be sure to close any sharer files that contain resource changes you don't want in the resource pool just yet. When those sharer files are ready for prime time, open them and the resource pool file, and then save the projects and update the resource pool.

If you select the "Do not open other files" option, then only the resources already assigned to tasks in your project appear in the Resource Sheet view. Likewise, you see only the assignments from your project. When you save the sharer file, the resource pool doesn't receive the resource assignments you make.

Tip: To make sure you're up to date with the most recent changes in the resource pool, in the Resource tab's Assignments section, choose Resource Pool→Refresh Resource Pool. Project immediately shows the most current information from the resource pool. Similarly, if you've made scads of resource assignments, then you can update the resource pool immediately by choosing Resource Pool→Update Resource Pool.

Detaching a Sharer Project from the Resource Pool

You can disconnect a sharer file from the resource pool, for example, if your project gets canned before it gets started or you no longer need the pool for viewing multiple assignments. On the other hand, if a project contains a lot of assignment information, keeping the sharer file and the resource pool connected helps you report on all resource assignments at once. For example, if you want to evaluate resource usage for the past year, you want to keep all projects—active, completed, and discontinued—connected to the resource pool.

To remove a project from the resource pool when the sharer file is open, do the following (you don't have to perform these steps in the sample project):

1. In the Resource tab's Assignments section, choose Resource Pool→Share Resources.

    The Share Resources dialog box opens.

2. Select the "Use own resources" option, and then click OK.

    Any resources assigned to tasks remain in the project and appear in the Resource Sheet view, but all other resource pool resources disappear from the Resource Sheet. In addition, the assignments from the detached sharer file (which is now just a regular Project file) no longer appear in the resource pool.

If the resource pool is open, it's easy to remove sharer files from the resource pool. Here's how (you don't have to perform these steps in the sample project):

1. With the resource pool open, in the Resource tab's Assignments section, choose Resource Pool→Share Resources.

    The Share Resources dialog box, shown in Figure 24-5, opens.

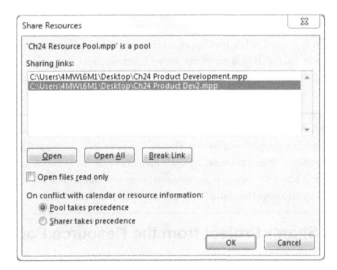

Figure 24-6. *If you choose Resource Pool→Share Resources when the resource pool is the active project, the Share Resources dialog box displays all the sharer files.*

2. Select the file you want to remove, and then click Break Link.

    This dialog box is helpful for troubleshooting sharer files, because it lists all the sharer files connected to the resource pool. In addition to removing files, you can also open one by selecting it, and then clicking the Open button beneath the list. Click Open All to open all sharer files.

3. When you're done removing sharer files, click OK. Save the resource pool and sharer files.

Editing Resource Pool Information

Once a resource pool is connected to at least one sharer file, you have three ways to open the pool. Sometimes you just want to see what's in the resource pool. Sometimes you need full read-write access—for example, when you're updating everyone's cost rates or work calendars. Project gives you options for each scenario.

When you open a resource pool file (choose File→Open, and then select the resource pool Project file), the Open Resource Pool dialog box appears with options that win the prize for longest option labels. Here's what your choices are, and when to use each one (you don't have to perform these steps in the sample project):

- **Read-only**: The "Open resource pool read-only allowing others to work on projects connected to the pool" option opens the resource pool as read-only. However, even if you choose this option, saving sharer files updates the resource pool with assignments you've made. The benefit of choosing this option is that everyone else who uses the resource pool can continue to work on their projects at the same time.

- **Read-write**: If you need to make changes to resources in the resource pool, select the "Open resource pool read-write so that you can make changes to resource information (like pay rates, etc.), although this will lock others out of updating the pool with new information" option. When you select this option, you can modify fields like costs and resource calendars. Of course, you want to use read-write mode for as short a time as possible, because no one else can access the resource pool while you're using it. That means other project managers can't see resource assignments and availability in any of the sharer files connected to this resource pool. If they open their Project files, they have to do so without opening the resource pool.

- **Create master project**: The "Open resource pool read-write and all other sharer files into a new master project file. You can access this new master project file from the View tab, Switch Windows command" option combines the resource pool and all sharer files into a brand-new master project file. If you work on several projects of your own, this is an easy way to build a master project. This master project is also useful when you want to produce reports that span all the projects your organization performs. Remember that the resource pool is read-write, so other project managers can't open their sharer files connected to the resource pool while you have it open.

Creating a Master Project

Setting up a master project is a matter of sharing resources from your resource pool file with each project you want to be part of the master project. Once you do that, you can open the resource pool file and choose the option that creates a master project from all the sharer files. (The less-common alternative is to create a master project when you already have a single large project that you want to break into subprojects. The note titled "Creating a Master Project from One Large Project" tells you how to do that.) If you create a master project to supervise several projects managed by others, be sure to store all the files in a shared location that all the project managers can access.

Follow Along Practice

Here's how you create a master project that includes several subprojects:

1. Open a project file that you want to be part of the master project, in this example, "Ch24 Product Development.mpp."

2. If the project isn't connected to your resource pool file, follow the steps described earlier to connect the file to the resource pool, in this example Ch24 Resource Pool.mpp.

3. Save the project and update the resource pool.

4. Repeat steps 1-3 for all projects that you want in the master project, in this example, open "Ch24 Product Dev2.mpp" and connect it to the resource pool. Close all the open files.

   When you open a master project, the program opens all the subprojects. As you add more subprojects to a master project, the demand on your computer's memory increases. Theoretically, a master project can contain up to 998 subprojects. However, if you try to include that many subprojects, your machine is likely to crash before you get close to that limit. A maximum of 50 subprojects is more realistic.

5. Open the resource pool file if it isn't already open. In the Open Resource Pool dialog box, select the option that begins with "Open resource pool read-write and all other sharer files into a new master project file." Click OK.

6. On the View tab, click Switch Windows, and choose the file that Project created (it will be named something like Project1).

7. Save your new master project. In this example, call it "Ch24 Master Project."

Now, you can work on the inserted projects as you would regular tasks. If you need help identifying tasks and resources from different subprojects, insert the Subproject File column into the view table. The Subproject File column contains the full path to the subproject file, which means the column's values are huge. Don't widen the column to show the entire path. Instead, you can read the full path simply by putting your mouse pointer over a cell in the column.

Note: When you insert projects into a master project, the ID cells for tasks seem to go crazy. Project assigns sequential ID numbers to each subproject, beginning with 1. However, the tasks that belong to inserted projects have ID numbers that *also* begin with 1. So you're likely to see several tasks with the same ID number. When you work with subprojects, ignore the ID numbers. Instead, refer to the WBS code with a project prefix (see the section "Setting Up a Custom WBS Code" in Chapter 21) to uniquely identify every task.

Suppose you supervise several newbie project managers and you want an easy way to review all the projects they manage, but you don't want to change those subprojects by mistake. You can insert projects into a master project as read-only. Then you can view the inserted projects from the master project, but you can modify them only by opening their source Project files. To insert projects as read-only, in the Insert Project dialog box, click the down arrow on the Insert button, and then, from the drop-down list, choose Insert Read-Only.

You can also change an inserted project to read-only *after* it's inserted. In a Gantt Chart table, click anywhere in the inserted project's summary task row, and then press Shift+F2 to open the Inserted Project Information dialog box (or in the Task tab's Properties section, click Information). Select the dialog box's Advanced tab, and then turn on the "Read only" checkbox. To quickly change several subprojects to read-only, insert the Subproject Read Only field in the Gantt Chart table (right-click in the table's heading area, and then choose Insert Column→Subproject Read Only). To make an inserted project read-only, change the field's value to Yes.

One exception to a subproject's read-only status occurs when you open the subproject and then open the master project while the subproject is still open. In that case, Project changes the read-only subproject file whether you make the change in the master project *or* the subproject source file.

Creating a Master Project from One Large Project

You've forged ahead on a massive project, putting all the tasks into one Project file. One day, you realize that this big, awkward file is making it harder for you to manage the project and, more importantly, delegate subprojects to other project managers. All is not lost—you can turn your gargantuan project into a master project with subprojects. Here's how (you don't have to perform these steps in the sample project):

1. Make a copy of the original Project file for each subproject within your large project.

2. In each new file, select all the tasks that don't belong to that subproject by dragging over their ID cells (the numbered cells in the table's first column). Then, in the Task tab's Clipboard section, choose Cut.

3. Save each subproject Project file.

4. Use the original Project file to create a resource pool as described earlier in this chapter.

5. Connect each subproject file to the resource pool.

6. Create a master project as described in the steps earlier in this section.

7. Create task dependencies between the subprojects to restore them to the chronological order they had in the original large project.

Removing a Subproject from a Master Project

If you no longer need an inserted project in your master project, then you can delete the inserted project task while keeping the original subproject file. Suppose another project manager takes over one of your projects, so you no longer need to see that project. Simply delete it from your master project. The new project manager then works on the original Project file. That's it.

To remove an inserted project, do the following (you don't have to perform these steps in the sample project):

1. In the master project's Gantt Chart view, click the ID cell for the inserted project's summary task.

    Project selects the entire row.

2. Press the Delete key on your keyboard, or right-click the task's row and choose Delete Task on the shortcut menu.

    The Planning Wizard dialog box appears and asks you to confirm that you want to delete a summary task and all its subtasks.

3. Make sure the Continue option is selected, and then click OK.

    Project removes the inserted project from the master project but leaves the original subproject file where it is. (If you change your mind, click Cancel instead.)

Working with Baselines in a Master Project

Baselines in a master project don't work quite like they do in individual Project files (Chapter 12). In a master file, the baseline values for the subprojects appear for each task within the subprojects. However, the project summary tasks for each subproject are empty: the subproject baseline values don't appear in the master file. (That's because each subproject could have been baselined at a different time.) You probably want to see baseline values in subproject project summary rows, so you can evaluate all your projects. You can do that by setting a baseline for the entire master project.

To set a baseline for the master project and all the subprojects within it, do the following (you don't have to perform these steps in the sample project):

1. In the master project, display a task-oriented view like the Gantt Chart.

2. In the Project tab's Schedule section, choose Set Baseline, and then choose Set Baseline on the drop-down menu.

    The Set Baseline dialog box opens.

3. Choose the baseline you want to use, for example, Baseline10.

    Choose a baseline that you haven't used in any of your subprojects. If you modify tasks within the master project and re-baseline using a baseline that's already been used, Project will overwrite that baseline with the new values from the master file. If you haven't made any modifications to the subprojects, this newly saved baseline rolls up baseline values in the subprojects to their project summary tasks.

4. Click OK.

> **Tip:** When you generate reports that use baseline values, those reports use baseline values from the master project. To tell Project to use the baseline you save in the master, choose File→Options. In the Advanced category's "Earned Value options for this project" section, choose the master file's baseline (Baseline10, in this case) in the "Baseline for Earned Value calculation" box.

Correcting Broken File Links

When you work with master projects, sharer files, and resource pools, the links between files can break for various reasons. For example, say you rename a sharer file or your resource pool. Or perhaps, you delete a sharer file, because the project has been cancelled. (As long as you keep all your linked files in the same subfolder, the links between files won't break if you move or copy the folder.) This section describes how to correct broken file links depending on what broke the link:

- **Resource pool can't be found**: Suppose you rename your resource pool without disconnecting sharer files from it. The next time you open a sharer file, Project displays a message that Project can't find the shared resource pool. Click OK to dismiss the message. In this situation, you have to reconnect the sharer file to the resource pool. To do that, follow the steps in the section "Connecting a Project to a Resource Pool" using the new resource pool file name.

- **Subproject in a master project can't be found**: If you move a subproject to a different folder or delete it, when you open the master project that links to that subproject, the master project opens without complaint. In fact, the summary task for the subproject still appears in the task list. However, when you click the white triangle to the left of the subproject name in the Task Name cell to expand the subproject, the "Cannot find inserted project" dialog box opens, which is basically a File Open dialog box so you can tell Project where the file is. If the file has been moved or renamed, simply navigate to the new folder, select the file, and click Open. On the other hand, if the file has been deleted, click Cancel. Then, in the task list, select the subproject summary task, and press Delete to delete it.

25

Exchanging Data Between Programs

Managing projects is much more about communicating with people than tweaking Gantt Charts. Project planning is a collaborative effort among you, the stakeholders, and the rest of the project team. For the duration of the project, people communicate continuously as they complete work, identify and resolve problems, and report statuses.

As you've already seen, Microsoft Project isn't the only program you need for managing projects, especially when it comes to communicating about aspects of your projects: Word documents, Excel spreadsheets, PowerPoint presentations, and other types of files are often better tools. For example, tracking issues and risks is easier in a spreadsheet, SharePoint list, or an Access or SQL database. (Project Server and Project Online have built-in features for tracking issues and risks, too.) And PowerPoint or Sway are great for presenting different views of project information at a status meeting.

Information flows in both directions—from other programs to Project and vice versa. For example, after you hammer out costs and estimates in Excel, you can bring them into your Project schedule. Similarly, looking at change request documents, specifications, or quality control graphs from within Project can save the time it takes to open other files in other programs.

In this chapter, you'll learn how to copy and paste data and pictures between files—the most straightforward way to exchange data. For example, you can copy task names as text or costs as numbers from a Project Gantt Chart table into an Excel spreadsheet, or vice versa. You'll also learn how to import and export data into and from Project.

An Overview of Information Exchange

With the various ways to exchange information, it's hard to know which one to choose. This is a quick guide to the ways you can exchange information between Project and other programs, and when to use each one.

- **Copy**: For small amounts of data and pictures, copying and pasting is the simplest way to get information from one program to the other. You can copy values and then edit them like any other data in the file. In fact, you can't even tell they came from another program and file. You can also copy and paste a picture of a Visio diagram into a Project timescale or copy a picture of your Project schedule into a PowerPoint presentation. Pictures land where you paste them (although you may have to resize them).

- **Import**: Since this book is about Project, the term "importing" refers to transferring data from another program into a Project file. For example, you can import cost estimates from an Excel spreadsheet into Project task fields or import tasks for a work breakdown structure from a Word document into a Project file; once the data is in Project, it acts as if you created it there. Imported data looks and acts like text and numbers you copy and paste into Project. The advantage of importing over copying is you have more control over the data you import and where it goes in your Project file. (Later in this chapter, you'll see how data types help you get the correct data into the correct fields in Project.)

- **Export**: Exporting data from Project converts the data into a format that other programs can read. For example, you can export task lists from Project to Excel to build a cost-estimating spreadsheet.

- **Synchronize**: Project and SharePoint have a special bond that helps when you want to collaborate with team members on small projects. You can synchronize tasks between these two programs to share project tasks with your team or to obtain status from them. Chapter 28 describes how synchronizing tasks works.

- **Link**: When you want changes in one file to appear automatically in other files, linking is the way to go, as you'll learn in detail in Chapter 26. It creates a lasting connection between the source data and its destination, so you can update the source data once and see the changes in every linked object. For example, suppose you use a PowerPoint file to present project status. You can insert a Gantt Chart view into a PowerPoint slide as a linked object to show the current schedule. In the other direction, you might link a risk-tracking spreadsheet to your Project schedule, so you can see where risk responses stand. When you double-click a linked object, the source file opens in the source program, so you *always* modify the original. The drawback to linking is that the links point to the source files, so if those files get moved, then the links break. In addition, links don't work if they point to a computer or network you can't access.

- **Embed**: This method (which is described in detail in Chapter 26) is a middle ground between copying and linking. When you embed an object from one program into another, you insert a package of data along with its source program into the destination file. The data isn't linked to the source file, so you don't see changes made in the original. When you double-click an embedded object, the commands from the source program appear, but you're editing the *copy*. Embedding data is ideal for sending the destination file to someone else. The person who receives the file has everything they need: the destination file, the embedded object, and the program commands for editing the embedded data. The downside to embedded data is that it inflates the destination file's size, sometimes to gargantuan proportions.

Copying Information

Copying and pasting moves small amounts of data quickly and easily. It's the way to go when you want to insert a few values from another file, copy a picture into a report, or reference details spelled out in a document. You can copy task data from a Project table and then paste it into Word to create an agenda for a team meeting. Copying numbers from an Excel column into Project table cells works equally well.

> **Note:** If you've downloaded files from the book website, you can follow along using the file Event_Ch25_start.mpp. This sample file does not include external links or a connection to a resource pool that was covered in Chapter 24.

Copying Project Data to Other Programs

Copying data from Project tables into another program is blissfully easy; it's like a simple form of exporting. You select the table cells you want in Project and then paste them into the destination file. Copying and pasting between Project and other Office programs brings formatting along with your data, which makes your job easier. For example, if you copy task data from Project to an Outlook email message to show task status, the tasks appear in the email message in a table with the same indenting, highlighting, grouping, and other formatting as the Project table, as shown in Figure 25-1.

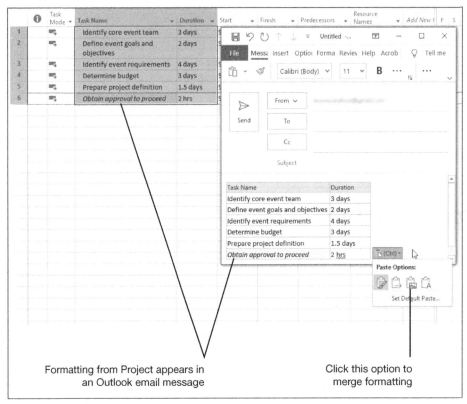

Formatting from Project appears in
an Outlook email message

Click this option to
merge formatting

Figure 25-1. *Office programs can exchange formatting from the source file (Project, say) to the destination file (Outlook, in this example).*

Follow Along Practice

Here are the steps for copying data from a Project table, using Excel as an example destination program:

1. In Project, display the view and table that contains the fields you want to copy, in this example, display the Gantt Chart view, and then display the Cost table.

> **Tip:** If necessary, add the fields you want to copy to the table by right-clicking a column header in the table and then choosing Insert Column from the shortcut menu. To simplify copying nonadjacent columns, drag the columns in the Project table into the order you want, and *then* select the cells or columns you want to copy. In this example, keep the Cost table as it is.

2. In the table, select the data you want to copy. In this example, drag from the Task Name cell in row 4 to the Remaining Cost cell in row 9.

You can select specific cells or entire columns. If the cells are adjacent, drag from the upper-left cell to the bottom-right cell. To select nonadjacent cells—for instance, when you don't want all the columns in the table—Ctrl-drag over each set of cells (in other words, hold the Ctrl key down as you drag over nonadjacent sets of cells). You can also Ctrl-click cells or columns to select nonadjacent values. Select entire columns by dragging across their column headings.

3. Press Ctrl+C (or right-click the selection and the choose Copy Cell on the shortcut menu), to copy the selected cells to the Clipboard.

    If you click the Copy down arrow in the Task tab's Clipboard section, you can choose Copy to copy data or Copy Picture to copy an *image* of your selection.

4. Switch to Excel and, in the destination spreadsheet (create a new blank one for this example), click the top-left cell of the destination cells.

    The cell you click is the starting point for the data you copy.

5. To paste the data into Excel, press Ctrl+V, or in the Home tab's Clipboard section, click the top half of the Paste button.

    The data copies from the cell you clicked in step 4 into cells to the right and below. Even data that's nonadjacent in Project pours into adjacent cells in the destination file. If you're using Office 2010 and later, column headers from the Project table paste into Excel, even if you don't select them in the Project table.

> **Tip:** If you click the bottom half of Excel's Paste button, you can choose between pasting the data using the formatting from the source file or the destination file.

Copying Data from Other Programs into Project

Copying data *into* Project requires more finesse than copying data out of the program because Project is fussy about the type of data that goes into its fields. For example, if you try to copy plain numbers from Excel into a Start date cell, Project complains about the mismatch in an error message. Values you paste into Start cells had better be dates if tasks are auto-scheduled—otherwise, you'll see an error message. You can also paste data into custom fields, as long as the data types match. For example, values you copy into a custom Project field like Duration1 must be a length of time like 2d.

To copy data into Project without that kind of drama, take the time to match up the data *before* you start the copy. For example, you may have to rearrange columns so they're the same in both files. Where you rearrange columns doesn't matter; you can rearrange the columns in the Project table or in the external file. Perhaps the easiest approach is to copy each column individually into its Project cousin. (Copying data between Project files works the same way, as the section "Copying Data Between Project Files" explains.) Otherwise, copying data *into* Project is the same as copying data from it:

Follow Along Practice

1. In this example, create a new blank Project file and set the Task Mode setting so new tasks are automatically scheduled (Chapter 3).

2. In the source program, open the file (in this example, Ch25 TaskList_in_Word.docx), and then select the data you want to copy (in this example, the entire table).

   You can copy data from a Word document, an Excel spreadsheet, or a table in an Access database. If necessary, rearrange the columns of data to match the columns in the destination Project table.

3. Press Ctrl+C or, in the Home tab's Clipboard section, click Copy.

   Ctrl+C works regardless of which version of Word, Excel, or Project you use.

4. In Project, open the Project file you want to paste the data into (the new one you created), and then apply the view and table you want (keep the Gantt Chart view and Entry table displayed).

   If you didn't rearrange the data before you copied it to the Clipboard, then you can insert, hide, or drag columns in the Project table to match the source file's column order. In this example, the columns don't have to be rearranged.

5. In the Project view's table area, click the top-left cell where you want to paste the data (in this example, the Task Name cell for task ID 1), and then press Ctrl+V or, in the Task tab's Clipboard section, click the top half of the Paste button.

   Pasting data into a Project table doesn't insert new blank rows, so the values you paste *overwrite* any existing values in the Project cells, starting from the cell you click to the right and down. If you don't want to overwrite data, then insert enough blank rows to hold the data you're pasting—or paste the data in blank rows at the bottom of the table.

   If the values you pasted match the data types in Project's columns, the data appears in the correct cells in Project, with no error messages. If the data from the source file doesn't match the data type in Project, then you see an error message like the one shown in Figure 25-2. The fastest way to resolve this problem is to click Cancel to stop the paste. Then correct the mismatch by rearranging either the Project columns or the columns in your source file, and then repeat the copy and paste.

> **Note:** If you paste content from a Word document or an Outlook email message into Project, Project can transform indents into outline levels, so lines of text automatically turn into summary tasks and subtasks.

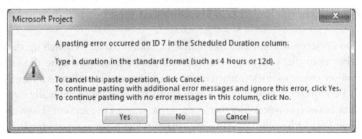

Figure 25-2. *Project displays an error message for every cell with the wrong type of data.*

Copying Data Between Project Files

Copying data from one Project schedule to another is handy when you want to reuse similar tasks from another project—for example, one you completed last year. Copying is the same whether you're copying within the same Project file, from one Project file to another, or from another program into Project. For example, to copy cells from a table in one Project file to a table in another file, select the cells in the source Project file and then, in the Task tab's Clipboard section, click Copy. In the destination Project file, select the first cell you want to paste the data into, and then in the Task tab's Clipboard section, click Paste. (Remember, when you copy cells, the paste starts at the first cell you click and continues to the right and down, overwriting any existing data in those cells.)

When you copy data within the same Project file or between two different Project files, you can also copy entire rows in a table. Unlike when you copy and paste cells, Project inserts *new* rows when you paste entire rows. Here are the steps (you don't have to perform these in the sample project):

1. In the table area, select the rows to copy by dragging over the row ID cells. You can select nonadjacent rows by Ctrl-clicking each ID cell.

2. Press Ctrl+C or, in the Task tab's Clipboard section, click Copy. If you're copying resource rows in the Resource Sheet view, you still head to the *Task* tab's Clipboard section and click Copy.

3. To paste the rows in the new location (within the file or in a second Project file), click the ID cell for the row below where you want to copy the data, and then press Ctrl+V (or, in the Task tab's Clipboard section, click Paste).

Creating Pictures of Project Information

From the time you initiate a project until you put the last tasks to bed, you communicate project information to stakeholders and team members. A *picture* of a project schedule shows where a project stands better than row after row of data. Project's Copy Picture command captures all or part of the current view and can create an image fine-tuned for displaying on a computer screen, printing, or publishing on the web. For example, you can create an image of the high-level schedule to publish on your Intranet or a Resource Graph to email to a functional manager (that is, the resource's manager outside the project). After you create the image, you can paste it into any destination you want.

Follow Along Practice

To create a picture of a Project view, follow these steps:

1. In this example, open the sample file Event_Ch25_start.mpp.

2. Display the view you want to take a picture of, in this example, Gantt Chart.

    Views like Gantt Chart, Team Planner (available in Project Professional), and Resource Graph are good candidates for a picture.

3. If you want to see specific rows in the view's table, then select them.

   In this example, collapse the Planning, Procurement, and "Event setup" tasks by clicking the black triangles to the left of their names. Select the rows you want by dragging over their ID cells (in this example, drag from task ID 0 to task ID 79 "Event setup"). You can also Ctrl-click the ID cells of nonadjacent rows.

4. Adjust the view's timescale to show the date range you want in the picture. In this example, keep the timescale as it is.

   Partially hidden columns in the table don't appear in the picture, so make sure the last column you want in the picture is displayed completely.

5. In the Task tab's Clipboard section, click the Copy down arrow, and then choose Copy Picture.

   The Copy Picture dialog box opens, as shown in Figure 25-3.

6. In the "Render image" section, choose the option for how you're going to use the picture (in this example, "For screen").

   Project automatically selects the "For screen" option, which is perfect for a picture you're copying into a program like PowerPoint. Select "For printer" instead if you're creating an image for a report most people will read on paper.

   The "For screen" and "For printer" options both create an image and place it on the Clipboard. To create an image file, select "To GIF image file," and then enter the path and filename. (Click Browse to navigate to the folder where you want to save the file.) For example, a GIF file format is what you need for publishing a picture on a web page.

7. Choose the option for the rows you want to include, in this example, "Selected rows."

   If you haven't selected rows in the table (step 3), Project automatically selects the "Rows on screen" option, which includes only the visible rows. If you want specific rows or all rows in the project, be sure to select those rows *before* you click the Copy Picture command; after you've done that, Project automatically selects the "Selected rows" option.

8. Choose the option to show the timescale that's visible in the view or a date range you specify.

   "As shown on screen" includes only the dates visible on the screen. To show a different date range, like the dates from project start to finish or the dates for a phase, select the From option, and then fill in the From and To boxes with the start and finish dates.

> **Tip:** If you want to save the image in another format, like .jpg or .png, choose the "For screen" option to copy the data, and then paste it into Paint (or another image-editing program). Then you can save the image in the file format you want.

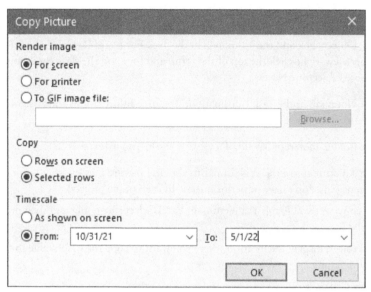

Figure 25-3. *The options you can select depend on the view that's displayed. For example, for the Gantt Chart view and usage views, you can specify the rows and timescale to include. The Resource Graph view doesn't have rows, so the row options are grayed out. And the Network Diagram view disables the options for rows and timescale.*

9. Click OK.

   If you selected the "For screen" or "For printer" option, Project copies the picture to the Clipboard. If you went with the "To GIF image file" option, Project creates the file instead.

10. In the destination file (in this example, create a blank Word document), click the location where you want to paste the picture, and then press Ctrl+V or, in the Home tab's Clipboard section, click Paste.

    For a GIF file, use the destination program's command for inserting a picture. For example, with Microsoft programs, in the Insert tab's Illustrations section, click Pictures.

Displaying Pictures in Project

You can copy graphics or pictures into Project to do things like display an Excel graph of bugs reported over time or photos of the customer's employees assigned to the project. Only certain places within Project can host these graphic files:

- A Gantt Chart view's timescale area.

- The Objects box and the Notes box in the Task Form and Resource Form (in either view, right-click the top of the form, and then, on the shortcut menu, choose Objects or Notes).

- The Notes tab in the Task Information, Resource Information, and Assignment Information dialog boxes.

- The header, footer, or legend of a view or report you print.

Copying a picture into Project is similar to copying picture files in other programs. Here are the steps (you don't have to perform these in the sample project):

1. To copy an Excel graph as a picture, in Excel, select the graph, and then press Ctrl+C.

2. In Project, display the location where you want to copy the graphic file (or Clipboard graphic).

3. Press Ctrl+V, and Project pastes the graphic at the selected location.

4. Drag a picture to reposition it. To resize it, select it, and then drag one of the resize handles at its corners or on its sides. You can't edit pictures in Project or open their source files.

Importing and Exporting Data

Arranging columns in the right order, selecting data, and copying it to the right place can be tedious and error-prone. A more dependable way to get data from one place to another is importing or exporting, depending on which direction the data is headed. In this book, "importing" means pulling data into Project from another program—for instance, importing data from an Excel spreadsheet or an Access database. "Exporting," on the other hand, refers to pushing data out of your Project file to another file format like Excel or XML. Unlike linking and embedding (Chapter 26), importing and exporting convert data from one file format to another, so the data is the same as what you enter directly in the destination program.

The great thing about importing and exporting is the control you have over the data you transfer and where it goes. Because you map fields in one program to fields in the other, you can make sure the right types of data go where you want.

Project provides wizards for importing and exporting data to and from your Project files. The wizards start automatically when you open a file in another format or save to another format (as explained in the next section). For example, if you open an Excel spreadsheet in Project, then the Import Wizard starts up. And if you save a Project file as a text file, the Export Wizard launches.

Maps are sets of settings that match up Project fields with fields or columns in the other program. Project comes with several built-in maps for doing things like exporting cost data, earned values, or basic task information. This section explains the basics of importing and exporting, no matter *which* programs you use to create and receive the data.

> **Note:** Updating actual values might be one reason that you consider importing data into Project. Unfortunately, importing task actuals is difficult; updating assignments by time period, for example, importing weekly time sheets you get from team members, is impossible with Project. If you want to update actual values, the best approach is to use a third-party application, such as Standard Time Timesheets (http://www.stdtime.com) or Planbridge (http://planbridge.ms/product/index).

File Formats for Importing and Exporting

Project can open different types of files, such as Excel files, tab-delimited text files, comma-delimited (CSV) files, and XML files.

You can save a Project file to other Project file formats, Excel workbooks, text-delimited files, comma-delimited files, and XML. Project doesn't save projects as web pages, because you can use an XML file to generate a web page (as well as for other purposes). Similarly, you can't save a Project file directly to a database format, although you can use a visual report (Chapter 18) to create a database file containing the data for the visual report.

The steps you take to open or save these files vary depending on the format. For example, you can open an earlier Project file format simply by choosing File→Open. However, when you choose File→Open with Excel file formats, comma-delimited files, and so on, the Import Wizard starts. Similarly, when you save files to formats other than the standard Project formats (.mpp, .mpt, .pdf, and .xml), Project's Export Wizard starts.

Importing Data into Project

Bringing data from other programs into Project is as easy as opening that file in Project. The Import Wizard guides you through mapping the data to the right Project fields and takes care of transferring that data.

> **Tip:** To understand the data Project accepts in various type of fields, export data from Project into an Excel spreadsheet before trying to import data.

Follow Along Practice

Although Project includes a few special tools for importing Excel data, the basic steps for importing any kind of data are the same:

1. In Project, choose File→Open. In the Backstage view's Open page, click Browse, and then select the location and folder that contains the file you want to import (in this example, the folder where you downloaded the sample files).

    The Open dialog box automatically sets the file type box (the unlabeled box to the right of the "File name" box) to Projects (the box says "Projects (*.mpp)" if Windows Explorer is set to display file extensions), so you have to tell Project which type of file you want to import.

2. In the file type box, click the down arrow, and then choose the file format you want to import—for instance, Excel Workbook, or "CSV (Comma delimited)." In this example, choose "CSV (Comma delimited)."

    In the Open dialog box, the file list shows only the files of the type you selected. So if the file you want is conspicuously absent, it might be a different format than you think. In that case, choose All Files to see every file.

3. In the file list, double-click the name of the file whose data you want to import (or click its file-name, and then click Open). In this example, use "Ch25 Estimated Tasks_csv."

    The Import Wizard starts. Click Next to bypass the welcome screen, which merely explains the process.

4. On the "Import Wizard - Map" screen, keep the "New map" option selected, and click Next.

    If an existing map (either a Project built-in map or one you've saved) matches fields the way you want, then select "Use existing map" instead. This option shortens the import process by several steps, as explained in the section "Using an Existing Map."

5. On the "Import Wizard - Import Mode" screen, select an option to tell Project where you want to import the data (in this example, keep "As a new project" selected), and then click Next.

    Project automatically selects the "As a new project" option, which creates a brand-new Project file from the data you're importing.

    The "Append the data to the active project" option is ideal when you want to import several files into the same project—for instance, when you receive tasks from several team leaders. This option tells Project to insert the appended data in the current Project table after the existing rows.

    The "Merge the data into the active project" option is perfect when you want to import values into existing tasks, like importing estimates into your Project file. To import values into existing tasks, Project needs a way to match the tasks in each file, as the note titled "Importing Data into Existing Rows" explains.

Importing Data into Existing Rows

If you're importing values and merging them into existing tasks or resources, like estimates of task work, Project needs to know how to identify matching tasks or resources. After you map the fields on the Import Wizard's Mapping screen (step 7 in this section) and then click Next, a message box might appear asking for a ***primary key*** so Project can merge the imported data. This message means you have to tell Project which field is a unique identifier for tasks (or resources). For example, a WBS code is an ideal primary key because every task has one, and you can tell Project to make them unique. (The Unique ID field is another candidate for a primary key. It is a unique identifier for tasks and resources. If you rearrange your task or resource lists, Unique ID values stay with their corresponding items.)

On the Mapping screen, in the table of matched fields, select the cell in the "To: Microsoft Project Field" column that represents the primary key, and then click Set Merge Key. Both cells in the row change to include the words "MERGE KEY:" in front of the field name.

6. On the "Import Wizard - Map" Options screen, select the type of data you want to import, in this example, Tasks, as shown in Figure 25-4. Then click Next.

    If the source file's first line or row includes column names, make sure the "Import includes headers" checkbox is turned on. (The "Include Assignment rows in output" checkbox stubbornly remains grayed out no matter what you do, because this checkbox applies only to ***exporting***.)

    Project automatically sets options on the "Import Wizard - Map Options" screen depending on the type of file you're importing. For example, importing a text file displays two additional boxes: the "Text delimiter" checkbox in which you can specify the delimiter as a tab, space, or comma; and the "File origin" option, which you can set to Windows (ANSI), MSDOS, or Unicode.

> **Note:** The Tasks and Resources options import data specifically for tasks or resources. The Assignments option imports information about tasks *and* who's assigned to them. When you exchange data with an Excel spreadsheet, these options are checkboxes so you can import more than one type of data at a time (you specify the worksheet that contains each type of data, as described later).

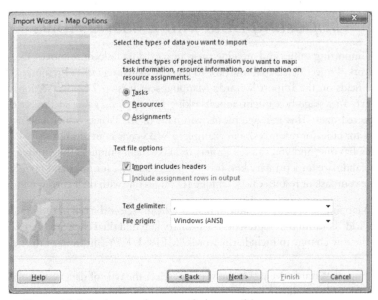

Figure 25-4. *In the wizard, you specify the type of data you want to import.*

7. On the Import Wizard's Mapping screen, map the import fields to their corresponding Project fields, as shown in Figure 25-5. (In this example, you have to specify the Project fields you want to use, which are shown in the figure.)

The exact mapping screen that appears depends on the data you selected to import: Task Mapping, Resource Mapping, or Assignments Mapping.

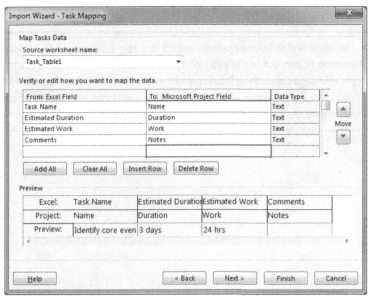

Figure 25-5. *You fill in Microsoft Project Field cells with the field that corresponds to the data you're importing.*

The "From: [source] Field" column (where [source] is Text File if you're importing a text file, Excel if you're importing from Excel, and so on) displays column headings from your import file, if they're present. Otherwise, the first cell in the "From: [source] Field" column displays the number 1.

For each field you want to import, choose the corresponding Project field in the "To: Microsoft Project Field" cell. Project makes educated guesses about mappings based on the imported column headings. For example, Project maps a Name field in the import file to the Name field in Project.

The value "(not mapped)" in the "To: Microsoft Project Field" cell is Project's way of saying that you need to tell it which Project field you want. To choose a field, click the down arrow in the "To: Microsoft Project Field" cell, and then choose the field. Leaving the value as "(not mapped)" is one way to tell Project not to import the field. (You can also click in a row and then click Delete Row to remove it from the table, which also removes it from the map.)

The Preview area shows a sample of the import. The first row in the preview shows the names of the selected source fields. The Project row identifies the fields into which the imported data goes. And the Preview rows show several values from that field in the import file.

> **Tip:** You don't have to import every field in an import file. Beneath the field table, click Delete Row to remove a mapping pair. Click Clear All to delete all the rows and start from scratch. Clicking Add All makes Project read the import file and insert rows for each import-file field. The Insert Row button inserts a blank row.

8. Optionally, to save the map you've defined, click Next (in this example, skip this step).

   The "Import Wizard - End of Map Definition" screen appears with the Save Map button sitting by itself mid–dialog box. Click Save Map to open the Save Map dialog box. In the "Map name" box, type a short but meaningful name for the map, like ***Import Tasks***. Clicking Save adds the map to your global template and closes the dialog box.

9. Click Finish.

   You may see a warning message if you're importing an older file format; click Yes to continue opening the file. Project imports the tasks into your Project file.

If you insert the Work column into the table, the imported tasks should look like the ones in Figure 25-6. Work values might not import if Project is set to create tasks as manually scheduled (Chapter 3).

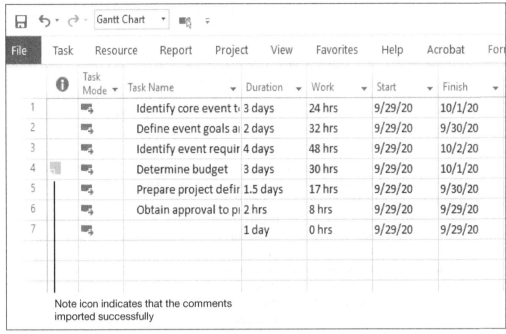

			ⓘ	Task Mode ▾	Task Name ▾	Duration ▾	Work ▾	Start ▾	Finish ▾
1				🖫	Identify core event t	3 days	24 hrs	9/29/20	10/1/20
2				🖫	Define event goals a	2 days	32 hrs	9/29/20	9/30/20
3				🖫	Identify event requir	4 days	48 hrs	9/29/20	10/2/20
4		🗏		🖫	Determine budget	3 days	30 hrs	9/29/20	10/1/20
5				🖫	Prepare project defir	1.5 days	17 hrs	9/29/20	9/30/20
6				🖫	Obtain approval to p	2 hrs	8 hrs	9/29/20	9/29/20
7				🖫		1 day	0 hrs	9/29/20	9/29/20

Note icon indicates that the comments imported successfully

Figure 25-6. *Project imports data into the fields you specify.*

Exporting Data from Project

A common reason to export data from Project is so you can work with the data in ways that Project doesn't handle well. For example, you might export comma-delimited data to another program to run Monte Carlo simulations on your schedule. Exporting data is also useful when colleagues don't have Project or just want to see the data in another format. See the section "Exporting Project Data to Excel" for the steps for exporting Project data to Excel. This section describes how to export data from Project to file formats *other* than Excel.

Follow Along Practice

The steps in the Export Wizard bear a strong resemblance to those in the Import Wizard, but there are a few key differences. Here's how you export Project data to another format:

1. Open the Project file you want to export (Event_Ch25_start.mpp) and choose File→Save As. On the Backstage view's Save As page, select the location and folder where you want to store the file with exported data (choose Desktop or the folder where you downloaded the sample files).

    The Save As dialog box opens.

2. In the "Save as type" drop-down list, choose the file format you want to use, in this example, choose "CSV (Comma delimited)."

If you save to one of the Project file formats (such as Project, Microsoft Project 2007, Project Template, pdf, xml, or Microsoft Project 2007 Templates), the Save As dialog box remains open. However, saving to an Excel workbook, a text file, or a comma-delimited file all start the Export Wizard.

3. In the "File name" box, type the name for the file (in this example, ***Event_Ch25_export***) and click Save.

   Project fills in the "File name" box with the Project file's name, but you can rename the export file to whatever you want. Project sets the file extension based on the file format you choose.

   > **Note.** If you choose an older file format, such as "Microsoft Project 2007," when you click Save, a message box may appear to tell you that the older file format may be less secure than a new file format. If you want to save the file to that format, simply click Continue. To quit, click Cancel, and then repeat steps 1 and 2 to choose a different format. If you see a message box that tells you that you can't save to older file formats, click OK to close the message box. Then Choose File→Options, click Trust Center, and then click the Trust Center Settings button. In the Trust Center dialog box, click Legacy Formats, and then choose the "Prompt when loading files with legacy or non-default file format" option.

4. When the Export Wizard starts, click Next to bypass the welcome screen.

5. On the "Export Wizard - Map" screen, select the "New map" option, and then click Next.

   To use an existing map to match up fields, select the "Use existing map" option instead (see the section "Using an Existing Map").

6. On the "Export Wizard - Map Options" screen, select the type of data you want to import (in this example, Tasks), and then click Next.

   Your choices are the same as the ones on the "Import Wizard - Map Options" screen (step 6 in the "Importing Data into Project" section), with one exception: The "Include assignment rows in output" checkbox is now active but turned off. If you want to export all the assignment rows for tasks, then turn on this checkbox.

7. On the Mapping screen, specify the fields you want to export. In this example, click the "Base on Table" button, choose Summary, and then click OK.

   You see the Mapping screen corresponding to the type of data you're exporting (Task Mapping, Resource Mapping, or Assignments Mapping). Compared with the Import Wizard, the Export Wizard's mapping pages have a few additional options, as you can see in Figure 25-7. The "Export filter" box lets you choose the items you want to export. For example, you might choose the Completed Tasks filter to export the final costs for tasks that are done.

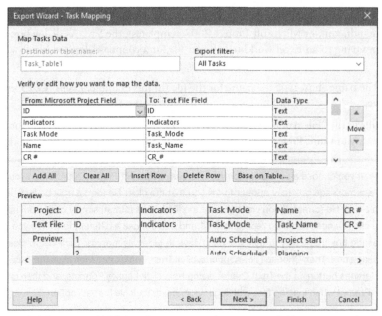

Figure 25-7. *Click "Base on Table" below the mapping grid to jumpstart field mappings with a Project table.*

Because you're exporting to a blank file, Project doesn't fill in the field table for you. Instead of selecting field after field, you can use a Project table like Entry, Cost, or a custom table you create to fill in the field cells. To do so, underneath the field table, click "Base on Table." The "Select Base Table for Field Mapping" dialog box opens, and you can select any table in your project. The granddaddy of all tables is the Export table, which fills in 84 fields. (If you're exporting tasks, the dialog box displays all the task tables; it lists resource tables if you're exporting resources.) Remember, you can edit the field names in the "To:" column to specify the headings you want in the export file.

> **Tip:** To export exactly the fields you want, use the Add All, Clear All, Insert Row, and Delete Row buttons to build a collection of fields.

The Preview area shows values in your Project by field. The Project and [destination] field names (where [destination] is the destination file format you choose—in Figure 25-7, for example, it's "Text File") are initially identical. To define the field names in your export file to match the needs of the destination program, change the field name in the "To: [destination] Field" cells.

8. Optionally, to save the map you've defined, click Next.

    The "Export Wizard - End of Map Definition" page presents the Save Map button, which saves a map exactly like the Import Wizard does. In this example, click Save Map. In the "Map name" box, type *C_Summary*, and then click Save.

9. Click Finish.

    Project exports the data to the file format you selected, but it doesn't open the file for you.

Using an Existing Map

There's no reason to manually map the same fields every time you import or export them for things like monthly reports you produce. Saving a map and reusing it in future imports and exports is a real timesaver. Moreover, after you apply an existing map, you can tweak the mapping if it isn't quite right.

Here's how to use an existing map (you don't have to perform these steps for this example):

1. When you start either the Import or Export Wizard, follow the steps until you get to the "Import Wizard - Map" page or the "Export Wizard - Map" screen.

    The wizards' screens vary depending on what you're importing or exporting.

2. On the "Import Wizard - Map" page or the "Export Wizard - Map" page, select the "Use existing map" option and then click Next.

    The Map Selection page appears, as shown in Figure 25-8.

3. Click the name of the map you want to use, and then click Next.

    If you want to review your settings or make minor adjustments to the map, click Next to step through the remaining wizard screens as described in the previous sections on importing and exporting.

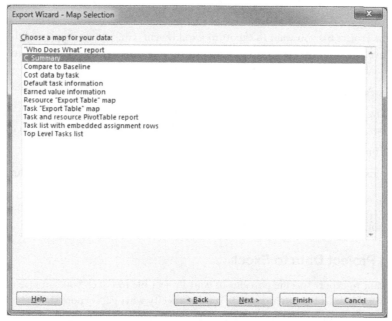

Figure 25-8. *If you're certain the map is exactly what you want, you can simply click Finish to immediately complete the import or export.*

Exchanging Data with Excel

Because Excel spreadsheets can contain more than one worksheet, the settings in the Import and Export Wizards are slightly different from the ones you see when you work with text files. For example, you can import and export tasks, resources, and assignments to Excel all at once. Moreover, when you have both Project and Excel installed on your computer, Excel includes two templates to jump-start your data exchange. When you create an Excel file using either of these templates, the column headings are set up to map to Project fields. To export Excel data without a hitch, see the section "Saving Projects to Other File Formats" in Chapter 3 to learn how to make Project work with older file formats.

> **Tip:** You can also exchange data between Project and Excel using visual reports. Chapters 18 and 19 have the full scoop on these reports.

Exporting an Entire Project to Excel

The Export Wizard contains an option for exporting all the task, resource, and assignment data in a Project file with a minimum of effort. Although the resulting export file doesn't include time-phased data (data that's broken down by time period), you can create an Excel spreadsheet with separate worksheets for tasks, resources, and assignments. Here are the steps (you don't have to follow along with this example):

1. Open the Project file you want to export to Excel (Event_Ch25_start.mpp), and then choose File→Save As. Select the location and folder where you want to save the new file (choose Desktop or the folder where you downloaded the sample files).

    The Save As dialog box opens.

2. In the Save As dialog box's "Save as type" drop-down list, choose Excel Workbook. In the "File name" box, type a name for the file (in this example, *Ch25_fullexport*), and then click Save.

    Project launches the Export Wizard. Click Next to start the wizard.

3. On the "Export Wizard - Data" screen, select the Project Excel Template option, and then click Finish.

    Project exports your project data to an Excel file that contains three worksheets: Task_Table, Resource_Table, and Assignment_Table.

Exporting Project Data to Excel

When you want to export specific portions of your Project file to Excel, you can save the Project file as an Excel workbook and use the Export Wizard to specify what gets exported. The steps are *almost* the same as exporting to other types of files. Here's how exporting to an Excel workbook works:

Follow Along Practice

1. Open the Project file you want to export to Excel (in this example, Event_Ch25_start.mpp).

   Display the view and table that contains the data you want to export, in this example, the Gantt Chart view and the Cost table. You can choose other views, like the Resource Sheet view to export resources or Task Usage view to export assignments.

2. In the view's table, select the rows or cells you want to export.

   You can drag over several ID cells to select multiple rows. Or you can drag over the cells you want to export. Ctrl-click rows or column headings if you want to export nonadjacent rows or columns. (For example, you could Ctrl-click Task Name, Total Cost, Baseline, and Variance.) To export *all* the data in the table, at the top of the ID column, click the blank Select All cell to select the entire table.

3. Choose File→Save As. On the Backstage view's Save As page, select the location and folder where you want to save the file containing the exported data (choose Desktop or the folder where you downloaded the sample files).

   The Save As dialog box opens to the folder you selected.

4. In the "Save as type" drop-down list, choose Excel Workbook. In the "File name" box, type a name for the file (in this example, Ch25_partialexport), and then click Save.

   If you have Project's Trust Center setting's set up to prompt you about legacy formats (Chapter 3) and you select Excel 97-2003 Workbook in the "Save as type" drop-down list, when you click Save, a message box warns you that the file may be less secure than a newer file format. Click Yes to save to the older format, or click No to cancel the wizard and go back to step 3.

   Project launches the Export Wizard. Click Next to get going.

5. On the "Export Wizard - Data" screen, the wizard automatically selects the Selected Data option, which exports the data you selected in the view. Click Next to continue.

   If you forgot to select data before you started the wizard, click Cancel and jump back to step 1.

6. On the "Export Wizard - Map" screen, keep the "New map" option selected and click Next.

   If you already have a map you want to use, select the "Use existing map" option instead, and then select the map as described in the section "Using an Existing Map."

7. On the "Export Wizard - Map Options" page, turn on the checkboxes for each type of data you want to export, and then click Next. In this example, turn on all three checkboxes: Tasks, Resources, and Assignments, and then click Next.

   Because Excel can handle several types of data on separate worksheets, this page includes checkboxes for tasks, resources, and assignments, as you can see in Figure 25-9.

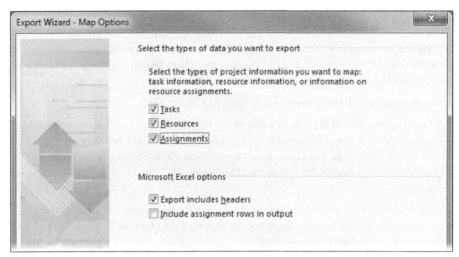

Figure 25-9. *If you selected an existing map, then the wizard initially sets the checkboxes to match the map's definition. The wizard displays a mapping page for each type of data you export.*

The wizard automatically turns on the "Export includes headers" checkbox. This setting exports Project field names to column names in Excel, which is usually what you want. If you want to export all the details about resources' assignments, then turn on the "Include assignment rows in output" checkbox.

8. On the first Mapping screen that appears, in the "Destination worksheet name" box, type a name for the Excel worksheet, in this example, ***Kickoff_Tasks***.

   The Mapping screen that appears depends on the checkbox(es) you selected on the "Export Wizard - Map Options" page. For example, if you turned on the Tasks checkbox, then the first Mapping screen you see is "Export Wizard - Task Mapping".

   The "Destination worksheet name" box automatically sets the worksheet's name to something like Task_Table1. You can stick with that or change the name to something else.

9. Set up the field mapping as you would for any other kind of export. In this example, in the From: Microsoft Project Field cells, choose Name, Cost, Baseline Cost, and Cost Variance. Keep the names that Project enters in the To: Excel Field cells.

   You can choose a filter in the "Export filter" box to export specific parts of your Project file—for example, choose the Critical filter to export data about critical tasks to see which ones you can shorten. The rest of the Mapping screen is the same as the one that appears for exporting to a text file or another format (described in section "Exporting Data from Project"). For instance, you can map fields based on an existing Project table or use the buttons below the table to insert and delete rows.

10. Repeat steps 8 and 9 for each Mapping screen that appears. In the Resource Mapping screen, choose Name and Standard Rate in the From: Microsoft Project Field cells. In the Assignment Mapping screen, choose Task Name, Resource Name, and Work.

The Mapping screens appear in the same order every time: tasks, resources, and then assignments. However, if you aren't exporting a type of data, that Mapping page doesn't show up. The wizard creates a separate worksheet in the Excel file for each type of data you export.

11. Click Finish.

Project exports the tasks into a new workbook (you have to launch Excel and open the file to see it).

If you saved the exported data to an older Excel format (Excel 97-2003 format, for example) but opened the spreadsheet in a newer version of Excel, then when you try to save it, you may see a message box asking if you want to overwrite the older Excel format with the current format. If you click Yes to update the format, Excel saves the spreadsheet to the version of Excel installed on your computer.

> **Tip:** The cells in an Excel export file are set to the General format, which doesn't apply any specific formatting to the values. To display data the way you want or to calculate values, you can change the data types for cells. For example, you can modify cost cells to the Excel Currency format to show dollar signs. To change the data type in Excel, select the column heading. Then, in the Home tab's Cells section, choose Format→Format Cells. In the Format Cells dialog box, choose the appropriate category, such as Number or Currency, and then click OK.

Importing Data from Excel

Importing data from Excel without a built-in template is almost identical to importing any other kind of data (see the section "Importing Data into Project"). In fact, you'll find only two exceptions:

* The "Import Wizard - Map Options" screen has checkboxes for each type of data you want to import, because Excel can create separate worksheets for each type of data.

* On the Mapping screens, Project enters the Excel worksheets' names in the "Source worksheet name" box. If the spreadsheet contains more than one worksheet for a type of data, then choose the appropriate worksheet from the drop-down list.

> **Tip:** Project used to provide two templates whose worksheets and columns are tailored to work perfectly with Project's Import Wizard. The Microsoft Project Task List Import Template (TASKLIST.xlt) is great for importing task lists that your team members give to you. The Microsoft Project Plan Import Export Template (PROJPLAN.xlt) helps you import information about tasks, resources, and assignments into Project. These templates are available to download on this book's web page (www.coldpresspublishing.com).

Working with Project and Visio

Most of the time, your work with Project and Visio revolves around visual reports, which send Project data to Visio pivot diagrams to dynamically display project information. (See Chapters 18 and 19 for more on Visio visual reports.) You can also turn to Visio to produce simpler pictures of your project, akin to the weather maps you see on television compared with the ones that meteorologists analyze. If Project's views are too complicated for your audience, try Visio's Schedule template category (on the New screen, click Categories, and then click Schedule), which includes templates for Gantt Charts, timelines, PERT Charts, and calendars:

- **Gantt Chart**: You can export task information from Project into a Visio Gantt Chart to make task bars look more interesting and to weed out the details that executive audiences don't care about. Although most project managers build even the quickest and dirtiest schedules in Project, you can also export any information created in Visio Gantt Charts and import it into Project to jump-start a new schedule.

- **Timeline**: You can produce high-level project views of tasks and milestones along a horizontal bar in both Project and Visio. However, if you want to produce a vertical timeline of your project, your only choice is Visio's Timeline template.

> **Tip:** Although Visio includes a PERT Chart template, you're better off using the Project Network Diagram view to show PERT boxes instead. That way, the tasks will be visible in other Project views, as well. The Visio PERT Chart template doesn't import or export data automatically, so it's difficult to display Project data with this type of drawing.

Because data exchange between Visio and Project takes place in Visio, this section switches the meaning of import and export from previous sections. In Visio, "importing" means bringing Project data into a Visio drawing, whereas "exporting" means creating a Project file from Visio data.

Every shape on a Visio Gantt Chart or Timeline drawing has its own sets of options, so you can make the drawing look just the way you want. To learn more about working with Visio schedule drawings, refer to *Microsoft Visio 2016 Step by Step* by Scott Helmers (Microsoft Press).

Displaying Project Data in a Visio Gantt Chart

A Project Gantt Chart can show a project summary, but it often contains too much information for most reports and presentations. Visio Gantt Charts are simpler renditions of their Project cousins, so they may be more suitable for audiences less versed in project management.

Project doesn't include tools for pushing its data to Visio, so importing Project data into a Visio Gantt Chart takes place within Visio. Here's how to do it (you don't have to follow along):

1. Make sure the Project file you want to import (in this example, Event_Ch25_start.mpp) *isn't* open in Project.

   The Import Project Data Wizard can't read a file that's already open.

2. In Visio, create a Gantt Chart drawing.

    To create a Visio Gantt Chart, choose File→New. In the Backstage view's New page, click the Categories heading (below the Search box), click Schedule, and then double-click Gantt Chart. In the Gantt Chart Options dialog box that appears, click OK to accept the settings as they are. You can modify them after you've imported your Project data.

3. In the Gantt Chart tab's Manage section, click Import Data.

    The Import Project Data Wizard starts. As a refreshing change, this wizard gets right to business with options on the very first page.

4. On the wizard's screen, leave the "Information that's already stored in a file" option selected, and then click Next.

    Despite the wizard's name, you can actually import data from Excel spreadsheets and text files, as well as Project .mpp and .mpx (an older Project exchange format) files.

5. On the "Select the format of your project data" screen, leave Microsoft Project File selected, and then click Next.

    To import from a different type of file, choose the format in the list.

6. On the "Select the file containing existing project schedule data" screen, open the file you want to import, and then click Next.

    On the page, click Browse. In the Import Project Data Wizard dialog box that appears, find and select the file you want to import (Event_Ch25_start.mpp), and then click Open. Back on the wizard screen, you see the path and filename filled in.

7. On the "Time scale" screen, choose the major and minor timescale units, as well as the time units you use to enter duration. In this example, set Major Units to Quarters and Minor Units to Months. Then click Next.

    Less robust than the timescale units in Project, Visio timescale units are days, weeks, months, quarters, and years. The duration units come in several variations. For whole numbers, you can choose Weeks, Days, or Hours. To show fractional values, choose Days Hours, Weeks Days, or Weeks Hours.

    Clicking the Advanced button opens a dialog box where you can specify the shapes for the Gantt Chart. However, changing the shapes once the drawing is complete makes it easier to see whether the results are what you want.

8. On the "Select task types to include" screen, select the category of tasks you want to import (in this example, "Top level tasks and milestones"), and then click Next.

    Initially, All is selected, which brings in every task in your Project file. Because you usually turn to a Visio Gantt Chart to produce an overview of your project, one of the other selections is usually more appropriate. "Top level tasks only" shows only the highest-level tasks. "Milestones only" shows milestones without any other tasks. "Summary tasks only" includes all levels of summary tasks so only the work tasks are eliminated. "Top level tasks and milestones" is a great summary with the highest-level tasks and all milestones.

> **Note:** Project tasks with 0 duration come in as milestones. Visio turns tasks designated as milestones that have a duration other than 0 into milestones with 0 duration.

9. On the last screen, review the settings you've chosen and then click Finish.

    Visio creates a new Gantt Chart from the imported data, as shown in Figure 25-10. If you import into an existing drawing, Visio creates a new page and then adds the imported Gantt Chart to it.

    To change any import settings, on the last screen, click Back until the appropriate screen appears, and then make the changes you want.

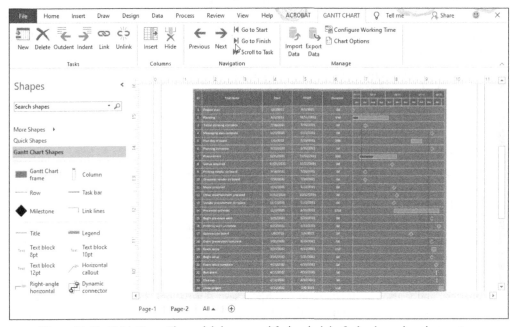

Figure 25-10. *Visio's Gantt Chart tab helps you modify the schedule, find tasks, and set chart options.*

10. To change the appearance of the Visio Gantt Chart, in the Gantt Chart tab's Manage section, click Chart Options. (You don't have to make any changes for the sample project.)

    The Gantt Chart Options dialog box has the same options the wizard presents when you click the Advanced button during the import process (see step 6). You can change the timescale dates, duration units, and timescale units. The dialog box's Format tab lets you choose shapes for task bars, summary bars, and milestones, as well as what the bar labels show.

> **Tip:** Visio's Gantt Chart tab helps you find task bars and dates. Click "Go to Start" or "Go to Finish" to move the timescale to the beginning or end of the project. Click Previous or Next to move to the previous or next time period. If you select a task and then click "Scroll to Task," the timescale moves to display the task's task bar.

Displaying Project Data in a Visio Timeline

Timelines are a great way to show when important events occur and how long phases last. Since Project can produce a timeline, you may not need to import project data into a Visio timeline drawing. However, Visio's timeline tools simplify importing different types of tasks: all tasks in the project or just top-level tasks, summary tasks, and milestones. To import information from Microsoft Project into a Visio timeline, follow these steps (you don't have to follow along):

1. Make sure the Project file you want to import *isn't* open in Project.

    The Import Timeline Wizard can't read a file that's already open.

2. In Visio, create a new Visio timeline drawing.

    To create a Visio Timeline, choose File→New, click the Categories heading, click the Schedule icon, and then double-click Timeline. Visio creates a new drawing and adds the Timeline tab to the Visio ribbon.

3. In the Timeline tab's Timeline section, click Import Data.

    The Import Timeline Wizard starts.

4. On the "Select a Microsoft Project file to import" screen, open the file you want to import (in this example, Event_Ch25_start.mpp), and then click Next.

    Click Browse to open the Import Timeline Wizard dialog box. There, find and select the file you want to import (it has to be a Project *.mpp* file), and then click Open. Back on the wizard screen, the path and filename appear in the box.

5. On the "Select task types to include" screen, select the category of tasks you want to import (in this example, "Top level tasks and milestones"), and then click Next.

    Initially, All is selected, which brings in every task in your Project file. Typically, "Top level tasks and milestones" is best for a summary of the highest-level tasks and all milestones. "Top level tasks only" shows only the highest-level tasks. "Milestones only" shows milestones without any other tasks. "Summary tasks only" includes all levels of summary tasks so only the work-package tasks are eliminated. Project tasks with 0 duration get imported as milestones.

6. On the "Select shapes for your Visio timeline" screen, review the default shapes, and choose different shapes if you want. In this example, keep the default shapes. Then click Next.

    The Timeline shape spans the dates for the full project schedule. Project milestones morph into Milestone shapes in Visio, and Project summary tasks become Interval shapes.

7. On the last screen, review the import properties you've chosen, and then click Finish.

    Visio creates a new timeline from the imported data, as shown in Figure 25-11. If you imported the data into an existing drawing, then Visio creates a new page and adds the imported timeline to it.

    To change any aspect of the import, click Back until you reach the appropriate page, change the settings you want, and then click Finish.

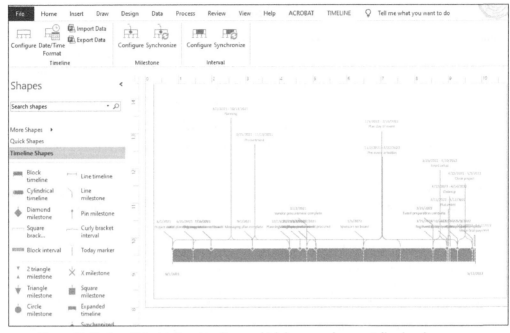

Figure 25-11. *On a Visio timeline, the callouts and labels may overlap, especially when dates are near one another. Click a milestone or timeline shape to display its yellow square control handles. Drag the control handles to separate the label from other labels nearby.*

8. To change the appearance of the timeline, right-click the shape you want to change and then choose one of the commands from the shortcut menu. In this example, you don't have to change anything.

   To change the time period for the timeline, right-click the timeline shape, and then choose Configure Timeline. You can also choose whether or not to show dates on the timeline. To modify milestones or intervals, right-click the appropriate shape and then choose Configure Milestone or Configure Interval.

   Changing the shape of an element like a timeline shape or milestone shape is as simple as clicking it and then, in the Timeline tab's Timeline, Milestone, or Interval section, clicking Configure. You can also right-click a shape, and then, on the shortcut menu, choose Timeline Type, Set Interval Type, or Set Milestone Type.

Exporting Visio Gantt Charts to Project

Suppose you used a Visio Gantt Chart to present a project proposal to the management team for their approval. The information in the Gantt Chart isn't much, but you can export it to Project to jump-start your schedule. When you do that, the tasks in a Visio Gantt Chart turn into tasks in Project with start dates, finish dates, and durations. Similarly, milestones in a Visio Gantt Chart become milestones in Project. (You don't have to perform these steps in the sample project.)

To export a Visio Gantt Chart to Project, follow these steps:

1. In Visio, open the Gantt Chart drawing you want to export, and select the Gantt Chart frame.

    Clicking within a Visio Gantt Chart selects individual task bars or task-name text boxes, which are subshapes within the Gantt Chart frame. To select the *frame*, click the very edge of the Gantt Chart. You can tell you've succeeded when selection handles appear at the frame's corners and at the midpoints along each side.

2. In the Gantt Chart tab's Manage section, click Export Data.

    The Export Project Data Wizard starts.

3. On the "Export my project data into the following format" screen, select Microsoft Project File and then click Next.

    You can also export to Excel files, text files, and Project .mpx files (an older Microsoft Project exchange format). However, you might as well export directly to Project.

4. On the "Specify the file to enter project schedule data" screen, click Browse and open the folder where you want to save the exported project file.

    The Export Project Data Wizard dialog box opens. Navigate on your computer or network to the folder you want.

5. In the "File name" box, type the name for the new Project file and then click Save.

    The dialog box closes and returns to the wizard, where the "Specify the file to enter project schedule data" box is filled in with the path and filename you specified.

6. Click Next.

    The last wizard screen shows that you're exporting a Gantt Chart, and it specifies the file you're creating.

7. Click Finish.

    A message box tells you that the data exported. Click OK.

8. Open the file in Project.

    You're ready to build a real schedule based on the data you exported from the Visio Gantt Chart. For example, you still have to create task dependencies between the tasks and assign resources.

Exporting Visio Timelines to Project

You can also export Visio timeline data to Project. Intervals from a Visio timeline turn into tasks in Project with start dates, finish dates, and durations. Milestones in Visio become milestones in Project. And the Visio timeline shape turns into a task with start, finish, and duration. You don't have to perform these steps in the sample project.

To export a Visio timeline to Project, follow these steps:

1. In Visio, open the timeline file and select the timeline shape.

   Select the timeline shape by clicking anywhere inside it.

2. In the Timeline tab's Timeline section, click Export Data.

   The Export Timeline Data dialog box opens. You can navigate on your computer or network to find the folder you want.

3. In the "File name" box, type a name for the new Project file, and then click Save.

   The "Save as type" box is set to Microsoft Project File. When you click Save, a message tells you that the data exported successfully. Click OK.

4. Open the Project file you created in Project.

   The timeline data turns into manually scheduled tasks in Project. After you create task dependencies in Project, you can switch these tasks to auto-scheduled (Chapter 5) so Project can do its job.

Integrating Project and Outlook

Outlook is Microsoft's email workhorse, but email is only one of the ways that Outlook and Project work as a team. When you're in Project, you can email Project files without jumping over to Outlook to do so. But because both programs can store lists of tasks and names, you can also export Project tasks to Outlook and vice versa. You can even use your Outlook address book to build your resource list in Project. This section explains how to use these features. (You don't have to perform these steps in the sample project.)

Adding Project Tasks to Outlook

If the old saying "Out of sight, out of mind" is all too true in your case, you can keep important Project tasks in sight by adding them (one at a time) to your Outlook Task List. By adding a reminder to these Outlook tasks, you can really stay on top of things. All you need to do is copy and paste. But before you get too attached to this approach, you should know that, when you add Project tasks to Outlook, you have copies of those tasks in two places—and they aren't linked. So if you mark a task as done in Outlook, it *isn't* automatically updated in Project, and vice versa.

If you decide to add tasks to Outlook as reminders, here are the steps:

1. In a task-oriented view like the Gantt Chart, select the Task Name cell for the task you want to copy to Outlook, and then press Ctrl+C. (Or right-click the cell and choose Copy Cell.)

    You can select only one task at a time. Project copies the task's name to the Clipboard.

2. In Outlook, display the Tasks list.

    Click the Tasks button, which looks like a clipboard with a checkmark in it) at the bottom of the Outlook window.

3. In the Home tab's New section, click New Task.

    The task-entry window appears with the heading "Untitled - Task."

4. Click the Subject box, and then press Ctrl+V.

    In the Subject box, the name of the task appears. If you want Outlook to remind you about the task's due date, turn on the Reminder checkbox, and then choose the date and time you want to be reminded.

5. On the ribbon, click Save & Close.

    Repeat steps 1–4 for other tasks you want to add to Outlook.

Importing Tasks from Outlook

Every once in a while, you may create tasks in Outlook that you later realize belong in one of your projects. You can import these tasks into a Project file as a head start. When you import tasks from Outlook, the imported tasks come in with the task names from Outlook and any notes you added. Although these imported tasks come in with the standard duration of "1 day?" (the question mark indicates estimated duration), they have no dependencies, resources, or dates.

To import Outlook tasks, follow these steps:

1. Open the Project file you want to import the tasks into, display a task-oriented view like Gantt Chart, and then in the Task tab's Insert section, click Task→Import Outlook Tasks.

    The Import Outlook Tasks dialog box opens. Outlook doesn't have to be running for this command to work, but you must have at least one incomplete task in your Outlook Task list. If you have no tasks in Outlook or they're all complete, a message box tells you there are no tasks to import.

2. Turn on the checkbox for each task you want to import, as shown in Figure 25-12.

    Any notes you typed in the Notes box in Outlook appear in the Notes cell in the table.

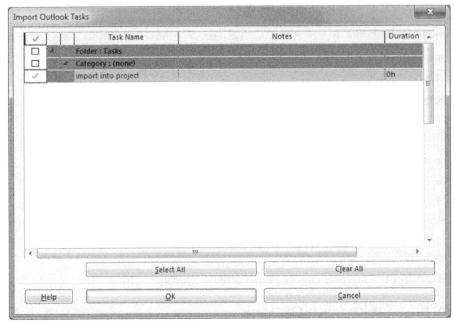

Figure 25-12. *To quickly select all the tasks, click Select All. Click Clear All to turn off all the checkboxes and start over. Don't turn on the checkboxes for folders and categories.*

3. Click OK.

    The tasks appear at the end of the list of tasks in your Project file.

Copying Tasks from an Email

If you copy an indented list of tasks from an Outlook email or a Word document, Project is smart enough to turn them into summary tasks and subtasks in your Project Task list. Copying and pasting tasks into Project is covered earlier in this chapter.

Building a Resource List from an Outlook Address Book

If you use Outlook at work, you probably already have information about team members in your Outlook address book or Contacts folder. Rather than retyping all this information in Project, you can import resource names from Outlook into Project. Here are the steps:

1. In Project, open the file into which you want to import resources.

    If you use a resource pool (Chapter 24), import the resources into the pool rather than into individual projects. Similarly, if you use Project Server, don't import resources directly into Project; import them into the enterprise resource pool instead.

2. In the View tab's Resource Views section, click Resource Sheet.

    Select the row where you want to insert the new resources.

3. In the Resource tab's Insert section, click Add Resources→Address Book.

   The Select Resources dialog box appears. If you select a Group in the Address Book, Project breaks the group into individual names.

4. Select the names of people you want to add to your project or resource pool.

   You can select several resources at a time by Shift-clicking the first name in the group and then the last name in the group. Select nonadjacent names by Ctrl-clicking each name.

5. Click Add.

   The names appear in the Add box.

6. Click OK.

   Project adds new rows in the Resource Sheet for the selected resources.

Sending Project Information to Others

You've probably emailed thousands of messages with attachments, so the concept of attaching a Project file to an email is nothing new. However, with Project, you can choose to send the whole project or only a few tasks and resources. And if your audience doesn't have Project installed on their computers, you can create a *picture* of the Project information and mail that instead. Project can send files using any MAPI-compliant (Messaging Application Programming Interface) email program. (You don't have to perform the steps in this section for the sample project.)

> **Tip:** If your organization uses SharePoint, that's a far easier way to share Project information. Chapter 28 shows you how.

Sending Project Files Via Email

With the plethora of cloud-storage and collaboration tools available, you might opt to share a file online (for example, in a OneDrive folder) and send reviewers or collaborators a notification email through the online service. Or you can print Project views as .pdf files to share with others (see the "Creating Pictures of Project Information" section earlier in this chapter). However, sharing a Project file with a few folks via email is easy (as long as the file size isn't ginormous), whether you send the message from your email program or directly from Project.

In Outlook, simply create a new message, and then, in the "Untitled - Message" window, head to the Insert tab's Include section, and then click Attach File to attach the Project file. (If you use a different email program, simply compose a new message and use the program's equivalent command to attach the Project file.)

On the other hand, if you tend to forget attachments (like most people do), you can create the email message in Project, which *automatically* attaches the file. Here are the steps for sending a Project file from within Project:

1. In Project, open the Project file you want to send, and then choose File→Share. On the Back-stage view's Share page, click Email, and then click "Send as Attachment."

    Your email program starts (if it isn't running already) and opens a new message window with the current Project file already attached. The Subject line contains the filename.

2. Click the "To:" box, and then, in the Select Names dialog box, choose the names of the recipients.

    You can also type email addresses directly in the "To:" box.

3. Edit the Subject box to tell your recipients why you're emailing them this file.

    In the message area, tell the recipients what you want them to do with the Project file, as shown in Figure 25-13.

4. Click Send or the equivalent button.

    The recipients receive your email message with the Project file attached.

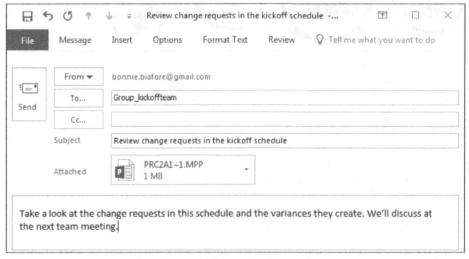

Figure 25-13. *The message form that you see is the same as the one that appears in your email program, so you can modify and format the message as you're accustomed to.*

26

Linking and Embedding

To manage projects, you usually need several types of information all at the same time. To see information without opening *every* program you use, you can take information created in one program and display an editable copy of it in another program. This exchange goes in either direction: Project data can appear in other programs like Excel and PowerPoint, or information from other programs can appear in Project.

You have three ways to make this happen: copying, linking, and embedding. As you learned in Chapter 25, you can copy data from one program and paste it into another. In a way, copying is a lot like embedding, because you create a copy of the data in the destination program, but embedding does more, as you'll learn shortly. *Linking* means connecting directly to information in one program from another program. For instance, a PowerPoint slide can display a high-level schedule from Project. Then, when you update the schedule in Project, that latest, greatest version of the schedule *automatically* appears in PowerPoint. On the other hand, *embedding* places a *copy* of an object (like a spreadsheet or Visio diagram) from one program into another. The embedded object and the original file aren't linked, so you don't automatically see changes made in the original. But embedded objects are ideal when you want to send self-contained files to colleagues.

The procedures for linking and embedding are usually almost identical—except for turning a Link checkbox on or off. However, a few linking and embedding techniques stray further from the typical path, depending on the type of data and whether you're displaying Project data in other programs, or vice versa. This chapter begins by describing the differences between linking and embedding in detail. Then you'll learn how to link and embed objects between programs, whether you want to place Project data into another program's files or vice versa.

This chapter concludes with another way you can link Project: adding hyperlinks to files, web pages, or other parts of your Project file. You'll learn how to add and modify hyperlinks, regardless of whether you're linking to a location in the same file, to another file, or to a web page.

Understanding Linking and Embedding

Linking and embedding both help you see data from one program in another program. However, these two methods for sharing data have their differences. By understanding what each one does, you'll be able to choose the right approach for what you're trying to do. This section describes the differences between linking and embedding and provides a side-by-side comparison to help you weigh the pros and cons.

- **Linking** means the data remains in the source file, and the destination file merely displays the source file's data. Linked objects get updated automatically, because the data you see in the destination file and the source data are one and the same, so the data in the destination file changes when the source data does.

  When you double-click a linked object, the source program starts and you can edit the source file. For example, suppose you link your Project schedule to a PowerPoint slide, and you spot a schedule change you want to make. Double-click the linked object in the PowerPoint slide, and Project launches and opens the source Project file. Any changes you make are saved in the source Project file *and* appear automatically in the PowerPoint slide.

- **Embedding** means that a separate copy of the source file (called an ***embedded object***) becomes part of the destination file. The source file still exists, but the embedded object is independent and doesn't change when the source data changes.

  In most cases, when you double-click an embedded object, the source program doesn't start. Instead, you see the source program's menus in place of the destination program's menus. For example, double-clicking an embedded Excel spreadsheet in the Project timescale pane replaces Project's menus with Excel's, and you see a hatched border around the object. (The menus revert to the destination program's menus when you deselect the embedded object.) Editing the embedded object doesn't affect the source file. In Project, embedded objects can also behave in another way, which the section "Editing Embedded Objects" explains.

> **Tip:** Linking and embedding work with any program that supports *Object Linking and Embedding* (OLE), a technology Microsoft developed specifically so that files can contain components created in different programs.

Whether linking or embedding is the better choice depends on what you're trying to do. Bottom line, linking is better if the source data is going to change. Embedding is better when you need to widely distribute the destination file, particularly to recipients who can't access your computers. Table 26-1 shows the pros and cons of each approach.

Table 26-1. *The differences between linking and embedding.*

Feature	Linking	Embedding
Updating	Linking keeps data up to date in both the source and destination files. You can edit the source file from either program and see the updated information in both places.	The destination file doesn't update along with the source file. If you want to update an embedded object to reflect a change in the source file, then you have to either make the same changes to the embedded object or re-embed the object after making the changes.
Copies of data	Linking means there's only one copy of the data, so you don't have to make the same changes multiple times. The link breaks if you move the source file, but you can repair it (described later in this chapter).	An embedded object is a second copy of the data. To show the most recent data in an embedded object, you have to edit the embedded object—or delete it and then re-embed it.
Distributing data	When you distribute a file with links, the recipients see the data *only if* they can access the linked files. If they can't, then the links break and they see an error message instead.	You distribute the destination file with the embedded object in it. The destination file contains everything the recipients need to view and edit the data.
File size	Destination files don't increase in size, because the data remains in the source file.	The size of a destination file increases because it contains the embedded object and all of its data.
Performance	When a file contains multiple links, it takes time to open the links (especially over a network). The file has to examine each source file for updates to the linked objects.	The additional data in embedded objects can make the destination file slower to open and respond.

Linking and Embedding Project Data

Project data comes in handy in lots of other programs. For example, a Project schedule shows project status whether it appears in a PowerPoint slide, a Word-based status report, or an Excel spreadsheet. Similarly, you might embed a Resource Graph into a memo requesting resources. This section describes how to link and embed Project data into other programs. It also explains how you can create a hammock task that spans a portion of your project by linking cells within a Project file. See the section "Working with Linked and Embedded Objects" to learn how to display, select, resize, and edit linked and embedded objects.

> **Note:** If you've downloaded files from the book website, you can follow along using the file Event_Ch26_start.mpp.

Linking Project Files to Other Programs

Sometimes, pictures of Project views aren't enough. For example, you might want to include a high-level Gantt Chart in your status report to show the up-to-date project schedule. When you link a Project file to another program, the linked object initially displays the portion of the view that you copied in Project. Once the linked object is in place, you can edit it to change the view, filter the tasks, and so on (as described later).

Follow Along Practice

Here's how you link a Project file to another program:

1. Open the Project file and the destination file. (In this example, open the file Event_Ch26_start. mpp. In Word, open the file Ch26 Report.docx.)

    You can link to a Project view in any program that supports OLE, including Excel, Word, and PowerPoint.

2. In Project, set up the view the way you want it.

    Select the view and the table you want. If necessary, insert or hide columns in the table. Filter the view to show only the tasks, resources, or assignments you want. In this example, display the Gantt Chart view and apply the Summary table. On the View tab, click Outline, and then choose Level 1 to show high-level tasks and milestones. In the View tab's Zoom section, select Months in the Timescale box.

3. Select the data you want to link (in this example, drag over the task IDs for all the tasks except for the project summary task), and then, in the Task tab's Clipboard section, click Copy (or simply press Ctrl+C).

    Whether you select entire rows by dragging over their ID numbers or cells in a table, the Copy command places what you've selected on the Clipboard.

4. Switch to the other program and, in the destination file, click where you want to place the linked view. In this example, in the Word document, click the blank row above the Cost Overview heading.

    Unlike pasting table cells, a view comes in as one object with its top-left corner at the location you click.

5. In the Home tab's Clipboard section, click Paste→Paste Special.

    If you're linking to a non-Microsoft program, the command may be Edit→Paste Special instead.

    The Paste Special dialog box opens.

6. In the Paste Special dialog box, select the "Paste link" option, as illustrated in Figure 26-1.

    Be sure to select "Paste link," since the Paste option *embeds* the object instead of linking it. If the "Paste link" option is grayed out, be sure to save the Project file, and then recopy and try "Paste link" again.

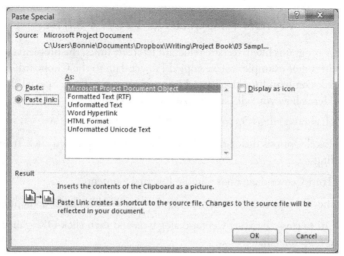

Figure 26-1. *Turn on the "Display as icon" checkbox to show an icon instead of the entire linked object. When you want to see the linked information, simply double-click the icon.*

7. In the As list, select Microsoft Project Document Object, and then click OK.

The Project view appears as a single object in the destination file (Figure 26-2). You can move the linked object around by dragging anywhere in the center of the object. To resize the object, click within it, and then drag the resize handles at the corners and the middle of each side.

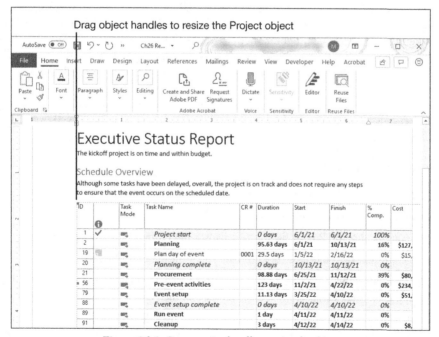

Figure 26-2. *Drag a resize handle to resize the object.*

When Programs Won't Link

If your Office programs like Excel are reluctant to create links, the problem could be your security settings. For example, you've copied Project data to the Clipboard, but in Excel, the Paste Link command (or the Paste Link option in the Paste Special dialog box) is grayed out. Here's how you tell Excel to play well with others:

1. In Excel, choose File→Options.

2. In the Excel Options dialog box, choose Trust Center, and then click Trust Center Settings.

3. In the Trust Center dialog box, choose External Content.

4. Select the "Prompt user on automatic update for Workbooks Links" option.

5. Click OK to close the Trust Center dialog box, and then click OK again to close the Excel Options dialog box.

If the "Paste link" option is *still* grayed out, try saving and reopening your files and then repeating the linking process.

Linking Project Table Data to Other Programs

If the other program's file has cells, such as an Excel spreadsheet, you can create links from portions of Project tables directly to the cells in the other program's file. Any portion of a Project table is fair game: You simply select the data you want (individual cells, groups of cells, entire columns, or entire rows) and then paste a link into the other file. Although the values in the other program *look* just like ones you type directly into that program, they're actually linked to Project cells. So when the Project values change, the linked cells in the other program display the updated values. For example, by linking Project cost cells to Excel, a financial analysis spreadsheet could show financial results at any time.

Linking and copying both work with Project table cells, but linked cells get their values directly from source Project cells. Copying pastes the text or numbers from the source Project cells into destination cells, as if you entered the values directly, and they don't get updated if the source data changes.

Follow Along Practice

To link Project table cells to cells in a program like Excel, follow these steps:

1. Open both the Project file and the destination file.

   In this example, use the Project file for this chapter and create a new Excel workbook.

2. In Project, display the table that contains data you want to link to Excel.

   In this example, in the View tab's Task Views section, click the Gantt Chart button. To change the table, in the View tab's Data section, click Tables, and then choose Cost from the drop-down list.

3. Select the data you want to link (in this example, drag over the columns in the table (from Task Name to Remaining Cost), and then in the Task tab's Clipboard section, click Copy (or right-

click anywhere within the selected cells, and then choose Copy from the shortcut menu, as shown in Figure 26-3).

Use any of the usual techniques for selecting data: dragging over column headings to select entire columns, dragging from the top-left to the bottom-right cell of a range, or Shift-clicking cells. The cells you select must be contiguous; if you Ctrl-click or Ctrl-drag to select nonadjacent cells, you can't paste-link that selection in the other program. If you select cells within a table, the shortcut menu entry that appears is Copy Cell, not Copy.

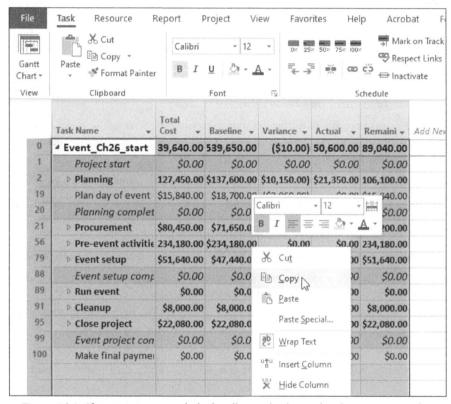

Figure 26-3. *If you want to create a link, the cells you select have to be adjacent to one another.*

4. In the destination file, click the top-left cell where you want to insert the linked data, in this example, cell A1 in the Excel worksheet.

    When you paste the data (in the next step), it starts at the cell you click, and then fills in cells to the right and below that cell.

5. In the destination program, in the Home tab's Clipboard section, click Paste→Paste Special. In the Paste Special dialog box, select the "Paste link" option and either HTML or Text, and then click OK.

    The linked data appears in the selected cells. If you can't see the full values, adjust the column widths in the destination file.

Creating a Hammock Task by Linking Cells in a Project Table

A hammock task is a task that spans a portion of your project, whether it's a phase or the entire project. For example, you might want to include a hammock task for the time someone from your project management office spends on supervision. Project doesn't have a built-in feature for creating hammock tasks. Fortunately, with OLE linking, you can build a hammock task by linking the hammock task's Start and Finish fields to other tasks' Start and Finish fields.

Follow Along Practice

Here's how to create a hammock task:

1. In your project, create a regular task for the supervisory effort.

    In this example, use the Project file for this chapter. In the first blank Task Name cell, type **PMO Supervision**. If necessary, change the task's Task Mode to Auto Scheduled. Change the task's Duration to **1d**. (Change the table in the view if necessary.)

2. To link the task's start date to the project start date, select the Start cell for the task that controls the hammock task's start date, and then press Ctrl+C (or right-click the cell and choose Copy Cell on the shortcut menu).

    In this example, select the Start cell for task ID 1 "Project start," and then press Ctrl+C.

3. Next, select the Start cell for the hammock task (in this example, task ID 101 "PMO Supervision"). In the Task tab's Clipboard section, choose Paste→Paste Special. In the Paste Special dialog box, select the "Paste link" option, and then click OK.

    When you select the "Paste link" option, the only type of data listed in the As box is Text Data.

    After you add the link, a small gray triangle appears at the cell's bottom right (Figure 26-4) to indicate that the field is linked to a field in another task.

4. To link the task's finish date to the project finish date, select the Finish cell for the task that controls the hammock task's finish date, and then press Ctrl+C (or right-click the cell and choose Copy Cell on the shortcut menu).

    In this example, select the Finish cell for task ID 100 "Make final payment," and then press Ctrl+C.

5. Select the Finish cell for the hammock task (in this example, task ID 101 "PMO Supervision"). In the Task tab's Clipboard section, choose Paste→Paste Special. In the Paste Special dialog box, select the "Paste link" option, and then click OK.

    A small gray triangle appears at the cell's bottom right to indicate that the field is linked to a field in another task. The hammock task's Finish date changes to the latest date in the project and its duration spans the entire project.

6. To test the link, in this example, click the Finish cell for task ID 100 "Make final payment," and type **5/18/18**. Press Enter.

    The Finish date for the hammock task changes to 5/18/18 and its Duration increases to 246.63 days.

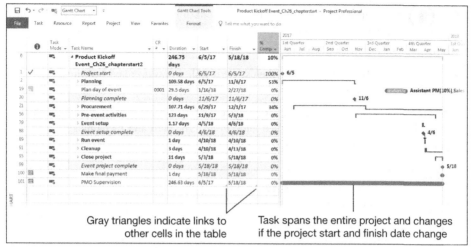

Gray triangles indicate links to
other cells in the table

Task spans the entire project and changes
if the project start and finish date change

Figure 26-4. *You can create a hammock task by linking its Start and Finish cells to the dates from other tasks.*

Note: If you want to remove or manage OLE links, see the section "Managing Linked Objects."

Embedding Project Files in Other Programs

Embedding Project files into another program creates a copy of your project in the destination file. Embedding data creates a self-contained file—for example, for the subcontractors who can't access your computer systems. If you sent them status reports with linked objects, they would see broken links, not data.

Note: You can't embed a *portion* of a Project file into another file. You can embed only an entire Project file into another file. Because embedding creates a copy of the data in the destination file, not a link, you can simply copy and paste a portion of a Project table into another file.

Follow Along Practice

To embed a Project file in another program, follow these steps:

1. Open the destination file, and then select the location where you want to embed your Project file (in this example, in the Ch26 Report Word document, put the cursor at the end of the Cost Overview section).

   Project doesn't have to be running to embed a Project file. Simply launch the destination program, and then put your cursor wherever you want the Project file to go.

2. In a Microsoft Office program, in the Insert tab's Text section, click Object.

The Text section is near the right end of the Insert tab. If the entire section isn't visible, click Text and then choose Object on the drop-down menu.

The Object dialog box opens.

3. Select the "Create from File" tab, and then select the file you want to embed (in this example, Event_Ch26_start.mpp).

To locate the file, click Browse. In the Browse dialog box, navigate to the folder that contains your Project file, click the filename, and then click Insert. The path and filename appear in the "File name" box, as shown in Figure 26-5.

Figure 26-5. *You can turn an embedded file into a linked file in no time flat simply by turning on the "Link to file" checkbox.*

4. To show an icon until you want to see the Project file, turn on the "Display as icon" checkbox. In this example, keep this checkbox turned off.

Turning on this checkbox displays a Change Icon button. Click this button to display the Change Icon dialog box, where you can select the icon and label you want.

5. Click OK.

The embedded file appears at the selected location in the destination file. If you chose to display an icon for the embedded file, then you can open the file by double-clicking its icon.

Note: When you insert an object into a file, the dialog box you use to do so (Object or Insert Object, depending on the program) offers a two-for-one option that lets you create an object *and* embed it in the destination file. (If the program you're using opens the Object dialog box (like Word or Excel), then select the Create New tab. If the Insert Object dialog box opens instead (like Project), then select the Create New option.) However, creating a Project file on the fly to embed in another program is a bad idea, because that Project file is then available *only within* the destination file. If, on the other hand, you create your Project file in Project, then you can work on the original file as you would normally and can also embed the file into another program. Just remember that the embedded Project file won't reflect any changes you make to the original file.

Linking and Embedding Data into Project

Linking and embedding data goes in either direction. Just as a Project schedule can provide information for a status report or presentation, other files can provide background information for the tasks in your Project schedule. For example, you might link information in a risk log spreadsheet to an at-risk task, so the most recent actions and results appear in the Notes tab of the Task Information dialog box. Likewise, you could embed a Word document for a change request in the Gantt Chart timescale.

You can link or embed entire files into Project, or link cells from an Excel spreadsheet to Project table cells. In addition, you can embed portions of other files, like Excel charts or Visio drawing pages. This section explains how to link and embed data into Project.

Linking and Embedding Entire Files into Project

Inserting an entire file into Project is one way to get easy access to additional information—for example, a specifications Word document or a change request tracking database. To see more of the file, simply drag the boundaries of the inserted object. To see a different part of the file, select the object and then edit it, as described in the section "Editing Linked Objects." (Another, even easier, way to access other files is by adding a hyperlink to the file within Project, as described later in this chapter.)

Follow Along Practice

When you work with entire files, the linking and embedding steps are almost identical:

1. In your Project file (in this example, Event_Ch26_start.mpp), select the location where you want to insert the other file. In this example, double-click the project summary task to open the Summary Task Information dialog box.

    Only some areas of a Project file accept inserted objects: the Gantt Chart timescale; the Notes or Objects boxes in the Task Form, Task Details Form, and Resource Form; and the Notes tab in the Task Information, Resource Information, and Assignment Information dialog boxes.

> **Note:** If you want to insert objects in the Gantt Chart timescale, you have to customize the ribbon to add the Object command to a custom group (see Chapter 22 for details). In the "Choose commands from" list, choose All Commands, and scroll until you see the Object command.

2.   On the Notes tab, click the Insert Object button immediately above the Notes area.

     The Insert Object dialog box opens.

3.   Select the "Create from File" option, and then choose the file you want to link or embed.

     Click Browse to navigate to the folder that contains the file you want. Double-click the filename, and the path and filename appear in the File box. In this example, select the Word document "Ch26 Change Requests.docx."

4.   To *link* to the file, turn on the Link checkbox (do this for the sample project). To *embed* the file instead, leave this checkbox turned off.

     What you do in this step is the only difference between linking and embedding; the rest of the process is identical.

5.   To display the file as an icon until you want to see it, turn on the Display As Icon checkbox (do this for the sample project).

6.   Click OK.

     The object appears at the location you selected in your Project file (Figure 26-6). To open the file, double-click it.

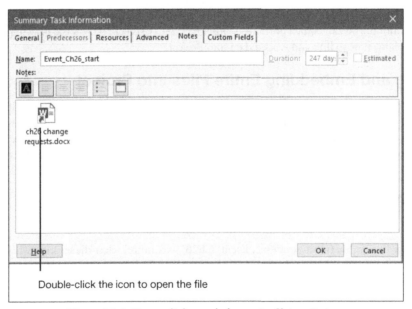

Figure 26-6. *You can link or embed an entire file into Project.*

Embedding Parts of Files in Project

With some programs, you can embed portions of a file into Project. A chart from an Excel spreadsheet, a slide from a PowerPoint presentation, and a drawing page from a Visio document are all candidates for inserting into a Project file. Although the embedded object represents only that portion of the file, the object still increases the destination file's size. And remember that the embedded object doesn't update to reflect any changes to the original file.

> **Note:** You can't *link* a part of a file. If you copy an Excel chart, PowerPoint slide, or Visio drawing page, and then use the Paste Special command in Project, the "Paste link" option remains grayed out.

Follow Along Practice

To embed a part of a file into your Project file, follow these steps:

1. In the source program, open the file and select what you want to show in your Project schedule (in this example, open the file "Ch26 ExcelChart.xlsx" and select the pivot chart).

    For example, in an Excel chart, click inside the chart. In Visio, drag across the shapes you want to embed in Project. (If you want to embed an ***entire*** Visio drawing page, make sure ***no*** shapes are selected.)

2. Press Ctrl+C to copy the selection to the Clipboard.

    Alternatively, in Microsoft Office programs, in the Home tab's Clipboard section, click Copy.

3. In your Project file, right-click the location where you want to place the object (in this example, double-click task ID 2 "Planning," click the Notes tab, and right-click in the Notes box), and then choose Paste Special.

    If you want to insert these partial objects in the Notes tab of the Information dialog boxes (see step 1 in the previous list for a full list of them), you have to right-click within the Notes area, because the ribbon is inactive while the dialog box is open. You can also insert partial objects in the Objects box in the Task Form or Resource Form view. (To display the Objects box in a form, right-click the top part of the form, and then, in the shortcut menu, choose Objects.)

    Project selects the Paste option, which embeds the object. The Paste Link option is grayed out, telling you that you can't link a part of another file.

4. In the As box, select the type of object you want to paste in, in this example, Microsoft Excel Chart.

    The choices vary depending on what you copied to the Clipboard.

5. Click OK.

    The object appears in Project at the location you selected. In this example, click OK to close the Summary Task Information dialog box.

Linking Tabular Data in Project

Just as you can link to Project table cells in other programs, you can also bring data from other programs into Project's table cells. When you link data to Project cells, the values look as if you typed them directly into Project, but they're actually linked to the source file and change when the source data changes.

Project demands the right types of data in some of its fields, so you have to make sure the data types are the same in both places. For example, you can link only dates in Project date cells. When you link tabular data from another program in Project, the links point to specific columns or cells in the source file (like column C or cells C5 through C12 in an Excel spreadsheet). If you rearrange columns or cells in the source file, the links in Project still point to the original linked locations, which could produce a data-type mismatch. The easiest way to keep data types in sync is to link column by column. Here's how (you don't have to perform these steps in the sample project):

1. In Excel or another table-based program, select the first column you want to link by clicking the column's heading, and then press Ctrl+C.

    Clicking the heading selects the entire column. You can also select several cells in a column that you want to link by dragging over them, and then press Ctrl+C.

2. In Project, display the view and the table in which you want to link the data. Then click the first cell for the linked data.

    Select the top-left cell for the linked data; Project will fill in the cells to the right and below it.

3. In the Task tab's Clipboard section, click Paste→Paste Special, and then select the Paste Link option.

    If you choose the Paste option, Project simply copies the values into the Project cells as text, numbers, dates, and so on.

4. In the As box, select Text Data.

    Selecting an object type like Microsoft Office Excel Worksheet inserts a linked object that you double-click to open and edit. By selecting Text Data, Project fills in individual cells with linked values. Each linked cell gets its value from the corresponding cell in the source file.

5. Click OK.

    The cells display values from the source file with a gray triangle at each linked cell's lower right (see Figure 26-4 earlier in this chapter). To link other columns in the source file, repeat steps 1–5 for each additional column.

Working with Linked and Embedded Objects

Linking or embedding information into another file is just the beginning. Linked and embedded objects are incredibly versatile, and this section explains all the things you can do with them.

Most of the time, you want the information in linked and embedded objects to be visible at all times, but these objects can just as easily keep a low profile as icons until you want to see what they have to show. Like other elements in files, you can move and resize objects—for instance, to get them out of the way of task bars in a Gantt Chart view or graphics on a Visio diagram. And the whole point of inserting a linked or embedded object instead of a picture is to edit it at some point. To get the most out of linked and embedded objects, you need to know how to manage the objects you insert as well as the links between files. This section explains all that.

Linked and embedded objects work like many other elements in your files. You can select them, move them around, change their size, and delete them. Here's how (you don't have to perform these actions in the sample project):

- **Resize an object**: When you select an object by clicking it, resize handles appear at each of its corners and at the middle of each side. You can drag these handles to change the size of the object. To change the object's dimensions while maintaining its proportions, drag a handle at one of the corners (the pointer changes to an angled two-headed arrow). To change the size in only one dimension, drag a handle at the middle of a side (the pointer changes to either a horizontal or vertical two-headed arrow).

- **Move an object**: You can move an object whether or not it's selected by dragging the middle of the object to the new location. The pointer includes a box at its lower right to indicate that you're about to move the object. If you drag too close to one of the object's edges, then you'll resize the object instead.

- **Delete an object**: Select the object, and then press Delete.

- **Display the object as an icon**: When you display an object as an icon, double-clicking the icon brings the full object into view. Dragging the icon moves the object, just as dragging the actual object does.

Editing Linked Objects

Whether you're working in the source program or the destination program when you edit a linked object, you always edit the same source file. Suppose you link an Excel spreadsheet in a task note. If you edit the spreadsheet in Excel, then your changes show up automatically the next time you open or update your Project file. Alternatively, you can double-click the linked object in Project to start Excel and open the source file for editing.

Follow Along Practice

Editing linked objects works differently from editing embedded objects in that you always edit ***the source file***. Here's how it works:

1. To edit a linked object, double-click it. In this example, double-click the project summary task to open the Summary Task Information dialog box. Then, double-click the "Ch26 Change Requests" icon.

    The source file opens in the source program. For example, double-clicking a linked Word document starts Word and opens the document—as if you'd started Word yourself and opened the file. (You need to have read-write privileges for the file in order to edit it, just as you would if you opened the file directly.)

    > **Tip:** If an error message appears when you try to edit a linked object (or when you open a file with links), a broken link is the most likely culprit. If the linked file moves to a different location, you have to edit the link to point to the correct file location (described shortly).
    >
    > Another cause of problems editing links could be that the source program isn't installed on your computer. For example, when you edit a linked Visio drawing, Visio starts and opens the file, which means you need to have Visio on your computer.

2. If you see a message box telling you that you're opening an OLE object that could contain viruses and other malicious code and you're ***sure*** it's safe, click Yes to open the file.

    If you have any doubts about the file, click No.

3. When you finish editing, save and close the file as you would normally. Close the object's program (Word in this example) if no other files are open in it.

    Back in the destination Project file, the linked object reflects the changes. If the linked object ***isn't*** up to date, you can tell the destination program to immediately check for updates, as described in the next section.

Managing Linked Objects

Linked objects require ongoing care and feeding. For example, you have to make sure that links can find the files they represent. If links are broken, then you can redirect them to the correct location for the source file. Conversely, you can ***intentionally*** break the link between an object and the source file to transform the object into an embedded object or picture. Finally, you can update a link immediately and tell the destination program whether you want it to update links automatically or wait for you to say when.

Out of the box, whenever you open a file that contains links, a message box asks if you want to re-establish the links. Click Yes to update the links. If you click No, Project opens the file with the existing values; that is, it doesn't check the source file to see if values have changed.

> **Tip:** If you want Project to re-establish links without asking you, choose File→Options. On the left side of the Project Options dialog box, click Advanced. In the Edit section, turn off the "Ask to update automatic links" checkbox, and then click OK.

If you want to perform more specific link-management tasks, you can use the Edit Links command to open the Links dialog box, shown in Figure 26-7. Unfortunately, the Edit Links command isn't on the ribbon, so you have to add it to a custom group (Chapter 22) before you can use it. In Figure 26-7, the Edit Links command is on a custom ribbon tab called Favorites in the custom Tasks group.

> **Note:** In other Office programs, the dialog box you use to edit links is named Edit Links; in Project, it's simply named Links. For other Office programs like Excel, open the Edit Links dialog box by selecting the ribbon's Data tab, and then, in the Queries & Connections group, clicking Edit Links.

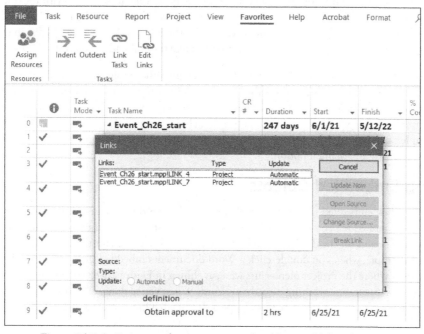

Figure 26-7. *In Project, you have to customize the ribbon to add the Edit Links command to a custom group.*

Here's how to use Project's Links dialog box to keep links in tip-top condition (you don't have to perform these actions in the sample project):

- **Review links**: The dialog box lists the links in your file whether they connect to other places in the same file or to different files altogether. Each link shows the source file's name, the type of file, and whether the link is set up to update automatically or manually. In this example, the links listed are the linked Project cells for the hammock task created earlier in this chapter.

Chapter 26: Linking and Embedding

- **Update a link**: To immediately update a link with changes from the source file, select the link, and then click Update Now.

- **Repair a broken link**: You can fix broken links by changing the folder or file that a link looks for. Click Change Source, and then in the Change Source dialog box, click Browse to find the file. Double-click the filename to update the path and name in the Source box. Click OK to save the link.

> **Tip:** If you want to move a source file without breaking its link in Project, open Project first, and then move the source file to its new location. That way, Project will automatically revise the link location.

- **Change a linked object into an embedded object**: Suppose you linked to a document during its development so you always saw the most recent version. Now that the document is approved, you want to embed the object so you can send your Project file to someone with the document attached. You can convert a linked object into an embedded object in the Edit Links dialog box by selecting the link and then clicking Break Link. The link disappears from the list in the Links dialog box, but the object remains—and now acts like the embedded object it is.

- **Specify when to update the link**: Initially, Project and other programs create links so they update automatically, which means that the destination program checks source files for changes and updates the objects with any changes it finds. All that checking and updating can slow your computer to a crawl, especially if the source files change frequently or are located on large or complex networks. In this situation, you can control when updates occur by selecting a link and then selecting the Manual option.

Editing Embedded Objects

You double-click embedded objects to edit them, just like you do linked objects. The result depends on where you embedded the object in Project. If you edit an embedded object in the Gantt Chart timescale, the menus for the destination program change to the menus for the embedded object's program. For example, when you double-click a Word document embedded in your Gantt Chart, Word menus appear where the Project menus just were, as shown in Figure 26-8. You can then work on the Word object as if you were working directly in Word. When you're done, click somewhere outside the embedded object, and the Project menus reappear. It's like having two programs at your fingertips!

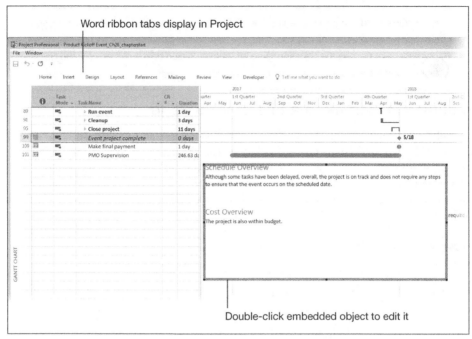

Figure 26-8. *When you're done editing, choose File→Save. Then press the Esc key. Resize handles appear on the embedded object, and the Project menus reappear.*

If you embed an object in a Project task's note (double-click anywhere in the task's row to open the Task Information dialog box, click the Notes tab, and then click the Insert Object icon), double-clicking the embedded object opens the object in its source program. If you can't remember whether an object is linked or embedded, click the File tab in that program. If the title bar says something like "Document in [your Project filename] - Word," you know you're editing an embedded object, not the source file.

> **Note:** When you double-click an embedded object, a message box may appear warning you that you're opening an OLE object that could contain viruses and other malicious code. If you're sure the file is safe, click Yes to open it. Otherwise, click No.

Hyperlinking to Information

Managing projects means keeping track of information stored in different places and different types of files. As a project manager, your nose is usually buried in a Project file, so why not access the information you need directly from Project? For example, you can add hyperlinks to tasks to access requirements Word documents, an Excel spreadsheet with financial figures, or the web page with your customer's mission statement. Project hyperlinks can also jump to tasks or resources within the Project file. This section explains all your options.

> **Note:** You can add only one hyperlink to each task, resource, or assignment. However, you can add as many hyperlinks as you want to a *note*. Simply double-click a task, resource, or assignment to open the corresponding Information dialog box, and then click the Notes tab and add the hyperlinks you want in the Notes box.

Creating a Hyperlink to a File or Web Page

Hyperlinks can connect to any kind of file—a Word document, an Excel spreadsheet, a web page, and so on. When you add a hyperlink to a task, resource, or assignment, Project displays a ***hyperlink indicator*** in that element's Indicators column, which looks like a globe with links of chain. Although the destination file can reside anywhere (anywhere that's accessible to the people who need it, that is), it has to ***remain*** in that same place. If the destination file moves to another location, the hyperlink can't find the file and becomes what's known as a ***broken link***.

Follow Along Practice

To create a hyperlink in a Project file, do the following:

1. In the project file for this chapter, display the view that shows the task, resource, or assignment to which you want to add a hyperlink. In this example, display the Gantt Chart view.

    You can insert hyperlinks in any view.

2. Right-click the task, resource, or assignment, (in this example, right-click the project summary task) and then choose Link. (Or click anywhere in the task, resource, or assignment's row, and then press Ctrl+K.)

    The Insert Hyperlink dialog box opens (Figure 26-9).

3. In the "Link to" section, select the type of data you want to hyperlink to, in this example, "Existing File or Web Page."

    The left side of the Insert Hyperlink dialog box has two vertical navigation bars for choosing what you want to hyperlink to: "Link to" and "Look in." In the "Link to" navigation bar, the aptly named "Existing File or Web Page" and "Place in This Document" are the most popular types of hyperlinks. (The next section describes the steps for linking to a location in your Project file.) You can also create a hyperlink to an email address, so you can easily email the person assigned to a task.

    Although you can simultaneously create a new document and hyperlink to it, creating the document outside Project is more expedient. Outside Project, you can create the document based on a template. Moreover, doing so keeps your multitasking to a minimum.

4. In the "Look in" section, navigate to the folder that contains the destination file, and then select the filename. In this example, navigate to the folder where you stored the sample files.

    The "Look in" drop-down list includes all the locations you can reach through Windows Explorer: drives on your computer, network drives, and removable drives. To look for the file you want, click the "Browse for File" button (whose icon is an open file folder) to the right of the "Look in" box. The "Link to File" dialog box opens.

The "Look in" section's navigation bar has three choices for finding files or web pages. Current Folder shows the files in the folder you've selected. Select Browsed Pages or Recent Files instead to hyperlink to files or web pages that you've used recently.

The "Browse the Web" button (its icon is a magnifying glass in front of a globe) to the left of the "Browse for File" button opens a browser window. Surf to the web page you want, select the URL in the browser's address bar, and then press Ctrl+C. Click the Address box in the Insert Hyperlink dialog box, and then press Ctrl+V to paste the URL.

5. In the "Text to display" box, type a brief description of what you're hyperlinking to, in this example, ***Change Request Info***.

The "Text to display" box is initially empty. When you position the mouse over a hyperlink indicator, a pop-up label containing the text from the "Text to display" box appears. If you type a description in this box, Project leaves it in place when you select a destination file. If you don't type a description in the "Text to display" box, Project fills in the path and filename of the destination file or the URL of the web page.

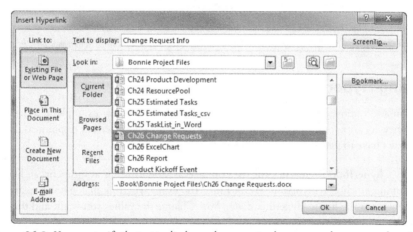

Figure 26-9. *You can specify the text to display and a screen tip that appear when you put the pointer over the hyperlink indicator.*

The Insert Hyperlink dialog box also has a ScreenTip button. When you position your pointer over a hyperlink indicator without clicking, a ScreenTip appears immediately below the description. If you type a meaningful description in the "Text to display" box, you may not need a ScreenTip, but it's handy if you want to see more information about a hyperlink.

6. Click OK.

A hyperlink indicator (Figure 26-10) appears in the task, resource, or assignment's Indicators column (depending on what type of element you chose in step 1). Click the indicator to open the hyperlinked file with its associated program.

If the Indicators column isn't visible, then you can't tell which elements have hyperlinks. However, if you know a hyperlink exists, you can follow it by right-clicking the task, resource, or assignment, and then, from the shortcut menu, choosing Hyperlink→Open Hyperlink. To insert the

Indicators column in the table, right-click a table heading, and then choose Insert Column. In the drop-down menu, choose Indicators.

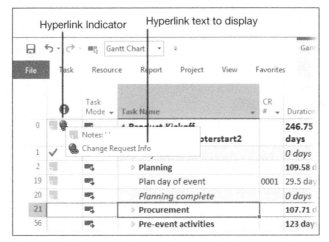

Figure 26-10. *You can specify the text to display and a screen tip that appear when you put the pointer over the hyperlink indicator.*

Modifying Hyperlinks

You can edit and remove hyperlinks to keep your files up to date. For example, if a destination file moves to a new location or a web page's address changes, edit the hyperlink to point to the new location (you don't have to perform these actions in the sample project):

- **Modify a hyperlink**: Right-click the hyperlinked task, resource, or assignment, and then, on the shortcut menu, choose Hyperlink→Edit Link. The Edit Hyperlink dialog box has all the same components as the Insert Hyperlink dialog box. Change the values you want, and then click OK to update the link.

- **Remove a hyperlink**: Right-click the hyperlinked task, resource, or assignment, and then, on the shortcut menu, choose Hyperlink→Clear Hyperlinks (this command is plural even though a task, resource, or assignment can have only one hyperlink at a time). Project deletes the hyperlink, and the hyperlink indicator disappears.

Creating a Hyperlink to a Location in the Project File

Hyperlinking from one place in a Project file to another is a great way to find related tasks or resources, or to jump to a view or report. For example, a hyperlink can take you from a work task to the corresponding approval milestone task or from a report to a view. Hyperlinks can point to tasks or resources. Moreover, to link to a task or resource, you need to know the task ID or resource ID that you want to link to *before* you open the Insert Hyperlink dialog box.

Follow Along Practice

To create a hyperlink to another location in the same Project file, do the following:

1. Right-click the task, resource, or assignment to which you want to add a hyperlink (in this example, task ID 95 "Close project"), and then choose Link on the shortcut menu.

    The Insert Hyperlink dialog box opens.

2. In the "Text to display" box, type a brief description of the hyperlink's destination, in this example, ***Cost Overview report***.

    Project keeps your description when you select a destination task or resource. If you don't fill in this box, then Project fills it in with the view name and ID that you select, which isn't particularly informative—for instance, "Gantt Chart!20" for task ID 20 in the Gantt Chart view.

    You can also add a ScreenTip to a hyperlink to another location. In the Insert Hyperlink dialog box, click the ScreenTip button. In the Set Hyperlink ScreenTip dialog box that appears, type the ScreenTip you want, such as what the hyperlinked location represents, and then click OK. Once you do that, when you position your pointer over a hyperlink indicator without clicking, the ScreenTip appears immediately below the description.

3. In the "Link to" section, click "Place in This Document."

    Project replaces the "Look in" area with a box for the task or resource ID you want to link to and a list of views and reports, as shown in Figure 26-11.

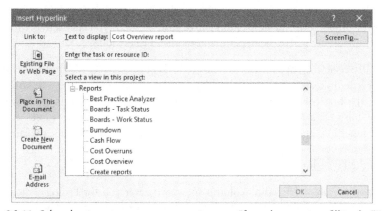

Figure 26-11. *Select the view or report you want to jump to. If you choose a view, fill in the "Enter the task or resource ID" box to jump to a specific task or resource.*

4. In the "Enter the task or resource ID" box, type the task or resource ID you want to link to (the number in the first column of the task's or resource's row in the task or resource table). In this example, leave this box blank.

    If you haven't filled in the "Text to display" box, then Project inserts the ID number in the "Text to display" box.

Project determines whether the number is a task ID or a resource ID based on the view you select in the next step. For example, it assumes you've entered a task ID when you select a task-oriented view like Gantt Chart; selecting the Resource Sheet view, for instance, changes the box to a resource ID.

5. In the "Select a view in this project" box, select the view or report you want Project to display when you follow the hyperlink (in this example, Cost Overview), and then click OK.

    If you haven't filled in the "Text to display" box, then Project inserts the view's name in that box in front of the ID.

    A hyperlink indicator appears in the hyperlinked task's, resource's, or assignment's Indicators column. Clicking this indicator switches to the view you chose in the Insert Hyperlink dialog box and selects the task or resource you hyperlinked to.

> **Tip:** You can insert hyperlinks in text boxes in a graphical report so you can jump to a view that provides more detail about what the report shows. To do that, select the text in a text box, such as the report name, and then right-click the text and choose Hyperlink on the shortcut menu.

Reviewing Hyperlinks

Checking that hyperlinks work is a good idea if some time has passed since you added them, because files may find homes in new locations. The "Text to display" hint and the ScreenTip pop-up box for hyperlink indicators show info you specify about the hyperlink, which typically isn't the file or location you're jumping to. If you click a hyperlink indicator, you don't know where the hyperlink goes until Project follows it.

To simplify reviewing hyperlinks, use Project's Hyperlink table, which displays the Task Name, Hyperlink, Address, and SubAddress columns. (If you're using a resource-oriented view, the first column is Resource Name instead.) To apply the Hyperlink table, in the View tab's Data section, click Tables→More Tables. In the More Tables dialog box, choose Hyperlink, and then click Apply. This table shows hyperlinks for the current file's tasks or resources; if tasks or resources don't have hyperlinks, then only their names are listed in the Hyperlink table.

The Hyperlink table's Hyperlink column shows whatever you (or Project) entered in the hyperlinks "Text to display" box. The Address column represents the Hyperlink Address field and shows the external files or web pages you hyperlinked to. For hyperlinks between locations within the file, the Address cell is empty. Instead, the SubAddress column represents the Hyperlink Subaddress field, which shows the view and ID for internal hyperlinks. All the entries in these cells are "hot," so you can click them to follow their hyperlinks

---

> **Note:** There is no sample file for the end of this chapter since links to files would break when you copy the files onto your computer.

27

Saving Time with Macros

You perform many of the same actions in Project day after day (sometimes several times each day). Some of these repetitive tasks might require different inputs each time you perform them, like choosing which baseline you want to see. Like doing the dishes, vacuuming the carpet, and washing the cat on the delicate cycle, some repetitive tasks are unavoidable—and timesaving tools sure would help. Instead of hiring a personal assistant to take the drudgery out of your Project work, you can write handy mini-programs called *macros*.

You don't have to be a geek to write your own macros. You can create a macro simply by recording the steps you want the macro to perform. Then you can run the macro to replay the steps again and again. However, for many repetitive tasks, you have to use Visual Basic for Applications (VBA) to get macros to do what you want.

This chapter explains macro basics: recording them, running them, adding them to the ribbon, and tying them to keyboard shortcuts. It also guides you through building a simple macro using VBA.

What You Can Do with Macros

A macro does one thing really well—it performs a series of steps each time you run it. For example, you can record a macro that hides summary tasks, turns on the critical path, and then sorts tasks by Duration in descending order. Macros are great timesavers because they can perform the equivalent of dozens of mouse clicks and key presses almost instantaneously. Moreover, macros reduce mistakes because you're not typing and clicking as much.

Any kind of repetitive task is a contender for building a macro. You can create a simple macro that sorts a task list or a sophisticated one that applies a view, filters and sorts the content, runs a report, and then prints it for your stakeholder status report. Since Project's creators couldn't anticipate *every* feature that organizations might need, macros let you create your own Project features, calculating project performance and evaluating your project in various ways. For example, a macro can calculate pessimistic task finish dates using custom duration fields containing pessimistic estimates.

Recording Macros

The best way to get started with macros is to record one. You don't have to write any code or invoke any arcane VBA spells. You simply start the recorder, click the same menus and press the same keys you always do, and then stop the recorder.

Recording a macro is like working a crossword puzzle in pen; your mistakes are indelibly saved along with what you got right. If you make a mistake, you have to rerecord the macro until you get it 100 percent right. So *before* you record a macro, take some time to figure out what you want to record. Then practice the steps a couple of times. (Write up a cheat sheet if you're recording more than a few steps.)

Before you start recording, make sure you perform any preliminary steps that you *don't* want to record in the macro—like opening a specific Project file or applying a view. In addition, the Project file must contain values that let you record all the steps you've planned. For example, if you're recording a macro that sorts tasks by their variances, then the Project file must have a baseline set.

> **Note:** If you've downloaded files from the book website, you can follow along using the file Event_Ch27_start.mpp. This file includes four baselines saved at different stages of the project.

Follow Along Practice

In this example, suppose you have three reports you produce in PDF format each week. You can record a macro that opens and prints each report. Now you're ready to record:

1. In the View tab's Macros section, click Macros→Record Macro.

    The Record Macro dialog box opens, as shown in Figure 27-1.

2. In the "Macro name" box, type a short name with no spaces, like *PrintWeeklyReports*.

    You can't include spaces in a macro name. If you want to separate words, insert underscores (_) between them or capitalize the first letter in each word. (Camel case means the first letter of the first word is uppercase, and then each subsequent new word is lowercase.)

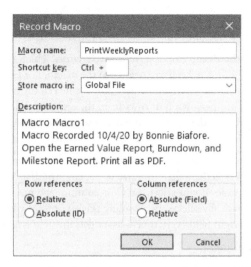

Figure 27-1. *Fill in the "Macro name" box with a meaningful name.*

3. In the Description box, fill in detailed information about what the macro does.

    Briefly describe what the macro does, any conditions that must be in place before you run it (like a selected task or a specific view), and what you end up with when the macro ends (views, filters, sort criteria, and so on). In this example, use this description: ***Open the Earned Value Report, Burndown, and Milestone Report. Print all as PDF.***

4. To assign a keyboard shortcut to launch the macro, type a letter (numbers aren't an option) in the "Ctrl+" box. In this example, type ***A***.

    The Ctrl key is the only key that works as a prefix for macro keyboard shortcuts in Project. However, as you can tell from the Keyboard Shortcuts Appendix, lots of keyboard shortcuts that combine Ctrl with letters of the alphabet are already taken (like the ubiquitous Ctrl+S for Save). Project doesn't give hints about which letters are still up for grabs (but it ***does*** complain if you try to type numbers or punctuation in the box). A, E, J, L, M, Q, and T are the only letters still available to combine with Ctrl in Project. In addition, if you set up a keyboard shortcut for the macro and then copy the macro to your global template, no other macros can use that keyboard shortcut.

    > **Tip:** Since you get so few letters to create keyboard shortcuts, save them for the macros you use the most. If you're a prolific macro builder, create a custom tab or a group on the ribbon (Chapter 22) to store your macros.

5. In the "Store macro in" drop-down list, select the file in which you want to store the macro.

    Project selects Global File, which stores the macro in your global template (***global.mpt***), so you can run the macro in any Project file you open from now on. To save a macro ***only*** in the current Project file, choose This Project (use this setting for the example). (The note titled "Where to Store Macros" explains how to choose the best place to store macros.)

6. If the macro includes moving around in the table area, choose options in the "Row references" and "Column references" sections. In this example, you don't have to choose these options.

   Project initially selects the Relative option for row references, which means that it moves the same number of rows from the selected cell when you run the macro. For example, suppose the first Task Name cell is selected, and you select the fourth Task Name cell during recording. Every time you run the macro, Project jumps down four rows from the cell that's selected. The Absolute (ID) option, on the other hand, tells the macro to move to the row with the same ID. So in this example, if you select the row with ID 4 while recording, then the macro always selects the row with ID 4.

   The Relative and Absolute options work similarly for columns. The main difference is that the Absolute (Field) option tells the macro to move to the column that contains the same field, as the name implies. For example, if you select the Cost column, the macro always jumps to the Cost column. Project automatically selects the Absolute (Field) option, which is the typical choice, because it gets you to the right field every time—as long as the field is somewhere in the view's table.

7. Click OK to start recording.

   The Record Macro dialog box disappears, and your Project file looks like it did before you created the macro. But the macro recorder is invisibly poised to record your every move.

8. Choose the commands and perform the actions you want to automate.

   For example, the steps for the PrintWeeklyReports macro include:

   a) Click the Report tab.

   b) Choose Costs→Earned Value Report.

   c) Choose File→Print.

   d) In the Printer box, choose Microsoft Print to PDF.

   e) Click the Print button.

   f) In the Save PDF File As dialog box, navigate to your report folder (in this example, you can choose the desktop or the folder where you store the sample files). In the "File name" box, type *EarnedValueReport*.

   g) Click Save.

   h) If necessary, click the Back arrow at the Print page's top right.

   i) Repeat the steps above for the Burndown and Milestone Report reports.

9. When the steps are complete, in the View tab's Macros section, click Macros→Stop Recording.

   You can't pause recording in Project like you can in Word and some other Microsoft programs—it's all or nothing.

10. To run your macro to make sure it works, in the View tab's Macro section, choose Macros→View Macros. In the Macros dialog box, select PrintWeeklyReports, and then click Run.

In this example, when the Save PDF File As dialog box opens, you can choose the folder you want to use and specify the file name for this copy of the report. For example, you can append the date you're running the reports to the file name.

> **Tip:** Once you've recorded a macro, you can fine-tune or fix it by editing its VBA code. In fact, the macro recorder can be your programming mentor. Record some macro steps in Project, and presto! The macro recorder dutifully logs the corresponding code. You can then study this code to learn about what you might do when modifying or writing macros from scratch.

Where to Store Macros

In most cases, storing macros in the global template (by choosing Global File in the "Store macro in" box) is the best option because you can run the macro whenever you're using Project in whatever Project file is open. In fact, anyone who uses the same global template (basically, anyone using your copy of Project) can use the macro.

On the other hand, storing macros in a specific Project file is useful in three instances:

1. If you need to send the Project file to someone who doesn't use your global template. In that case, storing a macro in the Project file lets your recipient run the macro.

2. If your macro works specifically with one Project file, selecting its unique tasks or resources, for example. In that case, the macro runs only when the correct Project file is open, and if you try to use the macro in any other Project file, it won't work.

3. Some organizations prevent users from writing information to the C: drive. In that case, you won't be able to save your macro to the global template, because it's located on that drive. However, you can save the macro in your Project file.

Running Macros

Project lists all the macros you create in the Macros dialog box (in the View tab's Macros section, click Macro→View Macros). You can run one anytime by selecting it and then clicking Run. But since the whole point of writing macros is to reduce time spent on repetitive tasks, clicking several times to run a macro defeats the purpose.

You can run a macro in any of three ways, each with its pros and cons. In the Macros dialog box, you can select a macro, and then click Run. Adding a macro to the ribbon or to the Quick Access Toolbar keeps it close at hand, and a click or two runs it. A keyboard shortcut is another way to run a macro, although the limited number of keyboard shortcuts available makes this method best for only your most popular macros. (Showoffs who edit code in the Visual Basic Editor: You can run a macro there, too, although doing so doesn't count as an everyday method.) This section explains your options.

Running Macros from the Macros Dialog Box

The Macros-dialog-box method requires the most mouse clicks, but it's ideal when you need a reminder about the macros you have available. Perhaps you've created so many macros that you can't remember them all. Or maybe someone else created the macros, and you want to see what's available. The Macros dialog box lists macros that are available in all open projects. To run a macro from the Macros dialog box, do the following (you don't have to perform these steps):

1. In the View tab's Macros section, click Macros→View Macros.

    The Macros dialog box opens. (You can also open this dialog box by pressing Alt+F8.)

2. In the macro list, select the macro you want to run, and then click Run (or press the F8 key on your keyboard).

    When you select a macro, the description appears at the bottom of the dialog box, in the Description area, as shown in Figure 27-2. Make sure the macro does what you want and that you've performed any setup the macro requires.

    You can do more than select and run macros in the Macros dialog box. Click Delete, for instance, to remove a hopelessly buggy macro you can't fix. Click Edit to open the Visual Basic Editor (described later in this chapter) so you can look at or modify the code directly. Click Step Into if you want to run the macro step by step, which helps you find the problem step when a macro isn't working properly.

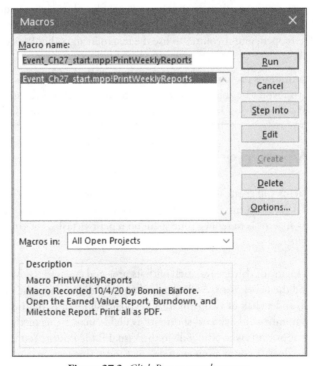

Figure 27-2. *Click Run to run the macro.*

Initially, the "Macros in" box is set to All Open Projects, which means you can run any macro stored in your global template or in any open projects. To see only the macros in the global template or in a specific Project file, in the "Macros in" drop-down list, choose Global Template, This Project, or the name of the Project file. The note titled "Setting Security" explains security features that make sure you run only the macros you want, not malicious ones that hitched a ride in a Project file.

Setting Security

Project's Trust Center has settings that make it harder for viruses and other malware to infiltrate your computer. The Trust Center lets you designate a list of people you trust so you can open only files that come from those sources. All other files stay unopened, keeping their malicious code to themselves. The security system also includes a way of creating digital *signatures*, so programs like Project can detect who created a given file. Here's how you set the level of security you want:

1. Choose File→Options.

2. On the left side of the Project Options dialog box, click Trust Center, and then, on the right side, click the Trust Center Settings button.

3. On the left side of the Trust Center dialog box, click Macro Settings.

4. Select the options for the security level you want. Project automatically selects "Disable all macros with notification," which is a good middle ground. It disables all macros but notifies you that it's doing so. (If you select "Disable all macros without notification," Project won't run any macros and doesn't tell you that it's disabled them because of your security setting.) To run macros with digital signatures, select the "Disable all macros except digitally signed macros" option.

5. Click OK to close the Trust Center dialog box. Click OK to close the Project Options dialog box.

Keep in mind that high security doesn't stop you from running macros *you* write. If you want to run a macro from someone else, the default option works well. It lets you tell Project on an individual basis whether or not to run a macro.

Running a Macro from the Ribbon

Buttons on the ribbon are probably the most popular way to run macros. They're quick. You don't have to remember another keyboard combination. You can show the macro name to jog your memory. And you can add as many macros as you want to a custom group on an existing tab, or a custom group on a custom tab.

Assigning a macro to the ribbon works almost exactly the same as adding other buttons or commands, as described in Chapter 22. You simply choose the macro to add from the Macros category.

Follow Along Practice

To add a button to the ribbon, follow these steps:

1. Choose File→Options. In the Project Options dialog box, choose Customize Ribbon.

   The "Customize the Ribbon" page appears.

2. On the right side of the page, select the tab and group to which you want to add the macro.

   In this example, if you created the Favorites tab in Chapter 22, click its + sign to expand the groups it contains, and then select the group you want (in this example, Tasks).

3. In the "Choose commands from" drop-down list, choose Macros.

   The available macros appear in the Commands list.

4. Select the macro (PrintWeeklyReports) and then click Add.

   The macro appears at the end of the group.

5. If you want to change the icon and text that appears in the ribbon, click the macro name in the group, and then choose Rename. In the Rename dialog box, choose the Printer icon. In the "Display name" box, change the name to *Weekly Reports*.

6. Click OK to close the Rename dialog box. Click OK to close the Project Options dialog box.

   The icon and name change on the ribbon.

Using Keyboard Shortcuts to Run Macros

If your brain has room to spare after memorizing Project's built-in keyboard shortcuts (Appendix Keyboard Shortcuts), you can assign keyboard shortcuts to run macros, too (see step 4 in the "Recording Macros" section). After you rule out the keyboard shortcuts that Project already owns, you have only seven letters of the alphabet left to combine with the Ctrl key (A, E, J, L, M, Q, and T). Yet nothing beats a deft two-key shortcut to run a macro you use all the time. To assign a keyboard shortcut, use one of the following two methods (you don't have to perform these steps):

- **While creating a macro**: In the Record Macro dialog box, in the "Ctrl+" box, type the letter you want to use.

- **When a macro already exists**: In the Macros dialog box, select the macro, and then click Options. In the Macro Options dialog box, in the "Ctrl+" box, type the letter you want to use, and then click OK.

> **Note:** You can't reuse keyboard shortcuts in the same file. For example, if you assign Ctrl+J to a macro you store in the global template, then no other macro in the global template can use Ctrl+J. However, Ctrl+J *is* still available in individual Project files. In fact, you can assign Ctrl+J to a different macro in every Project file you create by assigning Ctrl+J to a macro and then storing it in the current Project file (described in the "Recording Macros" section). When you press a keyboard shortcut, Project runs the macro assigned to that keyboard shortcut in the file you're working on.

Viewing and Editing Macro Code

Learning a programming language like VBA may be the last thing on your mind, but if you create your own macros, it pays to get familiar with—and even edit—some of your macro VBA code. For example, if you recorded a particularly long macro and made one little mistake, a quick edit in the Visual Basic Editor may be easier than rerecording the whole procedure. Similarly, if a macro references a specific name, which has since changed, then a surgical edit to change the name gets your macro working again. This section also guides you through creating a macro by writing VBA code.

The Visual Basic Editor is the place to look at and edit your macro code. Here's how you open it to create, edit, or inspect a macro (you don't have to perform these steps):

1. In the View tab's Macros section, click Macros→View Macros.

    The Macros dialog box opens.

2. Select the macro you want to tweak, and then click Edit.

    The Microsoft Visual Basic window opens, as shown in Figure 27-3. For simple edits, the code window is the only part of the editor you need. Because the module name appears in the macro's Run window, it's a good idea to rename Module1 to a more meaningful name.

    If you store your macro in the global template, then the module that contains the macro appears on the left side of the window (in the Project Explorer pane) underneath the ProjectGlobal entry. The VBAProject entry for a specific Project file contains macros stored in those Project files.

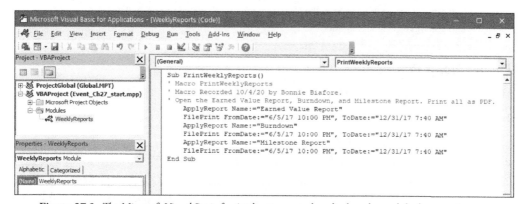

Figure 27-3. *The Microsoft Visual Basic for Applications window displays the module that contains your macro and the macro code.*

3. When you're done editing, choose File→Save Global.MPT.

    Visual Basic saves your macro to the global template. If you create the macro in a specific Project file, the File menu entry is "Save [Project filename].mpp," where [Project filename] is the file prefix.

4. To close the VBA window, choose File→"Close and Return to Microsoft Project."

The Microsoft Visual Basic window closes.

Creating a Macro with Visual Basic

Built-in baseline names (Baseline, Baseline1, Baseline2, and so on) don't tell you anything about what they represent. Suppose you want to save and display baselines in your projects using names that correspond to specific points during the project lifecycle. For example, Approval represents the initial baseline when stakeholders approve the project schedule; Planning represents when planning is complete; Procurement is the point when procurement is complete; and Implementation is when implementation is complete. This section steps you through using Visual Basic for Applications (VBA) to create a form and macro to do just that.

This example macro saves a copy of your project's current values into the Baseline fields (known as Baseline 0) as well as into the numbered baseline you choose (Baseline 1 up to Baseline10) from the drop-down list. In addition, it displays the baseline you choose for the baseline task bars in the Tracking Gantt view.

In this example, the first step is to build a form with buttons for each feature you want: Save Baseline, Show Baseline, and Close. You'll also need a box to choose the baseline you want to save or show. Then, you'll add code to the form's components to do the work.

> **Tip:** If you save baselines at different points in the project or save more than four baselines, you can modify the macro code to support those baselines. To support different names, you simply change the names in the Case statements. To include additional baselines, you can add more Case statements.

Follow Along Practice

Here's how to create a named baseline macro using VBA:

1. In the View tab's Macros section, click Macros→Visual Basic.

    The Visual Basic editor window opens.

2. Make sure the necessary Visual Basic References are turned on.

    In the Visual Basic editor, on the Tools tab, choose References and turn on the Microsoft Forms 2.0 Object Library check box. Make sure that the Visual Basic for Applications, Microsoft Project 16.0 Object Library, OLE Automation, and Microsoft Office 16.0 Object Library checkboxes are all turned on as well. Click OK to close the dialog box.

3. To add a form to the Project file (not the global template), in the Project – VBAProject panel, right-click "VBAProject [project file name]," and then choose Insert→User Form on the shortcut menu, as shown in Figure 27-4.

    Project opens a window for the form and a Toolbox window for selecting components to add to the form. Beneath the VBAProject entry, a Forms folder appears with UserForm1 in it.

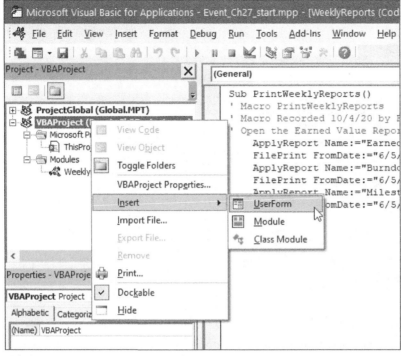

Figure 27-4. *To add a form to your Project file, right-click the entry VBAProject [filename], where [filename] is the name of the project.*

4. On the left side of the VBA window, in the Properties panel, in the cell to the right of the (Name) cell, replace UserForm1 with a name for the form, in this example, ***BaselineForm***.

5. In the cell to the right of the caption cell, type ***Named Baselines***.

    As you type the caption in the cell, over in the form window to the right, the caption appears as the form's title.

6. To add a List Box control to the form for choosing a baseline, in the Toolbox window, drag the List Box icon onto the form (the icon looks like a miniature list box).

    If the Toolbox window is not available, on the VBA window's View tab, click Toolbox.

7. To name the list box control, select it in the form. In the Properties panel, click the cell to the right of the (Name) cell, and type ***StageBox***, as shown in Figure 27-5.

    When you select a component in the form, its properties appear in the Properties panel on the left side of the VBA window. You can modify its properties by filling in the value cells in the second column.

8. To change the list box size, drag one of its corners to make it wider and shorter.

9. To label the list box, in the Toolbox window, drag a Label control (its icon is a large A) onto the form above the list box. In the Caption value cell, type ***Select a Baseline to show or save:***.

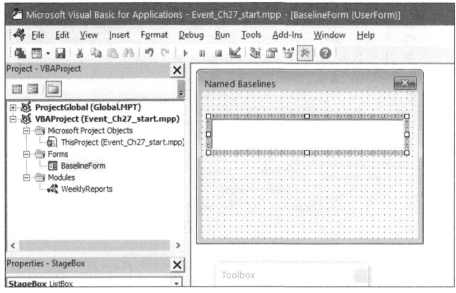

Figure 27-5. *Fill in properties in the Properties panel.*

10. To add code to the list box, right-click it in the form, and then select View Code.

    A code window opens. The control name appears in the box at the top left. The action that triggers the code appears at the top right. VBA automatically sets the action to Click.

11. In the code window, enter the following code, which defines the values that will appear in the list box's drop-down list when the form opens. In this example, the function Stagebox.AddItem adds an entry to the StageBox list box's drop-down list.

    Private Sub UserForm_Initialize ()

          'Define baseline names to display in the listbox.

          StageBox.AddItem ("Approval")

          StageBox.AddItem ("Planning")

          StageBox.AddItem ("Procurement")

          StageBox.AddItem ("Implementation")

    End Sub

    > **Tip:** Lines that begin with a single quote (') are comments. Use them liberally to explain what the macro does or why you wrote the code you did. (Project automatically adds whatever you type in the Record Macros dialog box's Description box to your macro's code as comments.)

12. Right-click the form name on the left, and then choose View Object. To add buttons, drag three CommandButton controls onto the form for saving a baseline, showing a baseline, closing the form. Figure 27-6 shows the button layout and labels.

13. Select CommandButton1 in the form. In the Properties panel, change its name to **ShowButton** and set the caption to **Show**.

14. Change CommandButton2's name to **SaveButton** and set the caption to **Save**.

15. Change CommandButton3's name to **CancelButton** and set the caption to **Cancel**.

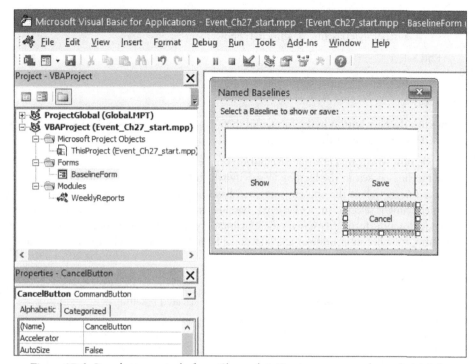

Figure 27-6. *Drag buttons onto the form. Change their Caption property to change the label that appears on the button.*

16. To add code to the Show button, right-click it in the form and then choose View Code.

    The Select Case code uses the name of the baseline you chose in the list box to specify which baseline bar style to display in the Tracking Gantt view. It closes the form after displaying the baseline. This code runs when you click the Show button on the form. If you change the StageBox item names in the BaselineForm_Initialize subroutine or add additional names, you have to change the names and cases in the following code.

17. In the View Code window, add the following code.

    Private Sub ShowButton_Click()

      'Changes the display to show the selected baseline in baseline bar styles

      Select Case StageBox.Value

      Case "Approval"

        GanttBarStyleBaseline Baseline:=1, Show:=True

```
    Case "Planning"
        GanttBarStyleBaseline Baseline:=2, Show:=True
    Case "Procurement"
        GanttBarStyleBaseline Baseline:=3, Show:=True
    Case "Implementation"
        GanttBarStyleBaseline Baseline:=4, Show:=True
    End Select
BaselineForm.Hide
End Sub
```

18. Right-click the Save button in the form, and then choose View Code. In the View code window, add the following code for the SaveButton.

This code runs when you click the Save button on the form. The Select Case code uses the name of the baseline chosen in the list box to specify which baseline to save. Current values are saved into Baseline as well as the chosen numbered baseline (Baseline1 through Baseline4 depending on which name is selected in the list box). Baseline is overwritten each time you run the macro. The code closes the form after it saves the baselines. If you change the StageBox item names in the UserForm_Initialize subroutine or add additional names, you have to change the names and cases in the following code:

```
Private Sub SaveButton_Click()
    'Copies the current values into Baseline0 and the selected baseline
    Select Case StageBox.Value
    Case "Approval"
            BaselineSave Into:=pjIntoBaseline
            BaselineSave Into:=pjIntoBaseline1
    Case "Planning"
            BaselineSave Into:=pjIntoBaseline
            BaselineSave Into:=pjIntoBaseline2
    Case "Procurement"
            BaselineSave Into:=pjIntoBaseline
            BaselineSave Into:=pjIntoBaseline3
    Case "Implementation"
            BaselineSave Into:=pjIntoBaseline
            BaselineSave Into:=pjIntoBaseline4
    End Select
```

BaselineForm.Hide

End Sub

19. Right-click the Cancel button in the form, and then choose View Code. In the View code window, add the following code for the CancelButton. This code closes the form if you don't want to click the form's Save or Show button.

Private Sub CancelButton_Click()

    BaselineForm.Hide

End Sub

20. You have to run a macro to display the form. To add a macro to the project, in the Project - VBAProject panel, right-click VBAProject [project file name], and then choose Insert→Module on the shortcut menu.

Beneath the VBAProject entry, a Modules folder appears with Module1 in it.

21. Rename Module1 to **SaveBaseline**. To open the code window for the module, double-click it in the Project – VBAProject panel. Add the following code to run the form:

Sub SaveBaseline()

    BaselineForm.Show

End Sub

22. To test the macro and the form, select SaveBaseline in the Project – VBAProject panel. On the menu bar, choose Run→RunSub/UserForm. In the Macros dialog box, select the SaveBaseline macro, and then click Run.

23. When the macro runs correctly, choose File→"Close and Return to Microsoft Project."

To add the macro to a custom group on the ribbon, see the section "Running a Macro from the Ribbon."

Learning More About Programming Project

Because this chapter barely scratches the surface of macros, you may want to learn how to do more with VBA and Project. As you'll learn in the Getting Help Appendix, Project Help doesn't provide much of that information. Instead, try the following resources and websites to get you going.

- **VBA Help**: In the Microsoft Visual Basic window, click Help→"Microsoft Visual Basic for Applications Help." On the left side of the Project MSDN page, click the "Project VBA reference" entry.

- **Microsoft Developer Network (MSDN)**: To reach the Project Developer Center directly, go to https://msdn.microsoft.com/en-us/library/office/fp161358.aspx.

28

Collaborating on Projects with SharePoint

According to the Project Management Institute (PMI), projects require 90% communication. With that guideline, it's clear you need a process for letting team members know the tasks they're assigned to, providing status to sponsors or executives, and more. In addition to the schedule, people need to discuss issues, track risks, communicate with one another, and share files like Word documents and Excel spreadsheets. Without a good communication plan and tools, information might fall through the cracks.

You already know how inefficient and overwhelming email has become. But what if you haven't graduated to needing enterprise-level project-management tools? You may want more tightly-knit team collaboration —a way to share project information with the entire team, to engage team members in solving problems, and to keep everyone in the loop about what's going on with the project.

If you're reading this book, chances are you use Project to plan and manage your project schedules. In that case, you may want an easier way to share task info with team members who ***don't*** use Project. You might begin by setting up a SharePoint ***team site***—a website you and your team members can use to share documents and other project information, track issues, and post status reports. You can also share info about project work by creating SharePoint ***Tasks Lists***. That way, team members can see what's on their to-do lists, send progress updates as they complete work, and make changes to tasks. And you can easily check the status of tasks and, if necessary, modify them.

You can create tasks in either a Project file or a SharePoint Tasks List. Then, you can synchronize the tasks between the two programs. This synchronization gives you the best of both worlds: you can use Project's scheduling features while still easily sharing tasks with your team. The updates that team members submit through SharePoint synchronize with your Project file, as well.

> **Note:** If your organization requires enterprise-level project management (coordinating an entire portfolio of projects and sharing enterprise resources, for example), this simple synchronization feature won't cut it. You need a solution that includes Project Server or Project Online and SharePoint for those types of project-management activities. In fact, when Project Professional is connected to Project Server/Project Online, the "Sync with SharePoint" option is disabled on the Backstage view's Save As and Share pages.

This chapter explains what you can do with SharePoint and Project, if you don't use Project Server/Project Online. You'll learn how to share Project files to a SharePoint site. You'll see how to create a Tasks List on a SharePoint site, publish tasks in Project to a SharePoint Tasks List, or convert a SharePoint Tasks List into a schedule in a Project file. This chapter then shows you how to synchronize tasks between Project and SharePoint. Finally, you'll learn how to handle task updates that team members submit.

> **Note:** The steps in this chapter are based on a SharePoint site created with default settings. However, SharePoint offers numerous options for customizing SharePoint sites, so your site might differ significantly from what you see here. If you can't find a command or element described in this chapter's steps, ask your SharePoint administrator for help.

SharePoint Editions

SharePoint comes in three editions: Foundation, Standard, and Enterprise. Foundation, which you can download at no charge, comes with Windows Server. It does not include some of the more advanced features that Standard and Enterprise have, but you can use it to complete the steps in this chapter. Standard edition works if you don't need Excel Services, PowerPivot, Power Query, Power View, or Visio features. If you subscribe to the Project Web Application, either on premise or in the cloud, the Enterprise edition is available. You can find out more at:

- **SharePoint online**: https://technet.microsoft.com/en-US/library/jj819267.aspx#bkmk_FeaturesOnPremise

- **Project Server/Project Online**: https://technet.microsoft.com/en-us/library/project-online-ser-
  vice-
  description.aspx

Understanding SharePoint Site Components

A SharePoint site is a group of related web parts where your team can work on projects, store data and documents, and share information. Your team might have its own site where it stores schedules, files, and procedural information. All SharePoint sites have common elements:

- **List** is a website component that helps you create a set of fields (columns) to capture information, such as a discussion board, calendars, and surveys.

- **Library** is a special type of list that stores files as well as information about files. You can view, track, manage, and create documents in a library.

- **Views** enable you to see items in a list or library, whether all items in a list or filtered to a set of items specific to a user. You can have multiple views for lists or libraries.

- **Web Part** is a unit of content that forms a basic building block for most pages on a site. If you have permissions to edit pages on your site, you can use web parts to customize your site display.

Working with Files on a SharePoint Site

A SharePoint site is a great way to keep all your project information in one centralized location. This section describes methods for sharing files on a SharePoint site.

Saving a Project File to a SharePoint Library from within Project

Say you just added the finishing touches to a Project schedule and you're ready to share the file with your team members. If the file is open in Project, you can save it directly to a SharePoint library. But before you can do that, you need to add your SharePoint site as a Save As location in Project. When you're signed into the Project application, click Account in the backstage to review your connected services (such as SharePoint sites).

> **Note:** If you know the path to a library on a SharePoint site, which is not part of Office 365 but is in your on premise or cloud environment, you can access it without adding it to the Save As list. Simply click Browse, and then type the site location using the format http://<site>/<subsite>/<library>/<filename.mpp>. If you use this approach, the site won't appear in the Save As list.

To add a Project file to the site, do the following:

1. Make sure that the file you want to upload to SharePoint is the active file in Project.

   A quick way to see which file is active is to look at the filename in the Project window's title bar.

2. Choose File→Save As, and then click the SharePoint site's name in the Save As list.

   The site's folders that you've opened recently appear on the Save As page's right, as shown in Figure 28-1.

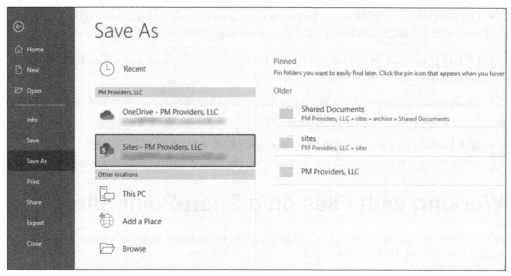

Figure 28-1. *If the site folder you want appears in the Save As page's list of recent folders, click it to open the Save As dialog box to that folder.*

3. To open a recent folder, click its name. If the SharePoint site folder you want isn't visible on the right side of the Save As page, click Browse instead and navigate to the folder.

   Either way, the Save As dialog box opens to your SharePoint site.

   > **Note:** Depending on the speed of your Internet connection, you might see a message box telling you that Project is contacting the server for information. You can remove folders from the Save As list by right-clicking the folder, and then choosing "Remove from list" from the shortcut menu.

4. In the Save As dialog box, select the library in which you want to save the file, and then click Open.

   The Save As dialog box displays the contents of the library, which is basically a collection of files in a digital repository.

5. In the Save As dialog box, click Save. (If you want to save the file with a different name, edit the name in the "File name" box first, and *then* click Save.)

   Project saves the file to your SharePoint site.

Adding Files to a SharePoint Site in SharePoint

Storing files on a SharePoint site makes it easy to share your files with others. As long as users have access to the SharePoint site and use the Project desktop client, they can download the files stored in the site libraries. A SharePoint site comes in handy in other ways. Imagine you travel to another office and your laptop dies en route. You can borrow a computer, go online, download the files you need from the SharePoint site, and continue working with a minimum of interruption.

You can upload any kind of file to a SharePoint site: Project files, Word documents, Excel spreadsheets, images, and so on. Here's how:

- **Upload a document:** You can add a document to a SharePoint team site right on its Home page. (You can also work with documents on the site's Documents page. To get there, on the Home page's left, click Documents.) Above the list where documents display, click Upload. In the "Choose File to Upload" dialog box, select the file you want to upload, and then click Open. Then click OK. (You can also drag and drop the file you want to upload onto the documents library list of documents to add it to the site.) Once the file is uploaded, it appears in the Documents list with the date and time it was last modified and who modified it.

- **Download a document:** To download a file to your computer, in the Documents list, click the three vertical dots to the right of the filename, and then choose Download from the shortcut menu. In the Opening dialog box that appears, select the Save File option, and then click OK.

> **Tip:** Opening a file created with an Office application (like Project, Word, and Excel) is as simple as clicking its filename in the Documents list, which opens the file in the corresponding Office Web App. For example, when you open a Word document, Microsoft Word Web App launches. On the Edit Document tab, choose "Edit in Word" if you want to take advantage of all the editing features Microsoft Word has to offer. For a few simple edits, choose "Edit in Word Web App" to edit the document in your browser instead.

Setting Up Tasks on a SharePoint Site

In SharePoint, a Tasks List is like a simple project plan with task names, dates, and so on. If you're putting together a to-do list and don't need all of Project's features, a SharePoint Tasks List might be just the thing. You can assign team members who are part of the SharePoint site to tasks. You can organize tasks into an outline with summary tasks and subtasks, view start and finish dates, and show progress. You can also use a SharePoint Tasks List to brainstorm with your team. This section shows you how to create a Tasks List within SharePoint.

Revving Up Your SharePoint Site

Keeping project information organized and up to date is even easier when you use Share-Point in conjunction with other programs like Outlook, OneDrive for Business, or Teams (Teams is a Microsoft product for communicating via instant message, video conference, online meeting, and other methods). On the main home page of the SharePoint site, click an item within the documents library web part to display the SharePoint ribbon. The SharePoint ribbon then appears at the top of the screen. Here are a few of the integrated features you might want to explore on the Library tab:

- If you use Outlook, you can connect a library with Outlook by using the "Connect to Outlook" button on the library ribbon.

- If you use OneDrive for Business, you can sync a library with the OneDrive folder by clicking the Sync button on the Library ribbon.

- From the Sharepoint library menu, you can add Alerts to receive emails on items that are added or changed.

- If you use Teams to communicate with team members, you can message or call them from within Project to follow up on status. To do that, put your pointer over the person's name in the Resource Name field and a Teams status box appears, showing the person's status, such as Away. Click the appropriate icon to send an instant message, call, initiate a video chat, or send an email.

Note: Once you add tasks to a Tasks List in SharePoint, you can also pull them into Project to build a schedule if you find out later that you need more features. In addition, you can publish a list of tasks that you built in Project to a SharePoint Tasks List for others to view and interact with.

Creating a Tasks List

To work with tasks on a SharePoint site, you need a Tasks List to hold them. In SharePoint, you add the Tasks app to create a new Tasks List. (Similar to apps on mobile phones, SharePoint apps are mini-applications that expand what you can do with SharePoint.) Here's how:

1. On the left side of the SharePoint site's Home page, click Site Contents, and then, on the Site Contents page, click New (beneath the SharePoint Home heading) and choose App on the dropdown menu.

    The Site Contents page displays several popular apps. You can also reach this page by clicking the gear icon on the SharePoint overall ribbon next to the login name, and then choosing "Add an app" from the drop-down list.

2. Click the Tasks app button.

    The Adding Tasks dialog box appears, as shown in Figure 28-2.

---

3. In the Name box, type a name for the Tasks List, such as ***WebsiteTasks***, and then click Create.

   When you click Create, the Site Contents page adds an entry with the name you specified. "Tasks list" appears in the Type column for that entry.

4. To create another Tasks List, repeat steps 1 through 3.

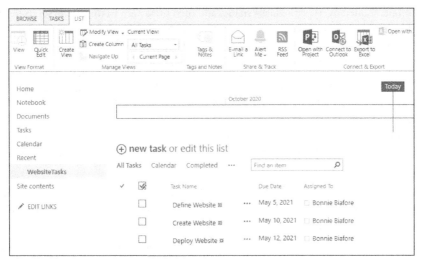

Figure 28-3. *The name you enter will appear in the Site Contents list when the Tasks List is created.*

> **Tip:** In the Name box, don't add spaces to names. Reporting and workflows work better when names don't include spaces in the URL. However, you can add spaces to the title of a Tasks List. To do that, click the Tasks List to open it. Then, on the List tab, choose List Settings. Beneath the General Settings heading, click "List name, description and navigation." Then, in the Name box, type the name including the spaces and click Save. That way, the site title includes spaces for readability, while the Tasks List URL will be space-free.

Adding Tasks to a Tasks List

Once you've created a Tasks List, it's time to add tasks to it. SharePoint Task Lists can be simple to-do lists or more sophisticated lists that include summary tasks and subtasks. In addition, you can link tasks to one another to define predecessors and successors for a schedule.

Here are the steps for adding tasks to a Tasks List:

1. On the left side of the site, click Site Contents, and then click the Tasks List you want to work on (WebsiteTasks, in this example).

   The Tasks List's page opens with the Tasks List's name at the top and a timeline and Grid view for editing tasks below it.

2. On the Tasks List page, click "new task."

    A task form (Figure 28-3) appears with several commonly-used fields, such as Task Name, Start Date, Due Date, and Assigned To (the fields you see may differ from these depending on how SharePoint is set up in your organization). You can display additional fields by clicking Show More below the Assigned To label. The Task Name box's border is highlighted to indicate that it's active.

3. In the Task Name box, type the task's name, and then press Tab. In this example, in the Task Name box, type *Define Website*.

    The asterisk (*) next to the field title indicates that the field is required.

4. Press Tab to jump to the Start Date box. To the right of the box, click the Calendar icon, and then choose the start date for the task (in this example, *5/1/2021*). Alternatively, type the date in the box. Then, press Tab.

    The Due Date box becomes active.

5. Enter the date that the task is due in the Due Date box (in this example, *5/5/2021*), and then press Tab.

    The Assigned To box becomes active.

6. To assign someone to the task, start typing the person's name or email address in the Assigned To box, and then click the name you want in the drop-down list.

    As you type, the Assigned To drop-down list shows matching names from the people who belong to the site.

Figure 28-3. *The Task Name field is the only field you have to fill in. To display additional fields, click Show More below the Assigned To label.*

7. Click Save.

    The task appears in the Tasks List.

8. To add another task, repeat steps 2 through 7.

    In this example, add two more tasks:

    Create Website with Start Date 5/8/2021 and Due Date 5/10/2021

    Deploy Website with Start Date 5/11/2021 and Due Date 5/12/2021

    The three tasks are shown in Figure 28-4.

Note: If you want to link a task to other tasks in the list, in the task form below the % Complete field, click Show More. In the Predecessors list box that appears, choose the predecessors to the task, and then click Add. The predecessor task appears in the list box on the right. To remove a predecessor, click the task in that list box, and then click Remove.

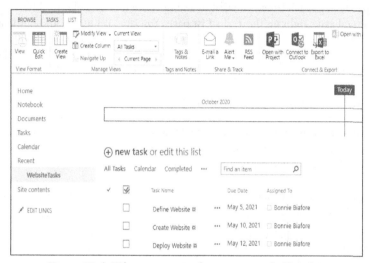

Figure 28-4. *When you save a task, it appears in the Tasks List.*

Tip: Say you want to rearrange tasks to put them in a different order. First, select the task you want to move: to do that, put your cursor to the left of the task's checkbox, and then click the checkmark that appears. Then, in the ribbon, click the Tasks tab. In the Hierarchy section, click Move Up or Move Down until the task is in the position you want.

Adding a Task to SharePoint's Timeline View

The SharePoint Tasks app offers many features that are available in Project, like the Timeline view. You can add key tasks to the Timeline View as bars or callouts. Here's how:

1. With the Tasks List page open, in the ribbon, click the Tasks tab.

    It contains commands that help you create new tasks, indent and outdent tasks into an outline, attach files to tasks, and so on.

2. Put your cursor to the left of the task's checkbox. When the checkmark appears, click it to select the task.

    SharePoint shades the background of the selected task's row. A checkmark appears to the left of the task's row, and the checkmark's background is shaded a darker hue.

3. In the Tasks tab's Actions section, click "Add to Timeline."

The task's name and date range appear in the timeline. (Tasks don't appear in the timeline unless at least one date field has a value.) If you want to change the task's appearance in the timeline, click the timeline to display the Timeline tab. Then, choose commands to format the task.

Adding, Editing, and Organizing Multiple Tasks

Opening a separate page each time you want to add or edit a task gets old quickly. With SharePoint, you can edit several tasks right on the Tasks List page. You can also indent and outdent tasks to create a hierarchy like the ones you've probably built in Project; or you can move tasks to reorder them. SharePoint also lets you change the way tasks are displayed. For example, you can display tasks in the Gantt Chart view to look at the schedule. This section explains all those techniques.

Editing Multiple Tasks

Initially, the fields in the list of tasks are editable. However if you leave the page, then to edit a task, you have to click its name to open the page with its info, and then, in the ribbon's View tab, click Edit Item. That's a lot of clicks to make a simple edit or two.

If you need to edit several task fields, Quick Edit view makes editing much more efficient. Here's how you edit tasks in Quick Edit view:

1. On the Tasks List page, click to the left of a task's checkbox to select the task, in this example, Deploy Website.

   In the ribbon, click the List tab, and then click Quick Edit (Figure 28-5).

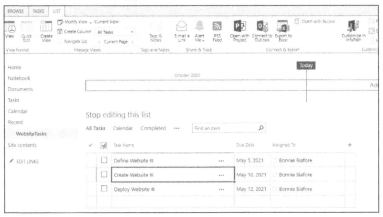

Figure 28-5. *Clicking Quick Edit on the List tab switches the Tasks List to Quick Edit view. Task values are displayed in a table, so you can click the cell you want to edit and change its value.*

2. Click a cell, and then edit its value.

   SharePoint outlines the selected cell with a bold border and displays a pencil image to the left of the task name.

3. Repeat step 2 to edit other cells in the table.

If you click a cell in a different row, SharePoint saves the edits you made in the row you clicked away from.

4. When you're finished editing, click Stop above the column headings or View on the List tab.

    The table disappears and the tasks revert to a read-only list.

Organizing a Tasks List into Summary Tasks and Subtasks

For most projects, a work breakdown structure helps keep tasks organized. By grouping subtasks below a summary tasks, it's easier to understand how the work is rolled up and how much of that work is complete. You can organize tasks in this same way in SharePoint. Although the steps are slightly different than the ones in Project, the resulting hierarchy is similar.

To organize your Tasks List, first open it (click Site Contents and then click the appropriate Tasks List). Here's how to create a new subtask under another task:

1. On the Tasks List page, click left of the task's checkbox to select it, in this example, Create Website.

    In the ribbon, on the List tab, click Quick Edit.

2. In the Quick Edit table, click the ellipsis (...) to the right of the task's name (Create Website), and then click Create Subtask. In this example, type *Finalize Image Placement* in the Task Name cell and set the Due Date to *5/11/2021*. Press Tab or click another row to save the task.

    SharePoint changes the task you selected into a summary task and inserts a blank row beneath it.

3. To create a second subtask (Figure 28-6), click to the left of the Create Website task's checkbox, click the ellipsis (...), and choose Create Subtask. In this example, the name is *Complete Final Testing* and the Due Date is *5/11/2021*.

4. To move the Complete Final Testing task so it comes after Finalize Image Placement, select that task if necessary. Then in the Task tab, click Move Down.

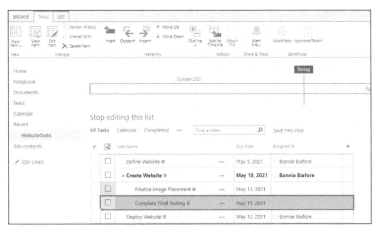

Figure 28-6. *The summary task's name is bolded and a black triangle appears to its left, just as it does for a Project summary task. Click this triangle to hide the summary task's subtasks.*

5.   When you're finished editing, click Stop above the column headings (or View in the List tab).

The table disappears and the tasks revert to a read-only list.

Here are other ways to work with summary tasks and subtasks in a SharePoint Tasks List:

- **Change a task into a subtask:** In your Tasks List, put the cursor to the left of the subtask's checkbox, and then click the checkmark that appears. In the Tasks tab's Hierarchy group, click Indent. SharePoint indents the selected task, and turns the task above into a summary task. You can expand and collapse summary tasks to show or hide their subtasks. Just like you do in Project, click the black triangle to the left of a summary task's name to hide its subtasks; click the white triangle to the left of a collapsed summary task to show its subtasks.

- **Outdent a task:** In your Tasks List, put the cursor to the left of the subtask's checkbox, and then click the checkmark that appears. Then, in the Tasks tab's Hierarchy group, click Outdent. SharePoint moves the selected task up one level in the hierarchy. If the task above was a summary task, it changes back to a regular task.

Working with SharePoint Task Views

SharePoint task views let you control how your tasks appear. For example, you can display tasks in the Gantt Chart view or choose Upcoming to filter the Tasks List to show the tasks that are on deck. Here are some of the things you can do with views in SharePoint:

- **Apply a different view to your Tasks List**: Within the Tasks List, click the ellipsis to the left of the "Find an item" box, and then choose the view you want. If you choose Gantt Chart, you'll see a Gantt Chart view like the one in Project. (It has a table with columns on the left and a timescale on the right. The table in the Gantt Chart view works much like the one in Project, so you can edit values directly in cells.)

- **Modify a view:** To modify the current view, click the ellipsis, and then, choose "Modify this View." The Settings→Edit View page that appears includes view settings like the ones in Project: the columns to include and their order, sorting, filtering, grouping, and so on. The main difference is that you choose the settings in a web page instead of a dialog box.

- **Create a new view:** To create a view from scratch, click the ellipsis, and then, choose "Create View." On the Settings→View Type page that appears, choose the type of view you want, such as Standard View for the read-only Tasks List, Datasheet View for an editable table, or Gantt View for a Gantt Chart presentation.

Exchanging Task Info Between Project and SharePoint

Project and SharePoint Tasks Lists play well together up to a point. You can publish tasks in a Project file to a SharePoint Tasks List or take tasks in a SharePoint Tasks List and add them to a Project file.

Once you set up the initial connection between a Project file and a SharePoint Tasks List, you can synchronize the info they contain so it appears in both places. That way, the entire team can see what's going on with the project at all times. This section explains how to do that.

Tasks Lists Have Their Limits

SharePoint doesn't have the scheduling engine that Project does. So before you synchronize your Project with SharePoint, see whether SharePoint's features satisfy your needs:

- **Task start and finish dates are set with date constraints**: SharePoint can't calculate project schedules, so tasks you synchronize appear in SharePoint Tasks Lists as manually scheduled. In Project, the tasks are still set to Auto Scheduled mode, but the task dates include partially inflexible date constraints like Finish No Later Than. That means you have to manage links between tasks as dates change, and resolve any resource overallocations that occur.

- **Resources assigned to tasks must be members of the SharePoint site**: The only resources you can see in a SharePoint Tasks List are people who are members of the SharePoint system. If you assign *other* resources to tasks, the Assigned To values for those tasks are blank. However, the resource assignments still exist in your Project file.

- **Custom fields that use formulas don't synchronize**: On the bright side, custom fields *without* formulas do synchronize to SharePoint. If you need a custom formula, you can build it in SharePoint.

Creating a SharePoint Tasks List from a Project File

If you build a project schedule in Project, chances are you want to share that schedule with your team, so they can see what they're supposed to do and what's happening in the project. Publishing your schedule to a SharePoint Tasks List makes your project tasks easily accessible on a SharePoint site (as long as the limitations described in the note above).

Note: If you've downloaded files from the book website, you can follow along using the file Ch28_simpleproject.mpp.

Here's how you publish tasks in a Project file to a SharePoint Tasks List:

1. Open the Project file you want to publish to SharePoint (Ch28_simpleproject.mpp), and then choose File→Save As→"Sync with SharePoint."

   The "Sync with SharePoint Tasks List" fields appear on the right side of the Backstage view's Save As page. If you want to add fields to the sync list, see the section "Managing the fields in SharePoint Task list."

2. To create a *new* SharePoint site for the project, in the "Sync with" box, keep New SharePoint Site selected. In the "Project name" box (Figure 28-7), type the project name you want to use for the site. In the "Site address" box, type the URL for the SharePoint site to which you want to add the project site and task list.

   If you've already set up the SharePoint site, skip to step 4.

3. Click Save, and then skip to step 6.

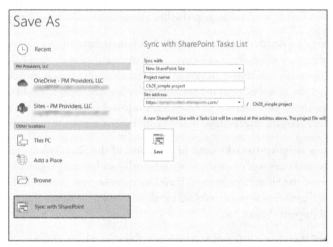

Fig 28-7. *Project creates a site with a Tasks List and populates the list with the project tasks.*

Note: If a SharePoint site's Tasks List already has entries, the SharePoint sync warns you that it will overwrite those entries. Project saves the .mpp file and creates a OneNote file with the same name in the Site Assets library within SharePoint during the Sync.

---

4. To sync with an *existing* SharePoint site, in the "Sync with" box, click the down arrow, and then choose Existing SharePoint Site (see Figure 28-8).

   If you choose this setting, you don't have to enter a project name, because the SharePoint site already has a name.

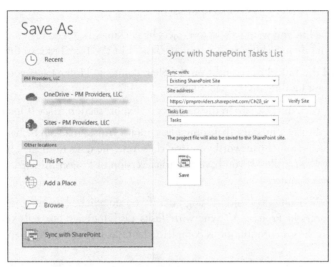

Figure 28-8. *When you fill in a SharePoint site address and click Verify Site, Project connects to the site, and then populates the Tasks List drop-down list with the existing Tasks Lists.*

5. In the "Site address" box, type the existing site's SharePoint URL. Alternatively, click the down arrow, and then, in the drop-down list, choose the SharePoint site you want.

    Don't include the name of the Tasks List in the URL.

6. Click Verify URL.

    Project connects to the site and retrieves the names of its Tasks Lists.

7. In the Tasks List drop-down list, choose the Tasks List you want to sync the Project file to.

    The Tasks List drop-down list contains existing Tasks Lists from the site you verified.

8. Click Save.

    A "Sync with Tasks List" message box keeps you posted on the synchronization process. If any of the resources you've assigned to tasks don't exist within SharePoint, a warning tells you that those resources won't be published. Click OK to continue. Although you won't see the resource names in the SharePoint Tasks List, the assignments remain in your Project file.

Your Project tasks are now published to the SharePoint site. You can see them by navigating to the SharePoint site in your browser.

Saving a SharePoint Tasks List to Project

Creating a list of tasks on a SharePoint site is an easy way to start a project schedule. For simple projects, creating and managing tasks on the SharePoint site may be enough. But if your simple project morphs into something bigger, you can save your SharePoint Tasks List to Project, and then use Project's more comprehensive tools to keep the schedule under control.

Here are the steps for saving a Tasks List to Project:

1. Open the Tasks List you want to save to Project by clicking Site Contents on the SharePoint site Home page, and then clicking the appropriate Tasks List (WebsiteTasks, in this example).

    If you opened the Tasks List recently, on the SharePoint site Home page, you can click its name below the Recent heading on the page's left.

2. In the ribbon, click the List tab. In the Connect & Export section, click "Open with Project."

    Project might display a message that some files contain viruses that can be harmful to your computer. If the file is from a trustworthy source, click Yes. The tasks from the SharePoint Tasks List open in a new Project file. (If you have an earlier version of Project installed, a message box tells you that you need Project.)

    You may see a Welcome to Project dialog box. If you do, click Skip Intro. Then the SharePoint Tasks List appears in Project. A "Sync with Tasks List" message box tells you the progress it's making. When the synchronization is complete, the tasks from SharePoint appear in the current Project view.

From now on, you can synchronize any changes you make in Project or SharePoint, as described in the next section.

Synchronizing Changes

When you connect a Project file and a SharePoint Tasks List, the process includes an initial synchronization that sends the info from one program to another. For example, if you publish a Project file to a SharePoint Tasks List, the synchronization pushes the tasks in Project into the SharePoint Tasks List. As you know all too well, a project is dynamic, so you'll want to synchronize future changes, whether they occur in Project or SharePoint. Fortunately, synchronizing is easy: once your Project file is connected to a SharePoint Tasks List, you can sync the two simply by saving the Project file within Project (choose File→Save). Or you can choose File→Info, and then click Save.

> **Note:** If you and someone on your team both modify the same field—one in Project and the other in SharePoint—when you synchronize, Project will display a Conflict dialog box, which includes a Microsoft Project Fields column and a SharePoint Fields column. The fields whose values differ between the two are highlighted. For each conflict, you can specify whether to keep the value from Project or SharePoint. To keep a value from Project, in the Version column for a conflict, click the down arrow and then choose Microsoft Project Version. To use the value from SharePoint, click the down arrow, and then choose SharePoint Version instead. After you've specified which version to keep for all the conflicts, click the Continue Sync button.

Managing the Fields in a SharePoint Tasks List

Once a connection exists between a Project file and a SharePoint Tasks List, you can specify the fields that appear in the Tasks List. For example, you can add the WBS field, Actual Start, or a custom field to the SharePoint view. Here's how to sync additional fields to a SharePoint Tasks List or edit the settings for existing fields:

1. In Project, choose File→Info.

    Once a Project file is linked to a SharePoint Tasks List, the Info page includes a Save button with the label "Save and Sync Your Project." In addition, you can see when the file and the Tasks List were last synchronized, as well as the site address and the Tasks List that the Project file is synced to.

2. Below the "Save and Sync Your Project" information, click Map Fields.

    The Map Fields dialog box opens, showing the fields in the Project table and in SharePoint. A checkmark in the Sync column indicates that the corresponding field synchronizes between the two programs. In the dialog box, some fields are grayed out to indicate that you can't change whether they synchronize. For example, the Name, Start, Finish, % Complete, Resources Names, and Predecessors fields are automatically synchronized.

3. To add a field, click Add Field. In the Add Field dialog box's Existing Project Field box, choose the Project field you want to add, such as WBS (as shown in Figure 28-9), and then click OK.

    The checkmark in the Sync column is turned on automatically. Project automatically copies the field's name to the SharePoint Column box. If you want the SharePoint column to use a different heading, then type the name in the box before you click OK.

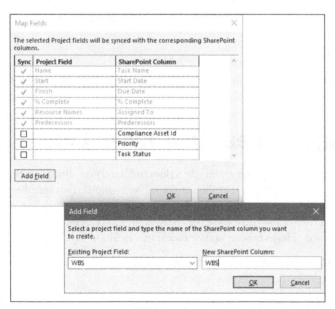

Figure 28-9. *To add fields to the map, click Add Field.*

4. To change the SharePoint column's name, in the Map Fields dialog box, type the new name. Turn the checkmark in a Sync cell off if you no longer want to synchronize the field.

5. When you're done mapping fields, click OK to close the Map Fields dialog box, and then click Save.

   You have to click Save to send the info from the new fields to SharePoint.

6. Back in the SharePoint Tasks List, click the ellipsis to the left of the "Find an item" search box, and then choose "Modify this View."

   The Settings→Edit View page appears.

7. To display a field in the view, turn on the field's checkbox. Then click OK.

   To reorder the columns in a view, in the "Position from Left" column, fill in the column number to specify the field's position in the table.

Keeping Tasks in Order

The "Sync with Tasks List" feature has an annoying idiosyncrasy: Sometimes when you synchronize tasks, they come across in seemingly random order. Links to predecessors don't help. In Project, you can easily sort the list by ID number, WBS code, or any other field to order it the way you want. Fortunately, you can do the same thing in SharePoint by adding the WBS field to a SharePoint Tasks List view. Then you can sort the Tasks List to match the order in your Project file. Here are the steps:

1. Add the WBS field to the SharePoint view, as described in the previous section.

2. In Project, synchronize your Tasks List to transfer the field values to SharePoint, as described in the Synchronizing Changes section.

3. In the SharePoint Tasks List, click the ellipsis to the left of the "Find an item" box, and then choose "Modify this View."

4. Turn on the WBS field's checkbox and click OK.

5. On the Tasks List page, put your cursor over the WBS heading, and then click the down arrow that appears. In the drop-down list, choose "A on Top."

Updating Progress in a Tasks List

You and your team members can view and edit values in SharePoint. But SharePoint doesn't offer the variety of progress update methods that Project does. For example, team members can change values in the % Complete field or change a finish date for a task. However, once you enter % Complete values or finish dates, you can synchronize the changes (in Project, choose File→Info→Save) to bring them back into Project. Here's how to update task status in SharePoint:

1. On the left side of the page, click Site Contents, and then click the Tasks List you want to work on.

   The Tasks List page opens.

2. If you want to see the tasks you're assigned to, click the ellipsis to the left of the "Find an item" box, and then choose My Tasks.

    The Tasks List displays only the tasks to which you're assigned.

3. Click the task to open it on its own page. Then, in the View tab's Manage section, click Edit Item.

    The fields on the page become editable.

4. Click Show More below the Assigned To label.

5. To flag a task as complete, in the % Complete box, type *100*. Change the Task Status to Completed, as shown in Figure 28-10.

    If you want to update other values, such as Finish Date or Work, you can add those fields to SharePoint as described earlier. Those fields then appear on the task's edit page. That way, you or your teammates can fill in the field values. When you sync the Tasks List and the Project file, those values propagate to your Project schedule.

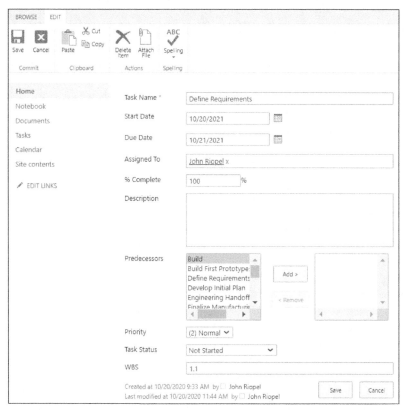

Figure 28-10. *Fill in the % Complete field with the current percentage complete. If you map additional fields from Project into SharePoint, you can fill in other status values, too.*

6.   Click Save.

The updated values appear in the Tasks List. If you synchronize the tasks with Project, the updated values appear in your Project schedule.

> **Note:** If you want to mark the task as complete quickly, on the Tasks List page, turn on the checkbox to the left of the task name. SharePoint draws a line through the task name in the list. If you click the task to review its details, % Complete is set to 100.

29

Managing Projects with Microsoft PPM Solutions

It's one thing to manage a single project with a dedicated team. You can create your project schedule, assign resources, track progress, and update the executive team mostly without worrying about what *other* projects are doing or sharing resources with those projects. However, you don't come across an environment like that very often. Usually, organizations undertake numerous projects, most of which compete for the same overworked pool of resources.

Portfolio project management (PPM) represents a software toolkit for managing and collaborating on an organization's portfolio of projects, which today could mean Agile or waterfall processes. Microsoft's PPM solution provides a framework for project management processes to help project managers adhere to the organization's project management standards and best practices. It also offers collaboration tools so everyone in the organization—project managers, team members, executives, and so on—can work together on numerous projects.

This chapter begins by describing some of the benefits organizations can achieve by using PPM tools. Next, you'll learn how Microsoft Project and Project Server (or Project Online) work together to help you manage projects in an enterprise environment.

This chapter also describes Planner and "Project for the web," which are additional tools in the PPM toolset. You'll also learn how to use Project Web Application (PWA) to manage projects in conjunction with the Project desktop client. The Project Web Application section describes how the Project Center provides an overview of enterprise projects and helps you work with them. You'll see how to define different types of enterprise projects, create, publish, and check in projects. This chapter also explains how to work with the Project cache.

You'll also learn about managing resources in an enterprise environment. You can add resources to the enterprise resource pool, build the project team from those enterprise resources, and finally, get status from team members using Tasks and Timesheets features.

This chapter wraps up with information on using project sites to collaborate on individual projects and how to use the Business Intelligence Center or Power BI to present project portfolio data effectively.

> **Note:** This chapter provides an overview of the Microsoft PPM solution. For more detail, check out the two courses on Project Server administration and Project Web Application in the LinkedIn Learning library (listed in the Credits at the beginning of this book).

Why Use Enterprise Project Management?

This section describes some of the benefits your organization can achieve by using Project Professional in conjunction with Project Server or Project Online:

- Project managers can create, update, and maintain project schedules in Project Professional or PWA. Project schedule information is stored in a project server so it's available throughout the organization.

- Team leads and team members can see all related task assignments regardless of project.

- Providing status updates and timesheets can be automated using Tasks or Timesheets. Team members submit status updates and timesheets. As project manager, you can approve or reject updates. Approved updates and time are automatically incorporated into the project schedule.

- Project managers can request status reports from team members and assemble them into a higher-level status report.

- Resources can be shared and managed across all projects through the enterprise resource pool. Project managers and team leads can review assignments and check resource availability.

- You can see the status of all projects simultaneously and drill down into individual projects for more detail.

- Project workspaces support document, risk, and issue management. You can upload files related to issues and risks to keep them in one place and easily accessible.

- Executives and project portfolio managers can review and modify the project portfolio. In addition, they can notify project managers whether projects are approved or denied.

- Business intelligence functionality can help generate standardized or ad-hoc reports.

Overview of the Microsoft PPM Solutions

Microsoft's PPM solutions are comprised of numerous components: Project for the web, Project Server or Project Online, Project Professional or Project Online Desktop Client, Power BI, and SharePoint. This section describes how the components work together.

> **Note:** Project Server is on-premise software that provides PPM functionality. Project Online is a Microsoft-hosted version with functionality similar to Project Server.
>
> When working in a Project Online environment, product compatibility is important. For example, you can't use Project Professional 2013 with Project Online. For a table that shows component compatibility requirements, head to www.coldpresspublishing.com/microsoft-project-compatibility.

Microsoft offers several tools for collaborating on projects, each providing different methods for managing project information. These tools include Planner, "Project for the web," Project desktop and Project Online. Project for the web is Microsoft's newest product for managing cloud-based project work. The following table shows how each tool supports project management work and the features it offers.

Feature	Planner	Project for the web	Project (Desktop)	Project Server/ Online
Task Management	X	X	X	X
Resource Assignments	X	X	X	X
Board view	X	X	X	X
Grid view		X	X	X
Gantt Chart view		X	X	X
Scheduling and Dependencies		X	X	X
Roadmaps		X	X	X
Baselines, Critical Path, Overallocations			X	X
Resource Management			X	X
Cost Management			X	X
Portfolio Management				X
Program Management				X

Planner

Planner is great for a small team that needs to collaborate on ad hoc tasks. It helps teams and guests work together without having to download and install software. With Planner, you can create task boards and organize tasks into buckets. You can categorize tasks based on their status or who is assigned to them. You can update status, buckets, and assignments by dragging and dropping tasks.

Project for the web

Project for the web is a step up from Planner and provides a predefined set of fields and views for users who need more capability than a simple ad hoc task list. You can add dependencies between tasks, assign work to users, and connect these projects into a Roadmap. "Project for the web" is a new product for cloud-based work and project management. It includes both task board and timeline views that project managers and team members can use to plan and manage work. This tool is built on the Microsoft Power Platform, which consists of PowerApps, Microsoft Flow, Power BI, and the Common Data Service (CDS).

Project Web Application

Project Server and Project Online use the Project Web Application (PWA) as a PPM system built on SharePoint with a SQL cloud server. PWA provides tools for managing projects, project portfolios, resources, documents, and other project and portfolio information. PWA also integrates with other Microsoft applications such as Business Intelligence, SQL Reporting Services, CRM, Power BI, and other SharePoint functions.

PWA supports project and portfolio management activities for project managers, portfolio managers, project team members, resource managers, and executives. It supports common methods and standardized processes and also serves as a distributed environment for collecting and sharing project information. PWA helps manage all the data needed to manage projects, programs, and portfolios.

Project Professional and Project Online Desktop Client

Project Professional is a desktop application that allows for detailed task and resource allocation planning. Project Online Desktop Client is the desktop client that comes with Project Online subscriptions. These serve as the desktop client that connects to Microsoft PWA. You can use either one to configure enterprise calendars, bulk-edit resources, and manage resource engagements. Of course, you can also use them for estimating; assigning resources; working with work, material, and cost resources; managing the critical path; and analyzing earned value as described throughout this book.

> **This** chapter uses "Project desktop" to represent both Microsoft Project Professional and Project Online Desktop Client.

Project Server/Project Online Security

There are two security modes available within Project Online and Project Server: SharePoint mode and Project mode. The SharePoint security mode is the default mode and provides a simpler security model. With the Project mode, you can set up additional detailed security, such as creating custom groups, adding users, and defining the data users can access.

PWA relies on Active Directory (AD) when on premise or Azure AD when in the cloud for managing security and user access management (Figure 29-1). In most cases, an organization's IT Department sets up AD Groups specific to PWA or SharePoint to create and manage user accounts. Users can be a member of one or more of these groups. Specific groups can be synchronized with the Enterprise Resource Pool. Project Server Groups also manage access to Project Sites. PWA enables access to capabilities based on the system configuration and the groups a user belongs to. With PWA, an organization can choose between the default SharePoint security or the enhanced PWA security model, which should be set up before users access PWA.

PWA security is flexible (and complex). The key point is that a user must have an AD Account (or Microsoft Account when using Project Online) and be a member of one of the application-specific groups to access PWA, the Project Sites, or be a member of the Enterprise Resource Pool, as shown in Figure 29-2.

With the SharePoint security model, the application is controlled by the Owners, Members, and Visitors groups. With this security model, you can manage users with the following groups: Administrators, Portfolio Managers, Portfolio Viewers, Project Managers, Resource Managers, Team Leads, and Team Members. These groups use security categories to apply permissions within the application: My Direct Reports, My Organization, My Projects, My Resources and My Tasks as defaults. Your organization can customize groups and categories to meet specific business needs.

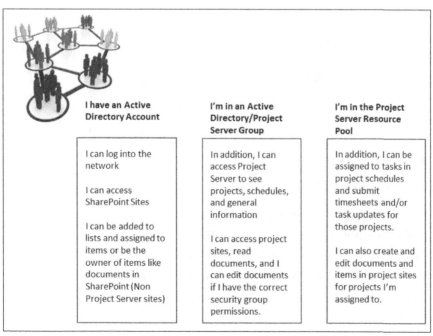

Figure 29-1. *An active directory account provides security permission to a Project Server or Project Online system*

Using Planner

Planner is a free tool for creating new plans that is available to anyone with Office 365. When you click Planner, it opens in the Planner hub (Figure 29-2) and displays recent and favorite plans. You can also connect Planner to a mobile device. If you integrate Planner into Microsoft Teams or Microsoft SharePoint, you can access Planner within those applications to make a more central access point for managing project work.

Figure 29-2. *The Planner hub*

Add a New Plan

To add a new plan, do the following:

1. Log into your Office 365 account.

2. Click the waffle icon at the top right, and then click Planner.

   If Planner isn't visible in the list, click All Apps, and then click Planner.

3. On the Planner screen, in the left navigation bar, click New plan.

4. In the Plan name area (Figure 29-3), type the Plan name. (To follow along, type "O365 rollout").

5. Select the Public option.

Public plans are visible to everyone within your organization. (Public plans are the only plans that appear in search results.) Private plans are visible only to people who have been added to the plan.

6. To tie an Office 365 group to the plan, click the Options down arrow and fill in a group description for this plan. (To follow along, type "Plan focused on 0365 rollout to production.")

    You can create a plan for an existing Office 365 group by selecting the Private option, and then adding to an existing Office 365 group.

7. Click Create plan.

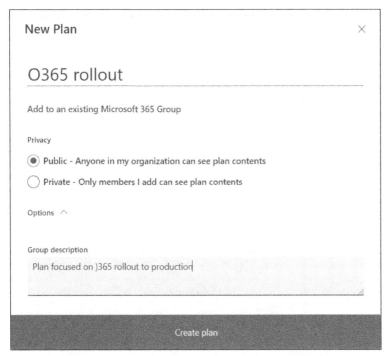

Figure 29-3. *Creating a new plan in the New Plan dialog box.*

Add a Task to the Plan

To add a task to the plan, do the following:

1. Click the Add task button.

2. Fill in the task name, choose a due date, and assign someone to the task.

    To follow along, fill in the name "Define Requirements" and set the due date to 03/03/2021. Do not assign anyone.

3. Click Add Task (Figure 29-4).

4.   Click the task name or image to edit an existing task.

The Detail dialog box opens (Figure 29-5).

You can add an attachment (file, link, or SharePoint location) to a task by clicking the task name, then clicking the Add attachment button. Turn on the "Show on card" checkbox to display the attachment icon on the task board. You can add multiple attachments to a task. With the "Show on card" option, you can link directly to a file with real-time co-authoring in Office for the web.

5.   When editing is complete, close the dialog box to save your edits or use the ellipsis to do additional tasks edits.

> **Note:** In Planner, you can include or omit details that appear with tasks and define how they appear on the task board.

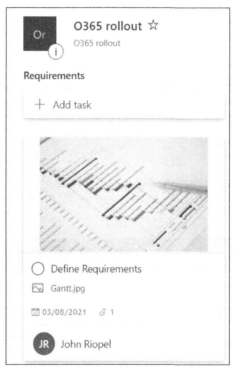

Figure 29-4. *Add a task to a plan.*

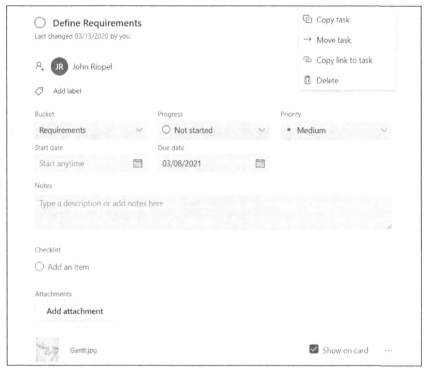

Figure 29-5. *Add detail in the Planner task detail dialog box.*

Categorize Tasks

You can categorize tasks into different buckets, each with its own color:

1. Click a task on the task board to display its details in a dialog box.

2. To categorize the task, hover over the color tabs at the dialog box's top right.

   The tabs expand and display labels.

3. Click the color you want to assign to the task.

4. Close the task dialog box.

5. To categorize tasks by their color, at the screen's top right, click Group by bucket, and then click Labels.

> **Note:** To create a bucket, on the task board, click Add new bucket, and then fill in the name, for example, "Requirements." Click Add new bucket again to create a second bucket, such as "Deployment." Click Add new bucket again, and type "Acceptance."

View Tasks

To review all your tasks across all plans, do the following:

1.   In Planner's left navigation bar, click My tasks.

2.   To group tasks (Figure 29-6), click Group by at the top right, and then choose Plan, Due Date, Priority, or Progress.

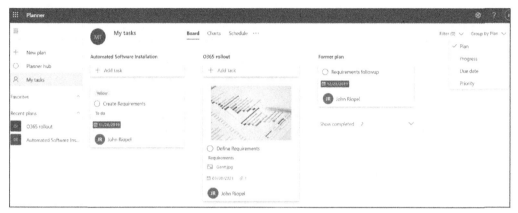

Figure 29-6. *My tasks grouped by Plan*

3.   To review tasks in different ways, at the top of the screen, click Board, Charts, or Schedule.

4.   To add "My Tasks" to your Outlook calendar, click the ellipsis to the right of Schedule.

Using Project for the web

Project for the web is available as an Office 365 app with a P3 or P5 license. (It uses modern sites and permissions associated with Microsoft groups.) It may look similar to Planner, but it offers more advanced features, such as dependencies and customizing the common data source with additional fields. Roadmaps are also available in the Project Home (Figure 29-7). (A Roadmaps description is available by downloading sample files from www.coldpresspublishing.com.)

> **Note:** Project for the web is a Power Automate app that allows creation of a project in the Common Source Dynamics 365 environment. By using this application, you can automate how projects can be created or integrate this application with other lines of business apps.

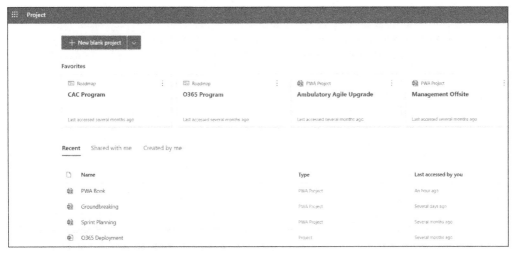

Figure 29-7. *The "Project for the web" screen.*

Create a New Blank Project

To add a new blank project, do the following:

1. In Office 365, click the waffle at the top left, and then click Project. (If necessary, click All Apps, and then click Project.

2. Click the New blank project button.

3. Type the project name (to follow along, type "O365 Deployment").

4. At the top of the screen, click Board to see a task board that looks much like the one in Planner. Click Grid to switch to a task table. Click Timeline to view tasks in a Gantt chart arrangement.

Add a Task to the Project

To add a task to the project, do the following:

1. Click the Add new task button.

2. If necessary, add columns such as Start, Finish, Dependents (after), Depends on, % complete, and Bucket.

3. Fill in the task name, assigned to, duration, and start and finish dates.

4. To link tasks, fill in Dependents after and/or Depends on.

5. To associate a task with a bucket, choose the one you want in the Bucket column.

> **Tip:** If you are familiar with Microsoft Project desktop predecessors and successors, Project for the web uses different terms for those elements. With Dependents after, the task numbers you specify represent tasks that occur after this task, in other words, successors. Depends on means that this task depends on when the tasks you specify occur – in other words, those tasks are predecessors to the task you're filling in.

To follow along, create these tasks:

Task name "Design." Duration 15 days. After all tasks exist, set Dependents (after) to 4.

Task name "Develop." Duration 10 days. After all tasks exist, set Dependents (after) to 3.

Task name "Test." Duration 15 days. After all tasks exist, set Dependents (after) to 4 and Depends on to 2.

Task name "Complete Milestone." Duration 0 days. After all tasks exist, set Depends on to 3,1.

> **Note:** Project for the web can display different columns for task details. In addition to including or omitting fields, you can define how they appear on the task board. To learn more, head to www.coldpresspublishing.com for downloadable articles.

6. To indicate progress, fill in the percentage complete in the % Complete column (Figure 29-8).

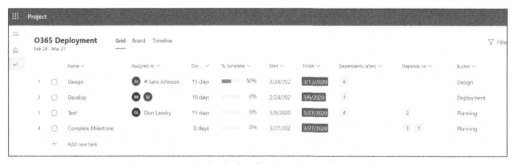

Figure 29-8. *Tasks displayed within "Project for the web."*

Using PWA to Manage Projects

Project Web Access (PWA) is command central for managing projects in an enterprise. You can create, publish, and check in projects, as well as review all the projects in your portfolio. This section describes how to access PWA and perform various project portfolio activities.

There are three licensing options (this may change in the future):

- With **Project P1 (formally known as Essentials)**, team members can review their assignments, update tasks, and fill out timesheets via the browser.

- **Project P3 (formally known as Professional)** includes the Project Professional client and access to Project Online or PWA.

- **Project P5 (formally known as Premium)** includes all the functions available in Professional in addition to resource engagement and portfolio selection features. This license is required to administer Project Online or Project Server for creating enterprise resources and other functions.

Accessing PWA via the Browser

Once your Active Directory account (or Microsoft account if you use Project Online) is added to a group, you can access PWA with Internet Explorer. Simply navigate to the URL that your system administrator provided (for example, http://<servername>/sites/pwa). The PWA Home Page that appears includes feature tiles by default. (A system administrator can customize the Home Page to display different features.) To access the PWA Home Page quickly, bookmark the page or create a desktop shortcut.

> **Note:** Google Chrome, Firebox and other browsers might not display some functions correctly.

Connecting to PWA with Project Professional

To connect Project Professional to PWA, do the following:

1. In Project Professional, click the File tab.

2. On the Backstage, select Info→Manage Accounts.

3. In the Project Web App Accounts dialog box, click the Add button. In the Account Properties dialog box (Figure 29-9), enter your account name.

    Depending on your environment, you might use an active directory account or a Microsoft account.

> **Note:** To set the account to be the default account when you connect Project Professional to PWA, turn on the "Set as default account" checkbox.

4. In the Project Server URL box, fill in the URL for the PWA site.

5. Click OK to close the Account Properties dialog box.

6. Back in the Project Web App Accounts dialog box, in the "When starting" section, select the "Choose an account" radio button.

    By choosing that radio button, you can choose an account that connects to PWA or choose a different account to use Project Professional without connecting.

7. Click OK to close the dialog box.

8. Close Project.

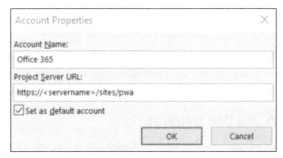

Figure 29-9. *To connect to PWA, fill in the Account Properties dialog box.*

To access PWA from within Project, do the following:

1. Open Project Professional.

2. In the Login dialog box's Profile box, choose the connection account you want to use. If you're prompted for a username and password, fill them in.

    The Backstage view opens. Above the templates on the right, you'll see an Enterprise tab to the right of the Featured tab.

3. Click the Enterprise tab to see your organization's Enterprise Project Type templates (Figure 29-10).

Figure 29-10. *The Enterprise tab appears when you're connected to Project Server or Project Online.*

Working with Projects in the Project Center

The Project Center is the main area in PWA for creating and accessing projects, and for working with project-related information. In the Project Center, you can review the overall portfolio using customized Project Center views. The Project Center also provides a Gantt Chart view of the portfolio schedule. Each task bar in this view represents the start and finish date of a project in the portfolio. The Project Center is like a dashboard where you can select a project and then drill down to see specific project information such as the Schedule, Project Detail Pages, Resource Plans, and the Project Site. The Project Center may contain different types of projects, including projects created within PWA using Project Professional, master projects (a collection of subprojects), or simple SharePoint Tasks List projects.

To obtain project information in the Project Center, do the following:

1. On the PWA Home Page, in the left navigation bar, click Projects.

    The Project Center page opens.

    > **Tip:** Microsoft refers to the left navigation bar as the Quick Launch.

2. In the Project Center web-part grid, click the empty cell to the left of the project's name.

3. Choose the function you want on the Projects tab.

    Features on the ribbon include views, filters, Project Permissions, and Build Team.

4. To open the project, click the Open button, and then choose either In Browser or In Microsoft Project

For more detail, do the following:

1. In the Project Center, click the project's Project Name cell.

    The Project Details page or the Project Information page opens depending on your system configuration.

2. In the left navigation bar, click Schedule.

    A project schedule appears like the Gantt Chart in Project.

3. Click the Task tab.

    You can click Edit and then choose In Microsoft Project or in Browser to open the project for editing. Or click Close to check in the project.

    > **Note:** Another way to obtain more detail is to click the Project Name (link). This method provides access to Project Detail page, which may include Custom Project Fields and the Project Schedule page.

Configuring Enterprise Project Types

Enterprise project types make it easier to create new enterprise projects by setting up standardized elements for new projects. When you create a new project in the Project Center, the project is based on an Enterprise Project Type (EPT). Enterprise Project Types can include several elements:

- **Project Schedule**: This template sets up the initial schedule for projects created using this EPT. You can set up multiple Project Schedule templates to create different types of Project plans. Each EPT can have one Project Schedule template.

- **Project Site**: An EPT might have a Project Site Template associated with it, which is used to create the Project Site for projects created using this EPT. You can set up multiple Project Site Templates to create different types of Project Sites.

- **Project Detail Page(s)**: An EPT can have one or more Project Detail Pages (PDP), which are used to access Custom Project Fields. You can set up multiple Project Detail Pages.

- **Governance Workflow**: An EPT might have a governance workflow, which includes a workflow for projects created using the EPT. You can set up multiple governance workflows.

You can define EPTs to support different project types such as small, medium, large, IT Marketing, Product Development, and so on. Each EPT might need a different type of schedule, Project Site, governance workflow, and different PDPs (containing specific Custom Project Fields). When you choose an EPT for a project, PWA provisions the corresponding elements based on the system configuration for your organization (see Figure 29-11).

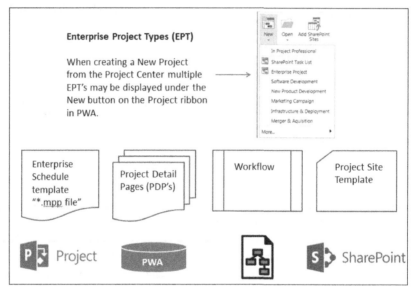

Figure 29-11. *Enterprise Project Types (EPT) provide template standards and make setting up projects easy.*

Creating a Project with PWA

To create a project within PWA in the brows, do the following:

1. In the PWA left navigation bar, click Projects.

2. Click within the Project Center to display the Project tab.

3. On the Project tab, click the New button, and then choose the appropriate Enterprise Project Type (in this example, Enterprise Project).

   The "Create a new project" page appears (Figure 29-12).

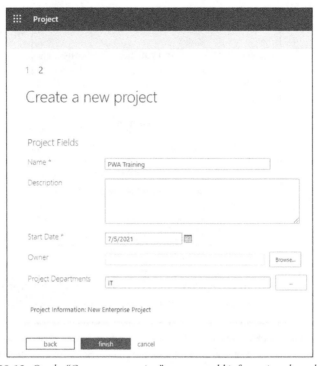

Figure 29-12. *On the "Create a new project" page, you add information about the project.*

4. Fill in the project information in the Project Details pages as needed.

   In this example, for the name type ***PWA Training***, and set the start date to ***7/5/2021***. You can add a description to describe what the project is about.

5. Click the Browse button to add the owner.

   The owner is the person who will manage the project and receive team member updates when the project is underway.

6. If your configuration has other fields, fill in them.

7. Click Finish.

   Progress messages tell you where the process stands.

8. Click entries in the left navigation bar to display Project Detail pages associated with the Enterprise Project Type.

   Pages could be schedule, Strategic Impact page, and so on.

9. On the Project tab, click Close. When the Close [project] message box appears, keep the "Check it in" radio button selected, and then click OK.

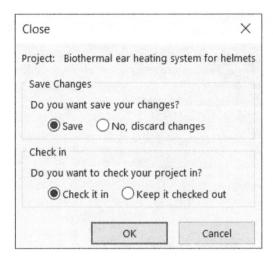

The project is now available in the Project Center. Depending on the Enterprise Project Type you chose, a Project Site may be available along with a preliminary Project Schedule.

> **Note:** You must check-in your project in order for others to see changes you've made. It's best to click Close. That way, Project prompts you to check-in the project. If you click another entry in the Quick Launch without closing the project, the project remains checked out and is only editable in PWA. If you forgot to close your Project, in PWA, click the project in the Project Center. Then, above the project information, you'll see text that begins "Status: Checked-out to you since." The version is set to Draft. To close the project, go to the Project tab, and click Close.

Publishing a Project

You can control when others see the changes you make to a project schedule. For example, you can wait until you've completed the schedule or finished all the changes someone requested. In PWA, you can save schedules in **_Draft format_**. When you're ready to make the schedule available, you publish the project, which saves it to **_Published format_**. Figure 29-13 shows the publishing workflow.

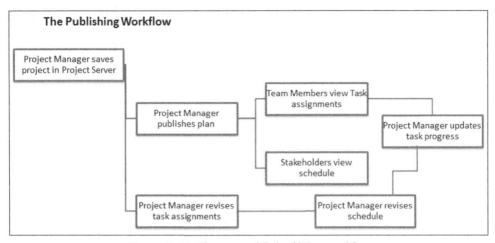

Figure 29-13: *This is a simplified publishing workflow.*

To publish a project schedule, do the following:

1. In PWA's left navigation bar, click Projects to open the Project Center.

2. In the Project Center web-part grid, click the empty cell to the left of the project's name.

3. On the left navigation bar, click Schedule.

   At the top of the Schedule page, you can see whether the project is checked in or out, and the version.

4. In this example, if the project Status is not Checked-out, on the Task tab, click Edit.

   The Task tab includes features like those in Project Professional, for example, you can set a baseline by choosing Set Baseline→Set Baseline→Baseline.

5. To save your changes and publish the project, click Publish. (To save changes without publishing, click Save.)

6. On the Project tab, click Close. When the Close [project] message box appears, keep the "Check it in" radio button selected, and then click OK.

Synchronizing Local and Server Project Data

When a project is checked out, the local version (stored using the Project cache), is updated as you make changes. When the project is checked in, the changes are synchronized with the server version. Saving also syncs the local version but does NOT post the changes to the server in the Project Center views. To update Project Server or Project Online Project Center views, on the File menu, click Info. In the Info section, click the Publish button.

By default, the cache is created in the profile for the user currently logged in to the local machine. To work with the Project cache, in Project Professional, choose File→Options, to open the Project Options dialog box, and then click the Save category. Project Professional must be connected to Project Server or Project Online to work with the cache.

View Cache Status

To view status and errors in the Project cache, in the Project Options dialog box's Save screen, click View Cache Status to open the Active Cache Status dialog box (Figure 29-14). Click either the Status or Errors tab to review details about the Project cache.

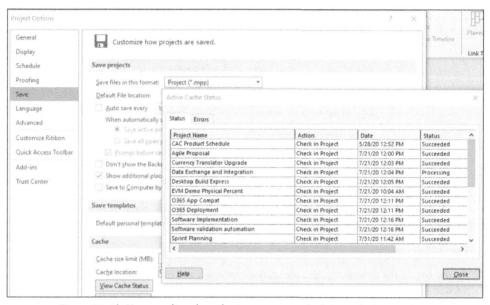

Figure 29-14. *You can adjust the cache size, or remove, check in, or check out projects.*

Adjust Cache Settings

You can adjust the disk space and memory allocated to the cache to open larger projects more quickly. In the Project Options dialog box, click the Save category. In the "Cache size limit (MB)" box, type the maximum amount of memory in megabytes that you want the cache to use the hard drive. In the "Cache location" box, fill in the path to the folder in which you want to store the cache.

Remove Projects from the Cache

You can remove projects from the cache that have been deleted from Project Server or Project Online. You can also remove projects if the local cache has become corrupted and can't open projects because of that. In the Project Options dialog box, click Clean Up Cache. In the Clean Up Cache dialog box, in the Project Filter drop-down list, select either "Projects checked out to you" or "Projects not checked out to you." Select a project in the list, and then click Remove From Cache. This dialog box also provides information about the cache like its size and the total size of the projects in it.

Checking In a Project from Project Professional

After working on a project in the Project Professional, you need to check the project in. That way, its information is available to others and timesheets and task updates submitted for the project can be applied to it. To check a project in, in Project Professional, choose File→Close. In the dialog box that appears, you can check-in the project, keep it checked out, or save or discard your changes.

> **Note:** If you click the Browse button to the right of Project Web App, the Open dialog box includes a Cache Status column which displays project status, as shown in Figure 29-15.

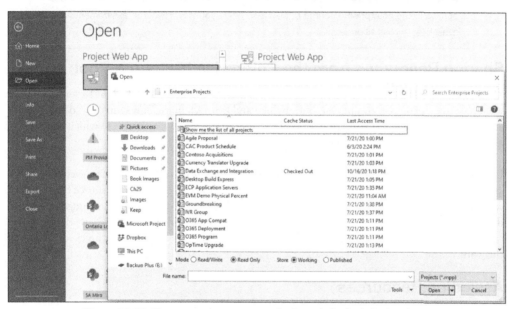

Figure 29-15. *You can see project status in the Open dialog box's Cache column.*

> **Tip:** It's a good idea to check-in and Publish a project after you work on it, instead of leaving it checked out. That way, others can see the changes you've made. If someone forgets to check-in a project, the PWA Settings page has a Force Check-in Enterprise Objects option. However, using that feature should be a last resort, because any changes that were made locally are lost.

Managing Resources and Status

Planned work (tasks that need to be performed), resource assignments for accomplishing those tasks, and what was actually accomplished (actuals) are closely related. One of the benefits of PPM is being able to manage resources shared among projects—analyzing resource commitments across multiple projects, viewing resource availability versus demand, and managing resources' workloads. Microsoft

Project and PWA have several ways to manage resource information, which deliver different results.

Resource management begins by storing information about shared resources in a common location—the enterprise resource pool. This pool contains information about people, equipment, materials, and other resources, like skill sets and resource availability. With an enterprise resource pool, you can find resources with the skills you need and sufficient available time. This section describes how to work with the enterprise resource pool to add your organization's resources, build a team for a project, and obtain status and timesheet updates.

> **Note:** In PWA, the Resource Center (in the left navigation bar, click Resources) provides access to the enterprise resource pool. It also helps you view resource assignments and availability across all projects.

Sharing Resources from the Enterprise Resource Pool

The Enterprise Resource Pool is a centralized repository of resource information. Resources include work resources (people or equipment, both named and generic), material resources, and cost resources. The pool contains resource information like resource rates, the departments to which they belong, group membership, team membership, and other attributes.

In PWA, you can use the Build Team function to add enterprise resources to a project team. Once enterprise resources are on your team, you can assign them to tasks or create a Resource Plan. Because resources are shared by projects from the Enterprise Resource Pool, the pool aggregates resource demand based on assignments and Resource Plans across all projects connected to the pool. You can compare overall demand to availability to see whether you have enough resources to perform all the work.

Assigning Resources

Just as in assigning resources in Project as a standalone tool, a resource assignment in an enterprise environment allocates a resource to a task. Here are additional things you need to know about resource assignments when you work with PWA:

- **Build your team first**: You have to add resources from the Enterprise Resource Pool to your project team by using the Build Team function before you can assign them to tasks.

- **Assign resources in PWA**: You can assign resources on the PWA Schedule page. With this assignment method, you can't set resource allocation—all assignments are created as 100% allocation over the task duration.

- **Assign resources in Project**: You can assign resources in Project and the publish them to PWA Assignments. With this method, you can choose the resource allocation (such as 25% or 50%) or contour the assignments.

Publish assignments: Only tasks with published resource assignments appear in a team member's task list and timesheet. Team members can then report time on tasks, projects, and non-project time using timesheets. Team members can also report time against a project (not tasks) with task updates. Whether data applies at the project or task level depends on PWA administrative settings. Timesheet and task updates can update the actuals in your project schedule.

Working with Resource Engagements

Resource Engagements are another way to plan for and allocate resources using high-level estimating from the top-down. With resource engagements, resources aren't assigned to specific tasks. Instead, you allocate them at the project level for specific time-periods to develop a high-level plan for the resources you need. Later, a project manager can then assign them to tasks and flesh out the details.

Resource engagements are useful early in project planning and evaluation, when you don't have detailed info to create task-level assignments or you need approval to acquire resources for your project. They also come in handy throughout the project lifecycle to project resource demand. Resource engagement plans were available in PWA and are available on the client side in Project Professional 2016 and later software versions. If an engagement request exists, the client software prompts you when you open that schedule.

Here is how you use resource engagement plans:

1. In PWA, click Resources to open the Resource Center. Click the Resources tab, and then turn on the Selected Resources checkbox.

2. Select resources in the Resource Center before you allocate them to a resource plan.

    In the Resource Center, turn on checkboxes to the left of resource names on the left side of the window, which is the pool. When you do that, the selected resources appear on the right side of the screen.

3. On the PWA Resources tab, click Resource Requests.

    A blank Resource Request list appears. In the ribbon, the Engagement and Options tabs appear.

4. On the Engagements tab, click Add Engagement.

5. In the New Engagement form (Figure 29-16), select the resource name, project, and start and finish dates for the request.

    Resources can be allocated by units or work. You can also add comments to document the engagement.

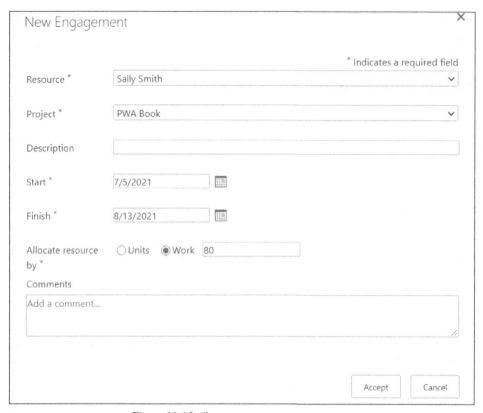

Figure 29-16. *Create a new resource engagement.*

6. Click Accept.

The Engagement appears in the Resource Request list (Figure 29-17). You can edit or delete engagements in this list.

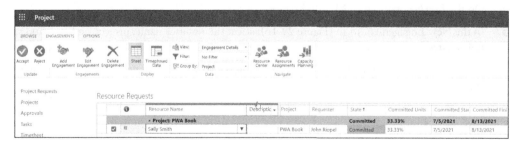

Figure 29-17. *The Resource Request list displays resource engagements.*

In Project Professional, an Update message appears below the ribbon that reads "New resources have been committed to your project." The View Engagements button appears to the right of the message. When the project is checked out, the Engagements tab appears so you can review engagement requests.

Here is how you work with an engagement within Project Professional:

1. To view your resource plan, click View Engagements to the right of the update message (Figure 29-18).

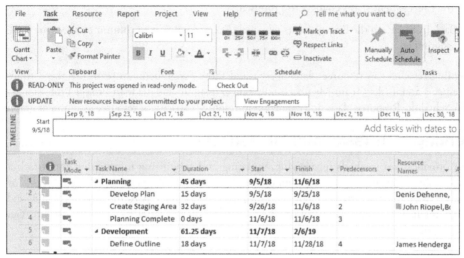

Figure 29-18. *The Resource Request list displays resource engagements.*

2. After that, you can return to the resource plan by clicking the Engagements tab in the ribbon. The Prop. Max Units and the Com. Max Units fields appear by default in the time-scaled grid on the right side of the Resource Plan view.

> **Tip:** You can also add engagements in Project desktop from the Engagements tab (figure 29-19.

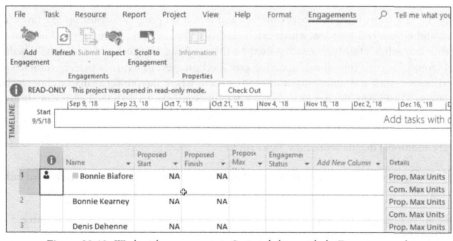

Figure 29-19. *Work with engagements in Project desktop with the Engagements tab.*

3. To modify a request, change the proposed start or finish date, or the proposed percentage allocation.

4. After you modify the request, click Submit on the Engagements tab.

    The Engagement status changes to Proposed.

5. Back in PWA, on the Engagements tab, click Accept or Reject to commit or reject the finalized assignment.

Assigning resources in resource plans doesn't add those assignments to team members' timesheets. Timesheets and Tasks (Team Members) only reflect assignments made in Project Professional or the PWA Schedule. Resource plans don't show up in resource capacity or resource assignment graphs.

Working with Tasks and Timesheets

PWA provides two methods for viewing, updating and submitting information about task assignments: tasks and timesheets. With timesheets, users can report actual work against task- or project-level assignments as well as report on non-project work such as Administrative Time, and non-work items like sick-time and vacation. Task updates, on the other hand, allow users to view and report progress only against assigned project tasks.

Your organization can choose either tasks or timesheets as the preferred method for task and assignment updates. Tasks and Timesheets can be configured to work independently to allow for more flexible reporting options or locked together to ensure that the task and timesheet data agrees.

Tasks and Timesheets have different approval workflows, Task updates are sent to the Status Manager whereas Timesheets are sent to the Timesheet Manager. Your system administrator can provide details on how task and timesheets are configured for your organization.

Updating Using Tasks View

On PWA's Task page, team members can view and report on progress against project tasks (assignments), and submit task progress, which can be approved by the project manager and used to update the project schedule. Task progress reported in this way can be synchronized to the schedule using Microsoft Project Professional, updating task level progress in terms of percent complete, hours worked, actual work and remaining work, or free-form where the project manager chooses data for each project. Tasks can also act as the source for timesheet data, or aligned with timesheets using Single Entry Mode, depending on your server configuration settings.

Here are additional details about how Tasks work:

- Team Member's Task lists only include tasks and projects in which they have published task assignments.

- Resource Engagements don't appear in Task lists, as described in the section on resource engagements.

- Some organizations use Administrative Projects to manage non-project work like training, support, and so on. In that case, Administrative Project tasks also appear in Task lists.

Updating Using the Timesheets View

Timesheets allow team members to report actual work against projects, tasks, non-project administrative work, and non-work time like sick time (Figure 29-20). Timesheets can provide actual work data to your Project schedule. When this feature is enabled, time reported in a team member's timesheet can be synchronized to the Project schedule using Microsoft Project Professional, updating task-level progress in terms of actual work and percent complete. If it isn't enabled, timesheets simply work as a stand-alone timesheet system with no impact on your project schedules.

Here are additional details about timesheets:

- Timesheets can be configured for time reporting at the task level only, or at the task and project level.

- Team members' timesheets only include tasks (and projects) in which they have published task assignments.

- Resource Engagements assignments don't appear in timesheets.

- Non-project work may be added to timesheets regardless of task assignments. However, some organizations use Administrative Projects to manage non-project work. In that case, resources must be assigned to tasks in the Administrative Project and those assignments must be published in order for team members to report time on those administrative tasks.

- Timesheets always include published task assignments, even when using Resource Plans as the source for resource utilization.

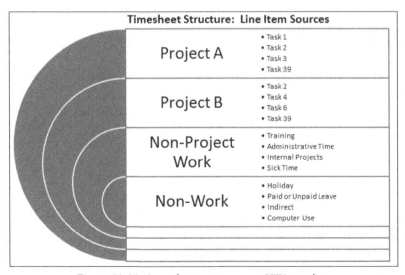

Figure 29-20. *Items that can appear on a PWA timesheet.*

Building and Using Project Sites

Project management produces many documents, risks, issues, and other information that you need to manage in addition to schedules. With PPM, you can set up sites to go with your projects. Enterprise Project Types can specify the project site template (PST) to use so you can the necessary details for a project. (Project site creation can be automatic or manual depending on your system configuration.) Project sites include standard SharePoint functionality including Document Libraries, Discussion Forums, Surveys, Blogs, and so on. Project Sites also include Project Management related lists including Issues and Risks.

Here are additional details about project sites:

- Project sites are SharePoint sites that contain webparts that work with Project to provide additional functionality. The Task list is one of PWA's enhanced lists that allows users to see published tasks.

- Project site permissions are automatically synced with the project schedule resource assignments to control user access.

- Project Site Owners have full control of the Project Site design and content.

- Team members have Contribute access for creating and editing content.

- Project Managers by default are owners of their project sites.

> **Note:** Task information is available in the project site, but the schedule is stored at the PWA level, not the project site level. That means users can see tasks within the project site but can't edit them.

Reporting in the Business Intelligence Center

The Business Intelligence Center is one way to deliver reports on project, task, or resource information that users can modify in an application like Excel. Three sample reports come with a Project Server or Project Online system: Project Overview Dashboard, Project Overview, and Resource Overview. The BI Center delivers data analysis and reporting capabilities across other line-of-business application databases, including PWA, by creating a data-connection to the underlying database information, and then presenting it in Excel pivot-tables, as shown in Figure 29-21.

The BI Center uses Excel Reporting Services, PowerPivot, and PerformancePoint services, which enable Excel spreadsheets, charts, graphs, and interactive features directly in Internet Explorer. Microsoft has also released Power BI, which is a graphical reporting tool that allows you to merge data from multiple data sources and employ graphics to build reports (Figure 29-22).

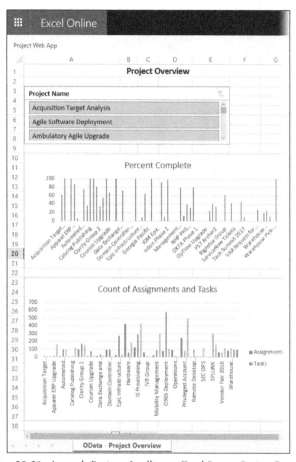

Figure 29-21. *A sample Business Intelligence Excel Report: Project Overview.*

Reporting in Power BI

You can use Power BI to create reports by connecting to Project Online, "Project for the web", Planner or SharePoint using an OData connection. Power BI reports are more engaging reports that can support your organization's reporting needs. To connect Project Online and Power BI, use the OData connection type and enter the URL in the following format: Error! Hyperlink reference not valid.. This will return all the reporting tables that you can use to build reports.

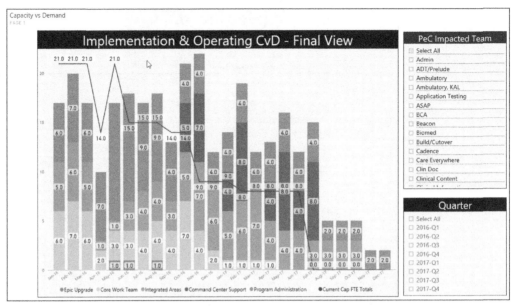

Figure 29-22. *A sample Power BI report of Capacity vs Demand*

30

Working with Agile in Project

Agile methodology is great when business needs change frequently. Agile produces value sooner by delivering a steady stream of product features. With this ongoing delivery, the customer can provide feedback on what's been delivered so far. That way, the team can respond to feedback, address changes easily, and deliver a better solution. This requires a different approach to managing and implementing work—agile project management.

With Agile, work is performed within iterations or sprints. Each iteration strives to deliver a complete, ready-to-use set of features. That way, the customer receives business value with each iteration. And when business needs change, those desired features are addressed in a future iteration.

This chapter starts with a brief overview of Agile project management, including Scrum and Kanban. It also explains why and how you might use a hybrid approach that combines both Agile and traditional waterfall project management.

If you have a subscription to Project Online, you can use Agile in your projects with Project Online Desktop Client's Agile features. This chapter walks you through managing Agile work with task boards and sprints. You add tasks to task board cards, which work with Project's Kanban and Scrum features. For Scrum, you can assign these cards to sprints. And finally, you can produce reports to communicate progress.

An Overview of Agile Project Management

The Agile approach empowers teams to respond to the ever-changing nature of business. It helps deliver business value sooner while welcoming change. It uses iterations (called sprints when using Scrum) that last from one to four weeks (sometimes longer). The objective for each iteration is to deliver a functioning ready-to-use set of features, which means the business gets value at the end of each iteration. Because iterations are relatively short, the team can address changing business needs in a future iteration.

At the heart of Agile project management is the work. Agile breaks delivery into small pieces, which are prioritized by the customer and team together. Teams regularly reflect on immediate needs in reviews and adjust the plan if necessary. This helps ensure that the customer receives business benefits and is satisfied with the results. In addition, collaboration is a key tenet. Customers are highly engaged in Agile projects. At the same time, people interact when there is a need. The Agile method also helps create a more efficient, sustainable and supportive environment so people can deliver their best work.

Agile isn't one-size-fits-all. The two most common approaches are Scrum and Kanban. This section briefly describes each approach. Some organizations use a hybrid approach to project management where Agile and the traditional waterfall methodology both play a part.

Scrum

With Scrum, the team shares responsibilities with others throughout the project lifecycle. Each sprint is supposed to produce a working deliverable. To ensure that the deliverable is done, part of each sprint cycle is defining the criteria that must be met for an item to be "done." Scrum sprints typically last from one to four weeks. (Once you define your sprint length, it applies to all sprints.)

Scrum teams are typically small with three standard roles:

- **Product Owner**: The product owner is the project's key stakeholder. This person performs several functions for the project: defines the project vision, manages the backlog of items to work on, maps out dependencies, eliminates obstacles to finishing work, explains prioritized customer needs to the team, manages customer requests, and acts as the customer-team liaison.

- **Scrum Master**: The Scrum master guides the team in implementing Agile in the organization and works with the team to organize meetings and monitor progress. This person also explains Scrum to the organization.

- **Team**: The team is a collection of individual contributors, a self-managing group with no formal leader. The team uses its expertise and resources to achieve the project's objectives. They work with the product owner to create the goal for each sprint and release. They then decide how to perform the work to meet that goal.

Scrum is lean, fast, and simple. Some of the benefits of this approach are:

- Constant feedback from the client or stakeholder helps the team understand needs and adjust accordingly.

- Shared responsibility by the team helps get more done in less time.

- Everyone is responsible for the product, which keeps the team motivated.

- Issues can be addressed and resolved during short, daily meetings.

- Speedy development means projects move along quickly.

Challenges of Scrum include:

- Scrum works best with a team of skilled, experienced, and committed members.

- Team members must be very knowledgeable to ensure features don't disrupt business while trying to expand business capabilities.

- Tight timelines mean that delays are likely if anyone gets sick or leaves mid-project.

- Excessive changes can lead to scope creep and delays from the original product goal.

- Team members in smaller organizations may work on multiple projects, delaying deliverables as priorities shift.

Kanban

The Kanban approach doesn't use fixed-length iterations. With Kanban, work is continuous and tied to the product delivery cycle. Taken from manufacturing, the idea is to keep the team fully productive at all times.

In theory, a Kanban board (task board) doesn't show a timeline for a project or task. Instead, it simply displays the items and when those deliverables finish. A release can occur without having to wait for a specific milestone. In addition, there are no set roles. No official "Kanban master" keeps things running smoothly (although someone usually takes on this function.) The entire team owns the board so they must be nimble and able to adapt to changing priorities.

With its loose structure, Kanban can help foster collaboration or create chaos. For that reason, it's critical to have a team that's communicative, committed and self-motivated.

Some of the benefits of this approach are:

- Kanban boards strictly limit the amount of work in progress, which helps focus the team on what's important and needed.

- New items can be added whenever capacity is available, not only when all tasks are completed.

- Daily meetings improve communication but aren't required.

- Team members have the ability to change direction if needed, without impacting a timeline.

- The board work contains everything necessary to create a releasable version, which allows for continuous improvement.

Challenges of Kanban include:

- Without timelines, team members may not feel a sense of urgency to complete tasks.

- In theory, no one person is responsible for making sure the team aligns with goals and best practices. (In reality, someone guides activity.)

- Without an owner, boards can become overly complicated and outdated. They must be maintained regularly.

- Continuous process improvement can lead to development issues and confusion by moving focus from the product to the process.

A Hybrid Agile/Waterfall approach

In many cases, a combination of Agile and traditional waterfall project management works well. With waterfall, project activities (tasks) are organized into project phases. Each phase may have a stage gate and may depend on the deliverables of the previous phase. The critical path represents the sequence of tasks with no slack—a delay on the critical path delays the entire project. By combining this traditional waterfall approach with Agile feedback mechanisms, you can uncover issues during development and address them quickly.

Here are a few examples where a hybrid approach might be beneficial:

- A short hardware/software project has defined deliverables and a fixed budget. The structure of waterfall supports the definition of the deliverables and a plan to complete the project within budget. Agile's speed and teamwork encourages collaboration between the team and the client/stakeholder to achieve the objectives.

- A hardware/software project needs to satisfy many stakeholders, while mitigating risks and delivering within a tight timeline. Agile is great for limiting risks and staying on deadline. Waterfall is often best for incorporating information and feedback from many stakeholders.

Some of the benefits of this approach are:

- Planning is performed early in waterfall, so teams gain valuable insight into the project's requirements and can give more accurate time and cost estimates.

- Work happens in short iterative segments, which makes it easy to adapt to changing needs and requirements.

- Collaboration is encouraged across teams and stakeholders.

- Fixed deadlines and budgets can be managed.

Challenges with this approach include:

- The approach seems restrictive to those used to the flexibility of Agile.

- The team must be committed to a collaborative approach.

- A skilled project manager is required to define and assign sprints.

- Too many stakeholders and changes can cause budget overages and missed deadlines.

- Defining the roles of Product Owners and Project Managers is critical with this method.

Where Are the Agile Features in Microsoft Project?

Microsoft Project includes built-in agile features, such as task boards and sprints—but only if you have the correct product. Agile features are available only when you have a subscription to Microsoft Project Online Desktop Client, which comes with a Project Online P3 or P5 plan.

> **Note:** To check your project version, in Project, click File, and then choose Account. Below the Product Information label, you'll see Subscription Product, Microsoft Project Online Desktop Client when you have the subscription product.
>
> In addition, some organizations set up targeted release options in Microsoft 365, so some functionality isn't introduced as soon as it's released. For that reason, what you see in your installation may be different than what's shown in this chapter. In addition, your software may vary from what you see here due to software updates that occur after the publication of this book.

Working with Task Boards

Task boards are the fundamental method for viewing work in Agile methodologies, whether you use Kanban, Scrum, or a hybrid traditional/Agile approach. A task board displays tasks as task cards in columns instead of rows in a table. The categories associated with columns help you track and manage tasks. You can change status or sprint assignments by dragging and dropping tasks into a different column.

> **Note:** If you've downloaded files from the book web site, you can follow along using the file Event_Ch30_start.mpp.

Display and Modify Tasks in a Task Board

Follow Along Practice

To display tasks in a Task Board, do the following:

1. In the View tab's Task Views section, click Task Board.

    The Task Board appears with tasks displayed as cards, as shown in Figure 30-1.

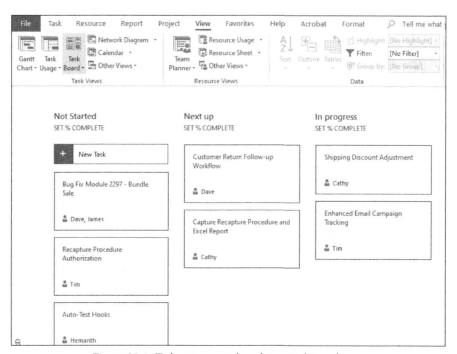

Figure 30-1. *Tasks appear as task cards in a Task Board view.*

2. If you don't see a task in the Task Board view, switch back to the Gantt Chart view.

    A task's Show on Board field must be set to Yes (the default setting) in order for the task to appear in the Task Board view.

3. Right-click a column heading in the table, in this case, Resource, and then choose Insert Column. Choose the Show on Board field.

    The Show on Board field is a Yes/No field. In this example, all the tasks are already set to Yes to display on a task board.

4. Repeat step 3 to insert the Board Status field into the table.

5. To change a task's Show on Board setting, click the task's Show on Board cell, choose Yes or No, and then press Enter (Figure 30-2).

6. To change a task's Board Status, click the task's Board Status cell, and then choose the status.

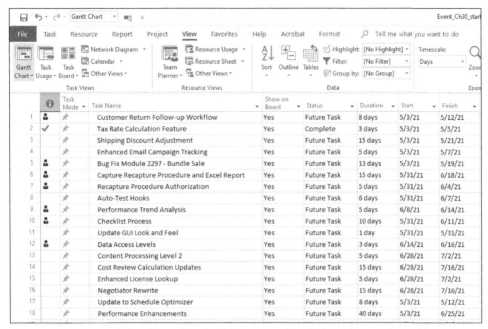

Figure 30-2. *Click Task Board on the ribbon's View tab to display tasks in Task Board boxes.*

Customize Task Board Cards

In a task board view, task cards display three base fields by default (task name, assigned resource, and a checkmark if the task is complete). You can add other fields to task cards with the Customize Cards feature. You can choose which base fields to display (for instance, task ID) and can add up to five additional fields.

Follow Along Practice

To customize task cards for a project, do the following:

1. On the Format tab, click Customize Cards.

   The Customize Task Board Cards dialog box appears.

2. In the Base Fields section, turn on the checkboxes for the Base Fields you want to display. In this example, turn on the Show Task ID checkbox.

   Task Name is always displayed on task cards. You can turn Task ID, Resources, and the checkmark on or off.

3. In the Additional Fields section, click one of the down arrows, and then choose the field you want. In this example, add % Complete, Duration, Start, and Finish.

4. Click OK.

   The task cards in every task board view (Task Board, Sprint Planning Board, Current Sprint Board, and so on) displays the fields you selected (Figure 30-3).

> **Note:** Card customizations are specific to the project in which you defined them. To use these customized cards in other projects, it's easiest to create a template. Otherwise, you need to redefine these customizations in each project you work on.

Figure 30-3. *You can choose the fields you want to display on task cards in task board views.*

Planning a Project with Sprints

If you use Scrum to manage work, you can manage and track work within sprints in Project. All you have to do is add tasks to your project, assign the tasks to sprints, and, if necessary, move the tasks to the sprint board. At that point, you can use sprint views to see the tasks assigned to a sprint.

Add Sprints to an Existing Project

Before you can assign tasks to Scrum sprints, you must create the sprints in your project. After adding sprints to your project, the Sprints tab provides additional sprints features.

Follow Along Practice

To add sprints to your project, do the following:

1. In the Project tab's Properties section, click Manage Sprints.

    The Manage Sprints dialog box appears with Sprint 1 added automatically.

    You can edit the Length and Start information provided for Sprint 1:

2. To modify the length and start date, simply fill in the Length and Start cells in the Sprint 1 row.

In this example, change the Length cell to 4w. Set the Start cell to 5/2/2021.

Length is the duration of the sprint. The Start field is the date on which the sprint starts.

3. Before you add additional sprints, in the Add Sprint section, specify the sprint start date and duration for the sprints you want to add. In this example, set the Sprint Start to 5/31/2021 and Duration to 4w.

4. To add a sprint, click Add Sprint (Figure 30-4).

    A new sprint appears in the table.

5. Click Add Sprint again to add the next sprint.

6. To close the Manage Sprints dialog box, click OK.

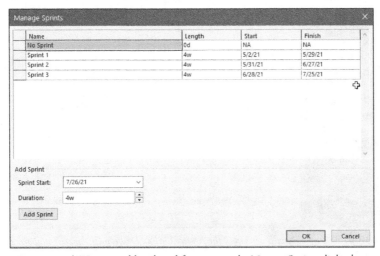

Figure 30-4. *You can add and modify sprints in the Manage Sprints dialog box.*

After you add sprints to your project, a Sprints tab appears in the ribbon, as shown in Figure 30-5. The Sprints tab includes tools for viewing and managing sprints.

Figure 30-5. *The Sprints tab appears in the ribbon after you add sprints to your project.*

Create a Project from a Sprints Template

The Sprints Project template makes it easy to create sprint-based projects. When you use this template, the project opens automatically to the Sprint Planning Board view.

1. Choose File→New.

2. In the Featured templates section at the top of the New screen, click Sprints Project (Figure 30-6).

The Sprint Planning Board appears (Figure 30-7) and the Sprints tab appears in the ribbon. (Three sprints are set up automatically.) You're ready to create tasks and assign them to sprints.

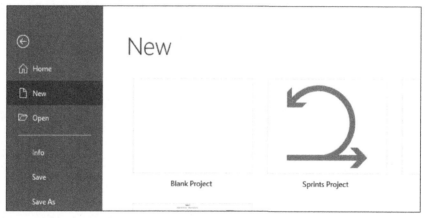

Figure 30-6. *When you have a version of the Project Online Desktop Client that supports Agile, the Sprints Project icon appears at the top of the New screen next to the Blank Project icon.*

Figure 30-7. *When you create a new sprints project, it opens to the Sprint Planning Board view.*

Tip: When you have a version of the Project Online Desktop Client that supports Agile, the Task Views section of the View tab includes a Task Board button. Click it to choose between the Task Board view and the Sprint Planning Board view.

Add Tasks and Details to an Agile Project

You can add tasks to a sprints project in the same way you add them to waterfall projects. With a sprints project, you have a few additional methods for adding tasks. Here's an overview:

- **Gantt Chart view**: When you add tasks in a Gantt Chart view table, they appear in the task list as they do for a traditional waterfall project. In addition, these tasks will also appear in the Task Board and Sprint Planning Board views.

- **Task Board view**: To create a task in this view, click the New Task button.

- **Task Board sheet view**: To create a task in this view, click the New Task button.

- **Sprint Planning Board view:** To create a task in this view, click the New Task button.

Follow Along Practice

To add tasks to your project, follow these steps:

1. On the Sprints menu, click Task Board, and then choose Task Board on the dropdown menu.

2. Click the New Task button.

3. Type the task name, in this example, "Scrum Task 1." Click Add.

   When you add tasks using any of these methods, they appear in the Task Board's Not Started column (Figure 30-8).

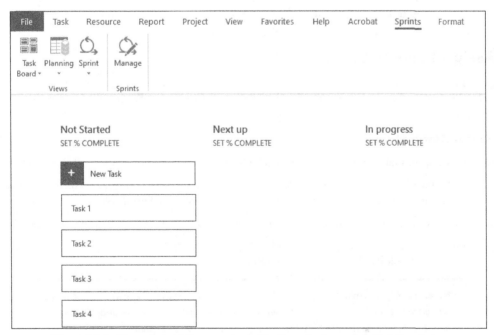

Figure 30-8. *New tasks initially appear in the Not Started column of the Task Board view.*

A table in the Gantt Chart view is the easiest way to add details to tasks even in a sprints project (Figure 30-9):

1. On the View tab, click Gantt Chart.

2. Select task ID 23 "Scrum Task 1", and then drag and drop it between task IDs 5 and 6.

3. In the Duration column, type 1 and press Tab. In the Start cell, type 5/20/21.

4. In the Resource Names column, check the box for Matt, and press Enter.

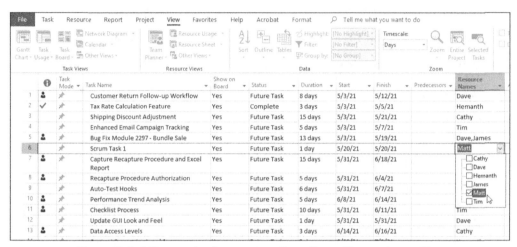

Figure 30-9. *Filling in task information in a Gantt Chart table is similar to adding info for non-Agile tasks.*

Assign Tasks to Sprints

As you begin to work on your sprints project, it's time to assign tasks to sprints based on when you want to complete them. For example, the tasks that the customer wants first will be assigned to the first sprint. Here's how you assign tasks to sprints:

Follow Along Practice

1. On the Sprints tab in the Views group, click Planning, and then choose Sprint Planning Board.

   The Sprint Planning Board displays tasks below the heading for the sprint to which they are assigned. Tasks that aren't yet assigned to a sprint appear in the No Sprint column.

2. Drag tasks from the No Sprint column to the sprint you want to assign them to (Figure 30-10).

   In this example, assign task ID 1 and task IDs 3 through 6 to Sprint 1, task IDs 7 through 13 to Sprint 2, and task IDs 14 through 17 to Sprint 3.

> **Note:** In reality, you might assign tasks to only one sprint at a time. That way, you can easily add additional tasks to the sprint if work is completed faster than estimated. Or you can assign any incomplete work from the previous sprint to the next sprint.

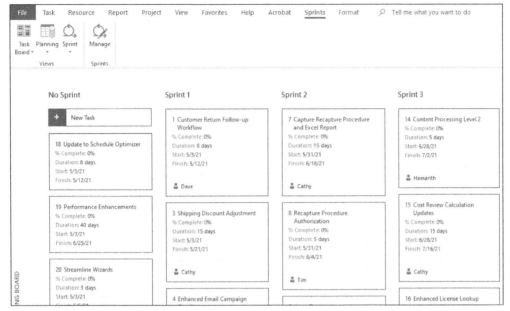

Figure 30-10. *Drag and drop tasks into a print column to assign them to that sprint.*

Tip: You can also assign tasks to sprints in the sheet view by clicking the dropdown in the Sprint column. To display the sheet view, on the Sprints tab, click Planning, and then choose Sprint Planning Sheet.

Track Progress in the Current Sprint

As your team works on tasks within a sprint, you can track task progress by changing their status. Project provides four status categories out of the box (Not Started, Next, In Progress, Done). However, you can add more and change the status names to match the ones your organization uses.

Follow Along Practice

To track sprint progress, do the following:

1. On the Sprints tab's Views group, choose Sprint→Current Sprint Board. Alternatively, in the View tab's Task Views group, choose Task Board→More Views→Current Sprint Board.

    The Current Sprint Board view applies the Current Sprint filter, which displays the tasks in the current sprint.

2. To select a specific Sprint, on the Sprints tab, click Sprint, and then choose the sprint you want, in this example Sprint 1.

    Tasks appear in the column that corresponds to their board status. In the sample file, a few tasks have already been assigned to status categories.

3.   Drag a task from the Not Started column to the appropriate status column. In this example, drag Bug Fix Module 2297 – Bundle Sale to the Next up column (Figure 30-11).

You can also change a task's status in a sheet view by changing the contents of the Board Status column. To display a sheet view, in the Sprints tab's Views group, click Sprint, and then choose Current Sprint Sheet. Or in the View tab's Task Views group, click Task Board, and then choose Task Board Sheet.

4.   Drag a task to the Done column with it is complete

A checkmark appears at the box's top right to indicate completion. In addition, if you look at task details, its % Complete field changes to 100%.

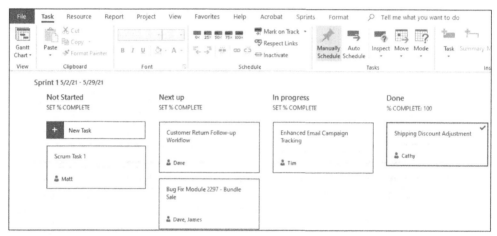

Figure 30-11. *Drag a task to the appropriate column to change its board status.*

Tip: To change the name of a column, right-click the column name, and then choose Rename on the shortcut menu. Type the new name and press Enter. To add more columns, to the right of the last column, choose Add New Column, fill in the name, and then press Enter.

Creating a Hybrid Waterfall/Agile Schedule

When you use both traditional waterfall and Agile approaches in the same project, you can view your tasks in either waterfall or Agile views. You can use Project's Agile features to manage a subset of your project. Task board views display a subset of task information, while all task details are still visible in Gantt Chart or Usage tables. In other words, you don't see all task details in a board view, but it's still there when you switch to other Project views.

Inserting a Traditional Project into an Agile Schedule

Suppose you have a large project and want to track a portion of it using sprints. You can specify which tasks appear in your task board views.

> **Note:** If you've downloaded files from the book web site, you can follow along using the file Event_Ch30_hybrid.mpp and Event_Ch30_waterfall.mpp.

Follow Along Practice

To add tasks from a waterfall project and modify the tasks that display on task board views, follow these steps:

1. On the Task ribbon, click the Gantt Chart button.

2. To insert another project as a subproject, first select the row where you want to insert the project. In this example, click the first blank task row beneath task ID 23.

3. On the Project menu, click the Subproject button.

4. In the Insert Project dialog box, navigate to the folder that contains the subproject file, in this example, the folder where you stored the book sample files. Select the project file you want to insert, in this example, Event_Ch30_waterfall.mpp.

5. Turn off the "Link to project" checkbox above the File name box (Figure 30-12), and then click Insert.

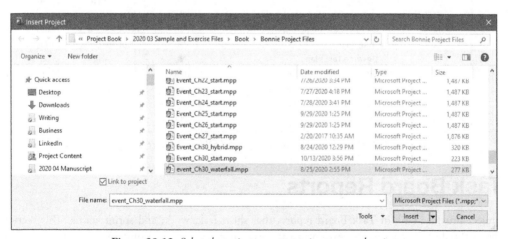

Figure 30-12. *Select the project you want to insert as a subproject.*

6. If the Show on Board field is not visible in the table, insert it.

7. To remove tasks from the Task Board, change their Show on Board cells to No. In this example, change the Show on Board cells for task ID 24 through the end of the Waterfall project to No, as shown in Figure 30-13.

Show on Board is set to Yes automatically. When you change Show on Board to No, the task no longer appears in all task board views. In this example, you can change task ID 24's Show on Board to No and then drag to copy that value to the end of the subproject.

	❶	Task Mode ▾	Task Name	Show on Board ▾	Board Status ▾	Duration ▾
22			Rework CodeGen	Yes	Not Started	100 days
23			AutoRun Enhanced Features	Yes	Not Started	13 days
24			⊿ **Waterfall**	No	**Not Started**	**105 days**
1			⊿ **Specification Phase**	No	**Not Started**	**35 days**
2			Begin Project X	No	Not Started	0 days
3			Develop Product Concept Document	No	Not Started	10 days
4			Write Product Proposal Document	No	Not Started	10 days
5			Create Requirements Spec	No	Not Started	15 days
6			Develop Functional Spec	No	Not Started	10 days
7			Write the System Architecture Spec	No	Not Started	5 days
8			Specification Phase Complete	No	Not Started	0 days
9			⊿ **Design Phase**	No	**Not Started**	**50 days**
10			Write Top Level Design	No	Not Started	10 days
11			⊿ **Develop Detailed Design**	No	**Not Started**	**40 days**
12			Produce Flowchart Diagrams	No	Not Started	10 days
13			Assign Software Modules	No	Not Started	15 days
14			Complete Mech Design Doc	No	Not Started	15 days
15			Design Phase Complete	No	Not Started	0 days
16			⊿ **Testing Phase**	No	**Not Started**	**80 days**
17			Develop Test Plan	No	Not Started	15 days
18			Develop Test Procedures	No	Not Started	20 days
19			Perform Integration Testing	No	Not Started	15 days
20			Ready for Quality Assurance Audit	No	Not Started	5 days
21			Project Complete	No	Not Started	0 days

Figure 30-13. *Change task Show on Board fields in a Gantt Chart table.*

Task Board Reports

Project provides built-in Task Board reports that show task, work, and sprint status. This section shows the default reports. However, you can customize them in the same way you can customize other reports (Chapter 19). To access Task Board reports, in the Report tab's View Reports section, click the Task Boards button, and then choose the report you want.

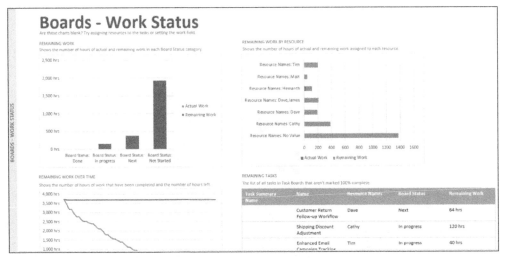

Figure 30-14. *On the Task Boards drop-down menu, choose Boards – Work Status to display this report.*

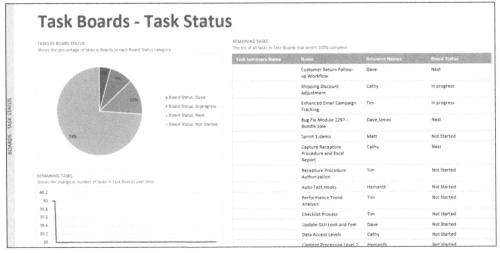

Figure 30-15. *On the Task Boards drop-down menu, choose Boards – Task Status to display this report.*

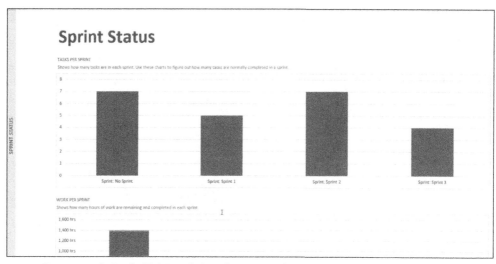

Figure 30-16. *On the Task Boards drop-down menu, choose Sprint Status to display this report.*

A

Getting Help

Microsoft Project may be your first introduction to project-management concepts like the critical path (Chapter 9) and work breakdown structures (Chapter 4). For you, Project presents a double challenge: learning what the program's commands and checkboxes *do*, and learning what to do *with them*. Or maybe you're a project-management expert and just want the dirt on how to use the program's features to get your work done: scheduling, budgeting, reporting, and keeping your project on course. For you, learning Project is a technical exercise: which features help you with the task at hand, where to find those features, how to get them to do what you want, and how to avoid the program's gotchas and limitations.

Whichever camp you're in, the first place you're likely to look for assistance is within the program itself. Project Help includes typical help fare like step-by-step instructions for using the program to perform various tasks. Help topics occasionally tell you why a feature is helpful, the best way to put it to use, and even give examples.

Finding the information you need is your biggest challenge. Project scatters tidbits of assistance throughout the program. For example, if you point to a column heading, a tooltip tells you what the field represents and may even show the formula Project uses to calculate it, as you can see in Figure A-1. Or if you point to an icon like the Insert Summary Task icon on the Task tab, you learn that the command inserts a summary task to help you organize the task list and that any selected tasks become subtasks of the new summary task. If you make changes to tasks and assignments, indicators and option buttons (Chapter 2) help you tell Project what you're trying to accomplish.

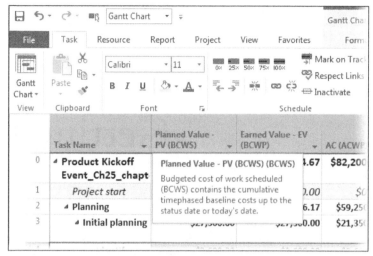

Figure A-1. *The tooltip for a field provides a brief description of the field and may include the formula Project uses to calculate it.*

Despite this helpful info, problems can arise when you try to use Project Help to learn the nitty-gritty. Say you aren't sure what the option to show task schedule warnings does. If you type ***show task schedule warnings*** into Project Help's Search box, about all you find out is a few entries describing warning related fields. Project Help is a work in progress, so typing in the "Tell me what you want to do" box or pressing F1 may take you to a specific help topic—or not. For example, clicking Help in the Task Information dialog box opens the Project Help window to top-level headings, not to the help topic about the field you're interested in.

This chapter explains how to make the best of the help that Project offers. These days, searching by keywords is the mainstay, so this chapter explains where to search for answers and how to ask the right questions. If you prefer scanning a table of contents, it's there, too—if you know where to look.

If Project Help leaves you in the dark, the silver lining may be discovering ***other*** resources and how helpful they can be. When an enigmatic Project feature is driving you crazy or you want to know how others use Project in the real world, search the Project discussion boards for the answer or post your problem. This chapter also identifies other websites and blogs that provide invaluable Project information.

In Search of Project Help

Naturally, Project Help is the first place you'll likely think to look for answers, and yet, finding them can be maddeningly difficult, as the note titled "Making the Most of Help" explains. But because Project Help is right there on your screen, you may still want to start there. This section tells you how.

You can choose from three ways to access Project Help's search feature:

- The **"Tell me what you want to do" box** (Figure A-2) streamlines getting help. When you click the box, it lists a few sample searches like "change the start date" and "set a baseline." As soon as you start typing in the box, a drop-down list displays likely related topics. For example, if you type *hide* in the box, the drop-down list includes Hide Window, Show Project Summary Task, Summary Task, Outline Number, and Table Data. If you continue to type *hide column*, the topics change to Select Column, Column Settings, Insert Column, and so on. If you see the topic you want, click it in the list and Project opens the Help window to that topic. To see additional related topics, click the last entry, which starts with "Get Help on."

> **Tip:** You can't type in the "Tell me what you want to do" box when a dialog box is open. In that case, click the Help button in the dialog box, or, if there isn't one, press F1.

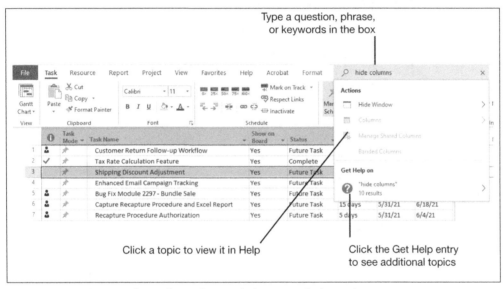

Figure A-2. *Type keywords or a phrase in the box to see info that might answer your question.*

- Click a **Help button** in a window or dialog box to open the Project Help window to a topic related to that feature. For example, if you click Help in the Assign Resources dialog box, Help opens to the assign resources topics.

- Press **F1** to open the Project Help window. When you press F1, Help opens to the "Project management goal: Create a new project schedule" topic. To see the top categories for Project Help, click the Home icon (which looks like a house) to the left of the Search box (Figure A-3).

Regardless of how you access Project Help, you end up in the Project Help window, shown in Error Reference source not found. Project Help works like a web browser, so you can hop from high-level topics to lower-level ones, or follow links within topics to related information. The Help window's icon bar includes several commands familiar to veteran web surfers: Back, Forward, and Home.

Clicking a category link on the Home page displays the help topics within that category. In turn, Help topic links lead to the nuggets of information each topic holds. You can type new or revised search terms in the Help window's Search box, and then click the search icon (it looks like a magnifying glass) or simply press Enter to see what Project Help has to offer.

Note: Regardless of which Project version you install, help results include topics that apply to both desktop and enterprise project-management versions (Project Server and Project Online). Unlike previous versions of help, beneath a topic's initial description, you'll see the versions it applies to.

Figure A-3. *Click the Home icon (it looks like a house) to the Search box's left to view top categories. To keep the Help window on top of other windows, click the pushpin icon at the bottom right.*

Tip: To get the full scoop on Project fields, type *field reference* in the Search box, and then click the search icon. The Help window displays a list of links that describe all of Project's fields.

> **Tip:** If you're interested in knowing things like the maximum number of resources per project, sharer files connected to a single resource pool, or filter tests per filter, in the Help window's search box, type *specifications*, click the magnifying glass, and then click the "Specifications for Microsoft Project" link.

Making the Most of Help

Because help is available only online, help topics are added and updated frequently, so instructions that are missing initially could show up later. Even up-to-the-minute online Project Help has a few issues:

- **No access to help if you don't have Internet access:** In the past, help was available both online and offline. Now, help is online only. That means you have to wait until you're back online to search for answers.

- **Finding the magic keywords or phrases**: Finding the help topic you want means using the right keywords or phrases, just like searching the web. For example, "manual scheduling" retrieves a topic titled "How Project schedules tasks" and then quickly digresses to topics like setting priorities for resource leveling. However, if you tweak your search slightly by typing "manually scheduled" instead, you see other topics such as linking tasks. So if you don't find the topic you're looking for, try changing your search terms. If one set of keywords doesn't do the trick, try synonyms or related terms; for instance, instead of "layout links," try "layout" or "format bars." Although one keyword usually isn't enough to pinpoint pertinent topics, too many keywords tend to add results that aren't related. Somewhere between two and seven keywords is usually about right.

- **Missing links**: Sometimes you click a Help link in a dialog box hoping to learn what turning on a checkbox does—but Project Help merely opens to the main Help window. You're left scratching your head over which keywords will give you the answer you seek.

Whether you find an answer or not, don't ignore the "Did this article help you?" buttons at the bottom of each help topic. Microsoft insiders will tell you that the company takes your votes seriously. Microsoft employees are rated by those responses, so content that no one finds helpful is likely to get an overhaul. If you click No, a text box appears giving you 650 characters to tell Microsoft what you'd like them to change. Clicking Yes opens a text box so you can describe what was helpful.

If the topic you choose isn't *quite* what you want, some topics include an additional section at the bottom of the topic, which may have what you're looking for.

Microsoft Office Online

You can also open your browser to Office.com and feast on its help, training courses, downloadable templates, discussion groups, and more. Type http://office.microsoft.com in your web browser. At the Office site, a set of tabs across the top of the page let you jump to different areas of the website, like Products, Support, and Templates.

To focus on Project-specific information, click the Support tab. On the page that appears, click the Project icon. (If you don't see it, click the right-pointing arrow to the right of the product icons to see more products.) To download project templates, click the Templates tab.

Interactive and In-Depth Assistance

Coming up empty-handed in Project Help is depressing. Then again, your problem may not be easily compartmentalized or described in a few keywords. Particularly gnarly problems often need some discussion and brainstorming. Because Project Help focuses on how-to, you may need other resources to learn how to put Project features into practice.

If you're lucky enough to have a Project know-it-all as an officemate, you know how refreshing it is to provide a quick summary and get a quick answer. For those of us who aren't so lucky, the online Project discussion groups are that know-it-all. Speaking of know-it-alls, many of them write *blogs* (web logs) about Project. Although some of the posts may be over your head, blogs are a great resource for learning how features, old and new, really work. This section tells you where to find all these resources.

> **Tip:** If Project behaves oddly, you see an enigmatic error message, or you have a gnarly project-management scenario you're trying to resolve with the program, you probably need more assistance than Project Help can give. Sure, you can go to the Microsoft Support website (http://support.microsoft.com), but the quickest way to find a solution is to use your favorite search engine: Google, Bing, Yahoo, and so on. In the site's search box, type the error message, error number, or keywords that describe your problem or question. Some of the results will be links to Microsoft's websites, but the answer you need may come from a Microsoft partner's website or someone's blog.

Discuss Among Yourselves

If you like a personal touch, Project forums can be very satisfying. You can search for an answer to your question in previous posts. If you don't find one, you can post a question and get an answer. Some group members are bona fide Project experts, but the answer you need could come from anyone. The two-way communication makes all the difference; you can describe your problem in detail and receive a detailed answer in return. And if you see a question *you* can answer, you can give back by helping out someone else.

Here are a few places you can find Project-related forums:

- **Microsoft Answers:** This site (http://answers.microsoft.com) has forums for all of Microsoft's products. To reach the Project forum, on the home page, in the Browse the Categories section, click Office. Below the "Browse by product or topic" heading, click All Topics. In the Office Topic drop-down list, choose Project.

- **TechNet forums**: Microsoft's TechNet forums (http://social.technet.microsoft.com/Forums) are usually a little geekier than other online communities. In many cases, that's exactly what you need. To get to the Project forums, on the TechNet Forums page, type *Project* in the search box, and then click the magnifying glass icon. Developers in the audience have their own Project-oriented forums: http://social.msdn.microsoft.com/Forums/en-US/category/project. For support with Project Server or Project Online, try http://social.technet.microsoft.com/Forums/en-US/category/project.

- **Microsoft Project User Group**: This user group (http://mpug.org) provides all sorts of support for Project, including forums, webinars, chapter meetings, newsletters, job boards, and so on. It does have an annual membership fee.

- **LinkedIn Project groups**: If you have an account with LinkedIn (www.linkedin.com), you can find dozens of groups dedicated to Microsoft Project. In the Search box at the top left of the site's home page, type *Microsoft Project groups*.

Project Blogs

Blogs tend to be informal and conversational, but don't let that fool you. They can provide a gold mine of in-depth information, in many cases from Microsoft employees. Go to https://www.microsoft.com/enus/microsoft-365/blog/, which is the official Project team blog. You can also find some great places for all kinds of Project info by searching online using the keywords "Microsoft project blogs."

Getting Social with Project

If you want to keep up with those in the know, you can connect with Project through its social networking channels:

- **Microsoft Project's Facebook page**: Connect with Microsoft Project and Project folks through Project's Facebook page: www.facebook.com/msftproject.

- **Microsoft Project's Twitter handle**: Use @msftProject to connect with the Microsoft Project team. To find all the Project-related tweets, use the hashtag #msproject.

- **Microsoft Project Help writer's Twitter handle**: To see what the people who write Project content for Office.com are tweeting, use @ProjectHelpTeam.

> **Tip:** When you find Project gurus who seem to have all the answers and explain things in a way that resonates with you, use social networking to connect with them, too. Follow them on Twitter, like their Facebook pages, or subscribe to their blogs.

From Your Authors

If you want to get in touch with us, head to the Credits at the beginning of this book for our email addresses, Twitter handles, and websites. Other books and training courses we've authored are listed at the end of the Introduction.

B

Keyboard Shortcuts

Keyboard shortcuts are tremendous timesavers, because your fingers can press a key combination in a fraction of a second compared with the seconds it takes to grasp the mouse and move the pointer to the correct location. Those saved seconds add up when you stick to the keyboard for your most frequent tasks—like saving a file regularly to make sure you don't lose any work or adjusting the position of tasks in the outline.

The only apparent disadvantage to keyboard shortcuts is learning their obscure keystroke combinations. If it takes you 10 seconds to remember that Alt+Shift+* displays all tasks in the project, then you really haven't saved any time. Mercifully, Project shares many keyboard shortcuts with other Microsoft programs, so you may not have to memorize as much as you think. On the other hand, a few minutes spent memorizing vital keyboard shortcuts can add up to *hours* saved down the line.

With Project, you have two ways to use keyboard shortcuts. You can press tried-and-true keyboard combinations like Ctrl+S to save a file just as you could in previous versions of Project. Or you can display KeyTips and press letters to move around the ribbon and choose the command you want. This chapter tells you how to use both methods.

How to Use Keyboard Shortcuts

Keyboard shortcuts can be a single key, like F3 to show all tasks or resources. But usually you have to press a combination of Ctrl, Shift, or Alt along with other keys.

If you don't know the keyboard shortcut for something you want to do, you can instead navigate through the ribbon, drop-down menus, and commands with KeyTips (the letters you press to choose a feature). Here's what you do:

1. To display KeyTips, press Alt.

    KeyTips appear over each feature in the current tab or menu. For example, if you press Alt and then press H to select the Task tab, you see letters next to each command on the tab, like the G next to the Gantt Chart command (as shown in Figure B-1).

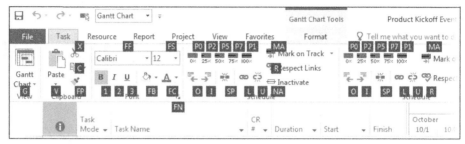

Figure B-1. *Pressing KeyTip letters to choose features works only when KeyTips are visible.*

2. To choose a feature, on the keyboard, press the letter in the feature's KeyTip.

    As you use KeyTips to switch between tabs and menus, additional KeyTips may show up. For example, if the View tab is visible and you press H, Project switches to the Task tab, which displays the KeyTips shown in Figure B-1.

3. Repeat step 2 until you press the letter for the command or feature you want.

    For example, if the Task tab is visible, press G to display the drop-down menu of Project views. Then press M to open the More Views dialog box.

4. To hide KeyTips, press Alt.

    When KeyTips are hidden, pressing KeyTip letters doesn't issue commands—it just types letters.

> **Note:** The keyboard shortcuts in Microsoft Help refer specifically to the US keyboard layout. If you use a keyboard layout for another language, your keyboard shortcuts vary depending on how characters map to the keys on your keyboard. For example, Ctrl+Z is the US keyboard shortcut to undo the previous action. However, the French keyboard layout has W located where Z resides on the US keyboard, so the French keyboard shortcut for Undo is Ctrl+W.

Project Keyboard Shortcuts

Some of the keyboard shortcuts in this section apply not only to Project but to every Microsoft Office program, so you can learn them once and then put them to work in all your favorite programs. Project doesn't come with flip cards to help you memorize these esoteric keyboard combinations, but if you memorize the ones for the tasks you perform most, then you can often save time without overtaxing your brain.

> **Tip:** If you memorize the shortcuts in this appendix and are still hungry for more, in the "Tell me what you want to do" box to the right of the ribbon tabs, type keyboard shortcuts, and then press Enter. One of the first help topic links should be "Keyboard shortcuts for Project." Click the link to view a complete list of keyboard shortcuts specific to Project, and many that apply to all Microsoft Office programs.

All-Time Keyboard Shortcut Favorites

These favorites apply to all Microsoft Office programs, and they're commands you use all the time. The keyboard shortcuts in Table B-1 should be at the top of your memorization list.

Table B-1. *Keyboard shortcuts you're sure to use all the time*

Task	Keyboard Shortcut
Create a new file (Project file, Word document, and so on).	Ctrl+N
Display the Open tab in the Backstage view.	Ctrl+O
Display the Open dialog box to open a file.	Ctrl+F12
Save the active file.	Ctrl+S
Display the Save As dialog box.	F12
Print the current view (such as Gantt Chart).	Ctrl+P
Close the active file.	Ctrl+F4
Undo the last action you performed.	Ctrl+Z
Redo the action you just undid. Ctrl+Y behaves differently in Project than in any other Office program. In Word, Excel, and so on, Ctrl+Y repeats the previous action. In Project, Ctrl+Y redoes the last actions you just undid by pressing Ctrl+Z.	Ctrl+Y
Copy a picture of the entire screen to the Clipboard (which you can then paste into a document or file).	Print Screen (might appear as Prnt Scrn or Prt Scr on some keyboards)
Copy a picture of the active window to the Clipboard (for pasting into another file).	Alt+Print Screen

Project Outlining

So much of working with a project schedule is adding tasks and placing them at the proper level in the Project outline. The shortcuts in Table B-2 help you view the outline and indent or outdent tasks.

Table B-2. *Outlining without touching the mouse*

Task	Keyboard Shortcut
Insert a new task above the selected task.	Insert
Indent the selected tasks.	Alt+Shift+right arrow
Outdent the selected tasks.	Alt+Shift+left arrow
Hide subtasks of the selected summary task.	Alt+Shift+hyphen (or Alt+Shift+minus sign on the numeric keypad)
Show next level of subtasks. Repeat this keyboard shortcut until you can see all the levels you want.	Alt+Shift+= (or Alt+Shift+plus sign on the numeric keypad)
Show all tasks.	Alt+Shift+* (or Alt+Shift+* on the numeric keypad)

Displaying Project Information

Whether you work on one Project file or several, the shortcuts in Table B-3 make it easy to see the information you want.

Table B-3. *Displaying Project windows and key dialog boxes*

Task	Keyboard Shortcut
Make the next Project file window active (when more than one file is open or when you use View→Window→Switch Windows).	Ctrl+F6
Make the previous Project file window active.	Ctrl+Shift+F6
Maximize all Project file windows within the main Project window.	Ctrl+F10
Open the Task Information dialog box with data for the selected task.	Shift+F2
Open the Resource Information dialog box with data for the selected resource.	Shift+F2
Open the Assignment Information dialog box with data for the selected assignment.	Shift+F2
Open the Field Settings dialog box to modify a column.	Alt+F3
Reapply the current filter.	Ctrl+F3
Reset the sort order to sort by ID and turn off grouping.	Shift+F3
Display all tasks or resources.	F3
Display smaller time units in the timescale, for example, switching from weeks to days.	Ctrl+/ (use / on the numeric keypad)
Display larger time units in the timescale, for example, from weeks to months.	Ctrl+* (use * on the numeric keypad)

Moving Around in a Project View

Whether you're setting up, modifying, or monitoring a schedule in Project, you're likely to move around within the table pane or timescale of the Gantt Chart and other Project views. The keyboard shortcuts for moving around in views, shown in Table B-4, are a little easier to remember because they use arrow keys as well as Home and End. For example, to move to the first field in a row, you press Ctrl+left arrow, whereas you press Ctrl+right arrow to move to the last field. The Ctrl key identifies shortcuts for moving within the rows and columns of the table area, and the Alt key applies to the shortcuts for the timescale.

> **Tip:** In Project, scrolling in the Timeline pane is an easy, mouse-driven way to scroll the timescale (Chapter 20).

Table B-4. *Moving within views*

Task	Keyboard Shortcut
Move to the first row.	Ctrl+up arrow
Move to the last row.	Ctrl+down arrow
Move to the first field in the current row.	Ctrl+left arrow (or Home)
Move to the last field in the current row.	Ctrl+right arrow (or End)
Move to the first field in the first row.	Ctrl+Home
Move to the last field in the last row.	Ctrl+End
Scroll the timescale to the beginning of the project.	Alt+Home
Scroll the timescale to the end of the project.	Alt+End
Scroll the timescale to the left.	Alt+left arrow
Scroll the timescale to the right.	Alt+right arrow
Scroll the timescale left one page.	Alt+Page Up
Scroll the timescale right one page.	Alt+Page Down
Scroll the timescale to display the task selected in the table area.	Ctrl+Shift+F5

Selecting Elements in a Project View Table

After you display the part of the schedule you want, your next step is often to select a field, task, or resource to perform some editing. Selection shortcuts use the arrow, Home, and End keys in similar ways to the shortcuts for moving within a view. The main difference is that selection shortcuts use the Ctrl+Shift combination. For example, moving to the first row is Ctrl+up arrow, whereas selecting from the current selection to the first row is Ctrl+Shift+up arrow. Table B-5 lists the keyboard shortcuts for selecting elements in a Project view.

Table B-5. *Selecting within views*

Task	Keyboard Shortcut
Expand the current selection to the first row.	Ctrl+Shift+up arrow
Expand the current selection to the last row.	Ctrl+Shift+down arrow
Expand the current selection to the first field in the current row.	Shift+Home
Expand the current selection to the last field in the current row.	Shift+End
Expand the current selection one field to the left.	Shift+left arrow
Expand the current selection one field to the right.	Shift+right arrow
Expand the current selection to the first field in the first row.	Ctrl+Shift+Home
Expand the current selection to the last field in the last row.	Ctrl+Shift+End
Expand the selection up one row.	Shift+up arrow
Expand the selection down one row.	Shift+down arrow

> **Note:** These selection shortcuts expand the selection based on the fields or rows that are already selected. For example, if a Task Name cell is selected, then expanding to the first row selects all the Task Name cells up to the first row. If the entire row is selected, then expanding the selection to the first row selects all the tasks up to the first row.

Editing Within a View

You're probably familiar with keyboard shortcuts for editing. Ctrl+X, Ctrl+C, and Ctrl+V cut, copy, and paste selected elements in Project, just as they do in Microsoft Word and other programs. But Project includes a few additional keyboard shortcuts for specialized editing, listed in Table B-6.

Table B-6. *Keyboard shortcuts for Project editing tasks*

Task	Keyboard Shortcut
Create a finish-to-start task dependency between the selected tasks.	Ctrl+F2
Remove all task dependencies from the selected tasks.	Ctrl+Shift+F2
Set the task mode for the selected task to Manually Scheduled.	Ctrl+Shift+M
Set the task mode for the selected task to Auto Scheduled.	Ctrl+Shift+A
Cancel changes without saving.	Esc
Activate a field so you can edit its text.	F2

Navigating Within Dialog Boxes and Forms

Of course, Project has dialog boxes like every other program, and the same keyboard shortcuts for navigating within them. The forms that appear in Project views, such as the Task Entry form, use some additional keyboard shortcuts to navigate within form fields and tables. Table B-7 lists these shortcuts.

Table B-7. *Navigating dialog boxes and forms*

Task	Keyboard Shortcut
Display the next tab in a dialog box.	Ctrl+Tab
Display the previous tab in a dialog box.	Ctrl+Shift+Tab
Select an option in a dialog box or toggle between turning a checkbox on and off.	Alt+the underlined letter in the option or checkbox
Move to a field in a table within a form (such as the Resources and Predecessors tables in the Task Form).	Up arrow, down arrow, left arrow, and right arrow

Help Shortcuts

You need just a few keyboard shortcuts, listed in Table B-8, to open the Help window and browse help topics.

Table B-8. *Keyboard shortcuts for viewing help topics*

Task	Keyboard Shortcut
Open the Help window.	F1
Display the previous help topic.	Alt+left arrow
Display the next help topic.	Alt+right arrow

C

Project Options Reference

The Project Options Online Reference file is part of the download available at www.coldpresspublishing.com.

Index

Made in United States
North Haven, CT
25 October 2023

43188537R00435